VOLUME 3

HISTORY OF THE INTERNATIONAL
1943–1968

VOLUME 3

HISTORY OF THE INTERNATIONAL

1943–1968

Julius Braunthal

*Translated by Peter Ford
and Kenneth Mitchell*

Westview Press/Boulder, Colorado

Geschichte der Internationale, Vol. 3, first published in
the Federal Republic of Germany 1971
Copyright © Verlag J. H. W. Dietz Nachf. GmbH., 1971

This translation first published in London, England, in 1980
Copyright © Victor Gollancz Ltd 1980, London, England

Published in the United States of America in 1980 by
Westview Press, Inc.
5500 Central Avenue
Boulder, Colorado 80301

Frederick A. Praeger, President and Publisher

Library of Congress Catalog Card Number 67-17667

ISBN 0-89158-369-6

Printed in Great Britain at
The Camelot Press Ltd, Southampton

Contents

List of Plates

Foreword

As this book is a work of contemporary or on-going history, a few words must be said here about the time-gap between its completion and its appearance in print.

The third and final volume of Julius Braunthal's *History of the International* was completed by him in February 1971. By May it had appeared in German, published by Verlag J. H. W. Dietz Nachf. GmbH., Hanover, and preparations for producing the English edition were well under way. It was originally planned for publication in the winter of 1972. However, Julius Braunthal died on 28 April that year, a week before his eighty-first birthday. A number of difficulties and delays cropped up, the translated typescript was mislaid, the Appendices were lost; it even seemed for a period of years as if the third volume was destined never to see the light of day. Nevertheless, Julius's wife Tini (who died in 1975), we, his sons, his nephew, Gerard Braunthal, as well as many friends, felt it essential that the final volume of this great work should become available in English and patiently strove to this end. Its publication, after this long delay, is for us a source of deep satisfaction, and we should like to express our gratitude for the encouragement and support we received in particular from Livia Gollancz and John Bush of Victor Gollancz Ltd and from Peter Marold of Verlag J. H. W. Dietz Nachf. GmbH.

The delay, however, posed a certain dilemma: should intervening events be taken into account? The book, for instance, contains detailed tables in the Appendices; they provide lists of congresses of the Socialist International, and of its leaders and officials up to 1969, and, in particular, figures for the state of Socialist and Communist parties for 1969–70 and of Socialist parties in power. These have patently and considerably changed over the years and, in revising the original typescript of Mr Peter Ford's translation, the question arose whether or not efforts should be made to bring it up to date at least in some respects.

Finally, on the advice of Mr J. R. van der Leeuw, Director of the International Institute for Social History in Amsterdam, we decided against incorporating changes; there have been too many of them to do them justice marginally. The only concession we made to the passing of time was to add where available the dates of death for some of the persons mentioned in the book who have died in the intervening years.

In revising the typescript, we have taken great care to ensure accuracy; however, in the absence of the author, and because of the dispersion of the original source material, which was written in several languages, an occasional minor error in such things as titles of organizations or books, or in the misspelling of transliterated names, may have slipped through: for these, we would ask the reader's forbearance.

Frederick G. Bonnart-Braunthal   Thomas O. Barry-Braunthal

Preface

With this volume the history of the first century of the International reaches its conclusion. Originally I had intended that the trilogy would come to a close with the centenary of the founding of the First International in September 1964. But before I could finish writing the third volume the tragedy of the Communist revolution in Czechoslovakia had played itself out. 'The Spring of Prague' of 1968, having set in motion a process of change from a Communist dictatorship to a Socialist democracy, was followed within a few months by the invasion of the armies of the five Warsaw Pact powers to forestall reformation in Czechoslovakia. Both revolution and counter-revolution were events of the utmost significance for the history of Socialism—the revolution, for showing that it was possible for a Communist system of totalitarian dictatorship to be transformed without resort to force; and the counter-revolution, for showing how the régime in the Soviet Union has remained essentially unaltered since Stalin's death. The invasion of Czechoslovakia brutally called in question any optimistic perspective of development within the Soviet Union itself.

It did not then seem possible that the present work could be concluded without any discussion of the historical significance of these two events. The chapter on 'The Spring of Prague' constitutes a postscript to the story of the first hundred years of international Socialism.

The history of the period covered by the present volume begins, as the first chapter describes, with the expectations of both Socialist and Communist parties that, in the aftermath of the catastrophe of the Second World War, the conflict between European Socialism and Russian Communism might be surmounted, the split in the international workers' movement repaired and a new Socialist Europe constructed on the ruins of the old continent.

These expectations were to founder on the profound mistrust existing between the Eastern and Western powers. The Soviet Union, fearing a new war with the United States and its European allies, sought security by expanding its power zone across the Eastern European countries which it had occupied during the war and afterwards changed into satellite states.

The process of Sovietizing Eastern Europe prompted fears in Western Europe and the United States that the Red Army might overrun the defenceless continent and place it under Russian rule—a fear which turned to panic when, in February 1948, the Communist party in Czechoslovakia seized power by a *coup d'état* and reduced the country to a satellite of the Soviet Empire.

The 'Cold War', developing out of the mutual mistrust between the great powers, governed the destiny of European Socialism. In Part Two an attempt has been made to describe the origins and the events of the 'Cold War' from the viewpoint of the Socialist movement so as to explain the reopening of the split, the founding of the Cominform and the re-establishment of the Socialist International.

Part Three is concerned with the amazing phenomenon of the spread of the Socialist idea throughout Asia, and how the concept of Socialism, which had developed in the tradition of European culture in a capitalist civilization, was able to put down roots in the pre-capitalist civilization of the Hindu–Buddhist and Islamic cultures and win mass followings for both Socialist and Communist parties.

Part Four describes the severe moral crisis suffered by the Communist world movement after the end of the war: the revolt of the Communist party of Yugoslavia against Moscow's overlordship, the rising of the Berlin workers in the Soviet Zone, the destruction of the myth of the Soviet Union as the ideological centre of the Communist world movement, the collapse of its moral basis as a consequence of Khrushchev's revelations at the Twentieth Congress of the Communist party of the Soviet Union about Stalin's reign of terror, the Polish October, the revolutions and counter-revolutions in Hungary and Czechoslovakia, and finally Peking's break with Moscow.

Finally, to close the trilogy, at the same time as trying to draw up an interim balance sheet of the historical achievements and failures of Socialism in the course of the first century of its history, I have had the temerity to enter into some reflections about its future.

The Appendices will be found to contain a statistical summary of the present state of the world Socialist movement in every shape of party—Social Democratic and Communist as well as those parties with Socialist leanings which are not formally allied to either of the two main groups; the basic documents of both the Socialist International and the Asian Socialist Conference; the manifesto of the inaugural congress of the Cominform, which was to become decisive in determining the attitudes in the Communist movement during the post-war period; and the declaration by the Fourteenth Congress of the Communist Party of Czechoslovakia over the invasion by the Warsaw Pact forces.

The work of which this is the last volume can by no means be regarded as comprehensive; with considerable misgivings I am only too aware of the yawning gaps which occur in my description of these hundred years. As Professor Adolf Sturmthal quite justly remarked in his review in the *American Political Science Review*, it lacks a detailed description of the relationship between the international Socialist movement and the international trade union movement; and as Professor Val R. Lorwin—certainly one of the work's most competent critics—very properly regrets in the *Annals of the American Academy*, it does not contain any comprehensive comparison of the structures of the Socialist and Communist parties, of their techniques of membership recruitment and election propaganda, their relationships with the trade unions, and most importantly, of their strategies and tactics in opposition, coalition or government.

But having said this, the list of gaps is by no means complete. Above all, it contains no study of Socialism in Africa or Central and South America, no examination of the ideologies and social structure of the parties in these continents which are professing to be Socialist parties, and no description of their histories. The movements of Central and South America have been treated in monographs in great profusion. African Socialism, on the other hand, is a barely-explored area of study. But however sparse or otherwise the sources, it would still have been desirable at least to sketch in the outlines of the currents of Socialism in these continents in any universal history of Socialism.

In return for his criticism of the work's imperfections, Professor Lorwin generously offered some gentle comfort. 'The task,' he wrote, in his discussion, 'which he [the author] has set himself' is most probably impossible, even if one spent a lifetime at it.'

Yet this qualification could never excuse such a prejudiced omission as that of which I have been accused by my critics in the Soviet Union: the omission of any appreciation of Lenin's role in the Second International as 'representative of the revolutionary line' in the fight against reformism. In their critique in the Moscow periodical *Voprosi Istoriki*, the authors, I. A. Bach, W. E. Kunina and B. G. Tartakovsk, stated that I had 'completely ignored the part which the Bolsheviks, with Lenin at their head, played in the Second International'.

The question of Lenin's role in the fight against reformism in the International is indeed of no small historical interest for it was Lenin who morally justified the fateful split, as the second volume showed, by asserting that since it was 'eaten up with opportunism' it had become incapable of carrying out its task in the revolutionary struggle of the working class against capitalism and imperialism. It would therefore have been dishonest of me had I, as accused, intentionally neglected to describe and assess his leading role in the International, before its collapse in 1914, as 'representative of the revolutionary line' in the struggle against reformism.

An examination of Lenin's activities in the Second International leads to an amazing result. Although he was a member of its Bureau, he appeared at no more than three of the nine congresses of the Second International (at Amsterdam in 1904, Stuttgart in 1907 and Copenhagen in 1910), and at none of these did he take the floor. In the chronicles of the International he puts in only three active appearances: at the meeting of the Bureau in 1908, with an explanatory additional statement in support of the admittance of the British Labour party to the International which Kautsky had proposed and for which he voted, even though it had not pledged itself to the class struggle; by a textural alteration to a resolution at the Copenhagen congress over the role of co-operatives in the battles for Socialism; and, lastly, at the Stuttgart congress with a supplementary statement to Bebel's resolution on the attitude of the working class to the war, drafted by Rosa Luxemburg and proposed by her also in the names of Lenin and Martov.

As is described in the first volume of the *History of the International*, the question raised by this resolution had been passionately debated at a number of congresses and was concerned with the possibility of averting the danger of war by a general strike, that is by revolutionary methods. Lenin's supplementary statement had left the question open. It had become critical when, at the beginning of November 1912, tensions between the European powers reached a climax, intensified by the Habsburg Empire's annexation of Bosnia and the Balkan War, both events giving rise to fears of an immediate outbreak of hostilities. An extraordinary congress of the International was hastily summoned to Basle on 24 November to discuss how the danger was to be averted. Victor Adler and Jean Jaurès in their speeches hardly disguised their threat of revolution which would follow in the wake of war. But Lenin's voice went unheard at the congress. He had not appeared. He even stayed away from the meeting of the Bureau of the International which was summoned to Brussels by telegraph with every sign of alarm for 29 July 1914— that tragic meeting five days before the outbreak of the First World War when the International should have resolved the important question of the attitude of the working class to the international crisis.

Consequently, in any account of Lenin's role in the struggle between the revolutionary and reformist lines in the International, there is only the Stuttgart additional statement to be recorded; this was naturally fully quoted in its proper place in the text, and its importance was discussed. Beyond this there is nothing to record of Lenin's struggle as 'representative of the revolutionary line' against reformism within the International.

Now a word of gratitude to friends who have assisted me in my work on the book. The chapter 'The Spring of Prague' was read in manuscript by Dr G. W. Brügel, author of the study *Tschechen und Deutsche 1918 bis 1939*, and the final section, 'The First Hundred Years', by W. L. Guttsmann,

Chief Librarian of Norwich University and author of the work *The British Political Élite*, and both were enriched by their suggestions. For the statistical material on the world Socialist movement I am much indebted to my young friend Alan Day, editor of *Socialist Affairs*. I am also grateful to the Librarian of the International Institute of Social History in Amsterdam, Miss Marie Hunink, and the Librarian at Chatham House, London, Miss Dorothy Hamerton, who both lightened my burden through their efforts to obtain books and periodicals; and Mr J. R. van der Leeuw, Head of the Archives of the International in the Amsterdam Institute, who has furnished me with various documents. For illustrative material, I am indebted to the picture archive of the Secretariat of the Socialist International, to the *Arbeiter-Zeitung*, Vienna, to the Amsterdam Institute, and to the chief editor of the Berlin daily newspaper *Telegraf*, Arno Scholz.

Teddington, 10 February 1971   Julius Braunthal

The Destiny of Socialism

Introduction

When Stalin concluded his pact with Hitler on 25 August 1939, the unity of the international labour movement was shattered. The United Front of Socialists and Communists against the menace of Nazism, for which the Communist International had campaigned so single-mindedly since 1935, was laid in ruins. While throughout the world Social Democrats stood firmly in the camp for war against Hitler, Stalin placed the Communist International at the disposal of Hitler's psychological war effort.[1]

It took Germany's invasion of Russia on 22 June 1941 to rectify Stalin's momentous blunder. Now the Soviet Union and the Western Allies found common cause in the fight for democracy against Fascism; once again Social Democrats and Communists stood shoulder to shoulder in the face of a common enemy. The heroism shown by the Red Army in first holding back the Nazis at the gates of Moscow and Leningrad, and then dealing them a numbing defeat at Stalingrad, aroused an enthusiastic response among Social Democratic workers everywhere. The bitter political quarrels of the past twenty years were forgotten. It seemed that an era of unity within the international labour movement had dawned at last.

The hopes entertained by many Socialists that the split could indeed be overcome received new impetus from the dissolution of the Communist International in May 1943. The Socialist International had ceased to exist after the last meeting of its Bureau early in April 1940,[2] and the disappearance of the Communist International seemed to remove the last obstacle to reconstituting a united International. Harold Laski (1893–1950), who was among the most renowned intellectual leaders in the British Labour movement, spoke for many thousands of its members when he welcomed the dissolution as 'one of the most hopeful political developments since 1919'

1. Julius Braunthal, *History of the International, 1914–1943*, pp. 504–26.
2. For the dissolution of the Communist International and the end of the Socialist International, see ibid., pp. 529–30 and 491–2.

from the viewpoint of re-establishing working-class unity throughout Europe and Asia.[1]

In all of Europe—with the exception of Britain, which had successfully resisted invasion, and Sweden and Switzerland, which were both spared invasion altogether—Fascism had crushed Socialist and Communist parties alike. Now, having participated in the defeat of Fascism, would they renew their struggle to lead the working class, or might a united workers' party at last emerge from their common ruin? This was the question which pre-occupied Socialists of every shade of opinion when, towards the end of the war, the outlines of a new Europe began to emerge.

The potentiality of a triumphant Socialist renaissance seemed very real. The old bourgeois parties had been discredited. World war had been preceded by a world economic crisis condemning millions in the leading industrial countries to the hunger and demoralization of long-term unemployment. And the bourgeois parties, confronted by this crisis, were at a loss how to overcome the disaster. They had also been surprisingly quick in abandoning their own liberal, humanitarian values when faced with a working-class threat to property and privileges. In Italy, Germany and Austria, they had joined forces with Fascism. In Hungary, Poland, Romania and the Baltic States, they had been ready to back semi-Fascist dictatorships. Nor could they avoid responsibility for the war itself. In Britain and France, instead of resisting Hitler, they had tried to appease him with concession after concession, and in France capitulation was followed by collaboration. In the lifetime of a single generation the old bourgeois parties had plunged Europe into two world wars. It seemed hardly conceivable that millions of people would ever again be willing to leave their fate in such hands, and to many it seemed far more likely that the finish of the war would witness the dawn of Socialism in Europe.

Against this background, the question of mending the split in the international labour movement took on new significance. No Socialist government emerging after the war could hope to revive exhausted economies on a fresh, Socialist basis without freely-given and self-sacrificing co-operation from the whole working class. Should the labour movement remain divided and the old pre-war rivalries be allowed to reassert themselves, then, it was clear, working-class governments would founder and the bourgeois parties return to power.

It is true that in Britain, whose Labour party had the unchallenged allegiance of the organized working class and whose Communist party was practically negligible, the question of the reunification of the labour movement was not crucial. But in France, Germany and Czechoslovakia there had been mass Communist parties before the war and it was impossible to predict

1. Quoted in Milorad M. Drachkovitch (ed.), *The Revolutionary Internationals 1864–1943* (Stanford, 1966).

the increase in strength likely to be obtained by the Communists in these and other countries which had experienced the war and Nazi occupation at close quarters and been affected by the immense prestige gained by the Soviet Union's war effort. The problem of reuniting the workers' parties had assumed the utmost importance.

This problem was, however, inextricably bound up with the issue of East–West relations. Most particularly, the continuing friendly relationship between Britain, the United States and the Soviet Union in the task of establishing a lasting peace settlement was essential to a united labour movement. For it became clear that, in the event of any conflict developing between the Soviet Union and a non-Communist country, then that country's Communists, even if they were within a united workers' party, would continue to pursue their policy of unquestioning allegiance to the Soviet Union, regardless of whether or not their country had a Socialist or non-Socialist government; for they would continue to see in the Soviet Union the leading genuinely Socialist state, on whose strength and survival, they believed, all the hopes of the world revolution depended.

The idea of reunifying the international labour movement could therefore only be realized on the solid foundation of a community of mutual interests existing between the Great Powers. Only if the great war-time alliance between the United States, Britain and the Soviet Union were to be carried over into the post-war world and made the basis of a lasting peace settlement could the international labour movement be reunited. But if the alliance broke down, then the split would inevitably recur.

The destiny of international working-class unity had therefore come to depend on friendly relations between Communist Russia and a United States whose social system and political ideology formed an antithesis to Communism. They were united only by the vaguely formulated agreements concerning the future division of Europe into spheres of influence that were reached at the Yalta Conference in February 1945. It was on the conflicting interpretations of these agreements, made as the war approached its climax, that the alliance was to founder within barely two years of peace. Cohesion between Socialists and Communists quickly followed suit. Their unity had not lasted long enough to put down roots, and the concept of an all-embracing International was buried beneath the rubble of the Grand Alliance.

It was not long, however, before the disintegration of the international labour movement reached a new stage. International Communism itself, whose monolithic unity had seemed forged in steel, began to break up. In Europe the Communist party of Yugoslavia, faced with the crucial choice between national independence and subjugation to Soviet imperialism, came into open conflict with Moscow. Of incomparably greater moment was the breach in relations between the Communist parties of the Soviet Union and China when, after a few honeymoon years of common triumph, they came into conflict over their rival claims to the leadership of the world Communist movement. Even as the disintegration of the Grand Alliance had broken the links between the Socialists and the Communists, so did the imperialistic rivalries between the two Communist super-powers, only thinly veiled by ideological slogans, destroy the unity of world Communism.

Socialism had emerged from the war with immense prestige and considerable political power. A Labour government was in command of the British Empire. Scandinavia had for long been under Social Democratic rule. Elsewhere in Europe, Socialists were prominent in coalition governments. And whereas Socialist movements had in the past largely been confined to the white races, now, for the first time in history, Socialism was to become influential in Asia and Africa. Yet, as had so often happened in the past, when the concept of international solidarity seemed to clash with national self-interest, it was the latter which was to triumph.

1 · The British Labour Initiative

The initiative for ending the split in the international labour movement was taken by the British Labour party. In their opinion the key lay in Moscow. As early as the spring of 1942, a year before the dissolution of the Communist International, the National Executive Committee of the Labour party had decided to send a delegation to Moscow in order to reach an understanding with the Soviet government towards solving the problems which had divided the international labour movement so as to lay down foundations for what Harold Laski, speaking at the party's annual conference in 1942, described as 'the permanent and unshakeable unity of the Labour movement for ever'.

The timing of the discussion had of necessity been left to the Soviet government, and it seemed improbable that any invitation would be issued in 1942. The German assault on Moscow had been halted in the winter of 1941, but in 1942 Leningrad was still under siege. That summer, German forces broke through into the Caucasus, while simultaneously in the Don basin forces were deployed against Stalingrad in a vast semi-circle that stretched from Voronezh to Rostov. In the autumn the decisive battles began for this fortress on the Volga. It was to prove one of the bloodiest battles in all the annals of war, and it ended, in January 1943, with the destruction of the German forces and the capture of 350,000 German soldiers. With this, Germany's power to take the offensive was broken and the way cleared for the Soviet counter-attack.[1]

Even if Stalin had wished for a discussion with the British Labour party,

1. Russian resistance in the face of overwhelming German might had won the world's admiration. 'In the course of my life,' General Douglas MacArthur wrote in February 1942, 'I have taken part in a number of wars and have witnessed others. I have also made a detailed study of operations conducted by great commanders of the past. In none of these wars did I find such an effective resistance against the heaviest blows of an enemy, till now regarded as invincible—a resistance which was followed by a devastating counter-attack which drove the enemy back into his own country. The extent and magnitude of this feat makes them the most distinguished military power in history.' Quoted in Robert E. Sherwood, *Roosevelt and Hopkins* (New York, 1948), p. 497.

this was hardly the most propitious moment. The British Labour party patiently awaited the Russian leader's decision. At its annual conference of June 1943, it reaffirmed its desire for a discussion to settle the main differences in the international labour movement. 'It would be a tragedy of the first order,' Laski declared in an address to the conference, 'if the twenty-five post-war years, like the twenty-five inter-war years, were to be characterized by destructive conflicts.'[1] In its Report to the next annual conference, in December 1944, the executive recorded that it had requested the Soviet Ambassador in London to arrange for the delegation's visit, and at its next conference, in May 1945, Hugh Dalton once again reaffirmed the executive's wish for talks with the Russians.

No such discussion was to take place. An official Labour party delegation, led by Harold Laski, did in fact visit Moscow in July 1946 and conducted an interview with Stalin. But the Soviet leader pointedly refrained from any mention of mending the split in the world labour movement.[2] While the Labour leadership genuinely wished to reach an understanding with the Russians, it had no particular desire to establish closer relations with the British Communist party. In Britain, the Communists had little popular support. The party had been badly compromised by its opposition to the war during the first two years, and its already small membership had dropped by a third. After the Soviet Union had been drawn into the war and international Communism changed its line, the British Communists had not had the chance given to their comrades in France, Italy and the other occupied countries to cancel out the stigma by a heroic record of resistance. While the heroism of the Red Army evoked immense sympathy, from which British Communists to some extent benefited, no Nazi occupation had occurred to consolidate solidarity between Socialists and Communists in the shared risks and sufferings of an underground movement. While the Communists no longer made open attacks on 'bourgeois democracy' or voiced their belief in proletarian dictatorship, this was seen as a temporary tactic, and most Labour party members considered the objectives of Communism as being incompatible with their own.

Yet there was no way of avoiding discussion with the Communists. As early as 18 December 1942, six months before the dissolution of the Communist International, the central committee of the Communist party had sent a letter to the Labour party executive requesting that Communist affiliation be placed on the agenda for the forthcoming annual conference.[3] This letter stated that the Communist party was willing 'to fulfil all the

1. Report of the Forty-Second Annual Conference of the Labour Party, 1943, p. 150.
2. For a record of the discussion of the British Labour delegation with Stalin, see Report of the Forty-Fifth Annual Conference of the Labour Party, 1946, pp. 218–19.
3. Because of its federal structure, which included trade unions, co-operative societies and Socialist organizations, the Labour party could accept affiliation from outside bodies, political parties included.

conditions of Labour party affiliation and to carry out loyally all conference decisions'.

This letter began a lively correspondence between J. S. Middleton (1878–1962) and Harry Pollitt (1890–1960), secretaries of the Labour and Communist parties respectively, which lasted for several months. It repays examination in some detail since it quite clearly illustrates the wider issues involved in restoring unity to the European labour movement.[1]

In replying to Pollitt's letter, J. S. Middleton, speaking for the Labour party, stated that he could not consider the Communists to be an autonomous party. As an affiliated section of the Communist International, they were, by the rules of that organization, bound to act on all its decisions. The British Communist party was not, therefore, a free agent, nor was it in any position 'to carry out loyally' the decisions of Labour party conferences.

Pollitt denied that this was the case. He stated 'categorically' that his party's policy was ruled solely by its 'democratically elected congress and its democratically elected leadership', and that any of its decisions were taken entirely in the light of 'prevailing conditions in Britain and in the interests of the British labour movement'.

Middleton then had no trouble in quoting six paragraphs from the Constitution of the Communist International, binding all its units to act on its decisions and to place themselves under the authority of its executive committee in every question of principle, programme, rules or tactics. Besides which, the principles of international Communism stood in glaring contrast to Labour party principles. And as to Pollitt's claim that his party enjoyed total autonomy, and that its policies were directed exclusively in the light of 'prevailing conditions in Britain and the interests of the British labour movement', this seemed hard to reconcile with the party's behaviour during the war, when, having denounced the fight for democracy in September 1939, it had performed a complete *volte-face* in June 1941. Such a change of line, he remarked, had had nothing to do with 'prevailing conditions in Britain'. It had been 'ordered by the Communist International and was not the result of a free decision by a democratically elected congress of the Communist party of Great Britain'.

Pollitt did not attempt to reply to Middleton's accusation directly. He simply repeated that the British Communist party was independent and autonomous. He also refrained from any attempt to justify its policy during the early stages of the war. Instead he quoted Léon Blum, who, at his trial before the Vichy authorities at Riom in February 1942, had told the court: 'The past opposition between the Communists and myself is no longer relevant; I have erased all that from my memory. All that matters now is

1. For the correspondence and related documents, see Report of the Forty-Second Annual Conference, pp. 9–19 and 227–31.

that the Soviet Union is participating in the common struggle and that the Communist party is making heroic sacrifices in the occupied zone.'

But then, Middleton could remind Pollitt, while 'Blum and thousands of his French comrades were being handed over to the mercies of the German Fascists', the British Communist party was denouncing its country's role in the war against Nazi Germany as 'imperialist', and had gone on to try to undermine it 'on direct orders from the Communist International'. 'The Labour party,' Middleton declared, 'does not accept that the blood of the French Communists and the Red Army has cancelled out the British Communist party's and the Communist International's share of guilt for the collapse of democracy and the spread of Fascist power.'

Again, in replying, Pollitt made no reference to his party's vacillations over the question of the war; it was clearly a subject which caused him some embarrassment. He did, however, repeat his earlier claims that, its membership of the Communist International notwithstanding, the Communist party of Great Britain was a self-governing body and that it was fully prepared to accept the Labour party's programme, principles and policy.

If that was so, Middleton asked, how was one to interpret the sudden 'overnight' switch in policy in September 1939, when the party had abruptly turned from a position of extreme anti-Nazism and support for the war to one of denouncing Britain as responsible for what it described as an 'imperialist war' in which the Communist position was tantamount to 'revolutionary defeatism'?[1] 'As you know,' Middleton wrote, 'this distortion of the facts was as stupid as the earlier description of the leaders and members of the Labour party as "Social Fascists"—at a time when they were fighting for an agreement with the Soviet Union on a system of collective security.'

He was quite sure that not one of these tactics had resulted from free decisions being taken by an autonomous party; rather they had been forced on it by the Communist International which, from its headquarters in Moscow, imposed an iron discipline on its affiliated members. Earlier, Pollitt had proposed an informal meeting between representatives of the two parties to clarify the disputed questions, but Middleton had said that his own executive declined to negotiate with a party which 'as a subordinate section of an international party has neither the authority to negotiate on its own behalf nor is in any position to carry out decisions without approval from a superior outside organization'.

The correspondence continued until the beginning of May 1942, when, having received a further letter from Pollitt on 30 April, the Labour party executive said there was no point in pursuing the discussion. But, it went on to state, 'Should conditions seem suitable for an attempt to bridge the gap

1. See Braunthal, *History of the International, 1914–1943*, pp. 500, 506–7, 512–13 and 522–3.

between the two Internationals, any discussion must take place on a broader, more representative and more responsible level.' In other words, the chances of reuniting the two sections of the international Labour movement depended entirely on the possibility of reaching an agreement with Moscow.

Three weeks later, on 23 May, the Communist International was dissolved, and on the very next day the Communist party renewed its application in a letter that proposed joint discussions. The unexpected dissolution of the Communist International had, indeed, brought about new conditions, and the Labour party acknowledged the necessity of a reassessment when it convened an extraordinary executive meeting on 28 May.

Hitherto discussion had, as we have seen, hinged on relations with the Communist International. Now that this had ceased to exist, it might seem possible that with the national Communist parties no longer bound by its statutes and resolutions,[1] the leading obstacle to Labour–Communist unity had been removed. In a new statement the Labour party executive went so far as to admit that 'certain circles' appeared to assume that no valid objection remained to Communist affiliation and that this could henceforth be regarded as inevitable.

A majority on the executive, however, took a different view. The dissolution of the Communist International, they reasoned, in no way implied that the Communists had either abandoned their support for a 'revolutionary dictatorship' or become loyal pillars of parliamentary democracy. Even if the Communist party were no longer bound by international commitments, this gave no reason for believing that it had jettisoned the principles on which it had been founded and which had subsequently guided its policy. And after all, the Labour party executive stated, had Communist policies been successful in the early phase of the war, 'we should all have been crushed by the Fascist hordes and the defeat of Russia would have followed. The entire world would have become a Fascist empire, and the Gestapo murderers would have strutted, in all their arrogance and brutality, through the streets of Moscow and London.'

The Communists were now professing their loyalty to the idea of labour unity, but the true test of their sincerity, in the view of the Labour executive, lay in their attitude to maintaining themselves as a separate organization. Should they insist on preserving themselves as a separate party, this would demonstrate that they pursued objectives different from those of the Labour party, in which case their entry into the Labour party could only be a cause of mistrust and dissension. If, on the other hand, they were genuinely concerned to foster unity in the British labour movement, they should follow the example of the Communist International and go into dissolution. For these reasons, the Labour party executive decided to oppose any affiliation of the Communist party as a separate organization. In its view, a separate

1. ibid., p. 528.

Communist party functioning within the Labour party could only be a source of weakness and disunity, and so it submitted a resolution in these terms to the party's annual conference.[1]

The conference met in London on 14 June 1943. The ensuing debate, during which eleven delegates spoke, lasted only a few hours. The Executive's resolution was moved by George Ridley, leader of the Railway Clerks, while the resolution supporting Communist affiliation was moved by Will Lawther, president of the powerful Miners' Federation. The executive submitted the entire correspondence to conference, and the debate covered much the same ground. The executive had chosen Herbert Morrison (1888–1965) to wind up. He enjoyed a large popular following, with all the prestige derived from his successful leadership of the Labour majority which had controlled the London County Council since 1934, and he received a tumultuous ovation as he mounted the rostrum. He added nothing new to the discussion, but confirmed the executive's readiness to hold discussions with the Communists, provided they first agreed in principle to dissolve their own party. In an emotional speech, he appealed to the Communist party to seize the historic opportunity presented to it by the dissolution of the Communist International and, in the interests of labour unity, to dissolve itself while calling upon its members to join the Labour party as individuals. After Morrison had spoken the motion was put to the vote, and the Communist party's application was defeated by 1,951,000 votes to 712,000.

Morrison's appeal to the Communist party evoked no response. It merely continued its campaign to affiliate to the Labour party as a separate organization, though no Labour conference debated the question again until June 1946. Meanwhile, the Labour party's massive victory in July 1945 undermined the argument that unity with the Communists could provide a decisive source of strength. Out of a total of 640 seats in the House of Commons, the Labour party held 394, the Communists only two. The new Labour government, with its substantial parliamentary majority, had no need of Communist support. In any case, the national membership of the Labour party was over sixty-five times that of the Communist party.[2]

Consequently, the debate at the 1946 Labour conference was brief and concerned only with conflicting assessments of the value of the Communist party's declaration of loyalty. The only speeches were one by Herbert Morrison, for the executive's point of view, and a second by Jack Tanner for

1. For the text of the resolution, see Report of the Forty-Second Annual Conference of the Labour Party, 1943, pp. 18–19.
2. In 1945, the Communist party had 45,435 members, the Labour party, 3,037,697. See Report of the Executive Committee to the Eighteenth Congress of the Communist Party of Great Britain (1945), p. 16, and Julius Braunthal (ed.), *Yearbook of the International Socialist Labour Movement* (1956), p. 234.

the Amalgamated Engineering Union, favouring Communist affiliation. This time the application was defeated by 2,678,000 votes to 468,000.[1]

This was the last occasion when the question was to be debated at any annual conference. The 1946 discussion had already been held in an atmosphere of worsening relations between Britain's Labour government and the U.S.S.R. Two years later, after the Cold War had come to dominate the international scene, the frail ambition to construct an international brotherhood on the foundation of Socialist–Communist unity was completely dead. The British Labour party's attempt to solve the problem of unity by a direct approach to Moscow had come to nothing. The trade unions, on the other hand, had a greater measure of success[2] and it was mainly as a result of the British Trades Union Congress (T.U.C.) initiative that the World Federation of Trade Unions came into being.

Britain did not, of course, have the problem of separate Communist unions. The Red International of Labour Unions (R.I.L.U.) established on Lenin's initiative at the Communist International's second congress in 1920,[3] never got off the ground in England. While in France, Germany and Czechoslovakia sections of the R.I.L.U. engaged in bitter conflicts with the Socialist-led unions, there was no serious attempt to set up splinter unions in the United Kingdom, where the idea of trade union unity was more deeply rooted.

As a result, Britain's union leaders had fewer inhibitions than their European counterparts when it came to working for international links. As early as 1925 the T.U.C. had tried to reach an agreement with the Soviet trade unions on establishing a comprehensive trade union international,[4] and it renewed its attempt during the war. The Trades Union Congress, meeting in Edinburgh in September 1941, three months after Hitler's attack on the U.S.S.R., authorized the general council to commence joint talks with the All Union Central Council of Trade Unions[5] with a view to establishing a single trade union international.

By the autumn of 1941, Russia's situation had become desperate. The German invasion had caught the Red Army unprepared, and initially it crumbled before the ferocity of the Panzer attacks. During the first three weeks some 620,000 Russian soldiers were taken prisoner by the Germans.

1. Report of the Forty-Fifth Annual Conference, 1946, p. 174.

2. It must be kept in mind that the British Labour party receives the bulk of its support from trade union affiliations, and that twelve of the twenty-seven seats on its executive are elected directly by the unions. Affiliated trade unionists outnumber individual members of constituency parties by more than seven to one, and the trade union block vote is thus the most important single factor determining conference decisions.

3. Braunthal, *History of the International, 1914–1943*, pp. 173–5.

4. For an account of the formation and break-up of the Anglo-Russian Trade Union Committee, see ibid., pp. 303 and 306–7.

5. Report of the Seventy-Third Annual Trades Union Congress, Edinburgh, 1941, p. 243.

During September the Germans captured Kiev and advanced to the gates of Moscow. Since France had capitulated and the United States had not yet entered the war, Britain was Russia's solitary ally, and the government of the U.S.S.R. naturally welcomed the T.U.C.'s declaration of solidarity with Russia in her time of greatest need.[1] Friendly messages were exchanged between the two trade union centres, and the Anglo–Soviet Trade Union Committee held its first meeting in Moscow in October 1941. In the following year the T.U.C.'s general secretary, Walter Citrine (b. 1887), went to the United States to seek the support of that country's two trade union organizations—the American Federation of Labor and the Congress of Industrial Organizations—for an international trade union conference.[2] The T.U.C., at its annual conference of September 1943 in Southport, which was attended by a Soviet trade union delegation led by N. M. Shvernik, decided to convene an international trade union conference to lay the foundations for a world trade union organization.

In November the invitations, signed by Citrine on behalf of both organizations, went out to seventy-one trade union bodies in thirty-one countries; the conference was intended to be held in London and to open on 5 June 1944.[3]

In fact the 'World Trade Union Conference', as it was officially called, began at County Hall, London, on 6 February 1945. This was the first occasion in over a quarter of a century that Socialists and Communists had been able to come together on a world scale for discussions on a friendly basis. It was an impressive gathering, representing sixty-three trade union organizations with a total of sixty million members from forty-six countries, even though the war was still in progress and a number of countries still under Nazi domination—notably Germany, Austria and Hungary—could not be represented. During talks which lasted eleven days,[4] the conference decided to set up a world organization at a congress to be held in Paris in September 1945. The conference also drafted a set of rules, a basic charter of trade union rights and a declaration on post-war reconstruction. In a manifesto to the international working class, the conference affirmed the right of the trade union movement to participate fully in laying the foundations of the post-war world. 'The organized workers,' it declared, 'who have

1. Another expression of solidarity was the strike which took place in British aircraft factories in September 1941 in protest against a remark made by a cabinet minister, J. T. C. Moore-Brabazon, who was responsible for aircraft production and who said that British interests would best be served by Germany and Russia inflicting maximum casualties on one another. Labour pressure, including pressure from Labour members of the cabinet, led to Moore-Brabazon's resignation.

2. The C.I.O. accepted the proposal. However, the A.F. of L. refused to take part in an international conference with the Soviet trade unions on the grounds that they were not so much genuine unions as agencies of the Soviet government.

3. The postponement of the conference occurred as a result of the opening of the Second Front, the name given to the Allied landing in Europe in June 1944.

4. See Report of the World Trade Union Conference, 6–17 February 1945, County Hall, London.

played such a great part in winning the war, cannot leave to others the sole responsibility for the peace settlement.'[1]

The inaugural congress of the World Federation of Trade Unions (W.F.T.U.) took place as planned in Paris in September 1945. The fratricidal conflicts which had largely undermined the power of trade unionism on an international scale were momentarily held in abeyance. 'The great experiment began in an atmosphere of widespread enthusiasm and a belief in mutual good faith,' as Arthur Deakin, the general secretary[2] of the T.U.C., recorded. But this experiment also failed within a few years as the Grand Alliance disintegrated. The W.F.T.U. had been founded on the assumption that friendship between the Soviet Union and the Western democracies could outlast the war and become permanent.

The progress of the common struggle of the United States, Britain, the Soviet Union and the other Allies [Arthur Deakin recalled] had given rise to a sentiment of international unity; feelings of allied solidarity were strengthened and a great hope swelled in all men's hearts. It was hoped that military victory over Fascism and National Socialism would be followed by an all-embracing and honest friendship which would fulfil the hopes for a fruitful co-operation between the nations of the world.[3]

These high hopes turned sour. On the very day following the German surrender, at the Potsdam Conference of the Big Three in July 1945, the gulf that separated Russia and the West became apparent. Over the next year or two it grew steadily wider, reaching its climax in the Cold War. At no point was there the remotest possibility that trade unions in the Soviet Union and the other Communist countries might remain neutral in any conflict between Russia and the West. And, from the outset, the influence of the Communist bloc in the W.F.T.U. was dominant. The Soviet trade union movement, with twenty-seven million members, was by far the largest single organization to be affiliated. The Communists, moreover, led the trade union movements of France, Italy, Latin America and China, while Louis Saillant, a Communist sympathizer, was elected general secretary of the W.F.T.U. and there was soon a Communist majority on the executive.

Disagreements between Communist and democratic elements on the executive were therefore inevitable, and as the breach widened between Russia and the West, so relations inside the W.F.T.U. grew worse. In November 1947, the Communists declared open war against their opponents in the executive; *Trud*, the official organ of the Soviet trade unions, demanded

---

1. ibid., pp. 230–50. For a summary of the decisions, see Hans Gottfurcht, *Die Internationale Gewerkschaftsbewegung im Weltgeschehen* (Cologne, 1962), pp. 169–80.

2. Arthur Deakin, *et al.*, *Free Trade Unions leave the World Federation of Trade Unions* (1949), p. 6.

3. ibid., p. 5.

the elimination of 'reformist' leaders.[1] Controversy over the Marshall Plan lasted for a full year before culminating in an open split.[2] The non-Communist unions seceded in January 1949, and at a meeting held in London in December 1949 set up the International Confederation of Free Trade Unions (I.C.F.T.U.).[3]

Thus, within four years of its restoration, the unity of the international trade union movement was broken up. Once again, two international federations—the I.C.F.T.U. and the W.F.T.U.—faced one another in bitter rivalry.

---

1. *Trud*, 16 November 1947. See Deakin, *et al.*, op. cit., p. 8.

2. See Gottfurcht, *Die Internationale Gewerkschaftsbewegung*, pp. 189–98. For the Communist version, see Saillant's speech in Report of the Proceedings of the Second World Trade Union Congress, Milan, 1949, pp. 21–30. G. Monmousseau, a French delegate, told the Congress that the 'split in the W.F.T.U. was planned and organized by Jouhaux on the order of the American billionaires with the object of furthering the anti-Soviet war aims of NATO' (p. 44). The Soviet leader, Kuznetsov, attributed the split to the pressure of the Labour government on the T.U.C. (ibid., p. 134).

3. See Gottfurcht, *Die Internationale Gewerkschaftsbewegung*, pp. 201–24. For the structure and development of the I.C.F.T.U., see Julius Braunthal and A. J. Forrest (eds), *Yearbook of the International Free Trade Union Movement* (1957–62), 2 vols.

2 · Socialists and Communists in France

In France, relations between Socialists and Communists were more complex than in Britain, and they developed along different lines. In Britain a minuscule party with hardly any political influence had sought unity with a giant. But in pre-war France the Communists had been a mass party which, with seventy-two parliamentary deputies, constituted a major political force. Like its British counterpart, the Communist party of France had been seriously compromised by its attitude during the war's early stages. If it could hardly be said that the record of the French Socialists represented a source of pride, the betrayal by the French Communists had been more serious and certainly more spectacular. After 1935 the party had called more stridently and persistently than any other in France for resistance to Hitler—the Communists were, indeed, the one parliamentary party to vote against the Munich Agreement—and, at the outbreak of war, it had thrown itself with patriotic fervour into the struggle to defend the mother country. But after a few weeks, when instructions were passed through from Moscow, it turned in its tracks to denounce the 'imperialist war', which, it said, was a consequence of the machinations of British capitalists. Like its sister party in Britain, it pursued this line right up to the Nazi attack on the Soviet Union. The entire inglorious episode was epitomized in the behaviour of Maurice Thorez, the party general secretary, who demonstratively joined his regiment at the outset of hostilities, only to desert within a few weeks and, from exile in the Soviet Union, called upon workers and soldiers to make peace with Germany.[1]

By contrast with the French Communist party, which had initially given unanimous support to the war and had then just as unanimously opposed it, only one section of the French Socialists jettisoned its anti-Fascist principles. At the time of Munich, the party became divided over the question of whether Hitler's aggression against Czechoslovakia should be opposed even at the

1. See Braunthal, *History of the International, 1914–1943*, pp. 507 and 510.

risk of war.[1] The party's leader, Léon Blum, stood for outright resistance, but another group, led by the general secretary, Paul Faure, wished for an understanding with Hitler in an attempt to avert war, and it was this pacifist section which had secured a majority. In the interests of party unity, Blum and his followers had bowed to the majority opinion and voted for the Munich Agreement.[2] While the Communists were condemning the agreement as an act of treason, the Socialists were giving it their official support. After war broke out, however, the Socialist party rallied whole-heartedly to the war effort, and denounced the Communist campaign for peace talks with Hitler, which began with the fall of Poland in September 1939, as a cynical betrayal.

But for France the serious fighting did not begin until eight months later with the German offensive in May 1940. Within five weeks the struggle was over. By-passing the Maginot Line, the German armoured divisions broke through the French defences on the Meuse, overran northern France almost unresisted and entered Paris on 14 June. The government, having evacuated itself to Bordeaux together with the deputies of both houses of parliament, had to decide in the midst of a nation-wide panic whether to abandon the mainland and continue the war from Africa or whether to sue for an armistice. On 16 June, two days after the fall of Paris, the Reynaud administration resigned, and the President of the Republic, Albert Lebrun, requested the eighty-four-year-old Marshal Pétain, the 'Hero of Verdun', to form a new government. Pétain personified the essence of the monarchist, clerical and social reaction. He represented those elements in French society which most loathed the Republic and which had hated above all the government of the Popular Front. Their hatred had run so deep that, once the possibility of war with Germany seemed to be growing, they had demanded an understanding with the Nazis under the slogan 'better Hitler than Blum'. Consequently, no sooner had Pétain been asked to form a government than he announced the cessation of the struggle and requested Hitler to grant an armistice. This was duly signed on 22 June, and under its terms Alsace and Lorraine were annexed by Germany while northern France, including Paris, was occupied by German troops.[3]

One group of Socialists, led by Léon Blum and Vincent Auriol, called for the war to be continued in the Jacobin spirit of 1792 and the Communard spirit of 1871. But a vast majority of the French people had had enough.[4]

This was the end of the Third Republic. Democracy had been assassinated, and reaction moved in to claim its inheritance. A joint meeting of senate and deputies on 10 July 1940 decided, by 569 votes to eighty, to appoint Philippe

---

1. For a detailed study of the pre-war split of the party, see Georges Lefranc, *Le Mouvement socialiste sous la Troisième République: 1875–1940* (Paris, 1963).
2. Braunthal, *History of the International, 1914–1943*, pp. 488–9.
3. In November 1942 German troops occupied the remainder of the country.
4. See Alexander Werth, *France 1940–1955* (New York and London, 1956), pp. 27–9.

Pétain head of state with almost unlimited powers. Among the eighty delegates voting against the new constitutional law, there were only thirty-six Socialists. A clear majority of the parliamentary Socialist party voted in support of the law[1] and several leading Socialists, including Paul Faure, the party secretary, Spinasse, who had been minister of commerce in Blum's government, and the trade union leader, René Bélin, shortly afterwards accepted appointments under Pétain.

But despite this betrayal by so many of its parliamentary representatives, the Socialist party nevertheless took up the struggle against the Vichy régime—Vichy being the seat of the French government under the Occupation. The party itself was suppressed and many of its deputies, senators and officials, including Léon Blum, Vincent Auriol and Salomon Grumbach, were arrested. It went underground, and by November 1940, within four months of the start of the occupation, it had launched one of the earliest resistance organizations under the leadership of Jean Lebas, the Socialist mayor of Roubaix. It also produced the monthly journal, *L'Homme libre*.[2] At about the same time, Socialists, in company with members of the illegal trade union movement, set up the *Fédération Libération-Nord* to co-ordinate the activities of underground groups within the occupied zone. The *Fédération* issued a clandestine weekly, edited by Christian Pineau and Jean Texier, which achieved an astonishing circulation of 50,000 copies an issue. Socialists likewise played a leading role in such underground groups as *Combat* and *Libération*.[3]

By January 1941 it had become possible to begin the reconstitution of the Socialist party in the shape of the *Comité d'Action Socialiste* C.A.S.), led first by H. Ribière, and then by Daniel Mayer, a friend and disciple of Léon Blum. By December 1941, they were able to publish a bulletin *Socialisme et Liberté*, and in May of the following year *Le Populaire* began to reappear.[4] By the summer of 1943, the party had re-established a nation-wide network of activists, and in July it issued a 'Charter' of demands to be implemented immediately following liberation. This became the charter for the whole

1. For a description of the political and psychological atmosphere, see Dorothy M. Pickles, *France Between the Republics* (London, 1946), pp. 13–16.
2. The paper was duplicated in a room which was separated from the German garrison headquarters only by a glass door. The duplicating machine, paper and vehicles for distributing it were all supplied by Lebas from the mayor's office. Lebas was arrested in May 1941, but the group continued its activities and a conference—the first such international gathering in occupied Europe—was held at Namur in May 1942, in company with Socialists from Belgium and Holland—see Werth, *France, 1940–1955*, p. 143.
3. For detailed descriptions of the Socialist resistance movements, see Robert Verdier, *La Vie clandestine du Parti Socialiste* (Paris, 1944); Daniel Mayer, *Les Socialistes dans la Résistance. Souvenirs et documents* (Paris, 1968); Jules Moch, *Le Parti socialiste au peuple de France* (Paris, 1945); and Jean-Pierre Bloch, *Mes jours heureux* (Paris, 1946).
4. The underground *Populaire* attained a circulation of well over 100,000. See Peter Novick, *The Resistance versus Vichy. The Purge of Collaborators in Liberated France* (London, 1968), p. 19.

resistance movement, and after the war it formed the programme for France's first liberation government.

On 9 November 1944, the party held its first conference since the outbreak of war. It met in an atmosphere of imminent victory. The tone of the conference was expressed in its concluding manifesto, which declared that: 'Steeled by sacrifice and reinforced in its beliefs, the Socialist party emerges from the resistance with a new spirit and a new structure.' Accordingly, the party had been completely overhauled, the manifesto continued:

So as to fulfil its national and international mission, the party has purged itself morally. Traitors, cowards and those who fell by the wayside have been removed from office and replaced by comrades who have earned our trust through their work in the resistance.

The conference expelled all those deputies and senators who had voted for the Pétain constitution,[1] and it elected Daniel Mayer, who had played a leading role in the underground, to be its general secretary. As a result, the Socialist party emerged from the war freed from the stigma it had acquired through the activities of Paul Faure and his fellow collaborators.

The Communist party, on the other hand, made no attempt to justify its policy during the first stage of the war[2] nor to make any kind of critical

1. The conference expelled ninety-six of the surviving 151 members of the party's parliamentary group. The groundwork for an out-and-out purge of the party after the Liberation had been laid during the war, in May 1941, by the *Comité d'Action Socialiste*, the party's underground executive committee, which had decided to expel not only those of the party's senators and deputies who had voted full power to Pétain, but also those who had abstained. After the Liberation every departmental federation carried out a root-and-branch purge, carefully examining old members and new applicants alike. 'No other party carried out a purge which even approached that of the Socialists in scope and rigor' —Novick, *The Resistance versus Vichy*, p. 108. The Communist party in the main purged only those members who had opposed the Russo-German Pact of August 1939. 'Many of these "renegades" were summarily executed both before and after the Liberation'—ibid., p. 109.

2. A defence of Communist policy was contained in a letter written to Pétain by François Billoux on 19 December 1940. Billoux was a leading Communist deputy who, together with a number of Communist deputies, had been arrested at the beginning of October 1939 and given a long prison term in April 1940. Writing from prison in Le Puy, in his letter (which proved a great source of embarrassment to the Communists when it was published after the war) he demanded the release of Communists from prison; he pointed out that their one crime lay in sharing the anti-war convictions of Pétain and his government. 'We were hauled before the Court,' he wrote, 'because we were the only ones with the courage to call for the overthrow of the Daladier government responsible for the war. . . . I told the Court that the war would be disastrous for France. If we lost, we should be slaves of Hitler; if we won, the lackeys of Chamberlain. We ought to have followed the Soviet Union and stayed neutral. Our country would then, like the Soviet Union, have kept out of the war'—quoted in Werth, *France, 1940–1955*, p. 193. For a Communist view of the period, see Florimond Bonté, *Le Chemin de l'honneur* (Paris, 1949). Bonté had been one of the imprisoned deputies. For another view, see Germaine Willard, *La Drôle de guerre et la trahison de Vichy* (Paris, 1960); and for a dissident Communist view, see Auguste Lecoeur, *L'Autocritique attendue* (St Cloud, 1955).

assessment of its own role. The devotion of its members to the resistance had been as fervent and self-sacrificing as their earlier 'revolutionary defeatism' had been total.[1] They had responded eagerly to the uncompromising anti-Fascist line as soon as it had once again become Communist orthodoxy, and their revolutionary background made them more effective members of an underground movement than did that of either the Socialists, Catholics or liberals. Consequently they secured many key positions in the resistance, particularly in its leading organizations: the *Front National* (F.N.), and its military wing, the *Francs-Tireurs Partisans-Français* (F.T.P.F.).

Recruitment to the resistance was greatly stimulated when, in February 1943, the *Service de Travail Obligatoire*, an agency of the Vichy government, began to deport thousands of French workers to forced labour in Germany. By the end of the war, the number of deportees may have run as high as 900,000.[2] It was a threat which caused thousands to join the *Maquis* in the woods and mountains of the Central Plateau as well as in the Pyrenees. During the course of the war, the numbers recruited in this way may have reached 100,000.[3] The Vichy government and its press denounced all members of the underground without distinction—those who opposed the régime on straightforward patriotic grounds as much as the Communists. Far from attaching any stigma to Communism, this inevitably became a great source of strength to the Communist party.

The underground resistance movement was not the exclusive confine of any one party. Politically, its membership ranged from the far left through the centre to the patriotic right, but the Communist party, with a certain degree of effrontery, declared itself to be *the* 'party of the resistance'. The Vichy régime as well as the Gestapo persecuted resistance members with ferocity and without any regard for ideological convictions: Communists suffered heroically in company with but, so far as the evidence goes, to no greater extent than did other sections of the resistance.[4] This did not

1. For an account of the underground, see Werth, *France, 1940–1955*, pp. 133–78. For the role of the Communists, see Franz Borkenau, *Der Europäische Kommunismus* (Berne, 1952), pp. 296–316. Though hostile the account contains valuable documentary material.

2. See Henry Ehrmann, *French Labor. From Popular Front to Liberation* (New York, 1947), p. 271. Val R. Lorwin estimates the number of Frenchmen deported to forced labour as being 600,000—see *The French Labor Movement* (Cambridge, Mass., 1945), p. 94.

3. Werth, *France, 1940–1955*, p. 157.

4. According to Domenach, some 350,000 Frenchmen died at the hands of the Germans —250,000 perishing in concentration camps and 100,000 being executed. The total number of Communists in the two categories is given as at least 60,000—see Jean-Marie Domenach, 'The French Communist Party', in Mario Einaudi (ed.), *Communism in Western Europe* (Ithaca, 1951), p. 99. The numbers seem exaggerated. The French government reported a total of 29,660 executions to the Nüremberg tribunal—*Agence France Presse*, 12 September 1947, quoted in Alfred J. Rieber, *Stalin and the French Communist Party, 1941–1947* (New York, 1962), p. 144.

inhibit the French Communist party from claiming a lion's share of the credit and describing itself as the 'party of the 75,000 executed'.

Co-operation between Communists and Socialists in the resistance led, on 27 May 1943, to the setting up in Paris of the *Conseil National de la Résistance* (C.N.R.), on which the Socialists were represented by André Le Troquer and the Communists by André Mercier. The C.N.R. assumed control over the eight federations into which the early free-ranging groups of resistance fighters had gradually coalesced, and also over the illegal trade union organiz- ations of Socialists and Catholics, represented by Louis Saillant. A year later, on 16 March 1944, the Socialists and Communists, together with the demo- cratic resistance groups, reached agreement on a mutual programme for post- war reconstruction, the 'Charter of the C.N.R.'. This was, to all intents, the programme of the revived Socialist party to which we have already referred.

The programme's key demand was for the restoration of the democracy which the Vichy régime had destroyed, including universal suffrage, freedom of thought and conscience, freedom of the press, freedom of speech and the 'absolute equality of all citizens before the law'. It called for the establishing of a 'genuine economic and social democracy', the destruction of those 'vast concentrations of economic and quasi-feudal financial power' which effec- tively controlled the country's economy, the nationalization of the great private monopolies 'created by the people's labour', and, specifically, for the nationalization of mines, the electric power industry, banks and insurance companies. The programme also demanded the setting up of a Welfare State with guaranteed minimum earnings compatible with security, dignity and a fully human existence, full employment and a comprehensive programme of social benefits.[1]

Under the Vichy government, the trade union federations as well as political parties had been made illegal, and in November 1940, the *Confédération Générale du Travail* (C.G.T.) had been formally abolished and its general secretary, Léon Jouhaux (1879–1954), deported to Germany. The Com- munist unions had been expelled from the C.G.T. as early as the end of September 1939, when their party reversed its policy towards the war. After that, Communists and Socialists ran their separate underground unions. But the general unification of the resistance made it feasible to think in terms of the Communists re-entering the C.G.T. On 17 April 1943, represen- tatives of both sides reached agreement at Le Perraux to annul the expulsion of the Communists from the C.G.T. The balance of voting power on the executive was restored to that prevailing in September 1939, with the Jouhaux section holding five votes to the Communists' three.

1. For the text of the Charter, see David Thomson, *Democracy in France: The Third Republic* (London, 1946), pp. 299–301.

The Communists had been working towards reunion with the C.G.T. as a result of their conviction that their efficient methods for forming cells in trade union branches and factories would enable them to win complete control of the organization and utilize it for party purposes. Their confidence proved to be well founded. When the C.G.T. held its first post-war congress at Toulouse in March 1946, with an impressive total membership of five million, the real balance of power became obvious during a vote on a Communist proposal that seven of the largest trade union federations should be allowed a voting strength equal to their affiliated membership.[1] The proposal was carried by a majority of four to one, or 21,238 votes to 4,872.[2] Ever since its foundation in 1895, the C.G.T. had made a point of remaining free of any political control. Now, for the first time in its history, it had become the instrument of a political party, the Communist party.[3]

The Socialist party had made no attempt to adjust its traditional attitudes to the conditions prevailing in post-war France. The historical division of the political spectrum into parties of left and right was complicated by the emergence of a new Catholic party of the left, the *Mouvement Républicain Populaire* (M.R.P.) in association with a broad Catholic trade union movement. The possibility of an alliance with the new party, however, ran counter to the traditional anti-clericalism of the French Socialist party. The question was debated at the latter's first post-Liberation conference, at an extraordinary meeting on 9 November 1944 in the *Palais de la Mutualité*, where the delegates tried to reassess their fundamental principles in the new era of the history of France.

The traditional anti-clericalism of the Socialist party had its origins in the struggle for democracy as it had developed in France ever since the Revolution of 1789. For over 150 years, the Catholic Church had sided consistently with the forces of reaction.[4] The Catholic hierarchy had supported the Fascist Vichy régime and had, as a result, formed one of the main targets of the resistance.

But with France subjected to a Fascist régime, a broadly-based Catholic workers' movement had repudiated the political leadership of the Catholic Church for the first time in French history and worked shoulder-to-shoulder

1. The seven federations—metal-workers, miners, textile workers, railwaymen, building workers, farm workers and workers in the food industry—were all Communist-led. In all, twenty-one of the thirty largest unions came under Communist control.

2. Lorwin, *The French Labor Movement*, p. 109.

3. At the Toulouse congress the rules adopted were in accordance with the foundation statutes of 1895, confirmed by the Amiens Charter of 1906, insisting on 'the complete independence of the trade union movement from . . . political parties, philosophical sects and other groups outside the labour movement'. Nevertheless, within eighteen months the Communists had the C.G.T. under firm control. For the text of the preamble, see Ehrmann, *French Labor,* p. 283; for the story of the Communist capture of the C.G.T., see Rieber, *Stalin and the French Communist Party*, pp. 220–4; Novick, *The Resistance versus Vichy*, p. 134.

4. See Braunthal, *History of the International, 1863–1914*, pp. 161–2.

with other anti-Fascist organizations in the resistance. The illegal Catholic trade unions, in co-operation with Socialist resistance groups, had affirmed their support for democratic and Socialist principles.

In all this Léon Blum saw the possibility of creating in France a non-sectarian workers' organization modelled on the British Labour party—a labour movement founded on mutual political and social ideals but treating ideology as the 'private concern' of its individual members and taking no specific line on Church–State relations.

But, in France, the role of the Church within the state was not to be divorced so easily from party politics, if only because *laicité*—the secular character of the state schools—had for so long been at the centre of party controversy. Nearly a quarter of all school children at the primary level attended Catholic schools, and throughout the history of the Third Republic the question of state subsidies to these schools had formed a subject of hot controversy between the anti-clerical parties of the left and the clergy, who enjoyed the support of conservative parties on the right. Whenever right-wing parties came to power, they made a point of subsidizing Catholic schools, and Pétain, heading the most reactionary French government in a hundred years, had given very substantial subsidies. Now the Socialists had to decide whether, as a matter of principle, they should stand firm on the policy of *laicité*, or whether they should make concessions in return for an alliance with the Catholic labour movement.

While this question was being debated at the party congress, Léon Blum was still in Germany as a prisoner of the Gestapo. He would certainly have supported concessions to the Catholic workers, but an overwhelming majority in the party was less flexible, and wished the party to remain as uncompromisingly anti-clerical as it had been since its inception. In the words of the resolution carried by the congress, 'Whatever alliances may be considered, it is essential that the Socialist Party should remain totally committed to *laicité*. . . .' 'This Congress,' the resolution continued, 'demands the repeal of the Act of 1942, decreed by Pétain, under which government money was given to private schools.'[1]

The party's desire to remain uncompromising in its traditional viewpoint became clear during the debates at its first regular post-war congress (the thirty-seventh), which met in Paris in August 1945. Léon Blum, who had returned from Germany in May, put forward a draft for a new 'Declaration of Socialist Aims and Principles'. This was intended to supersede the declaration of principles by which the Marxist *Parti Socialiste de France*, led by Jules Guesde, had joined with the reformist *Parti Socialiste Français*, led by Jean Jaurès, to form the united *Parti Socialiste: Section Française de l'Internationale ouvrière* (S.F.I.O.) at the Paris congress in April 1905. The

1. Quoted in Ronald Matthews, *The Death of the Fourth Republic* (London, 1954), p. 172.

declaration had contained elements both of Marxism and reformism, but he party's description of itself as 'a class party which stands for the socialization of the means of production . . . a party of class struggle and revolution' was unmistakably Marxist.

During his time in prison, Blum had had leisure to reflect on the party's principles in the light of his suspicion that somehow it had lost its way.

> I have asked myself [he wrote], after very many years [of party activity] and after many months of careful thought, whether the blame [for the party's failures] did not lie with the leaders in whom the workers had placed their confidence. Did they really understand their mission? Did they really grasp the significance of what Jaurès had made out of Marx's initial insights? Marx gave the workers' movement tremendous vitality by convincing them that the currents of history were on their side. . . . But Jaurès went on to show that social revolution is not simply the inevitable result of economic development; it is also the end product of humanity's eternal, basic strivings and beliefs.[1]

In the revision of the 1905 declaration which he submitted to the congress, Blum had tried to incorporate something of the spirit of Jaurès in an attempt to transform his party into a party of freedom and human rights—a party concerned not only with 'the political freedom and rights of the working class', but with broadening its objectives to include a social order working in the interests of the entire human race, for, as he expressed it in his draft, 'individual rights and free institutions are inseparable'.

In his speech supporting the proposed revisions, Blum argued that the aims of Socialism went far beyond mere economic and social change.

> Social change [he insisted] is not an end in itself. It is a means. It should be regarded as a condition for a more fundamental change in the way men live. The aim of the revolution is not only to free men from economic and social exploitation and all the derivative forms of human servitude. It must also guarantee to each member of the collective society the full enjoyment of human rights and freedom to follow his personal inclination. The aim of the revolution [he concluded] is to restore harmony between the individual as a social unit and the collective society of which he forms an essential part.

Blum's draft was inevitably opposed by many delegates as a watered-down version of the traditional Marxism on which they had been reared. In particular, his suggestion that the term 'class struggle' should be replaced by 'class action' had, as Blum admitted in his speech to the congress, 'caused grave offence to many of our brothers'. He went on to plead with his critics that 'tradition does not mean blindly repeating the actions of our predecessors. It means, rather, trying to act as they would act if they stood here in our place.' He asked the congress to bear in mind that, 'we have to reconstruct the party from scratch. Have all the years of underground struggle taught us

1. Léon Blum, *À l'Échelle humaine* (Paris, 1946). The book had been written in prison in 1941.

nothing?' What he had intended, he argued, was not so much to revise as to adapt Marxism to prevailing political and social conditions. His draft was quite compatible with the basic ideas of Marxism, and, indeed, his analysis was based entirely on the Marxist theory of the class nature of capitalism. But he was trying to present a concept of revolution which would have a more universal appeal than that put forward in the 1905 declaration. The objective of the revolution must be presented not only as 'social upheaval' and the simple replacement of one economic system by another. It had to be much more—'the transformation of the conditions of human life . . . not just an end to economic exploitation and domination but a guarantee of fundamental human rights'.

After a heated debate,[1] the congress decided to refer Blum's draft to the federations (regional organizations) of the party for comment and to authorize an editorial committee to prepare a new document, so far as possible reconciling majority and minority views. The proposal was considered by a conference of federation secretaries in February 1946, and it was adopted by 3,053 votes to 768, with 639 abstentions.

The new statement managed to incorporate the essence of Blum's draft without apparently impairing the party's commitment to Marxism. The party was to remain what it had been from its inception: a party of 'proletarian class struggle', not merely a party of 'class action'. As a result, the relevant paragraph in the new statement declared:

The Socialist party is by its nature a revolutionary party. It aims at replacing capitalist private property by a society in which natural resources and the means of production are socially owned and classes have been abolished. Such a revolutionary transformation, though in the interests of all mankind, is to be achieved only by the working class. Irrespective of the means by which it is brought about, it constitutes a social revolution. In this sense the Socialist party is a party of class struggle founded on the organized working class.

Having reaffirmed the party's commitment to Marxism, the statement proceeded to incorporate the spirit of Blum's draft by emphasizing its democratic character and insisting on the necessity of fighting for social reforms within the capitalist system. It declared:

The Socialist party is by nature a democratic party. Individual rights and class freedom are inseparable. The workers can only be free in a society which guarantees full freedom to all citizens. Complete democratic freedom is an essential part of any Socialist society. It also provides favourable conditions in which the workers can fight for reforms within a capitalist society, so raising their standard of living and simultaneously increasing their revolutionary fighting strength.[2]

But while the Socialist party was wrestling with its conscience and battling

1. For a review of the congress proceedings, see the excellent study by D. B. Graham, *The French Socialists and Tripartisme, 1944–1947* (London, 1965), pp. 87–114.

2. *Bulletin intérieur*, February–March 1946, quoted in Graham, *The French Socialists and Tripartisme*, p. 158.

out its differences in the open, the Communists experienced no such qualms. References to Marxism, let alone to Marxism–Leninism, disappeared from its public pronouncements.[1] The term 'class struggle' completely vanished from its vocabulary. When speaking directly to workers, it continued to describe itself as the party of the working class. But, in its general publicity, it made its appeal to every social class as the 'Party of Anti-Fascism', or the 'Party of the Resistance'. It beat the big drum of patriotism as 'the party of French renaissance', declaring its aim to be the restoration of the *grandeur* of France.[2] It denounced its critics not only as enemies of the working class but also as enemies of the nation. It was an approach which paid dividends. The party conference held in June 1945 was able to announce a membership of 545,900, as compared with a membership of 335,705 for the Socialist party; and at the first elections to the National Assembly, in October 1945, it gained 5,005,000 votes as against the Socialists' 4,561,000.

Both parties were represented in the two successive governments which followed—the Provisional Government, set up in Algiers in April 1944, and the 'Government of National Unity' which General de Gaulle formed on 10 September 1944, two months after the liberation of Paris. For the first time in its history, the French Communist party participated in a coalition government with Socialist and capitalist parties.

Now Socialists and Communists were working together in government as they had previously worked together in the underground. It seemed to many that the fratricidal strife which had been the bane of the labour movement for so long was at last finished. The pressure grew to consummate the alliance by merging the two parties—an idea which had a particular appeal to thousands of active Socialists.

But many Socialist leaders, including Léon Blum and Daniel Mayer, viewed the proposal for organic unity with more scepticism. While they were concerned to avoid any recurrence of pre-war conflicts and to establish a good relationship with the Communists, their experience of co-operative work in the days of the Popular Front had left its scars. The Communists had campaigned with the Socialists for a Popular Front government. But when Blum formed such a government following the election victory in April 1936, the Communists chose to stand outside rather than to share responsibilities with their allies. They had thus been able to claim credit for the government's social reforms while attacking the unpopular measures

1. According to one conservative critic, 'Capitalism has received a splendid camouflage. Communism hardly dares to use its own name'—*Le Figaro*, 11 April 1945, quoted in Pickles, *France Between the Republics*, p. 19.
   2. Jacques Duclos (1896–1975), after Thorez the most prominent member of the party, appealed at the Congress of the National Front, which was dominated by the Communists, for the 'unity of all Frenchmen of good will, wherever they come from, prepared to work for the renaissance and greatness of France'—quoted in Werth, *France, 1940–1955*, p. 244.

adopted to deal with the economic crisis. In parliament they had voted for Blum's policy of non-intervention during the early stages of the Spanish Civil War, but then had denounced his 'betrayal of Spanish freedom' in the streets. It was hard for Socialists who had lived through these experiences to place much faith in Communist loyalty.[1]

The question of closer links between the two parties first arose during the second half of 1944 while Blum was still in a German concentration camp. When, at the beginning of that December, official discussions were held between representatives of each organization, they agreed to lay a foundation for unity by trying to create an 'atmosphere of mutual understanding and co-operation', and a *comité d'entente* was set up to co-ordinate activity. Yet, when the committee held its first meeting a few days later, the question of fusion was immediately revived by the Communists.

The question came up for decision at the August 1945 congress of the Socialist party. In the meantime, Blum had returned from prison camp with his prestige among party members standing higher than at any other time during his career. The reforms achieved by the Popular Front during his premiership were unforgotten, and all France had been moved by his memorable and dignified address to the special court at Riom in February 1942.[2] He had become a national hero overnight. We have already referred to his analysis of the crisis of Socialism and democracy, written during the early period of his imprisonment in 1941, which was to have such a profound influence over the development of Socialist ideology in France.

Blum was seventy-three when he returned from prison, broken in health but with his enthusiasm and his faith in the victory of Socialism stronger than ever. He even believed that the Socialist era had already begun, and in *À l'Échelle humaine* he wrote:

> Socialism is approaching its final victory. The system it has consistently opposed is crumbling in ruins, and, where it survives, has lost faith in itself. Men and parties who were among Socialism's most intransigent opponents are now adopting its views and principles. Whether deliberately or otherwise, society will be rebuilt on Socialist foundations.

He had been able to write in these terms in 1941 at the height of Nazi power in Europe, and it was in the same spirit that he proclaimed to the party congress after it had given him a rapturous welcome, 'Socialism is now in the ascendant: one day it will control the world.'

Two months before the Socialist congress the Communists had published in *L'Humanité*, their party organ, a 'Charter of Alliance' proposing the fusion

---

1. Julius Braunthal, *History of the International, 1914–1943*, pp. 435 and 438.
2. *Léon Blum before his Judges*, with an Introduction by Félix Gouin and a Foreword by Clement Attlee (London, 1943).

of the two parties into a *Parti Ouvrier Français* to be based on 'the dialectical materialism of Marx and Engels, as developed by Lenin and Stalin'. The objective of the party was to be 'the conquest of power by the working class', and its organization would be founded on 'the principles of democratic centralism' which had governed the original Bolshevik party, and by which the executive controlled the whole organization, including its parliamentary representatives and its press. And while it was prepared to recognize the prime need to popularize the 'great achievements of Socialism in the U.S.S.R. under the leadership of the Communist party of the Soviet Union', it would, according to the Charter, remain independent of all governments, even including that of the U.S.S.R.[1] What the Charter was proposing in principle was a virtual takeover of the Socialist party by the Communists.

The Charter was vigorously discussed at regional conferences of the Socialist party, and the executive decided to place it on the congress agenda.

Before the congress took place, however, Blum made his opposition to organic unity clear in a series of articles in *Le Populaire*. He claimed from the outset that there was no question of the Socialist party ever participating in any domestic anti-Communist alliance, nor would it ever support French membership of an anti-Soviet bloc. The party was, moreover, committed to joint action with the Communists in the struggle for a new social order and in the fight against domestic reaction. But, he maintained in his articles, and subsequently repeated in his speech to congress, organic unity was impossible until the differences existing between the two parties had been examined and eliminated.

During the congress Blum laid great stress on these differences. First, since Communist principles were incompatible with democracy they were also incompatible with ideals for which the Socialist Party had stood from its foundation. It was true, he agreed, that the Communists had kept to the Charter of the C.N.R. which had called for the restoration of all the democratic rights destroyed by the Vichy régime. But serious doubts still stood about the sincerity of the Communists' devotion to democracy. And as long as such doubts remained, he argued, any fusion of the two parties had to be seen as 'impossible'.

There was secondly, said Blum, the further and probably decisive consideration of the French Communist party being virtually under the domination of the Soviet Union. He reminded delegates of the party's *volte-face* over the war in September 1939. Certainly Thorez had fervently proclaimed his patriotism after his return from Moscow under de Gaulle's amnesty in November 1944. Certainly, also, the Communists had played a respected role in France's post-war rehabilitation. But Communist professions of loyalty to France had not in any way weakened the party's fundamental loyalty to

---

1. *L'Humanité*, 12 June 1945, quoted in Graham, *The French Socialists and Tripartisme*, pp. 97–8; see also Rieber, *Stalin and the French Communist Party*, pp. 212–14.

the Soviet Union. This might do no great harm so long as the interests of the Soviet Union and France coincided. But how might the Communists be expected to act in the event of a future conflict between the two? Would they not, Blum asked, automatically take the side of the Soviet Union against France? And what would they do in the event of future disagreements between Russia and the new Socialist International? To judge from past experience, and from what he knew of the Communist cast of mind, it seemed only too likely that, given such an eventuality, they would persist in their apparently unshakeable support for the Soviet Union whatever its actions. In such a situation a reunified workers' party would once again experience an agonizing split. A merger between the two parties was therefore, in Blum's view, out of the question while the intellectual and emotional bonds linking French Communism to the Soviet Union remained intact.[1]

Representatives of the Socialist party's left wing, speaking at the conference, objected that should unification not take place, then the Socialist party would find itself forced further and further towards the right, and that, under the existing electoral system, it would have to depend on right-wing and centre votes to get its candidates returned.[2] Moreover, the separate existence of two working-class parties could only weaken the left and increase the danger of reaction.

In the end, a resolution submitted by the conference resolution committee and supported by Jules Moch (b. 1893) was carried by 9,921 votes to 274. This stated that the unity of the labour movement was one of the Socialist party's prime objectives. But no merger with the Communist party could develop before a prolonged period of successful joint activity had had time to generate the necessary atmosphere of loyalty and mutual trust. At all events, there were certain conditions which would first have to be satisfied: a frank statement of the principles of the two parties, guarantees of democracy within the united party, an unambiguous commitment to democracy and to the need to defend it against enemies at home and abroad, and complete freedom from any special relationship with a foreign government. Since the Communist 'charter of unity' did not satisfy these conditions, it did not provide a basis for discussions which could lead to a merger. The congress was not, however, in any way opposed to working in conjunction with Communists. Therefore, as a first step, it authorized the executive to reach an agreement with the Communist leadership in the *comité d'entente* on co-

---

1. Léon Blum, *Le Problème de l'unité* (Paris, 1945).
2. Under French electoral law, a candidate must receive an absolute majority of the votes cast in order to be returned on the first ballot. In the event of a second ballot, the candidate is returned who obtains the largest number of votes. This system lends itself to the formation of electoral alliances between parties, who agree to withdraw after the first ballot in favour of whichever member of the bloc obtained the largest number of votes.

operation in the forthcoming election campaign, and, after the elections, to renew discussions on the continuation of joint activity.[1]

On 21 October 1945, two months after the Socialist congress, the elections to the Constituent Assembly took place. In June, at their tenth congress, the Communists had discussed their electoral programme. Maurice Thorez, who as we saw returned from Moscow in November 1944 and was back in France for the first time since his desertion from the army, delivered a speech which left no room for doubt that the Communists saw themselves as a government party and intended to remain so after the election. It was, however, a moderate speech, based on the party's acceptance of responsibility for the reconstruction of France, and it contained a thoroughly realistic approach to the problems of economic and foreign policy.[2] 'We are,' Thorez claimed, 'a party participating in government responsibility. Two of our members have seats in the government. Communists hold responsible posts in public administration, the army and industry. We control thousands of local authorities. . . . We must not lose sight of the weight of responsibility we carry for both party and nation.'[3] The tone of the passage was typical of Communist pronouncements at this time. 'Yesterday we were in opposition,' said Gaston Monmousseau, a brilliant Communist trade union leader, in a speech to a C.G.T. conference, 'and did not need to be too fussy in our choice of tactics. But now it is the big capitalist magnates who are in opposition while we hold responsible positions.'[4]

During this period the Communist party's actions were consistent with its fresh conception of its role. It threw enormous energy into restoring industrial production. During the hard winter of 1944–5, output fell to less than a third of its pre-war level and large numbers of workers found themselves in desperate straits.[5] The Communist trade unions, however, responded to the crisis by opposing the workers' demands for pay rises and insisted that production must first be increased. 'Only through work can we win the battle for democracy,' ran the slogan in huge letters across the hall in which the C.G.T. held its congress in 1946. 'The highest expression of our duty as a class is the development of production to the maximum,' one of the miners'

1. See Graham, *The French Socialists and Tripartisme*, pp. 98–101.
2. For the text, see Maurice Thorez, '*Une Politique française: renaissance, démocratie, unité*', in *Rapport au Xe Congrès du P.C.F.* (Paris, 1945).
3. ibid., p. 59.
4. *Vie ouvrière*, 28 March 1946, quoted in Lorwin, *The French Labor Movement*, p. 106.
5. Having suffered devastation during the course of the fighting, France had then been bled white during the ensuing occupation. 'Occupation costs' of 400 million francs a day were imposed on a country whose harbours, bridges and railways had been destroyed by the Germans, before being subjected to repeated bombing by the Allies and finally sabotaged by the resistance. By the end of the war, every bridge across the Seine and the Loire had been destroyed, while France had lost in all 1,900 railway bridges and 1,850 miles of track—see Matthews, *The Death of the Fourth Republic*, p. 178; Dorothy Pickles, *French Politics. The First Years of the Fourth Republic* (London, 1953), p. 48.

leaders declared at the congress. Another claimed that 'only the big capitalists want to hinder the development of production so as to sabotage the
reconstruction of our economy, increase the misery of the people and, on
the basis of the resulting discontent, replace our democratic government by
one which is reactionary'. The congress manifesto made the same point when
it said: 'The first duty is to increase production.'[1] And when, in January
1946, the printers of Paris came out on strike for more pay, they were
denounced in a broadcast by Ambroise Croizat, the Communist leader of the
metal-workers and minister of labour, while Monmousseau stated: 'It is no
accident that such a notorious Fascist organ as *L'Époque* [a Paris daily]
defends the right to strike at a time when production has become by far the
most crucial issue facing our people.' In similar vein, the theoretical journal
of the Communist party wrote:

> In the recent past we have seen manoeuvres designed to create splits in certain
> sections of the working class—manoeuvres which, needless to say, have been
> applauded by the worst type of reactionary. We have seen sinister elements setting
> out to provoke strikes through demagogic tactics. We have seen *agents provocateurs*
> trying to stir things up. . . .[2]

Talking to miners in July 1945, Thorez, himself an ex-miner, said: 'I tell
you frankly, comrades, speaking for the central committee and in accordance
with the decisions of our party—we cannot countenance the smallest strike,
particularly after it has actually broken out.'[3] And, indeed, there were no
significant strikes in France through 1945 and 1946.

Under the leadership of Maurice Thorez (1900–1964), the French Communists stuck to this policy as consistently and for as long as was practicable.
Naturally the party still aimed at achieving political power, but Thorez had
opposed the policy of seizing power by force which had been advocated by the
party's left wing, led by André Marty and Charles Tillon, at the moment when,
in September and October 1944, German power was collapsing and it seemed
as though the Communists might move swiftly into the vacuum created.[4]

The question became critical when de Gaulle's government ordered the

1. *C.G.T. Congrès, 1946, Compte rendu* . . . , pp. 52 and 373, quoted in Lorwin, *The
French Labor Movement*, p. 106.
2. *Cahiers du Communisme*, September 1946.
3. Quoted in Rieber, *Stalin and the French Communist Party*, p. 231.
4. 'A number of leading comrades,' according to a declaration by the party's central
committee in October 1952, 'believe that the workers should have seized power at the
moment of liberation.' That, the statement continued, 'would have been a serious error.
It would have ended in a bloody defeat and would have left the party isolated in France'—
L'Humanité, 4 October 1952. When, in December of that year, Marty and Tillon were
expelled from the party for opposing Thorez, it was alleged against them that their 1944
policies would have led to a catastrophic worsening in relations between the Soviet Union
and the West. Marty had also opposed the decision to dissolve the *Milices patriotiques*
and had gone on to criticize the Communist participation in the governments from 1944
to 1947, 'in the thoroughly irresponsible, romantic spirit of Blanqui, which was strongly
condemned by Marx as well as by Lenin'—quoted in Werth, *France, 1940–1955*, p. 588.

dissolution of the *milices patriotiques,* which were under Communist control, and the 'liberation committees'—equally dominated by the Communists—which had taken over in many towns and villages in the chaos following the German withdrawal. The militias had represented the party's armed wing, the 'liberation committees' its political instrument for taking over local administration. The Communists at first protested strongly against the decree. *L'Humanité* spoke of a virtual return to Pétainism. Jacques Duclos called for millions of recruits to the *milices* so as to prevent their dissolution and the two Communist ministers threatened to resign. Yet, in the end, the party took no action and allowed the militias to be dissolved. To the party's great surprise, Thorez on his return approved the dispersal of militias and liberation committees. De Gaulle, he said, had acted correctly. Thorez was convinced that they would attain power by legal and constitutional means, particularly if they succeeded in infiltrating and absorbing the Socialist party, as had in effect been done with the C.G.T. The policy of merging the two parties thus became of supreme importance in the Communist party's overall strategy.

The Communists emerged from the election of 21 October 1945 as the strongest individual party, with five million votes (26 per cent of the total) and 161 seats in the Constituent Assembly. Next came the Socialist party, with over four and a half million votes (24 per cent of the total) and 150 seats. The two parties together held an overall majority of 311 out of 586 seats.

The third party of the left, the Catholic *Mouvement Républicain Populaire* (M.R.P.), which polled about the same number of votes and obtained the same number of seats as the Socialists, had been formed only in January 1944, at Lyons, the centre of the Catholic underground, through the merging of several Catholic organizations. By August 1944 it had a membership of 100,000.[1] It had campaigned on a moderate Socialist programme and declared its support for the C.N.R. charter.[2] Among its active members it could count on a large number of genuine Christian Socialists and left-wing democrats. But the bulk of its four and a half million voters were conservative; finding their previous leadership compromised through collaboration with Vichy, they turned to the M.R.P. as the one substantial non-Marxist force in politics and a potential bulwark against Communism.

But one decisive influence over the M.R.P.'s character, and it was a factor which tended to direct it towards the left, was its close association with the Catholic trade union movement, the *Confédération Française des*

1. See Gordon Wright, *The Reshaping of French Democracy* (London, 1950), p. 76.
2. The M.R.P. programme included a passage which read: 'An economic and social democracy . . . must ensure the participation of the workers in leading posts in the economy through the strengthening of the trade union movement, participation in control at the place of work and profit-sharing.' It declared itself unambiguously in favour of the nationalization of enterprises, 'in both the management and profits of which employees will participate'—*Feuilleton de l'Assemblée Nationale,* 29 November 1945.

Travailleurs Chrétiens (C.F.T.C.). From having unkindly been dubbed 'a crowd of choir-boys' in 1919, with a mere 150,000 members as late as 1936 (compared with over five million in the C.G.T.), this had grown by 1945 into a mass movement with some three-quarters of a million members.[1] It had held back from joining the Popular Front in 1935 but when in 1940, despite its being 'unsullied by Marxism', the Vichy government dissolved it together with the C.G.T., the two organizations co-operated in illegal actions. In occupied Paris, nine leading members of the C.G.T. and three from the C.F.T.C. had produced a joint 'Manifesto of the Twelve' protesting against the withdrawal of 'the inalienable right' of the workers to organize freely, and, at the same time, to lay down as a principle common to both organizations: 'The French workers' movement cannot tolerate anti-Semitism, religious persecution, violation of the freedom of thought and the confiscation of personal property on any pretext or in any circumstances.'[2]

From this joint publication stemmed co-operation between the two federations in the resistance, and when, in August 1944, the Allied armies, having broken through the German front and advanced swiftly across France, began to approach Paris, the C.G.T. and C.F.T.C. issued a joint call for a general strike. 'Brothers in factories and farms,' it ran, 'unite . . . to win back our lost freedom.'[3]

The C.F.T.C.'s attitude under the occupation conflicted sharply with that of the Catholic hierarchy, which not only supported Pétain's régime as the *de facto* legal authority, but had even gone out of its way to sing its praises as a gift of Providence. Many priests who had performed years of work in the Catholic trade unions turned propagandist for the 'Christian social order' which Fascism had introduced into France.[4] The leading Catholic paper, *La Croix*, appointed itself as the political voice of Vichy. It glorified Pétain as a 'redeemer' who had rescued France from the evils of anti-clericalism, freemasonry and democracy.

Following the Liberation, the C.F.T.C. had every intention of maintaining its working alliance with the C.G.T., though without wishing in the least to fall in with the Communist proposal for a merger. This, in the C.F.T.C.'s view, was out of the question in the light 'of the very great differences in the principles and policies' existing between the two organizations.[5]

For the first time in French history, the country's predominantly petty-bourgeois agrarian electorate had given the Communists and Socialists a

1. See Lorwin, *The French Labor Movement*, p. 101; for the relation of the C.F.T.C. to the M.R.P., see ibid., pp. 294–8.
2. Quoted in Lorwin, *The French Labor Movement*, p. 91.
3. *L'Humanité*, 21 August 1944.
4. See Ehrmann, *French Labor*, p. 265. See also Novick, *The Resistance versus Vichy*, pp. 130–1.
5. Rieber, *Stalin and the French Communist Party*, pp. 224–6.

clear majority.[1] More than anything else, this bore witness to the depth of the crisis in French society, in both towns and villages, which had resulted from defeat and occupation. The electorate was expressing an overwhelming desire by French people to see a new France, and not merely a restoration of the democracy they had experienced under the Third Republic. They longed not only for political freedom, but also for social justice, and they were inspired by the prospect of a Socialist France.

After the Liberation, however, neither the Socialists nor the Communists took up the slogan that had been popularized by the militant underground paper *Combat* under Albert Camus's editorship: 'From Resistance to Revolution!' The Socialist and Communist parties alike visualized a complete transformation of the economic and social system, but, in the words of the Communist slogan, it was to be a 'revolution based on law' and carried through entirely by constitutional means.[2] Nothing was further from the minds of the Communists than to precipitate a civil war. The unity of the French nation, for which they had striven during the heroic years of underground struggle, was to be preserved. And while the Socialist and Communist parties enjoyed a small overall majority in parliament, neither wished to exclude non-Socialist parties from the government. The Communists hoped for a coalition with the Socialists as well as the Radical Socialists, a republican, anti-clerical party which had represented the middle-class element in the Popular Front government, although its representation in the chamber had now dropped to twenty-five. The Socialist party, on the other hand, while naturally desiring a coalition with the Communists, also wanted one with the M.R.P., whose trade union wing appeared as a useful source of support for carrying through social reforms, and particularly because a coalition extending to the M.R.P. would be founded on a broader social basis and thus ensure

1. In the local elections, held six months earlier on 29 April and 6 May 1945, the Socialists and Communists either separately or jointly had won a majority in half of the 957 communes of France with over 4,000 inhabitants. They had also won majorities in a number of smaller communes. Altogether, the Socialists had control of more than 4,000 local authorities compared with 1,400 before the war, while the Communists controlled 1,400 against a pre-war total of 300. The tremendous increase in the influence of both parties was reflected in the increase in the numbers of their respective newspapers and their circulations. The number of Socialist newspapers grew from ten in 1939 to twenty-five in 1944, and their share of total circulation from 6·2 to 21 per cent; the number of Communist newspapers increased in the same period from three to thirty-one, and their share of total newspaper circulation from 5·2 to 26·8 per cent—see Jean Mottin, *Histoire politique de la presse: 1944–1949* (Paris, 1949), p. 143. In 1939, the Radicals and the parties of the right controlled newspapers with 46·2 per cent of the total newspaper circulation; the Socialist and Communist press combined accounted for only 11·4 per cent of the total readership. In 1944, the share of the Radicals and the right dropped to 12·7 per cent; the Socialists' and the Communists' share rose to 47·8 per cent; see Novick, *The Resistance versus Vichy*, p. 118.

2. Marty was highly critical of the party leadership on this point. He considered it to have 'adopted a Social Democratic position, aiming at the peaceful and painless transition from capitalism to Socialism'—André Marty, *L'Affaire Marty* (Paris, 1955), p. 248, quoted in Rieber, *Stalin and the French Communist Party*, p. 166.

greater stability in government. The Communists were prepared to accept this. They voted for a Socialist, Félix Gouin, to be President of the chamber even though, as the largest party, they could have claimed the post for their own nominee. General de Gaulle was also elected 'Head of State' with the aid of Communist votes in the Constituent Assembly.

The coalition formed by de Gaulle—with Auriol and Thorez as vice-premiers—was made up of the three great parties of the left: Communist, Socialist and M.R.P., and these, between them, held nearly 80 per cent of the seats in the chamber. The government was faced with two main tasks: to carry out the reform programme contained in the Charter which intended to pave the way for Socialism in France; and to draft a new constitution, which was to be approved by referendum.

The three government parties therefore constituted a left-wing bloc within the chamber. Their overwhelming majority meant that they encountered hardly any resistance. Mines, electricity, gas, the merchant navy, air transport, the Bank of France and the other four leading banks together with thirty-four of the largest insurance companies were all nationalized, while the great automobile firm of Louis Renault, who had collaborated with the Nazis, was taken over without compensation. The social security system was reorganized, works councils were made compulsory by law in large companies and a National Economic Council for the planned reconstruction of France was set up in co-operation with the two trade union federations.[1]

The new constitution presented more formidable problems. The draft, having been approved by the three government parties after prolonged discussion, was opposed by General de Gaulle.

De Gaulle's whole cast of political mind was aristocratic. He had rebelled against the government of Pétain when it capitulated to Hitler and he sought to arouse the spirit of France against the disgrace of capitulation to foreign rule. He felt himself to embody in his own person a renaissance which would restore to France all her former greatness and glory. But the new France, as he saw it, could not be a democratic republic with a government responsible to a parliamentary majority. He envisaged instead a constitution which granted full power to the Head of State independent of parliament, which was thus to be relegated to a largely advisory role. In such a system, the Head of State would derive his authority from the people by direct election—not indirectly from a parliamentary majority.

Such an authoritarian constitution was, as a matter of course, rejected by all three of the left-wing parties.[2] They insisted on a fully sovereign chamber

1. Pickles, *French Politics*, pp. 52–4; Lorwin, *The French Labor Movement*, pp. 102–5.
2. There were also considerable differences between Socialists, Communists and the M.R.P. over the draft constitution. For the Socialist point of view, see Graham, *The French Socialists and Tripartisme*, pp. 74–87 and 131–7; for Communist policy, see Rieber, *Stalin and the French Communist Party*, pp. 270–3, 284–9, and 297–9.

with the President of the Republic elected by parliament. De Gaulle, having failed to impose his will on the majority of the chamber, resigned as Head of State on 20 January 1946.

A new government then had to be formed, and the Communist party proposed a Socialist–Communist coalition under its leadership. The Socialists, however, insisted on the participation of the M.R.P. There were immense problems of economic reconstruction that needed to be solved if the country was to recover from its war-time devastation, and the Socialists did not wish to share this responsibility with the Communists alone. Consequently the government of the left was re-formed with Gouin as prime minister, while Thorez retained his post as one of the two vice-premiers.

The Constituent Assembly had completed its task once it had agreed on the draft of a new constitution. But, in the referendum held on 5 May 1946, the draft was rejected by 10,500,000 to 9,000,000 votes and a second Constituent Assembly had to be elected. At these elections, held on 2 June, the Communists improved their position by adding another 150,000 votes to their previous total, bringing their poll to 5,154,000; the Socialist vote fell to 4,199,000. But, on this occasion, the M.R.P. emerged as the strongest single party, having won nearly 5,500,000 votes—an increase of 900,000.

The second draft proved more acceptable and received a majority of votes by referendum, after which the first parliament of the Fourth Republic could be elected.[1] The Communists increased their vote by a further 300,000 while the Socialists lost almost another 700,000 votes and the M.R.P. vote dropped by 600,000. Once again the Communists were the strongest party in the Chamber, with 183 deputies compared to the Socialists' 105 and the M.R.P.'s 167.

Three days after the election, the Communist party officially demanded that it should lead the next government, putting forward Maurice Thorez's nomination for the prime ministership. The prospect of a French government actually being led by Communists provoked great alarm among businessmen in Britain as well as in France. Thorez, giving an interview to *The Times* of London, went to great pains to reassure the capitalist world. He stated that his party had no intention of setting up a proletarian dictatorship.

It is clear [he said] that the Communist party, as a member of the government working within the framework of a parliamentary system which it has itself helped to establish, must adhere strictly to the democratic programme by which it has won the support of the mass of the people. Despite rare exceptions which confirm the

1. For a full analysis of the constitution, see O. R. Taylor, *The Fourth Republic of France* (London, 1951), pp. 18–76. For the text of the constitution, with appendices, see Philip Williams, *Politics in Post-War France. Parties and the Constitution in the Fourth Republic* (second edition, London, 1958), pp. 423–36. For the position of the various parties during the discussion, see Pickles, *French Politics*, pp. 37–46.

rule, the progress of democracy throughout the world . . . permits us, in the march of Socialism, to foresee other roads than those travelled by the Russian Communists. In any case, the road is necessarily different for each country.[1]

Meanwhile, the M.R.P. had nominated its own leader, Georges Bidault, for the post of prime minister. The Socialists, who remained allied to both the M.R.P. and the Communists in the Assembly, decided to vote for Thorez. But since neither Thorez nor Bidault received the necessary majority, it fell to Blum to form a purely Socialist government with the support of the other two parties. He announced that, as soon as a President of the Republic was elected, he would hand in his resignation.

The election of the first President of the Fourth Republic took place on 16 January 1947, a month after the formation of Blum's caretaker government. The Socialists had nominated Vincent Auriol (1884–1966), one of the party's old guard, who had been secretary of the parliamentary party, finance minister in the pre-war Popular Front government and a vice-premier in de Gaulle's post-war administration. A joint session of both chambers, meeting in Versailles, elected him by an absolute majority which included the votes of the Communist deputies.

His first task was to form a new cabinet as soon as Blum, who was now nearly seventy-five, had announced his resignation. Auriol selected another Socialist, Paul Ramadier (1888–1961), to form a government, which, on the insistence of the Socialists themselves, was again to consist of a coalition of the three parties of the left: Socialists, Communists and the M.R.P.—an arrangement that was termed 'Tripartism'.

The system of Tripartism, by which France had been governed since the end of the war, apart from the brief period of Blum's caretaker government, was reinstated by Ramadier. But it broke down after only five months. It had proved unduly costly to the Socialist party, which during the year following the elections of October 1945 lost nearly a million votes—half to the Communists, half to the M.R.P. In fact it got the worst of both worlds, for while its own left wing distrusted the M.R.P. its more bourgeois supporters were terrified by the Communist alliance. One group of its supporters found it too conciliatory; the other too revolutionary.

Yet, even though the coalition system was involving them in costly concessions to both the Communists and the M.R.P., the Socialists saw the maintenance of a stable government of the Left in office as an essential alternative to de Gaulle's return. In no respect had the general renounced his political ambitions, and a dangerous assortment of reactionaries and

1. *The Times*, 18 November 1946. Thorez confirmed this view as late as November 1960 in a speech to the Conference of the Eighty-one Communist and Workers' parties in Moscow, quoting his statement of November 1946. For the text of his speech, see Alexander Dallin (ed.), *Diversity in International Communism. A Documentary Record, 1961–1963* (New York and London, 1963), p. 837.

nationalists had rallied to his side. The Socialists considered that the sacrifices which Tripartism involved were justified to counter this threat, and they paid the price by a considerable loss of popularity. Commenting on the drop in the Socialist vote, Blum claimed that 'the electorate held us, and us alone, responsible for the three-party coalition and blamed us for all the difficulties inherent in the situation'.[1]

For the success of Tripartism, the Socialists had had to presuppose that there would be no lack of loyalty from the Communists, with whom they had established particularly close relations. The *comité d'entente*, formed by the two parties in December 1944, had, it was hoped, been created to prepare the way for a united party of the working class. The committee had met regularly for over a year and had sponsored a certain amount of joint activity. But it had not succeeded in its main task of establishing an atmosphere of mutual trust. Disagreements within the committee had grown, and during the elections of October 1945 there had been public disputes, including mutual attacks in the press.

The Communists sat in the government and in theory shared responsibility for its policies. But as a party they did not consider themselves as bound to support the government outside the chamber. To the public at large, they often appeared to be the most vigorous section of the opposition. As a government party, for example, the Communists were committed to a policy of wage stabilization as part of the struggle to check inflation, and at one stage Benoît Frachon, the C.G.T. general secretary, gave his official support. In April 1946, he even went so far as to denounce as 'traitors' those who were 'demanding that wages be linked to prices on a sliding scale, a policy calculated to undermine France's economic recovery'. But scarcely a month later, during the election campaign of June 1946, the Communist-controlled C.G.T. demanded a general wage increase of 25 per cent with the full backing of the Communist party.[2] By such methods the Communists managed to increase their vote by another 150,000. 'Their attitude in Cabinet discussions,' said André Philip (b. 1902), finance minister in the coalition government in a speech to the Lyons congress of the Socialist party at the end of August 1946, 'is governed entirely by electoral considerations. They table demagogic proposals which are sure to be rejected by their colleagues so as to provide themselves with ammunition for subsequent use against those same colleagues.' Co-operation with the Communists was extremely difficult, he added, since they seemed to lack the necessary minimum of intellectual honesty.[3] In fact the congress had already come to the conclusion that any attempt to find a basis for fusion with the Communists into a single party would be a waste of time.

1. *Le Populaire*, 4 June 1946.   2. Pickles, *French Politics*, p. 26.
3. *Le Populaire*, 2 September 1946; quoted in ibid., p. 25; see also Lorwin, *The French Labor Movement*, pp. 114–15.

However, the question of relations with the Communist party was now only part of a much wider problem concerned with the future of the coalition of the left, and, more immediately, with whether the Socialist party could remain in coalition with the M.R.P.[1] The growing strength of the conservative section within the M.R.P., which opposed further social reform, made the continuation of Tripartism of very doubtful value to the working class. It had already forced the Socialists to make compromises which had alienated large numbers of workers and driven them into the arms of the Communists. Follcwing the loss of votes in the elections of October 1945 and June 1946, the Socialist left wing, led by Guy Mollet (1905–75), called on the party to leave the government and to go into opposition with a clear Socialist programme. Guy Mollet, with his distinguished record as a fighter in the resistance, represented the Pas de Calais—the party's strongest federation (he was also mayor of Arras, eternally associated in French history with Robespierre). His uncompromising advocacy of a strong, Marxist line created a powerful impression at the congress. Daniel Mayer pleaded in vain that, failing the participation of the Socialist party, there could be no stable democratic government in France; that, if the Socialists returned to opposition, one of the main pillars of the Fourth Republic would be broken and the way laid open for de Gaulle and the reactionary authoritarianism which he represented. Mayer, Blum's closest associate, was defeated as general secretary, and Mollet was elected in his place.

This change in the Socialist party leadership did not have any immediate effect on its position in the coalition. There still seemed to be no escape from its basic dilemma. It remained reluctant to staunch the flow of voters to the Communists by resigning and so to risk handing the Republic over to a government of the right. It seemed that it must remain within the government, if only to block de Gaulle's return to power. Consequently Guy Mollet, after his election to the general secretaryship of his party, joined Blum's government as a vice-premier; and after Blum's resignation, Ramadier, with the approval of the party's executive, undertook to revert to a coalition policy.

Similar pressures were mounting within the Communist party to put a finish to the coalition. It was true that, in many ways, the system of Tripartism had paid off handsomely. The party had gained votes at each election and won positions of considerable state influence. Several key positions in the administration of the nationalized industries had been filled by Communists, and there were Communist ministers of mines and aviation. But it had been prevented from holding the key positions of power in the state: the ministries of interior and defence. It was the strongest party in the Chamber, representing over a quarter of the electorate and an overwhelming majority of wage-

1. For the congress debate on Tripartism, see Graham, *The French Socialists and Tripartisme*, pp. 197–219.

earners. But by this stage a point had been reached where continued participation in government with the clerical M.R.P., which was capable of blocking any further concessions to the working class, was endangering the Communist party's popularity as a party of the left. In its public pronouncements it had never hesitated to dissociate itself from unpopular government measures, but the Socialists had always been there to remind it that its members continued to form part of the government. The Communist party wished to attain state power but once the attempt to build a united party with the Socialists had failed there was no further hope for them of obtaining power through parliament. André Marty, one of the leaders of the Communist old guard, urged the party to withdraw from the government and commence a struggle for power by extra-parliamentary methods. But in the light of the threat to the Republic posed by de Gaulle, the executive decided in favour of continued participation. 'When the Republic is in danger,' said Jacques Duclos, 'it is better for us to be in than out.'[1]

The threat represented by de Gaulle was real enough. He had declared himself to be a contender for power and, at a speech made at Bruneval in Normandy on 29 March 1947, he made it clear that he intended to replace the parliamentary system of the Fourth Republic with an authoritarian régime based on presidential power. A fortnight later, on 7 April, he launched the *Rassemblement du Peuple Français* (R.P.F.) at a meeting in Strasbourg to which hundreds of thousands rallied. Members of the middle classes and small shopkeepers flocked to the party in great numbers, and more than 800,000 were enrolled during its first few weeks.[2] Within scarcely six months the R.P.F. was winning nearly 38 per cent of the votes in the local elections and securing majorities in thirteen of the largest towns.

Yet even in the face of the threat posed by de Gaulle and his massive following in the country, the three parties of the left coalition remained deeply divided. Towards the end of April 1947, a government crisis was sparked off by a strike for higher wages by engineers in a number of departments in the nationalized Renault car works. At first it was denounced by the C.G.T. as a wild-cat strike. Benoît Frachon (b. 1893), the Communist general secretary of the C.G.T., condemned it outright, while the Communist secretary of the Paris section of the C.G.T. referred to the strike leaders as 'Hitlerites and Trotskyists in the pay of de Gaulle'.[3] But as soon as the strike spread to all the 30,000 employees in the vast concern, the C.G.T., with full Communist party support, placed itself at the head of the movement. Indeed, it had little alternative since the metal-workers' union was the most powerful of the

1. Quoted in Werth, *France, 1940–1955*, p. 352.
2. Taylor, *The Fourth Republic of France*, p. 100.
3. Pickles, *French Politics*, p. 77. According to *L'Humanité*, the strike was 'led by a handful of Trotskyists who had succeeded in pulling out 1,500 of the 30,000 workers'— *L'Humanité*, 27–8 April 1947.

C.G.T.'s federations while the Renault works represented a Communist stronghold.

This strike, occurring as it did in one of the largest nationalized industries, carried clear political implications, because it placed the government's entire economic policy in jeopardy. During the months preceding Blum's entry into the government in the middle of 1946, inflation, which had been a problem in France even before the outbreak of war, had increased rapidly. Prices had risen by 50 per cent in six months; higher living costs provoked claims for higher wages which raised costs and hence prices. To break the vicious spiral, Blum's government had, as a temporary measure, decreed a general price reduction of 5 per cent, accompanied by a wages standstill agreed to by the C.G.T. Ramadier's government continued this policy and on the assumption that wages would remain stabilized, ordered a further price reduction of 5 per cent. The Renault strike cut across this policy by attempting to force the government to violate its own wage freeze in a nationalized industry.

When the strike was debated in the chamber, the Communists, who now fully supported the strike, argued that it was not necessary for wage increases to be followed by price increases if they were paid for out of profits. The Communists also made it clear that they no longer felt bound to support the government's incomes and prices policy.

A second occasion was to arise within a few weeks to bring the Communists into conflict with Ramadier. In French Indo-China a war of national independence had broken out in February, and at the end of March an uprising took place in another French colony, Madagascar, which ended in widespread and merciless slaughter by French colonial troops. The Communist cabinet members had threatened to resign, and had made it clear that Communist deputies no longer felt committed to voting for the government's colonial policy. Then, on 4 May, when the chamber held a debate on incomes and prices policy and the Communists emerged openly to oppose government policy, Ramadier asked the House for a vote of confidence; whereupon the Communist members, including the ministers, voted against the government.

It would have seemed logical in these circumstances for the Communist ministers to resign from the government, but they did nothing of the sort and had to be relieved of office by Ramadier on the following day.[1] This was the end of Tripartism, and 5 May 1947 became a landmark in the history of

1. For a description of the government crisis, see Taylor, *The Fourth Republic of France*, pp. 162–4. On the day when the Communist ministers were dismissed, the National Council of the Socialist party met and Guy Mollet proposed that the Ramadier government should be forced to resign. He argued that the left-wing and working-class pressure which had forced the Communists to break with Ramadier must operate equally on the Socialist party. But Blum and Ramadier urged the need to continue the coalition under Socialist leadership in view of the threat of Gaullism. Blum's resolution was carried by a narrow majority (2,529 votes to 2,125).

the Fourth Republic as the day on which the Communists, as the largest party in the Republic, were excluded from an active share in the government of France.

A number of historians have seen these events as a victory for the Fourth Republic in the 'struggle for Prague',[1] as though the French Communists, like their Czech counterparts, had hoped to win control by infiltrating the state apparatus and awaiting a favourable opportunity to seize power. However, this view is very difficult to reconcile with the actual behaviour of the party at the time. No evidence exists to show that the leaders of the French Communist party were thinking in terms of violent revolution. While their followers did hold prominent posts in the state apparatus, the party had kept strictly to legal methods, whatever its motives.[2] At the time when the Vichy régime was collapsing into chaos, a genuinely revolutionary situation had existed in France. The state machine had ceased to function, production had ceased, the country, devastated by war, had faced the threat of famine and the workers were in a mood of revolutionary ferment. In this confused situation the Communists had held important bases of power. They had their armed militia units, and through the liberation committees were in control of local government in a number of towns. They had objected to the dissolution of the militia units, but had offered no armed resistance when the government insisted.[3]

In fact the policies of the party were concerned not so much to foment revolutionary situations as to prevent them from arising in the first place. It was the driving force for the reconstruction of French industry immediately after the war. As late as December 1946, the Communist party had stated its belief in a democratic road to Socialism.

The great advances made by democracy throughout the world (despite certain exceptions which tend only to confirm the general trend) [said an article in its theoretical journal] allow us to envisage other paths to Socialism than that trodden by the Russians. In any case, each country has its own route. We have always believed and stated that the French people, enriched by their unique and glorious traditions, will find their own means of building on our past achievements a society with ever-widening democratic rights, progress and social justice—though history shows that progress is always won as a result of conflict. . . .[4]

1. e.g. Williams, *Politics in Post-War France*, p. 20, and Rieber, *Stalin and the French Communist Party*, p. 354.
2. 'Though the Communists were fond of condemning revisionism verbally and laying great stress on their party's revolutionary traditions, they made full use of the legal, parliamentary and constitutional means of gaining power'—Rieber, p. 361.
3. Documents which some historians have used, and which purport to show that the Communists were planning a violent seizure of power, are, as Rieber has shown, forgeries. He acknowledges that some local organizations of the party contained leftists who, defying instructions from the centre, printed and distributed calls for revolution. But 'not even the most painstaking scholar or the most intransigent of the party could quote more than one or two such documents'—ibid., p. 151.
4. *Cahiers du bolchévisme*, December 1946, quoted in Borkenau, *European Communism*, p. 447.

Even after the Communists had voted against Ramadier in the vote of confidence on 4 May, and had taken up a position of 'constructive opposition', Duclos stated that they would persist in their previous policy and would continue to struggle for higher production and against industrial conflicts. 'While we are no longer in the government,' he said, 'we are still a government party.'[1]

Nevertheless, another major strike occurred within a few weeks. At the end of May, 80,000 dockers, gas and electricity workers came out on strike and in June they were joined by the railwaymen, miners, Paris bakery workers, bank employees and other workers.[2] Ramadier described the strike wave, as it spread from industry to industry, as an 'orchestra with a hidden conductor' whose object was clearly 'to undermine the authority of the government'.[3]

In fact the services of a 'hidden conductor' were scarcely necessary to bring the workers out on strike. They had suffered untold hardships during the war and the early post-war years. The policy of wage and price restraint which Blum had introduced, though generally welcomed at the outset, had begun to founder. In April, prices again began to rise, and in May the bread ration was cut. In the end, the strikes broke out as the spontaneous result of a cumulative resentment that had been building up over a long period. Though the Communists supported the strike movement once it had broken out, they had done nothing to incite it. The strike movement had no political objectives; its demands were purely industrial and, as it happened, its duration was short-lived. It ended as soon as the unions reached an agreement with the government on a revised scale of minimum wages.

Until the autumn of 1947 the Communists continued to avoid any serious conflict with government or state. They intended to proceed with their role of a thoroughly national party, a 'party of the French renaissance'. And, having been forced out of the government, their first objective was to get back in again.

In November 1947, however, Communist tactics underwent a drastic change. The party unleashed a strike movement on a massive scale that was clearly aimed at paralysing the French economy. It began following an incident in Marseilles. De Gaulle's R.P.F. had just supplanted the Communists as the majority party in the town's council chamber, and when the new local administration pushed up tram fares as one of its first acts, the Communist party called a protest demonstration in front of the town hall where four youths were arrested. A few days later, demonstrators stormed

1. Pickles, *French Politics*, p. 78; Matthews, *The Death of the Fourth Republic*, p. 245.
2. The strike wave during May and June 1947 caused the loss of 6,416,000 working days, or twenty times the loss during the whole of 1946—see Lorwin, *The French Labor Movement*, p. 118.
3. Quoted in Pickles, *French Politics*, p. 78.

the court, freed two of the prisoners, broke into the offices of the public prosecutor and destroyed the prosecution files. Simultaneously there were severe clashes between Communists and Gaullists, and as a result of these one Communist was killed. The Communists retaliated by calling a strike. Forty thousand workers stopped work, troops were called out and Marseilles seemed poised on the brink of civil war.

While the strike in the south was still in progress, in the north miners in the *départements* Nord and Pas-de-Calais came out in protest against the dismissal of an official who had refused to raise the price of coal after the ministry had instructed him to do so. The resulting strike was supported by stoppages in other Communist-controlled unions, metal workers, railwaymen, building workers, dockers, gas workers—a movement which, according to a C.G.T. estimate, embraced three million workers.[1] This movement also stemmed from genuine economic grievances. Rising prices had reduced the level of real wages. The C.G.T. demanded a rise of 25 per cent, and entrusted leadership of the strike movement to a national strike committee led by Communist trade union leaders.

In opposition to the Communist-controlled C.G.T. the Socialists and the unions which were under their influence organized a movement through the weekly journal *Force Ouvrière* (Workers' Force), led by Léon Jouhaux. This group also demanded higher wages, but it criticized the Communists for subordinating an industrial movement to political ends and refused to recognize the national strike committee. When the committee rejected concessions offered by Daniel Mayer, the Socialist minister of labour, and refused to accept them even as a basis for discussion, the non-Communist unions ordered their members back to work.

The movement now degenerated into bitter three-way strife between strikers and non-strikers on the one hand and strikers and the state authorities on the other. The Communists occupied factories, railway stations and mines to prevent the resumption of work, and troops were called in to clear occupied premises. In the mining areas striking miners clashed with troops in heavy fighting; street battles were fought in Lyons when about 1,000 Communists tried to storm the central police station; the Paris–Lille express was derailed by sabotage and twenty lives were lost. At the end of November, the government counteracted by introducing an emergency Bill which imposed heavier sentences for acts of sabotage for a limited period; at the same time it called up 80,000 reservists. By early December the strikers' determination was exhausted and two-thirds of them had returned to work. On 9 December the national strike committee called off the strike; in order, it said, 'to gather our strength for the hard struggles which lie ahead'.[2]

By comparison with what it had been during the immediate post-war period, the Communists' strategy had obviously undergone a drastic change.

1. *Le Peuple*, 13 December 1947.   2. *Le Peuple*, 13 December 1947.

The strike movement which they had set in motion was not primarily concerned with wage demands. The conflict had broken out initially in Marseilles with a general strike accompanied by street fighting following the arrest of four young men. In the mining areas of the Pas-de-Calais, the general strike had been called as the result of the dismissal of a Communist official. Such comparatively minor incidents could not, in normal times, have been claimed as justifying a nation-wide upheaval on such a scale. Nor, if the movement had been mainly for higher wages, would the national strike committee have dismissed so peremptorily the concessions offered by the government; it would at least have been prepared to use them as a basis for discussion. The Communists were now, it seemed, ready to undermine the French national economy, and to this end to prolong strikes as far as was possible.

Despite the defeat of the strike movement, the Communists considered that a 'positive result' had been attained by the opening of a rift between workers and government as well as between workers and the Socialist party. 'The brutality of the government,' wrote Benoît Frachon, 'and the reactionary attitude of the Socialist leadership ... have both done much to open the eyes of the workers. ...'[1] It had therefore been one of the objectives of the strike movement to discredit the Socialist-led coalition and to 'expose' the Socialist party.

Following the Liberation, the Communist party of France had assiduously courted the Socialist party, treating it as a 'fraternal party' with which it wished to establish the closest possible relationship. Now the Socialist party was being unequivocally classified as an enemy. It is a change that can only be understood in the light of the Soviet Union's foreign policy and the growing rift between Russia and the Western Allies, particularly with the United States. The beginnings of what was to be known to history as the 'Cold War' had destroyed the chances of working-class unity, not only in France but also throughout Europe.

But before examining the reasons behind this wider conflict and the subsequent developments in East–West relations, it may be as well to look at the relations existing between the working-class parties in two other major European countries—Italy and Germany.

1. Benoît Frachon, '*Une Étappe de la lutte des classes en France: Les grandes grèves de novembre–décembre 1947*', in *Cahiers du Communisme*, January 1948, quoted in Lorwin, *The French Labor Movement*, p. 125.

3 · Unity and Division in the Italian Socialist Movement

By the time Socialism had been forced underground in Italy in 1925 after enduring four years of Fascist persecution, it was already split in three directions. Increasingly intensive attacks by the Fascist authorities had brought about its fragmentation. A number of heroic individuals had maintained a degree of organization within small units to keep up the apparently hopeless struggle against repression, but their leaders, threatened with imprisonment and death, had fled abroad one by one—Togliatti to Moscow; Modigliani, Treves, Nenni, Saragat, and eventually Turati, to Paris—overwhelmed by the débâcle which had destroyed their formerly powerful movement. In 1921 the Socialists had made up the strongest parliamentary group, with several hundreds of thousands of members, and membership of Socialist-led unions ran into millions. The party controlled the civil administrations in Milan, Bologna and Turin as well as almost half the municipal authorities in Italy. It had seemed to stand on the brink of power. Yet within four years its organization lay in ruins.

The reason behind such a dramatic reversal of fortune was all too obviously the three-way split in the Socialist movement—first by the formation of the Communist party in January 1921, and then by the expulsion of the reformist wing, led by Turati, in October 1922. These breakaways to left and right left the movement defenceless in the face of a Fascist offensive.[1]

However, after such a disaster the disagreements over ideology and tactics which had been the cause of the schism became insignificant when, under conditions of exile, the task was clearly to mobilize all anti-Fascist forces in the struggle against the régime in Italy. As a result, in 1927, the two

1. For the history of the split and the consequent defeat, see Braunthal, *History of the International, 1914–1943*, pp. 208–13. The split stemmed from the ideology of the Socialist party, which was close enough to Bolshevism to advocate a revolutionary struggle for power culminating in the 'dictatorship of the proletariat'. Italian Socialism, therefore, made no attempt to co-operate with non-Socialist democratic forces in the defence of parliamentary democracy threatened by the rise of Fascism.

Socialist parties, the revolutionary 'Maximalists' (*Partito Socialista Massimalista*) and Turati's reformist followers (*Partito Socialista Unitario*) joined forces with the émigré leaders of the trade union federation (*Confederazione Generale del Lavoro*) and the middle-class radical Republican party at a congress in Nérac to form the *Concentrazione Antifascista*, a broadly-based anti-Fascist coalition which published from Paris the weekly *Libertà*, edited by Claudio Treves (1869–1933), a close friend of Turati.

Another group which shortly joined the *Concentrazione* was the émigré *Giustizia e Libertà* ('Justice and Freedom'), founded by Carlo Rosselli (1899–1937) in 1929. Rosselli was an unusually gifted and dedicated anti-Fascist revolutionary who, in 1927, together with Ferruccio Parri—subsequently a prime minister in post-Fascist Italy—had got Turati out of Italy in a motor-launch, taking him from Savona to Corsica. For this action a Fascist court had, after he had made a courageous speech, sentenced him to incarceration in the concentration camp on the island of Lipari. Rosselli escaped in 1929, and eventually after many vicissitudes reached France by way of Tunisia. While deprived of his freedom he had worked out in his book *Socialismo Liberale* a somewhat eclectic version of Socialism in which great emphasis was laid on the value of personal freedom and which attracted a group which gathered about him in exile. He saw his group as the nucleus for a future Italy, a 'microcosm of a new, completely liberal state', as he put it, 'a new world of justice and freedom which will rise on the morrow of the revolution—a cell capable of infinite expansion, the germ of a new society encapsulated in the present'.[1]

Rosselli was not, however, destined to live to see his country's liberation. He fought with the International Brigades in Spain, became ill and went with his brother, Nello, a historian, to Normandy to convalesce, where both were murdered by Fascist agents.

By working together in the *Concentrazione*, the two émigré Socialist parties grew closer to one another. Yet, at the same time, the gulf between Socialists and Communists had widened. Following the fiasco of the German uprising in October 1923, the Communist International had made increasingly bitter attacks on Social Democracy, culminating in its definition of Social Democrats as 'Social Fascists' at its Sixth World Congress in the summer of 1928—the Congress which had, under the slogan 'Class against Class', denounced all non-Communist Socialists as enemies of the working class.[2] In such circumstances, the Italian Communists could not consider co-operating with the Socialists either in the *Concentrazione* or in any other organization.

The problems of unity were therefore faced only by the two Socialist

---

1. Quoted in W. Hilton-Young, *The Italian Left. A Short History of Political Socialism in Italy* (London, 1949), p. 155.
2. See Braunthal, *History of the International, 1914–1943*, pp. 337–40 and 423–4.

groups which had split in 1922. There could be no questioning the wish of Turati and his reformist wing to see the achievement of reunification.

For Filippo Turati (1857–1932), the unity of the Socialist movement was of the utmost importance, and to preserve it he was ready to make fundamental sacrifices. Although he had rejected the Bolshevist ideology which had permeated the Socialist party after the triumph of the October revolution in Russia and opposed the party programme founded upon it as well as the adoption of Bolshevist tactics, he had never resigned from the party voluntarily. To avoid hazarding party unity, he had accepted the majority decision of the 1919 party congress—which he had uncompromisingly opposed—to seek entry into the Communist International, loyally representing in Parliament a policy which he had personally condemned as fatal. He did not found his opposition party—the *Partito Socialista dei Lavoratori Italiani*, organized in exile as *Partito Socialista Unitario* (Socialist Unity party)—until, despite his pleading, his group had been expelled.[1] Reunification with the parent party, which after the split called itself the Maximalist party, was for him and his followers the realization of a sincere ambition.

But the same wish was not held unanimously within the Maximalist party. According to their programme they were a Communist party, but despite all their efforts they had never been accepted into the Communist International because of their refusal to expel Turati, who, as founder of the party and its spiritual leader over three decades, was held in the highest esteem by the working classes. Their sympathies with the Communist International cooled notably, however, after the pro-Moscow faction split off to re-constitute itself as a Communist party and to commence a bitter struggle with the Maximalists for working-class leadership. An attempt made in 1923 by Giacinto Serrati (1872–1926), the leader of the Maximalists, to unite the Maximalists with the Communists, was rejected by a majority in the party. Serrati acted as a consequence of this defeat; he joined the Communist party. And when, soon afterwards, Mussolini suppressed all Socialist parties in Italy, any talk of unification became merely academic.

The theme was, however, taken up by the exiles in France, where many active members of local organizations had fled in the face of threats. Here they organized themselves into groups aligned along the old divisions. Many Maximalist émigrés had slowly come to realize that, since the Socialist movement had been the victim of its split, only a united Socialist movement could effectively combat the Fascist dictatorship. Yet many, still in the grip of the Bolshevist ideology, opposed any partnership with the reformists.

The most passionate advocate of unity was Pietro Nenni (b. 1891), who had begun his political career before the First World War as a revolutionary Republican, becoming a Socialist only after 1918. During the years 1919 to

1. See Braunthal, *History of the International, 1914–1943*, pp. 211–12 and 228–9.

1921, when ideological conflicts shattered and finally split the Socialist party, he had been Paris correspondent for the party's daily newspaper, *Avanti!* He saw clearly how the split, occurring at the historic moment when Fascism went on to the offensive, was a genuine disaster; that healing the split was consequently the most urgent task. He had returned to Italy in 1922 to attempt the then impossible reunification of the Socialist movement. For Serrati, reuniting the Maximalists with the reformists was out of the question; his aim was affiliation with the Communist International through union with the Communist party. Nenni, on the other hand, persuaded a majority of Maximalists that fusion with the Communist party and their consequent bondage to the Communist International would perpetuate the split in the labour movement. His first priority was unification with Turati's party, which, supported by most of the trade unions, represented a large mass of the working class. But a majority of the party, having rejected Serrati's proposal under the impact of Nenni's speech, threw out Nenni's proposal for an understanding with the reformists just as decisively. Thus the Socialist movement remained split in three.

After Serrati left the party, Nenni became his successor as chief editor of *Avanti!*; and he continued to edit the paper in exile. The experience of the tragic ideological confusion that had manifested itself in the Socialist movement—and which he described in an intriguing book, *Storia di quattro anni, 1919–1922*,[1] influenced his attitude to the problem of the split, particularly in exile. In the *Partito Socialista Unitario* he found sympathy for the idea of reuniting with the Maximalists. Turati, as we have seen, stood consistently for unity in the labour movement, and one of his most prominent followers, Giuseppe Saragat, canvassed the question among the reformists.

Nenni's attempt at reunification met the biggest resistance from the Maximalist left wing, since the question of unity also raised the question of joining the Socialist International. The party had split from it in 1918, hoping to join the Communist International, but had been rejected. The left wing of the Maximalist party in exile still felt ideologically bound to the Communist International. Turati's party had in the meantime joined the Socialist International, so providing one more reason for the left to resist unity. It even resorted to physical force to prevent it. When, in 1930, a congress was called in Grenoble to decide on the question, the dissidents occupied the hall and locked the gates. But later in the year, when the congress met in Paris, Nenni was able to win a majority.

Thus reunited, the party called itself, as it had before the schism, the *Partito Socialista*. The splinter group continued to publish *Avanti!* in Lugano, but the organ of the united party, edited by Nenni, reappeared under the name of *Nuovo Avanti!* (New Forward). The united party then affiliated

1. See Braunthal, *History of the International, 1914–1943*, p. 213.

formally to the Socialist International, being represented in the executive by Nenni for the Maximalists and Giuseppe Modigliani (1872–1947) for the reformists.

An unexpected change of policy within the French Communist party towards the French Socialist party also brought about a change in the attitude of the émigré Italian Communists to the Italian Socialists. In June 1934, a conference of the French Communist party at Ivry proposed an 'anti-Fascist united front' with the French Socialists.[1] Until this point the Communists had been in fierce conflict with the Socialists as the party of 'Social Fascists'. Overnight they came to see them as a fraternal proletarian party with which they would hope to form an active alliance.

This obscure change of attitude may be explained by the change of direction in his foreign policy which Stalin undertook in the spring of 1934. Since Hitler came to power at the end of January 1933, Stalin had been genuinely concerned that friendly relations should exist between Germany and Russia. He did not, however, discover any warm response on Hitler's part, and so approached France with a view to a Franco–Russian alliance against Hitler's Germany. If this was to succeed, however, he needed the support of the highly influential French Socialist party.

The Italian Communist party in exile could therefore no longer perpetuate its hostility towards the Italian Socialists, but had similarly to seek an understanding. The French Socialist party accepted the Communist proposal of an anti-Fascist 'action group', and on 27 July 1934 signed the agreement. Three weeks later, on 17 August, a 'united action' agreement between the Italian Socialists and Communists was concluded.[2]

This agreement was rudely shattered, however, when, in the summer of 1939, Stalin once again abruptly turned about his foreign policy and signed the Nazi–Soviet Pact on 23 August as an immediate prelude to the Second World War. While Nenni condemned the pact in *Nuovo Avanti!*, he continued to do all he could to avoid a total break with the Communists, remaining mindful of the fateful consequences which had attended the labour movement's split into Socialists and Communists in Italy, Germany and France[3]—

1. See Braunthal, *History of the International, 1914–1943*, pp. 425–6.
2. For Stalin's wooing of Hitler's Germany, see ibid., pp. 396–9; for the change of policy by the French Communist Party, see Cecil and Albert Vassart, 'The Moscow Origin of the French "Popular Front"', in Milorad M. Drachkovitch and Branko Lazitch (eds), *The Comintern—Historical Highlights* (New York, 1966), pp. 234–52. Albert Vassart was a member of the central committee of the Communist party and its representative in the executive committee of the Communist International. For the conclusion of the Italian 'united action' agreement, see Braunthal, *History of the International, 1914–1943*, p. 476.
3. As in Italy, so in Spain, where he was a political commissar of the International Brigade, Nenni had witnessed the tragedy of the split at first hand; for the history of the split during the Spanish Civil War, see Braunthal, *History of the International, 1914–1943*, pp. 447–9, 453–4 and 463–7.

all quarrels which had led to a mutual downfall. When the party executive decided despite his opposition to dissolve the Socialist–Communist 'united action' pact and to sever all connection with the Communist party, he resigned as party secretary and from the editorship of *Nuovo Avanti!*

The turning-point of the war, marked by Hitler's defeat before Stalingrad in January 1943, eventually created conditions in which the fight against the Fascist régime in Italy could commence. The myth of Hitler's invincibility had been destroyed, the spirit of resistance, atrophied by many years of dictatorship, reawakened. On 5 March 1943 more than 20,000 workers of the Fiat–Mirafiori works in Turin went on a strike which spread like wildfire through Northern Italy and brought engineering works in Milan, Piedmont, Lombardy and Liguria to a standstill. It was a strike for bread and peace. In vain the government brought in troops and military tribunals against the strikers. Work did not begin again until 2 April when the government sanctioned increases in wages and food rations. This defiance of Mussolini's militia represented the first sizeable blow against his régime.[1]

Another was to follow shortly. While the Red Army threw back the Panzer divisions in Russia, the Western Allies began their European offensive. On 10 July 1943 Allied troops landed on the southern coast of Sicily, and on the 22nd they occupied Palermo. The days of the Fascist régime were drawing to their close. On 25 July, Benito Mussolini was dismissed by King Victor Emanuel III and arrested; Marshal Pietro Badoglio was appointed prime minister in his place.

It was now only natural that Socialists and Communists should once again move closer as the struggle began for Italy's liberation. Divisive enmities had already been bridged in a common sympathy felt for the Soviet Union as a victim of Hitler's treachery, the earlier conflict becoming insignificant in the face of a common cause. Italy stood on the threshold of at least a political revolution. And if this was to develop into a social revolution, unity within the working classes would be an essential factor.

As early as 26 July, the day after the fall of Mussolini, representatives of the Socialist, Communist and anti-Fascist middle-class parties met in Milan and formed a 'Committee for National Liberation' (C.N.L.). Socialists and Communists thus once again became united in their aims. On 4 August 1943 they renewed the pact for mutual Socialist–Communist action. This entrusted a joint permanent committee with the task of unifying the reborn Socialist and Communist organizations. Both parties, the pact stated, 'recognize the Soviet Union ... as the people's most certain friend in the struggle for independence and freedom against the reactionary, imperialist

---

1. See Roberto Battaglia, *The Story of the Italian Resistance* (London, 1957), pp. 32–3; Maurice F. Neufeld, *Italy: School for Awakening. The Italian Labor Movement in its Political, Social and Economic Setting from 1800 to 1960* (New York, 1961), p. 449.

powers, and place their faith in the solidarity of the British Labour party'.[1] Nenni, once again leader of the Italian Socialist party, aspired to an even closer unity: an alliance sealed with a contract. The Communists accepted, and a 'pact of alliance' was signed on 8 August 1944 by both Nenni and Togliatti.

The armistice signed between the Allies and Badoglio's government on 8 September 1943 had divided Italy into two areas: the South, to which king and government had fled, now occupied by the Allies and administered by Badoglio's government; and the North, continuing as a war zone and occupied by twenty-five German divisions, under whose protection Mussolini, escaped from incarceration, had set up in Salo on Lake Garda a so-called 'Social Republic'. Thus the focal point of Italy's internal politics was centred on the South. As in the North, the anti-Fascist factions of the South had come together in a national liberation committee, which met on 23 January 1944 at a congress in Bari to formulate its political programme.

The Socialists, Communists and *Partito d'Azione*—the Action party led by Ferruccio Parri which had emerged from Rosselli's group, *Giustizia e Libertà*—made up the left wing, while the Christian Democratic party (*Democrazia Cristiana*), led by Alcide de Gasperi and previously known as the *Populari* (the Catholic People's party), together with the Liberal party, led by Bededetto Croce, the historian, and Count Carlo Sforza and a 'Democratic Labour party' formed the right. At Bari the congress was unanimous in demanding the eradication of Fascism and the restoration of civil and political freedoms. The left wing, however, went further, demanding an immediate coalition government made up of all the anti-Fascist parties, the overthrow of the monarchy and the establishment of a republic. The parties of the right, on the other hand, wished to preserve the monarchy. While prepared to sacrifice King Emanuel, who had assisted at the birth of Fascism and continued as its protector through twenty-two years, they demanded his abdication in favour of his son, Crown Prince Umberto. For this reason they declared themselves with the left against participation in Badoglio's government, which had been installed by the king.

That was how the situation stood when, at the end of March 1944, Palmiro Togliatti (1893–1964) returned to Naples from Moscow after his eighteen-year exile. Following the death of Gramsci, he had been accepted as leader of the Italian Communist party, representing it in the executive of the Communist International. He now appeared as a well-briefed delegate of the Soviet government. His arrival on the scene signalled a dramatic *volte-face* in the Communist camp. For seven months the Italian Communists had repeatedly stated in accord with the whole of the left wing that, before a

1. Quoted in Hilton-Young, *The Italian Left*, p. 170.

free democratic régime could be installed in Italy, a government had to be formed from which every trace of the king's influence had been erased. They had vigorously demanded the dismissal of Badoglio, the marshal who had conquered Abyssinia for Mussolini. But then, in March 1944, Stalin recognized Badoglio's government and thus effectively disarmed the Italian Communists in their opposition to the king and his prime minister. It was significant that Togliatti, in his propaganda broadcast from Moscow after the fall of Mussolini, had avoided touching on the question of the monarchy—undoubtedly in line with the directives of the Soviet government.[1]

Now, armed with Moscow's authority, Togliatti bluntly opposed the earlier policies. The question of democracy, freedom or form of government, he stated to a conference of the national council of the Communist party in Naples on 1 April, was one for the future so long as the war against Germany continued. 'It is impossible,' he stated, 'to grant the Italian people any guarantee of freedom until the Nazis have been banished from our country.'[2] Nothing mattered beyond the present war of liberation. But this demanded, he insisted, total co-operation between all forces within the nation—a national government of all the anti-Fascist parties, irrespective of whether they were capitalist or clerical, monarchist or republican, with or without Badoglio. The Communist party was in any case, he declared, itself prepared to join a Badoglio government.

Togliatti's 'elastic tactic', as an anonymous Communist historian has called it,[3] broke the front of the opposition to Badoglio. The Socialists, surprised by such a drastic shift in Communist policies, found themselves faced with a *fait accompli*. Leaderless in the South—Nenni had left for the North—they joined the Communist line so as not to jeopardize their hard-won unity. And now none of the other parties represented in the C.N.L. could persist in opposition. They agreed to co-operate with Badoglio on condition that the king declared himself at least willing to abdicate in favour of his son as regent after the liberation of Rome. This being agreed to, Badoglio formed his second government on 24 April from representatives of the six parties of the C.N.L., Togliatti becoming a minister without portfolio. In its first announcement the government declared that it was necessary for the decision of the character of the Italian state to be postponed until the war had ended.

Togliatti's 'elastic tactic' determined the policy of the Italian Communist party until 1947, when its participation in the government came to an end. Revolutionary tactics were at all events out of the question so long as the

---

1. See Paolo Robotti and Giovanni Germanetto, *Dreissig Jahre Kampf der italienischen Kommunisten 1921–1951* (Berlin, 1955), p. 204; Isaac Deutscher, *Stalin* (London, 1966), p. 505.
2. Quoted in Battaglia, *The Story of the Italian Resistance*, p. 109.
3. *Die Kommunistische Partei Italiens* (Berlin, 1952), p. 88.

Allied forces faced German divisions in Italy. And so the Communist party had to try to win power and influence by democratic means. They reached an understanding with the monarchy and the army—regardless of how these institutions had been compromised as the organs of Fascism—to safeguard their position in the government. Their policies were thus aimed at retaining the power they held as members of the government, and since they went to some lengths to avoid serious conflict with any of the bourgeois coalition parties which might have questioned their participation, any talk of measures to attain social revolution was severely discouraged. For this reason Togliatti, even after the liberation of northern Italy in April 1945, continued to reject as 'utopian' demands for a planned economy and he recognized private enterprise as a driving force for economic development, setting a limit to the control of the economy by the state. 'The only way out of this present difficult situation,' he still stated a year and a half later, in September 1946, in a resolution of the Communist party central committee, 'lies in this: that a "new course" be set in economic policies, in which private enterprise is offered an extensive freedom, the state interfering only to prevent speculation which might lead to the collapse of the monetary system and threaten the people with starvation so that it can act to achieve complete economic rebuilding in the national interest.'[1]

The Communist party did not even flinch from a striking betrayal of its principles when, to stay on an equal footing with the strongest party, the Christian Democrats, as well as to gain the sympathies of the Catholic electorate, it voted for the inclusion in the new constitution of the Lateran Treaty, concluded between Mussolini and the Holy See in 1929, which safeguarded the Catholic Church's territorial and financial imperatives as well as its privileged position within the state.[2]

This was hardly a policy to fulfil the expections of the workers in the factories or of the guerrillas who had fought so heroically in northern Italy. Their hopes had been for a new Italy, a 'second *Risorgimento*', rising from the ruins of the Fascist régime. What they expected was a radical political revolution which would not be satisfied simply with the king's abdication, but which would demolish the whole institution of the monarchy and firmly establish true republican democracy: a social revolution which would give Socialism its place in the economic system. 'Socialism,' Nenni had stated in a speech in September 1944, 'is no longer in Italy a matter of propaganda,

1. Quoted in *Die Kommunistische Partei Italiens*, p. 105; see also Aldo Garosci, 'The Italian Communist Party', in Mario Einaudi (ed.), *Communism in Western Europe* (New York, 1951), p. 186.

2. The Communist group in the constituent assembly was prepared even to vote for an article in the constitution stipulating the prohibition of divorce. Togliatti, who had been in Sicily on an election campaign when this decision was taken by the Communist deputies, convinced his fellow members that, in their worthy attempts to win Catholic votes, they had drifted a little too far from party principles and had the decision negated; see Hilton-Young, *The Italian Left*, p. 197.

of the sun in the future of which Garibaldi spoke, but a problem of the day in the most concrete and positive sense.'[1]

Thus the revolution had been postponed to a remote future. The constitution, adopted at the end of 1947, did, to be sure, state in Article III that it was a task of the state 'to remove those economic and social obstacles which, in that they *de facto* curtail the freedom and equality of the citizen, hinder the full development of the human personality and the participation of every worker in the political, economic and social organization of the country'. But it was only a promise, and one which in the event was never redeemed.[2]

The conflict between Nenni's and Togliatti's views on the task of the working class during the crisis did not, however, shake the Socialist–Communist alliance. Though other conflicts inevitably developed from time to time, they all left the new concept of unity intact.

In November, soon after the conclusion of the pact, Ivanoe Bonomi, who had formed the June 1944 government of the six parties represented in the C.N.L., resigned. But he handed his resignation not to the Committee of National Liberation, which had nominated him, but to the newly installed regent. For Nenni this represented a question of high principle (as it must have been for the Communists), since he saw the Committee of National Liberation as the nation's representative and the organ of its sovereignty. Now, in handing the regent his resignation, Bonomi had acknowledged the royal prerogative and denied the people's sovereignty. Nenni at once issued a manifesto stating that if Bonomi was again entrusted by the regent to form a government, the Socialists would withdraw their participation. But when Bonomi was appointed as prime minister by the regent, the Communists, not unduly alarmed by conflicts over questions of principle, joined his government without hesitation. The Socialists went into opposition, as they had said they would, but even so the pact for joint Socialist–Communist action remained in force.[3]

Not even the open conflict which arose between the Socialists and Communists over the question of the Lateran Treaty succeeded in jeopardizing the pact. Nenni protested bitterly against any revival of the Treaty, and the Socialist faction voted against its inclusion in the constitution—a provision ironically achieved with Communist votes.

The initiative for the policy of the Socialist–Communist alliance was to remain with the Communist party from the moment when Togliatti arrived

1. Quoted in ibid., p. 171.

2. 'To compensate the left for the lack of a revolution, the powers of the right agreed to incorporate a guarantee of revolution into the constitution'; see Piero Calamandrei, *Cenni introduttivi sulla Costituente e i suoi lavori* (Florence, 1950), quoted in Hans Hinterhäuser, *Italiener Zwischen Schwarz und Rot* (Stuttgart, 1956), p. 23.

3. For a description of this episode, see Hilton-Young, *The Italian Left*, pp. 172–5.

on the political scene in Italy in April 1944 up till the dissolution of the alliance in 1965. Under Nenni's leadership, the Socialist party periodically opposed Togliatti's policies, but was careful to avoid any open break.

This predominant position of the Communist party did not stem from the actual ratio of power between the two parties alone. In the first election after the war—the election to the constituent assembly on 2 June 1946—the Socialists received 4,758,192 votes (21 per cent of votes cast), to the Communists' 4,356,686 (19 per cent of the total vote). But it was of small account that the Communist party should have collected 2 per cent fewer electors to support them than had the Socialist party, and of great account that in terms of power they were pressing the Socialist party so closely.

The rapid rise of the Italian Communist party to a party of mass support, soon to leave the Socialist party far behind, is a remarkable phenomenon.[1] When in 1921 the Communists had separated from the Socialists at Leghorn and formed their own party, they represented 42,000 members against a quarter of a million Socialist supporters; and in the elections of May 1921, the last free election before Mussolini seized power, they gained only thirteen seats in parliament against the Socialists' 128. The Fascist dictatorship had forced both parties underground and had worn down their underground movements by a brutal twenty-year suppression. Neither party had been able to express itself through an underground organization,[2] and both, after the fall of Fascism, had to build new foundations. In competing with the Communists, however, the Socialists had the advantage of their tradition as a workers' party representing a heroic past. Furthermore, the industrial centres of northern Italy, among which the movements of both parties restarted, were Socialist strongholds.

But, at the elections of 18 April 1948, in which the Communists and the left wing of the Socialist party led by Nenni stood jointly under the title Democratic People's Front (*Fronte Democratico Popolare*), the Communists won 135 seats to Nenni's fifty-one, the splinter right wing of the party,[3] led by Giuseppe Saragat, winning only thirty-three. Within two years the balance of power between Communists and Socialists had shifted heavily in the Communists' favour.

1. The Italian Communist party, according to its own figures, had in 1926 only 'about 20,000 members', and until 1944 'the Communist ranks remained thin'. But by 1945 it could claim 1,800,000, and by 1947 2,252,000 members. See Robotti and Germanetto, *Dreissig Jahre Kampf der italienischen Kommunisten*, p. 254.

2. D. Manuilsky reported to the eighteenth congress of the Russian Communist party in the spring of 1939 as a representative of the Communist International, that it was necessary to 'recognize a certain weakness in the Italian Communist party. In all the long years of Fascist dictatorship, it has been in no position to form a strong underground organization'—*Imprecorr*, 1939, p. 381, quoted in Franz Borkenau, *Der europäische Kommunismus. Seine Geschichte von 1917 bis zur Gegenwart* (Berne, 1952), p. 268.

3. For the history of the split of the Socialist Party, see pp. 63–65.

Both parties were reborn in the struggles of the underground movement in the north, Socialists and Communists organizing illegal cells in the factories and guerrilla fighters in the field—the Socialists, the Matteotti Brigades, and the Communists, the Gramsci Brigades. The clandestine factory cells had created recurring waves of strikes involving many thousands of workers. The mass strike of March 1943 was followed by a general strike in March 1944 embracing over a million workers[1] and another on 25 April 1945 which incited the workers to rise as the Allies prepared for the last decisive blow against the Germans in northern Italy. And while the resistance movements in the industrial centres were paralysing by strikes and sabotage economic life in the districts occupied by the Germans, the guerrillas, with Allied arms, met German as well as Italian Fascist troops in full-scale battles. At the height of the fighting the partisans had an army of 200,000 to 300,000 men[2] formed from followers of every political alignment, Christian Democrats fighting in the 'Brigade of the Green Flame', members of the Action party in the 'Rosselli Brigade' and liberals and neutrals as well as Socialists and Communists in the Garibaldi Brigade. The resistance movement in Italy was a political as well as a national liberation movement; its history forms a major epic of modern times.[3]

The leadership of the guerrilla groups and the clandestine factory cells rested with the Communist party. It was superior to every other party in its organizational techniques, in the discipline of its members, and in its spirit of daring and self-sacrifice. It had taken the initiative in organizing the guerrillas, founding the first group—the Garibaldi Brigade—in November 1943 under the command of two veteran Communists, proven in battle: Luigi Longo and Pietro Secchia. Longo, one of the founders of the Communist party, had been a political commissar of the International Brigades in the Spanish Civil War, and Secchia had been one of the leading organizers of the Communist underground during the years of Fascism, imprisoned for seventeen years until released in 1943 under the Badoglio government's amnesty. Even in those brigades not under direct Communist leadership, the Communists represented the most active and daring elements. 'They organized,' as one unbiased historian reported, 'the strongest partisan brigades and won, through their bravery, the respect of most of the patriots.'[4]

1. See Neufeld, *Italy: School for Awakening*, p. 452.

2. See Hilton-Young, *The Italian Left*, p. 178. A report prepared by a member of Mussolini's general staff on the 'danger of rebellion' estimated the strength of the partisans in the summer of 1944 to be 82,000; see Battaglia, *The Story of the Italian Resistance*, p. 166.

3. For a detailed description, see Battaglia's standard work; the author was a member of the Action party and commander of a guerrilla division. See also Leo Valiani, *Dopo dieci anni* (Florence, 1946). Valiani, a historian who was imprisoned for several years under the Fascists, was one of the leaders of the resistance movement in northern Italy and one of the organizers of the Milan uprising in April 1945; he represented the Action party in the provisional government in northern Italy, and after the liberation joined the Socialist party.

4. Neufeld, *Italy: School for Awakening*, p. 458.

They were also the most forceful and effective element in the factories. Among the 20,000 workers in the Fiat–Mirafiori works in Turin, whose strike in March 1943 unleashed the mass strike which followed, they counted only eighty members.[1] But it was by their initiative that the strike had been called in association with the Socialists. And while the majority of politically active workers in northern Italy most probably felt themselves in sympathy with the Socialist party, the Communists maintained an initial responsibility in the wave of strikes during the resistance campaign. Their revolutionary dynamism won the Communist cause thousands of followers.

It was moreover admiration for the Soviet Union that in Italy as well as in France had moved countless numbers of workers and intellectuals alike to join the Communist party as the party standing closest to Communist Russia. 'The myth of October,' one historian of the Communist party of Italy commented in describing the attraction that was generated by Russia, 'the figure of Stalin, the five-year plans, the hydroelectric power stations growing like mushrooms, the Red Army which had smashed Hitler's invincible forces: all held a fascination for intellectuals outside the Soviet Union as a great epic, and it attracted the mass of the people who saw in the strength of a country which had proclaimed itself as a Socialist country and abolished injustice and exploitation, a beacon for the oppressed and a weapon for the realization of their ambitions.'[2]

It also won the Communist party a predominant place in the trade union movement. The Italian trade union congress, the *Confederazione Generale del Lavoro* (C.G.L.), had been unaffected by the split in the Socialist party; the Communists did not, as in France, start their own. But side by side with the Socialist-led trade union movement was the Catholic trade union federation, the *Confederazione Italiana dei Lavoratori* (C.I.L.), founded in March 1918 and grouping many thousands of workers. Both these trade union movements had been ruthlessly suppressed by the Fascist régime.

Their reconstruction began when Bruno Buozzi (1881–1944), leader of the metal workers' union and General Secretary of the C.G.L. before its suppression, returned to Italy in 1943 from exile in France. Commencing his illegal activities in a Rome still occupied by the Germans, he strove to achieve a single trade union movement for Socialist, Communist and Catholic workers by bringing together the Socialist C.G.L. with the Catholic C.I.L. In this he was supported by the most distinguished trade union leader in the Catholic movement, Achille Grandi (1883–1946), who canvassed for this unity in the Catholic camp. In February 1944, both federations constituted

1. See Battaglia, *The Story of the Italian Resistance*, p. 32.
2. Giorgio Galli, *Storia del Partito comunista italiano* (Milan, 1958), pp. 258–9, quoted in Donald L. M. Blackmer, *Unity in Diversity. Italian Communism and the Communist World* (Cambridge, Mass., 1968), pp. 28–9.

themselves, initially in congresses in Salerno but entering without delay into discussions regarding their unity. On 3 June 1944, the day before the Allied troops approached the outskirts of Rome, Emilio Canevari for the Socialists, Giuseppe di Vittorio for the Communists, and Achille Grandi for the Christian Democrats, signed a 'declaration affirming the unity of the workers'—the Pact of Rome. Buozzi's signature was missing from the document, which he had seen as the crowning glory of all his endeavours; as the Allies were approaching he had been arrested by the Fascists to be murdered by the Germans on 4 June—the day after the signing of the declaration.

The trade union federation which emerged from this merger under the title of *Confederazione Generale Italiana del Lavoro* (C.G.I.L.) was pledged by the declaration to respect democratic principles at every level of the hierarchy, to ensure proportional representation for minorities and to guarantee political and religious freedom of thought. The statutes, promulgated later at the inaugural congress, specifically guaranteed participation by representatives of the three main political streams as well as of minorities in any resolution of outstanding importance. The declaration emphasized the C.G.I.L.'s independence of any party, while reserving the right 'to co-operate with the democratic parties—the representatives of the working masses—in any act necessary to preserve the people's liberty or to defend the interests of workers and country'.[1]

A provisional executive committee consisting of a general secretariat and five representatives for each of the three political alignments—Oreste Lizzadri as member of the secretariat for the Socialists, di Vittorio for the Communists and Achille Grandi for the Christian Democrats—was formed. On 28 January 1945, the C.G.I.L. constituted itself at its inaugural congress in Naples in the presence of fraternal delegates of the International Federation of Trade Unions as well as leaders of the British, American and Russian trade union movements.[2]

Yet in less than two years the Communist party had gained full control of the C.G.I.L. It was hardly their radical spirit which won them a majority. Togliatti continued to sit with the middle-class parties in the coalition, stepping carefully so as not to endanger the position of the Communists in the government; and di Vittorio's policy was openly reformist, trying to raise the workers' living-standards by traditional methods of negotiation with employers and government to gain wage increases and improve social conditions. But, simultaneously, di Vittorio was attempting to transform the C.G.I.L. into an instrument of the Communist party.

Giuseppe di Vittorio (1892–1957) had served the party faithfully since its inauguration and, like Longo, had been a political commissar in the Spanish

1. Neufeld, *Italy: School for Awakening*, p. 455.
2. See ibid., pp. 451, 454–5 and 457.

Civil War, moving on to edit a Communist newspaper in exile in France. He was by far the most powerful personality in the triumvirate of the secretariat. His colleague, Oreste Lizzadri (b. 1896), the representative of the Socialist party, faced the tasks which confronted him helplessly; he had neither trade union nor political experience and could only submit himself passively to di Vittorio's leadership. As for Achille Grandi, the Christian Democrats' representative, he was hindered from action by the ravages of cancer. In these circumstances the leadership soon fell to di Vittorio. Trained in the Bolshevik techniques of conspiracy in organizing the masses, he systematically infiltrated key positions in the trade union movement with Communist sympathizers and so won control over an enormous organization embracing many tens of thousands of Social Democratic as well as Christian Democratic workers.[1]

At length, like the C.G.I.L., the Socialist party also became a Communist auxiliary. This was clearly how Togliatti saw its function when, at the end of April 1945 in the Communist national council, he proclaimed the concept of a 'party of a new type'. 'We have today arrived at a point,' he said, 'where it is important not only to propagate an idea, but also to renew the country through that democratic idea, to save it from its ruin and defeat. We therefore need, besides party members and officials, to find a way for us to lead the mass of the people'[2]—as, for example, the masses of trade union workers by infiltrating the organizational machines of the trade union movement and the Socialist party through the united action pact.

Ideology had to adapt to Togliatti's 'elastic tactics'. Of the dogmatic inflexibility which had split the Socialist movement before the war there was now no sign. Article II of the statutes which the Communist party formulated at the end of December 1945 allowed 'all honest workers ... regardless of race, religious belief or philosophical conviction' to become members of the Communist party. The statutes showed, wrote *Unità*, the official party organ, that 'the Communist party is not the party of atheism' and that belonging to it by no means involved embracing 'the philosophical teachings of materialism'—namely, the teachings of Marxism. Pietro Secchia, the party's vice-secretary, explained the statutes to be the 'statutes of a national party ... a party of a new type ... a party of unity'.[3] It was therefore necessary, Longo

1. The transformation of the C.G.I.L. into an instrument of the Communist party illustrates the role that chance as much as personality may play in history. Had Bruno Buozzi not been murdered, he would have represented the Socialist party in the triumvirate of the general secretariat, and the independence of the trade union movement would most probably have been preserved. Buozzi was a veteran trade union leader with an integrity comparable to Ernest Bevin's in Britain and capable of fighting off any attempt at a political takeover.

2. *Die Kommunistische Partei Italiens*, p. 91.

3. Quoted in Garosci, 'The Italian Communist Party', in Einaudi (ed.), *Communism in Western Europe*, pp. 201–2.

stated at the party congress, to extend the united action pact with the Socialists into a pact to combine the very organizational machinery of each party, since without proletarian unity it would be impossible to create a spearhead for democratic action.

While the Socialist party had pledged itself at its first congress after the war, in April 1945, to the principle of proletarian unity, the fundamental question of organic fusion between the two parties had been left open. And at the next congress, in April 1945 in Florence, even the principle of united action with the Communists was questioned vehemently in debate by the group known as the Saragats—the 'pure Socialists'.

Giuseppe Saragat (b. 1898) had worked as a financial expert in a bank before he left Fascist Italy in the 1920s and had played no part in the ideological struggles of 1921 between the majority party, led by Serrati, and the reformists who gathered about Turati. He did, however, share Turati's reformist convictions, which had made an even deeper impression on him through his studies during his exile of the history of the English labour movement. Elected after his return from exile to be president of the constituent assembly, his position in the executive as well as his writings in *Critica Sociale*, the periodical founded by Turati, stood out clearly for a split away from the Communists; he was supported in this by Ivan Matteo Lombardo, a representative of the party's right wing, as well as by Ignazio Silone and Angelica Balabanoff. Silone and Balabanoff, however, were not reformists. Silone (b. 1900), whose distinguished novels and stories had established his name abroad as a writer,[1] was a former ardent Communist who had only left the party when, as he wrote, he came to the realization that Communism was 'no more than a new version of that inhuman reality against which we, as Socialists, had originally been inflamed'.[2] Angelica Balabanoff (1876–1966), a disciple of Lenin's who had worked with him and been secretary of the Communist International during the year following its inauguration, had also turned away from the Communist movement in disillusion.[3]

Opposition to united action also came from a group of adamant anti-Communists of the younger generation of Socialists—the 'Young Turks', as they were known. They had assembled about the periodical *Iniziativa Socialista* under the leadership of Mario Zagari and Matteo Matteotti, whose father had been murdered in 1924 at Mussolini's instigation. This group likewise demanded the dissolution of the pact and a break with the Communists.

At the same time, on the left wing, a group of Communist sympathizers,

1. Above all his novels *Fontamara* (London, 1934) and *Bread and Wine* (London, 1934), neither of which could appear in Italy before the fall of the Fascist dictatorship.
2. See in R. H. S. Crossman (ed.), *The God That Failed* (London, 1950), p. 103.
3. For her strange biography, see her *Erinnerungen und Erlebnisse* (Berlin, 1927).

the 'Fusionists', stood with their periodical, *Compiti Nuovi*, for organic fusion with the Communist party, while a group of the old majority party, close to the Communists, whose organ was *Quarto Stato* and who were led by Lelio Basso, demanded at least a continuation of the concept of united action.

Nenni himself took up a central position. Elected at the 1945 congress as president of the party, his wish had been to see an organic unification of the left. The question of proletarian unity was one that had always occupied him profoundly, representing a principle that he had stood for constantly and uncompromisingly in *Avanti!*. But he also knew that the majority of even his most faithful followers would refuse to follow him into a united party and that any decision by congress to impose unification would inevitably split his party asunder. So for the sake of unity he avoided laying the resolution before congress. In an alternative resolution he proposed as a compromise that the question be postponed and that, with no prejudice to the autonomy of the party, the current policy of united action be continued.

In the event, the group surrounding Saragat and the *Critica Sociale* also sought a compromise, declaring themselves against organic unity with the Communist party—a question left open by Nenni's resolution—but in favour of retaining the united action pact so as not to endanger party unity. The *Iniziativa Socialista* group, however, stood by their demands for an annulment of the pact and a separation from the Communists.

Nenni's resolution in fact received the most votes (338,000), but since the resolutions by Saragat's group and the 'Young Turks' had received 300,000 and 83,000 respectively, this did not represent an absolute majority. Therefore, to avoid a crisis, the congress also had to find a compromise solution for the party's leadership. It re-elected Nenni as president, but at the same time elected Lombardo as its general secretary to represent the right wing.

The congress met, as the *Bulletin* of the Socialist International recorded, 'in an atmosphere of fanaticism difficult to describe. A majority of delegates supported the "unionists" [Nenni, Basso and the "Fusionists"], but a minority, raving and shouting, demonstrated continously.'[1] But the majority had hardly been short on the quality of 'fanaticism', forcing, for example, Angelica Balabanoff to leave the stand under a hail of abuse after she had accused Nenni of complacency towards the Communists, criticized the Soviet dictatorship and attempted to expose the seemingly democratic façade of the Communist party.

Before the congress had even begun to debate the relationship with the Communist party, it had considered the programme for the election to the constituent assembly arranged for 2 June 1946: a programme in the tradition

1. *S.I.L.O. Bulletin*, III, February 1947, published by the Socialist Information and Liaison Office.

of democratic Socialism causing no differences of opinion. Then, when the conflicts in attitudes towards the Communist party were later resolved by a compromise between left and right, it seemed as though the badly shaken unity of the party had been fully restored. And success in the elections was not denied to the Socialist party. Five weeks later it emerged as the second strongest party in the constituent assembly and as the strongest party in the Socialist–Communist alliance, winning 115 seats against 104 for the Communists.

But, within a few more weeks, the quarrel between left and right had broken out afresh. Under the influence of the Florence congress, the Socialist party executive had to some extent held aloof in its relationships with the Communist party. Togliatti moved to make a public attack on the Socialists. Evidently, he stated, relations with the Socialist party were poor, the united action pact had remained ineffective for several months, and this was 'the fault of the group of reformist opponents of unity who in fact control the Socialist party'.[1]

Instead of contradicting Togliatti, Nenni, anxious for the future of the Socialist–Communist alliance, hurriedly discussed the revival of the pact with the Communist party leadership. The proposed result was a pact which would bring still closer the relationship between the two parties, while envisaging a 'joint executive committee'. The pact, Togliatti announced, 'would create a solid block of two fraternal parties . . . Socialist and Communists would work together to create a policy of concord'.[2]

But this 'joint executive committee' was in fact only mentioned in the pact as a desirable expectation, Nenni being well aware that, unless he were to take the risk of gambling with the unity of his party, any such expectation must remain unfulfilled. The Communist party, however, began without hesitation to build the United Front 'from below'. Pietro Secchia, its secretary, circulated to all cells and branches of the party an instruction, 'in agreement with our Socialist brothers', to seize the initiative in calling meetings in factories, urban districts and villages for the purpose of 'creating joint executive committees'[3]—in other words, those instruments by which the Communist party could gain a direct influence over the great mass of Socialist party members in factories and local organizations and so infiltrate the party organization. The Saragat group at once accused Nenni of disregarding the decisions of the congress in Florence and thus of endangering the party's autonomy. The differences between the left, whose policy was aimed at unification with the Communist party, and the right, which

---

1. *Gazzettino*, 17 September 1946, quoted in Garosci, 'The Italian Communist Party', in Einaudi (ed.), *Communism in Western Europe*, p. 212.
2. *Gazetta*, 1 November 1946, quoted in ibid., p. 213.
3. Quoted in ibid., p. 213.

strove for a clear-cut division, were forcing events towards an explosive crisis.

The crisis broke when an ordinary congress called by the party executive met in Rome on 19 January 1947. While the majority of party delegates assembled in the university building, a counter-congress of the opposition groups met in the Palazzo Barberini under the banners of Marx, Turati and Matteotti—the group Saragat, and the *Critica Sociale* and *Iniziativa Socialista* groups. Saragat himself did not appear at the congress until the fifth day, when he made a vehement speech to the majority in the university hall condemning the party leadership for its sanguine attitudes towards the Communists. He then returned to the Palazzo Barberini to announce the formation of a new Socialist party—'The Socialist party of Italian Workers' (*Partito Socialista dei Lavoratori Italiani*—P.S.L.I.); this was the name that Turati had chosen for the party he had founded after his group's exclusion from the Socialist party in 1922.

Meanwhile the main congress of the P.S.I. went on to discuss the question of a unified list of candidates with the Communists in the forthcoming parliamentary election. The idea of a 'People's Front' and a unity list had been mooted between the Communist party and Nenni before the congress had reached an understanding with Togliatti. The debate on unity lists ended with three resolutions. The first, put by the party executive and seconded by Lelio Basso, the party secretary, proposed the acceptance of a unity list and a People's Front. Against this, the second resolution, put by Lombardo, declared itself against a People's Front, and the third, put by Giuseppe Romita (1887–1958), while in favour of a common struggle with the Communists in a 'People's Front', wished to see the party retain its individual list. The executive's resolution received nearly two thirds of the votes (525,332), while Romita's received 257,099 and Lombardo's a mere 4,337. Thus the left, led by Nenni and Basso, triumphed at the congress.

The initial effect of this victory of the Socialist left wing was the splitting away of the group led by Lombardo and Silone, which thereupon constituted itself as 'Alliance of Socialists', canvassing in association with Saragat's party on one list—the *Lista dell'Unità Socialista*. In the event, the elections of 18 April 1948 ended for the Socialist party in deep disappointment. The unity list of the People's Front gained 8,137,000 votes, but only about one third of these had been cast for the Socialist party; this gave them fifty-one seats to 135 for the Communists.[1] The Communist party had outflanked its Socialist confederates.

1. In the elections to the constituent assembly on 2 June 1946, the Socialist party had won 4,758,000 votes and 115 seats against 4,356,000 votes and 104 seats going to the Communists. Saragat's party, which had separated itself from the Socialist party in the interim, received 1,858,000 votes and thirty-three seats in the elections of April 1948.

The disappointment of defeat worked itself out in a stormy five-day debate at a congress in Genoa at the end of June, two months after the elections. While Basso defended the policy of the party executive, Romita demanded the break up of the People's Front; this policy, he stated, as had been shown by the experience of countries in Eastern Europe, was one of suicide. He proposed the dissolution of the pact with the Communist party. Riccardo Lombardi, who had been secretary of the Action party, also demanded the breaking up of the People's Front, but insisted that the pact should be preserved.

In the voting on these three resolutions the executive suffered a decisive defeat. Nenni's and Basso's resolution received only 161,000 votes against 240,000 for Lombardi's resolution; Romita's received 141,000. Nenni resigned as president of the party and as chief editor of *Avanti!*, but retained the presidency of the parliamentary group; Basso gave up the secretaryship. Riccardo Lombardi's group thereupon took over the party's leadership with A. Z. Jacometti as secretary and Lombardi as chief editor of *Avanti!*. The party's relationship with the People's Front was dissolved at once, but the united action pact was left intact. The right, led by Romita and Carlo Spinelli, separated itself during the course of the next few months from the P.S.I. and eventually joined the P.S.L.I.

In both parties, as well as in the Socialist International, efforts were continuously being made to bring about a reunification, but the gulf which separated them widened in the same degree as the Cold War conflict between the Soviet Union and the Western powers increased in intensity. Solidarity with the Soviet Union had been a tradition of the P.S.I., but it was one which had preserved the freedom to criticize Moscow, as when it had, for example, opposed the policy of the Stalin–Hitler Pact. The same sympathy with the Soviet Union had been reborn as Russia, in alliance with the Western powers, had faced the treachery of Hitler's Germany. In the clash between the Great Powers following the war, the P.S.I., under Nenni's leadership, had, even before its split, leaned towards identifying its foreign policy with that of the Soviet Union (this had indeed been one of the reasons for the split). And following the split, it agreed unreservedly with each manifestation of the Soviet Union's foreign policy, regardless of any criticisms made by the other Socialist groups. It declared its solid sympathy with Russia's policies in Poland, Romania, Greece and Czechoslovakia as well as with its attitudes towards the Marshall Plan and the North Atlantic Treaty. In the view it took of the Soviet Union, the Socialist party did not stray one inch from that displayed by the Communist party. As a member of the Socialist International, the P.S.L.I. under Saragat stood in the camp of democratic Socialism; the P.S.I., though it was a party of democratic Socialism, found itself in the Communist camp because of its foreign policy.

In the light of this fundamental disparity, any attempt to bring about a reunification of the Socialist groups was bound to fail.

A change of course in Alcide de Gasperi's government in May 1947 finally provoked a radicalization of the Communist policy and led to the breaking up of the trade union movement. The government had, until then, rested on a coalition of the Christian Democrats with the Socialists and Communists. While restructuring his government, de Gasperi dismissed his Socialist and Communist ministers without further explanation. It soon became clear that this surprising change of policy had been suggested to him in the United States, where he had gone a few months before to discuss a possible loan and where it had been hinted that Italy could expect generous American aid were he to exclude Communists and Socialist left-wingers from his coalition.[1] And, indeed, a month after their exclusion Italy received over $600 million as a first instalment from Washington.

Over the years, Togliatti had supported the principle of a government coalition between the three democratic parties and, by an impressive display of statesmanship, had sought to prove the value of Communist co-operation in the rebuilding of democracy and the country's economy. Now the Communists found themselves removed from the government for no apparent concrete reason. By inciting unrest they therefore tried to show how, lacking their co-operation in the government, the country would be threatened with chaos. From July until the middle of December 1947 there was a series of short-term strikes, combined with stormy street demonstrations, in town after town: Milan, Ancona, Leghorn, Lecco, Messina, and above all, in Rome. All these, however, fell short of confrontations with the armed forces of the state, and it was obviously not a part of Togliatti's plan to push the struggle as far as a violent revolutionary uprising. With the general strike which began in Rome on 11 December and which, in the face of massive police opposition, was broken off on the second day, the strike movement was for the moment exhausted.

It began again on a greater scale on 14 July 1948, triggered off by an attempt made on Togliatti's life as he left the parliamentary building by a young Fascist; Togliatti, struck by four pistol bullets, was seriously wounded. The general council of the C.G.I.L. at once called for a general strike, and, above all in the north, but also in the south, street demonstrations led to violent clashes with the forces of the state. The indignation of the working classes against the de Gasperi government's tolerance of an undisguised Fascist movement, the *Movimento Sociale Italiano*, had, as in the strikes of 1947, broken out once again. De Gasperi's party had, however, won a clear majority in parliament in the election in April and the prime minister felt himself strong enough to defy the storm evoked by the attempted murder.

1. See Neufeld, *Italy: School for Awakening*, p. 470.

The strike was broken off after thirty-six hours without any concessions being made.

The political character of the strikes from July until the middle of December as well as of the general strike was obvious; they were organized by the Communists in their fight against de Gasperi's government. The C.G.I.L., whose general council carried responsibility for the strike movement, was, however, a confederation not only of Communist and Socialist trade unions, but also of the Catholic unions. Giulio Pastore (1902–1969), the leader of the group of Catholic trade unions after Achille Grandi's death, had protested in the general council of the C.G.I.L. against the strikes of 1947 as a political movement, had denounced the general strike of July 1948 as being in breach of the Pact of Rome and had asked the Catholic-organized members to return to work. He and his followers were branded by the Communists and Socialists as traitors, whereupon the Catholic trade unions separated from the C.G.I.L. and reconstituted themselves at a congress in Rome in October 1948 as a trade union federation under the title of *Libera Confederazione Generale Italiana del Lavoro* (L.C.G.I.L.).

The great achievement of the Pact of Rome of 1944 had been to unite the trade union movements of every alignment; this unity had now been broken, but it was not yet the end of the splitting process. A month later, in May 1949, the trade unions led by Saragat's party left the C.G.I.L. to form the Italian Workers' Federation (*Federazione Italiana del Lavoro*—F.I.L.)[1] at a congress in Rome.

The Italian labour movement, its political as well as its trade union wing, was now split three ways. In the last analysis, it was the break-up of the alliance between the Western powers and the Soviet Union which had broken the unity of the labour movement in France as well as in Italy. The struggle between Communists and the Social Democrats was not about the question of a Communist *versus* a democratic form of constitution or whether the working-class struggle for power should be achieved through democracy or revolution; nor about differing economic and socio-political demands. As in France, the Communist party in Italy during the period 1944 to 1948 (or at any later date) neither proclaimed the setting up of a Soviet dictatorship as the objective of its efforts, nor attempted to seize the reins of power by revolutionary means. At each step it declared itself in favour of democracy and, in common with the reformist Socialists, directed its policies towards social reform rather than towards revolution. It remained profoundly aware, however, of its deep-rooted alliance with the Soviet Union, and thus it became necessary for it to call into being impassable barriers between itself and Social Democracy, which was once again outlawed by Moscow as traitor of the working classes. And when in the autumn of 1947 Moscow

1. For the strike actions of the Communists and the splitting of the trade union movement, see Neufeld, *Italy: School for Awakening*, pp. 470–6.

finalized its breach with the Western powers with the founding of the Cominform and called upon the Communist parties of all countries to begin a revolutionary offensive,[1] the Italian Communist party aligned its policy with the rest. It took up its position of solidarity with the Soviet Union opposing the Marshall Plan—the offensive's actual objective—and thus placed an unbridgeable chasm between itself and the democratic trends in the working classes.

1. See pp. 144–46, 148–51.

4 · The Problem of Unification in the German Labour Movement

The split in the German labour movement had a more profound significance than in any other European country. In Britain, Belgium, Holland and Scandinavia, as in Austria and Switzerland, the Communist movement remained largely sectarian and powerless to influence political developments. Even in those countries in which Communism enjoyed a mass following, such as France (until the coming of the Popular Front in 1935) and Czechoslovakia, the split, while it weakened any influence the working classes might have had on political processes, hardly amounted to a full-scale catastrophe. In Italy, Hungary and Bulgaria it was not the split itself which precipitated the defeat of the Socialist movement, but the spectre of the 'dictatorship of the proletariat'.[1]

It was in Germany, however, that the struggle for alignment between the Social Democrats and Communists degenerated into a bitter internecine strife—a struggle waged with passionate hatred between worker and worker in assembly halls, factories, mines, on the streets and even on the barricades. Only in Germany did the split become the tragedy of the working class and indeed of the country and the whole world. When the collapse of the imperial régime gave the working class its opportunity of state power, it was its dissensions which prevented the restructuring into a Social Democracy governed by the working class of a country hitherto controlled by an alliance of capital and the Junkers. While the working class bled to death in fratricidal struggle, the counter-revolution organized itself and, in its triumph, destroyed the whole Socialist labour movement—with dreadful consequence for all mankind.

From this utter defeat at the hands of the new Nazi régime, the realization slowly dawned on Communists and Socialists alike that the split in the labour movement had been a tragic error of enormous dimensions. Thus a determination grew among the broad mass of Socialists that, once the Nazis

1. For the struggle between Communists and Social Democrats, see Braunthal, *History of the International 1914–1943, passim.*

had been overthrown, the unity of Socialist interests should never again be hazarded for the sake of theoretical or tactical conflicts.

This was the solemn attestation behind the first statement put out by the Social Democratic party executive in exile at the end of January 1934 in Prague, where they had fled in 1933. The so-called 'Prague Manifesto of 1934' was drawn up by Rudolf Hilferding (1877–1941). It outlined a programme for a revolutionary struggle to overthrow Hitler together with the policies to be followed after this had been achieved. It stated:

We have shown the way; we have shown the aim of the struggle. The differences within the labour movement have been annulled by the enemy. The reason for the split has become void. . . . The unification of the working class becomes a priority, which history itself demands. German Social Democracy, having freed itself from sectarianism, is awake to its mission to unite the working class in a party of revolutionary Socialism. . . . It refuses to sanction the self-destruction which others have sought to perpetuate, since victories can hardly be gained while the division of the working class remains the [Nazi] dictatorship's surest safeguard.[1]

The Communist International, however, maintained its implacable hostility towards Social Democracy. Its May appeal, appearing three months after the manifesto, once again denounced Social Democracy as the ally of Fascism;[2] underground Communist propaganda in Nazi Germany continued to direct its spleen against Social Democracy as a leading enemy of the working class.

But the hope of the manifesto, that revolution would prove the force to forge the working class together, remained unfulfilled. During the course of three years, the power of Hitler's police state destroyed all cells of resistance and broke down any fighting spirit which may have remained. And, after the Nazi–Soviet Pact in August 1939, the gap between Social Democrats and Communists became absolute. Communist propaganda savagely attacked the Social Democrats as agents in the service of British imperialism who were 'against the working people' of Germany.[3]

Only after the Soviet Union itself had fallen victim to Hitler's duplicity did the unification of all the enemies of Fascism under one banner to fight Hitler's dictatorship become the Communist watchword. When Stalin dissolved the Communist International in May 1943, it seemed as if the last obstacle in the way of working-class unity had disappeared. The question became urgent when, in the spring of 1945, the defeat of Hitler's Germany became only a question of time. With the fall of Fascism close, the Socialists

1. *Neuer Vorwärts* (Prague), 28 January 1934. The manifesto was issued under the title: *Kampf und Ziel des revolutionären Sozialismus. Die Politik der Sozialdemokratischen Partei Deutschlands.* For the text, see Wolfgang Abendroth, *Aufstieg und Krise der deutschen Sozialdemokratie* (Frankfurt, 1964), pp. 114–22.

2. See Braunthal, *History of the International, 1914–1943*, pp. 394–6.

3. For Ulbricht's article, see *Die Welt* (Stockholm), 9 February 1940, quoted in ibid., p. 532.

faced the problem of rebuilding the labour movement to carry out its tasks in the new Germany which would rise from the ruins.

Again, the initiative for unification came from the Social Democrats—in fact from inmates of Buchenwald concentration camp. Hermann Brill, sentenced by a people's court in 1939 to twelve years' hard labour, had been brought after four years of his sentence to Buchenwald, and there, in April 1945, with Benedikt Kautsky, who had already been in the concentration camp for almost seven years, drew up a manifesto outlining the measure which they saw as 'necessary to save Germany from this historic and unprecedented collapse'.

It is a moving document, coming, as it does, from martyrs for the cause of Socialism.

We have [it states as an introduction] borne prison and concentration camps because we have believed that even under dictatorship it was essential to work for the ideals and aims of Socialism and for the preservation of peace. In prison and concentration camps we have continued with our conspiratorial activities despite the daily threat of a terrible death. . . . In the spirit of those victims of our ideals who died at the hands of Hitler's executioners . . . we feel duty-bound to inform the German people of measures which we see as necessary if Germany is to be saved from unprecedented historical collapse.

The thirty-three signatories of the manifesto identified themselves as representative of the whole spectrum of Socialist prisoners. The measures which they proposed for transforming the Fascist state into a truly 'Socialist people's republic' therefore carried the marks of democratic Socialism. To realize its ideals, the manifesto stated, 'the unity of the Socialist movement is indispensable. . . . Founded on the ideals of the class struggle and of internationalism,' it continued, 'and on the fact that the realization of Socialism is not a question of a future state but an immediate task, we wish to establish the unity of the labour movement as a unity of practical, proletarian action.' In particular, the manifesto appealed to those 'parties and trade unions who are at the roots of the class struggle' urgently to set up after initial discussion a preparatory committee which would have the task of organizing a constituent congress to determine the statutes of a Socialist Unity party and to set up the party organs.[1]

Unity in the Socialist movement following the fall of Fascism in fact became a dominant theme at both Socialist and Communist meetings. Kurt Schumacher first formulated this viewpoint on 6 May 1945—two days before the capitulation of Germany when former officials of the Social Democratic party assembled in Hanover to form a local party. Hanover had been

1. For the text of the Buchenwald Manifesto, see Benedikt Kautsky, *Teufel und Verdammte. Erfahrungen und Erkenntnisse aus sieben Jahren in deutschen Konzentrationslagern* (Zürich, 1946), pp. 299–304; Abendroth, *Aufstieg und Krise der deutschen Sozialdemokratie*, pp. 123–7.

occupied by American troops on 10 April, and within nine days the group had passed a resolution to rebuild the party organization, though they could, of course, concern themselves initially only with rebuilding at local level. With the collapse of totalitarian rule, the social and economic structure of the state collapsed also in a dissolution unparalleled in modern history. The land was divided by the Allies into four occupation zones, each closed to the others, the highest power of state devolving to the appointed military governors, who, apprehensive that the forces of National Socialism might regroup inside camouflaged organizations, at first forbade the founding of any party. For this reason, the local association in Hanover was only able to constitute itself in secrecy.

Kurt Schumacher (1895–1952), who had called this local group into being and who in his report developed the future aims and policies for German Social Democracy, had been a leader of the *Reichsbanner* (a para-military Social Democratic force for the defence of the Weimar Republic) and a Socialist deputy before suffering ten years in prison and concentration camps. Severely wounded in the First World War, his right arm had been amputated, and through an eye-infection picked up in the concentration camp, he had lost his full vision. His appearance seemed to personify Germany's tragedy: crippled and emaciated, glaring eyes and a face drawn with pain. But his speech, which developed his thought on the destiny of German Social Democracy, shone with inspiration. Through the rare gifts of personality that he displayed, it became obvious that he would be the one called upon to lead the party.[1]

As in Hanover, so in other towns, above all in Berlin, former Social Democrats began to reconstitute their local groups. But the inaugural assembly of the organization in Hanover had a particular significance for the history of Social Democracy in Germany, since it established the basis for the renewal of its ideals.

Schumacher considered that one of the most important tasks facing the party was to safeguard its intellectual and political independence from the forces of occupation. 'The Social Democratic party,' he wrote in the summer of 1945, 'aligns itself with the political and social needs of the German working population. It cannot and will not agree to becoming the manipulated instrument of any one of the victorious powers. Even as it is independent internally, it must remain independent of foreign influence. Our party is neither Russian nor British, French nor American.'[2]

1. See Friedrich Heine, *Kurt Schumacher. Ein demokratischer Sozialist europäischer Prägung* (Göttingen, 1969); Lewis J. Edinger, *Kurt Schumacher. A Study in Personality and Political Behaviour* (Stanford, 1965); Fried Wesemann, *Kurt Schumacher. Ein Leben für Deutschland* (Frankfurt, 1952). For a biographical essay, see Werner Blumenberg, *Kämpfer für die Freiheit* (Berlin and Hanover, 1959), pp. 163–71.
2. Arno Scholz and Walter G. Oschilewski (eds), *Turmwächter der Demokratie. Ein Lebensbild von Kurt Schumacher* (Berlin, 1953), vol. II. *Reden und Schriften*, p. 33.

Pursuing this theme, he went on to examine the question which, as he said, was 'closest to our hearts as Socialists in co-operating with other parties': the future relationship between Social Democrats and Communists. While admitting that a Socialist Unity party appeared to many workers to be 'the ideal and, for the German experience, the most suitable solution', he turned decisively against it. The Unity party idea, he stated, was impracticable owing to power-political factors and external ties. The dividing line arose from the obligations of the Communists towards a single one of the major victorious powers, that is Russia as a state and its external policies. 'But we, as Social Democrats,' he continued, 'will not depart from our belief that we must take notice of the political and social needs of the German working classes, and from this first principle, must work for international co-operation between every workers' party. We cannot,' he stated, 'and do not wish to become the puppet instrument of foreign imperialist interests.'

This was also, it will be remembered, the cardinal argument used by Léon Blum against an organic unification of the French Socialist party with the Communists.[1] In France, however, the argument had only had a theoretical significance. In Germany, on the other hand, partly occupied by Russia, it carried direct political import for the country's future social and political make-up. 'The Communists,' Schumacher stated, 'with their complete orientation towards Moscow, hope to graft the example and method of one country on to the political and economic conditions prevailing in other countries and to declare this as the orthodox method to be used in the struggle. But we do not wish for any such one-sided tie of obedience, nor do we recognize any categorical pattern of class struggle or any absolute rules which could be valid for all countries and at all times.'[2]

Schumacher's attitude to the principle of a Unity party, however, represented a conflict with the prevailing general mood, especially in Berlin and the cities under Soviet rule in the Eastern Zone. Conquered by a revolutionary Socialist power, as the Soviet Union appeared in the eyes of many, the workers believed that now at last the era of Socialist revolution had dawned in Germany and that therefore, as had been laid down in the Prague Manifesto of the S.P.D. executive, the reasons for the split had become invalidated and the solidarity of the working class was now the top priority. At its conference in Berne on 1 February 1939 the Communist party in exile had also declared itself in favour of a 'united revolutionary party', asking Communists working with the underground 'to create a united organization for a single future party of the German working class'.[3]

1. See p. 26.
2. Quoted in Wesemann, *Kurt Schumacher*, p. 73. The book contains a shortened transcript of the report; the complete manuscript text is in the S.P.D. archives in Bonn.
3. For the text of the resolution, see *Zur Geschichte der Kommunistischen Partei Deutschlands. Ein Auswahl von Materialien und Dokumenten aus den Jahren 1914–1946*, (Berlin, 1955), pp. 393–410, subsequently referred to as *Materialien und Dokumente*.

So while in Hanover a majority of Social Democrats, apparently under the impact of Schumacher's speech, declared themselves against any union of the two Socialist factions, the group of Social Democrats in Berlin emerged strongly in favour. Schumacher's Hanover speech could hardly have been known to the party members in Berlin; and Berlin represented a special claim to authority in expressing the wishes of all German Social Democrats. It was not, of course, an authority that lay exclusively in the hands of the Berlin group either but, simply as a result of Berlin's position as the former capital and as the traditional centre of Social Democracy, their action carried special weight.

Berlin fell to the Red Army a few weeks after the taking of Hanover. Immediately after the capitulation had been signed on 8 May, a Social Democrat group, led by Otto Grotewohl (b. 1894), a former member of parliament and minister of state in Brunswick, Max Fechner, at one time a Prussian parliamentary deputy, and Gustav Dahrendorf, a member of parliament who had been sentenced by the Nazis to seven years' hard labour, attempted to contact Walter Ulbricht who had been leader of the Communist party under the Weimar Republic. Ulbricht had arrived in Berlin on 1 May in a Soviet aircraft direct from Moscow, and the Social Democrats were anxious to commence discussions on the founding of a Socialist Unity party as soon as possible. But, to their intense surprise, Ulbricht was not available.[1]

In repeatedly refusing invitations to discuss the founding of a Unity party, Ulbricht was acting, according to Wolfgang Leonhard, in line with directives that he had received before departing from Moscow.[2] According to these, not even the rebirth of the Communist party was envisaged as being part of the original plans for the Soviet Union's political strategy for Germany. In every country at that time occupied by the Red Army, the Communists had been instructed not to appear as an independent party, or even as a 'workers' party', but to create broadly based anti-Fascist organizations which under oblique Communist leadership were to become the basis of Communist-

1. The following account is based on a detailed study by Albrecht Kaden, *Einheit oder Freiheit. Die Wiedergründung der S.P.D. 1945–46* (Hanover, 1964); and on Waldemar Ritter, *Kurt Schumacher. Eine Untersuchung seiner politischen Konzeption* (Hanover, 1964); Carola Stern, *Porträt einer bolschewistischen Partei. Entwicklung, Funktion und Situation der S.E.D.* (Cologne, 1957); *Dokumente und Materialien der deutschen Arbeiterbewegung*, Series 3, vol. I: *Mai 1945–April 1946* (Berlin, 1959). The preface to this collection (subsequently referred to as *Dokumente*) outlines the official Communist view of the rise of the S.P.D. See also Hermann Weber, *Von der S.B.Z. zur D.D.R. 1945–1958* (Hanover, 1966), Chapter 1. For accounts from a Communist viewpoint, see Horst Lipski, *Deutschland und die deutsche Arbeiterbewegung 1945–1949* (Berlin, 1963); Hans Müller, *Die Entwicklung der S.E.D. und ihr Kampf für ein neues Deutschland 1945–1949* (Berlin, 1961).

2. Wolfgang Leonhard, *Die Revolution entlässt ihre Kinder* (Cologne and Berlin, 1955), p. 327. Leonhard, who had grown up in the Soviet Union and been educated in the Comintern school, was a member of the ten-man 'Ulbricht group' which arrived in Berlin on 1 May 1945. Before its departure, a selected group of German emigrants had been given their directives for working in the Soviet state system; Leonhard became a member of the Central Bureau of the Communist party.

controlled government 'blocs'. This, as we shall see, happened with the 'Democratic Bloc' in Poland, the 'National Democratic Bloc' in Romania and the 'Fatherland Front' in Bulgaria.[1] In the Soviet Zone of Germany the 'Bloc of Fighting Democracy' was intended to fulfil the same task.

But then, a month after Ulbricht's return to Berlin, a further delegation of important party dignitaries under the leadership of Wilhelm Pieck (1876–1960) arrived from Moscow with fresh instructions. These reiterated the necessity of forming a 'bloc', but at the same time instructed the immediate formation of a new Communist party while rejecting the concept of Socialist unity which had been supported at the Berne Conference of the Communist party in February 1939.[2] By 10 June, the right to form political parties had been granted by Marshal Grigori Zhukov, the military governor of the Soviet Zone, and on the following day the announcement of the forthcoming formation of the Communist party appeared in the Berlin press; it constituted itself on 12 June in the Big Hall of the Berlin Senate.

Grotewohl and his colleagues were taken unawares by this turn of events. Their hope had been that from the very start of the struggle to build a new Germany, a single Socialist Unity party would stand at the head of the working classes instead of a Social Democratic party and a Communist party; but now this plan had been thwarted by the Communists. At once Grotewohl's group constituted itself as the 'Central Committee of the S.P.D.' and dispatched Dahrendorf to the inaugural meeting of the Communist party, at which he was to state in 'the name of the reborn Social Democratic party the wish to bring about the organizational unity of the workers' and to affirm a readiness 'to talk on every question of unity with Communist friends'.[3]

It was Ulbricht's speech which opened the debate, and it made no reference to Socialist unity. In bringing about the rebuilding of a new Germany, the co-ordination of all the anti-Fascist democratic factions was, he stated, an absolute necessity; the Communist party would suggest to the 'S.P.D., the Christian Democrat party and the other anti-Fascist democratic organizations' that they should consider forming a bloc with the Communists.[4] Yet every speaker who followed Ulbricht in the discussion was in support of the idea of forming a single united Socialist party.[5]

Three days after the Communists' inaugural meeting, the S.P.D. central committee issued a proclamation announcing the formation of the new

1. For Poland, see p. 103; for Romania, p. 114; for Bulgaria, p. 117.
2. See Leonhard, ibid., pp. 389–90.
3. Quoted in Kaden, *Einheit oder Freiheit*, p. 38.
4. For the text of Ulbricht's speech, see *Dokumente*, pp. 21–4.
5. See Leonhard, *Die Revolution entlässt ihre Kinder*, p. 399. In the report which Leonhard, who attended the inaugural meeting, wrote for *Deutsche Volkszeitung*, the central organ of the Communist party, all references by speakers to the necessity for a unified Socialist party were deleted.

Socialist party, and posters were put up in the streets inviting all Socialist representatives to attend an inaugural meeting called for 17 June. Thus, as in Hanover, the labour movement in Berlin was with reluctance divided into two parties.

The inaugural manifesto of each party already showed conflicts of intention. The Social Democrats' appeal was for the party to aim at forming the new Germany on a truly Socialist basis: 'Democracy in state and community, Socialism in economy and society'. The manifesto ended its explanation of the immediate measures needed to realize this aim with the slogan: 'Fight Fascism, for the people's freedom, for democracy and for Socialism.'[1]

In the inaugural manifesto of the Communist party, however, no reference is to be found to the word 'Socialism'. It openly acknowledged the capitalist economic system; it demanded a 'completely uninterrupted development of free trade and private employers' initiative on the basis of property ownership'. As Leonhard recorded, the Communist officials selected to go to Germany had been instructed in Moscow that they were not to consider either the realization of Socialism or the preparation for Socialist development as being their immediate task.

Socialism [the directive instructed] must be condemned as a damaging tendency and one which must be fought. Germany is now facing a democratic middle-class transition which, in content and spirit, is a culmination of the democratic middle-class revolution of 1848. It is important to support this culmination actively while resisting any Socialist solutions, since under present conditions they would amount to complete demagogy.[2]

The task as defined by the Communist party's manifesto was 'to bring to a conclusion the move towards a democratization of the middle classes which had begun in 1848'. But this avowal of democracy was not completely unqualified, the next paragraph going on to state:

We are of the opinion that to force the Soviet system on Germany would be to take the wrong path, because this path does not correspond with *present* development conditions in Germany. We are rather of the opinion that the paramount interests of the German people in the *present* situation prescribe a different path, namely the path of the resurgence of an anti-Fascist democratic régime, a parliamentary republic incorporating democratic rights and people's freedom.[3]

1. For the text of the manifesto, see *Dokumente*, pp. 28–31.
2. Leonhard, *Die Revolution entlässt ihre Kinder*, p. 325. The official Communist attitude to this question can be found in the Foreword to *Dokumente*: 'After the defeat of Fascism, many honest Communist and Social Democratic workers, who were not sufficiently familiar with Marxism–Leninism, felt that the time was right to erect Socialism forthwith. The right-wing S.P.D. leaders of Schumacher's group tried to exploit this confusion by attempting to cloak their co-operation with the imperialist forces of occupation and reactionary elements in Germany, to sabotage working-class unity and prevent democratic development under the demagogic phrase, "Socialism as a daily task" ' (pp. 12–13).
3. For the text of the appeal, see *Dokumente*, pp. 14–20. (The italics are the author's.)

Democracy was therefore in no way acknowledged as a fundamental principle but rather as being suitable for the 'present situation', while the system of dictatorship—the so-called Soviet system—was by no means discarded, but simply reserved for possible future 'development conditions'.

In this way the German Communist party reoccupied the stage of history with a programme which, on the face of it, any democratic, middle-class, capitalist party might support without qualm, since it guaranteed the pre-eminence of a middle-class, capitalist social order.[1]

The content of the programme, however, had been composed not in Berlin but in Moscow; Wilhelm Pieck had brought it in his luggage, together with the new directives.[2] It spoke not with the voice of the 'honest Communist worker' of Germany, but with the voice of Joseph Stalin. His evident intention was to convince Truman and Churchill at the Potsdam Conference, due to take place in the middle of July and which could play a decisive part in the plans he had for Eastern Europe and the Balkans,[3] that nothing was further from the Soviet Union's mind than the concept of world revolution. Moreover, the approval of capitalist economics in the inaugural manifesto was no doubt aimed at winning German middle-class parties over to the idea of a 'bloc'.

In complete contrast to the Communist programme, that of the Social Democrats demanded that the way to Socialist change should be paved by the nationalization of banks, mines, power industries, insurance companies and mineral deposits.[4] Socialism, it declared, now had a direct appeal to all 'honest Social Democratic workers', as the obvious consequence of the fall of Fascism, for, with it, Schumacher stated in Hanover, 'German capitalism . . . has itself collapsed together with its political systems and parties'. Therefore the realization of Socialism had become the task in hand for the working class. 'The crucial necessity,' he wrote, 'is to bring about the abolition of capitalist extortion and to take the means of production out of the hands of the tycoons to make of it a common property, the direction of the whole economy then being not in the interests of private profiteering but following the necessities of required planning'. And, speaking in harmony with Grotewohl's group in Berlin, he defined the nationalization of all large industrial enterprises and high finance as well as the redevelopment of landed property as being absolute essentials. 'Above all,' he wrote, 'the mines, heavy industries, power industries, transport, a large section of the manufacturing industry as well as the insurance and banking economies are not

1. Even with such agrarian reform as the Communist programme visualized, only the 'great estates of the Junkers, counts and dukes' were to be included. 'It will be obvious,' it stated, 'that these measures will in no way affect the land or the economy of the big farmers'—*Dokumente*, p. 19.

2. See Leonhard, *Die Revolution entlässt ihre Kinder*, p. 392.

3. See the next chapter, 'The Origins of the "Cold War" '.

4. *Dokumente*, p. 30.

only ripe for socialization, but must be nationalized if the German economy is to function effectively.'[1]

It was inevitable that the whole idea of a Unity party should founder, considering the one fundamental conflict in the respective aims of the Communist and Social Democratic parties, for, as Schumacher wrote, it would become 'a playground of the most bitter internecine quarrels and of reciprocal deceit'. Yet, even so, Schumacher did not turn against an action alliance with the Communist party. 'We accept without reservation,' he stated, 'a practical co-operation with the Communist party on all social questions and all aspects relating to the stamping-out of Fascism. This co-ordination will be organized in such a way that the Social Democratic and Communist parties will retain their respective ideological and organizational independence.' Such a co-ordination of effort, 'with no attempts at reciprocal deceit', would, he believed, bring about an atmosphere suitable for creating 'improved conditions for a possible union in the future, instead of forcing through the idea of unity.'[2]

On the other hand, Otto Grotewohl (1894–1964), as chairman of the central committee of the S.P.D. in Berlin, wished to see the immediate founding of a Unity party without waiting for the processes of co-operation between the two parties to bring about an atmosphere of mutual trust. For his group the Unity party seemed to be the one effective guarantee against a resurgence of the schism which had proved such grave disaster to the German working class. And whatever doubts the Berlin Social Democrats felt about the Communists' policy, they believed it would be possible to bring sufficient influence to bear for the Social Democrats to form a working majority in any such party.[3]

Yet while in Britain the Communist party executive was striving for representation in the Labour party, and in France pressing hard to bring about a fusion of the two Socialist parties, in Germany it dismissed any proposal for organizational unification as untimely.

In their understandable haste to see an organizational unity being created within the workers' movement as quickly as possible [the justification in the official history ran], it was overlooked by certain comrades that, despite an extensive agreement over many questions that were soon to be solved, there were nevertheless politico-ideological differences, and this prejudice and mistrust would have had to be removed. . . . Failing a modicum of politico-ideological understanding, any

1. Quoted in *Turmwächter der Demokratie*, vol. II, pp. 37 and 38.
2. Kurt Schumacher, *Politische Richtlinien* (Hanover, 1945), quoted in Kaden, *Einheit oder Freiheit*, pp. 79 and 80. This memorandum was submitted as a basis for the state conference of the S.P.D. in October 1945.
3. And, indeed, a few months after the rebirth of the S.P.D., in the elections of a works council of thirty-two members in the Leuna works, twenty-six Social Democrats, five centre parties' representatives and one Communist were elected; see Kaden, *Einheit oder Freiheit*, p. 84.

fusion of the two workers' parties would have been useless. A unification which neither rested on a solid Marxist basis nor made it possible for a Unity party to evolve into a party of a new type would, from its very inception, have carried within itself the seed of a renewed split.[1]

On 19 June, the central committees of the two parties, however, agreed at least to form an action alliance, and they set up a joint committee to work for 'closer co-operation in the building of an anti-Fascist democratic society' as well as 'to clarify ideological questions'. The S.P.D. had also, on 14 June, joined the constituted 'bloc of anti-Fascist democratic parties' (the bloc embracing, apart from the two worker parties, the Christian Democratic Union and the Liberal Democratic party). But the central committee of the Communist party still declined to discuss the formation of a unified party with the Social Democrats; for them this had to remain a 'distant objective'.

It was an attitude which they maintained for six months, up till the beginning of November 1945. One can only speculate on what their motives may have been, since the official archives remain sealed. But it does not seem unreasonable to suggest that Moscow would have been prepared to sanction a unified party only provided it could have been guaranteed as a willing instrument of Soviet policy. This being so, the Communists would have had to change in their favour the balance of power between themselves and the Social Democrats before giving consideration to the formation of a unified party in whose structure they would be ensured a dominant influence.

The Soviet occupation forces naturally spared no pains in attempting to promote such a development. In filling administrative positions in the provincial and district councils, they favoured Communist applicants; they impeded the licensing of Social Democratic newspapers while making concessions of newsprint allocations to the Communist press.[2] Above all, they supplied the Communist party apparatus with officials carefully schooled in Russia—German prisoners of war repatriated *en masse*.

For the Social Democratic central committee, however, a unified party remained the 'immovable aim', as Grotewohl had expressed it at a mass meeting of 3,000 S.P.D. officials in Berlin on 14 September. But he could not suppress his disappointment at the predominating lack of encouragement for true co-operation with the Communists. The ideological differences between Communists and Social Democrats had hardly been spanned by the ambiguous gesture towards democracy which was contained in the Communist inaugural manifesto, for in practical terms this remained no more

1. *Dokumente*, p. 16.
2. While the Communist press was enjoying at the turn of the years 1945–6 a total circulation of more than four million copies, the whole circulation of the Social Democratic press was restricted to under a million issues; see Stern, *Porträt einer bolschewistischen Partei*, p. 84.

than lip service. 'Our friends in the Communist party central committee,' Grotewohl protested with careful diplomacy, 'are experiencing a degree of difficulty in convincing their followers that acknowledging the application of democracy has become a historic necessity.' The Social Democrats, he said, 'could only harbour doubts about an honest conviction being contained in a Communist orientation'. Mistrust between the two parties had not by any means been overcome, and Social Democrats were being slandered by the Communists. Yet, if the quest for a common workers' party were to be fulfilled, the Communists should not look towards 'their Social Democratic comrades in any search for traitors'. Grotewohl also complained of the breach of the agreed principle of parity through the preferences being given to Communists in filling vacant posts at the top of the civil service as well as in local government. From both sides, he stated, 'opinions against minor eccentricities and petty jealousies must be expressed, because without the genuine mutual trust of true comradeship any unified organization will be condemned to inaction'.[1]

Grotewohl went on to develop the idea of how he saw the historical destiny of Social Democracy in the new Germany. As the standard-bearer of Socialist tradition, it was the party's duty to stand up for democratic principles in face of Communist opposition, and for Socialist principles in face of objections by the bourgeois parties. Its historic function must be to act as a mediator between the varied concepts of the 'bloc' parties now, as in government and state in the future, as a focal point for all the political ideas and aims of the other parties in general. This function would win for the party the leading role in the future German Republic.

But the Communist executive was not prepared to grant the Social Democrats any leading position in the new state. It demanded that function exclusively for the Communist party, which, Ulbricht stated, 'had proved itself through the fight it had carried out against German imperialism', and was therefore entitled to claim its role as the 'dynamo of democratic reconstruction' with special responsibilities. He also decisively rejected Grotewohl's concept of Social Democracy as playing the mediator in ideological strife. 'The action unity of the K.P.D. and S.P.D. allows for no "middle position",' he said. 'Any attempt to occupy such a middle position must weaken the unity of the working class and only aid the infiltration of reactionary influences into their numbers.'[2] And Franz Dahlem, also a member of the Communist central committee, replied to Grotewohl's complaint at the damage being done by unfairness in filling official posts by saying 'that for us Communists the question of any numerical equality between the K.P.D. and S.P.D. in

1. Otto Grotewohl, *Wo stehen wir, wohin gehen wir ? Der historische Auftrag der S.P.D.*, (Berlin, 1945), quoted in Kaden, *Einheit oder Freiheit*, pp. 81–2.
2. *Deutsche Volkszeitung*, 14 October 1945, quoted in Stern, *Porträt einer bolschewistischen Partei*, pp. 26 and 27.

filling positions is less important than the necessity of establishing a strong, democratic and anti-Fascist sense of direction.[1]

These high-handed rejections of Grotewohl's statement and protest were hardly calculated to fire enthusiasm for a Unity party among the Social Democratic factions; but the Communists remained unconcerned, for the Unity party concept did not feature on the agenda they were laying down, in which it remained a 'distant objective'.

Then, three weeks later, the Communist executive underwent a startling *volte-face* in its attitude to the whole question. At a mass rally in Berlin on 9 November to celebrate the anniversary of the revolution in Germany, Wilhelm Pieck, supreme leader of the Communist party, declared that now it must strive 'with all its strength' to bring into being 'a unified German workers party. Only in this way will the decisive influences in anti-Fascist democracy be safeguarded for the working class.'[2] Unification with the Social Democrats to form a single party, hitherto regarded as merely a 'distant objective', was now all at once to be realized 'as quickly as possible'.

The reasons for this sudden turnabout in Communist tactics are again a matter for speculation; since it had been ordered by confidential directives from Moscow, it could hardly be otherwise. Evidently Stalin had begun to realize that he had miscalculated how the ratio of power between the Social Democratic and Communist parties would develop. Considering the mood of the hard-pressed population in the Russian occupation zone, it was a remarkably elementary mistake. The excesses of the Red Army soldiers when they had entered Germany, the dismantling of plant and machinery undertaken by the Russians and the reparations which they had secured as a toll out of current production would hardly have awoken warm sympathies for the Soviet Union; and the Communist party was clearly regarded as a tool of the Soviet Union, as the Russian party.

When Moscow directed that, for the time being, no united workers' party was to be formed with the Social Democrats, the view prevalent there, as it was for the Communist executive in Berlin, was that eventually the people would come to accept the Russian occupation as a permanent factor in their lives, would recognize that their future depended upon the benevolence of the Soviet Union and would then come to see the Communist party as their most effective guardian. But as symptoms of the prevailing public temper became more obvious as, for example, in the works' council election at the Leuna works,[3] so this illusion was progressively destroyed. However, local elections had already been proposed by the Allies for all the zones in Germany

1. *Deutsche Volkszeitung*, 26 October 1945, quoted in ibid., p. 26.
2. *Deutsche Volkszeitung*, 10 November 1945, quoted in Stern, *Porträt einer bolschewistischen Partei*, pp. 27–8.
3. See p. 77.

to take place in 1946. Moscow could not face the risk of elections which would not secure the Communist party its claim to leadership of the working class because all Stalin's plans for Germany depended on Communists holding leading positions in the new state. Now that it had become doubtful whether the Communist party could ever emerge with effective power from an election in the Soviet Zone, the Social Democrats had to be called on to act as 'blood donors', as Schumacher put it, and to be wooed to join with the Communist party. Hence the sudden urge of the Communists to see the formation of a proletarian Unity party.

But now it was the Social Democratic party's central committee which hesitated to launch itself precipitately into a Unity party enterprise. At their celebration of the revolution, which took place two days after that of the Communists in Berlin, Grotewohl formulated the conditions for alliance. It could not, he said, be brought about as a result of a decision by the party leadership, as the Communists seemed to think, but could only emerge if it was the 'will of all German comrades' that it should do so; nor could it come about as 'a result of external pressure or indirect force'—a warning against possible Communist attempts to force unity by terrorist techniques. Moreover, any unification of the parties must apply throughout the whole German state and not in the Russian Zone alone. So after Pieck had, two days earlier, called for a total unification of the two parties as quickly as possible, Grotewohl now described this as a 'distant goal' which might 'one day' be brought about.[1]

Meanwhile, for the first time since the catastrophic year of 1933, Social Democratic delegates from all over the country had assembled on 6 October 1945 for a conference at Wennigsen, a small village near Hanover. Seventy-six delegates had come from the three Western Zones, with Grotewohl, Fechner and Dahrendorf from the Eastern Zone, and, from London, Erich Ollenhauer and Fritz Heine, two of the surviving members of the party executive who had left the country in 1933. But while the Allies had approved the formation of political parties at the Potsdam Conference, these were not to be permitted at a national level; as a result the conference could not undertake a formal restoration of the German Social Democratic party. Since no overall party leadership could be established, it was agreed temporarily to give responsibility for the leadership of the party in the Eastern Zone to the central committee in Berlin, and that for the three Western Zones to Kurt Schumacher, as political representatives.

The question of a Unity party was dealt with at the conference as one of great significance, but the delegates abstained from committing the party to any decisions that belonged to the future. Grotewohl advocated the necessity

1. See Kaden, *Einheit oder Freiheit*, pp. 188–9; Stern, *Porträt einer bolschewistischen Partei*, p. 29.

of eventual unity for the workers' movement, while Dahrendorf feared disaster if, following reunification of the state and of the parties, 'the unity of the labour movements were not also established; our fight would then have been in vain'. According to the official report, however, the delegates were unanimous in agreeing that the question of organic unity with the Communist party could be decided only at a state congress for a binding decision which represented the view of the whole party. Neither was it a decision which could be made in isolation from the influence of developments in the international labour movement. 'The question of unification,' the report stated, 'is not a German but an international one.' Emphatic in their wish to overcome the split in the workers' movement, the delegates were nevertheless of the 'opinion that a lasting and effective unity can only be achieved when there is agreement on the main Socialist aims and if the party is founded on a true democracy, submitting its leadership and policies exclusively to the control and decisions of its members'.[1]

What made the Unity party a theme of burning urgency for the Communist leadership was an event in Austria: the devastating defeat of the Austrian Communists in the elections to the constituent national assembly of 25 November 1945. Until only a few months previously and for seven years before that, Austria had been the *Ostmark* (Eastern Province) of the Third Reich and was now partly occupied by the Red Army. If the Communists had been defeated there so decisively in spite of the Russian occupation forces, how could the German Communists expect to emerge as the dominant party from free elections, even in the Russian Zone?

But while Austria, like Germany, was subjected to military occupation by the Allied powers—the Russian Zone in Austria embraced the districts of Vienna and Lower Austria where industry was concentrated and the working class was a decisive factor—unlike Germany it was not a vanquished country; rather, like Poland, it was one which had been 'liberated'. In the Moscow Declaration of 30 October 1943 the Allies had declared Germany's annexation of Austria to be null and void, defining the restoration of Austria's independence as a war aim. Thus the question of forming a provisional government arose as soon as the German army was beaten in mid-April 1945 and Austria freed.

In liberated Poland, Stalin had installed a 'Soviet-friendly' government the moment the Red Army was across its eastern borders and still facing a long, heavy fight to gain control of the country;[2] the Polish government was, so to speak, smuggled in on the Red Army's baggage train. In Austria,

1. '*Die Wiedergeburt der deutschen Sozialdemokratie*'. *Bericht über die Vorgeschichte und den Verlauf der sozialdemokratischen Parteikonferenz von Hannover vom 5. bis 7. Oktober 1945* (manuscript in the S.P.D. Archives in Bonn), pp. 13–14; see also Kaden, *Einheit oder Freiheit*, pp. 132–53; Wesemann, *Kurt Schumacher*, pp. 90–4.
2. See p. 94.

however, Stalin caused general astonishment by appointing Karl Renner (1870–1950) as head of the provisional government.

Renner was one of the leading but most controversial figures in Austrian Social Democracy. During the First World War he had supported the German position and the Habsburg Monarchy;[1] he led the Social Democratic right wing in the First Republic and in Hitler's plebiscite of March 1938 had declared himself publicly for the *Anschluss* annexing Austria to Germany. In calling him to the leadership, Stalin had, as Renner's biographer Jacques Hannak stated, 'a sly chess tactic in mind'. Simply because Renner appeared 'tainted' by his past, Stalin believed he would evidently be 'an ideal sort of puppet for the role of president in a satellite government'.[2]

Renner, however, was equal to Stalin's cunning. He unhesitatingly showed Stalin the required deference. In a letter written on 15 April 1945, the day after his summons to office, he paid him homage as the 'highest leader, crowned with glory' of the Red Army. 'Without the Red Army,' he wrote, 'none of my moves [in taking over office] would have been possible; and for this not only I, but the future Austrian "Second Republic" and its workers, remain indebted to you and your victorious army for all time.' And he finished the letter with the declaration:

> Due to Russia's astonishing demonstration of her power, our whole country has come to see through the falsehoods of twenty years of National-Socialist propaganda and to be filled with admiration for the great Soviet achievement.
> The trust of the Austrian working class in particular in the Soviet Union has become boundless. The Austrian Social Democratic party will consult together with the Communist party in fraternal affection and they will work together as equals in the establishment of the new republic. That the country's future lies with Socialism is beyond question and need no longer be stressed.[3]

According to the instructions of the commander of the Russian forces of occupation, Marshal F. Tolbuchin, Renner was to form a coalition government from among the three 'anti-Fascist parties': the Social Democrats, the Communists and even the Austrian People's party, as the Christian Democratic party, which had destroyed the First Republic and installed a Fascist dictatorship, now called itself.[4] Under Tolbuchin's pressure, Renner agreed to allow the Communists to take control of the Ministry of the Interior with power over the political and civil police as well as of the Department of Education and Information with influence over the press and public opinion. But on one point he remained adamant: he insisted that there should

1. See Braunthal, *History of the International, 1914–1943*, pp. 17–18 and 142–3.
2. For, Hannak reasons, 'what trust could they [the Russians] place in a man who had been classified by Lenin as one of the "most despicable lackeys of German imperialism" and as "a traitor to Socialism"?'—Jacques Hannak, *Karl Renner und seine Zeit* (Vienna, 1965), pp. 670–1.
3. For the full text of the letter, see Hannak, *Karl Renner und seine Zeit*, pp. 672–5.
4. See Braunthal, *History of the International, 1914–1943*, pp. 403–14.

be the earliest possible calling of elections for a constituent national assembly.

Marshal Tolbuchin, having sought to delay the holding of elections as long as possible, finally gave in to Renner's insistence, confident of the rapidly growing influence of the Austrian Communist party. The Communists had been a very small party at the time of the First Republic; in no general election had they been able to win more than 20,000 votes against 1,500,000 for the Social Democrats, or to gain a single seat in Parliament. But in the eight months between the beginning of Soviet rule and the date of the elections, they had succeeded in capturing strong positions under the wing of the Soviet occupation forces. Through the Ministry of the Interior they controlled the police force and gendarmerie of several thousand men and the administrative apparatus of the state; through the Department of Information, they controlled the radio and a large part of the press. They controlled the factories, impounded as reparations by Russia, with their tens of thousands of workers and staff; with financial aid from the occupying Soviet power they were able to flood the country with journals and leaflets. They felt they could view the outcome of the elections with confidence.

But it was all to culminate in a catastrophic defeat for the Communist party, which received only 174,000 votes, against 1,435,000 for the Social Democrats; 5 per cent of votes cast, and only four seats out of 165 in the assembly.

Marshal Tolbuchin was naturally profoundly disappointed. The failure of the Communist party, Renner recorded, 'startled the Russian occupation régime, disillusioning it considerably and providing a lasting irritant. The hope that its party would force back Social Democracy in the workers' esteem and take over the leadership had thereby been rendered null and void . . .'[1]

This catastrophe for the Austrian Communist party cast its shadow over the situation in Germany. Any assurance that the Communists might emerge as

---

1. Karl Renner, *Österreich von der Ersten zur Zweiten Republik* (Vienna, 1953), p. 239. Later the Communists tried to reverse their failure at the polls by violent tactics. On the morning of 5 May 1947 they called workers out of the factories and on to the streets, and during a battle with police forces attempted to occupy the offices of the Federal Chancellor. A second attempt at an uprising, in September and October 1950, which had the support of the Soviet forces of occupation, was more serious. A conference of Communist shop stewards had called a general strike to take place on 26 September and had presented the government with an ultimatum, due to expire on 3 October, demanding the fulfilment of certain economic conditions. The Communists sent out raiding parties in attempts to bring the factories to a standstill, block the railways and erect road blocks and barricades in the streets of Vienna. This action was also to falter on the resistance put up by the Social Democratic workers, who defended the factories against the invading Communists and finally forced the abandonment of the strike. See Adolf Schärf, *Österreichs Erneuerung 1945–1955* (Vienna, 1955), pp. 161–3 and 254–9; Alfred Migsch, *Anschlag auf Österreich. Ein Tatsachenbericht über den kommunistischen Putschversuch im September–Oktober 1950* (Vienna, 1950).

the leading party in a German election was now finally dispelled. A unified party had therefore become for the Communists a vital and urgent necessity.[1] The Communist executive suggested to the Social Democratic central executive that there should be a joint conference of thirty representatives from each party to discuss the whole question.

The 'conference of the sixty' sat on 20 and 21 December in Berlin. The S.P.D. (Social Democratic party) central executive had submitted a memorandum to the K.P.D. (Communist party) central committee before the meeting to serve as a basis for discussion and to explain the Social Democratic attitude to unification. According to this concept, both parties were initially to retain full organizational autonomy until fusion was completed; each party was to pledge itself 'to attempt everything possible, and also to lobby the occupying powers, to ensure a cessation of any preference for or prejudice against any one of the parties, be it in respect of the freedom of the organization, be it in respect of the provision of agitation'.[2] Each of the two parties should, 'at least in the first round of elections,' have their own candidate list. Furthermore, favouritism towards Communists in filling administrative positions and 'all inadmissible pressure on the S.P.D. and its individual members' was to cease. Also, the question of unification would have to be decided by a national party congress representing all Social Democrats in Germany.

Yet in the event it was not the Social Democratic memorandum but a Communist draft which served as a basis for discussion. According to this, the parties were to head the election campaign from the outset with joint candidate lists; and they were to 'reach a fraternal understanding' in respect of the selection of candidates and the holding 'of political positions within the joint administration'. The Unity party programme was at its least to achieve 'the fulfilment of a democratic revival in Germany in the spirit of building an anti-Fascist, democratic and parliamentary republic', and, at its most, 'the realization of Socialism . . . through working-class political rule in the spirit of the teachings of Marxism'. The Social Democrats' demand that any decision on the merger of the parties should be reserved for a national party congress was rejected by the Communists since, 'in view of

1. Leonhard recorded: 'The Austrian election and its consequences were the main topic of discussion with us in the central committee. . . . From that day the great unity campaign began. There was only one theme: unity. At every discussion the question of unity was always at the top of the agenda . . .'—Leonhard, *Die Revolution entlässt ihre Kinder*, p. 425.

2. How things stood regarding 'freedom' for the Social Democrats, even in the 'honeymoon' months of Social Democratic–Communist co-operation, was illustrated by Gustav Klingelhöfer, a member of the S.P.D. central executive, during the conference debate. 'You, comrades of the K.P.D.,' he said, 'you can speak openly. You have nothing to fear. You can talk anywhere, and say what you like without even being taken to task. It is a fact that many of our comrades do not feel able to speak what they feel in their hearts, since they wish to exercise restraint because of certain fears resulting from past experience . . .'—quoted in Stern, *Porträt einer bolschewistischen Partei*, p. 44.

the situation in the whole of Germany' it would, they said, 'mean a delay for many months', while on the other hand, 'the fusion of the organizations of both parties in the respective zones is immediately possible.'

In the speech he made on the Communist draft, Grotewohl made it clear that the S.P.D. rejected joint lists for the impending elections; it would be through these elections that the true ratios of party strength would be defined, since the parity demanded by the Communists could not possibly be reached by purely mechanical considerations. He also emphasized that for the organizational fusion of both parties, a national unified organization and the assembly of national party congresses were essential conditions, while on this question 'conflicting concepts may arise for which there can never be a bridge unless the central committee of the K.P.D. insists less strictly on its point of view'.

In the resolution passed by the conference, however, the presence of conflict remained unacknowledged. Each party pledged itself to an 'extended and deepened unity of action' as a 'prelude to the realization of political and organizational unity within the labour movement which would lead to the coming together of the German Social Democratic and Communist parties into one organization'.[1]

But a few days later, Max Fechner reaffirmed the Social Democrats' condition for unity. 'Decision on unity can only,' he wrote, 'be made in the name of the whole party within the German state. Such a decision may only be realized following confirmation by a national party congress . . . if necessary by referendum among its members.'[2]

The referendum was decided upon at the end of December by an enlarged Berlin S.P.D. district executive, and three weeks later a conference of regional delegates in Berlin called on Social Democrat party members in the Soviet Zone to declare by ballot whether they wished for an immediate amalgamation of both labour parties, or only for an alliance which would 'safeguard the task before them and avoid fraternal strife'.

This decision, however, ran contrary to the policy of the S.P.D. central executive which, while it had indeed formulated conditions for the fusion, had held firm to seeing unity as an 'ultimate aim'. But now this policy met strong opposition, organized by Franz Neumann, who unconditionally rejected a Unity party and proposed to force a decision by referendum. The Berlin district executive, whose majority stood in opposition to the central

1. See Kaden, pp. 196–213; Stern, pp. 30–3; for the text of the resolution, see *Dokumente*, pp. 346–54.

2. *Tägliche Rundschau*, 1 January 1946, quoted in Kaden, p. 216; this paper was the organ of the Soviet occupation. On the other hand, the decisions of the central executive of 15 January, that national parties must first be founded before unification could be accomplished, was suppressed by the Russian military government censor in the press of the Soviet Zone. The Social Democratic paper in Dresden which published this decision had to be pulped; see Kaden, p. 228.

executive, called a conference of Social Democratic functionaries for 1 March and, by an overwhelming majority from the 2,000 delegates, sanctioned the decision to hold the vote and stipulated 31 March as the day for the ballot.

The central executive attempted to undermine the decision, seeking through appeals and meetings to influence party members against taking part. In the Soviet Zone the ballot was forbidden by the Russian military government, and so it took place only in the three Western Zones of Berlin. Of the 33,247 members entitled to vote, 23,755 participated. Of these, 2,937 voted in favour of amalgamation while 19,529 (or over 82 per cent) rejected it.

This vote was of deep concern to the Communist party leadership, who could no longer anticipate that a national Social Democratic party congress would come out in favour of unity. They therefore urged the central executive to settle the question of a Unity party without further delay in the five districts of the Soviet Zone.

Grotewohl had also come round to the view that, were the question of a Unity party to be decided by a national party congress, it would never see the light of day.[1] In company with many Social Democratic supporters, he was honestly convinced that it was imperative to overcome the split in the labour movement through the organizational integration of the two workers' parties. The tragic experience of fraternal strife at the time of the Weimar Republic had embedded itself deeply in the consciousness of Germany's workers. 'We could never wish to experience again,' he stated at a Communist conference, 'what we went through between 1933 and 1945. We could never wish to find ourselves once again stepping side by side to the scaffold or into the penitentiary. Our wish is to work jointly together.'[2] Divided, the German working class had been powerless; united, it would form the leading force in the coming Germany.

At the same time many Social Democrats felt that Germany's future would depend economically and politically upon the occupying powers and that they would have to choose between orientation towards capitalist America or Communist Russia. Orientation towards the West was likely to lead to a renaissance of German capitalism, but orientation towards the East at least held out a hope of seeing Socialism realized.

1. In a number of districts within the Soviet Zone—in Saxonia, Thüringen, Mark Brandenburg and Mecklenburg–Pomerania—the Social Democratic party organizations had declared themselves in favour of integration; and in some towns in the Western Zones—Hamburg and Bremen—there was a strong feeling in favour of fusion. On the other hand, a conference of Social Democratic delegates in the British Zone and the district executives of the three districts in the American Zone rejected the fusion by, respectively, a unanimous vote and 144 against six votes. It may therefore be assumed that at any national conference of the party a majority would have declared themselves against unification.

2. See *Dokumente*, p. 522.

In any case, a fusion of the two workers' parties in the five districts of the Soviet Zone appeared inevitable since the Soviet government would hardly tolerate an independent Social Democratic party. As long as discussions on integration continued the Russians would sanction their existence. Once they declared themselves against integration however, they would clearly stand in opposition to the occupying power and would inevitably be suppressed. This was certainly a factor in the views developed by many Social Democrats in the Soviet Zone.

There was one further consideration behind the thinking of the central executive. Should it continue to resist an early integration of the two parties, the Soviet authorities would arrange for the executive to be voted out and replaced by more pliant officers. But if, on the other hand, the executive was to offer its full co-operation, it could expect, as Grotewohl said, to be able 'to co-ordinate Social Democratic thinking organizationally, and to be able to utilize it'.[1]

For these reasons the central executive decided upon co-operation. They agreed with the Communists that a party congress on unification should be called for 21 April 1946. Two days earlier separate conferences of the S.P.D. and K.P.D. were held—the Social Democratic conference representing only the Social Democratic organizations within the Soviet Zone and East Berlin— to define every aspect of unification. Then, at the main conference, the joint congresses agreed unanimously on the integration of each party into the German Socialist Unity party (S.E.D.).[2]

With this decision the seal was set on the fate of Social Democracy in the five districts of the Soviet Zone. In these areas the S.P.D. had been able to claim 619,000 members, many thousands of whom were no doubt against integrating their organization with the Communist party. But now there would never be any question of their being able to separate out again from the S.E.D. and to reconstitute themselves as the S.P.D., since the Soviet occupation authorities would have refused them the necessary recognition. In effect the re-establishment of a Social Democratic party had been banned throughout a third of all German territory. Only in the Russian sector of Berlin which, with the three sectors under Allied administration, was administered by the Allied Control Authority, was the S.P.D. unaffected by the ban.

The actual ratio of power between the S.P.D. and the S.E.D. became clear in the municipal elections that took place in all four sectors of the city on 20 October 1946. The S.P.D. obtained 48 per cent of all votes and the S.E.D. 19 per cent; even in the Russian sector 43 per cent of votes were cast for the

---

1. Quoted in Kaden, p. 290.
2. For the history of the conflict in the S.P.D. on the question of unification, see a detailed report in Kaden, pp. 220–40, 242–56; Stern, pp. 30–40; see also Leonhard, pp. 431–6. For the resolution at the party congress, see *Dokumente*, pp. 623–33.

S.P.D. against 29 per cent for the S.E.D.[1] The results left no room for doubt that an overwhelming majority of Social Democrats in the Soviet Zone had been against integrating their party with the Communists and that the issue of unification had been forced upon them.[2]

Less than three weeks after the founding of the S.E.D., German Social Democracy reconstituted itself during the course of a party congress in Hamburg from 9 to 11 May 1946 at which 258 delegates represented Social Democratic organizations in the three Western zones of occupation and the western sector of Berlin. No reference to the question of integration with the Communists appeared on the agenda. The only mention came in a resolution by Schumacher on the 'tasks and aims of German Social Democracy'. In this he justified a rejection of the concept of unification by drawing attention to the sharp contrasts of attitude existing between each party on points of principle.

The German Communist party, he said, had once again emerged with nationalistic slogans, 'and this fact alone,' he stated, 'that a unification [of the S.P.D. and the K.P.D. into the S.E.D.] has taken place under a nationalistic banner, is enough for us to say no. . . . We can never reconcile ourselves with nationalism.' He reminded the congress of Léon Blum's words, as appropriate to the situation in Germany as they had been to that in France. 'The French Socialists,' Blum had said, 'are French patriots and international Socialists, but the French Communists are French chauvinists and Russian patriots.' 'But we,' Schumacher continued, 'do not wish for politics with

1. The actual ratios of votes between the S.P.D. and S.E.D. in each of the four sectors were:

	S.P.D.	S.E.D.
	%	%
American Sector	52·0	12·7
British Sector	50·9	10·3
French Sector	52·5	21·7
Soviet Sector	43·6	29·8
For the whole of Berlin	48·0	19·0

—Weber, *Von der S.B.Z. zur D.D.R. 1945–1958*, p. 44.

2. The integration of the Social Democratic party with the Communist party could be imposed only because the country was under Russian rule. 'The creation of a Unity party of the working class in Germany,' Melnikov admitted, 'was only possible thanks to the great victories of the Soviet Army. . . . Stalin's clever tactics in the German question laid the foundations for the advance forces of the German working class to create a single workers' party'—D. Melnikov, *Borba*, quoted in Rieber, *Stalin and the French Communist Party*, p. 336. For the part played by the Russian authorities in Berlin in bringing about the amalgamation of the two parties, see Erich W. Gniffke, *Jahre mit Ulbricht*, with a preface by Herbert Wehner (Cologne, 1966). Gniffke was a member of the S.P.D. Berlin central committee in 1945 and had been from April 1946 a senior official of the S.E.D.; in October 1948 he fled to West Berlin. From his first-hand experience of the events which led up to the fusion, he asserts that it is General Bokov, the Chief of Staff in the Soviet military administration, and Colonel Tulpanov, the head of its information department, who should be regarded as the real founders of the S.E.D.

principles where the principles have become simply a tactic leading on to adaptable opportunist manoeuvres.'

But even if integration remained out of the question in the three Western Zones where Social Democracy could continue to exist unhindered, 'a definite working basis with the Communist party remained quite possible,' he said, always provided that there were no attempts to 'try to lie to us, undermine us or to take over our leadership'.[1]

The conference unanimously agreed with Schumacher's views on the Unity party, as it showed during the debate which followed his resolution. Not a single delegate supported union with the Communists. Gustav Dahrendorf, who had earlier, as a member of the Berlin central executive, strongly pleaded the cause for unification, now described from direct experience how it had been forcibly imposed in the Russian Zone 'as one move in carrying through a political design which had, as its aim, the subjection of all Germany by means of political and pseudo-national propaganda, and under the influence of which the Soviet Zone had already succumbed'.[2] Schumacher's undisputed position as party leader was confirmed when he was unanimously elected as chairman; Erich Ollenhauer, a former member of the party leadership in exile, was elected as his deputy.

For Germany the whole question of the amalgamation of the Socialist with the Communist party was of far more vital significance than it was perhaps for any other country in Europe. It is imaginable that in Britain, even in France or Italy and certainly in the smaller countries of Western Europe, an integrated Socialist–Communist Unity party might not necessarily succumb to Communist control and might succeed in asserting its independence of the Soviet Union. This was unthinkable, however, in countries under Russian occupation since in the long run the Soviet authorities would never have tolerated the existence of a party which remained free of Communist control. A united party in these countries could never be more than a thinly disguised Communist party, irrespective of the number of Social Democratic members that it might contain. And no Communist party in any of these countries could hope to maintain its independence from the Soviet Union or be anything other than an instrument of Soviet policy.

What might have been the consequences of such an amalgamation of the two parties throughout the whole of Germany? The Soviet Union controlled a third of the German state, their area embracing such traditional working-class strongholds as central Germany and Berlin. Based on these areas, the Communist-dominated Unity party would have been able—but for the counterprevailing weight of the Social Democratic party—to seize control of

1. *Protokoll der Verhandlungen des Parteitages der Sozialdemokratischen Partei Deutschlands* (Hamburg, 1947), pp. 47, 200 and 30–1.
2. *Protokoll*, p. 113.

the labour movement throughout the whole of Germany and thus ensure the predominance of the Communist party over the entire state.

For those Socialist parties in other Western European countries contemplating integration with the Communists, the question of what the relationship of a future Unity party should be towards the Soviet Union was of no great significance. In Germany, on the other hand, it was a critical factor involving the extension of Russian influence across the whole German state as far as the Rhine. Thus, short of sacrificing the ideal of independence for a future Germany, the concept of a Socialist Unity party was bound to fail.

So once again the German labour movement had entered the stage of history in a state of schism. And even as the conflict between the Western powers and the Soviet Union intensified and degenerated into the Cold War, so the conflicts between the two workers' parties increased and degenerated into a passionate hostility.

5 · The Origins of the 'Cold War'

1

During the course of the Second World War, relations between the Western powers and the Soviet Union had remained on the friendliest possible terms. Roosevelt kept himself free of any suspicions towards Stalin's plans and, apparently, Churchill's trust in Stalin remained unshakeable. As he reported in the speech that he made in the House of Commons on 27 February 1945 after returning from the Yalta Conference:

> The impression I brought back from the Crimea, and from all my other contacts, is that Marshal Stalin and the Soviet leaders wish to live in honourable friendship with the Western democracies. I feel also that their word is their bond. I know of no Government which stands to its obligations, even in its own despite, more solidly than the Russian Soviet Government. I decline absolutely to embark here on a discussion about Russian good faith. It is quite evident that these matters touch the whole future of the world. Sombre indeed would be the fortunes of mankind if some awful schism arose between the Western democracies and the Russian Soviet Union.[1]

And a few weeks later, on 29 April, he wrote to Stalin: '. . . there has grown up throughout the English-speaking world a very warm and deep desire to be friends on equal and honourable terms with the mighty Russian Soviet Republic'.[2]

The United States was similarly motivated by a warm sympathy for Russia. 'Two months ago,' Harry Hopkins told Stalin in conversation on 26 May 1945 when sent to Moscow by President Truman, 'there had been overwhelming sympathy among the American people for the Soviet Union . . . primarily because of the brilliant achievements of the Soviet Union in the war.'[3]

---

1. Winston S. Churchill, *The Second World War*, vol. VI: *Triumph and Tragedy* (London, 1954), p. 351.   2. ibid., p. 431.
3. Robert E. Sherwood, *The White House Papers of Harry L. Hopkins*, vol. II (London, 1948), p. 876. See also James F. Byrnes, who recorded in his notes: 'If one remembers the attitude of the peoples in the days of the German defeat . . . everyone will agree that the Soviet Union possessed a treasure of good will in the United States as great if not greater than in any other country'—*Speaking Frankly* (New York, 1947), p. 71.

But Hopkins's objective in describing America's sympathies for Russia was to convey to Stalin the fact that there had been a change of the mood. American opinion was now, he stated, 'seriously disturbed about [the deterioration in] their relations with Russia'. Churchill's long letter to Stalin of 29 April similarly indicates the presence of a conflict which carried within it the seed of a split in the Western alliance and which related to the interpretation of agreements over Poland at the Yalta Conference.

Four months before the Yalta Conference took place, Churchill had agreed with Stalin in Moscow in October 1944 that there should be a division of the spheres of influence between the two powers in the Balkans: a 90 per cent predominance in Romania was to go to Russia while Britain took a 90 per cent predominance in Greece; a 75 per cent Russian predominance was to be accepted in Bulgaria, while each was to exercise a 50 per cent influence in both Yugoslavia and Hungary.[1] But the question of Poland's future had been left in abeyance, reserved for decision at the Yalta Conference itself.

At the Yalta Conference, which began on 4 February 1945, Stalin soon reached an agreement with Churchill and Roosevelt on the eastern border of the future Poland.[2] The Soviet Union was to keep the eastern half of the

1. Churchill's own description of how his agreements with Stalin were arrived at provides an illustration of the way in which the fate of a people and their country may be decided. Churchill and Eden had reached Moscow on the afternoon of 9 October, and both had withdrawn after supper for a discussion with Stalin and Molotov. They had hardly sat down at the table when Churchill raised the question of the future of the Balkans. 'Don't let us get at cross-purposes in small ways,' he said. 'So far as Britain and Russia are concerned, how would it do for you to have ninety per cent predominance in Romania, for us to have ninety per cent of the say in Greece, and go fifty-fifty about Yugoslavia?' Then, while this was being translated, he wrote on a half-sheet of paper:

> 'Romania
>   Russia 90%
>   The others 10%
> Greece
>   Great Britain 90%
>   (in accord with U.S.A.)
>   Russia 10%
> Yugoslavia 50–50%
> Hungary 50–50%
> Bulgaria
>   Russia 75%
>   The others .. .. .. 25%'

Churchill pushed the list across to Stalin, who had by then heard the translation. There was a slight pause. Then he took his blue pencil and made a large tick upon it, and passed it back to us. It was all settled in no more time than it takes to set down. . . . After this there was a long silence. The pencilled paper lay in the centre of the table. At length I said, 'Might it not be thought rather cynical if it seemed we had disposed of these issues, so fateful to millions of people, in such an offhand manner? Let us burn the paper.' 'No, you keep it,' said Stalin—Churchill, *Triumph and Tragedy*, p. 198.

2. For a documentary description of the discussions on the territorial new order for Poland, see Boris Meissner, *Russland, die Westmächte und Deutschland. Die sowjetische Deutschlandpolitik, 1943–1953* (Hamburg, 1953), pp. 40–4.

country up to the Curzon Line, which Russia had been conceded by the Western powers after the First World War and which it had annexed in the Nazi–Soviet attack on Poland in September 1939, while Poland was to be 'compensated' with German provinces. But the actual definition of Poland's western borders—the Oder–Neisse Line, as proposed by Stalin—was to be held in reserve for the peace conference.[1] The prior concern at Yalta was to discuss the character of the provisional government in liberated Poland.

But in the event the Yalta Conference faced a *fait accompli*. Stalin had already established a pro-Soviet government—a 'Polish Committee of National Liberation'—which on 22 July 1944 proclaimed itself the provisional government and declared that it would take over the administration of the provinces liberated by the Soviet army;[2] its seat was in Lublin, and it therefore became known as the Lublin government.

But, long before the Lublin government appeared on the scene, the Polish government in exile, with General Wladyslaw Sikorski as prime minister, had constituted itself in London following the fall of Poland in September 1939. Sikorski's government was recognized by the Western Allies, and, after Russia's entry into the war against Germany, by the Soviet Union as well; it had organized guerrilla forces in Poland as well as an army of 150,000 men under British command.[3] Stalin, however, had broken off relations with the London government in exile on 25 April 1943[4] and had formed a counter-

1. As early as the Tehran Conference at the end of November 1943 Churchill and Roosevelt had recognized the Curzon Line in principle as Russia's western border. See W. D. Leahy, *I Was There* (London, 1950), p. 249; see also Stanislav Mikolajczyk, *The Pattern of Soviet Domination* (London, 1948), pp. 107–8.

2. The manifesto to the 'Poles in the country, in foreign lands and in German captivity' stated: '. . . The National Council [of the Polish Committee of the National Liberation] . . . is the only authority of Poland's sovereignty . . . based on the constitution of 1921, which has been legally approved and is valid'; the London government, on the other hand, 'is a self-nominated body based on the illegal Fascist constitution of 1935'—quoted in Brian Ireland, 'Poland', in R. R. Betts (ed.), *Central and South-East Europe, 1945–1948* (London, 1950), pp. 132–3.

3. See Churchill, *Triumph and Tragedy*, p. 330.

4. The reason for breaking off relations was the crisis precipitated by the 'Katyn massacre'. The Germans claimed that in April 1943, on their retreat through the woods of Katyn, near Smolensk, they had found a mass-grave containing the corpses of several thousand Polish officers. Nazi propaganda at once accused the Soviet government of having allowed them to be murdered three years previously through the 'Jewish executioners of the G.P.U.' The Russian government naturally countered that the Polish officers had been murdered by the Nazis. When, however, the Polish government in London took up the Nazi accusation, the Soviet government broke off all relations with it. No impartial examination could convincingly apportion the blame for the massacre. That, however, Hitler and Stalin were equally capable of having done it requires no special proof; both had systematically exterminated people who were embarrassing them in hundreds of thousands. For the attitude of the Polish government in London, see Mikolajczyk, *The Pattern of Soviet Domination*, pp. 30–42; for the text of the Soviet note, see ibid., pp. 294–5. Alexander Werth, who had as the correspondent of the *Sunday Times* of London taken part in the investigations into the incident and carefully examined the evidence, took a very sceptical view of the Russian version despite his sympathies for the Soviet Union; see *Russia at War* (New York, 1964), pp. 661–7.

government, which, on 4 January 1945, a month before Yalta, was officially recognized by the Soviet government in all its forms as the legal provisional government of Poland.

As a result, the Yalta Conference found itself with two Polish governments to deal with: the one in Lublin and the one in London. Stalin had persuaded Roosevelt and Churchill that the Soviet Union would only tolerate in Poland a government which was friendly towards it. 'To this we are pledged,' Stalin wrote in a letter to Churchill, 'apart from all else, by the blood of the Soviet people, which has been profusely shed on the field of Poland in the name of the liberation of Poland.'[1]

There was also the issue of the security of the Soviet Union. 'For our people,' Stalin told the Yalta Conference, 'the question of Poland is a question of security.'

Poland has throughout her history been a corridor through which the enemy has driven into Russia. Twice in the past thirty years have our enemies the Germans passed through that corridor. It is in Russia's interests that Poland should be strong and powerful enough to be able to close that corridor by its own strength. . . . For the Soviet Union this is a question of life and death.[2]

No special show of friendship towards the Soviet Union could, however, be expected from the Polish government in London, which was made up of a coalition of the Polish National party, a nationalist party of the bourgeoisie, the conservative Polish Peasants' party, the Christian Democrats and the Socialists. Stalin's main problem was that, the Polish Communists apart, not a single Pole could be found who felt genuine friendship towards the Soviet Union.[3] Hatred of Russia, which had governed Poland as a province for over 150 years, suppressing all national freedom movements with fire and sword, was a national tradition deeply rooted in the thought and feelings of the Polish people.[4] It had been drastically revived at the time when the Soviet Union had joined with Hitler's Germany to attack the young republic in 1939, so destroying the Polish state and dividing the country between

---

1. Quoted in Churchill, *Triumph and Tragedy*, p. 430. Churchill, however, reminded Stalin of his reply of 29 April 1945, that Great Britain had declared war on Germany in 1939 for the sake of Poland's independence.

2. Quoted in Byrnes, *Speaking Frankly*, pp. 31–2; Churchill, *Triumph and Tragedy*, pp. 322–3.

3. Even the Polish Communists harboured few exuberant sympathies for the Soviet Union. In May 1938 Stalin had dissolved the Polish Communist party and exterminated almost all of its leaders—among them Henryk Walecki, Adolf Warski, Wera Kostrzewa and Julian Lenski. Only Wladislaw Gomulka and Boleslaw Bierut escaped this 'purge'. See Branko Lazitch, 'Stalin's Massacre', in *The Comintern—Historical Highlights*, pp. 146–51. For the dissolution of the party, see Braunthal, *History of the International, 1914–1943*, pp. 336–9.

4. 'There is no people,' Lenin said, 'which has suppressed Poland as much as the Russians'—speech on the national question to the Seventh Congress of the Russian Communist Party, 12 May 1917, *Sochineniya*, XXIV, pp. 264–5, quoted in David J. Dallin, *From Purge to Coexistence* (Chicago, 1964), p. 171.

Germany and Russia for the fourth time. The régime of bloody terror which Russia had then established in eastern Poland to match that of the Nazis in western Poland in no way helped to pacify Polish hatred of the Russian nation.[1]

Then, finally, one towering catastrophe had heaped glowing coals on to their already burning hatred. Towards the end of July 1944, the Soviet army of Marshal Rokossovsky was advancing up to the River Vistula. The Germans had withdrawn to the western bank and were entrenched in a suburb of Warsaw. While Soviet fighter planes bombarded the German positions, Moscow radio on 29 July appealed to the people of Warsaw to rise to meet the hour of their liberation.[2] Upon this, General Tadeuz Bór-Komorowski, commander of the Polish underground army, in agreement with the Polish government in exile, gave orders that the armed uprising in Warsaw was to take place on 1 August.

It began in the early hours of the morning. The Polish underground army, with 46,000 men in its ranks, rose, expecting that the Soviet Army, only twenty miles distant, would support them by an advance across the Vistula. Instead, Marshal Rokossovsky halted the offensive, the Russian artillery fell silent, and the Soviet army maintained its inactivity during the city's nine-week death-struggle. When the uprising began, Warsaw contained only bare reserves of food and ammunition. Mikolajczyk, who had been appointed prime minister of the Polish government in exile following Sikorski's death, had arrived in Moscow two days before the start of the uprising to ask Stalin for help.[3] This Stalin not only refused; he also blocked help from the British and United States air forces by forbidding their landing on the Russian-occupied airport near Warsaw, since 'the Soviet government did not wish', as the Russian note to the Allies stated, 'to associate itself either directly or indirectly with the adventure in Warsaw'.[4] Roosevelt and Churchill telegraphed a joint appeal to Stalin on 29 August to consider the moral effect on world opinion. Stalin, however, remained obdurate; the incident, he replied, concerned a 'group of criminals who have embarked on the Warsaw adventure in order to seize power. . .'.[5] And so the city of a million inhabitants

1. Wladyslaw Gomulka, secretary general of the Communist party, which had reorganized after Hitler's attack on the Soviet Union under the name of the Polish Labour party, emphasized this on 12 January 1944 in a letter to the Polish Communists, who had formed a Federation of Polish Patriots in Moscow; quoted in Hansjakob Stehle, 'Polish Communism', William L. Griffith (ed), *Communism in Europe* (Massachusetts, n.d.), vol. I, p. 93.

2. 'The hour of liberation has arrived! People of Poland, take up arms! Don't hesitate for one moment!' Thus ended the appeal. For its text, see Mikolajczyk, *The Pattern of Soviet Domination*, p. 76.

3. For his discussion with Stalin, see Mikolajczyk, *The Pattern of Soviet Domination*, pp. 79–82.

4. Quoted in Churchill, *Triumph and Tragedy*, p. 118.

5. For the text of the two documents, see ibid., pp. 119–20.

was left to its fate. On 2 October, after sixty-three days of bitter fighting, Bór-Komorowsky capitulated. Three hundred thousand Poles had been killed or deported and the city was one vast ruin.

The motive which governed Stalin in his attitude towards the Warsaw rising was to be found in his reply to Roosevelt and Churchill. He saw the leaders of the uprising as men who, owing allegiance to the Polish government in London, formed 'a group of criminals' who had plotted the insurrection in order to 'seize power'. It was exactly this which he wished to avoid—that the Polish government in exile should gain a foothold in Warsaw. Consequently he wished to see the failure of the uprising and the destruction of the Polish underground. In his plans for the future of Poland, Warsaw was not to be allowed liberation under the aegis of the government in exile.

The Yalta Conference devoted six of its seven full meetings to the question of the future character of the Polish government.[1] Stalin wished to gain recognition for the Lublin government, at whose head stood men—he named Bierut, Osóbka-Morawski and General Rola-Zymierski[2]—who had been in the resistance movement and who, he asserted, were highly popular with the Polish people. Churchill and Roosevelt demanded that the basis of the Lublin government should be widened by the inclusion of members of the London government and that there should be elections for a democratic people's parliament at the earliest moment. Following lengthy discussion, the conference finally agreed on a declaration by which the Soviet government undertook responsibility for reorganizing the Lublin government.[3]

Upon this, Roosevelt asked Stalin what the earliest possible date would be for the election. 'Within a month,' Stalin replied, 'unless there is some catastrophe on the front, which is improbable.'[4]

Stalin gave this assurance on 11 February 1945, two and a half months before the entry of the Soviet army into Berlin and the end of the war in Europe. No election took place in Poland, however, until almost twenty-three months later, on 19 January 1947.

Churchill and Roosevelt had expected from their agreements with Stalin that developments would take place in Poland along the pattern of the Western democracies—that they would see the creation of a Poland that would ideologically and politically fall within the Western powers' sphere of influence.

1. For a review of the discussions, see ibid., pp. 320–4 and 329–39.
2. Boleslaw Bierut was a leader of the Polish Communist party who had been its representative at the Communist International; Edward Osóbka-Morawski was a left-wing Socialist who, in December 1943, together with a group from the Socialist party of Poland, opted out to join forces with the Communist party.
3. For the text of the declaration, see Churchill, *Triumph and Tragedy*, p. 338.
4. Quoted in ibid., p. 333.

These expectations were, however, in total conflict with the demand made by the Soviet Union—recognized in all its implications by both Churchill and Roosevelt—for a Poland friendly to the Soviet Union. They had sought a tempering of the Lublin government through the acceptance of representatives of the bourgeois parties. These were not, however, sympathetically disposed towards the Soviet Union, but regarded it with loathing. The Polish government in London, of which they were a part, had accepted with alacrity the German districts of East Prussia and Silesia up to the Oder which had been given to the future Poland at Yalta, but had refused to recognize any concessions to Russia in the eastern parts of the country. It could not therefore be expected that a Poland influenced by men of the London government and their parties would become Russia's friendly neighbour. Poland remained a Catholic country, and the Church was the arch-enemy of Bolshevism; it governed the attitudes of the peasants, who formed a predominant majority, while the middle classes were equally anti-Soviet. Therefore it was unthinkable that any pro-Soviet government could emerge from free and secret democratic elections. Moreover, Stalin feared that an independent Poland, founded on democratic principles, might actually become a hostile force, the object of whose foreign policies would be to regain the Polish provinces east of the Curzon Line lost at Yalta in a future war in alliance with anti-Soviet powers. So he refused to allow in the Warsaw government the presence of any middle-class politicians whose attitudes towards the Soviet Union might be questioned.

Then, two months after Yalta, an event occurred which decisively changed the foreign policy of the United States towards the Soviet Union. Roosevelt who throughout the war had honestly striven for a friendly relationship between America and Russia, out of his conviction that the peace of the world could only be safeguarded by a permanent agreement between these two great powers, died on 12 April 1945. With his successor, Harry S. Truman, an anti-Bolshevik strain of feeling emerged within the United States government. Truman himself, in any case, felt as little sympathy for Bolshevik Russia as he had for Nazi Germany; as he had publicly declared a few weeks after Hitler's attack on the Soviet Union, his wish was to see a battle of attrition and the destruction of both sides.[1] Now Russia had won her war with tremendous aid from the United States, and Truman was obliged to accept this fact. However, he remained determined as far as was within his power to prevent the subjection of Russia's neighbour states to the dominance

1. *New York Times*, 24 July 1941, quoted in David Horowitz, *The Free World Colossus. A Critique of American Foreign Policy in the Cold War* (London, 1954), p. 61. Roosevelt, on the other hand, had assisted the Soviet Union even before America entered the war after Pearl Harbor. Harry Hopkins, sent by Roosevelt to Moscow, had on his orders pledged the United States unconditionally 'to grant Stalin all possible aid in tanks, aeroplanes and whatever was required'; see Robert Sherwood, *Roosevelt and Hopkins* (New York, 1948), pp. 327–8, 333.

of the Soviet Union and, above all, of Poland. Only forty-eight hours after Roosevelt's death, even before the funeral of the deceased president, Truman wrote to Churchill suggesting they should dispatch a joint note requiring Stalin to invite representatives of the Polish middle-class parties to Moscow to agree on the formation of a new Polish government.[1] Then, a few weeks after the entry of the Red Army into Berlin, he called a halt to aid—as heavy a blow for Russia as for Britain.[2]

When the American Secretary of State, Harry Hopkins, arrived in Moscow towards the end of May to discuss the candidates for the Warsaw government proposed by Truman and Churchill, Stalin rejected them all,[3] with the exception of the leader of the Polish Peasants' party, Stanislaw Mikolajczyk, who had become the prime minister of the Polish government in exile after the death of General Wladyslaw Sikorski in July 1943, and who had agreed to Poland's new territorial order. In his attitude he stood alone in the cabinet, however, and so resigned from it in November 1944. Furthermore, he had openly stated that he considered 'a close and lasting friendship with Russia' to be 'the keystone of future Polish policy' and that he recognized the borders of Poland as they had been agreed at Yalta.[4] As a result of this declaration of loyalty, Stalin consented to accept him as a member of the 'Provisional Government of National Unity'. He became its vice-premier.

It represented a compromise on Stalin's part, and now Truman and Churchill could no longer reject a government which, while it was evidently ruled by Communists, included a representative of the Polish Peasants' party and, quite apart from the Socialists, representatives of a 'democratic party' even though it had been founded and was led by Communists. This government was recognized by Britain and the United States on 5 July 1945.

1. See Churchill, *Triumph and Tragedy*, pp. 424–6.
2. Hugh Dalton, the British Chancellor of the Exchequer in the new Labour government, remarked in his memoirs on the effect of the cessation of 'Lend-lease'. 'This very heavy blow struck us without warning and without discussion . . . now we faced . . . total economic ruin.' Britain, he continued, had to reckon with a deficit in its trade balance of £1,250 million ($5,000 million)—Hugh Dalton, *High Tide and After. Memoirs 1945–1960* (London, 1962), pp. 68 and 72. The blow which struck Russia was, however, a great deal harder because Russia had been far more devastated by the war than Britain. The Germans had partially destroyed fifteen large cities, 1,710 smaller towns, 70,000 villages and 31,850 industrial complexes. For a summary of the Russian war damage, see D. F. Fleming, *The Cold War and its Origins 1917–1960* (London, 1961), vol. I, p. 252.
3. Stalin stated his position very clearly in a letter to Churchill of 5 May 1945: '. . . we cannot be satisfied that persons should be associated with the formation of the future Polish government who, as you express it, "are not fundamentally anti-Soviet", or that only those persons should be excluded from participation in this work who are in your opinion "extremely unfriendly towards Russia". Neither of these criteria can satisfy us. We insist, and shall insist, that there should be brought into consultation on the formation of the future Polish government only those persons who have actively shown a friendly attitude towards the Soviet Union and who are honestly and sincerely prepared to co-operate with the Soviet state.' For the text of this letter, see Churchill, *Triumph and Tragedy*, pp. 435–7.
4. For the text of the declaration, see ibid., pp. 426–7.

Yet Truman and Churchill were not fully confident. A delegation from the Provisional government was invited to the Potsdam Conference—assembling in the middle of July 1945—so as to bring home to the Russians the prime importance which Britain and the United States attached to the holding of free elections in Poland. The promise that such elections would be held was renewed in the Potsdam Declaration, while Churchill asked Boleslaw Bierut, the Communist president of the Provisional government, for a *tête-à-tête* in order to subject him to a 'strict' explanation. He asked him whether Poland would plunge into Communism, and Bierut assured him that nothing was further from their intentions than a Communist Poland. Poland, he said, wished for friendly relations with the Soviet Union, but it had no wish to imitate the Soviet system, and whoever attempted to impose this by force would encounter resistance. 'Poland,' he said, 'will develop on the principles of Western democracy'; it would, in fact, become the most democratic state in Europe, while elections in Poland would be more democratic than those in England itself.[1]

Yet the calling of elections was once again delayed, for soon after Mikolajczyk's return to Poland, where he was received by vast, jubilant crowds, there occurred a series of heavy and frequently bloody battles between his followers and the Communists causing thousands of casualties on both sides. The Polish People's party (*Polskie Stronnictwo Ludowe*—P.S.L.), which he had founded after his return, and of which he was the leader, had become a rallying point for all those who were afraid of Soviet Russia and the Communists—the aristocrats, big landowners, peasants, the middle and upper classes, and, above all, the Catholic hierarchy with its legion of priests. Mikolajczyk believed that his party could, in free elections, collect at least 60 per cent of the votes.

Of the consequences of such an election result there could be no doubt. An anti-Communist middle class, united in its bitterness towards the Soviet Union and in control of Parliament and the government, and even despite Mikolajczyk's declaration of loyalty, would come into sharp conflict with the Soviet Union.[2] The principles of democracy were incompatible with the principle of Russia's security under Stalin's definition, which had been agreed to at Yalta by Britain and the United States: a Poland friendly towards Russia. For only a Communist-led Poland could ensure a permanent alliance

1. For Churchill's talk with Bierut, see ibid., pp. 575–7.
2. In fact Gomulka, making an election address in Lodz as the general secretary of the Workers' party, as the Communist party now called itself, stated that the Soviet Union would not tolerate any government in which the Workers' party was not the leading element; should the P.S.L. emerge from the elections as the leading party, the Red Army would occupy Poland—*Glos Ludu* (Warsaw), 5 January 1947, quoted in 'R.', 'The Fate of Polish Socialism', in *Foreign Affairs*, vol. xxviii (October 1949), p. 132. The Red Army had been withdrawn from Poland in June 1945, but Soviet troops remained in Poland to maintain a 'line of communication' between the U.S.S.R. and the Red Army occupying East Germany.

of friendship with the Soviet Union, while the Communists, as a political minority,[1] could not expect that free elections, even in alliance with the Socialists, would win them a parliamentary majority.

Thus it was unimaginable from the outset that any election might take place in Poland which had any regard to the spirit and methods of democracy. The Communist leadership made no attempt to conceal the fact. 'Democracy,' Zambrowski, a Politbureau member, declared, 'can never mean freedom for the enemies of freedom. While powerful organizations of political bandits remain active and infiltrate the judiciary as well as the State administration, we can allow such people none of the privileges of democratic freedom.'[2] The Communists, in command of the powers of the state—the minister of the interior, with authority over the civil and secret police, was naturally a Communist, apart from the actual presence of Russian divisions in the country—had ruthlessly invoked these powers to ensure the suppression of their opponents. Active members of Mikolajczyk's party were arrested in large numbers, while the party's press was stifled, its election meeting broken up and its list of candidates declared void in ten out of twenty-five constituencies.

The only other opposition party in Poland, the Polish Socialist party or P.P.S. (*Polska Partia Socjalistyczna*) had by the time of the election already joined the Communist camp. As early as December 1943, when, as we have seen, a group under the leadership of Edward Osóbka-Morawski and Stanislaw Szwabbe split off from the P.P.S. to constitute itself as the 'Workers' party of Polish Socialists' (*Robotnicza Partia Polskich Socjalistow*—R.P.P.S.) and formed an alliance of action with the Communist Polish Workers' party (*Polska Partia Robotnicza*—P.P.R.) under Wladyslaw Gomulka's leadership.[3]

1. The Polish Communist party at the height of its recruiting drive in 1931 could claim 12,000 members, and in 1941 (in the areas occupied by the Russians as well as by the Germans) 20,000 members; see *Nowe Drogi*, January 1951, quoted in Richard F. Staar, *Poland 1944–1962. The Sovietization of a Captive People* (Louisiana, 1962), p. 72. The party, shaken by internal crisis, was dissolved by Stalin in March 1938 under the accusation of having been infiltrated by 'Fascist agents in the leadership'; see Braunthal, *History of the International, 1914–1943*, pp. 316–17. In 1955, however, J. Dzierzynski declared in the *Great Soviet Encyclopedia*, vol. 34, 'any suspicion that the leadership of the Polish Communist Party had been saturated by enemy elements . . . has proved to be unfounded. The Polish Communists stood during this period at the head of the anti-Fascist struggle by the Polish nation for their country's freedom and independence'—*Pravda*, 3 September 1955. The Communists had had to cease their struggle, however, when Stalin and Hitler reached agreement to destroy and divide Poland between them; see Braunthal, *History of the International, 1914–1943*, p. 531. After the entrance into Poland of the Soviet army, the number of party members rose to 364,000 in July 1946 and to 848,000 in July 1947; see Staar, *Poland, 1944–1962*, p. 167.

2. Roman Zambrowski, 'The Party before the Elections', in *Nowe Drogi*, January 1947, quoted in ibid., p. 49.

3. For the bringing into line of the P.P.S., see Adam Ciolkosz, 'Poland', in Denis Healey (ed.), *The Curtain Falls*, with a Foreword by Aneurin Bevan (London, 1951), pp. 38 and 56; 'R.', 'The Fate of Polish Socialism', in *Foreign Affairs* vol. xxviii (October 1949), pp. 125–42.

A national conference in September 1944 declared itself to be the representative of the 'official' P.P.S. Osóbka-Morawski, installed by Moscow as president of the Lublin Committee, was elected chairman, with Józef Cyrankiewicz as general secretary.

Two parties of the P.P.S., the 'official' and the 'original', thus existed side-by-side and it was the original which had led the guerrilla resistance and the Warsaw rising. Its general secretary was Kazimierz Pužak, one of the foremost figures in the history of the Polish Socialist movement. He had joined it in its early years in 1904, had in 1910 been sentenced as an active revolutionary by a Tsarist court to eight years' hard labour, and been imprisoned for seven years in chains and solitary confinement in the infamous Schlüsselburg Fortress until released in March 1917 by the onset of the Russian Revolution. As general secretary of the P.P.S. in the period between the wars and during the German occupation, he had been the symbol and inspiration of the underground. Then, in March 1945, his arrest by the Soviet authorities excluded him from having any influence over the realignment of the P.P.S.[1]

The party's leadership now fell to Zygmunt Zulawski, who had been general secretary of the Polish trade union confederation in the period between the wars. The original P.P.S. now found itself under heavy pressure from the state machinery, legal promotion of its activities being almost impossible. Zulawski therefore tried to organize under the title of 'Social Democratic party of Poland', but Osóbka-Morawski, who had meanwhile been made prime minister of the Lublin government, refused to allow its registration as a lawful party. So Zulawski asked all members of the 'original' P.P.S. to join the 'official' party in the hope it would prove possible to preserve its Social Democratic character. And as it happened, a great many members of the original party did in fact transfer their allegiance. The original P.P.S. having thus vacated the public scene, the official party was recognized in May 1946 by the International Socialist Conference (COMISCO)—the forerunner of the post-war Socialist International—as representing the Socialist movement in Poland.

But Zulawski's hopes never materialized. The Communist dominance within the party became more and more evident. Even Osóbka-Morawski, who had promoted the pact to form a United Front with the Communists and who had defended this move against Zulawski's wing of the party, was moved to protest against the domination which the Communist party exerted. 'A United Front should not rest on the principle,' he wrote in August 1946,

---

1. After imprisonment and a remand for an eighteen-month period, Pužak was sentenced in November 1948 with five other leading officials of the P.P.S. by a military court 'as agents of Polish and international capitalism' to ten years' hard labour; see *The Trial of Polish Socialist Leaders*. Report presented by the Polish Socialist Party to the International Socialist Conference, Copenhagen (1950), Archives of the Socialist International, Amsterdam.

'that one [member of the front] governs, while the other subordinates itself; that one decides the policy, while the other obligingly nods its head.' This conflict between the Socialist and Communist elements was settled by a discussion in Moscow in November 1946, to which representatives of both parties were summoned, which formulated a new pact on a United Front basis, declaring the Socialist party and the Communist Workers' party to be 'separate, independent and equal organizations', which would 'mutually respect their organizational structures'.[1]

This pact did not, however, hamper Communist efforts to drain power away from the Socialist party so as ultimately to incorporate it by fusion with the P.P.R. On 1 May 1947, Wladyslaw Gomulka declared both parties to be 'on the road towards complete working-class unity', and any resistance by the Socialist leaders was broken by pressure from Moscow. At a joint conference in Warsaw on 15 December 1948, the two parties coalesced to form the 'Polish United Workers' Party' (*Polska Zjednoczona Partia Robotnicza*—P.Z.P.R.).[2]

Zulawski, who had strongly resisted the absorption of the Socialist party by the Communists, had left the organization two years before in November 1946 and stood in the elections as an Independent Socialist. The elections were held on 19 January 1947 in a general atmosphere of fear. The result was not unexpected. The 'Democratic Bloc', formed by the Socialists with the Communists, received 80 per cent of the votes, representing 394 of the 443 seats in the Polish parliament, while Mikolajczyk's P.S.L. received only 10 per cent of the votes and twenty-seven seats; the remaining 10 per cent were distributed among a group of smaller parties. The Polish Socialist party, canvassing in tandem with the Communist party, had already agreed before the elections to a distribution of seats in the Polish parliament, each party being allotted 119 seats. Together they formed a combined majority.

At Yalta and Potsdam Stalin had given his personal pledge that the Polish government would hold 'free, unimpeded elections', and on the basis of these pledges it had received recognition from the British and United States governments. The elections as they were in fact held were

1. *Robotnik* (Warsaw), 6 August and 29 November 1946, quoted in 'R.', 'The Fate of Polish Socialism', pp. 130–1 and 132.

2. See page 350. The third Socialist party of Poland, the Polish Jewish Social Democratic party, the 'Bund', which had counted 100,000 members before the war, so far as it had escaped Hitler's destruction in the western half of Poland, was exterminated by Stalin when the Red Army occupied the eastern half of the country in 1939. 'Bundists' were killed *en masse* or deported to the slave camps in Siberia, while two of the Bund's most important leaders, Heinrich Erlich and Victor Alter, members of the Bureau of the Socialist International, were executed in December 1942 under the fantastic accusation of having, as Ivan Maisky, the Soviet Ambassador in London, informed the British Labour party, 'appealed to Russian troops to cease from bloodshed and to make peace with Germany without delay'. For Maisky's letter, see the Report of the Forty-Second Annual Conference of the Labour Party (London, 1943), p. 41.

neither free nor unimpeded.[1] Both Britain and the United States denounced them in protest notes as being in clear breach of the Yalta and Potsdam agreements.

2

The delays to the holding of elections in Poland and their consequent falsification were not the only grounds on which the conflict between the Western powers and the Soviet Union reached a crisis. President Truman had stated bluntly in a memorandum to the Potsdam Conference, assembled on 17 July 1945, that the Soviet Union had failed to fulfil the Yalta agreements concerning conditions for peace in the whole of Eastern Europe.

The agreements represented a solemn 'declaration concerning liberated Europe'. The three Great Powers had pledged themselves, 'under joint responsibility', to solve 'by democratic means' the urgent political and economic problems of the liberated countries, to instal provisional governments representative of 'all democratic elements in the population', and, 'as early as possible, to establish through free elections responsible governments which will comply with the wishes of their people'.[2]

The declaration naturally contained no mention of Churchill and Roosevelt having recognized at Yalta, upon Stalin's insistence, Russia's right to friendly governments in the countries bordering on the Soviet Union—governments which, according to Stalin's concept, could only be Communist-dominated.

When Truman raised at Potsdam the question of the form governments were to take in the countries of Eastern Europe, he had already, as we saw, come to accept a compromise concerning the government in Poland in the light of Stalin's guarantee of 'free, unimpeded elections'. It was the form of government that was to prevail in Romania, Bulgaria and Hungary which Truman now placed on the agenda. No power, he stated, owned a sphere of influence in those three countries, and he proposed that there should be joint action to reorganize the Communist-dominated governments in Romania and Bulgaria so as to safeguard the participation of 'all democratic groups therein'.

However, Truman's statement that no power had a sphere of influence in Romania or Bulgaria ran contrary to the agreements reached between Churchill and Stalin at the Moscow Conference in October 1944, which

1. Zulawski, elected as the only Socialist independent, stated in his first speech in the Parliament: 'These were no free elections. It was no election at all, but an invocation of organized brutality against the voter and his conscience'—quoted in Ciolkosz, 'Poland', in Healey (ed.), *The Curtain Falls*, p. 47.
2. Quoted in Byrnes, *Speaking Frankly*, pp. 49–50.

divided the powers' respective spheres of influence in the Balkans.[1] It will be remembered how, according to these agreements, the Soviet Union was to enjoy a 90 per cent predominance in Romania and a 75 per cent predominance in Bulgaria. 'Thus,' Churchill wrote in the report he sent back to his Cabinet, 'it is seen that quite naturally Soviet Russia has vital interests in the countries bordering on the Black Sea, by one of whom, Romania, she has been most wantonly attacked with twenty-six divisions, and with the other of whom, Bulgaria, she has ancient ties. Great Britain feels it right to show particular respect to Russian views about these two countries, and to the Soviet desire to take a lead in a practical way.'[2]

3

When Churchill conceded the Soviet Union a 90 per cent predominance in Romania and 75 per cent in Bulgaria, he had secured for Britain the 90 per cent predominance in Greece. As he reported to his Cabinet, he had agreed with Stalin that Great Britain would 'take the lead in a military sense and try to help the existing Royal Greek government to establish itself in Athens'.[3] To put it in less diplomatic language, this meant that Churchill and Stalin had reached an agreement whereby they were to promote governments according to their judgement, if necessary under military pressure, in the Balkan countries occupied by their respective armies—the Russians in Romania and Bulgaria and the British in Greece.

At the time when Churchill was discussing in Moscow the division of spheres of influence in the Balkans, the British invasion of German-occupied Greece had already begun. At the beginning of October 1944, British troops occupied Patras on the southern coast and entered Athens on the 18th to be greeted with warm enthusiasm by the population. By the end of the month the Germans had been driven from the country. The return of the Greek king from exile now became a critical question.

George II had fled to London in May 1941 at the start of the German invasion of Greece, settling in Cairo two years later. In the meantime, a Greek army of about 20,000 men had been built up from Greek refugees and Greeks living in Egypt who were liable for military service. But at the time of the British invasion Greece itself, with the exception of the state of Epirus,

1. It should be remembered that the Balkans were not the only area to be divided into spheres of influence. A 1941 agreement between Britain and the Soviet Union had divided Persia into British and Russian spheres of influence, while the Yalta Conference divided Manchuria and the Kuril Islands; then a few months later, North Korea up to the 38th parallel was assigned to the Soviet Union as a sphere of influence, Japan and the Pacific Ocean going to the United States. The Mediterranean, Turkey, Greece and Italy were similarly recognized as British spheres of influence; see Leahy, *I Was There*, pp. 173 and 264.

2. Churchill, *Triumph and Tragedy*, p. 203.   3. ibid., p. 204.

was firmly under the control of the E.A.M. (*Ellenikos Apelevtherotikon Metopon*), or 'National Liberation Front' formed and led by the Communist party.[1] This was a federation of all Greek republican and democratic groups, including the Socialist party led by Alexander Svolos, and the Democratic People's Union, led by Elias Tsirimokos. It was a mass movement of some 100,000 men and women out of a population of seven million, and it had, during the course of German occupation, built up a formidable guerrilla army—the E.L.A.S. (*Ellenikos Laikon Apelevtherotikon Straton*) or 'National People's Army of Liberation'—which had been recognized by the Allied High Command in the Near East as a regular force of the Allies and was armed by them. With about 30,000 to 40,000 men[2] it was by far the most strongly armed underground group in Greece, besides being, according to Brigadier Berker-Bentfield, head of liaison service between the British High Command and the guerrillas, the most effective group in the fight against the German occupation forces. 'We would never,' he told a press conference on 18 October 1944, 'have been able to gain a foothold in Greece without the brilliant achievements of the E.A.M. and E.L.A.S.'[3] Among non-Communist guerrilla-groups, only the E.D.E.S. (*Ellenikos Dimikratikos Ethnikos Syndesmos*), formed by Napoleon Zervas, had made any sort of mark as an armed organization of the right.

The National Liberation Front set up a provisional government in March 1944 with the Socialist leader, A. Svolos, as president. During the following month the Greek army in Egypt as well as the Greek fleet, stationed in Alexandria, rose in an anti-royalist mutiny and demanded the recognition of the provisional government. The mutiny was put down by the combined forces of the British army and navy; almost 10,000 of the mutinous troops were rounded up and interned in Eritrea.

George Papandreou, summoned to be prime minister of the Royal Greek government in Cairo after the mutiny, reached an understanding between the left and the right to promote the formation of a coalition government in

1. Since its formation in 1924 under the leadership of Georgios Siantos and Nicolas Zachariades, the Communist party of Greece, *Kommunistikon Komma Ellados*, had won over the majority of the working class. At the 1936 election—the last election before the outbreak of the war—they had won fifteen seats. The Socialist Labour party, founded in 1911, had never developed into a party with a mass following; it had no representation in parliament.

2. See William Hardy McNeill, *The Greek Dilemma. War and Aftermath* (London 1947), p. 92. McNeill, an American historian, was in Greece from November 1944 until June 1946, and had witnessed the events that occurred.

3. Quoted in Fleming, *The Cold War and its Origins*, vol. I, p. 183. According to an estimate by Anthony Eden, Foreign Secretary, 75 per cent of the guerrillas came under E.L.A.S. leadership—Speech in the House of Commons, 5 April 1944. Field Marshal Alexander, Commander of the British Forces in the Mediterranean, reminded Churchill during the course of the struggle between British troops and the E.L.A.S. in a letter dated 21 December 1944 that the E.L.A.S. 'had during the German Occupation six to seven Divisions on the mainland and a further four divisions in the Greek Islands' in the field. For the text of this letter, see Churchill, *Triumph and Tragedy*, p. 269.

which the left-wing Liberation Front and the right-wing E.D.E.S. were each represented. The provisional government dissolved itself, and a pact was negotiated—the Caserta Agreement—to share out control of the liberated districts: the command of the regular Greek forces in Athens and Attica was handed over to a British general, Ronald M. Scobie, while Salonika and Thrace came under Papandreou's government and by far the largest part of the country was controlled by the E.L.A.S.

However, immediately after the liberation of the country, a bitter struggle broke out between the royalist right and the republican left over the issue of the form of government in Greece. The right wished to see the king's return from exile, while the left opposed his re-establishment and demanded that there should be a plebiscite to decide the form of government. The Greek people had not forgotten how in 1936 George II had flouted the constitution to dissolve Parliament and install a Fascist dictatorship under the leadership of the since-deceased pro-German general Ioannis Metaxas. The National Liberation Front, carefully veiling its Communist roots and leadership by electing as its general secretary the respected Socialist George Elonomau, had gained a surprisingly wide following also among the middle classes and especially among the intellectuals,[1] as the most effective party of republican patriotism in the fight against the Germans. The mutiny of the army and the navy in Egypt had similarly demonstrated the republican attitude prevailing among the Greek regular troops.

Support for the cause of the throne came only from the E.D.E.S. on the Greek mainland and from the royalist 'Mountain Brigade' in Egypt, which had been organized after the mutiny by General Vendiras, a sworn enemy of Communism. The Mountain Brigade was landed immediately after the liberation. But the king had a far mightier ally at his side: Winston Churchill.

Churchill did not consider the form of government in Greece to be in any way a question for the Greek people alone. As decisively as Stalin had made it known that he would not tolerate anti-Soviet governments in Russian neighbouring states, so Churchill moved to block the development of an anti-British government in Greece—or, at any rate, to ensure that British predominance in a Greece, destined to be a base for the British Fleet in the Mediterranean, was in no way endangered by any decision made by the Greek people. He now feared that, should the E.A.M. come to power, Greece would fall under a Soviet-Communist régime. 'If the powers of evil prevail in Greece, as is quite likely,' he wrote on 22 December 1944 in a

1. In a letter to the Foreign Secretary Anthony Eden of 21 December 1944, Harold Macmillan, sent by Churchill to Greece as political adviser, warned against underestimating the sympathies of the Greek people for the E.A.M. 'I am sure,' he wrote, 'that the E.A.M. has a great volume of sympathies in Greece'--Harold Macmillan, *The Blast of War 1939–1945* (London 1967), p. 622.

letter to Field Marshal J. C. Smuts, 'we must be prepared for a quasi-Bolshevized Russian-led Balkan peninsula, and this may spread to Italy and Hungary.'[1]

Such danger could, in his opinion, only be prevented by reducing the power of the National Liberation Front and re-establishing the monarchy. With this aim in view he intervened in the internal political struggle between the royalists and republicans. On 7 November he had written in a minute to Anthony Eden, who visited Athens on his return trip from the Moscow conference: 'We should not hesitate to use British troops to support the Royal Hellenic Government. . . . I hope the Greek Brigade [the royalist Mountain Brigade] . . . will not hesitate to shoot when necessary.'[2]

Three weeks later when the government attempted to disarm the National Liberation Front, civil war broke out. Papandreou had demanded soon after the landing of British troops that the E.L.A.S. should be disarmed and, at the same time, organized a National Guard. The Front, which was represented in the government, agreed to the demobilization of the E.L.A.S. on condition that the Mountain Brigade should also be dissolved. But at this the British Ambassador, Sir Reginald Leeper, acting on Churchill's instructions,[3] raised a protest, and General Scobie, as Commander of the Allied Forces in Greece, decreed towards the end of November that the dissolution of the E.L.A.S. was to take place by 10 December. Upon this, the Liberation Front resigned from the government and called upon the workers of Athens to attend a protest demonstration on Sunday, 3 December, while it also proclaimed a general strike for the following day. The enormous crowds which streamed into Constitution Square on Sunday to take part in the protest demonstration broke through a police cordon, whereupon the Greek police opened fire. Troops of the E.L.A.S., who were being held in reserve, at once stormed the police station, and then the British troops swung into action.[4]

Churchill had issued instructions that British troops were to intervene in the Greek Civil War on his own initiative and without consulting the Cabinet, which contained Labour party representation.[5] On 5 December he had wired to General Scobie: 'You are responsible for maintaining order in Athens and for neutralizing or destroying all E.A.M.–E.L.A.S. bands approaching the city. . . . Do not . . . hesitate to act as if you were in a conquered city where a local rebellion is in progress. . . . We have to hold and dominate

1. Churchill, *Triumph and Tragedy*, p. 270.
2. ibid., p. 250.
3. See Leland Stowe, *While Time Remains* (New York, 1946), p. 249; see also McNeill, *The Greek Dilemma*, p. 131; C. M. Woodhouse, *Apple of Discord* (London, 1948).
4. For an eye-witness report, see McNeill, *The Greek Dilemma*, pp. 137–42.
5. See Churchill, *Triumph and Tragedy*, p. 251.

Athens . . . without bloodshed if possible, but also with bloodshed if necessary.'[1]

The events of 3 December were the prelude to civil war. The next morning General Scobie ordered the withdrawal of all E.L.A.S. troops from Athens and the Piraeus within seventy-two hours, upon which the leadership of the National Liberation Front, under pressure from the Communists and against Socialist protest—whose representative Alexander Svolos resigned as president—decided to seize the parliament building and to proclaim itself as the government.

Their attack began in the early hours of the morning of 6 December.[2] General Scobie's troops had occupied the government buildings, and during the course of the battle, which lasted for several days, they systematically stormed street after street in the workers' districts of Athens. The numbers of dead in the street-fighting among both insurgents and British soldiers ran into many thousands.[3] Hundreds of houses were destroyed and well over 10,000 suspects arrested and deported to North Africa. In a desperate act of vengeance, the E.L.A.S. seized as hostages close on 15,000 men and women whom they suspected of holding right-wing views and transferred them to the north of the country; about 4,000 perished miserably on this march.[4]

The intervention of British troops in the Greek Civil War raised a storm of protest in both Britain and the United States. In the House of Commons debate on the war on 7 and 8 December 1944, Aneurin Bevan and Emanuel Shinwell attacked the government and, although the Labour party was a member of the Coalition, a vote of confidence found only twenty-three out of 154 Labour M.P.s to support the government.[5] Roosevelt, as his son recorded, was disgusted by the British intervention,[6] and the American Secretary of State, Edward R. Stettinius, dissociated the United States from

1. For the wording of the telegram, see ibid., p. 252. Churchill, who had accompanied Eden to Athens on their return from the Moscow Conference to attend the conference of Greek party leaders arranged by Macmillan for 26 December 1944, 'stated categorically that Stalin supported [British] intervention'—see Macmillan, *The Blast of War*, p. 682.

2. For a description of the battle, see McNeill, *The Greek Dilemma*, pp. 145–50.

3. See Stowe, *While Time Remains*, p. 242; the British lost more than 1,000 men. See also Churchill's letter to Roosevelt of 25 December 1944, *Triumph and Tragedy*, p. 278.

4. See McNeill, *The Greek Dilemma*, p. 155; see also Macmillan, *The Blast of War*, pp. 600–1, 608 and 638. Macmillan blamed the Greek king as much as the Communists for the catastrophe, since he had refused to make his return to Greece dependent on a plebiscite. In a diary entry for 11 January 1945 he noted: 'I have the feeling that apart from the Communist plotters, the King of the Hellenes is the real villain of the drama. . . . One must remember that Greece had always been divided equally between republicans and monarchists. The King was the head of a party . . . not of the state'—ibid., pp. 638–9.

5. At the Labour Party Conference, meeting three days later on 11 December, Churchill's policy in Greece was outspokenly condemned. Only Ernest Bevin, as a member of the war-time cabinet, came to its defence, mainly with the argument that, 'The British Empire cannot surrender its position in the Mediterranean'—Report of the Forty-Third Annual Conference (London, 1944), p. 147. For Bevin's attitude, see Alan Bullock, *The Life and Times of Ernest Bevin*, vol. II: *Minister of Labour 1940–1945* (London, 1967), pp. 340–7.

6. See Elliot Roosevelt, *As He Saw It* (New York, 1946), p. 222.

the events in Athens in open criticism. 'The vast majority of the American press,' Churchill reported, 'violently condemned our action, which they declared falsified the cause for which they had gone to war.'[1]

Churchill found some consolation for his embarrassment in Stalin's attitude. '*The Times* and the *Manchester Guardian*,' he wrote, 'pronounced their censures upon what they considered as our reactionary policy.[2] Stalin, however, adhered strictly and faithfully to our agreement of October, and during all the long weeks of fighting the Communists in the streets of Athens not one word of reproach came from *Pravda* or *Izvestia*.'[3] Even in neighbouring Yugoslavia, under Tito's rule, the Communist press observed an aloof silence.[4] When Mackenzie King, the Canadian prime minister, sent a number of dismayed telegrams to inform Churchill of the indignation invoked in Canada by the British action in Greece, Churchill referred to Stalin's 'verbal approval of our entering Greece and liberating Athens. Although I concluded [in the reply to Mackenzie King] Communists are at the root of the business, Stalin has not so far made any public rejection of our action.'[5]

The first phase of the civil war ended with defeat for the Communists. On 11 January 1945, the E.L.A.S. stopped fighting and asked for a ceasefire. This was confirmed on 12 February in the Treaty of Varkiza; the E.L.A.S. agreed to surrender its arms and to vacate Athens, Salonika and Patras. An amnesty for 'political crimes' committed during the period of occupation and the civil war was guaranteed. Furthermore, the government pledged itself to submit a decision on the question of the constitution as early as possible and to call elections for a constituent assembly.

Alexander Svolos and Elias Tsirimokos, who had opposed the decision to seize power by armed struggle, withdrew their respective followers from the E.A.M., the two groups constituting themselves as the 'United Socialist party'. As a result, the E.A.M. lost its character of a National Front; it was now openly a Communist party organization.

British forces remained in the country until the spring of 1947, when they were relieved by American troops. The triumph of the right in the civil war enabled it to take power and, in breach of the Treaty of Varkiza, it took its

1. Churchill, *Triumph and Tragedy*, p. 255.
2. *The Economist* accused Churchill of justifying his policies in Greece by invoking the 'Bolshevik bogey', commenting: 'A British policy which stands in open hostility to the Left would place our country into the position of Metternich—without a Holy Alliance which could support us'—*The Economist*, 9 December 1944.
3. Churchill, *Triumph and Tragedy*, p. 255. According to the minutes of Churchill's War Cabinet, after he returned from the Yalta Conference he reported to his colleagues on the Russian attitude to the British military intervention in Greece as follows: 'As regards Greece, the Russian attitude could not have been more satisfactory. There was no suggestion on Premier Stalin's part of criticism of our policy. . . .'
4. After the outbreak of the Greek Civil War in autumn 1946, Tito supported the insurgent Communist troops and therefore came into conflict with Stalin; see Vladimir Dedijer, *Tito Speaks: His Self-Portrait and Struggle with Stalin* (London, 1953), p. 331.
5. Churchill, *Triumph and Tragedy*, p. 266.

revenge for the left's acts of terrorism during the civil war. The new government issued 80,000 arrest warrants and the military tribunals which it set up passed hundreds of death sentences and imprisoned many thousands.[1]

In this general atmosphere of persecution of anyone suspected by the police of holding left-wing views—Socialists and Republicans as well as Communists—the Communists rekindled the civil war in the autumn of 1946. The struggle began a year before the establishing of the Cominform,[2] which signalled a change of direction in the Soviet Union's policies towards the Western powers, and it lasted for almost three years.[3]

The elections had in fact been called under the régime of white terror to take place on 31 March 1946, and the E.A.M., with all other parties of the left, had boycotted them. As a result, the Royalist People's party easily succeeded in winning an overwhelming parliamentary majority, taking 231 out of 354 seats. Under its rule, the plebiscite of September 1946 yielded a majority vote for the return from exile of George II.

The counter-revolution which now unfolded itself was by no means, as has been generally believed, aimed solely against the Communists. The right, as A. Gregoroyannis, a member of the Greek Socialist party executive, reported in the spring of 1948, turned 'with the same savagery against the Socialists as against the whole working class. All local Socialist party organizations, with the exception of those in the three large towns and Crete, were disbanded together with a number of trade union organizations, the distribution of the Socialist press being suspended in the provinces while many Socialists were imprisoned or deported'.[4] And a year later a party

1. The official figure for the number of death sentences issued between 1945 and 1948 for acts performed during the liberation and civil war was 2,961 — *Machi*, 24 May 1948. For the wording of this survey of persecutions, see Circular No. 111, S.I.L.O. (Socialist Information and Liaison Office).

2. See pp. 144–5.

3. The rising was obviously not started on Stalin's initiative, since in the autumn of 1946 an easing of the difficult relationship between Russia and the Western powers seemed imminent. They had agreed on finalizing the peace treaty with Bulgaria, Hungary and Romania, who all came within the Russian sphere of influence; also the quarrel over the Trieste question had been patched up. In any case, Stalin had no illusions about the likely outcome of the uprising in Greece. In a discussion with Kardelj on 29 February 1948, at which Djilas was present, he remarked: '. . . This uprising has no hope whatsoever of success. Do you [Kardelj] believe that Great Britain and the United States—the United States, the mightiest state in the world—would allow the endangering of its lines of communications in the Mediterranean? Rubbish! We have no Navy. The uprising in Greece must come to an end as quickly as possible'—quoted in Milovan Djilas, *Conversations with Stalin* (London, 1962), p. 164. A motion of solidarity with the Greek insurgents, proposed by the Yugoslav delegation at the inaugural conference of the Cominform in September 1947, was rejected by the Russian delegates on Stalin's orders; see Eugenio Reale, 'The Founding of the Cominform', in *The Comintern—Historical Highlights*, p. 264.

4. A. Gregoroyannis, 'The Socialist Movement in Greece', in *Socialist World*, vol. I, March–May 1948. This quarterly publication was the official organ of the International Socialist Conference.

resolution stated: 'The régime of political persecution is becoming worse by the day. . . . Techniques of despotism, typical of a Fascist police rule, have stripped away all the liberties of the individual and swept aside elementary civil rights. . . .'[1]

Thus, as Churchill expressed it in closing his account of the episode, ended the struggle for 'freedom in the Western world'.[2]

4

When Churchill decided on military intervention in Greece so as to prevent the country from falling under Communist rule and becoming a Soviet base in the Mediterranean, he had not reckoned that this action would present Stalin with the political justification for Russia's military intervention in Romania, Bulgaria and, ultimately, Poland.[3]

In Poland, Stalin's use of military pressure to obtain the formation of a government to his liking had remained covert. In Romania, on the other hand, a new government was imposed by a Soviet commissar backed by the presence of Russian tanks in the streets of Bucharest. But then Romania was a vanquished enemy, having proclaimed a 'Holy War' against Russia immediately in the wake of Hitler's attack on the Soviet Union, on 22 June 1941. It had invaded the country with twenty-six divisions to recapture Bessarabia,[4] which Russia had seized in June 1940, and had annexed and systematically plundered south-western Ukraine, including Odessa. In General Rodion Malinovsky's counter-offensive in 1944, Soviet troops liberated the occupied territories and entered Romania, which then capitulated in the armistice of 12 September 1944, while Russian troops occupied the country.

Romania was hardly a democracy, having been subjected from September 1940 to the brutal Fascist rule of General Ion Antonescu and his 'Iron Guard'. On the day of the capitulation, Antonescu's government was overthrown by a *coup d'état* and Constantin Sanatescu charged by King Michael

1. Resolution of the Third National Conference of the Socialist Party of Greece E.L.D., 27–28 February, Circular No. 15/49 of the Socialist International. The martial law imposed at the start of the war was rescinded only at the beginning of 1950—when the number of political prisoners amounted to 10,000, among them 3,000 who had been sentenced to death; see A. Svolos's Report on the Situation in Greece, COMISCO Conference, Hastings, March 1950, Circular No. 74/50.

2. Churchill, *Triumph and Tragedy*, p. 283.

3. Stalin had earlier formulated a theoretical justification for the military intervention when, in conversation with Tito in April 1945, he had commented on the special character of the war: 'Whoever occupies a district, subjects it to his own social system. Everyone enforces his own system as far as his army is able'—quoted in Djilas, *Conversations with Stalin* p. 105.

4. See Braunthal, *History of the International, 1914–1943*, pp. 517–18.

with the formation of a government to represent the four anti-Fascist parties which had combined during the war within the underground movement as the 'National Democratic Front' (F.N.D.): the Social Democratic party, the National Peasants' party, the Liberals and the Communist party.

But, the Communists apart, none of these parties represented a reliable ally for Soviet Russia. The Peasants' party, led by Juliu Maniu, was conservative; the Liberal party, led by Ion Bratianu, was an anti-Socialist party of the middle class, and the Social Democratic party (*Partidul Social Democrat din Romania*), led by Constantin Titel Petrescu, had for two decades fought for democratic principles against Communism and was certainly no friend of Russia. Admittedly it had combined in April 1944 with the Communist party in the F.N.D. to fight Fascism and the war, and had reached mutual agreement with them on a programme of reform to be carried through in the early days of peace. But it included no agreement on Romania's future relations with the Soviet Union.

Thus the government promoted by King Michael was by no stretch of the imagination one which might be termed pro-Soviet. Within the course of a few weeks, the king had changed the government twice, finally at the beginning of December nominating as prime minister General Nicolae Rădescu, a declared enemy of Communism. While the Communists with the other parties of the National Democratic Front continued to be represented the government's character remained remote from Stalin's ideas or wishes.

So Stalin took a hand. The general secretary of the Communist party, Gheorghe Gheorghiu-Dej, a government member, was invited to talks in Moscow and returned to Bucharest on 16 January with instructions to promote mass demonstrations by the Communist-dominated F.N.D., to demand the sacking of Rădescu and the setting up of an exclusively F.N.D. government, and to eliminate Maniu, the Peasants' party's leader, from political life.[1] The mass demonstrations commenced at the beginning of February, while the Communist-dominated press—papers of other sympathies having been suppressed by the Soviet mission—demanded Rădescu's overthrow. During a mass demonstration in Bucharest on 24 February, eight demonstrators were killed in clashes with troops, and Rădescu was at once branded by the Communist press as a criminal. The psychological moment for Rădescu's overthrow had been reached. On the next day Russian troops occupied the Romanian General Staff H.Q. and other government buildings and disarmed all Romanian troops in the city. The scene had been set for a Communist *coup d'état*.

It is interesting to see how, in fact, the change of government ordered by Stalin took place. In the late afternoon of 27 February 1945, the deputy

1. See E. D. Tappe, 'Roumania', in *Central and South-East Europe*, p. 6.

people's Commissar for foreign affairs, Andrei Vishinsky, arrived at the Royal Palace in Bucharest direct from the Moscow plane and demanded that the king should instantly dismiss Rădescu's government and nominate a government of the National Democratic Front as representing the 'true democratic power in the country'. When the king hesitated, Vishinsky, with a glance at his watch, told him that he had until 8 o'clock to make a public announcement on the dismissal of Rădescu's government and the nomination of its successor, which gave him two hours and five minutes. Vishinsky then left the king, but the ultimatum having expired without the demands being fulfilled, he returned the next day to inform him that the Soviet government requested that the leader of the 'Ploughmen's Front', Petru Groza, should be appointed to form a government. When the king raised objections, Vishinsky banged his fist on the table and declared that, in the event of a government led by Groza not having been nominated by the following afternoon, he would wash his hands of any responsibility for the continuation of Romania as an independent state. Upon which he left the room, slamming the door loudly. Meanwhile Russian tanks and troops had occupied strategic positions throughout the city.[1]

Groza was nominated a few days later, the provisional government of the 'National Democratic Front' which he formed resting on a coalition of the Communists with the Communist-dominated 'Ploughmen's Front', a farmers' movement founded in 1934, the Social Democrats, and a group of Liberals sympathetic towards Russia. As a government it was, of course, completely Communist-controlled. Communists occupied all the key political positions: the Ministry of the Interior, with command over the civil and political police, the War Ministry and the Ministry of Justice. Also, as the American note of 18 August 1945 stated, there were 'important elements of democratic public opinion' which remained unrepresented. Under pressure from Truman, Stalin agreed in discussion with Byrnes, the American Secretary of State, that he would accept into the government representatives of the conservative National Liberal party and the National Farmers' party and would, in answer to Truman's demand, hold elections as 'early as possible'.

The elections were originally called for May 1946, but postponed until November when the Allies protested that they were clearly being prepared in Romania's political tradition—the tradition by which the party in control of

1. See Byrnes, *Speaking Frankly*, pp. 50–2; Churchill, *Triumph and Tragedy*, p. 368; Tappe, p. 7. The Russian *coup d'état* had 'deeply disturbed' Churchill as a prelude of things to come. 'The Russians,' he wrote, 'had established the rule of a Communist minority by force and misrepresentation. We were hampered in our protests because Eden and I during our October visit to Moscow had recognized that Russia should have a largely predominant voice in Romania and Bulgaria while we took the lead in Greece. Stalin had kept very strictly to this understanding during the six weeks' fighting against the Communists and the E.L.A.S. in the city of Athens, in spite of the fact that all this was most disagreeable to him and those around him'—*Triumph and Tragedy*, p. 369.

the apparatus of government invariably emerged from the polls as triumphant victor.[1]

The Romanian Communist party (*Partidul Comunist din Romania*), having been banned for twenty years since 1924, began its rise to power after the end of the war in September 1944 with only 1,000 members. A year later, at the party's first national conference on 16 October 1945, it was able to report a membership of 800,000. The miracle of this 800 per cent increase in party membership during the course of a year had been brought about by Anna Pauker, second in command of the party hierarchy. She won over not only industrial and agricultural workers, but also, as she later had to answer for, members of the middle classes, generals and bishops, members of Antonescu's secret police and, above all, members of the Fascist Iron Guard.[2] A party card meant bread, work and, in certain cases, a career, and in others immunity from prosecution for past misdeeds.

However, the fundamental task facing the Communists was the absorption of the Social Democratic party. This had always been by far the stronger of the two labour parties in Romania and had developed its traditions in the course of an honourable history over half a century. But now it found itself overtaken in terms of membership by about 600,000. When both parties had agreed in April 1944 on the formation of a 'United Labour Front', it was an arrangement which left their respective autonomy untouched. Now, however, the Communists wished to create a closer relationship with the Social Democratic party, and in particular to form joint lists for the elections due to take place in 1946. This proposal was declined on 1 December 1945 by a

1. On the influence of governmental powers on the results of Romanian elections, see the following examples collected by Fleming. In 1926, General Averescu was nominated as prime minister and won 280 seats against 105 for the opposition. In the following year, Stirbey became prime minister, who, while having won only 7 per cent of the votes in the 1926 elections, now gained 62 per cent. In 1928, Maniu, the leader of the National Farmers' party, became prime minister, winning 85 per cent of the votes and 385 seats. In 1931 he was relieved of office by the king, and Jorga, leader of a nominal party, was nominated: upon which he received 48 per cent of the votes and two thirds of the seats. In 1933, the National Liberals came to power, the number of seats which they won leaping from that of 30, which they had held up till then, to 274; see *The Cold War and its Origins*, vol. I, p. 308.

2. 'Elements foreign to the working class', so the June 1948 resolution of the central committee of the party stated, 'have infiltrated the party ranks—elements previously active in the Iron Guard movement, opportunists and those aiming at personal advancement, whose attitudes do not confirm with proletarian morality and who do not belong within the party'—quoted in Ghita Ionescu, *Communism in Rumania 1944-1962* (London, 1964), p. 119. In the process of purging the party over the next two years, 192,000 'Fascists', 'opportunists' and 'careerists' were expelled; see Stephen Fischer Galati, *The New Rumania. From People's Democracy to Socialist Republic* (Cambridge, Mass., 1967), p. 39. At a conference of the central committee on 15 December 1961, Alexandru Draghici, a Politbureau member, accused Anna Pauker of having, through her delegate, Teohari Geogescu, made a pact with the leader of the Iron Guard, Nicolae Patrascu, which made it possible for a considerable proportion of the members of the Fascist organization to enter the Communist party—see Ionescu, *Communism in Rumania*, p. 98.

party conference under the leadership of C. Titel Petrescu and Serban Voinea despite the opposition of the party's pro-Communist wing led by Lotar Radaceanu and Stefan Voitec.

The Communists now began to work to split the Social Democratic party. In their propaganda they differentiated between Petrescu and Radaceanu Socialists—fighting the first and supporting the latter—and gained control of the party by infiltrating its ranks up to the highest levels with their own secret members. By 1946 over half those sitting on the central and executive committee of the Social Democratic party were undercover Communist party members.[1]

The split finally occurred during a congress on 10 March 1946 over the question of unity lists with the Communists. The Communist undercover influence in the party secretariat guaranteed a pro-Communist majority, but Petrescu refused to accept the decision and withdrew from the congress, accompanied by his followers, to form the Independent Social Democratic party (*Partidul Social Democrat Independent din Romania*). The parent party thereupon formed a 'Democratic Bloc' with the Communists and fought the elections with joint lists. The election results of 19 November 1946 were as anticipated. The joint lists of the pro-Communist parties—the Democratic bloc—won 347 seats, while the two middle-class parties counted thirty-six and the Independent Social Democrat party, while receiving 66,528 votes (10 per cent of votes cast), gained not a single seat. Six weeks later, on 30 December 1947, the monarchy was overthrown and a 'People's Democracy of Romania' proclaimed. In this way Stalin secured the 90 per cent predominance in Romania promised to him by Churchill.

To gain total rule over the country, however, the absorption of the Social Democratic party into the Communist party was a necessity. The impetus for this action was given by the formation of the Cominform.[2] Four days after the end of the inaugural conference, both parties declared in a joint statement that they were in favour of amalgamation into a 'Romanian Workers' party'. A few days later, on 5 October 1947, the congress of the official Social Democratic party decided upon fusion with the Communist party; it had, as Barber Solomon, one of the party secretaries, reported to the congress, 560,201 members and a further 193,000 members in youth and women's organizations.[3] The amalgamation of both parties into the Romanian Labour party took place at an ordinary congress of 23 February 1948. The programme resolution passed by the congress declared that 'the teachings of Marx, Engels, Lenin and Stalin' would provide the ideological basis for the party.

1. See ibid., pp. 122–3.   2. See pp. 144–5.
3. *Scanteia*, quoted in Ionescu, *Communism in Rumania*, p. 150.

5

By contrast, the case of Bulgaria demanded other methods of subjection to Russian influence than those applied in Romania. Russia had been able to occupy Romania as an enemy country. Bulgaria, although it had been an ally of Hitler's Germany and had served as a base for the German campaign against Yugoslavia and Greece, had never actually entered into a state of war with Russia; it had declared war on Britain and the United States, but not on the U.S.S.R. But since Stalin deemed the military occupation of Bulgaria to be indispensable for its transformation into a Russian satellite state, the Soviet Union declared war on Bulgaria, though not until 5 September 1944, ten days after Bulgaria had asked Britain and the United States for a cease-fire. Now Bulgaria also asked Russia for an immediate cease-fire and the Soviet army occupied the country without opposition.

Three days before the entry of Russian troops into Bulgaria, the national committee of the National Front ordered an armed insurrection against the government. The National Front (*Otechestven Front*) had been founded in June 1942 by the Communist party under the leadership of Traichko D. Kostov as an underground fighting organization against Fascism and the war; the left wing of the Social Democratic party, led by Grigor Cheshmedzhiev, joined it, as did the radical Peasants' Union, under Nikola Petkov (which had in 1931 split off from the conservative Agrarian Alliance), and the *Zveno* Group, an organization of middle-class intellectuals allied with the powerful Military League. Colonel Kimon Georgiev, leader of the *Zveno* Group, had organized volunteers in an underground movement grouping approximately 10,000 men.[1]

In the early hours of 9 September 1944, a few hours before the Russian troops entered Sofia, the National Front undertook its planned *coup d'état*. Detachments of volunteers occupied government buildings while a group of Military League members invaded the building of the Presidency of the Ministers Council, surprised the government in the conference room, where it had assembled for discussion, and arrested the ministers. A government of the National Front was proclaimed, representing a coalition between the Communists and the *Zveno* Group, with Colonel Georgiev as prime minister and Petkov as deputy prime minister; the Social Democrats were represented in the government by Cheshmedzhiev.

But even though the parties of the farmers and the middle class were admittedly represented, Truman withheld his recognition; its Communist character was only thinly disguised and it had attained power by means of a *coup d'état* in the shadow of the Soviet army's occupation of Sofia. In a memorandum submitted to the Potsdam Conference, Truman declared the

1. See L. A. D. Dellin (ed.), *Bulgaria* (London, 1957), p. 116.

formation of the government to be in breach of the Yalta Declaration and demanded as a condition for its recognition that it should be re-formed by the inclusion of representatives of those conservative middle-class national parties not represented and that elections should be called.

The government was not, however, re-formed, and the elections, originally fixed for 26 August 1945, but postponed under pressure from the Western powers, were not held until 18 November. Meanwhile, in the period following the cease-fire, the Bulgarian army had been purged of 'unreliable elements' and, by a decree of 6 October 1944, 'people's courts' set up to prosecute war criminals. Rumours indicated the execution of between 20,000 and 100,000 during their first six months of activity, but according to official details only about 11,000 of the accused had been sentenced by March 1945.[1] Either way, disagreeable enemies of the régime had been eliminated from public life. Furthermore, by a decree of March 1945, the right to political activity was granted only to those parties represented in the National Front.

Soon afterwards the 'purging' of the member parties of the National Front commenced. At the request of the Communists, Petkov was removed from the leadership of the Farmers' Alliance and replaced by the more reliable Alexander Obbov; and Kosta Lulchev, the general secretary of the Social Democratic party, was displaced by Dimiter Neikov.[2] Both these parties had split into separate pro-Soviet and opposition parties. Furthermore, in the elections only candidates who had been entered on the joint list of the National Front were acknowledged. Therefore the opposition parties—the breakaway Social Democratic party and the split Farmers' Alliance as well, of course, as the middle-class national parties—were unable to nominate candidates.

The November elections, so thoroughly prepared, resulted in an over-whelming majority for the government; it received 86 per cent of all the votes cast. But the United States and Britain refused to recognize the elections and demanded as a condition for signing a peace treaty that new elections should be held in the letter and spirit of the Yalta Declaration. These were called, but for a date almost a year ahead, 27 October 1946. Soviet troops remained in the country and, with their support, the Communists, their hands on the reins of power, entrenched their rule against any threatening opposition. They were therefore able to fulfil the demands of the Western powers for free elections to the extent of granting at least the Social Democratic splinter group and the Farmers' Alliance an independent canvass. The

1. According to official details, 10,897 accused were found guilty in 131 cases, 2,138 being sentenced to death and executed, 1,940 being sentenced to twenty years' imprisonment, 962 to fifteen years, 727 to ten years and 3,241 to shorter terms; see Phyllis Auty, 'Bulgaria', in R. R. Betts (ed.), *Central and South-East Europe* (London, 1950), p. 30.

2. Kosta Lulchev and seven other members of the executive of the Social Democratic party were in 1948 sentenced to a heavy term of imprisonment in a mock trial involving fantastic accusations; they received between ten years and life imprisonment according to the extent of their prestige with the working class.

result of the elections was, as could only be expected, a victory for the parties of the National Front. Of the 465 seats in the *Sobranje* (the Bulgarian parliament) they won 364 to 101 for the opposition parties, the Communist representation rising from ninety-four at the elections of 1945 to 277; the Social Democrats won only nine seats.[1]

With the Communists enjoying an absolute majority in the *Sobranje*, Vassil Kolarov, Communist party leader, became president, while Georgi Dimitrov, the last general secretary of the Communist International—he had returned from Moscow in November 1945—was made prime minister.

To fulfil the conditions for its recognition laid down by the United States and Britain, the government had allowed the opposition parties to nominate independently. The Western powers therefore confirmed their recognition, and now that formal obstacles to peace treaty negotiations had been removed, they were brought to completion on 10 February 1947. On the day following the ratification of the peace treaty by the United States Senate, on 4 June 1947, Petkov was arrested, the opposition Farmers' Alliance dissolved, and he himself executed within a few months. The Social Democratic party, led by Neikov, already a part of the National Front, was amalgamated with the Communist party in February 1948; the Social Democratic party splinter group was demolished by administrative methods. The Constitution, proclaimed on 4 December 1947, declared Bulgaria to be a 'People's Democracy', and now Moscow could also feel secure in the knowledge that there existed in Bulgaria a completely reliable pro-Soviet government.

6

By the time Truman, Churchill and Stalin had assembled with their foreign ministers on 17 July 1945 at the Potsdam Conference, Poland, Romania and Bulgaria were in effect already ruled by pro-Soviet governments. These were Communist coalition governments, each containing a nominal representation of the parties of the Social Democrats, peasants and the middle class. They were not governments which had sprung from a democratic demonstration of the people's will in free elections, but had been installed by Stalin. At the heads of these governments stood leaders of non-Communist parties—in Poland the Socialist Osóbka-Morawski, in Romania the peasants' leader, Petru Groza, and in Bulgaria Colonel Georgiev, leader of the radical middle-class *Zveno* Group; but the real power lay in Communist hands. In none of these three countries had the Communist party enjoyed mass support before the war. In Poland, it had been dissolved in May 1938 on instructions from Moscow;[2] in Romania, even before the setting up of the Fascist dictatorship, it had been hardly more than a sect; and in Bulgaria, after an insurrection in

1. See Auty, 'Bulgaria', in Betts (ed.), *Central and South-East Europe*, p. 37.
2. See Braunthal, *History of the International, 1914–1943*, pp. 316–17.

September 1923 and their attempt to blow up the cathedral of Sofia,[1] the Communists had been practically extinguished in bloody persecutions.

They had now received their impetus from the Soviet army which had entered their countries and was keeping them under occupation in accordance with the cease-fire arrangements agreed with the Western powers. As agents of the Soviet government, Communists were thus able to secure the crucial positions of power, even though they were a minority in each country: the Ministry of the Interior, with its command of the civil and political police and the state administrative apparatus, and the Ministry of Defence, with its command of the army. In each country occupied by the Soviet army the government was committed by the cease-fire agreement to purge the police, army and state administration of Fascist and anti-Soviet elements. Therefore, during the sanitation process and without openly infringing the cease-fire agreements, the Communists were able to transform the armed power of the state and its administration into the instrument of a Communist dictatorship.

This was the situation existing in the three Russian-occupied countries at the time of the Potsdam Conference, and it could only alarm and provoke the mistrust of the Western powers. 'Like you,' Churchill wrote to Truman a few weeks before Potsdam, 'I feel deep anxiety because of their [the Russians'] misinterpretation of the Yalta decisions, their attitude towards Poland, their overwhelming influence in the Balkans.'[2]

But Churchill, in company with Roosevelt, had recognized the principle of installing 'pro-Soviet' governments in the states bordering on Russia and had, in his separate agreement with Stalin, legalized that very 'overwhelming influence in the Balkans'. Any protest against Russian policy in the occupied countries could therefore only come from Truman, and he, as we have seen, demanded a change of government in these countries and the implementation of the Yalta Declaration. This meant, in principle, the setting up of bourgeois democracies in some form, though these would unavoidably—in Poland and Romania at least—come into sharp conflict with the Soviet Union, which with Allied approval had annexed parts of their countries.

Stalin interpreted Truman's demands as a breach of his agreement with Churchill. As he told Churchill at Potsdam, he felt hurt by the American demand for a change of government in Romania and Bulgaria. He was not meddling in Greek affairs, he stated, and the demand was unjust. Furthermore, he assured Churchill, 'in all the countries liberated by the Red Army the Russian policy was to see a strong, independent, sovereign State. . . . They would have free elections, and all except Fascist parties would participate.'[3]

To this disagreement between the Western powers and the Soviet Union on the Russian policy in Poland, Romania and Bulgaria, was added disagreement

1. ibid., pp. 289, 290.   2. Churchill, *Triumph and Tragedy*, p. 498.   3. ibid., p. 550.

on Poland's western borders. At Yalta, Churchill and Roosevelt had 'in principle' agreed to Stalin's proposal that Poland should be compensated for the loss of her regions east of the Curzon Line by the German districts in East Prussia and Upper Silesia.[1] But any final decision on the extent of these districts and, above all, on Poland's western border—the future eastern German border—had been reserved for the peace conference. Under the terms of the Yalta agreements, East Prussia and Upper Silesia fell within the Russian zone of occupation and were to be transferred to Poland by the peace treaty.

Without any reference to the Western powers, Stalin had already handed over these districts to Poland, and not only those east of the Oder allotted to Poland at Yalta, but also the region west of the Neisse against the separation of which from Germany Churchill had objected.

Therefore the Western powers found themselves at Potsdam facing a *fait accompli*, which, as Truman declared, was in breach of the Yalta agreements. Stalin admitted that no settlement of boundaries had been reached at Yalta, apart from the plan to grant Poland an increase in territory; he emphasized, however, he had by no means transferred these districts to Poland as an occupation zone but, since the Germans had fled from the Russian troops and someone had to administer the districts, had allowed the Poles to take over their administration. After all, he said, the Soviet government must be allowed to ensure 'orderly conditions in the rear of the Red Army'.[2]

The Western powers, unable, of course, to appeal to force of arms, were therefore powerless to alter the situation created by Stalin in the districts occupied by the Red Army and colonized by the Poles. They thus agreed to a 'temporary' administration of these districts by the Poles, but refused to recognize the Oder–Neisse Line as Poland's future western border. Any border settlement, they insisted, must, as had been agreed at Yalta, be kept for the peace conference.[3] President Truman was extremely annoyed. 'At Potsdam,' he wrote, 'we were . . . forced by the circumstances to agree to the Russian occupation of East Poland and the Polish occupation of the German districts east of the Oder. It was an arrogant act of violence.'[4]

Shortly afterwards a new Russian demand further inflamed the mistrust of the Western powers towards Stalin's plans. At the first meeting of the Council of Foreign Ministers in London (10 September to 2 October 1945),[5] which had been arranged in Potsdam for the drafting of the peace treaty, Molotov surprised the assembly with the totally unexpected Communist demand for

1. See page 94.　　　2. See Byrnes, *Speaking Frankly*, p. 204.
3. For the Potsdam discussions on this question, see Meissner, *Russland, die West-mächte und Deutschland*, pp. 62–8.
4. Harry S. Truman, *Memoirs* (New York, 1955), vol. 1: *Year of Decisions, 1945*, p. 552.
5. At this meeting the following were present: Bevin (Great Britain), Byrnes (U.S.A.), Molotov (U.S.S.R.) and Bidault (France).

a colony in Africa. Italy had lost its African colonies in the war, and when the conference discussed their future Molotov demanded the cession of Tripolitania to the Soviet Union. Russia, he declared, had earned the right to one of the Italian colonies in Africa since it had had to fight against ten Italian divisions; furthermore, he declared, the Russians were exceptionally successful in civilizing backward peoples. 'But,' he continued, 'if you won't give us one of the Italian colonies, we should be quite content to have the Belgian Congo.'[1]

Already at Yalta, as five years earlier from Hitler,[2] Stalin had demanded a Russian base in the Dardenelles—the fulfilment of one of Tsarism's most cherished ambitions, and one which Britain had always frustrated through war or diplomacy. The possibility of Soviet Russia now installing itself in the straits of the eastern Mediterranean and so, under certain conditions, being in a position to threaten Britain's lines of communications with India, could only produce in Churchill feelings of acute anxiety. But Stalin, whose Red Army was of overwhelming importance for ending the war in Europe, could not be antagonized by a flat refusal; and so the whole question had been left open at Yalta.

Now Stalin had put forward his demand either for Tripoli on the southern edge of the Mediterranean, or alternatively the Congo in the heart of Africa. Britain could hardly take the demand seriously,[3] but the refusal to recognize Russia's colonial ambitions introduced a further element into the tension already existing between the Soviet Union and the Western powers.

Then a new conflict broke out over Russian policy in Persia. Russia and Britain had, in August 1941, deposed Shah Reza Khan of Persia, a friend of Hitler's, by a combined invasion and had occupied the country—the British taking the south and the Russians the province of Azerbaijan in the north. It had been mutually agreed that both would withdraw from the country within six months of the end of the war but, while the British duly withdrew their troops in December 1945, the Russians had remained.

In the social unrest which developed after the fall of Reza Khan, the Communists had, in 1942, formed the party of the *Tudeh* ('Party of the Masses'), an apolitical democratic movement which attracted a tremendous mass following from among the Persian proletariat and the radical intellectuals. In Azerbaijan the movement had organized itself under the leadership of Jaafar Pishevari[4] as the Democratic party, and in December 1945, with

1. Quoted in Dalton, *High Tide and After*, p. 56; Byrnes, *Speaking Frankly*, pp. 95–7.
2. See Braunthal, *History of the International, 1914–1943*, pp. 520–1.
3. General Smuts was, as Dalton reported, 'horrified by the idea of having the Russians in Africa, since he thought they would stir up the tribes everywhere'—*High Tide and After*, p. 56.
4. Pishevari had, under the name of Sultan Zadeh, been commissioner for internal affairs in the Persian Soviet Republic of Ghilan, proclaimed after the Soviet conquest of

the connivance of Russian occupation troops, had begun an insurrection in Tabriz, the capital of the province, and proclaimed Azerbaijan an independent republic.

The proclamation of the republic took place a few days after the opening of the second Foreign Ministers' Conference, which assembled on 16 December 1945 in Moscow. There Molotov repeated his request for a Soviet base on the Dardenelles and additionally demanded that Russia should be given the Turkish districts of Kars, Ardahan and Trapezunt on the Black Sea coast. It had, in any case, become clear that Stalin was not going to pull his Russian forces out of the Azerbaijan Republic at the agreed date.[1]

Truman reacted to Russia's policy in the Near East by introducing a switch in American policy towards the Soviet Union—one which he had, in fact, been planning for some time. In a memorandum dated 5 January 1946, three weeks after the establishment of the Republic of Azerbaijan, he directed Byrnes, the Secretary of State, 'to protest as forcibly as possible against Russia's schemes in Persia. Nothing can justify them. . . . They are in line with the assumptions and arbitrary methods by which Russia has operated in Poland. . . . We have been faced in Persia with a *fait accompli*. . . . I have no doubt that Russia proposed to invade Turkey and to conquer the Black Sea straits to the Mediterranean. If Russia does not find itself confronted with an iron fist . . . it will come to a new war . . .'[2]

But Truman's memorandum, a secret state document, ran counter to the frame of mind prevalent in the United States and in Britain. Popular admiration for the heroism of the Red Army had not by any means evaporated at this time, nor had sympathies towards the Soviet Union cooled; general confidence in Russia as an ally of Western democracy remained unshaken. The strife between Allied ministers at their conferences over the form government was to take in the states bordering on Russia appeared insignificant beside the overwhelming importance of attaining lasting friendship between East and West as an indispensable guarantee for world peace. In the hostile language of his memorandum, the President of the United States could speak only for himself and was in no way reflecting popular opinion, which would have been shocked and disgusted at the very thought of a possible war against Russia.

In the event it was Churchill who took upon his own shoulders the task of awakening America to the 'Bolshevist danger'. Defeated in the 1945

Azerbaijan in 1920 by the Persian rebel Kushik Khan with the support of the Russian troops. After the defeat of the Ghilan Soviet Republic in 1921 by Reza Khan, Pishevari fled to Moscow and worked there in the Secretariat of the Communist International as adviser on the Near East.

1. They were actually withdrawn in March 1946.
2. Truman, *Year of Decisions*, p. 552.

elections, succeeded by a Labour government and freed from responsibilities of government, he made a visit to the United States. In a speech delivered at Fulton, Missouri, on 5 May 1946, he denounced in Truman's presence Russia's expansionist ambitions, calling on the United States and Great Britain to set a limit by means of military co-operation to Soviet territorial ambitions. 'Nobody knows,' he said, 'what Soviet Russia and its Communist international organization intends to do in the immediate future, or what are the limits, if any, to their expansive and proselytizing tendencies. . . .' But, in order to do justice to the prevailing mood of the people of Britain and America, he emphasized his feeling of 'high esteem and admiration for the brave Russian people and my comrade from war-time, Marshal Stalin'; he also mentioned the feelings of 'sympathy and well-wishing' which Britain—'and surely America too,' he added—'harbours for the people of Russia' and that he was determined 'in spite of all differences and set-backs to work unflinchingly for the construction of a lasting friendship with Russia'.

But then he turned to describe the 'Bolshevist danger'. 'From Stettin in the Baltic to Trieste in the Adriatic,' he said, 'an iron curtain has descended across the continent of Europe. Behind this line lay all capitals of the central and eastern European countries: Warsaw, Berlin, Prague, Vienna, Budapest, Belgrade, Bucharest and Sofia. All these famous cities lay within the Soviet sphere and all are in one form or another exposed not only to the Soviet Russian influence, but in ever increasing degrees subjected to the control of Moscow. . . . The Communist parties, which had in all these countries been very small until now, have been cultivated everywhere, they have achieved incongruous power and now aim to seize everywhere total rule. In almost every case there now exists a police state.' He did not believe, he said, that Soviet Russia wished for war. 'What they desire,' he stated, 'is the fruits of war and the indefinite expansion of their power and doctrines.' For defence against this danger he recommended an Anglo-American policy of military strength. Because 'there is nothing for which they [the Russians] have less respect for than . . . military weakness'.[1]

Churchill felt it to be important that any conflict of interest between Russia and the Allies should appear a conflict between irreconcilable ideologies: Communism and 'freedom and democracy'. So long as the Soviet Union was fighting on the side of the Western powers in the name of 'freedom and democracy' against Hitler's Germany, there had been no talk of the 'danger of Communism'. Russia's system of government had been accepted as a fact with which the world had to come to terms, and no Western statesman had paid a more respectful tribute to the Communist dictator,

1. Quoted in Desmond Donnelly, *Struggle for the World. The Cold War from its Origins in 1917* (London, 1965), pp. 211–12; Meissner, *Russland, die Westmächte und Deutschland*, pp. 79–80.

Stalin, than Churchill. But now Churchill called upon the United States and Britain to defend the principle of democracy throughout the world by opposing the Communist threat posed by the Soviet Union with military force.

But those who had just passed through the hell of the Second World War were in no mood to receive with applause Churchill's call to arms in preparation for a Third World War. Byrnes hastened to explain that the United States government had not been consulted by Churchill over the content of the speech, and that it 'had nothing to do with it'; 105 British Labour Members of Parliament condemned the speech, stating in a motion to the House of Commons that it constituted a 'hostile attack on the cause of world peace'. Even the conservative London *Times* criticized Churchill's theory of the conflict between 'western democracy and Communism'. 'Although western democracy and Communism,' it wrote, 'contradict each other in many aspects, both [systems] have to learn a lot of each other—Communism from the experience of political institutions and the justifications of the right of the individual, western democracy from [the Communist system's] economic and social planning.' 'It would,' it continued, 'be a counsel of despair to assume that western democracy and Communism are condemned to a struggle to the death.'[1]

Stalin was understandably exercised over Churchill's speech. He denounced it as 'a dangerous act aimed at dividing the Allied governments and preventing their co-operation. . . . I do not know,' he continued, 'whether Churchill and his friends will succeed after the Second World War in organizing a new armed camp against Eastern Europe; but should they succeed, it may confidently be said that they may expect to receive a hiding. . . '[2] He was concerned that America's monopoly of the atom bomb might tempt them into contemplating an attack on Communist Russia. Barely five months after the end of the war, the Moscow *New Times* had given a warning of this danger. 'The atom bomb,' it wrote, 'is a signal for reactionaries throughout the world to agitate for a new crusade against the Soviet Union.'[3] Ernest Bevin, who as British foreign secretary was fairly well informed of the political trends in Washington and Moscow, was under the impression, as he said in conversation with Hugh Dalton, that 'both the Americans and the Russians' were each 'afraid of the other'; both were 'too bomb-minded'. And he confirmed that in certain American circles it was felt that 'since they had the bomb now and the Russians hadn't, they had better have a show-down at once'. 'Stalin,' he explained, 'has, since Churchill's Fulton speech, convinced himself that the Tories, who the Russians thought

1. Quoted in Wilfrid Knapp, 'The Partition of Europe', in Evan Luard (ed.), *The Cold War*, (London, 1964), pp. 53–4.
2. *Pravda*, 13 March 1946, quoted in Donnelly, *Struggle for the World*, pp. 212–13.
3. *New Times* (Moscow), 18 November 1945, quoted in Fleming, *The Cold War and its Origins*, vol. I, p. 329.

would soon return to power in this country, would get in line with the Americans to oppose them.'[1]

Truman, however, still hesitated to show the Soviet Union the 'iron fist' and Stalin strove not to lay down a challenge. In an interview with Alexander Werth on 24 September 1946, he declared that he believed absolutely 'in the possibility of friendly and lasting co-operation between the Soviet Union and the Western democracies. . . . I do not doubt,' he said, 'that the possibilities for peaceful co-operation are likely to increase rather than decrease.'[2] And then, a few weeks later, in December 1946, Molotov demonstrated the desire of the Soviet Union to avoid a break with the Western powers when, in the closing discussions of the New York conference of the Council of Foreign Ministers on the peace treaties with Italy, Hungary, Romania and Finland, he made a number of surprising concessions.

7

The most outstanding question facing the Allies and emphasizing the differences between them was the problem of Germany—how to prevent this country which, twice in the lifetime of a single generation, had unleashed a world war, from becoming a renewed menace to the world. When the Allies first discussed this question at Tehran at the end of November 1943, Churchill, Roosevelt and Stalin had all agreed that Germany should be divided so that it might never again challenge the world by force of arms. Roosevelt's plan, submitted to the conference, suggested a division into five autonomous states. Not unexpectedly, it was Stalin who spoke most decisively for the dismantling of Germany, since it was Russia which had suffered most from the war caused by Germany. As he told the conference, he was convinced that Germany would quickly recover from the war and might 'start on a new one within a comparatively short period'. Therefore, he said, it would be 'far better to break up and scatter the German tribes. Of course they would . . . always want to reunite. . . . Germany should at all costs be broken up so that she could not reunite.'[3] Even at the Yalta Conference in February

1. Quoted in Dalton, *High Tide and After*, pp. 155–6. For the mutual mistrust between the former allies which erupted shortly after the end of the war, the memorandum which Molotov submitted to the Foreign Ministers' conference in Moscow in December 1945 provides a good illustration. In this he charged the British government—the government of the Labour party!—with rebuilding the Austrian army and organizing military groups of Nazis and anti-Communist Russian White Guards, with the evident intention of employing them against the Soviet Union. Bevin, in his counter-statement, said that the accusations were, of course, 'completely without foundation' and that he 'denied them categorically'; see Byrnes, *Speaking Frankly*, p. 163.

2. *Sunday Times* (London), 25 September 1946.

3. Winston S. Churchill, *The Second World War*, vol. v: *Closing the Ring* (London, 1952), pp. 317 and 356.

1945, the partition of Germany remained a unanimous war aim of the Allies.

Then, three months later, on 9 May 1945, Stalin declared that the Soviet Union had no intention of 'dismembering or destroying Germany'.[1] And at the Paris conference of the Council of Foreign Ministers (June–July 1946), which had been called to prepare the ground for the peace treaties, Molotov not only turned against the partition or even a forced federation of Germany, but also against the cession of the Rhineland, the Ruhr and the Saar, as France demanded. 'It has lately become fashionable,' he said, 'to speak of German partition as separate "autonomous" states, of German federalism, of the cession of the Ruhr districts from Germany. All such proposals spring from the same aim: to destroy Germany and to transform it into an agrarian state, for it is certainly clear that without the Ruhr Germany could hardly exist as an independent, viable state. But as I have already said, our task must not be the destruction of Germany if the interests of peace and quiet are dear to us.'[2]

A number of historians have taken the view that Stalin retracted his demands for German partition and began to plead for a unified German state after coming to believe that the Communists, or at least such segments of the middle classes as were ready for a return to the Rappallo policy against 'Anglo-American capitalism', would attain power.[3]

Yet, while Molotov declared his opposition to any cession of the Ruhr, he proposed a four-power control for the Ruhr industry—a control by the United States, Great Britain, France and, of course, Russia. Bevin, on the other hand, proposed that the Ruhr should remain a political part of Germany, but that its industry—Germany's most powerful war potential—should be internationalized by being transferred to the ownership of an international consortium of governments—not only of the four great powers but also of the smaller states which had united in alliance against Hitler's

1. Quoted in V. M. Molotov, *Questions of Foreign Policy* (Moscow, 1949), p. 427.
2. ibid., pp. 70–1.
3. This consideration might have played a part in Stalin's well-known order of the day of 23 February 1942, when he emphasized that nothing was further from the Soviet Union's intention than the destruction of Germany. 'In the foreign press,' he said, 'there is talk about the Red Army's aim to exterminate the German people and destroy the German State. . . . The Red Army has no such idiotic aims, and never can have. The Red Army has set itself the aim of dislodging the German occupants of our country. . . . It is quite possible that the war for the liberation of our country will lead to the expulsion or destruction of the Hitler clique. We would welcome such a result. But it would be laughable to compare the Hitler clique with the German people, with the German state. The experiences of history foretell that the Hitlers will come and go, but the German people, the German state, will remain'—J. Stalin, *Over the Great National War of the Soviet Union* (Moscow, 1946), pp. 49–50. The purpose of this speech was the founding of the 'Free Germany' National Committee in July 1943 and of the 'Federation of German Officers' in September. Both organizations were dissolved on 2 November 1945. It was, of course, kept from the public that Stalin, at the same time as he pledged himself to the retention of the German state, was demanding its partition in confidential discussions with Churchill and Roosevelt.

Germany, such as Belgium and Holland.[1] The United States, however, rejected both proposals, being anxious to prevent a Western European sphere of influence opening out to the Soviet Union as a consortium member, and perhaps also to secure an investment market in Germany's heavy industry for American capitalism.

Besides blocking Stalin's plans for the Ruhr, the United States also strove to check his demands for German reparations. At Yalta he had proposed that Russia should receive total reparations in the form of goods and means of production to the value of $10,000 million, a demand he renewed at Potsdam. But at neither of the two conferences did the Allies agree to reparation settlements for Russia. Byrnes was therefore able to deny at the Paris conference of the Council of Foreign Ministers[2] that any binding agreements had been made, and implied that the Soviet Union was already sufficiently compensated, having won an increase in 'taxable wealth' in Königsberg and the northern part of East Prussia, allocated to it at Potsdam, as well as in the districts given to Poland, which far exceeded the reparation sum demanded. The United States was not, of course, able to prevent the Soviet Union from collecting their reparation demands in the Russian-occupied zone, but in May 1946 it blocked the delivery of reparations to the Soviet Union from the American zone.

The attitude of the United States government to the question of a joint administration of the Ruhr and to Russia's reparation demands demonstrated symptoms of a change in American thinking towards the Soviet Union. It accorded with the humiliating response which met Russia's request for American loans.

When, during the course of the war, Stalin had raised the possibility of an American loan to rebuild Russia's ruined cities and industries after the war, he found Roosevelt sympathetic; it was not to be forgotten, as Churchill had said, how the Soviet Union had carried 'the brunt of the war'. Thus encouraged, the Soviet Union early in January 1945 submitted a formal application for a post-war loan of $6,000 million. It was, however, a request which could only be discussed after the war had ended, and by then Roosevelt was dead, while his successor, Truman, was in no mood to help the Soviet Union to overcome economic ruin. Not only did he stop Lend-Lease three weeks after the end of the war in Europe but, in a memorandum of January 1946, he directed his Secretary of State to 'enforce' settlement of Russia's Lend-Lease debt.[3] There was no further talk of Russian requests for a loan.

1. See Dalton, *High Tide and After*, pp. 105–6.
2. The questions of Russian reparation demands and the Ruhr were discussed at two further conferences of the Council: in Moscow in March 1947 and in London in November–December 1947. For a detailed report of the discussions, see Meissner, *Russland, die Westmächte und Deutschland*, pp. 105–6.
3. See Truman, *Year of Decisions*, p. 552.

8

On 12 March 1947, President Truman startled the world with an open declaration of war against Communism as the instrument of the Soviet Union's expansionist policies. In a message to both houses of Congress he stated that the United States government had made a decision to curb the spread of Communism in the world and to check the expansionist ambitions of the Soviet Union.[1]

Truman's statement was prompted by the decision of the British Labour government in the spring of 1947 to withdraw its troops from Greece. The country was still witnessing the terrible civil war unleashed by the Communists in the autumn of 1946,[2] and its disrupted economic life and government administration was only being kept from collapse by military and economic help from Britain. But Britain, bled dry by the war and burdened with the crippling cost of feeding the population in the British occupation zone in Germany, felt itself unable to continue with the financial burden of an occupation in Greece. London informed Washington that it would withdraw its troops on 31 March.

Hugh Dalton, the Labour Chancellor of the Exchequer, described in his memoirs the panic which the cabinet decision unleashed in Washington. 'The Americans,' he wrote, 'took fright lest Russia should overrun the whole of the Balkans and the Eastern Mediterranean.' He quoted a radio address by Joseph Harsh in Washington, which explained the motives which moved Truman to announce his 'policy of restraint'. Should Greece go Communist, he said, 'it might mean the spread of Russian influence to Italy in one direction and as far as the borders of India in the other'. The expansion of Russia, he continued, 'would not require a single Red Army soldier or a single overt act by the Russian State, and here also was the type of possible Russian expansion which could not be answered by any atomic bomb'.[3]

The United States government undertook responsibility for Greece, Truman justifying the decision by a principle which has gone down in history under the name of the 'Truman Doctrine' and which was to direct the future international policy of the United States: the principle of resistance to Communist revolution wherever it may appear. 'In a number of countries,' Truman said, 'totalitarian régimes have been forced on to nations. . . .' He mentioned Poland, Romania and Bulgaria which, in spite of repeated protests by the United States government, had been subjected 'through force and intimidation' to totalitarian rule. In Greece a belligerent minority had been able to create chaos by exploiting the poverty and misery which so far had made the country's economic recovery impossible. 'I believe,' Truman

1. Truman, *Year of Decisions*, p. 552. 2. See pp. 108–111.
3. Dalton, *High Tide and After*, pp. 207–8.

stated, 'that it must be the policy of the United States to support free peoples who resist attempted subjugation by armed minorities or by outside pressure.'[1]

The Truman Doctrine rested on the assumption of an irreconcilable antagonism between states with democratic and Communist systems of government. But this was in fact only an ideological cover for the struggle by the United States and its allies to restore in Europe the balance of power overthrown by the war. The collapse of the countries of Eastern and Central Europe had created a vacuum and in trying to fill as much of it as possible, the Soviet Union was driven by its paramount need for strategic security. It was not so much the idea of a Communist world revolution which provoked Russia into subjecting Poland, the Baltic and eastern Balkan states, as the fear of encirclement should these countries ever come under the rule of hostile powers. The Communist ideal served the Soviet Union simply as an ideological cover for its power policy and as a moral justification for the imperialistic methods it harnessed to subject other countries—methods which in fact stood in such sharp contrast to the ethos and fundamental principles of Socialism. The rule of Communism set up under the system of Soviet dictatorship in the countries occupied by the Soviet Union was not the object of their subversion, but only a means towards strengthening Russia's predominance in these states. In fact there was at that time nothing further from the interests of Stalin, that most pragmatic of politicians, than the expansion of Communism by world revolution. What he strove for was a balance of power in Europe which would ensure the security of the Soviet Union.

Yet, because the power policy of the Soviet Union cloaked itself in the ideology of Communism, the expansion of Russia in Eastern Europe and the Balkans appeared as a prelude to world revolution. This was the myth upon which Truman founded his doctrine. Its object was to contain not only Russian expansion in Europe but also, by threat of war if necessary, to prevent the spread of Communism wherever in the world it attempted to seize power. It represented a turning-point in the history of the alliance between the Western democracies and the Soviet Union, putting an end to any exuberant hopes that the peoples of all the nations had felt for a lasting, friendly co-operation between the Great Powers in a world of peace and prosperity. It triggered off the 'Cold War' and the years of stock-piling colossal atomic arsenals which have swallowed up the peacetime wealth of the people, who would in any case be destroyed by their actual use in war. It suggested the possibility of armed conflict between East and West, giving impetus to the development of an atmosphere of international tension in which each power bloc seemed to threaten the existence of the other.

1. On 22 May, nine weeks after Truman's declaration, Congress passed $400 m. for military and economic support of the Greek and Turkish governments, which, as Truman said, were threatened by the danger of Communism.

In the atmosphere of the Cold War, any hopes of overcoming the split in the international Labour movement could only remain unfulfilled. Whatever the rights or wrongs of the situation, Communists naturally aligned themselves with the Soviet Union in the face of the general threat, while Socialists identified themselves with their own countries, which in turn felt threatened by the Soviet Union.

PART TWO

The Reopening of the Split

6 · The Revival of the International

The Socialist Labour International did not survive the Second World War; its bureau met for the last time on 3 April 1940. Six days later the German army invaded Norway and Denmark, and, a month later, overran Belgium and Holland and had begun its offensive against France. When French resistance collapsed after a few weeks, only three European countries remained whose labour movements had escaped destruction by Fascism: Great Britain, Switzerland and Sweden. The International had been ineffective ever since the Munich agreement of October 1938;[1] then the catastrophe of war, swallowing up almost all its members on the Continent, put an end to its effective existence. It had not, however, been entirely dissolved. While no death certificate had been issued in the name of the International,[2] it had departed from the stage of history.

The vacuum thus created had been filled, however sparsely, by a small international group of leaders from the suppressed European Socialist parties who had found asylum in Great Britain. Their meetings, convened by the British Labour party, were, however, held *in camera* and they issued no statements.[3]

The first Socialist International conference since the beginning of the war did not meet until early March 1945 in London under the chairmanship of Hugh Dalton. It was called by the British Labour party, but was attended by representatives of only thirteen Socialist parties. The Socialist parties of

1. See Braunthal, *History of the International, 1914–1943*, pp. 487–92.
2. The formal dissolution of the Socialist Labour International did not take place until November 1946 by a decision taken at an international conference in Bournemouth.
3. *International Supplement*, a supplement to the Labour party's *Labour Press Service*, which appeared at the beginning of 1942, established contacts between émigré Socialist groups in Britain. To discuss the peace aims of Socialism and the problem of the future International, *International Socialist Forum*, a monthly periodical, was founded in 1941 by Julius Braunthal in association with Harold Laski, a member of the Labour party executive, and Louis de Brouckère, a former president of the International. Its editorial board represented almost all Socialist groups of exiles, and it appeared as a supplement to the *Left News*, edited by Victor Gollancz.

those countries which were fighting the Allies in the war—Germany, Austria and Hungary—were not invited, while representatives of other parties were unable to attend owing to the difficulties of travel imposed by war-time conditions. This conference was not therefore able to speak in the name of the International. But it did assume some importance, for it was the first occasion since the beginning of the war that any form of the International had appeared in public and expressed opinions on the political and economic problems facing the world in constructing the imminent peace.

The focal point for discussion[1] was the problem of Germany, which had been at the centre of passionate debate in the British Labour party as well as among Socialist émigré groups during the war. At the time of the conference the seal had still to be set on the defeat of Nazi rule. What was to happen to Germany afterwards? This was the question for debate.

The conference's resolution on Germany reflected the mood which the outrages of National Socialism had evoked in the world at large. It declared that the German people had, under Hitler, 'burdened itself with a collective guilt greater than that of any people in history'. Although it should never be forgotten that large sections of the German population had opposed Hitler's rise to power and many had become victims of its terror, it remained impossible to take measures which would not strike Germany as an entity; 'the whole German people must suffer the consequences' of the deeds of the Third Reich. As a result of the outrages of Hitlerism and its barbaric methods during the war, the German people had forfeited their right to self-determination which, up till now, 'the civilized world' had acknowledged. Germany must, the resolution insisted, place itself for a while under the control of the United Nations and submit to military occupation by the four Great Powers until such time as it became clear that Fascism had indeed been purged from the national consciousness. The country must be totally disarmed, the landed estates of the German aristocrats broken up, the captains of heavy industry dispossessed, and the industrial complexes of the Ruhr and the Rhineland internationalized. On the other hand, the conference declared against any division of Germany into several states, though it did not oppose 'necessary adjustments of borders' or the setting up of special régimes in the Rhineland, Ruhr and Saar.

The main concern of the British Labour party in calling the conference was, however, the renewal of the Socialist International. The conference instituted a steering committee charged with drawing up a plan on the basis of its memorandum to re-establish the International, with its principles,

---

1. No minutes are available for any Socialist International conference up to 1950. This account is based on documents and resolutions of the conference in the Archives of the Socialist International, International Institute for Social History, Amsterdam.

structure and main functions to be discussed and approved at a general conference to follow 'in the near future'.[1]

More than a year elapsed, however, before an international Socialist conference met again. Once more it was called by the British Labour party and it met in May 1946 at Clacton, the seaside holiday town on the Essex coast not far from London.

It seemed as though a conference to discuss the re-establishment of the International could hardly have met under more hopeful auguries. For the first time in history, the working class had entered the scene as a decisive factor in world policy. In Britain the Labour party had attained power in the triumphant election victory of July 1945; in Sweden, Norway, Australia and New Zealand there were Labour parties in sole control of government, and in almost every other European country the Social Democratic parties participated in coalition governments. And while the fundamental split in the International Labour movement had not yet been overcome, in most of Europe, as in France, Italy and Czechoslovakia and all other Eastern European countries, Socialist parties were co-operating with Communist parties in joint action alliances or coalition governments. An International, based on the power and influence of the European Socialist parties, was for the first time in a position to become a true power factor capable of direct influence over world policy.

But it could only attain a reality as a power factor provided that the reopening of the split in the international labour movement could be avoided. This realization had already shown itself in a declaration of the London conference of March 1945, which had stated: 'The conference recognized the urgent need to unite the working class.'

Unity in the international labour movement could only be preserved by an understanding between the Social Democratic International and the Soviet Union. Such an understanding was seen to be simply the precondition for the development of Socialist power. 'If there were to be collaboration between Russia and the Socialist International,' Harold Laski commented in a memorandum which he laid before the Clacton conference,[2] 'then Europe would become a Socialist continent within twenty years.' But if collaboration with Russia should fail, he added, then the greater part of Europe would become prey to monopoly capitalism, which carried within itself the seeds of a Third World War. 'To prevent this catastrophe at the same time as uniting the working classes of the world,' he stated, 'the new International must

1. For the text of the declaration and resolution, see Report of the National Executive Committee, in Report of the Forty-Fourth Annual Conference of the Labour Party, 1945, pp. 163–70 and 13.
2. The memorandum may be found in the Archives of the Socialist International, Institute for Social History, Amsterdam.

strive to gain the friendship of the Soviet Union.' This, he said, was its central task.

However, the chaotic world situation which followed the end of the war threw up political and ideological conflicts between the Socialist parties which were not easily reconciled. These stemmed from contrasting attitudes towards the conflict between the Western powers and the Soviet Union which had already become apparent at the Potsdam Conference in July 1945. The French and British Socialist parties, as ruling parties responsible for their own governmental policies, were guided by loyalty to the position of the West, while Socialist parties of countries within the Russian sphere of influence—Poland, Romania, Bulgaria, Hungary and Czechoslovakia— supported the alliance of their states with the Soviet Union as being the most effective guarantee of security against a possible threat posed by Germany. Thus differences of aims between the governments of the Western powers and Russia—as, for example, over the question of Germany's future—threw up differences between the Socialist parties of the West and East.

To these were added differences of ideology. The Western Socialist parties were traditionally Social Democrat, while those of the East, now carrying joint responsibility for government with Communist parties, found themselves unable under prevailing conditions to act in the spirit of Social Democracy to carry through social and economic changes if they were to avoid the return to power of the old ruling class. Each one of these countries, with the exception of Czechoslovakia, was a country with no democratic tradition, always subjected to one form or other of dictatorship by the landed gentry, the aristocracy or the officer caste. They were agrarian societies in which the industrial proletariat—the traditional catalyst for social revolution— formed only a minority of the population, while the great mass of peasants, still at an early stage of political development, remained subject to the reactionary influence of the Church. The Socialist parties in Eastern Europe were thus honestly convinced that a system of genuine democracy, on the model of the Western states, would undermine the social revolution which they had undertaken in alliance with the Communists. It would permit the forces of reaction to regain power by manipulating parliamentary democracy; it would demolish democracy, as had happened between the wars in Poland, and even in states with democratic traditions, such as Germany and Austria, and would, as it had then, subject the working class to a Fascist dictatorship.

The dilemma faced by Socialist parties in these countries was impressively described by Emanuel Buchinger, a Hungarian Social Democrat leader, in the speech of welcome which he made to the German Social Democratic party congress in July 1947:

We are [he said] about to build up democracy in Hungary. But it cannot be like English democracy which has developed in the course of centuries. Let us assume that the British Labour government were defeated at the next election. Its defeat would, at worst, slow down the pace of Socialist transformation in Great Britain. However, should the old reactionary classes regain power in Hungary, there would not be enough trees in the forest of Bakony on which to hang honest democrats and Socialist workers, who would be doomed by a counter-revolutionary régime. The three million landless peasants who have been settled by a land reform on the vast estates of the big landowners, would again be reduced to serfs, the coal mines and foundries which have been nationalized would be returned to their former capitalist owners, and the industrial workers would be thrust back into the misery from which they have now emerged. Our country, which had never known freedom under the Habsburg domination, was poisoned by the reactionary spirit of the Horthy counter-revolutionary dictatorship and Fascism, which ruled it for a quarter of a century.[1]

What the Socialist parties of these countries visualized was a somewhat modified form of parliamentary democracy which would, on the one hand, realize the principle of the political equality and democratic right to freedom for every citizen, while, on the other, ensuring a leading role in the state for the alliance of Socialist and Communist parties as representing the working class.

It was a system which, as our survey of the development of parties in these countries has shown,[2] could not avoid terrorist methods in imposing a Communist dictatorship and so met with criticism from the West. The British Labour government protested against the system as being in breach of the Yalta Declaration, while the Socialist parties of the West in general protested in their press against the excesses of these systems of government as a violation of democratic principles.

It was on these differences of ideology and political methods that the first attempt to re-create the International foundered. Only the Socialist parties of France, Belgium and Austria were in favour of its renewal in all its forms. The Labour parties of Britain and the Scandinavian countries, which all happened to be in power, were reluctant to accept the proposal for re-creating the International at this stage, since it might infringe their autonomy. The strongest resistance, however, came from the Socialist parties of the Eastern European countries. For these parties, directly allied with the Communists, and with their policies closely attuned to friendship with the Soviet Union, any formal alliance with an international organization that would inevitably be led by the parties of the West was unacceptable. They pleaded at the conference for the creation of a labour international embracing both Socialist and Communist parties along the lines of the World Federation of Trade Unions, founded in Paris in September 1945.[3] Pietro Nenni, leader of the

1. *Protokoll der Verhandlungen des Parteitages der Sozialdemokratischen Partei Deutschlands, Nürnburg, 29 Juni–2 Juli 1947* (Hamburg, 1947), p. 29.
2. See pp. 100–103, 116–119. 3. See page 13.

Italian Socialist party, then closely allied with the Communist party in a joint action pact, was also in favour of this idea, as were a number of French Socialist party members and Louis de Brouckère, representing the Belgian Labour party. It did not, however, meet with the approval of a majority of the conference, and the question of renewing the International was once again postponed.

On the other hand, a positive decision was taken at the Clacton conference to create a forum by organizing periodic conferences between Socialist parties so as to hold confidential discussions on international problems. It was agreed that any political resolutions taken by this body would require unanimity, that only one party from any one country was to be eligible to participate and that no Socialist parties in exile were to be invited—a rule insisted upon with particular emphasis by the Eastern European representatives, whose parties had split over the question of joint action with the Communists. Finally it was agreed to set up a small secretariat in London—the Socialist Information and Liaison Office (S.I.L.O.)—whose sole function was to pass information reports to the parties and to prepare the administration of future conferences. The British Labour party placed its international department at the disposal of the S.I.L.O., and its secretary, Denis Healey, was responsible for the secretariat of the S.I.L.O.

The renewal of the International was once again brought up for debate at the next international Socialist conference, held in Bournemouth in early November 1946. Again the conference was almost unanimously of the opinion that any 'new organization of Socialist International is impractical at the moment'. Crucial for this decision was the attitude taken by the Socialist parties of Eastern Europe, which made it absolutely clear that they would not be able to join a formally constituted International. The result would have been an International geographically split between West and East, and the British Labour party was seeking above all to avoid breaking with the Socialist parties of Eastern Europe who had representation in their respective governments—in order, as Dalton put it, 'to avoid a split between West and East Europe'.[1]

At the centre of the discussion at Bournemouth, however, loomed the question of admitting the German Social Democratic party into the international community of Socialist parties. The enormity of the crimes which the Nazi régime had committed in the name of the German people had engendered a profound hatred, at first only for the Nazis themselves, but which, during the course of the war, as the Nazis invaded country after country in Europe, came to be transformed into a hatred for the entire German people. What those whose countries had been attacked and torn by Hitler saw was, to all effects, a united German people supporting a barbaric

1. Report of the Forty-Sixth Annual Conference of the Labour Party, 1947, p. 107.

dictatorship and condoning a war against all the peoples of Europe. The phenomenon of the apparent total unity of the German people during the war was explained in the hate propaganda directed against Germany as a pre-eminent characteristic in the psychology of the German people—a people described as possessing an inherent love of war and greed of conquest and who, as history had demonstrated down the centuries, would willingly and obediently submit themselves to the dictatorship of war-like leaders. Thus not only the Nazis were responsible for the misdeeds of Hitler's régime: the whole German nation must carry the burden of a collective guilt.[1] Hence, Germany had to be destroyed.

This blanket condemnation of the whole German nation was, of course, in sharp contrast with the principles of international Socialism. But in spite of this, many prominent Socialists, in particular those from nations which had suffered most from the brutality of the Nazi régime—for example, Camille Huysmans (1872–1968), the Belgian president of the Socialist Labour International[2]—declared themselves uncompromisingly for the outlawing of the whole German people. They were prepared to make no differentiation between Nazis and anti-Nazis, between German reactionaries and German Social Democrats. The blood sacrifices of those who had fallen in the struggle of German Social Democracy against the Nazi movement were forgotten. Because there had been no visible signs of mass resistance to Hitler during the war, they declared that the German Social Democrats had, with other Germans, supported the war efforts of the Nazi régime. They accepted the thesis of the collective guilt of the whole German people and rejected any common ground with German Social Democracy.

The British Labour party had certainly not remained unaffected by the propaganda of hate, but at its party congresses both during the war and even more so afterwards, an overwhelming majority had declared in favour of a policy of conciliation with the German working class. The attitude of most other Socialist parties towards German Social Democracy being in dispute, however, the British executive had decided not to invite German representatives to the first formal conference at Clacton, but to leave any decision to admit German Social Democracy over till the following conference at Bournemouth. When a majority there spoke out against admitting the

1. For a report on the propaganda of hate and its consequences, see Julius Braunthal, *Need Germany Survive?*, with an Introduction by Harold J. Laski (London, 1943). One source of a passionate propaganda of hate was Radio Moscow, stirred by Ilya Ehrenburg. This propaganda did not, however, start until after Hitler's attack on Russia and it fell silent after the capture of Berlin. It was, however, continued by the Austrian Communist party, which held fast to the thesis that 'the German working class had opposed Fascism with no more real resistance than any of the other classes of the German nation', and that it had, 'with the rest of the German nation supported Hitler's war of conquest'—Otto Langbein, 'Our Attitude to Germany', in *Weg und Ziel*, January 1947, p. 23.

2. See Julius Braunthal, 'The Socialist International and Its President', in *International Socialist Forum*, January 1945.

German Social Democrats, a decision was once again postponed and it was simply decided initially to invite a number of German Social Democratic representatives to the following conference so that they could answer for their attitude.

This conference had been called for 6 June 1947 to take place in Zürich. Three hundred and eighty delegates representing twenty-four parties assembled on the last day to interrogate the German delegates, Kurt Schumacher, Erich Ollenhauer and Fritz Henssler. Somehow the conference had managed to get itself involved in the role of a historical tribunal when it called upon the German delegation, practically as defendants, to answer the question: 'Why was Germany the only state in which no attempt was made to overthrow the Nazi régime?'

Schumacher began his reply by describing the internal differences in conditions for resistance in Germany as opposed to those in the German-occupied countries.

'In the countries occupied by Germany,' he said, 'the resistance movements certainly contained men and women who were motivated solely by the ideals of Social Democracy and freedom. But the mainspring of these resistance movements was the fact that an enemy army, personifying Hitler's Germany, had invaded the country and oppressed the population. No such motive for resistance existed in Germany. . . . Also the web of security extended by the Gestapo was incomparably tighter in Germany than it had ever become in France, Norway or Czechoslovakia. . . . In Germany,' he continued, 'the Gestapo installed its agents in every factory, beside every desk, inside every house, and in many thousands of cases even within individual families. This is a fact to prevent false comparisons.'

Despite these conditions, Schumacher told the conference, there *had* been resistance among the German Social Democrats. 'I will not,' he said, 'lay before you a list of the mass trials that took place in many German towns; I do not intend to produce the death sentences and imprisonments.' He wished only to recall a personal experience. At the first meeting of Social Democrats held after the war, on 6 May 1945, a day after Germany's capitulation, about a hundred men and women from the resistance movement had gathered in Hanover.[1] They were asked to write nothing more on a piece of paper than the lengths of the sentences passed on them by the Nazis. 'I looked at these pieces of paper,' Schumacher said, 'and over a thousand years of imprisonment faced me.'

'Do not speak to me of the weakness of the resistance movement among German Socialists,' he told the delegates. 'No one without personal experience of the Nazi system can imagine how deeply it infiltrated the whole of society, even private family life, and so allowed the unthinkable to

1. See page 70.

happen—mothers denouncing their children, fathers their sons, and sending them to concentration camps. Even so, a resistance movement did exist, though unlike those in the occupied countries it lacked the incentive of a struggle for national freedom.'

In conclusion, Schumacher commented that a refusal to admit the German Social Democratic party (S.P.D.) into the new International could only 'cause pain, though we would not react to this with bitterness,' he said. 'The spirit of internationalism which flows through our movement will remain alive under every circumstance.' He requested of the delegates one thing only: 'That you do not use towards us a double standard of justice and do not further delay your inquiry. This we should find unbearable. If differences of opinion on this question turn out to be so insurmountable that they could endanger international Socialist co-operation, then we are prepared to withdraw. . . . But my appeal is to the principles of Socialist ethics. Either we are to be respected as international Socialists, enjoying equal constitutional rights, or we can find no place in the international Socialist community. . . .'

Following on the discussion the conference appointed a commission consisting of Louis de Brouckère (Belgium), Salomon Grumbach (France), Joe Reeves (Great Britain), Vilem Bernard (Czechoslovakia), Franz Jonas (Austria), W. Thomassen (Holland) and John Sannes (Norway). When it appeared, their Report, drafted by de Brouckère in his position as chairman of the commission, reached the following decisive conclusions:

The S.P.D. differs in its programme neither in word nor deed from the Socialist parties of other countries. It is therefore a fraternal party.

It has been stated that the S.P.D. has never dissociated itself from Hitler's policies of conquest and cruelty. This stands in contradiction to the facts. The resolutions by the S.P.D. party congresses and the speeches of its members have invariably denounced Hitlerism in the strongest possible terms.

It has been said that S.P.D. members did not offer enough resistance to the Hitler régime. This statement is contradicted by the fact that very many among present active Social Democrats suffered for years in concentration camps—Schumacher himself over ten years. These officials are the survivors of an élite which did not hesitate to risk torture and death for the sake of their ideals.

Accusations and recriminations have been voiced against the attitude taken by the S.P.D. before the war. The S.P.D. has a great history behind it, a history with many glorious and some less glorious pages. . . . International Socialism has more urgent problems to solve than to pass a verdict on shortcomings which have been revealed in the past in the Socialist party of Germany or any other country.

There is one party only which can effectively help to create a Germany with a more fruitful, democratic and, above all, peaceful future. This is the S.P.D.

Are we ready to assist the S.P.D. in the fulfilling of these tasks, which are also ours? Or do we wish to refuse the S.P.D. our help and abandon them to a struggle with the German Communists, supported by the Communists of all countries, with the German Catholics, supported by the Catholics of the whole world, and with German capitalism, supported by our old enemy, international capitalism?

If international labour refuses to assist the S.P.D. we shall have to carry the moral responsibility for the consequences, and these consequences will be highly dangerous.[1]

Acting in the spirit of the report, the Socialist International Conference meeting at Antwerp, at the end of November 1947, agreed to admit the S.P.D. as an equal member.[2] A broad gap in the representation of Europe's Socialist Labour movement in the International Conference had been closed. The Zürich conference had also appointed a commission to study the possibility of re-establishing the International and had committed it to submitting its proposals to the next conference, planned for the beginning of December 1947 at Antwerp. The commission, meeting twice in Paris, had looked at the question mainly from the viewpoint of the relationship existing between the Western powers and the U.S.S.R. The intensification of the conflict between the United States and the Soviet Union was threatening the world with a division into a confrontation of two hostile power blocs—a development carrying the danger of a Third World War. In such a situation it appeared particularly important to preserve relations between the West European parties and Socialist parties in countries within the Russian sphere of influence, because these parties collaborated with Communists in governments closely allied with the Soviet Union and so represented a potential link between Western and Eastern Socialism. But, as we saw earlier, the Socialist parties of Eastern Europe were not able to affiliate themselves with a revived International, and so its re-establishment appeared to the commission to be untimely.

It did, however, suggest changing the over-loose structure of the S.I.L.O. into a tighter organization: a permanent committee of the International—the Committee of International Socialist Conferences, to be known by the title COMISCO—in which all member parties would be represented by the mandates of their representatives. The Zürich conference therefore appointed a select committee to act as executive committee to COMISCO under the chairmanship of Morgan Phillips, secretary-general of the British Labour party. The committee was made up of one delegate each from the parties of Great Britain, France, Belgium, Holland, Austria and representation for the Scandinavian parties by a delegate they had nominated.

1. For the text of Schumacher's speech at the Zürich conference and the commission's report, see Julius Braunthal, '*Kurt Schumacher und die Sozialistische Internationale*', in *Turmwächter der Demokratie*, vol. I, pp. 510–22.
2. The admission of the S.P.D. into the International was decided by twelve votes to four (Palestine, Poland, Czechoslavakia and Hungary), with two abstentions (Switzerland and Italy). For a short survey of the debate on the question, see COMISCO Circular 88/47, pp. 21–3, Archives of the Socialist International, Institute for Social History, Amsterdam.

But, by the time the Antwerp conference met, Moscow had already broken with Social Democracy. Two months earlier Stalin had re-created the Communist International, which had been dissolved in May 1943, in a new guise—the 'Cominform', which entered into existence with a declaration of hostility towards Social Democracy and the Western powers.

But, by the time the Antwerp conference met, Moscow had already broken with Social Democracy. Two months earlier Stalin had re-created the Communist International, which had been dissolved in May 1943, in a new guise — the 'Cominform', which entered into existence with a declaration of hostility towards Social Democracy and the Western power.

7 · The Founding of the Cominform

1

The founding of the 'Cominform', a 'Communist Information Bureau', by a select group of Communist leaders at a conference, meeting from 21–27 September 1947 in Szklaraska Poreba in Poland, is a crucial factor in the history of the Communist movement.

The event itself was veiled in secrecy. To those Communist parties who had not been invited it came as much as a surprise as it did to the rest of the world. The conference was held in a castle in the middle of a huge estate ringed by police guards; only nine parties were represented, and not all of these, the Italian Communist party, for example, had been informed of the purpose of the conference.[1]

The basis on which parties had been selected for the conference was also cryptic. Except for the Russian Communist party, which had, of course, called the conference, only countries under Communist governments— Poland, Romania, Bulgaria, Hungary, Yugoslavia and Czechoslovakia and only two Western European Communist parties—those of Italy and France— were represented. Conspicuous by their absence, therefore, were those parties which were at that time of special importance in the Communist world movement, such as the Greek Communist party, then involved in an armed struggle for power[2] and relying on the moral and material support of its fellow parties, or the German Communist party in the Russian Zone of Occupation, to whom a special task had been allotted in Stalin's strategy. Neither were any non-European Communist parties invited to take part, not even the powerful Chinese Communist party, which had now entered the critical phase of its struggle against Chiang Kai-shek. Whatever plans Stalin

1. See Eugenio Reale, 'The Founding of the Cominform', in Milorad M. Drachkovitch and Branko Lazitch (eds.), *The Comintern—Historical Highlights* (New York, 1966), p. 259. Eugenio Reale, jointly with Luigi Longo, represented the Italian Communist party at the inaugural conference of the Cominform.
2. See pp. 108–111.

was pursuing with the Szklaraska conference, its peculiar make-up did not indicate anything resembling a revival of the Communist International in its old form.

The idea of such a revival had been mooted by Tito in discussion with Stalin in 1945 shortly after the end of the war, and he had welcomed it 'with open arms'.[1] Yet not until a year later, in June 1946, did Stalin take up the suggestion. Tito had arrived in Moscow for Kalinin's funeral with a Yugoslav delegation, while Dimitrov, the last Secretary of the Communist International, had arrived with one from Bulgaria. At a dinner given by him for both delegations, Stalin raised the subject of the Communist International without in any way attempting to hide from his guests his true feelings—namely contempt—for Lenin's creation. 'What made me feel deeply hurt,' Alexander Ranković, who was sitting next to Tito, commented, 'was the aggressive, almost spiteful tone in which he spoke of the Third International and the way he directed his shafts at Dimitrov. The blood shot to the head of the aged Dimitrov . . .'.[2] Stalin explained to his guests that reviving the Communist International in any form was out of the question. On the other hand, an organization for exchanging information could be founded, the members of which could meet at conferences from time to time to compare experiences and pass resolutions. These resolutions would not 'of course', he added, 'be binding on those parties which did not vote for them'.[3]

Stalin then hesitated for one further year before consolidating the idea. In the summer and autumn of 1946 it had seemed as if an understanding between the Western powers and the Soviet Union was still possible. In his interview with Alexander Werth in September 1946, as was seen earlier, Stalin declared that he 'believed absolutely' in the possibility of their future peaceful co-existence.[4] Obviously he wished to prevent any action, such as setting up an international Communist organization, which would exacerbate the impression that he was trying to revive the concept of world revolution.

Stalin's good faith, if genuine, was evidently badly shaken by the Truman Doctrine announced in March 1947. Yet it seems remarkable that he accepted this declaration of America's hostility towards Communism without making a counter-declaration or any evident change in his foreign policy. Oddly

---

1. See Vladimir Dedijer, *Tito Speaks. His Self-Portrait and Struggle with Stalin* (London, 1953), p. 300.

2. Dedijer, *Tito Speaks*, pp. 284–5. Reale recorded as a 'deceitful omission' the fact that the word 'Comintern' was not mentioned once during the six days of the Szklaraska Poreba Conference—'clearly an intentional taboo,' he remarked—Reale, 'The Founding of the Cominform' in Drachkovitch and Lazitch (eds.), *The Comintern*, p. 258. It may be recalled that Stalin, on the eve of Lenin's funeral, had solemnly declared: 'In leaving us, Comrade Lenin enjoined on us fidelity to the Communist International. We swear to thee, Comrade Lenin, to devote our lives to the enlargement and strengthening of the Union of the workers of the whole world, the Communist International'—quoted in Boris Souvarine, *Stalin. A Critical Survey of Bolshevism* (New York, 1939), p. 352.

3. Dedijer, *Tito Speaks*, p. 301.   4. See page 126.

enough, he took a generous United States scheme for economic assistance to Europe—the Marshall Plan—as his excuse for making such a change, and deciding to revive an organ of the Communist world movement, he summoned the Szklaraska Poreba conference.

The Marshall Plan had been outlined by George Marshall, Byrnes' successor as Secretary of State, at the beginning of January 1947, in a speech delivered at Harvard University on 5 June 1947. The United States government was, he said, prepared to finance a programme for rebuilding the ruined economies of the European states, provided the governments of Europe would together grasp the initiative to carry out the programme. Marshall emphasized that this assistance was by no means intended to be a weapon for the United States administration to use against any system of government. 'Our policy,' he declared, 'does not turn against any one country or doctrine, but against hunger, poverty, despair and chaos. . . . Every government,' he said, 'which is prepared to collaborate in the task of rebuilding would find full support with the government of the United States.'[1] He therefore made it clear that Communist-governed countries could participate as well as all others in the aid action. He added, however, that 'no government attempting to hinder the economic rebuilding of other countries could expect any help from us'. And in a vague phrase, the meaning of which was, however, unmistakable, he stated, in the spirit of the Truman Doctrine: 'Governments or political parties which attempt to perpetuate the state of misery of people, in order to profit by it either politically or in other ways, will encounter the opposition of the United States.'[2]

While the Marshall Plan in no way excluded Communist-ruled states or questioned their doctrines or attached any conditions to the granting of American financial aid, it was undoubtedly intended as a factor to stem Communist expansion in Europe. Under the impact of the general strikes in France and Italy during the spring of 1947,[3] Ernest Bevin, the British foreign secretary, had written to Marshall a few days before his speech to say that, unless the United States government could at once produce a huge and comprehensive plan for Europe, it was going to be too late. Bevin believed that, in the face of the desperate situation in most Western European

---

1. George F. Kennan, an adviser to President Truman, had insisted in a memorandum on active American aid for Europe, that this should not be allowed to appear as an act aimed at the Communists; on the contrary, it was intended to cancel the impression created by the Truman Doctrine that the economic assistance of the United States was only a 'side-product' of its 'defensive reaction towards the Communist pressure', and not an action to establish healthy economic conditions in Europe. Therefore, the memorandum insisted, economic aid was to be offered to all European states, and, he added, 'should anyone wish to split the European continent, then this should be Russia by its attitude [to the aid action] and not through our offer'—*Memoirs 1925–1950* (London, 1968), pp. 341–3.
2. Quoted in Louis J. Halle, *The Cold War as History* (London, 1967), p. 130.
3. See Chapters 2 and 3.

countries, the Soviet Union was working to unleash a civil war, starting with strikes; a beginning could be seen in the general strikes in France and Italy.[1]

The Marshall Plan, the declaration of which may have been accelerated by Bevin's alarm call, was meant to soothe a general desperation with promises of easing the misery of the masses for the present and of creating prosperity in the immediate future, thus immunizing them against Communist propaganda.

However, as long as the possibility of co-operating with the Western powers had seemed open to him, Stalin had in no way incited the Communist parties of France or Italy, by unleashing strikes and unrest so as to sabotage economic revival in their countries, to create a revolutionary situation which would allow them to seize power. On the contrary, he had instructed them to co-operate with the non-Communist parties[2] in reconstructing their countries, and the Communists, particularly in France, were not lacking in patriotic zeal.[3] A change of attitude towards the state began only after Stalin had presumably been convinced by the Truman Doctrine that United States policy was directed at breaking with the Soviet Union.

The Marshall Plan could not, however, be regarded as a hostile act against the Soviet Union meant to set the seal on a permanent rupture. It might rather be interpreted as an invitation to avoid a break between East and West by participating in a plan for the economic reconstruction of Europe.[4]

Stalin at first appeared in doubt as to how he was to interpret it and react towards it. When Bevin, with Georges Bidault, the French foreign minister, on 19 June invited the Soviet government to a conference in Paris on the 27th to plan preliminary discussions between the three powers on how the rebuilding of Europe was to be achieved by means of the Marshall Plan, Molotov accepted at once. The amazing number of advisers—twenty-three in all—that he brought with him to the conference seemed a clear indication of the Soviet Union's willingness to co-operate in implementing the plan.

1. Desmond Donnelly, *Struggle for the World. The Cold War from its Origins in 1917* (London, 1965), pp. 242–3.
2. Mathias Rákosi, leader of the Hungarian Communist party, who, like Thorez and Togliatti, had returned at the end of the war from a Moscow exile, remembered Stalin's instructions. 'After the liberation of 1945,' he said, 'we, in common with all Communist parties in the Hitler occupied countries, followed Stalin's instructions and set up the Hungarian National Independent Front, a coalition with other anti-Fascist parties'—*Társadalmi Szemle*, February–March 1952, quoted in *Socialist International Information*, 17 May 1952.
3. See Chapters 2 and 3.
4. The speech in which Marshall announced the plan, was, as André Fontaine, the foreign editor of *Le Monde*, observed, 'very different from Truman's speech three months earlier. It contained no accusations [against the Soviet Union] and no appeal for a crusade [against Communism]. It was a call for reconciliation and collaboration for the common weal'—André Fontaine, *History of the Cold War. From the October Revolution to the Korean War, 1917–1950* (London, 1968), p. 327.

But, to general astonishment, Molotov left the conference after only two days, explaining that the Marshall Plan threatened the independence of the European states and was not, therefore, acceptable to the Soviet Union.[1]

But this was not, of course, the impression gained by a number of Communist parties. When, on 4 July, the British and French governments invited the governments of every European state [except Russia and Spain] to Paris for a conference on the 12th for the realization of the Marshall Plan, the Communist-controlled governments of Czechoslovakia[2] and Poland accepted and the French Communists' theoretical journal declared: 'Of course France, like England, must not reject American aid, but its independence must, as Comrade Thorez made clear, be jealously protected.'[3]

For Stalin, who regarded the Communist parties as agents of the Soviet Union and looked upon those countries governed by them as satellite states, this 'deviation' by the Czech, Polish and French Communist parties from the line he had laid down was intolerable. There was an immediate 'correction'. On Stalin's order,[4] Klement Gottwald, prime minister of Czechoslovakia, had to revoke the unanimous decision his government had taken to participate in the Paris conference. Wladislaw Gomulka, in the name of the Polish government, did likewise. A rejection of the invitation on behalf of the other Communist-ruled countries of Eastern Europe was made over Radio Moscow before a number of their governments had in fact reached any decision.

It was at this point that Stalin, as shortly became obvious to the whole world, decided on a new direction in his foreign policy, and therefore called together those Communist parties, which would have to play a part in his 'cold war' strategy, to the conference at Szklaraska Poreba so as to inform

1. Isaac Deutscher assumes that Stalin rejected the Marshall Plan because he did not want to disclose the economic state of Russia; in the framework of the Marshall Plan, the requests of states seeking aid was to be worked out on the report of their exact economic situation and their resources. Russia had during the war lost twenty million people, not seven million, as Stalin said; moreover in 1946 the country was in the wake of the worst climatic disasters for over half a century and afflicted by a severe economic crisis. A report of the actual economic condition of the Soviet Union would have disclosed its military weakness; see *Stalin* (London, 1966), pp. 559–60 and 567. Not until 1963 in the *Statistical Yearbook of the Soviet Union* (Moscow, 1963), p. 8, were Stalin's figures for the loss of Russian lives during the war corrected; it recorded a loss of twenty millions.

2 . Gottwald said in a discussion with Sir Robert Bruce Lockhart, in May 1947, that Czechoslovakia would welcome American credits, provided they were granted without political strings. See 'The Czechoslovak Revolution', in *Foreign Affairs*, vol. XXVI (July, 1948), p. 636.

3. *Cahiers du Communisme*, 9 September 1947, quoted in Val R. Lorwin, *The French Labor Movement* (Cambridge, Mass., 1954), p. 118.

4. Two days after the decision by his Cabinet, Gottwald was summoned by Stalin to Moscow. Of their discussion he told the two cabinet ministers, Jan Masaryk and Prokop Drtina, who had accompanied him: 'I have never seen Stalin so angry. He remonstrated bitterly on our accepting the invitation to the Paris conference. He could not understand how we could do it. He said we had acted as if ready to turn our backs on the Soviet Union' —see Hubert Ripka, *Le Coup de Prague* (Paris, 1949), pp. 58–9.

them of the special tasks allocated to them in the coming struggle. He did not himself put in an appearance, but he was, as Reale reported, the conference's 'absolute ruler'. Andrei Zhdanov and Georgi Malenkov, as members of the Politbureau, had been entrusted with the task of informing the parties of the new policy direction; further instructions were issued during the course of the conference over a direct telephone line from the Kremlin.[1]

The most important requirement in Stalin's strategy was to consolidate his control over the Communist parties whose countries fell within the Russian sphere of influence and the two Western European parties which represented power factors in their own countries. This was the whole purpose of the Cominform, the founding of which was to be achieved by the conference. The dissolution of the Communist International had, as it were, created a vacuum; Moscow no longer enjoyed the use of an instrument by which it might exert direct influence over the organization and policies of other Communist parties. 'Many comrades,' said Zhdanov, giving the reasons for the setting up of the Cominform, 'have taken the dissolution of the Communist International to mean the breaking of all connections and every contact between Communist brother parties. But experience has shown that this kind of isolation of the Communist parties one from another is wrong, harmful and at bottom unnatural.'[2]

Yet the Cominform, whose foundation the conference promulgated, was by no means an organization of all Communist parties, but simply of the nine parties represented. As the conference resolution declared, it was to form an 'organization for the exchange of information and, where necessary, to co-ordinate the activities of Communist parties on the basis of mutual consent'.[3]

But the true function which Stalin in fact envisaged for the Cominform emerged in a letter to Tito on 22 May 1948 when he was involved in conflict with him. 'During the organization of the Cominform,' he said, 'all the

1. Reale, 'The Founding of the Cominform', in Drachkovitch and Lazitch (eds.), *The Comintern*, pp. 258–9.
2. *For a Lasting Peace and for a People's Democracy*, 10 November 1947. This periodical was founded at the conference to be an organ of the Cominform; it appeared bi-monthly, its first issue printed in Russian, French and English, from 1 November 1947. It was edited and printed in Belgrade. It actually came under Stalin's direct control. He had installed Pavel Yudin as chief editor, and arranged a direct radio-telephone link between Belgrade and Moscow. Several copies of each number were flown to Moscow by special plane before issue to be censored 'personally by Stalin and Molotov'. 'Sometimes there were so many alterations [to be made] in articles, that the paper had to be recomposed, made up again and returned to Moscow, whereupon new corrections would arrive from there. It also happened that when a number had already passed all the phases of censorship and its French, English and Russian texts had already been printed, the order would come from Moscow to withdraw the number. . . . It was burnt in an oven during one complete day and night under the supervision of Yudin's assistant. . . . The reason for the destruction of the number was an article by the general secretary of the Communist party of Greece, whom Stalin disliked'— Dedijer, *Tito Speaks*, pp. 307–8.
3. *For a Lasting Peace and for a People's Democracy*, 10 November 1947.

Communist parties were agreed on the unequivocal principle that each Communist party should be responsible to the Cominform. The Cominform,' he explained, 'is the party-political basis of our united international front; any deviation from it leads to betrayal.' What he had in mind in founding the Cominform was the restoration of his direct control over the Communist parties at large. Dimitrov spoke for him when he said in his declaration of 8 December 1948: 'All the Communist parties of the world form a single front under the direction of the most powerful and most experienced Communist party, the party of Lenin and Stalin. In Comrade Stalin all Communist parties possess a universally recognized leader and teacher.'[1]

The conference agreed that Prague should be the Cominform's headquarters, but following telephone instructions from Stalin, the choice was altered to Belgrade.[2] The purpose behind Stalin's choice was soon to become obvious.[3]

The resolution on the political tasks before the Communist parties was based on Zhdanov's analysis of the world situation, as seen by Stalin. Since the end of the war, Zhdanov said, the world's political powers had coalesced more sharply into two camps: 'the imperialist, anti-democratic camp [gathered about the United States] on the one hand, and the anti-imperialist, democratic camp on the other'. United States' imperialism had, since the end of the war, followed an aggressive, expansionist course; both the Truman Doctrine and the Marshall Plan, he declared, 'embodied America's plan to enslave Europe'. Both plans interfered with the internal concerns of other states and were an attack on the principle of national sovereignty.

By contrast, he said, the Soviet Union had interceded 'unflaggingly for the principle of real equality and to safeguard the sovereign rights of all countries'; it formed 'a reliable bastion against interference in the rights of equality and self-determination of nations'; it stood 'as a bulwark in the path of America's attempts at world domination'. This was why, he said, 'the expansionist and reactionary policy of the United States is directed against the Soviet Union . . . against the working-class movement in every country and against the anti-imperialist forces of freedom everywhere'. The American imperialists, Malenkov added in his own speech, were 'hatching new plans for war against the Soviet Union. . . . The clearest indication of their policy can be seen in the Truman and Marshall Plans.'

'The Soviet Union,' Zhdanov announced, 'will harness all its forces to defeat the Marshall Plan.' This was also to be the task of the other Communist parties. They must, he said, 'take the lead in every field—governmental,

1. Quoted in the declaration of the COMISCO secretariat, 20 December 1949.
2. See Milovan Djilas, *Conversations with Stalin* (London, 1962), p. 129. Djilas had attended the conference as delegate of the Yugoslav Communist party.
3. See Chapter 18.

political, economic and ideological—in the campaign of resistance to those imperialist plans for expansion and aggression. They must close their ranks, unite their efforts on the basis of a common anti-imperialist and democratic platform and gather around them all democratic forces of the people.' And, he emphasized, to the Communist parties of France, Italy and Britain he allocated 'a special task'. They must, he stated, 'raise the banner of defence for the national independence and sovereignty of their countries . . . in the struggle against all attempts at the political and economic enslavement of their countries'.[1]

The resolution passed by the conference confirmed Stalin's theory that the world had been divided into two camps: the imperialist camp, whose aim was world domination and the destruction of democracy through the imperialist power politics of the United States; and the anti-imperialist camp, whose objective was to undermine imperialism and strengthen democracy. The Truman Doctrine and the Marshall Plan, the resolution stated, were only part of a larger all-embracing plan to extend the power of the United States to all parts of the world. 'The plan to bring about the economic and political enslavement of Europe by American imperialism,' it continued, 'is supplemented by plans for the economic and political enslavement of China, Indonesia and the Latin American countries,' while the 'right-wing Socialists,' such as 'Blum, Attlee and Bevin', were supplying a 'democratic mask' for American imperialism. To thwart the imperialists' plans to enslave the world, the 'anti-imperialist camp' must above all mobilize its strength 'against the main force of the imperialist camp'— 'American imperialism and its British and French allies'.[2]

2

To comply with the spirit of the Szklaraska Poreba resolution, the Communist parties of France and Italy faced a radical change of policy. Up till then, as has been seen, both parties had co-operated in coalition governments with Social Democrats and middle-class democratic parties to achieve the economic and political rebuilding of their respective countries; and even after their expulsion from government in May 1947, their immediate goal had been to regain admission. It was beyond question that Thorez and Togliatti had

1. *For a Lasting Peace and for a People's Democracy*, 10 November 1947. For the text of the resolution, see Appendix Seven, pp. 549–51. For comprehensive reports on the conference, see Dedijer, *Tito Speaks*, pp. 301–6; 'The Foundng of the Cominform', in Drachkovitch and Lazitch (eds.) *The Comintern*, *passim*; Günther Nollau, *International Communism and World Revolution* (London, 1961), pp. 216–26; Halle, *The Cold War as History*, pp. 150–2 and 155–6.

2. *For a Lasting Peace and for a People's Democracy*, 10 November 1947. The Cominform's resolution gave the parties of southern Asia the signal for armed uprising in India, Burma, Malaya and Indonesia. See Chapters 10, 12, 13.

guided the policies of their parties in line with instructions received in the Kremlin before returning from exile in Moscow.

Even so they found themselves being severely criticized at Szklaraska Poreba by Zhdanov, Kardelj and Djilas, who accused them of having unreservedly supported parliamentary democracy; of having pinned their hopes upon impotent parliamentary action by a 'revision of Marxism–Leninism'; of having, 'out of opportunism', worked with the bourgeois elements in governments while only feebly attacking Blum and Ramadier in France and, in Italy, seeking favour from de Gasperi and subserviently fulfilling the wishes of the Vatican. By allowing the dissolution and disarming of the resistance movements and granting the forces of reaction concession after concession, finally accepting their exclusion from government without a fight, they had exposed their countries to the mercies of American imperialism. They showed no understanding of the United States' true motivations, which were to dominate the world—a danger, as Djilas said, worse even than Fascism. The Italian Communist party had even coined the opportunist slogan: 'Neither London, nor Washington, nor Moscow!'[1]

Togliatti, however, was not prepared to change the policies which, without invoking the methods of intimidation or terror resorted to by the Communists in those countries which they ruled, had won for his party a considerable measure of mass support. Its aim remained parliamentary democracy, not the dictatorship of the proletariat. Its undertaking, as the programme of its first congress after the end of the war in January 1946 stated, was to bring about 'a democratic republic of workers and intellectuals . . . governed by parliamentary rule'. Togliatti emphasized the distinction between the 'Italian road to Socialism' and the Russian. 'International experience,' he said in a speech made in Florence in January 1947, 'shows us how at the present stage of the class struggle in the world, the working classes can find new paths to Socialism—namely that development of democracy to its farthest borders which is nothing other than Socialism. These paths,' he continued, 'differ from, for example, that of the proletariat in the Soviet Union.'[2]

It was notable that Togliatti made no appearance at the inaugural conference of the Cominform—obviously he had no wish for the 'Italian path to Socialism' to be questioned. The adoption of the more aggressive tactics which he undertook following the expulsion of the Communists from the Italian government in July 1947, and which he intensified under pressure of Cominform decisions in October and November, consisted of short-term general strikes and rowdy street demonstrations in northern Italy and Rome,

1. *For a Lasting Peace and for a People's Democracy*, 10 November 1947; for a comprehensive report of the debate, see Reale, 'The Founding of the Cominform', in Drachkovitch and Lazitch (eds.), *The Comintern*, pp. 265–6.

2. *Rinascita*, July 1947, quoted in Georgio Galli, 'Italian Communism', in *Communism in Europe*, vol. II, pp. 305–6.

but which nevertheless carefully avoided clashes with the powers of the state[1] and represented hardly more than a gesture of loyalty towards Moscow. Apart from this he avoided the challenge of criticism by the Cominform and kept to the 'Italian path to Socialism'.

On the other hand, Thorez, without hesitation, aligned the policy of the French party with the course of Stalin's new foreign policy. He set in motion his change of policy by acknowledging 'tactical errors' committed by the party. 'As a result of these mistakes,' he wrote, 'we failed to unmask ruthlessly the attitudes of Socialist leaders.'[2] Neither had the party, he told the central committee in a speech of 30 October 1947, recognized in time the danger to France's independence which was threatened by the Marshall Plan—that 'attempt by war-mongering American capitalism . . . to enslave Europe.'[3] The National Committee of the Communist-controlled French trade union federation, the C.G.T., meanwhile condemned the plan as 'part of a scheme to subject the world by capitalist trusts and to prepare for a new world war'.[4]

The party now prepared itself for a struggle on the grand scale. At the beginning of November 1947 it took, as we have seen,[5] an insignificant event in Marseilles as the occasion for inciting a national strike movement which embraced three million workers. For the workers, hard hit by economic distress, the motive was to win a settlement for their wage demands. But what were the true intentions of the Communists? They had tried to extend the action into a general strike; they had put forward demands that were economically impossible; they had sabotaged wage negotiations; they had provoked clashes with the state powers. What was their actual aim? 'The taking of power by force; their reinstatement in the government; a dress rehearsal for a later uprising; the sabotaging of American aid?'—Georges Lefranc, the contemporary historian of the French trade union movement, in formulating these questions could find no answer. 'Perhaps,' he wrote, 'the leaders themselves did not know it.'[6]

But even if the Communist party leadership was not setting itself any concrete aims, it was at least achieving a powerful demonstration—a demonstration to show a changeover from its earlier policy of 'opportunism', now condemned by the Cominform, to a policy of revolutionary action. Obviously nothing beyond this was planned, since in any case the party leadership drew back from pressing the general strike to the point of a revolutionary rising. Thus the strike exhausted itself after only a month and had to be broken off without any gains being won.

1. See page pp. 65–6.   2. *Cahiers du communisme*, October 1947.
3. Quoted in Domenach, 'The French Communist Party', in Mario Einaudi (ed.), *Communism in Western Europe* (Ithaca, 1951), p. 78.
4. Quoted in Lorwin, *The French Labor Movement*, p. 121.
5. See pp. 42–3.
6. Georges Lefranc, *Histoire du syndicalisme français* (Paris, 1947), vol. I, p. 190.

An intense expenditure of energy had been wasted and what suffered most was the unity of the French trade union movement. Once the strike's political character had become obvious, the Socialist and syndicalist trade union leaders in the C.G.T., centred around the periodical *Force Ouvrière*, refused to continue with it.[1] After the collapse of the strike, a split in the C.G.T. became inevitable. During the strike it had shown itself to be a Communist party weapon directed against the Social Democratic party; its attacks had been concentrated upon the Socialist ministers in the coalition government—Ramadier, the prime minister, and Daniel Mayer, the minister of labour—and it could not be expected that the Socialist trade union leaders would capitulate. Several leading Socialist trade union federations severed their link with the C.G.T. and at a congress in April 1948 founded the trade union federation *Confédération Générale du Travail—Force Ouvrière* (F.O.).

The F.O. embraced the railwaymen's trade union as well as the unions of municipal workers, civil servants and splinter groups of textile workers, dockers and metal-workers; according to official statistics, it counted a million members.[2] While this estimate may be on the high side, the numbers of workers embittered by the strike débâcle who fell away from the trade unions was even higher. The C.G.T., which in 1946 grouped five million members, had lost almost half its membership through a mass desertion by disillusioned workers.[3]

Yet despite this strike defeat, the Communist leadership returned within a year to the tactics of revolutionary action. Like all Communist parties, it was committed by the resolution of the founding congress of the Cominform 'to use every means to wreck the Marshall Plan'—a somewhat difficult task, since the Marshall Plan represented relief from unprecedented misery and its announcement, as Alexander Werth reported, had been 'received with feelings of relief and gratitude by practically the whole of France'.[4] It was hard for the Communists to make out a convincing case for the Marshall Plan as an imperialist conspiracy. In fighting against it, they could not count on rousing the passions of the workers; it was hardly a suitable target for revolutionary action.

One was found, however, in the miners' strike of October 1948. The reasons for this were measures introduced by the new Socialist minister of labour, Robert Lacoste, to strengthen working discipline and reduce the level of employment in the coal industry. The Communist-led miners' union rejected these measures as breaches of the miners' statute and a strike ballot produced a majority vote in favour of striking. Miners' conditions were hard; their

---

1. See pp. 43–4.   2. See Lorwin, *The French Labor Movement*, p. 127.
3. Domenach, 'The French Communist Party', in Einaudi (ed.), *Communism in Western Europe*, p. 125.
4. See Alexander Werth, *France, 1940–1955* (New York and London, 1956), p. 396.

wages were low and the defeat which they had suffered a year before had embittered them.

When the strike began on 4 October 1948 under C.G.T. leadership, the government condemned it as politically motivated and refused to negotiate with the C.G.T. The C.G.T. thereupon called on the pit safety teams to cease work. This was the first time in the history of the French miners' struggle that safety measures had been placed under dispute. And the mines were now no longer privately owned; they had been nationalized. They were no longer administered by the mine-owners' directors, but were run collectively with participation by shop stewards and trade unions. Yet the C.G.T. introduced a weapon to threaten the mines with floods and gas.[1]

Again the question was raised: what was the objective of Communist tactics? Could it have been to attain a maximum weakening in the public economy so as to annul the benefits of Marshall Aid; or to provoke clashes between state and strikers and so place the Socialists in the government in an antagonistic position towards the miners? It could certainly be anticipated that the government would use force to prevent the destruction of the mines.

The strike dragged on for seven weeks until the miners were completely exhausted. The Socialist minister of the interior, Jules Moch, had had the mines occupied by security troops, and in violent clashes three strikers were killed and hundreds injured. The prisons were filled with many more hundreds of workers.[2] The country lost 5,000 million tons of coal, while one eighth of the value of Marshall Aid was negated within the year by indirect losses to the nation's economy. And a new element of embitterment intensified the conflicts between the Communists and Socialists.

3

The British Communist party received no invitation to the founding conference of the Cominform, even though Great Britain was the United States' most powerful ally, and the Labour party held sole governmental power. The conference did, however, describe how the 'right-wing Socialists' of England, such as Attlee and Bevin, 'supported loyally the imperialists in every respect, dividing the ranks of the working classes and poisoning their outlook'.[3] Thereupon, the Communist party executive did not hesitate

1. Even the left wing of the workers' movements protested against this action. *Révolution prolétarienne*, for example, wrote: 'If it was really only concerned with gaining its demands, how could it [the C.G.T.] decree the senseless order by which it called on men of the safety service to strike? Such an unbelievable idea would never enter the minds of French trade unionists, who feel at one with the cause of the working class. It is foreign to our movement, standing in contrast to its thought and traditions'—*Révolution prolétarienne*, 20 November, quoted in Lorwin, *The French Labor Movement*, pp. 129–30.

2. See Werth, *France, 1940–1955*, pp. 404–5.

3. *For a Lasting Peace and for a People's Democracy*, 10 November 1947.

to line up with the new direction in Russian policy. 'Since the world is clearly divided into imperialist and anti-imperialist camps,' the report of its general secretary, Harry Pollitt, due to be discussed by the executive in December 1947, stated, 'and the Labour government is an active partner in the imperialist camp, important changes in the policy of the Communist party are necessary.'[1]

Until this point the British Communist party had loyally supported the Labour government's efforts to further the economic reconstruction of the country; it had encouraged increased productivity and had tried to contain any strike outbreaks. This policy, Pollitt stated in his report, had been 'absolutely correct'; but it was 'correct' no longer, for, he continued, 'it would lag behind the government's reactionary policy'.[2]

During the winter of 1947, when the Communist party began its open opposition to the Labour government, Britain was afflicted by the most severe economic crisis in its history. The country had emerged from the war completely drained of its lifeblood. On 17 August 1945, the United States had stopped deliveries of food and raw materials under Lend-Lease, and Britain was faced, as a Treasury memorandum recorded, by 'an economic Dunkirk'. It had an unsecured foreign debt of £2,879 million, and by 1946 the deficit in its trade balance ran to almost £300 million. Lacking considerable American aid, Britain would have been bankrupt. In 1945 the United States and Canada had granted her a loan of $5,000 million to reconstruct the means of production and transport which had been damaged or destroyed. Within two years, however, this loan had been exhausted in buying food and raw materials. An unusually hard winter with a series of heavy snowstorms at the beginning of 1947 had crippled transport and the coal mines. Quotas of coal to industry were cut by half, and the electricity supply to private dwellings had to be rationed to five hours daily. In many districts industry came to a standstill owing to the shortage of coal, and at a stroke five million workers became unemployed.[3]

It was in these circumstances that the Communist party began the fight against the Marshall Plan to which it felt committed by the Cominform conference. 'Official declarations of the British Communist party,' stated a resolution of the General Council of the Trades Union Congress in October 1948, 'prove without doubt that it has as its aim the sabotage of the European programme of reconstruction. . . . It is trying [by strikes] to bring industry to a standstill.'[4] And Jack Tanner, president of the metalworkers' union, which before the war had stood close to the Communist party, declared that, 'The Communists hope and work for the economic collapse of the

---

1. *World News and Views*, vol. XXVII, p. 584.　　　2. ibid., p. 585.
3. See A. J. P. Taylor, *English History 1914–1945* (Oxford, 1965), p. 599; Halle, *The Cold War as History*, pp. 112–13.
4. Quoted in Henry Pelling, *The British Communist Party* (London, 1958), p. 154.

country, the weakening of the Labour movement and the Labour government.'[1]

It was not a tactic to win the workers' sympathies for the Communist cause as the elections of 1950 were to reveal. The Labour government had kept its promises. It had, in the face of terrible economic problems, constructed a welfare state. It had considerably raised the living standards of the working class. It had nationalized a massive sector of the country's productive industries—the coal-mines, the electricity and gas companies and the whole transport system—and it had taken the Bank of England into public ownership. It had also set in motion the dissolution of the British Empire. While the Communist government of the U.S.S.R. was significantly enlarging Russia's empire—during the war it had annexed half Poland and Bukovina, the whole of Bessarabia, the three Baltic states of Estonia, Latvia and Lithuania, and part of East Prussia with the German city of Königsberg—the British Socialist government had freed the peoples of India, Pakistan, Burma and Ceylon from subjection under British imperialism. Communist statements calling the Labour government 'reactionary' and 'imperialistic' did not carry much conviction. But the Communist party, obsessed by this surprising self-deceit, was so confident of support at the polls that, in 1950, it opposed Labour party candidates with its own in a hundred constituencies—almost four times the number of opposition candidates in 1945. Yet, in these hundred constituencies, only 91,000 electors gave them their vote, while the number of Labour votes increased from twelve to thirteen million. The Communists lost even the two seats which they had won in 1945. They were thus and remained during subsequent decades without parliamentary representation.

4

Stalin had founded the Cominform to be an instrument in his Cold War strategy. In Western Europe the two Communist parties with a mass following—the French and the Italian—had been immediately subordinated to Moscow's leadership, and in Eastern Europe the countries were brought into line under the Russian sphere of influence.

At the time of the Cominform's founding congress, in none of these countries—Poland, Romania or Bulgaria—had the process of Stalinization been completed, since Social Democratic parties continued to exist there, though they were, admittedly, allied with Communists in coalition governments, if not subjected to Communist leadership. The process of their elimination through fusion with the Communist party had begun before the founding of the Cominform; now it was intensified. All Socialist parties were 'purged' of those who opposed fusion with the Communist party, and

1. ibid., p. 156.

by February 1948 unification congresses in Bucharest and Sofia had set their seal on the end of the Social Democratic parties in Romania and Bulgaria; they had been merged with the Communist parties, in order, as was intended, to be finally absorbed.

By contrast to the Romanian and Bulgarian Socialist parties, that in Poland put up a more stubborn resistance. The Polish Socialists represented a mass party with a deep-rooted tradition—and consequently the terror invoked by the Communists in the government to break its resistance was that much harder. In the summer of 1947, 200 Socialist leaders were arrested on suspicion of espionage, and by the autumn of 1948, 82,000 out of 800,000 members had been expelled from the party. Only then was the drastically 'purged' party ready for self-dissolution; as we have seen, it merged on 15 December 1948 with the Communist party[1] at a congress in Warsaw.

With the liquidation of the Socialist parties in these three countries, the final obstacle to constructing a totalitarian system under Stalin's dictatorship was removed; they became, if not in constitutional form, at least in terms of political and economic reality, provinces of the Russian empire.[2]

It seems idle to speculate whether Stalin had planned to destroy sovereign independence in these countries at Yalta when he had claimed Russia's right to 'pro-Soviet governments' in her neighbouring states. Moscow's predominance in those countries occupied by the Red Army was never called in question, even under the coalition régimes, since in each country state power was in the hands of Communists and the non-Communist coalition parties were, in fact, pro-Soviet; they genuinely wished to see the closest friendly relationship between their countries and the U.S.S.R.

But under the system of coalition governments, Moscow's rule fell short of being absolute, since the elements of democracy on which they rested, however mutilated, allowed the non-Communist participant parties a certain right in joint decisions and, through independent associations and newspapers, to make this right effective. Also, as members of the COMISCO, the participant Eastern European Socialist parties in coalition governments enjoyed in its conferences a world forum.

1. See Adam Ciolkosz, 'Poland', in Denis Healey (ed.), *The Curtain Falls*, with a Foreword by Aneurin Bevan (London, 1951), pp. 48–56. Stalin's agent in this process was Josef Cyrankiewicz, general secretary of the Socialist party; he had been installed as prime minister in February 1947.

2. Ministers in these governments were the Kremlin's representatives, and if they lost the confidence of Moscow they were disposed of. Thus, for example, Osóbka-Morawski was deposed in 1947 as prime minister of Poland for having objected to the unification of the Socialist with the Communist party; and Gomulka was relieved of his joint position as vice-president and general secretary of the Communist party in August 1948 for having held out for a limited Polish independence and for trying to circumvent the absorption of the Polish armed forces and industries into the Russian apparatus. He was finally arrested and imprisoned for many years; only the Polish rising against Moscow's dictatorship in October 1956 freed him from prison and returned him to power.

As long as Stalin had believed in the possibility of peaceful co-operation with Britain and the United States, it had appeared that, for the countries concerned, he had come to terms with a system of rudimentary democracy under Communist party rule. His change of policy came with the announcement of the Truman Doctrine in March 1947. Now he saw the United States as planning to encircle Russia in preparation for war. His fears were not entirely without foundation. The United States had a monopoly of the atomic bomb, and an influential circle was actually agitating for a preventive war against the U.S.S.R. before it could make itself into a nuclear power.[1] Stalin did not hesitate to secure the countries under the Russian influence, not only as a bridgehead in the event of war, but also for their full war potential. What had been undertaken in the Stalinization of these countries was their incorporation into the war apparatus of the Russian empire.

5

Of greater importance than the Stalinization of the three Russian neighbouring states was that of Hungary and Czechoslovakia.

Churchill and Roosevelt had accepted Russia's demand for pro-Soviet governments in Poland and Churchill had agreed to Russia's predominance in Romania and Bulgaria.[2] The right of the Soviet government to exercise direct influence on the composition of their governments was thereby conceded, and so their sovereign independence was limited from the outset. However, the Soviet Union had pledged itself by the Yalta Declaration to establish democratic governments in the countries concerned—a condition which remained unfulfilled. While the Allies had protested against the breach of the declaration by rigged elections, they finally recognized the Communist-controlled governments and concluded peace treaties with them. The transformation of these semi-independent states into Russian satellite states therefore seemed inevitable.

But Hungary and Czechoslovakia did not fall within the Russian sphere of influence as recognized by the Allies. They did, however, fall within the Soviet occupation zone agreed at Potsdam; both countries had been occupied by the Red Army.

In Hungary, which had been occupied by Germany during the war, Marshal Klementi Voroshilov had, soon after the Red Army offensive began in

---

1. The distinguished journalist Walter Lippmann disclosed several years later that, 'in the late forties' (probably 1947 or 1948), a 'high official' of the War Department of the U.S. government had tried to persuade him 'to stand up in his articles for a preventive war against the Soviet Union'—*New York Herald Tribune*, 25 June 1965, quoted in Halle, *The Cold War as History*, p. 170.

2. See page 93.

October 1944, installed in Debrecen a provisional government made up of Communists, Social Democrats and representatives of the farmers' parties. After the conclusion of the campaign at the beginning of 1945, this government had removed to Budapest and, supervised by the Allied Control Commission, had undertaken to administer the country under Voroshilov's presidency. It decreed an electoral law based on democratic principles and called elections to form a parliament for 4 November 1945.

The Hungarian Communist party, Stalin's policy instrument, came into existence only after the invasion of the Red Army began. A Communist party had effectively been formed in November 1918; but within ten months it was wiped out in bloody persecutions at the hands of the triumphant counter-revolution[1] and was finally suppressed by law. Hungary had therefore had no legal Communist party for a quarter of a century. Unlike the Italian Communist party, for example, which had also been officially suppressed for over two decades, it was not reborn in any heroic war-time resistance movement—there had been no armed resistance in Hungary—but was rather resurrected by Hungarian Communists returning from exile in Moscow in the wake of the Red Army.

Its leader was Máthiás Rákosi (1892–1963), a strong personality and a master of political manoeuvre. He had received his initial Communist schooling as a Russian prisoner of war during the First World War and then became prominent after his return as one of the leaders of the young Communist party. Invited by Béla Kun to be commissar for the Hungarian Soviet Government, he had been entrusted with the command of a Red Army division. After the collapse of Kun's republic, he had fled to Moscow and become active in the Communist International. During a clandestine visit to Hungary in 1922, he had been arrested and sentenced to death. Under pressure from an international Socialist protest movement, the sentence was commuted to life imprisonment, and only after fifteen years was he released through an exchange agreement for Hungarian prisoners still in Russia.

The Communist party was fostered and protected by the Red Army. It was, as Antal Bán wrote, 'a refuge for the guilty', for 'opportunists of all kinds and classes'.[2] The Communist party membership card provided a safe-guard against arbitrary arrest by Red Army soldiers and secured living accommodation, work and food rations. It was not long before the masses had rallied to the Communist party, drawn, not by a tradition, for it had not

1. Hundreds of Communists and Socialists were murdered, 27,000 were brought to trial, 329 were executed, 70,000 were interned and 100,000 fled abroad. See Julius Braunthal (ed.) *Yearbook of the International Socialist Labour Movement 1956–1957* (London, 1956), p. 262. See also the Report of the Commission of Inquiry dispatched to Hungary by the British Labour Party: *The White Terror in Hungary* (London, 1921).

2. Antal Bán, 'Hungary', in *The Curtain Falls*, p. 66. Bán was a leader of the Hungarian Social Democratic party and Minister of Industry, 1945–8.

inherited any, but by the power which it radiated as an apparent arm of the Red Army. The Communist party membership grew from about 2,000 in the autumn of 1944 to 30,000 in February 1945 and to 150,000 during the following three months. In 1947 there were 700,000 card-carrying members.[1]

The Socialist party (*Magyarországi Szociáldemocrata Párt*) had for over six decades—it was founded in 1869—stood against the semi-feudal aristocratic régime under the Habsburgs and the semi-Fascist régime under Horthy. In the revolutionary ferment which gripped the country after the fall of the Habsburgs, it had joined with the Communist party in March 1919[2] and been dragged into the catastrophe which followed. But it reorganized, and in the first parliamentary election, in 1922, won twenty-four seats. By 1939 it counted several hundred local organizations and about 150,000 members. Thus, unlike the young Communist party, it had the backing of a tradition developed through decades of hard battle and firmly established organization.

But the Communist party, with the backing of the Russian occupation forces, had caught up with the Social Democratic strength within a year. In the November 1945 election it won 802,000 votes, against 823,000 for the Social Democrats, both taking 17 per cent of the total poll.

As was to be expected in a predominantly agrarian country, the victor emerging from the elections was the 'Party of the Small Farmers', which received 2,697,000 votes, or 57 per cent of the total poll, and 245 out of the 409 seats. The Communists gained sixty-nine seats and seventy went to the Social Democrats.

Even though the Small Farmers' party had won an absolute majority in parliament, only a coalition between it and the Communists and Social Democrats could be considered under the conditions of the Russian occupation. The Small Farmers' party did, of course, take precedence in the administration. Its two leaders, Zoltán Tildy and Ferenc Nagy, were respectively elected president and prime minister of the Hungarian republic. But in the praesidium of the Cabinet the Communists were represented by Máthiás Rákosi and the Social Democrats by Árpád Szakasits as vice-premiers; and under pressure from the Kremlin[3] a Communist, Imre Nagy,

1. See Paul E. Zinner, *Revolution in Hungary* (New York and London, 1962), p. 75.
2. See Braunthal, *History of the International, 1914–1943*, pp. 149–50.
3. The Ministry of the Interior was originally allotted to the Small Farmers' party. Rákosi then, however, demanded it for the Communists, threatening to withdraw from the government otherwise. To the objections of Ferenc Nagy, he replied: 'You do not seem to understand! Have a look at the whole of eastern Europe and see if you can find a country there in which the Ministry of the Interior is not in the hands of the Communist party.' 'We have been given to understand,' Nagy added to the report of the discussions, 'that the Communists raised their demand on instructions from the Soviets'—Ferenc Nagy, *The Struggle behind the Iron Curtain* (New York, 1948), p. 163. Antal Bán, Social Democratic minister for industry, who took part in the discussions, confirmed that, 'the Russians insisted that a Communist should be nominated as Minister of the Interior'—Bán, 'Hungary', in *The Curtain Falls*, p. 68.

was nominated as minister of the interior, though he was soon relieved by Laszlo Rajk.[1]

The coalition government was the instrument of a social revolution which began soon after the cease-fire. The Small Farmers' party did not obstruct its course, being only interested in agrarian reform—equally urgently wished for by the Social Democrats and the Communists—and so the fate of industry was left in the hands of the two working-class parties. The semi-feudal landed estates, on which the rule of the Hungarian aristocracy had rested for 1,000 years, were abolished and the land—about 3,200,000 hectares—divided among 642,000 agricultural workers and small landholders.[2] Simultaneously the mines, heavy industry, electricity plants, the whole transport system and the National Bank together with the largest private banks were nationalized.[3]

But the over-riding question remained Hungary's independence. Could it be maintained or would it fall under Russian domination? The heavy reparations imposed by the peace treaty, the trade agreements which Russia forced on Hungary, and the seizing of German property in key industries to which she was empowered under the Potsdam Agreement, appeared to be symptoms of a policy aimed at achieving Hungary's economic dependence upon Russia. And was not Stalin's successful endeavour at Potsdam to secure a common border between the Soviet Union and Hungary in the western Carpathians also an indication of his intention to submit Hungary to the Russian sphere of influence?

The Social Democratic leaders, meeting in secret in March 1946 to discuss trends in Russian policies, came to the conclusion like the majority of the population that the Soviet Union intended to 'create a situation to bring Hungary into total dependence upon the Soviet Union'.[4]

Stalin, however, tried his best to dispel such fears. In April 1946 he explained to the Hungarian prime minister, then on a state visit to Moscow in the company of Rákosi and Szakasits, that nothing was further from the Soviet Union's intentions than to tamper with Hungary's independence. 'In my opinion,' he told them, 'it is easy enough to create friendly relations between Russia and Hungary. . . . The Soviet Union has no wish to interfere in Hungary's internal affairs. The peoples of smaller nations have no reason to fear Soviet oppression. The Soviet Union would be betraying Lenin's ideology and revoking its former practice if it were to subject or influence smaller nations. . . . We believe,' he continued, 'that true friendship between a great power and a small country is possible without hazarding the latter's

1. Both were sentenced to death by a Communist court and executed some years later.
2. Zinner, *Revolution in Hungary*, p. 51. The Act of Land Reform, by which the aristocratic landholdings were abolished and redistributed, was promulgated on 15 March 1945.
3. See *Socialist World*, vol. i, No. 4, p. 313.
4. Bán, 'Hungary', in *The Curtain Falls*, p. 68.

independence.'[1] Nagy now became convinced, as he wrote, 'that Hungary no longer needed to fear that it would be forced to become a member of the Union of Soviet Socialist Republics'.[2]

It is possible that Stalin's assurance of April 1946 for Hungary's independence was sincere. But, from the spring of 1947, when the break in relations between the United States and the Soviet Union became evident, and Stalin saw Russia being threatened with war, it became obvious that his intention was total rule over Hungary.

A time limit was set for this objective. The Hungarian peace treaty was signed on 10 February 1947, to come into force on 15 September. On that day direct Soviet influence on the Hungarian government, granted by the Potsdam Agreement, was to be terminated, the Allied Control Commission dissolved and the occupation of the country to cease. So, by the time the Soviet army was to be withdrawn in September 1947, it was necessary for the Communist party to have secured a position which would give it the power to transform Hungary into a Russian satellite state.

But the Communist party had rallied only 17 per cent of the electorate. Under the country's democratic constitution, it could only attain a ruling position if it could reduce its two rival parties to total impotence—the Small Farmers' party, representing a majority of the people, and the Social Democratic party, rooted in the industrial working class.

The Communists were able to initiate their fight against the Small Farmers' party in the name of democracy, since it was the party not only of the conservative farmers, who had not yet awoken to political consciousness, but also of all reactionary elements in society—the expropriated landed aristocracy, the Church, the discharged officers, old civil servants[3] and the conservative wing of the middle classes—all, in fact, who detested democratic Socialism no less than totalitarian Communism. Like the Christian Social party in the Austrian Republic, it represented no guarantee for democracy. It was thus also opposed by the Social Democrats, but by normal democratic methods.

The Communists, on the other hand, as in all Russian-occupied countries, in fighting opposition invoked their tactic of terror combined with disintegration and schism. Following the occupation of Hungary more and more active members of the Small Farmers' party were arrested by the Russian secret police, the N.K.V.D., and by the Hungarian state police under accusations of Fascist machinations. At the beginning of January 1947, Rajk, the Communist minister of the interior, announced the discovery of a conspiracy by high-ranking officers and members of parliament of the Small

---

1. Nagy, *The Struggle behind the Iron Curtain*, pp. 212–13.
2. ibid., pp. 216–17.
3. Ferenc Nagy admits that his party had opened its doors 'to the aristocrats, the priests and the old officials'; see *The Struggle behind the Iron Curtain*, p. 450.

Farmers' party, among them its general secretary Béla Kovács. Now a general terror against the Small Farmers' party was set in motion. 'We demanded the expulsion of the reactionary elements from the party of the Small Farmers', and under the pressure of the terror '21 members of parliament were expelled as a start,' reported Rákosi, when describing, during a course of instruction to the Communist party a few years later on 29 February 1952, the political miracle that had enabled the Communist party, starting with the support of only 17 per cent of the population, to seize power within two years. 'Naturally,' he emphasized, 'from the very beginning the state police were under our control.'

This provided one explanation of the success of terrorist methods. 'After this success'—namely the decimation of the Small Farmers' party in parliament—Rákosi continued in his speech, 'we adopted salami tactics. That is, we continued, so to speak, to reduce the power of the Small Farmers slice by slice.' The Communists fragmented the party by introducing farmers' parties which they both called to life and controlled: 'The party of the farm labourer and small farmer' and the 'National Peasant party', also called the 'Party of the New Landowners', i.e. those farmers who had received land under agrarian reform; and they also founded, under the leadership of Father Stephan Barankovics, a Roman Catholic party. 'The camp [of the Small Farmers' party], which three years ago represented the overwhelming majority in the country,' Ferenc Nagy concluded his account, 'has shrunk to nothing. Their leaders submit obediently to the instructions of Moscow and the Communists.'[1]

'Then it was the turn of the Social Democratic party,' Rákosi reported. 'We had to fight harder and harder against them.'[2]

The Social Democratic party was divided into three groups in its attitude towards the Communist party. One small group, which was the furthest to the right and was led by Karoly Peyer, rejected any relations with the Communist party whatsoever. Peyer's origins were in the trade union movement, and after the collapse of the Hungarian Soviet Republic he had been general secretary of the trade union federation and leader of the Social Democratic party. With the Hungarian prime minister, Count Stephan Bethlen, one of the leaders of the counter-revolution, he had made the 'Bethlen–Peyer' pact, by which the party pledged as the price of its legal recognition as a 'loyal opposition' to refrain from propaganda among the peasants and to limit its activity to industrial workers. It had been a secret pact, not unveiled until later and then evoking a serious crisis within the party; it had naturally proved objectionable to the Socialist International. Opposition to Peyer's leadership within the party had been powerless under

1. ibid., p. 441.
2. *Társadalmi Szemle*, February–March 1952. For the text of Rákosi's speech, see *Socialist International Information*, 17 May 1952.

the Horthy régime. An opposition party did, on the other hand, organize itself abroad—the Hungarian Socialist party in exile (*Világosság*)—under the leadership of men who had stood at the head of the old party and who had been members of the Hungarian Soviet government: Siegmund Kunfi, Zoltán Ronai and Wilhelm Böhm.

Peyer had only returned in the summer of 1945 from the Mauthausen concentration camp, where he had been deported by the Gestapo in 1944. Meanwhile Árpád Szakasits, chief editor of its journal *Népszava*, had been elected general secretary of the party. He stood to the far left, supporting the closest co-operation with the Communists.

The centre was led by Wilhelm Böhm, army commander of the Red Army in the Hungarian Soviet Republic, Imre Szelig, a prominent trade union leader, Anna Kéthly and Antal Bán; it represented the majority. It saw co-operation with the Communists as essential for succeeding in building a new Hungary through social and economic reform as well as for preventing the revival of Fascism, a serious latent danger. It strove to construct a true democracy in Hungary—which had never in fact known democracy—and rejected the 'dictatorship of the proletariat' for which the Communists stood. It sincerely wished for friendly relations between the Soviet Union and an independent Hungary, but not, as the Communists did, for her incorporation into the Russian empire. It fought above all to preserve the party's independence as a guarantee for the independence of Hungary itself against Communist attempts to swallow it in the process of unification.

'The fight against Social Democracy,' Rákosi reported in the lecture already quoted, 'lasted longer and was more severe.' The Communist party advanced under the slogan of the unity of the proletariat. It infiltrated Social Democratic organizations, in particular the left wing of the party executive,[1] and simultaneously attempted to terrorize Social Democratic opponents of unity; among others, Gyula Kelemen, a member of the executive, was sentenced to life imprisonment on a ludicrous charge of treason, and Sari Karik, leader of the party secretariat, was deported by the N.K.V.D. to Siberia.

The Communist party's dominance in the country rested, as its leader freely admitted, on the Russian forces of occupation. As Joszef Révai, the Communist minister for culture, commented when describing the metamorphosis of democracy in Hungary into a 'dictatorship of the proletariat',

We were a minority in parliament and in the government, but at the same time we represented the leading force. We had decisive control of the police forces. Our

1. Gyorgy Marosan, deputy general secretary of the party, Zoltán Ronai and Stephan Ries, members of the party executive and members of the government, were secret members of the Communist party. See Bán, 'Hungary' in Healey (ed.), *The Curtain Falls*, pp. 72–3. Marosan publicly admitted that members of the illegal Communist party had been instructed during the war 'to continue with their work inside the Social Democratic party'. See *For a Lasting Peace and for a People's Democracy*, 15 June 1949.

forces, the force of our [the Communist] party . . . was multiplied by the fact that the Soviet Union and the Soviet army were always there to support us with their assistance.[1]

But to maintain that dominant position after the withdrawal of the Soviet army, it was essential that new elections should be held *before* the direct influence of the occupying power was ended so as to secure parliamentary rule by an appropriate manipulation of the ballot. Under Soviet pressure, new elections were called for 1 August 1947, and an apparently harmless clause was added to the electoral law which, however, enabled the Communists to carry out election rigging on a tremendous scale. The clause allowed electors who were absent from their place of residence on the day of the elections to vote with special voting slips in any other electoral district. The Communist minister of the interior then had hundreds of thousands of these slips printed and distributed throughout the Communist party, whose trusted members voted dozens of times; 300,000 such voting slips were counted.[2]

From these elections so openly manipulated the Communist party emerged as the strongest in parliament and the majority party of the coalition. It had increased its representation from sixty-nine to 100 seats, but these tactics had not weakened the Social Democratic party significantly; they lost only three of their seventy seats.[3] The Small Farmers' party was, however, routed, having lost 177 out of 245 seats. The remnant which escaped 'submitted,' as Nagy said, 'obediently to instructions from Moscow and the Communists'. The National Peasant party, which had gained thirty-two seats, was in reality an auxiliary arm of the Communist party.[4]

Now it became important to destroy the last obstacle to the Stalinization of Hungary—the Social Democratic party. Up until the elections, Communist propaganda had done no more than try to slander the 'rightist leaders' of the party[5] as 'dollar imperialists' and 'anti-Soviet agents'. But following the elections all opponents of unification with the Communists—the whole active membership of the party supporting the centre—were simply defamed 'as

1. Joszef Révai, 'On the Character of our People's Democracy', in *Társadalmi Szemle*, March–April 1949; for the text, see *Foreign Affairs*, vol. xxviii (October 1949), pp. 143–51.
2. See Bán, 'Hungary', in Healey (ed.), *The Curtain Falls*, p. 73.
3. In the process of Stalinization, however, thirty-five of the sixty-seven Social Democratic deputies were expelled from parliament by the 'salami-tactic'; see ibid., p. 75.
4. Concerning the infiltration by secret Communist party members of the National Peasant party, which participated in the Communist-dominated coalition government, Joszef Révai reported to the founding conference of the Cominform: 'The secretary [of the party] is Communist, fifteen of the thirty-two deputies are Communists, and eight are close to the Communists'—quoted in E. Reale, *Avec Jacques Duclos au Banc des Accusés* (Paris, 1958). As was mentioned earlier, Reale attended the founding conference of the Cominform as delegate of the Italian Communist party.
5. Peyer and his group had parted with the party before the elections and aligned themselves with the middle-class Radical party. It was the leaders of the centre who were now the 'rightist leaders'.

traitors to the working class'; an odium meant to serve as both warning and threat.

The psychological moment for an all-out attack on the centre Social Democrats had arrived. Szakasits, now a puppet in Communist hands, submitted to their instructions and called a meeting for 18 February 1948 of the active party members in Budapest, at which Marosan announced the resignation of the leaders of the centre—Szelig, Bán and Kéthly—and an imminent amalgamation with the Communists. In fact, none of these leaders had actually resigned; on the contrary, the party executive had only recently agreed, with Szakasits' and Marosan's approval, that at their forthcoming congress they should propose the preservation of the party's independence. But the ruse met with extraordinary success. The great majority of party members, believing that their leaders had capitulated under Communist pressure, thought that unification was in fact agreed upon. Bewildered, demoralized and afraid, they deserted by the tens of thousands—often as intact party organizations—into the Communist ranks; according to official Communist statistics, 200,000 Social Democrats were, during the course of a few weeks, admitted into the Communist party, while a further 40,000 applied for admission. Before the Social Democratic party congress could assemble on 6 March 1948 to take its formal decision, the Social Democratic party was already swallowed up by the Communist party. A joint congress of the two parties on 12 June 1948 ratified their formal union into the 'United Workers' party'.[1] Thus Révai was able to record accurately: '[Hungary's] development into a dictatorship of the proletariat was crowned in June 1948, and finally secured by the destruction of the right wing of the Social Democratic party and by the founding of the United Workers' party.'

6

The setting up of a Communist dictatorship in Hungary was justified by its apologists as being essential for securing the achievements of the social revolution against the threat of counter-revolution. That this was a latent danger cannot be denied. Hungary had, until the day of the Red Army's entry, known nothing beyond a thousand years of autocratic rule by the aristocracy and the Catholic church.[2] It had, in fact, remained untouched by

1. See Antal Bán, 'The Last Months of Social Democracy in Hungary', in *Socialist World*, vol. I, No. 5; Lázló Révész, '*Die Liquidierung der ungarischen Sozialdemokratie*', in *Die Zukunft*, June 1968. Szakasits became chairman and Rákosi general secretary of the United Workers' party; one of its three deputy secretaries was Marosan, the other two were the Communists János Kádár and Mihaly Fárkás.

2. The nine-month revolutionary interim period between November 1918 and August 1919 can be disregarded; the failure of the revolution strengthened rather than weakened the power of the aristocracy and the Church.

the vast social and political upheavals which had taken place during the century and a half since the French revolution in the countries of Europe west of the River Leitha. In no other European country had church and aristocracy been so freely able to maintain their vast landed estates while keeping the peasants in semi-feudal servitude.[1] The social traditions of feudalism were so deeply rooted in the villages that even the agrarian reform left the dominant influence of the church over the peasants unbroken. And the church remained a reactionary power, while the peasantry formed an overwhelming majority in the population. Therefore the pre-eminence of industrial workers, which in Marxist thought formed a prerequisite for Socialist development, could not be hoped for in Hungary under democratic conditions. Democracy in Hungary presented the traditional conservative and reactionary forces—the dispossessed aristocracy in alliance with the church, the peasantry, the petty bourgeoisie—with the possibility of using democratic means to destroy the predominant position of the working class and ultimately to destroy democracy itself and construct on its ruins a counter-revolutionary dictatorship.[2]

In Czechoslovakia, by contrast, the social revolution was threatened by no latent counter-revolution. Czechoslovakia was a highly developed industrial state with a mass labour movement and a middle class which had, in the Czech nation's struggle for independence under the Habsburg monarchy, evolved a democratic tradition; and which had, after the fall of the Austro–Hungarian Empire in October 1918, built up in alliance with the working class a genuine democratic republic. History had destroyed the breeding-grounds of social reaction among the Czech people. After the battle at the 'White Mountain' in 1520, the Czech aristocracy had been exterminated, the Hussite religious movement suppressed and the Catholic church forced upon the people from outside. Czechoslovakia itself possessed, as Thomas Masaryk recalled, 'no dynasty, no national aristocracy, no venerable military tradition and no church which, as in the old absolutist states, was politically recognized'.[3] The strongest party of the urban middle class, the party of Masaryk and his successor Beneš, was a progressive party of social reform, calling itself the National Socialist party—and the rural Catholic People's

1. A description of the social relationship between dependence and conditions of life for the land-starved farmers can be found in Gyula Illyés, *People of the Puszta* (Budapest, 1967).

2. But even if, from a Socialist viewpoint, a dictatorship of the proletariat to defend the achievements of a social revolution can be historically justified in a country which had never known democratic traditions, there could never be any justification for a Communist party dictatorship destroying democracy within the labour movement and subjecting the working class to rule by a Communist politbureau. The alternative in Hungary to a parliamentary democracy based on the English example did not necessarily imply the imposition of a Communist dictatorship patterned on the Russian model.

3. Thomas Masaryk, *The Making of a State* (London, 1947), p. 436, quoted in Paul E. Zinner, *Communist Strategy and Tactics in Czechoslovakia, 1918–1948* (London, 1963), p. 5.

party, though conservative, was by no means reactionary, as, for example, the Christian Social party was in Austria.[1]

These then were the characters of the two middle-class parties, urban and rural, with whom the two Socialist parties had to share the power of the state.

The leading roles of the two Socialist parties were beyond question. They had been the strongest parties in the First Republic. The Czecho-slovak Social Democratic party (*Československá Sociálni Demokracie*, Č.S.D.) had emerged with 1,500,000 votes as the strongest individual party in the republic's first elections; and the Czechoslovak Communist party (*Komunistická Strana Československá*, K.S.Č.) could at the time of its formation in 1921 call on 350,000 members. Shaken by a severe internal crisis, it lost 300,000 members between then and 1938, but it maintained its strength in elections, and in 1935, in the last election before the war, it won 850,000 votes, as against 1,034,000 votes which went to the Social Democrats.[2]

The balance of power between these two parties shifted rapidly after the country's liberation by the Red Army. The Czech people were conscious of a long-standing sense of relationship with the people of Russia as members of the broad Slav community. Further, the Soviet Union had, before the war, been an ally of the Czechoslovak Republic, renewing during the war an agreement for mutual aid and friendship towards the Republic, which was signed in Moscow on 12 December 1943 by President Eduard Beneš. The majority of Poles, Romanians and Hungarians had viewed the Red Army with fear, hatred and contempt when it entered and occupied their countries. The Czechs, on the other hand, had greeted the Red Army with demon-strations of enthusiasm. In Poland, Romania and Hungary, the Communist party was the 'Russian party' in a disparaging sense. But in Czechoslovakia, the sympathy felt by the broad masses towards the Soviet Union, which had smashed the arch-enemy Germany, was a source of strength to a Communist party with close connections with Moscow.[3] In May 1945, when Marshal Ivan Koniev's armoured division entered Prague, the Communist party

1. Even the right-wing Agrarian party was, until the time of the Munich Agreement in September 1938, free of Fascist tendencies. But since it later collaborated with the Nazi government during the German occupation, its revival was prohibited in the Second Republic.

2. For the membership shift in the Communist party, 1921–38, see Zinner, *Communist Strategy and Tactics in Czechoslovakia*, Table 1, p. 250; and for the respective numbers of voters for the two parties, 1920–35, see ibid., Table 5, p. 253.

3. The Communist party in its propaganda tried to present itself to the Czech people as the party and even the organ of the Soviet Union. In its policy guide-lines, party officials were instructed 'to emphasize at every opportunity the strength and power of the Soviet Union and its army; at all assemblies to use not only Czech but also Soviet flags and emblems, and to try to convince the people that the real master of the country was the Soviet Union and the local representative the local section of the Communist party'—quoted in Jan Stransky, *East Wind over Prague* (London, 1950), p. 45.

counted 37,000 members;[1] a year later, immediately before the post-war elections, it could claim 1,159,264 members.[2] It was not the use of terror, as had occurred in Romania and Hungary, nor opportunism alone[3] which could explain this general shift to the Communist party; at the constituent national assembly elections on 26 May 1946—which were genuinely free elections as in the Western democracies—the Communists won 2,695,000 votes against 855,000 for the Social Democrats.

The Communists had thereby gained 114 seats; the Social Democrats thirty-nine. Both parties had joined together in an alliance back in 1944. With 153 seats, this alliance now held a slender majority in the constituent national assembly, which contained 300 delegates; together they had won 51 per cent of votes cast—representing more than 47 per cent of the total electorate (3,550,000 out of 7,583,000 voters had exercised their prerogative).[4] The alliance between Communists and Social Democrats had, moreover, been strengthened in June 1945 by a further association with the National Socialist party, all three committing themselves to social reform—'a Socialist bloc of workers in town and country', now shown, as claimed, to represent 'clearly a majority of the people'.[5] The National Socialist party, with fifty-five seats, had emerged as the second strongest individual party; and thus the 'Socialist Bloc' counted a majority of fifty-eight deputies in Parliament.

The firm foundations for a Socialist order in Czechoslovak society were already well laid before the elections. The instrument for social revolution had been the 'National Front', a provisional coalition government formed by President Beneš in Košice, the capital of Eastern Slovakia, on Communist initiative in March 1945 when Prague and Brno were still in German hands. The provisional coalition government had embraced six legally recognized parties: Communists, Social Democrats, National Socialists, the People's party and two Slovak parties. On a proposal made by the Communists, the leader of the Social Democratic party, Zdeněk Fierlinger, who had been Czechoslovakia's Ambassador in Moscow, was elected prime minister of the provisional government, Klement Gottwald, leader of the Communist party, becoming deputy prime minister. The Communists took for themselves the

1. See Zdeněk Eliaš and Jaromir Netik, 'Czechoslovakia', in William Griffith (ed.), *Communism in Europe*, vol. II (Massachusetts, n.d.), p. 124.
2. See Zinner, *Communist Strategy and Tactics in Czechoslovakia*, p. 124.
3. Not surprisingly, many thousands joined the strongest party for reasons of self-interest. But they did not find themselves in a comfortable position. In a 'new registration of members', 177,000 'unreliable elements and enemies, self-declared opportunists and profiteers, who had crept into the party' were expelled between June 1946 and January 1947. See *Dějiny Komunistické Strany Československá* (Prague, 1961), p. 150, quoted in Eliaš and Netik, 'Czechoslovakia', in Griffith (ed.), *Communism in Europe*, p. 199.
4. See R. R. Betts (ed.), *Central and South-East Europe 1945–1948* (London, 1950), p. 179.
5. *Pravo Lidu*, 12 May 1945, quoted in Zinner, *Communist Strategy and Tactics in Czechoslovakia*, p. 150.

ministry of the interior, and with it gained control over the police as well as a dominant influence over the army through the nomination of General Ludvik Svoboda—who was a Communist sympathizer and who had commanded the First Brigade in the Soviet Union—to the post of minister of defence.

The coalition parties had agreed on a rebuilding programme for the republic—the 'Košice Programme'. The republic was to be based on political rights of freedom as well as on a comprehensive system of social welfare and on economic democracy based on trade union participation. The programme promised an agrarian reform by distributing the land and property of Germans and Hungarians who had been expelled from the country as well as that owned by the church and the Counts Schwarzenberg, Thun and Waldstein. The key industries—the mines, electric power stations and banks —were to be nationalized.[1]

The provisional government did not hesitate to carry through its programme, signed by the representatives of the six coalition parties in Košice on 27 March 1945. Within ten days of the country's liberation, on 19 May, the Communist minister for agriculture, Julius Ďuriš, publicly announced the guide-lines for agrarian reform: by a decree of 21 June nearly three million hectares were to be appropriated without compensation and divided among over 300,000 small farmers.

A few weeks later, on 18 July, the Social Democratic minister for industry, Bohumil Laušman, submitted to the president the decrees worked out by a commission for the nationalization of industry: 3,119 companies, including particularly the mines, the iron, steel and engineering industries, were to be taken into public ownership.[2]

This was not, however, a social revolution taking place under conditions of parliamentary democracy. The sovereign power of the state rested in the hands of the National Front central committee, in which the parties were represented by their respective leaders. All decisions taken by the central committee were given legal effect by an Act passed by the provisional assembly. Yet even this assembly had not been elected, but was made up from forty delegates from each party and sixty representatives from special-interest groups. The provisional government itself, nominated by President Beneš in agreement with the National Front parties, was really no more than an executive organ of the central committee, representing and executing the committee's decisions following formal agreement.

This system of government, established in the emergency brought about

1. For a comprehensive description of the Košice Programme, see W. Diamond, *Czechoslovakia between East and West* (London, 1947), pp. 1–7.

2. For a short review of the agrarian reform and the nationalization of industry, see Zinner, *Communist Strategy and Tactics in Czechoslovakia*, pp. 171–5; see also Betts (ed.), *Central and South-East Europe*, pp. 173–4.

by the collapse of the administration of the state and its economic life, could be defined as a system of dictatorship—a dictatorship by the central committee of the National Front. However, it was a dictatorship founded not on the exclusive rule of a single party, but on a coalition of the legal parties that left democratic rights fundamentally untouched. Such rights had been withdrawn with the authority of the Allies at the Yalta Conference only from those parties which had co-operated with the Nazi régime—the Agrarian party and the Czechoslovak German minority.

Moreover the dictatorship was intended, even by the Communists, to be no more than a temporary measure precluding full parliamentary democracy. During this period no serious consideration was given to the possibility of a dictatorship on the Russian pattern. The Communists had in no way attempted to obstruct or manipulate elections to the constituent National Assembly. And upon entering parliament as the strongest individual party, they had, together with all the other parties, voted for Beneš's re-election as prime minister of the republic and had joined the coalition with Klement Gottwald as deputy prime minister. What they sought was the construction of a Socialist order of society on a democratic basis—a 'particular Czechoslovak path to Socialism', as Gottwald defined it to the Communist central committee after the elections in September 1946; and, he added, it was a 'path' which Stalin had approved in conversation with him.[1] When, in January 1947, the approved government plan for 'rebuilding the Czechoslovak Republic' was put into action—a detailed plan by which the 1937 industrial productivity figures were to be overtaken by 110 per cent[2]—Gottwald again emphasized the party line: 'We advance towards Socialism along our own Czechoslovak path.'[3]

During the twelve months following the election there were no overt indications of any possibility of the Communist party departing in the near future from the 'Czechoslovak path to Socialism' and opting for the 'Russian way'. Immediately after the elections, the Communist leader Jiři Hronek explained the policy his party had decided upon. 'Further revolutionary upheavals,' he declared, 'are neither anticipated nor necessary.' This, he

1. Quoted in Eliaš and Netik, 'Czechoslovakia', in Griffith (ed.), *Communism in Europe*, p. 179. Tito, however, stated in a conversation in the summer of 1946 with W. Rust, then chief editor of the British *Daily Worker*, that Gottwald had fallen 'into disgrace' as a result of his policies. For Tito is alleged to have said, 'whilst the other new democracies introduced a régime which aims at the classic dictatorship of the proletariat . . . the Czechoslovak party claims that under the special conditions of its country it could progress to Communism by a democratic form of organization. . . . This,' Tito said, 'the other Communist leaders considered to be pure heresy, which makes things difficult for them. The matter will soon reach its final conclusion.' For the conversation, see Douglas Hyde, *I Believed* (London, 1951), p. 234. Hyde was then news editor of the *Daily Worker*.

2. See Betts, (ed.), *Central and South-East Europe*, pp. 180–2.

3. Quoted in Eliaš and Netik, 'Czechoslovakia', in Griffith (ed.), *Communism in Europe*, p. 179.

stated, was not only the view of the majority of the population, but also, he emphasized, 'was shared by the leading men and women of Czechoslovakia's strongest party, the Communist party. . . . The party,' he continued, 'has as its programme the consolidation [of revolutionary achievements] and future development.'[1]

They held to this line, which had already proved itself. The Czechoslovak Republic was indeed on the road to Socialism. Two thirds of the industrial means of production and the whole basis of finance had been nationalized, capitalist *laissez-faire* in the production of goods having been overcome by a Socialist planned economy. Industrial production had rapidly developed, coming close to fulfilling the two-year plan target of increasing production by 110 per cent over 1937. A comprehensive social security scheme and the basic law of the constitution, which solemnly confirmed rights to democratic freedom, were in the final stages of preparation. It seemed as though Czechoslovakia was on the way to becoming an example to the world of how, even under Communist leadership, a Socialist commonwealth might be founded on a democratic basis.

Moscow in the event respected Czechoslovakia's independence up until July 1947. While in Hungary the Soviet army remained in occupation until the end of 1947, being employed as the instrument of its Stalinization, it had been withdrawn from Czechoslovakia as early as the end of 1945. Stalin had, according to Gottwald's evidence, approved Czechoslovakia's 'path to Socialism'; at any rate, he had made no attempt to block it. Perhaps he hoped to demonstrate to the world through Czechoslovakia's example that the Soviet Union would even leave freedom and independence intact in a country under Communist rule.

The change in his policy towards Czechoslovakia came with the change in his policies towards the United States and Britain. When, at the end of June, at the Paris conference, Stalin rejected Marshall Aid, he broke his bridges with the West. And when the Prague government, on 7 July, nevertheless unanimously accepted Marshall Aid, as has already been mentioned, Gottwald was 'summoned to Moscow' on the following day,[2] where Stalin unhesitatingly confronted Czechoslovakia with the necessity of choosing between Marshall Aid and an alliance with the Soviet Union. Faced with such a choice, Czechoslovakia could only capitulate, for it was politically and psychologically unthinkable that its alliance with Russia should be hazarded. In the eyes of most of the Czechoslovak people Russia represented the only true friend of the republic and its only reliable ally against the danger of a 'German revenge'. As Poland had been chained to Russia by the annexation of East Prussia, so was Czechoslovakia through the expulsion of

1. Quoted in Betts (ed.), *Central and South-East Europe*, pp. 183–4.
2. See page 148.

the Sudetenland Germans. Thus the Prague government, under pressure from Stalin, repealed its decision. But having rejected Marshall Aid, it could now expect economic help only from Russia. On 12 July Gottwald signed a five-year trade agreement which brought Czechoslovakia into economic dependence upon the Soviet Union.

By his intervention on the issue of the Marshall plan, Stalin had incorporated Czechoslovakia into the Soviet economic bloc.[1] The founding conference of the Cominform in September 1947 set in motion the process of its incorporation into the bloc of Soviet-dominated states. 'The decision to set up the Cominform,' the Communist historian Karel Kaplan reported on these events in retrospect, 'influenced the entire development of the Socialist camp, the individual countries and their Communist parties.'[2]

The first priority in the Stalinization of Czechoslovakia, as in Hungary and Poland, was to destroy the independence of the Social Democratic party and finally to see it absorbed by the Communist party. Even before the liberation of the country the Communist leadership had set itself the task of fusing the two Socialist parties. Fierlinger tells in his memoirs of how the question of fusion had been raised as early as the winter of 1942–3:

In the discussion [with the Soviet leaders] on the joint action to be taken by our country's two parties of the left after the liberation, which we had in Kuibyshchev [as has been mentioned, Fierlinger was at the time Czech Ambassador to Russia], each side was of the opinion that the economic and social programmes of the Communist party and the Social Democratic party would certainly coincide and joint action between the parties would not be a temporary make-shift arrangement. It would lead to its logical conclusion—a co-ordination of tactical principles and in the end to the fusion of both parties.[3]

Zdeněk Fierlinger, chairman of the Social Democratic party after the liberation, had no doubt wished for the merger between the two Socialist parties from the beginning; but it was also the aim of the majority in government and parliament. 'The idea of Socialist unity,' Václav Majer, an eminent trade union leader, who had been in the provisional as well as in Gottwald's government, reported, 'was very popular and accepted from the outset as a natural consequence of new life in the liberated republic.'[4]

But after the elections Fierlinger's policy of close co-operation with the Communists met with growing opposition from the party leadership as well as from the rank-and-file. The party's defeat at the polls—they had won less than a third of the votes gained by the Communists—was attributed to its alliance with the Communists which had resisted its policy of independence.

1. See Betts, (ed.), *Central and South-East Europe*, p. 183.
2. Karel Kaplan, 'Class Struggle after February 1948', *Příspěvky*, No. 3, 1963, quoted in Eliaš and Netik, 'Czechoslovakia', in Griffith (ed.), *Communism in Europe*, p. 207.
3. Zdeněk Fierlinger, *In the Service of the Czechoslovak Republic* (Prague, 1949), pp. 124–5, quoted in Václav Majer, 'Czechoslovakia', in Healey (ed.), *The Curtain Falls*, p. 89.
4. Majer, 'Czechoslovakia', in Healey (ed.), *The Curtain Falls*, p. 87.

A document published on 12 September 1947, jointly signed by three leading Social Democrats (Fierlinger, with the party secretary Blažej Vilím, and a member of the party executive, Frantisek Tymes) as well as three leading Communists, engendered a crisis in the party. It amounted to a Social Democratic–Communist pact, committing both parties to a united attitude on any decisive political problem. Fierlinger had negotiated and signed it in secret since he feared opposition to the pact from the party executive but believed that it would be approved by a majority at the party congress. However, the party congress, meeting in an excited mood on 16 November 1947 in Brno, rejected the pact, deposed Fierlinger and elected Bohumil Laušman in his place as party president by 283 votes against 162.

Fierlinger did not, however, abandon the fight; he was now determined to lead the Social Democrats into the Communist camp. He organized within the party a general staff to work to seize control: a six-pronged political directorate, a three-pronged political secretariat, an organizational secretariat, and a left-wing group within the party executive and the parliamentary group.

While Fierlinger's fall had been a set-back for the Communist party, Laušman's election to the party presidency by no means implied a breaking-off of relations with the Communists, for Laušman was a left-wing Socialist. On the other hand, the party conference made it perfectly clear that the Social Democrats intended to defend their autonomy. The Communists could therefore no longer, as had been the case under Fierlinger's leadership, count on their unconditional support in the government and the national assembly. Their predominant influence could therefore now be called in question, since it was only with the votes of the Social Democrats that they constituted an overall majority in the cabinet and parliament. It was also now in doubt whether they could maintain their earlier strength in the elections due to be held in the spring of 1948. An official public opinion poll taken in January 1948 indicated a Communist loss of 10 per cent of votes; a similar poll before the 1946 elections had been accurate to within half of one per cent.[1] The Communist party could not, in any case, expect to gain a majority at the elections and maintain their domination of the country on a parliamentary basis.

Yet even a decrease in the parliamentary strength of the Communist party would hardly have obstructed the 'Czechoslovakian path to Socialism'. It would have remained the strongest individual party. Its membership outstripped the membership of any other party; it controlled the trade unions and also enjoyed a mass following among the small farmers, who had, through the agrarian reform, gained land holdings. It was, above all, the

1. See Tana Adam Smidt, *Anatomy of a Satellite* (Boston, Mass., 1952). The Institute of Public Opinion polls came under the Ministry of Information, headed by the Communist minister, Václav Kopecký.

party trusted by the Soviet Union, the protector of Czechoslovakia against the possibility of a German revenge. It would have continued to be the most influential element in the government and would have been able in alliance with the Social Democrats and unhindered by the party of the National Socialists, which had participated in the coalition government since the liberation, to carry on the process of constructing the new social order.

But it was not the danger of a counter-revolution threatening Socialist developments which, in February 1948, provoked a Communist insurrection. In Bohemia and Moravia—the republic's industrial centres—a successful counter-revolution was unimaginable in the face of a powerful labour movement. One source of reaction, however, was Slovakia, culturally and socially backward, a predominantly agrarian country with a predominance of Catholic, conservative peasants. Under the leadership of Father Joseph Tiso and with Hitler's help, it had broken away from the republic and constituted itself as an independent state in March 1939. In the autumn of 1944, however, the separatist Fascist régime had been swept away by a revolutionary uprising and Slovakia was once again incorporated with certain autonomous rights into the republic. Until the autumn of 1947 there had been no signs whatsoever of a separatist revival in Slovakia. Then, in September, a conspiracy to assassinate Beneš and overthrow the republic came to light. The conspirators were arrested, and there the matter ended.

This episode had occurred before the founding conference of the Cominform in September 1947, and had no effect on the Communist party's course. But, two months after the conference, on 29 November, a speech by Gottwald to the Communist party central committee indicated a change in its policy. Czechoslovakia would have to reckon 'in the coming weeks and months', he said, 'with increasing pressure from foreign reaction'. To contain this attack, the Communist party would have to eliminate 'agents of reaction and counter-revolution in the National Front, and in its foreign policy it must suppress all signs, tendencies and actions which could damage Czechoslovakia's relationship in its alliance with Soviet Russia'.[1] 'Foreign reaction' was, according to the resolution of the Cominform conference, 'American imperialism'. Ten days after Gottwald's speech, the Communist minister of the interior, Václav Nosek, announced the arrest of 'spies' on the Bohemian–Bavarian border who, it was hinted, had been recruited in Bavaria by the American occupying power. Communist propaganda now declared the republic to be threatened by the intrigues of foreign powers, Slovak separatism and Czech counter-revolutionaries.

Nevertheless, during the course of the next three months, these pronouncements in no way disturbed the concord between the parties in the coalition

1. *Svobodné Noviny*, 30 November 1947, quoted in Betts (ed.), *Central and South-East Europe*, p. 187.

government. It was only at the beginning of February 1948 that disagreements between the Communists and other parties in the cabinet began to take on a hectic tone; but these did not involve any fundamental ideological differences. In one case it was a question of whether the date for the forthcoming elections should be settled for April or May; in another it was whether the salary increases for civil servants, approved by all parties, should be fixed proportionately or equally for all grades. None was the kind of conflict to place the coalition in jeopardy.

Then, on 17 February, a conflict arose between the Communist ministers and those of other parties in the cabinet which unleashed a fateful government crisis; it was fateful because it was selected by the Communist party as a justification for seizing state power. The conflict centred on the nomination of Communists to senior positions in the police by Václav Nosek, the Communist minister of the interior. With the votes of the Social Democrats, a majority in the cabinet decided to instruct him to cancel these appointments. Yet on the same day the Communist party central committee issued a manifesto accusing 'certain parties' of having deliberately precipitated a government crisis, mainly to cause internal political chaos which might seriously threaten the elections. It was planned, the Communists asserted, to instal before the elections by unconstitutional means a government of civil servants 'which would attempt to snatch power out of the hands of the sovereign people and, in the service of reaction, in an atmosphere of political and economic unrest, prepare undemocratic elections'. The manifesto called upon 'all true Czechs and Slovaks, irrespective of their party loyalties, to nip in the bud these infamous plans of the reactionaries'.[1] Gottwald had stated earlier in his speech of the end of November 1947 that 'reactionary forces would at the critical moment create a government crisis and try to form a government of civil servants. Such a step,' he declared, 'would politically speaking be the equivalent of a reactionary *putsch*, a reactionary *coup d'état*'.[2]

When the Cabinet next met on 20 February, Gottwald avoided answering a question on whether the countermanding of the police appointments had been carried out, and the ministers of the National Socialists, the People's party and the Slovaks announced their resignations. The Communists now demanded that Beneš should form a new government under Gottwald but excluding the three parties whose ministers had resigned. Beneš, however, refused to accept the resignations and appealed to the Communists to solve the crisis 'by parliamentary means'. 'It is clear to me,' he wrote to Gottwald, 'that the prime minister will be the president of the strongest party, Mr

1. *Svobodné Noviny*, 18 February 1948. For the text of the manifesto, see Betts (ed.), *Central and South-East Europe*, pp. 189–90.

2. Quoted in Eliaš and Netik, 'Czechoslovakia', in Griffith (ed.), *Communism in Europe*, pp. 202–3.

Klement Gottwald. It is also clear to me that Socialism is the pattern of life which a majority of our people desire.' Freedom and unity, he continued, were the main principles of national life, and compatible with Socialism. He asked Gottwald to prevent the division of the nation into two camps at one another's throats.[1]

The Communists declared, however, that the three parties whose ministers had resigned had ceased 'to represent the interests of working people in town and country'; they had 'betrayed the fundamental principles of a people's democracy . . . and had taken up a position of seditious opposition'. Co-operation with these parties was therefore out of the question.

Meanwhile the Communist party had mobilized the masses. A workers' militia was organized and armed and action committees were set up in towns and villages; a series of mass demonstrations took place in streets and squares and on 24 February the workers in the factories held a one-hour general strike to demonstrate their support for the Communist demand that Beneš should accept the ministers' resignations and form a new government. On the next day, a crowd 100,000 strong gathered in St Wencelas Square to await the president's decision. Beneš capitulated, fearing that refusal to meet the demands might unleash civil war, or even a war between the Great Powers. (An intervention by Russia, or the United States, whose troops were stationed in Bavaria, was within the scope of possibilities.)[2]

Gottwald formed his government on the same day. It was a Communist government. Twelve of its twenty-four members were Communists, and only three were Social Democrats—Fierlinger, Laušman and E. Erban, secretary of the trade union council. The remainder were nonentities from the middle-class camp who had placed themselves at the service of the Communists.

Fierlinger's participation in the government was a logical consequence of the views he had advanced since 1942 on co-operation between the two Socialist parties, convinced from the beginning that the correct course was to lead the Social Democratic party into the Communist camp. After his rejection by his party in November, he had organized his plans to take it over. As the crisis began, he prepared to seize control. When, on 24 February, the day before the Communists took power, the party executive met to express its

---

1. For the Beneš–Gottwald correspondence, see *What Happened in Czechoslovakia?* (Prague, 1948), pp. 40–6.

2. Whether the U.S. government had ever considered intervening in Czechoslovakia is unknown. But the Truman Doctrine had indicated the possibility of intervention in countries where the Communists seized power by insurrection. This was probably the contingency that one Communist historian had in mind when he wrote: 'At the moment when the Czechoslovakian reaction attempted an internal overthrow, it was the Soviet Union which by its authority prevented any interference in internal matters in Czechoslovakia and thereby objectively helped to solve the government crisis constitutionally and without loss of blood'—Jaroslav Sedivy, 'February and the Bourgeois World', in *Příspěvky*, No. 1, 1962, quoted in Eliaš and Netik, 'Czechoslovakia', in Griffith (ed.), *Communism in Europe*, p. 203.

attitude to the situation, an armed group of the left wing broke into the party headquarters and reinstalled Fierlinger as party chairman.

Laušman's participation, on the other hand, was seen as an attempt to preserve the party independence. The Communists had always been anxious to encourage official participation of Social Democrats in the government. 'It is essential,' they had stated in their proposals for a Communist–Social Democrat government, 'that our parties . . . form a solid Socialist core to which all democratic and socialistic forces can rally.' They anticipated that 'the Czech Social Democratic party, together with ourselves, will, on a basis of co-operation between equals, take its place on the side of peace, order and the consolidation of the state'.[1]

However, Laušman very soon became aware that he had been nursing an illusion. On 9 April 1948, six weeks after the Communist seizure of power, the central committee of the Communist party, as the Communist historian Jaroslav Nedved revealed twenty years later, reached a decision to eliminate the Social Democratic party. 'After February 1948,' he wrote in explanation of this decision, 'it had gone beyond any possibility that the Communist movement . . . would tolerate the existence of a rival Socialist force.'[2]

Fierlinger, as an accomplice of the Communist plot, now held back no longer. He called a conference of those left-wing members of the central committee of the Social Democratic party who had approved the fusion with the Communist party. 'The unification of the Social Democratic party with the Communist party was decided,' Nedved recorded, 'not by a congress of the party, but by a central committee in the absence of the right-wing leaders who had been expelled.' This action, as he emphasized, was 'unquestionably a gross breach of the statutes'.[3]

In fact there was no genuine fusion between the two parties. Only local fusion committees, composed of Communists and Fierlinger's left-wing Socialists, were set up and in an impetuous campaign members of the Social Democratic party were urged to join the Communist party as individuals. Up until 31 July 1948—the date set for the termination of the campaign—no more than 22,201 Social Democrats had joined the Communist party, and by the end of the year the total was 118,104.[4] Thus, of the 371,580 members of the Social Democratic party registered on 1 January 1948, more than two thirds had refused to join the Communist party in spite of being subjected to political and economic pressure.

1. *What Happened in Czechoslovakia?*, p. 48, quoted in Zinner, *Communist Strategy and Tactics in Czechoslovakia*, p. 212.

2. Jaroslav Nedved, '*Cesta ke slouceni socialni demokracie s kommunistockou stranou v roce 1948*', in *Academica* (Prague), vol. VIII, 1968, p. 72. See also Vilem Bernard, 'Czecho-Slovakia: The Spurious Unification of the Labour Movement', in *Labour's Call*, March 1961.

3. Nedved, '*Cesta ke slouceni . . .*', in *Academica*, vol. VIII, 1968, p. 70.

4. ibid., p. 79.

Laušman, in protest against the Communist action, resigned from the government. He fled to Austria under threat of arrest in 1949. In 1953 he was kidnapped by Czech secret police agents in Salzburg, and after being detained in prison awaiting trial for four years, was sentenced to seventeen years' imprisonment on 2 September 1957; he died in mysterious circumstances in prison in 1963.

Meanwhile the National Assembly declared eighty-two of the 300 deputies to have forfeited their seats and called elections for 30 May 1948. Only joint lists of National Front candidates were permitted. The Communists won 214 of the 300 seats; the Social Democrats twenty-three. Within a few weeks of the elections, the parliamentary group of Social Democrats had been absorbed into the Communist group.

Nothing now stood in the way of the transformation of the Czechoslovak Republic into a Russian satellite state through the Stalinization of its Communist party. The process was completed in less than four years. The climax to Stalin's triumph came in 1952 with the trial of Rudolf Slánsky, the general secretary of the Communist party and the strongest man in the party after Gottwald.[1] He was arrested at the beginning of December 1951 and sentenced to death a year later as a 'Trotskyist-Titoist, Zionist, bourgeois national traitor', together with ten other top Communist leaders, including the foreign minister, Vladimir Clementis, and was hanged.[2] These trials were the high point to the 'great purge' of those party leaders whom Stalin found uncongenial.[3]

Socialism in Czechoslovakia became the tragic victim of Stalin's power policy. Conditions for its development had been more favourable in Czechoslovakia than in any other country of Eastern Europe. The working class there was numerically superior to every other class and its size and strength were developing steadily with the rapid growth of industry. The peasants, like the capitalistic middle class, were a minority. The social atmosphere was permeated with the ideas and ideals of Socialism. Socialism was, as Beneš had said, 'the pattern of life which the majority of the people wish for'.[4] Thus it was possible, while fully preserving rights to freedom, to accomplish under the conditions of democracy within three years a social revolution which had, before the Communist power seizure in February 1948, transferred into

1. Slánsky held the Order of Communist Socialism, and only six months before his arrest, on the occasion of his fiftieth birthday, he had been fêted in *Rude Pravo*, the party's central organ, as 'a devoted and fiery fighter under the flag of Lenin and Stalin' and as 'a distinguished example of a Communist revolutionary'—see Edward Taborsky, *Communism in Czechoslovakia 1948–1960* (Princeton, 1961), p. 103.

2. See *Proceedings against the Leadership of the Centre of Conspiracy Hostile to the State with Rudolf Slánsky at the Head* (Ministry of Justice, Prague, 1953), p. 8.

3. See Eliaš and Netik, 'Czechoslovakia', in Griffith (ed.), *Communism in Europe*, pp. 210–16.

4. See page 178.

public ownership 80 per cent of industry, reckoned by the numbers of workers employed.[1] In every other country of Eastern Europe in the Soviet Union's zone of power, the social revolution had taken place under the auspices of the Red Army's bayonets. In Czechoslovakia, a country evacuated by the Soviet army within six months of its liberation, the social revolution had been the fruits of a genuine national movement. In every other East European state the Communists had, before the war, represented no more than a small minority of the people; the Russian forces of occupation then installed them in positions of power which they could maintain only by imposing the system of dictatorship. In Czechoslovakia, by contrast, the Communist party had before 1939 enjoyed the status of a national movement representing about half the working class, and had after the war rallied an overwhelming majority of the workers to its support to become by far the strongest party. It did not need the power of a dictatorship to consolidate its predominant influence. Nor, under the existing ratio of class strength, was the leading role of the Communist–Social Democrat alliance in the state ever in question.

Thus Czechoslovakia could have developed a genuine Socialist society on the basis of civil rights and democracy. Such a society had, indeed, been the solemnly proclaimed goal of the Communist party. Until the founding of the Cominform in September 1947, it had striven for 'a Czechoslovak path to Socialism'—a way of peaceful transition to Socialism under conditions of democracy. Its shift to a policy aimed at seizing power had been ordered by Stalin when he decided to switch his policy *vis-à-vis* the Western powers. Stalin's concern was not with the fate of Socialism in Czechoslovakia, but with the power and security of the Soviet Union. Since he believed in the contingency of a war by the United States against the Soviet Union, he wished to secure for Russia Czechoslovakia's war potential.

The sequels to Stalin's action were disastrous. The Truman Doctrine had declared the Cold War. The Communist seizure of power in Czechoslovakia had commenced it. And it was the *coup d'état* in Prague in September 1948 which destroyed any attempt to bridge the gulf between democratic Socialism and the Communist movement.

1. See Taborsky, *Communism in Czechoslovakia*, p. 357.

8 · The Reconstitution of the Socialist International

1

The Communist *coup d'état* in Czechoslovakia unleashed panic throughout Western Europe and the United States. 'The Prague *coup d'état* had destroyed the last illusion [that peaceful co-existence with Russia was possible]. . . . The Soviet Union was about to conquer the rest of Europe'—thus ten years later Paul-Henri Spaak, the general-secretary of the North Atlantic Treaty Organization (NATO), described the mood from which the pact had stemmed.[1] The most impressive illustration of the reaction in the West to the international tension of those weeks and months appears in the much-discussed letter of the great British humanist philosopher Bertrand Russell, written on 5 May 1948, a few weeks after the *coup d'état*. In the danger, as he saw it, of the Soviet Union overrunning Western Europe, he 'urged that all nations favouring international control of atomic energy should form an alliance, and threaten Russia with war unless Russia agreed to come in and permit inspections'. In the opinion of 'professional strategists' whom he had consulted, 'at present neither air power nor atomic power could prevent Russia overrunning all West Europe up to the Straits of Dover'. Europeans, he wrote, were 'more vividly conscious than Americans of that danger'. For, he continued,

> If Russia overruns West Europe, the destruction will be such as no subsequent reconquest can undo. Practically the whole educated population will be sent to labour camps in Siberia or on the shores of the White Sea, where most will die of hardships and the survivors will be turned into animals (see what happened to the Polish intellectuals). . . . Unless West Europe can be preserved from invasion, it will be lost to civilization for centuries.

He was aware that, in such a war, 'the Russians, even without atomic

1. Quoted in Paul E. Zinner, *Communist Strategy and Tactics in Czechoslovakia 1918–1948* (London, 1963), p. vi.

bombs, will be able to destroy all the big towns in England . . .'. Yet, 'even at such a price I think war would be worthwhile'.[1]

But the reaction of the United States government was an even graver matter, since any decision for war or for peace depended upon its evaluation of the danger. General Lucius Clay, military governor of the American Zone in Germany, had tried for months to convince Washington that fears of an imminent Russian war of aggression were without basis and that an armed conflict with the Soviet Union 'appeared improbable for at least ten years'. But a week after the *coup d'état*, on 5 March, he cabled Washington that a change in the Soviet attitude had become clear, 'which makes me feel that it could develop with dramatic speed'.[2] The war panic in Washington became so acute that, to quieten it down, the Central Intelligence Agency (C.I.A.), the intelligence arm of the United States government, reported to President Truman on 16 March that, the way they saw it, an outbreak of hostility was at least 'not likely within sixty days'.[3]

The foundation of the Cominform was looked upon in the West as an act to resurrect the concept of Communist world revolution. Before the war, the Soviet Union had been seen as a power watching for, encouraging and working for such a revolution, and for this reason Stalin had dissolved the Communist International during the war in an attempt to obliterate this image.[4] Now, in founding the Cominform, he had once again raised its spectre. The general strikes unleashed by the Communists in France and Italy in the autumn of 1947, following hard on the founding of the Cominform, helped to confirm the West's belief that the Soviet Union had returned to its policy of pursuing the world revolution, and that the analysis of the world situation put forward at the Cominform conference[5] reflected Russia's

1. For the text of the letter, see *Saturday Review*, 16 October 1954. For the history of the letter, see *The Autobiography of Bertrand Russell* vol. III: *1944–1967* (London, 1969), p. 18. On the mood in France, Alexander Werth reported from his own experience: 'It must be said that during the years 1948–49 the French non-Communist left had been forcefully anti-Communistic. . . . The political strikes towards the end of 1947 were very unpopular. . . . It also seemed as if Russia had taken up the position through the Cominform, that the war is more or less unavoidable and the liquidation of the Beneš régime in Czechoslovakia was considered as a strengthening of this attitude. Czechoslovakia appeared until then as a life symbol of the adjustment [of conflicts] between the East and West and the east-west co-existence within one country; it had now been ruthlessly destroyed. . . .' —*France 1940–1955*, p. 409. In her autobiography, Simone de Beauvoir described how the *coup d'état* in Prague, like the establishment of the Cominform before it, intensified the mood of anti-Communism among French intellectuals and generated a general war psychosis. 'There was much talk of [the possibility of] a Russian invasion'—*Force of Circumstances* (London, 1965), p. 146.
2. Quoted in Walter Millis (ed.), *The Forrestal Diaries* (New York, 1951), p. 387.
3. ibid., p. 395.
4. For the dissolution of the Communist International, see Braunthal, *History of the International, 1914–1943*, pp. 528–9.
5. See Appendix Seven.

view that a war between the 'imperialist' and 'anti-imperialist' camps—or between the Western powers and Russia—appeared inevitable.

The Russian *coup d'état* in Czechoslovakia seemed to the West to herald the opening of a Russian offensive intended to carry the Communist revolution across Europe with the Soviet army as its spearhead. Certainly the Soviet Union possessed the forces to overrun Europe to the Atlantic coast, for while the United States and Britain had demobilized their armies, leaving only token troop units on the Continent, 180 Russian divisions stood ready in the East to march into what was militarily speaking practically a vacuum.

In a speech in the House of Commons on 22 January 1948, a month before the Prague overthrow, Ernest Bevin, foreign secretary in the British Labour government, deeply disturbed by the Communist-led strikes in France and Italy,[1] had called upon the countries of Western Europe—France, Belgium, Holland and Luxembourg—to join with Britain in a defence alliance—the 'Western Union'. The Prague *coup* hastened the realization of this plan; it was ratified on 17 March by the signing of the Treaty of Brussels. On the same day, President Truman welcomed the conclusion of the Treaty before a combined meeting of both Houses of Congress, declaring, 'That the decision of the free countries of Europe to defend themselves will find a comparable determination [in the United States] to help in their defence.'[2] Two weeks later, on 31 March, Congress voted $6,000 million in foreign aid, mainly to arm the western states of Europe.

The fever of rearmament even gripped the Scandinavian countries. 'The *coup d'état* in Czechoslovakia,' Tage Erlander, Sweden's Socialist prime minister, declared in a speech of 1 May 1948, 'was a test not only for Prague, but also for Stockholm.'[3] He withdrew a proposed law intended to decrease the armament budget and asked Parliament instead to approve a 50 per cent increase to the air force with a doubling of air-force personnel. Similarly, Norway's Socialist government and the Socialist coalition in Denmark hurried to rearm.

A few weeks after the Prague *coup* an event occurred which had the effect of intensifying the international anxiety psychosis—the Russian blockade of Berlin. When General Clay announced a currency reform for the three Western Zones of Berlin on 30 March, Marshal Vassily Sokolovsky, commander-in-chief of the Soviet occupation forces, first barred the access roads traversing the Russian Zone surrounding Berlin and then, on 23 June, announced a total blockade of the city.[4] Now it seemed as if the world faced an

1. See pp. 42–3.
2. Quoted in George F. Kennan, *Memoirs 1925–1950* (London, 1967), p. 401.
3. Quoted in Howard K. Smith, *The State of Europe* (New York, 1949), p. 185.
4. The blockade of the two million Berliners lasted from 23 June 1948 until 12 May 1949. For a detailed description of the confrontation, see Boris Meissner, *Russland, die Westmächte und Deutschland* (Hamburg, 1953), pp. 158–81.

immediate outbreak of war and that Stalin had invoked the blockade to provoke war and overrun Western Europe.

Yet Stalin's attempts during the blockade to ensure a peaceful conclusion lent weight to the interpretation that, in reality, nothing was further from his mind than the plan of 'overrunning' Western Europe, and finally he lifted the blockade without any concessions having been made. In his memoirs General Clay recollected that, 'The care with which the Russians avoided anything that might have provoked resistance by force convinced me that the Soviet Union had no wish for a war, even though it believed that the Western Allies would rather surrender an essential point in their position than risk war as an alternative.'[1]

To damp down the war scare in the United States, Stalin told Kingsbury Smith, director-general of the U.P.I. press agency, in an interview on 27 January 1949 that he was prepared in conjunction with the United States to issue a declaration 'to confirm that neither government had any intention of venturing into a war against the other'.[2] And a few days before, on 21 January, *Pravda* had quoted from an open letter from Stalin to a prospective presidential candidate, Henry A. Wallace: 'Despite the differences in the economic systems and ideologies of the U.S.S.R. and the U.S.A., the co-existence of these systems and the peaceable removal of differences of opinion between them is not only possible, but absolutely necessary in the interests of general peace.'[3]

But Stalin's protestations of innocence had been spoken to the wind. The U.S. government, as well as the people of the United States and Western Europe, were obsessed by a fear of Russia and with the possibility of the Soviet Union starting to move its million-strong army to establish a Communist reign over Western Europe. On 22 January 1949, President Truman laid before both Houses of Congress the draft treaty for a pact to cover the 'collective security of the North Atlantic area'; it was signed on 4 April by twelve countries. By the pact the partners in the North Atlantic Treaty Organization (NATO) pledged themselves 'to consider an armed attack against any one or more [treaty powers] in Europe or North America to be an attack against them all'. The publicity for NATO declared it to be a bastion to protect the 'free peoples of Europe' against the threat of Communism.[4] 'The pact,' declared Belgium's Socialist prime minister, Paul-Henri

---

1. Lucius Clay, *Decision in Germany* (London, 1950), p. 174.
2. For the text of the interview, see Meissner, *Russland, die Westmächte und Deutschland*, p. 180.
3. Quoted in ibid.
4. It must, however, be remembered that, among the twelve governments who had signed the pact, pledging themselves to the collective defence of the 'free peoples' against attack by Communist Russia, were, apart from the United States, Canada and the five countries of Western Europe with Denmark and Norway, three countries in which any popular freedom movements were instantly suppressed—Portugal, Greece and Turkey.

Spaak, 'is a shield, but not a sword . . . a pact of defence aimed at no one.'[1]

The Soviet Union, however, saw the pact as the 'weapon of an aggressive Anglo-American bloc in Europe . . . whose objective was the setting up of Anglo-American world rule'.[2] 'The North Atlantic Treaty,' a note from the Soviet government to the signatory powers stated, 'has nothing to do with the self-defence of the participant states, which are threatened by nobody and whom nobody intends to attack. On the contrary, the pact has an obvious aggressive character and is aimed against the U.S.S.R., a fact not even concealed in public declarations by the official representatives of the participant states.'[3]

The pact's consequences were disastrous. It sealed the split of Germany, of Europe and the world. It represented the ultimate link in a chain of illusions and misinterpretations. The Yalta Declaration, which had envisaged the setting up of democratic governments in Poland and the Russian border states, rested on misapprehensions that the Soviet Union's demand for governments friendly to the Soviet Union in these countries could be fulfilled under a democratic system. But an overwhelming majority of the people of Poland and Romania was far from being 'Soviet-friendly', hating Russia with an enmity rooted in their historical tradition, while the Russian annexation of large areas of these countries, sanctioned at Potsdam by the Western Allies, was bound to deepen and perpetuate their resentment. Little support for a 'Soviet-friendly government' could therefore be expected from the democratic elements in these countries. So the Soviet Union had, not unexpectedly, subjected the countries under their administration to a Communist predominance, for only by placing Communists in power could Russia ensure the governments it wished for.[4]

---

1. Quoted in D. F. Fleming, *The Cold War and its Origins 1917–1960* (London, 1961), vol. I, p. 616.

2. *Soviet Press Translation*, July 1949, p. 401, quoted in Fleming, *The Cold War and its Origins*, vol. I, p. 515.

3. Quoted in Meissner, *Russland, die Westmächte und Deutschland*, p. 183. The protest of the French Communists was particularly outspoken. The executive committee of the C.G.T. issued a 'solemn declaration' announcing that the French working class would never feel 'itself bound' by the government's signing of the North Atlantic pact—*Le Peuple*, 17 May 1949. And Thorez declared that the French people would welcome the Soviet army if it were to occupy Paris in the lawful 'pursuance of an attack'—*L'Humanité*, 23 February 1949, quoted in Val R. Lorwin, *The French Labor Movement* (Cambridge, Mass., 1954), p. 283.

4. Finland was the one Russian border state which, even though it came within the Soviet sphere of influence and could have been transformed into a Russian satellite state, remained free of Communist party rule. The Communist party, which operated an electoral front organization called the 'Finnish People's Democratic League' (S.K.D.L.), had emerged from the March 1945 election as the strongest party with fifty-one out of 200 seats (the Social Democrats gaining fifty seats). In 1946 the S.K.D.L. leader Mauno Pekkala succeeded Juho Kusti Paasikivi as prime minister, and it seemed that the danger of a Communist takeover was imminent. In February 1948, a week after the Communist

Yet the actions undertaken by the Soviet Union out of concern for its security to prevent the growth of hostile states along its borders were interpreted by the United States as a stage in a policy of spreading its sphere of influence across the whole of Europe right up to the Atlantic coast. The Truman Doctrine was a reply to the Stalinization of the Russian border states.

The Truman Doctrine was basically intended to contain Russia's desire for expansion: it was a warning directed at the Soviet government: 'Thus far, and no further'. But it had the very opposite effect. The Soviet Union saw in it an advance warning of a war of aggression planned by the United States, and so countered by establishing the Cominform to enable Moscow to regain control over the world Communist movement and by incorporating Hungary and Czechoslovakia into the Russian orbit, to strengthen its war potential and advance its outposts in the event of war. The Prague *coup*, however, hardened fears and attitudes in the West, which replied with the North Atlantic Treaty.

2

The Communist *coup* in Prague set a term to the history of endeavours to reach an understanding between the international Socialist labour movement and the Communist movement. Until Prague the International Socialist Conference had, as it stated at its London meeting on 20 March 1948, worked for 'a fraternal relationship' with all Socialist parties in general, but in particular with the Socialist parties in the countries of Eastern Europe, for in each of these countries the Socialist parties were coalition partners in predominantly Communist régimes. As members of the International Socialist Conference—the only common platform for Socialists in the East and West—they formed at the same time a bridge of understanding across the gulf which had opened between East and West. Because of the particularly difficult position of its Eastern European member parties, the International Socialist Conference had hesitated to revive the Socialist International in all its

---

coup in Czechoslovakia, the Finnish government received a note from Moscow calling for the signing of a mutual aid treaty. Street riots followed. Finland seemed on the verge of incorporation into the Communist bloc. But suddenly the crisis was overcome. The Finnish army took steps to curb the disturbances. In Moscow, Stalin acceded to President Paasikivi's terms for the friendship treaty, by which Finland preserved her independence and neutrality. This Soviet-Finnish treaty of mutual assistance, signed on 6 April 1948, pledged Finland to come to the defence of the Soviet Union should it be attacked through Finland— but even then only on Finnish territory. In the elections of July 1948, the Communists lost thirteen of their seats and the Social Democratic party formed a minority government under the leadership of Karl August Fagerholm, which was subsequently transformed into a coalition government with the Agrarians and which lasted until 1959. The Social Democrats were then excluded from government for almost a decade, until the elections of 1966, from which they emerged with fifty-five out of 200 seats as Finland's largest party in the Diet. Under Rafael Paasio's leadership they formed a 'grand coalition' government in which Communists were represented again for the first time since 1948.

aspects,[1] and had refrained from any criticism of Russia's terrorist policies in the countries it occupied. The conference had even kept silent on the declaration of war against Social Democracy made at the founding conference of the Cominform.[2]

But this declaration of war was shortly followed by hostile acts in the form of a 'co-ordinated action by the Soviet Union and the Cominform', as the conference resolution ascertained: the enforced merger by terror of all Social Democratic with Communist parties in those countries under the power of the Soviet government, and finally by the *coup* in Prague. Now Moscow had completed its alienation from the parties of democratic Socialism. The International Socialist Conference could no longer remain silent. 'The Communist parties have been ordered to destroy democratic Socialism,' it declared. The International Socialist Conference now faced 'the problem of defending democracy'.

First the resolution defined the dividing-line between the parties of democratic Socialism and of Communism. It stated that the parties in Romania, Bulgaria and Hungary, which had agreed to merge with the Communists, had by this action excluded themselves from the community of the International Socialist Conference. From the Czechoslovak Socialist party, which had supported the *coup d'état*, it withdrew recognition as a representative of Socialism. It appealed to the Polish Socialist party to withstand fusion with the Communist party 'as long as it was able', and to demonstrate through its attitudes 'its belief in the active solidarity of international Socialism'.

This was the first occasion since the end of the war that the International of democratic Socialism had come into the open to challenge the Communist movement. The illusion that any understanding might be reached with Moscow on co-operation with the Communists had finally been destroyed. The resolutions of the International Socialist Conference in London, in March 1948, confirmed the renewal of the schism. Responsibility for the split, the conference had declared, 'lies alone with the Cominform, whose

1. See page 137.
2. The International Socialist Conference in Antwerp, meeting at the end of November 1947, two months after the founding of the Cominform, was the last conference at which the Socialist parties of Eastern Europe (Poland, Hungary and Czechoslovakia) were represented. To avoid breaking with them, the conference refrained from condemning the Cominform, which had called for a struggle against the 'reactionary right wing of the Social Democratic leadership in the West'. It passed a resolution against the attacks on Social Democracy, but without mentioning the Cominform or the Communists. It declared its solidarity with 'the people's struggle to defend democracy, being kept alive at a cost of so heavy a sacrifice and destruction', but without pointing directly at the Communists who endangered it. Harold Laski did, however, indicate the danger in the debate. 'In France,' he said, 'democracy is threatened by the strategy, tactics and manoeuvres of the Communist party. It is as much in danger from the Communist camp as from the camp of de Gaulle.' The most detailed description of the conference discussions may be found in a report by Madhu Limaye of India's Socialist party, who took part; see Socialist Party of India: Report of the Nasik Conference (Bombay, 1948), pp. 122–38.

policy has been guided exclusively by its interests in serving the Soviet Union'.[1]

The defence of democracy against attempts at its destruction by the Soviet Union had now become a central policy for the Socialist International. Two months after the London meeting, there was another conference in Vienna on 4 June 1948 to formulate its attitude towards the 'people's democracies', as the Communist governments in Eastern Europe, the Balkans, Hungary and Czechoslovakia were now described.

These 'people's democracies', the conference resolution stated, were in reality 'dictatorships'. 'They are governments which deny by political means the fundamental rights of the citizen and which seek the economic replacement of private enterprise by state capitalism. They betray democracy as well as the Socialism which they claim to represent. . . .' And, in exceptionally solemn words, the resolution declared: 'The parties represented at this conference are determined to stand together in their struggle to preserve and extend political democracy.'

The resolution next formulated the concrete guarantees necessary for the personal rights to freedom—in fact, putting them down in black and white for the first time in the International's history, for from its foundation it had regarded the personal rights to freedom, as the French Revolution of 1789 had proclaimed them in the declaration of the human rights as obvious basic tenets of Socialism which required no further specific definition. It had protested against the suppression of these rights by the Communist dictatorship in Russia, but had never explicitly codified the principles in a document. In Russia itself, rights to freedom remained suppressed in the name of 'the dictatorship of the proletariat'; and now in those countries under the Soviet Union's subjection they were suppressed by the system of a 'people's democracy', which camouflaged a dictatorship by the Communist party within a one-party state. The Conference therefore considered it appropriate to restate the principles of political democracy. It declared in its resolution:

The parties represented at this conference are opposed to the one-party state and all systems of government based upon it.

They are of the opinion that a system of political democracy must combine in itself a recognition of the pre-eminence of the individual which is to be guaranteed by the following freedoms:

Freedom of thought, opinion and speech; security in law and protection against interference by other individuals; . . . equality before the law and protection against political tampering with the machinery of justice; unimpeded freedom and guarantees of rights in elections; the right to an opposition; the political and lawful equality of all citizens, irrespective of class, race or sex.

The decision by the International Socialist Conference to oppose the

---

1. The circular, with the text of the resolution, can be found in the archives of the Socialist International; it is dated 20 March 1948, but is unnumbered.

Cominform in a clearly defined battle front did, however, encounter resistance from Nenni's *Partito Socialista Italiano*. This was one of the largest member parties of the International, having emerged from the June 1946 elections with 4,760,000 votes as the second strongest party in Italy. As we saw earlier, it had in the spring of 1944 entered into open struggle against Fascism after two decades of underground activity. Then, in August 1944, it had concluded the 'pact of alliance' with the Communist party which had been renewed in November 1946 in the face of protests from Saragat's anti-Communist wing. The party had split on the whole question in 1947.[1]

Before the Prague *coup* the Socialist International Conference had made no criticism of the pact between the P.S.I. and the Communists, even though the formation of the Cominform as an active opponent to Social Democracy had raised the whole question of whether a Social Democratic party *could* maintain an alliance with Communists. But the conference had, as we have already seen, decided to enter into open conflict with the Cominform only after the Prague *coup*; and at its London conference in March 1948 it appealed to the Italian Socialists 'to demonstrate by their attitudes how, faced with a choice between subjection by the Cominform and free Socialist co-operation in the reconstruction of Europe, they had chosen the Socialist path'. Yet upon the resolution being read out, the Italian delegates left the conference in protest. The P.S.I. executive drafted a memorandum to the conference rejecting its interference in the internal policies of the party and stating that it had no intention of dissolving the alliance with the Communists, which remained necessary to combat the forces of reaction in Italy.

When the conference met in Vienna, in June 1948, it suspended the P.S.I. and accused its leaders of having 'preferred, even after the Cominform had declared open war against international Social Democracy, and even after democracy in Czechoslovakia had fallen victim to totalitarian tyranny, rather to forfeit the sympathies of their foreign brethren than to break off relations with international Communism'.

The P.S.I. executive reacted with an open letter to the conference, in which they again justified their alliance with the Communists as an indispensable instrument for united action by the forces of democracy in Italy against the alliance between Italian and foreign capitalism and the Vatican, which aimed at setting up a conservative–clerical Italy.[2]

1. See pp. 60–65.
2. For the text of the open letter, see *Avanti!*, 18 July 1948. The Catholic hierarchy had, in fact, already made clear its position in its opposition to Socialism and Communism. Pope Pius XII had made a speech on 1 June 1946, the day before the plebiscite to select the form of government in Italy, to agitate in favour of monarchy; in July 1949 he excommunicated all Marxists. Cardinals and bishops instructed priests to refuse the sacrament to Catholics who, in the April 1948 election, voted for the Socialist-Communist unity list. 'Never in the history of unified Italy had the Catholic Church been so powerful and influential as in the two decades following the end of the war'—see Norman Kogan, *A Political History of Postwar Italy* (New York, 1966), pp. 37, 51–2, 53, 124–5 and 217.

The International Socialist Conference at their meeting in Clacton-on-Sea early in December 1948 now addressed a 'final appeal' to the P.S.I. Unless they had by 10 March 1949 declared their willingness to be reunited with the Social Democrats on terms 'acceptable' to the Socialist International, they would be excluded from membership of the conference. The P.S.I. should understand, Morgan Phillips, executive chairman of the International Socialist Conference, said in an open letter to the P.S.I. executive, that democratic Socialism was 'incompatible' with totalitarian Communism. 'The offensive against international Socialism begun by the Cominform,' he continued, 'excludes any common ground between a democratic Socialist party and a party which continues at every level to liaise with a Communist party.'

The P.S.I. executive, however, persisted in their view that the political fight in Italy was not between Communists and anti-Communists, but between a conservative–clerical reaction which stood in opposition to the working classes. 'The united action pact,' they said, 'despite its unpleasantness and danger, keeps the solidarity of the workers alive—a solidarity without which it would be impossible to defend democracy.'[1]

As a consequence the International Socialist Conference, at its meeting in Baarn, Holland, in the middle of May 1949, expelled the P.S.I. for having 'refused to dissolve the pact with the Communists'.[2] The P.S.I. did not return to the Socialist International until almost two decades later when it reunited itself with the *Partito Socialista dei Lavoratori Italiani* at a mass meeting in Rome on 30 October 1966.[3]

Meanwhile leading Socialists who had fled from the Soviet-dominated countries of Eastern Europe had organized émigré groups and founded, in

1. For the text of the two letters, see COMISCO, Circular No. 11/49.
2. See COMISCO, Circular No. 27/49. In 1956, after Khrushchev's disclosures of Stalin's crimes at the Twentieth Congress of the Russian Communist party, Nenni had placed responsibility for the degeneration of Communism on the system of the Communist dictatorship. After the crushing of the revolution in Hungary in October 1956 by the Soviet army, which he strongly condemned, Nenni handed back the Stalin Peace Prize awarded to him several years earlier. The pact with the Communists had, in fact, been ineffective since the early 1950s and had in reality, if not officially, become meaningless. The party congress in February 1957 condemned the Communist dictatorship in a resolution which Nenni sponsored and which laid down that democracy and freedom were questions equal in importance to the nationalization of the means of production, and that democracy founded on a plurality of parties was not only a means to an end, but an end in itself. But in October 1958 the majority of the party's central committee voted against Nenni's resolution to dissolve the pact, and so he resigned the general secretaryship. He did, however, win a majority vote from the party congress on 19 January 1959; the pact was formally dissolved and Nenni re-elected as general secretary. The left wing of the party eventually separated itself from the party in January 1964 over the question of participation in government; it formed the *Partito Socialista Italiano di Unità Proletaria* (P.S.I.U.P.). See Kogan, *A Political History of Postwar Italy*, pp. 101, 103, 137–8 and 198.
3. In August 1956 Nenni had proposed the reunification of the two Socialist parties during a discussion with Saragat in Pralogna; as Nenni intimated, Saragat was then not yet ready for it.

Paris, a *Bureau International Socialiste* (B.I.S.). But the parties in exile were themselves divided into two hostile camps: of Socialists who had opposed participation in Communist-dominated coalition governments and those who had approved of them. It was a conflict which was to reduce the B.I.S. to impotence.

Until that point the parties in exile had not been invited to attend the International Socialist Conferences in accordance with a decision taken by the Clacton conference of 1946[1] upon the insistence of the Socialist parties in Eastern Europe which had refused to recognize émigré groups that had split away over the question of co-operation with the Communists. But now these Socialist parties themselves had been dissolved during the process of merging with the Communist parties. The parties in exile had therefore in fact come to represent the Socialist oppositions of their respective countries. The recognition of their right to representation in the International Socialist Conference could no longer be withheld. The Clacton conference which met at the beginning of 1948 proposed that a centre be set up for the splinter groups of Socialists in exile and that their parties be incorporated into the International as advisory members. The International Socialist Conference (the resolution stated) 'refuses to recognize as permanent the division of Europe into a free region and an enslaved region. It considers that the East European Socialist parties will some day recover their right to full organization and activity. In this belief the International Socialist Conference calls on the Socialist parties of Poland, Czechoslovakia, Hungary, Bulgaria and Yugoslavia to set up a common centre in exile to meet under its auspices.'[2]

The centre was founded at a conference of parties in exile in London in July 1949. It adopted the title Socialist Union of Central-Eastern Europe and elected as chairman Zygmunt Zaremba, with Vilem Bernard as secretary. The member parties of the Socialist Union were now recognized as consultative members of the International Socialist Conference.[3]

The depths of conflict existing between Social Democracy and the Soviet Union which came to a head over the Prague *coup* explain their attitude to

1. See page 138.

2. See Julius Braunthal (ed.), *Yearbook of the International Socialist Labour Movement 1956–1957* (London, 1956), pp. 92–3.

3. See COMISCO, Circular No. 38/49. The founding members of the Socialist Union were the exiled Socialist parties of Bulgaria, Poland, Czechoslovakia, Hungary and Yugoslavia; soon afterwards those of Estonia, Lithuania, Romania and the Ukraine also joined. The decision to incorporate these parties into the International apparently caused the Cominform great alarm. Its press release stated that the Clacton conference did in fact nothing less 'behind closed doors' than 'to lay plans for the organization of a widespread net of espionage and terror against the democratic régimes of Eastern Europe'. This organization 'under the leadership of the British Labour party and the right wing of European Social Democrats', it reported, 'would co-ordinate the action of the reactionary "socialist" emigrants from Eastern Europe with the already existing espionage system organized by the German Social Democrats in the closest co-operation with the British and

the Brussels Treaty of March 1948 and, a year later, to the North Atlantic Treaty.

It must be remembered that the Treaty of Brussels had been proposed by the British Labour government and that seven of the twelve governments which signed the North Atlantic Treaty had been directly Socialist governments or coalition governments in which Social Democrats played a prominent role.[1] If the Western Union founded by the Treaty of Brussels already appeared as a thinly disguised military defence alliance ranged against Russia, the North Atlantic Treaty left no further doubt about its character of a defensive alliance between Western Europe and the United States—a pact of collective security against the eventuality of a Russian attack.

The Soviet Union had emerged from the war immensely strengthened, while Western Europe had become a military and defensive vacuum. The Prague *coup* had thrown further doubts on the practicality of containing solely by diplomatic means Russia's expansionist drive, already made manifest by the incorporation of Poland and the Russian border states into her sphere. It seemed essential to balance the might of the East with a corresponding war potential in the West; but a parity of military potential could only be achieved through an alliance of the countries of Western Europe with the United States. This was the problem which faced the Socialists of Western Europe, who now took a heavy share of responsibility within Western European governments and whose decisions had given rise to the North Atlantic Treaty.

Yet the very idea that Social Democracy might approve an alliance with the capitalist United States against the Soviet Union had been unthinkable before the Prague *coup d'état*. Despite their fundamental differences with the system of Communist dictatorship, the Social Democratic parties regarded the Soviet Union as the world's leading revolutionary power—the first and only state which had genuinely abolished capitalism and had established conditions for the development of a Socialist society. In 1923 the inaugural congress of the Labour and Socialist International had declared that it 'considers it the duty of workers throughout the world to throw their full weight into the struggle against attempts of the imperialist powers to intervene in the internal affairs of Russia'. And whenever Russia was threatened by an intervention by the imperialist powers, it had urged the working classes to resist such designs, calling on them in resolution after resolution 'to fight the policies of aggression aimed against the Soviet Union'.[2] This was an

American espionage machine in Europe . . .'—*Daily Worker* (New York), 19 December 1948; this article also appeared in a number of Communist papers in Eastern Europe. For the text, see also COMISCO, Circular No. 3/49.

1. See page 184.
2. For the attitude of the Socialist International to the question of intervention by capitalist governments in Russia, see Braunthal, *History of the International, 1914–1943*, pp. 268–70 and 338–40.

attitude rooted not only in the natural solidarity which linked the European with the Russian working class, but also in the conviction that the overthrow of the revolutionary régime in Russia through a war by the imperialist–capitalist powers would usher in an age of counter-revolution that could set back the international Socialist movement for decades.

Yet in the meantime the Soviet Union had itself become an imperialist power; it had annexed the countries of Eastern Europe or subjected them to an imperialist type of domination. It had become a super-power in its own right—the most powerful state in the world after the United States. It no longer appeared, as it had in the pre-war period, to be vulnerable to the old capitalist–imperialist governments but, since the Prague *coup*, to have become a positive threat to the independence of the peoples of Western Europe.

This, at all events, was the image of itself which Russia displayed to the world after 1945. It was enough to explain the fundamental change in attitude of European Social Democracy towards the Soviet Union, as shown by its support for the North Atlantic Treaty.[1]

3

The renewed outbreak of open hostility between Social Democracy and the Cominform once more threw up the whole question of the reconstruction of the International. It had already in effect been reborn under the title 'International Socialist Conference' in May 1946: first as a loose union, to be consolidated a year later by the setting up of its permanent executive, COMISCO; and secondly by the election of an official secretary in December 1949. As a forum for exchanging opinion between Socialist parties and as an organization to co-ordinate common policies it was in any case already essentially fulfilling the function of an International. But the International Socialist Conference did not possess that moral authority which had, as it were, been inborn in the historic International.

1. While the International Socialist Conference did support the treaty's principle of collective security, it refrained from placing the treaty itself on the agenda, since the Swedish and Swiss Socialist parties supported their own countries' neutrality and thus the unanimous approval needed for a resolution in favour of the treaty would not have been forthcoming. The Swedish Social Democratic party's congress of May 1948 unanimously approved the declaration of Sweden's Socialist foreign secretary Oesten Unden: 'We not only reject any alliance with Western or Eastern power-blocs, but also any indirect alliance with a Great Power, which could lead to involvement in a future conflict.' A congress resolution of the Swiss Social Democratic party in April 1948 declared: 'The party categorically defends Switzerland's neutrality as the basis of its foreign policy and pursues a policy of independence from any bloc, irrespective of whether it is of the Eastern or Western powers.' In Italy, not only did the Socialist Party under Nenni declare against the Atlantic Treaty but also did a majority in the executive of Saragat's party, as its general secretary, Ugo Mondolfe, informed the International Socialist Conference in a circular of 25 June 1948. See COMISCO, *Italy* File, in the Archives of the Socialist International, in the International Institute for Social History in Amsterdam.

Its revival was requested by a majority of parties, though as we have seen,[1] it met with initial resistance from the Socialist parties of Eastern Europe, which had co-operated with the Communists in coalition governments. The dissolution of these parties after the founding of the Cominform had, however, removed this particular obstacle.

But still doubts expressed by several parties—above all by the British Labour party and the Scandinavian parties—concerning the possible infringement of their autonomy by decisions of the International delayed its reconstitution. Decisions taken by the Second International had not been mandatory, though they had been morally binding upon its member-parties. But its successor—the Labour and Socialist International founded in 1923—though it left untouched the parties' autonomy concerning their own internal policies, had made decisions on foreign policy binding in Article 3 of its statutes; it stated:

The Labour and Socialist International can be a living reality only in so far as its decisions on all international questions are binding on all its members. Every decision of the international organization thus represents a voluntarily accepted limitation of the autonomy of the parties in the individual countries.[2]

Yet that rule necessarily remained ineffective whenever it involved passionately contended matters as, for example, the question of joint action with the Communist International during the years 1936–8; a majority decision for a United Front would at that stage have broken the International asunder.[3] In practice the Labour and Socialist International—like the International Socialist Conference—could only take decisions in agreement with all its member parties. Article 3 was never in any case invoked during the course of its history.

In the event, the impetus to reconstitute the International came from the Belgian Labour party, which proposed it at a congress in December 1950. Their resolution in no way sought to change the workings or structure of the International Socialist Conference, as Victor Larock, a member of the Belgian party's executive committee, stressed in an open letter to Morgan Phillips, then secretary of the British Labour party; what it asked for was simply to restore the historical name to the international organization of the working class, for 'the profoundest and most strong inspirations were associated with the name Socialist International which crystallized its international solidarity'.[4]

The British Labour party executive, to which the Belgian party had appealed, accepted the Belgian motion on condition that the autonomy

1. See page 137.
2. See Braunthal, *History of the International, 1914–1943*, p. 266.
3. *ibid.*, pp. 391–3.
4. *Le Peuple* (Brussels), 5 January 1951; *Le Populaire* (Paris), 5 January 1951; *Socialist International Information* (*S.I.I.*), vol. I, No. 2.

of individual parties would remain untouched. The Belgian and British parties then together submitted to the International Socialist Conference in London, in March 1951, the following resolution, which was accepted unanimously:

For nearly five years the International Socialist Conference has organized co-operation between the democratic Socialist parties of the world. Its members are a major force in the affairs of their countries and the world.

The International Socialist Conference has proved the value to Socialists of regular consultations on common problems. There is now general agreement that the best method of co-operation between Socialist parties is pursued in the International Socialist Conference.

Socialist co-operation must be based on consent. The resolutions passed by an international Socialist body must reflect agreement freely reached. They cannot constitute a binding command on parties which are individually responsible to their own members and to a national electorate. An international Socialist body cannot claim mandatory power.

The achievements of the International Socialist Conference justify it in assuming the moral authority of the Socialist International. No change is required in the principle of co-operation by consent whose virtue has now been proved to the satisfaction of all parties.

The resolution moved that the formal foundation of the Socialist International be placed on the agenda for the forthcoming full meeting of the International Socialist Conference.[1]

4

The congress called for the reconstitution of the Socialist International assembled on 30 June 1951 in the Congress Hall at Frankfurt-am-Main. The choice of a German city to be witness to the rebirth of the International was deliberately symbolic. A great majority of the delegates gathering in Frankfurt were from countries which the German armies had invaded and occupied, and from which many thousands of human beings had been deported to be incarcerated or murdered. Only six years had gone by since the end of the Nazi reign of terror. They had not been forgotten. But not forgotten also were the innumerable German Socialists who had fallen in resisting Hitler's barbaric régime. The choice of a German city was meant to demonstrate the solidarity of the Socialists of all countries with the German Social Democrats. The feeling of solidarity manifested itself in the election of Kurt Schumacher as president of the congress on a proposal by Guy Mollet, general secretary of the French Socialist party, who had been one of the French resistance leaders against the German forces of occupation. The choice, he said, was a token of 'deep gratitude to a man who had pledged his

1. COMISCO, Circular No. 71/51.

life to defend democratic Socialism'. Erich Ollenhauer was elected deputy president.[1]

The congress was attended by 106 delegates, representing thirty-four individual parties with 9,783,000 members altogether, and the aggregate votes of 43,534,000 electors. The International actually encompassed all Socialist parties from countries in Europe which were not subjected to Communist or Fascist dictatorships, as well as the Socialist parties of the Argentine, India, Japan, Canada, Malta, Uruguay, and the United States of America and finally the International Union of Socialist Youth with 466,000 members.[2]

The first act of the congress was formally to re-establish the International by passing the following resolutions: The International Socialist Conference, assembled in Frankfurt-am-Main on 30 June 1951 for its eighth meeting:

in consideration that the International Socialist Conference has attained by its activity the moral authority of the Socialist International,
grants hereby the proposals of the committee of the International Socialist Conference (COMISCO), agreed at its London Conference, 2–4 March 1951,

- (a) that the International Socialist Conference change its name to 'The Socialist International';
- (b) that the committee of the International Socialist Conference (COMISCO) change its title to 'General Council of the Socialist International';
- (c) that the sub-committee of COMISCO change its title to 'Bureau of the Socialist International'.

In accordance with this decision, the conference here assembled is to be entered in the minutes as the First Congress of the Socialist International.[3]

Victor Larock, who seconded the resolution, emphasized in his speech the principle of the parties' freedom in their choice of tactics adapted to their individual situation—a principle which had to remain inviolate. 'What matters,' he added, 'is the will to act in common in Europe and throughout the world, the determination to stand together and to leave behind all purely national considerations. . . .' It aroused, he said, 'a tremendous hope in the hearts of millions of workers. Now it has been reborn at the moment when it may well play a decisive role in the political and social history of the peoples. It is up to all Socialist parties, to every one of their leaders and members, not to disappoint the new hope generated by the Socialist International.' And he concluded with a warning derived from the experience of the Second International. This, he said, had had 'a deep influence over the masses and events

1. See Report of the First Congress of the Socialist International held at Frankfurt/ Main, 30 June–3 July 1951, Circular No. 100/51, p. 8, subsequently referred to as Report (Frankfurt). The minutes of the congresses of the Socialist International never appeared in print; they were circulated to member parties and delegates. A collection of the minutes may be found in the archives of the Socialist International in the International Institute for Social History, Amsterdam.
2. For a list of the parties and their strength, see report of the secretariat, Circular No. 71/51.
3. See Report (Frankfurt), p. 104.

so long as its responsible leaders put the Socialist cause above all considerations of mere expediency or purely national interest'.[1]

The act of reconstituting the Socialist International by the formal adoption of the resolution was, as the minutes recorded, received by the Congress with enthusiasm. While the chairman announced the decision, a huge red flag, carried by four 'Red Falcons' (members of the youth movement) was brought into the congress hall while the delegates rose to their feet to sing the *Internationale*.[2]

Two documents for the re-establishment were then laid before the congress: a draft of the statutes and a declaration of principles.

In the statutes the Socialist International was described as an 'association of parties which seek to establish democratic Socialism as formulated in the declaration of the Aims and Tasks of Democratic Socialism'. Its purpose was 'to strengthen mutual relations between the affiliated parties, and to co-ordinate their political attitudes and actions by consent'.

Four agencies were defined to carry out its functions:

(a) The Congress of the Socialist International.
(b) The Council of the Socialist International.
(c) The Bureau of the Socialist International.
(d) The Secretariat of the Socialist International.

The congress is the supreme body of the Socialist International. It proclaims its principles, determines its statutes and decides by a two-thirds majority of all members the admission and status of new members and of organizations in relation to the Socialist International. The congress, to be convened by the council, assembles every second year. The statutes differentiate between full members and consultative members and observers (i.e. parties in exile or international organizations such as the International General Council of Socialist Women or the International Union of Socialist Youth); consultative members and observers have the right to speak but not to vote. Each party entitled to vote has only one vote at its disposal irrespective of strength, as was the rule in the First and Second Internationals. The statutes of the Labour and Socialist International had, on the other hand, allotted votes to member parties according to the size of their membership.

The General Council assembles at least once a year. Its task is to co-ordinate the attitude of the member parties towards current political issues, to elect the chairman of the International, the vice-chairmen and the secretary, to approve the budget and stipulate membership fees. Since every party is represented on the General Council, it forms in effect a miniature congress.

The executive function within the International is the preserve of the

1. ibid., pp. 14–15.   2. ibid., p. 18.

Bureau, whose members are to be the chief executive figures in the International; its secretary, as head of the secretariat, is responsible to the bureau.[1]

The general council elected Morgan Phillips, former chairman of the Bureau of the International Socialist Conference, as president, Erich Ollenhauer and Louis Levy as vice-presidents and Julius Braunthal as secretary; the latter had previously been elected secretary by the International Socialist Congress in Paris in December 1949.

5

The *Frankfurt Declaration*, the 'Declaration of Aims and Tasks of Democratic Socialism' which the congress now considered, stands with the *Communist Manifesto* of 1848 and the *Inaugural Address* of the First International of 1864 as a fundamental document in the history of the International. In a number of resolutions and manifestos, the Second International and the Labour and Socialist International had formulated their basic attitudes to political and economic questions, but neither of the two earlier Internationals had proclaimed the fundamental ideas on which they were based and the objectives which they were trying to achieve.

The *Communist Manifesto* and the *Inaugural Address* originated from a single man—Karl Marx. The *Frankfurt Declaration* is, by contrast, a collective work of all member parties. There is no other document in the history of the International which was the fruit of so much intensive collective work by individual parties. Never before had any resolution or manifesto been submitted to the parties for previous discussion; they had always received the texts of proposed resolutions on arrival at the congress assembly and had left their formulation to discussion by the resolution committee.[2]

The *Frankfurt Declaration* was, on the other hand, discussed between the

1. For the structure of the International, see *Yearbook of the International Socialist Labour Movement*, vol. I: *1956–1957*, pp. 15–17; for the German text of the statutes, see Report (Frankfurt), pp. 111–13.

2. This had also been the procedure of the Communist International. Lenin's major thesis on *Bourgeois Democracy and Proletarian Dictatorship*, for example, which formulated the principles and objectives of the Communist International, and was submitted to the first Comintern Congress in March 1919, as well as the *Manifesto of the Communist International*, drafted by Trotsky, and read out by him on the last day of the inaugural congress (6 March 1919), were approved without any previous discussion, and even without debate. The only voice to oppose this procedure was that of Hugo Eberlein, delegate of the German Communist party, who had been instructed by his executive to protest against the founding of the Communist International without discussion between the parties concerned. He 'insisted', as an official announcement stated, 'that the guide-lines accepted here should first be submitted to the workers in the various countries; not until they have accepted these established guide-lines can the official founding of the Third International take place. . . .'—quoted in Hermann Weber, *Die Kommunistische Internationale. Eine Dokumentation* (Hanover, 1966), p. 29; see also Braunthal, *History of the International, 1914–1943*, pp. 163–4.

member parties in the course of nearly a year and a half. Its history began with a resolution moved by the French Socialist party in mid-December 1949 at the Paris conference of the International Socialist Conference. This called for the appointment of a commission to work out a declaration of the basic ideological principles common to all the parties. A few weeks later, in early January, a draft by the secretary of the principles of democratic Socialism was circulated to individual parties, inviting them to submit memoranda stating their views. At the same time the subject of the projected declaration was placed on the agenda for the International Socialist Conference to be held in mid-June 1950 in Copenhagen, and the submitted memoranda circulated before the debate. Not until after the debate, introduced by Guy Mollet, was a commission of twelve parties elected to incorporate the comments and suggestions of the member parties into the draft. The corrected draft was then again submitted to the parties and, acting on their criticisms, further corrections were made. In all, three further drafts went through the same 'long-drawn-out and painstaking process of inserting additional material and alterations, and repeatedly restyling the text', as the French Socialist, Salomon Grumbach, chairman of the editorial commission, reported to the congress. The draft laid before the Frankfurt Congress was the fourth, and was the one which the parties finally voted for.[1]

The *Frankfurt Declaration* represents a synthesis of the basic principles common to all Socialist parties, irrespective of whether their ideology rests on Marxism or on any other of the theoretical systems prompted by humanitarian or religious thought.

It condemns capitalism, which, despite its enormously developed powers of production, which 'could be made to provide a decent life for everyone', is by its nature incapable of satisfying the elementary needs of the world's population.

It has proved unable (the declaration continued) to function without devastating crises and mass unemployment. It produced social insecurity and glaring contrasts between rich and poor. It resorted to imperialist expansion and colonial exploitation, thus making conflicts between nations and races more bitter. In some countries, powerful capitalist groups helped the barbarism of the past to raise its head again in the form of Fascism and Nazism.

Socialism, it continued, had originated in Europe as a movement of protest against the inbred evils of the capitalist system of society; as a mass movement by those workers 'who suffered most from capitalism'. Socialism appeals to all men 'who believe that the exploitation of man by man must be abolished'.

1. Report (Frankfurt), p. 21. The congress revised the suggested title from *Declaration of the Principles of Democratic Socialism* to *The Aims and Tasks of Democratic Socialism. Declaration of The Socialist International, resolved in Frankfurt-am-Main on 3 July 1951.*

Socialism aims to liberate the peoples from dependence on a minority which owns or controls the means of production. It aims to put economic power in the hands of the people as a whole and to create a community in which free men work together as equals.

The declaration was headed by a statement on the principle of freedom: 'Without freedom there can be no Socialism. Socialism can be achieved only through democracy. Democracy can be fully realized only through Socialism.'

With its statement on the principle of freedom and democracy the Socialist International said its final word on the question which had so deeply disturbed the Socialist movement from the beginning of the Bolshevik Revolution in Russia to the outbreak of the Second World War: the question whether a Socialist reorganization of society was possible only on a foundation of democracy, or whether it necessitated the establishment of a system of dictatorship; whether the capitalist society could be changed by a process of evolution into a Socialist society, or whether it required revolutionary methods.

The example of Soviet Russia had demonstrated the consequences of the theory of dictatorship. While it had shown that a dictatorship of the proletariat was indeed an effective instrument for destroying the bourgeois-military organization of the capitalist state, it had also shown how the 'dictatorship of the proletariat' inevitably developed into a dictatorship by the party which holds power, and that the dictatorship of the monopoly party ultimately deteriorated into a reign of despotic terrorism.

The example of Bolshevism further showed that while a Communist dictatorship was indeed capable of destroying the capitalist structure of bourgeois society, it destroyed at the same time the creative potential for development in a Socialist community, because it suppressed the freedom of the people to participate in the process of building the new society. The Communist dictatorship in fact replaces private capitalism with state capitalism, and the capitalist wages system—which at least leaves the workers their personal freedom—with a system of state servitude which suppresses all the individual's rights.

The lesson of Russian Communism was therefore that the abolition of private capitalism by a Communist dictatorship could be done only at the expense of fundamental human rights. The 'dictatorship of the proletariat', which the Bolshevik Revolution had established, had degenerated inevitably into despotic tyranny. Rather than a society of justice, freedom and equality, which had been the objective and justification for the revolution, it had produced a totalitarian system of state power, based on a hierarchical bureaucracy imposing universal economic, political and spiritual subjugation. And then, following the Second World War, international Communism had, as the declaration said, become 'the instrument of a new imperialism'—the 'imperialism of the Soviet Union'.

Above all it was those parties which, in memoranda and during the debate, acknowledged their own basis in the Marxist tradition, which demanded that the declaration should condemn Communism and its claim to derive its moral justification from Marxism.

In summing up its indictment, the declaration stated that Communism, which had split the international labour movement and set back the realization of Socialism for decades in many countries, 'falsely claims a share in the Socialist tradition. In fact it has distorted that tradition beyond recognition. It has built up a rigid theology which is incompatible with the critical spirit of Marxism.'

In the light of the experience of the Communist dictatorship, the principle of political democracy and the value of freedom assumed a new significance in the struggle of the Social Democratic parties for a Socialist society; they recognized political democracy and civic rights as essential prerequisites for Socialism. They had in fact as a matter of course fought from the very beginning for the individual's right to freedom and democracy as essential elements of Socialism. But in the struggle against capitalism their theory and propaganda emphasized its economic and social aspects under the assumption that, by the overthrow of capitalist class rule, freedom and democracy would automatically be attained. At all events, prior to the Bolshevik Revolution in Russia, Socialist society had been visualized by Socialists of every shade, including the Bolsheviks, as a fully developed democratic society founded on the principles of individual freedom.

In Communist countries capitalist class rule had indeed been destroyed, but freedom and democracy had gone along with it. It was in protest against this fundamental aspect of the so-called 'peoples' democracies' that the Vienna International Socialist Conference of 1948 had passed its resolution affirming the principles of political democracy.[1]

The *Frankfurt Declaration* supplemented these with a list of basic political rights—an outline followed by a programme for realizing social and economic democracy, covering the various forms of common ownership of the means of production and the democratic control of economic power.

One other reaction to totalitarian Communism was a revival within the Socialist parties of their humanitarian tradition. The roots of Marxism, like any other Socialist alignment, lay in the European tradition of the Judeo-Christian and liberal philosophical ethics. English Socialism had sprung from a long tradition of religious nonconformity and political radicalism, while in the Socialism of France, Belgium and Italy, which had developed under the impressive influence of Jean Jaurès, Émile Vandervelde and Filippo Turati, the philosophical liberal tradition was predominant.

1. See pp. 188–9.

In its affirmation of humanitarian Socialism the newly constituted Socialist International stated:

Socialism means far more than a new economic and social system. Economic and social progress have moral value to the extent that they serve to liberate and develop the human personality.

Socialists oppose capitalism not only because it is economically wasteful and because it keeps the masses from their material rights, but above all because it revolts their sense of justice. They oppose totalitarianism in every form because it outrages human dignity.

In contradiction to Marx's theory of the realization of Socialism as an imminent 'economic necessity', the declaration stated in Article 13 of the preamble: 'The achievement of Socialism is not inevitable. It demands a personal contribution from all its followers.'

As Willi Eichler, the S.P.D. delegate, commented during the debate, this represented 'a break with the beliefs of the past'.[1] The theory that Socialism would come about as a necessary result of the processes of history had been hotly disputed since the great debate on revisionism at the turn of the century, but never before had this theory been questioned by a congress of the International. It had been a source of inspiration for the Socialist movement, holding out the hope of ultimate triumph. Yet during the last few decades events had shown how barbarism could in all its horror become an alternative to capitalism.[2] The declaration wanted to impress upon Socialists the realization that only by their concerted efforts could the danger of barbarism be averted and Socialism achieved.

Socialism was international from its inception, the declaration stated, 'for it aims at liberating all men from every form of economic, spiritual and political bondage'. It called for transcending the system of absolute national sovereignty and urged the establishment of democracy on a world scale under an international order of law, guaranteeing freedom for nations and respect for human rights. It rejected any form of imperialism, and demanded a new distribution of the world's wealth in favour of the economically under-developed countries. Above all, it recognized the maintenance of peace as the supreme task of our time.

The declaration closed with the following appeal:

Socialists work for a world of peace and freedom, a world in which the exploitation and enslavement of men by men and peoples by peoples is unknown, for a world in which the development of the individual personality is the basis for the fruitful development of mankind. They appeal to the solidarity of all working men in the struggle for this great aim.[3]

1. Report (Frankfurt), p. 31.
2. Marx had touched upon this point in the *Communist Manifesto* when he had commented on the class struggle of the past, 'a fight that each time ended either in a revolutionary reconstitution of society at large or in the common ruin of the contending classes'.
3. For the full text of the declaration see Appendix Two, p. 531.

The declaration made no attempt to develop a theory of Socialism. As Article 11 of the preamble says:

Socialism is an international movement which does not demand a rigid uniformity of approach. Whether Socialists build their faith on Marxist or other methods of analysing society, whether they are inspired by religious or humanitarian principles, they all strive for the same goal—a system of social justice, better living, freedom and world peace.

Even so, the question of the attitudes of individual parties to the Marxist tradition had been thrown up in memoranda and debate—a question which had never before been a theme for discussion in any congress of the International.

The debate on Marxism took place at the Copenhagen conference on 1–3 June 1950, and was introduced by Guy Mollet as chairman of the programme commission to which the memoranda had been submitted.[1]

The Dutch Labour party's memorandum asserted that, since two world wars had separated European Socialism from Marx, even 'if European Socialism does not go to the length of excluding those who are convinced that the Marxian doctrine is still important, it must in any case make room for those who feel nearer to Jaurès and Thomas Masaryk [than to Marx]'.[2]

The sternest rejection of Marxism, however, came from Morgan Phillips, secretary of the British Labour party. The British party had, in fact, in its official memorandum already stressed that the intellectual make-up of British Socialism had been shaped not under the influence of Marxism, but rather by the radical ideas of John Stuart Mill, the teachings of the Fabians, Sydney Webb and Bernard Shaw, and the social reformers within the Anglican Church;[3] there existed a contrast between the ideology of the British Labour movement and that of Marxism.

'British Socialism,' Phillips declared, 'owes little to Karl Marx, either in theory or in practice, or in its methods of organizing the working class.' 'Marx's conception of the political organization required for the waging of the class war', he continued, 'is not accepted by the British Labour movement.' British Socialism, he said, pointed 'the way to the achievement of the rarest phenomenon in history—a revolutionary change in political control and class relations without physical conflict'.

Phillips emphasized 'the profound influence of religious thought' upon the Labour movement and the example of the Methodist Church upon its structure. 'The essential point,' he said, 'is that Marxism as a philosophy of materialism, as an economic theory and as a form of political organization

1. Report of the International Socialist Conference at Copenhagen, Circular No. 155/50, subsequently referred to as Report (Copenhagen).
2. ibid., p. 54.
3. For a history of the ideas behind British Socialism, see Hugh Gaitskell, '*Die ideologische Entwicklung des demokratischen Sozialismus in Grossbritannien*', in Julius Braunthal (ed.) *Sozialistische Weltstimmen* (Berlin and Hanover, 1958), pp. 108–38.

with revolutionary intention and aim, is historically an aberrant in the development of British Socialism.'[1]

Morgan Phillips's blunt rejection of Marxism met with no response from the congress. When all was said and done, for all the parties of the European continent Marxism had been the source of inspiration most deeply influencing their ideology, and it remained an element of a tradition to which they felt indebted. Even the British Labour party had officially acknowledged this by deciding to celebrate the centenary in 1947 of the publication of the *Communist Manifesto* with a new edition and commissioning Harold Laski to write a historical appreciation as a foreword. Laski's foreword ran[2] somewhat in contradiction to Morgan Phillips's statement:

'In presenting this centenary volume of the *Communist Manifesto* ... the Labour party acknowledges its indebtedness to Marx and Engels as two of the men who have been the inspiration of the whole working-class movement.' The foreword referred to the peculiar English sources which had formed the ideology of English Socialism but, it added, 'the British Socialists have never isolated themselves from their fellows on the continent of Europe. Our own ideas have been different from those of continental Socialism which stemmed more directly from Marx; but we too have been influenced in a hundred different ways by European thinkers and fighters and, above all, by the authors of the *Manifesto*.'[3]

In fact it was only Dutch Social Democracy which had broken with its past. Under the leadership of Koos Vorrink, it had founded a new party at a congress in Amsterdam in February 1949—the *Partij van de Arbeid* (Labour party), representing a merger between the old Social Democrats and a number of religious Socialist parties and groups: the Calvinist Christian Democratic Union, the Progressive Democratic movement, the Dutch People's movement and the Christophorus movement, a Catholic group.

But no single party, irrespective of its views on Marxism, had categorically dissociated itself from Marxism at the congress. At the least they were, like the Swedish party, 'not interested in discussions on theory', as Tage Erlander openly confessed. But he admitted that from its inauguration it had been strongly influenced by Marxist ideas, though it had never built up a body of doctrines.[4]

So far as the parties were able to define their attitudes towards Marxism, they confessed themselves to be its standard-bearers. In France, Guy Mollet said, 'the entire party—including Guesde, Jaurès and more recently Léon

1. Report (Copenhagen), pp. 57–60.

2. The official nature of this declaration is indicated by its title: 'Foreword by the Labour Party'.

3. See *Communist Manifesto. Socialist Landmark*, A New Appreciation written for the Labour Party by Harold J. Laski together with the original text and prefaces (London, 1948).

4. Report (Copenhagen), pp. 62–4.

Blum and Alexandre Bracke—had accepted without reserve the analysis of capitalist society made by Marx.

No French Socialist was bound, he continued, to avow himself to dialectical materialism as a philosophical method, though many do it freely, but 'all French Socialists consider historical materialism to be a marvellous application of that method to the history of human society'.[1]

For the Italian Socialist party, Angelica Balabanoff stated, Marxism was not simply a method for recognizing the social forces within society, but also a source of faith and strength for the working class. 'If the working class,' she said, 'does not understand its proper role in society, if it does not acquire a historical sense of its own mission, if it does not understand that it is an instrument of the historical change from capitalism to Socialism—how on earth can we develop the strength and confidence of the working classes?'[2]

The Austrian Socialist party, Oscar Pollak declared, 'considers itself to be the very modest heirs to the school of Austro-Marxism'.[3]

6

In concluding this survey of the congress reconstituting the Socialist International, the attitude of the Cominform towards this event has yet to be recorded. This was formulated in its official organ, *For a Lasting Peace and for a People's Democracy*, in an article headed: 'International Traitors and Accomplices of Warmongers'. The article which followed stated:

> Last week, Frankfurt-am-Main (Western Germany) witnessed a gathering of hardened Wall Street agents—the right-wing Socialist leaders who, with much noise, announced the re-creation of a 'Socialist International'.
>
> Among the motley crew represented in this newly formed agency of traitors and accomplices of the warmongers, intimately linked with the general staffs, intelligence services and ruling cliques of the capitalist countries, were the Labour party secretary, Morgan Phillips, European loudspeaker for the American-British armaments drive, Jules Moch, chief American policeman in France, Schumacher, leading American agent provocateur in Western Germany, Saragat, inveterate betrayer of the Italian working class, and Spaak, who has waxed rich by selling to the transatlantic atom-bomb makers uranium mined by slave labour in the Belgian Congo. Others present included 'representatives' from the countries of Eastern Europe, right-wing Socialists, that is, exposed and played-out American and British intelligence agents who fled from the countries of People's Democracy to escape the wrath of the people.

The article further stated that 'the main premise of the Frankfurt rally of traitors was: not imperialism, but Communism is the main enemy. . . . Speaking from the Frankfurt rostrum, the orators complained that rearmament was proceeding too slowly.' They had, the article claimed, demanded the

1. ibid., p. 55.　　　2. ibid., p. 68.　　　3. ibid., p. 27.

acceleration of rearmament, and 'the Fascist Tito came in for special praise' for having 'mobilized more divisions than the whole of Western Europe put together'. Then the question was raised: 'Why did the American–British warmongers decide to stage the disgusting farce of an international 'Socialist Congress' precisely at this moment?'

Because, the article offered its explanation, 'the growth and consolidation of the world camp of peace, democracy and Socialism . . . seriously alarm the imperialists and force them to bring their main reserves into action—the right-wing Social Democrats—in a desperate endeavour to split the world peace movement and the unity in the ranks of the working people—a unity which is growing stronger every day'.

But, the article concluded, 'these calculations are doomed to failure! . . . The working people of the world spurn with contempt this police international, created for the purpose of justifying and supporting the monstrous plans for world domination by the U.S. imperialists. . . .'[1]

7

During the debate at the Frankfurt congress on the report of the programme commission, the S.P.D. delegate Willi Eichler had complained that in rejecting totalitarianism in the form of Fascism and Communism the declaration had neglected its much older form—the hierarchical totalitarianism of the Roman Catholic Church; a totalitarianism which, he said, was based on a theory of the state which was definitely anti-democratic, which as a principle rejected the idea of the people's sovereignty and which was therefore in essence an enemy of democracy and freedom as well as of Socialism itself as the bearer of the idea of freedom. He reminded the congress of the treaty which the Vatican had made with Hitler, as it had made one earlier with Mussolini, and of how the Church had supported Franco in the Spanish Civil War. To oppose this enemy of democracy, a common attitude among Socialists was needed, based on a dialectical argument with theocratic theory.[2]

The matter which Eichler had raised prompted a declaration of faith by a Christian Socialist, sanctioning the principles of Socialism. The Dutch delegate, Geert Ruygers, who as a member of the programme commission had participated in drafting the declaration, stated that the declaration contained no single word which he could not support as a practising Christian. This fact, he said, was 'of great significance in view of the serious and tragic conflict between Socialism and the Christian churches existing in many

1. *For a Lasting Peace and for a People's Democracy*, No. 28. For a transcription of the full text, see *Socialist International Information*, 1 September 1951.
2. Report (Frankfurt), p. 30.

countries of Continental Europe. It was a conflict delaying the development of Socialism, and one which had to be overcome. The *Frankfurt Declaration* represented the 'first great step' towards this objective and hence was 'a matter of great historical importance for our Continent'.[1] This was the first occasion at a congress of the International that a Christian Socialist had taken the floor to defend Socialism on behalf of Christianity.[2]

Since the Second World War the question of the relation between Social Democracy and the churches had become a matter for serious examination for many Socialist parties. In France, Belgium, Austria and Holland, Social Democratic parties were partners in coalition governments with Catholic parties which had won for themselves considerable support from the workers and, above all, from the rural proletariat. These could only be won for Socialism if they could be persuaded that Socialism did not contradict the Christian faith. In many countries Socialists had sought a dialogue with Catholic circles to bridge Socialist and Christian conviction.

In the Netherlands such attempts had been especially lively, for in the deeply religious country the whole structure of political and social life was built upon religious foundations. There are both Protestant and Catholic political parties, as well as Protestant and Catholic trade unions, and a barrier divided religious workers from Social Democracy. The transformation of Dutch Social Democracy into the *Partij van de Arbeid* had represented an experiment to try to break through this barrier. The party changed not only its name, but also its structure; its party organization allowed for special representation for Protestantism, Catholicism and Humanism, and its party programme recognized the 'profound relationship between the deeply religious convictions of the people and their political beliefs', declaring them valid, if their members express their basic convictions clearly in their work for their party. And to free the party from the stigma with which it had been marked by Church propaganda as representing anti-religious and anti-Church ideas, the Church should, the programme stated, 'be free to fulfil its calling and to preach Evangelism at the same time as giving its service to the world. The churches are also to have complete freedom to state their attitude to political and social life for the spiritual and ethical welfare of the people.'

Acting on a proposal of the Dutch party, the Bureau of the International called a special conference to discuss the relationship between Democratic

---

1. Report (Frankfurt), pp. 36–7.
2. A number of delegates with religious affiliations had been present at earlier congresses of the International. Arthur Henderson, for example, the president of the Labour and Socialist International, was also a Methodist lay preacher, and F. Domela Nieuwenhuis, founder of the Anarcho-Socialist movement in Holland, had been a priest of the Lutheran Church in The Hague. But neither Nieuwenhuis nor Henderson nor any other religious Socialist had made a statement linking their political ideas with their religious convictions to any congress.

1 *First Congress of the Socialist International in Frankfurt, July 1951*

2   *Congress of the Socialist International in Milan, October 1952.*
Clement Attlee speaking; next to him Angelica Balabanoff.
In profile in the foreground (from left to right)*: Koos Vorrink,*
Paul-Henri Spaak, Guy Mollet, Giuseppe Romita

Socialism and its ethical and religious sources. It met from 9 to 11 March 1953 in Bentveld in Holland, and was the first occasion since the founding of the International that the relationship between Socialism and Christianity, and between Social Democracy and the Church, had formed a theme for an international congress.

The Declaration on Socialism and Religion adopted by the Bentveld Conference should not be seen as a declaration of principles of the International, which could only be issued by a congress. Yet it is important because it presents an aspect of the Socialist ideology which had actually been an effective element from the beginning, but which had never been officially defined. It augments the usual definition of Socialism as a social and economic movement with the characteristics of a great moral and cultural movement.

> Socialism, [the declaration stated], is a moral protest against the debasement of man in modern society. It proclaims human dignity and the right of every man and woman to equality of opportunity, to spiritual, intellectual, political and economic freedom and to the exercise of responsibility in decisions affecting work and life. . . .
> Socialist policy, inspired by these principles, is therefore the practical working out of an ethic which may be derived either from religious or non-religious sources. The ethical principles on which Socialist ideals and policies are based are associated with the finest traditions of creative culture. Socialism which uplifts those who have been deprived of their human rights, is becoming a world-wide force for the enriching of life.

The declaration stressed, however, that 'Socialism is in itself neither religious nor anti-religious; it is a political movement for the transformation of society,' and that 'there should be no denominational parties'.[1]

8

The Frankfurt declaration had outlined the ideas prevalent among the parties of the Socialist International on the principles and tasks of Socialism; the declaration of Bentveld emphasized the ethical and religious elements which are manifested in those principles. These are ideas, ideals and principles which are rooted in the cultural and religious tradition of Western civilization. The task which the parties had set themselves was to realize those ideas by changing the capitalist order of society in the industrialized countries.

1. For the text of the declaration, see Appendix Three, p. 537; for the discussions of the Bentveld Conference, see Report of the Special International Socialist Conference on Socialism and Religion, Circular No. 80/53; for the memoranda submitted by the parties to the conference, see *Socialist International Information*, vol. III, Nos. 12, 13, 14 and 15.

But since the end of the Second World War the Socialist movement had turned into a world-wide movement which had also gripped the peoples and races of Asian civilization in pre-capitalist countries. The Frankfurt declaration additionally called for a statement on the principles and duties of Socialism in pre-capitalist countries, especially those of Asia and Africa. This was discussed at the second congress of the newly constituted International.

The Frankfurt declaration had laid down the attitude of the Socialist International towards imperialism particularly clearly. 'Democratic Socialism,' it stated, 'rejects every form of imperialism. It fights the oppression or exploitation of any people.'

But the declaration did not only assure those countries still subjected to imperialism and colonialism of the moral and political solidarity of the International; it also called for the active solidarity of all Socialists with the people liberated from imperialism and colonialism in their struggle against poverty and want. 'A negative anti-imperialism is not enough,' the declaration states:

Vast areas of the world suffer from extreme poverty, illiteracy and disease. Poverty in one part of the world is a threat to prosperity in other parts. Poverty is an obstacle to the development of democracy. Democracy, prosperity and peace require a redistribution of the world's wealth and an increase in the productivity of the underdeveloped areas.

The second congress of the International, which met in Milan from 17 to 21 October 1952, undertook to define a programme of Socialist policy for the underdeveloped countries. A conference of experts, called by the Bureau to study the economic and social problems involved, assembled in Vienna in November 1951. It submitted to the general council the results of its examination in a memorandum, and a programme was thereupon instituted to be drawn up on the basis of the memorandum. Suggestions from the member parties and from the Socialist parties of Asia were then incorporated into three consecutive drafts. The final wording of the draft submitted to the congress was, with certain amendments moved during the debate, accepted unanimously.[1]

1. The Vienna conference of experts, presided over by Karl Waldbrunner, minister for nationalized industries in Austria, met with the participation of ten parties: Austria, Belgium, France, Germany, Great Britain, Greece, Holland, Norway, Sweden, Switzerland and the International Union of Socialist Youth. For the wording of the memorandum, see *Socialist International Information*, vol. II, No. 8; for the discussions of the commission under the chairmanship of Hein Vos, and the drafts repeatedly amended according to proposals from the Socialist parties of Ceylon, Japan, India and Canada and a number of European member parties, see the minutes submitted by the congress secretary, Circular No. 65/52, pp. 19–21; for the congress debate on the declaration, see Report of the Second Congress of the Socialist International, Milan, 17–21 October 1952, Circular No. 1/53, pp. 95–117.

In its preamble, the declaration of 'Socialist Policy for the Under-developed Territories' formulated the basic principles determining the attitude of the Socialist International to imperialism and colonialism:

The Socialist International aims at the liberation of all men from economic, spiritual and political bondage and the creation of a world society based on the rule of law and voluntary co-operation between free peoples.

In accordance with these basic principles, it continued:

It seeks to establish in every country equal citizenship and democratic institutions through which to maintain and expand the political freedom and economic wellbeing of all the people. It rejects every form of racial discrimination. It seeks to create between countries relationships which express the fundamental unity of mankind. . . .
The Socialist International therefore rejects without reservation capitalist imperialism which binds peoples in the chains of political domination and economic exploitation and which creates the disastrous myth of racial superiority. . . . The oppression and exploitation of any people, whatever ideological justification may be sought for it, is diametrically opposed to the principles of democratic Socialism.

The declaration further stated the International's solidarity with the freedom movements in those countries not yet liberated from colonial rule, and pledged all Socialists 'to work for the earliest possible creation of conditions under which full self-government may be achieved'.

The elimination of poverty and misery in the underdeveloped countries, the declaration said, was 'a moral responsibility for the peoples of those countries in a more advanced stage of development'. Far-reaching economic and social changes would be necessary to create living conditions worthy of humanity for those millions who were oppressed by misery. And since the accumulation of capital in the underdeveloped countries was totally inadequate to bring about speedy developments in their economies, financial assistance from the advanced countries was an essential condition.

In a 'World Plan for Mutual Aid', the declaration laid down in detail the methods and international organizations which would be necessary to bring about improvements in the material and cultural conditions of life for the masses of the underdeveloped countries and 'to close the gap between living standards in the different parts of the world'. It would, the declaration stated, make 'an all-out attack on misery everywhere and would express in action the international solidarity of working people the world over'.[1]

At its third congress, meeting in Stockholm in July 1953, the Socialist International defined its attitude towards colonialism anew, stating in its resolution:

The Congress of the Socialist International expresses once again that the abolition of the colonial system in all its forms is a main objective for democratic

1. For the text of the declaration, see Appendix Four, p. 538.

Socialism. . . . It welcomes the awakening of national consciousness among the peoples of the colonial countries and declares the Socialist International support for them in attaining independence and democratic self-government.[1]

Thus, during the first three years following its reconstitution, the International had formulated the main ideological principles behind its policy, which now gained a new dimension with the spread of Socialist ideas in Asia and Africa.

1. Report of the Third Congress of the Socialist International, Stockholm, 15–18 July 1953, Circular No. 115/53.

PART THREE

Socialism and Communism in Asia

9 · Oriental Key Positions in the World Revolution

One of the most amazing phenomena in contemporary history has been the rapid spread of Socialist ideas throughout Asia and Africa following the end of the Second World War. Socialist parties had, it is true, been formed in Japan and Indonesia before 1914, and in India and China between the world wars. Only in China, however, then enmeshed in the prevailing chaos of civil war, was the Communist party able to win a mass following.[1] Elsewhere in Asia, Socialist and Communist parties represented only small groups of intellectuals.

Thus the Second International had, in reality, been no more than an International for the white races of the industrial countries, and had made no attempt to encourage life in Socialist movements in pre-industrial areas. According to accepted dogma, genuine Socialist parties could never put down roots in a social structure of a feudal, pre-capitalistic kind, for Socialism —as the antithesis of capitalism—could only make a mass appeal in capitalist countries as a concept of the struggle for liberation by a modern industrial proletariat. And of all the countries of Asia, at that stage only Japan and India stood at the beginning of industrial development and the creation of a new proletarian class. The national freedom movements existing under colonial rule in Asia were not social but political movements; they aimed at the overthrow of their European masters, but not at the change of the structure of society.[2]

1. See Braunthal, *History of the International, 1914–1943*, pp. 321–8.
2. The view which motivated the attitude of both the Second International and the Socialist Labour International had been formulated by Otto Bauer in an article of 1911: 'The revolutionary movements of the peoples of the Orient,' he wrote, 'are, in origin and aim, completely different from that of the European proletariat. Even if, at times, Turkish, Egyptian, Persian, Indian or Chinese movements in these countries are adopting certain slogans of the European Social Democrats, they remain unrelated to the class movement of the proletariat. None the less, it is our duty to give these movements serious attention. The world-political change for which they are preparing in the world of Islam, in the Indian and the Mongol world, will influence the conditions under which the European proletariat must lead the struggle'—Otto Bauer, '*Orientalische Revolutionen*,' in *Der Kampf*,

The attitude of the Second International towards colonialism and imperialism was clear; it had rejected colonialism and imperialism without reservation and so supported the cause of the Asian peoples against foreign rule in a moral and political sense,[1] even though it had not identified itself with the national freedom movements concerned. It had never attempted to associate those movements with the Socialist movement.

Yet from its very inception Lenin set the Communist International the task of making the cause of the national freedom movements in the colonies its own. In his *Theses on the National and Colonial Questions*, submitted to the Second Congress of the Communist International in July 1920, he declared that

our policy must be to bring into being an alliance of all national and colonial liberation movements with Soviet Russia. . . . All Communist parties are to support by action the revolutionary liberation movements in these countries. . . . Above all, efforts must be made to give the peasant movement as revolutionary a character as possible, organizing the peasants and all the exploited wherever possible in soviets and thus to establish as close a tie as possible between the West European Communist proletariat and the revolutionary peasant movement in the East, in the colonies and in backward countries.

Soviet Russia was embattled and threatened by the leading imperialist powers. 'All events in world policy,' Lenin stated in his theses, 'are necessarily concentrated on one central point, the struggle of the world bourgeoisie against the Russian Soviet Republic, which is rallying round itself both the Soviet movements among the advanced workers in all countries, and all the national liberation movements in the colonies and among oppressed peoples, convinced by bitter experience that for them there is no salvation except in

vol. v, p. 115. In commenting on the repercussions that revolutionary movements in Asia were likely to have on those in Europe, Marx observed in an article on the Taiping peasant uprising in China in the *New York Daily Tribune*, 14 June 1853: 'It may seem a very strange and a very paradoxical assertion that the next uprising of the people of Europe, in their next movement for republic freedom and economy of government, may depend more probably on what is now passing in the Celestial Empire—the very opposite of Europe—than on any other political cause that now exists'—Dona Torr (ed.), *Marx on China 1853–1860* (Bombay, 1951), p. 1.

1. The guide-lines for the attitude of the Second International to colonialism had been laid down by the London congress of 1896 in resolutions demanding 'the full autonomy of all nationalities' and declaring 'its sympathy with the workers of any country at present suffering under the yoke of military, national, or other despotism'. It condemned colonialism as an aspect of capitalism. 'Whatever the religious and civilizing pretexts invoked to support colonial policies,' the resolution stated, 'the extension of capitalist exploitation has the exclusive interest of the capitalists as its aim'—*International Socialist Workers and Trade Union Congress* (London, 1896), p. 31. The question of colonialism in general and imperialism in particular in connection with militarism and the dangers of war was debated at the next three congresses (Paris, 1900; Amsterdam, 1904; Stuttgart, 1907). For a review of the debates and the attitudes of individual parties, see Braunthal, *History of the International, 1864–1914*, pp. 305–19.

union with the revolutionary proletariat and in the victory of the Soviet power over world imperialism.'[1]

Lenin believed, as he stated in the debate which followed, that it was by no means necessary for people in a feudal, pre-capitalistic colony to pass through a capitalistic phase of development, as Marx had presumed, before conditions became right for a Socialist order of society. 'If the victorious revolutionary proletariat organizes systematic propaganda and the Soviet governments give them all the help they can, it is incorrect to assume,' he said, 'that such people must pass through the capitalistic stage of development.'[2]

The congress not only supported the theses, but also laid down the duty of individual parties—as the eighth of the twenty-one conditions for membership of the Communist International—to fight against colonialism and imperialism. 'Every party which wishes to join the Communist International,' it declared, 'is obliged to expose the tricks and dodges of its imperialists in the colonies, to support every colonial liberation movement not merely in words but in deeds; to demand the expulsion of their own imperialists from these colonies, to inculcate among the workers of their country a genuinely fraternal attitude to the working people of the colonies and the oppressed nations. . . .'[3]

The importance attached by Lenin to the congress decisions was echoed in the pages of *Izvestia*.

Hundreds of millions of Indians, Chinese, Negroes, Malays and other suppressed nationals [it wrote] will receive news of the decisions of the second congress of the Communist International as a message of good fortune and also as a call to a renewed and broadened struggle against their exploiter, capitalism. . . . The fact that the Communist International was first to raise the flag of battle and to rally to this cause the suppressed peoples together with the organized proletariat will remain a living act of service.[4]

The Communist International's executive committee had, prior to the Second Congress, called a 'Congress of Eastern Peoples' to take place on 1 September 1920, at Baku, so as to mobilize them in the anti-imperialist struggle.'[5]

1. Jane Degras (ed.), *The Communist International 1919–1943*, 2 vols. (London, 1956), pp. 141 and 143.
2. Quoted in ibid., p. 139.
3. ibid., p. 170. See also Braunthal, *History of the International, 1914–1943*, p. 540.
4. Quoted in Frank N. Trager (ed.), *Marxism in Southeast Asia* (Stanford, 1960), p. 246.
5. Trotsky had supported immediate action in Asia in a letter he wrote to Lenin on 5 August 1919, immediately after the collapse of the Hungarian Soviet Republic. 'Until now we have paid too little attention to agitation in Asia,' he wrote. 'However, the international situation is evidently shaping in such a way that the road to Paris and London lies via the towns of Afghanistan, the Punjab and Bengal.' He suggested the setting up in the Urals or Turkestan of a 'Revolutionary Academy'—a 'political and military headquarters of the Asian Revolution, which,' he continued, 'in the period immediately ahead may turn out to be more effectual than the Executive Committee of the Third International'. For the text of the letter, see *Trotsky Papers 1917–1922* (The Hague, 1964), vol. I, pp. 621–7.

In its call 'to the oppressed popular masses in Persia, Armenia and Turkey', the executive committee had appealed for them to attend the congress 'in as large numbers as possible'. 'Every year,' it continued, 'you make a pilgrimage across deserts to the Holy Places. Now make your way across deserts and mountain and river to meet together, and to deliberate together, how you can free yourselves from the chains of servitude, how you can join in brotherly union and live as free and as equal men.'[1]

According to Zinoviev's report, 1,891 representatives from thirty-two nations attended the congress, mainly from the Caucasus and the Central Asian districts of Russia, but also including many Turks and Persians; two thirds of the delegates, Zinoviev alleged, were Communists.

In his opening speech Grigori Zinoviev (1883–1936) stated: 'We are ready to help any revolutionary struggle against the English government.... Our task is to help the East to liberate itself from English Imperialism.... Our task is to kindle a real holy war against the English and French capitalists.' In its manifesto the congress called on the peoples of the East 'to raise themselves as one man in a holy war against the British capitalists'.[2]

Yet, except in Turkey, the congress awoke no responses among the peoples of the Near East. It was planned to assemble the congress annually; but the first congress remained an isolated occasion. The congress had elected a 'Council of Propaganda and Action of the Eastern Peoples', attached to the Executive Committee of the Communist International, but it was never assembled. The one practical outcome was the foundation of an Institute for Oriental Studies in Moscow in 1920, and, in the following year, of the 'University of the Toilers of the East'.[3]

The Baku congress had, however, given an impetus to the founding of the

1. Degras (ed.), *The Communist International*, p. 109.
2. See ibid., p. 105.
3. See ibid., pp. 105–9. But by then the Soviet government had during negotiations for a trade agreement with Britain pledged itself to refrain from anti-British propaganda in the East. L. B. Krassin, the Soviet representative in London, was charged by a note of 18 April 1921 to assure the British government that 'From our point of view the signature of the agreement is a turning-point in our relations with Great Britain. ... We always considered that we had no obligations in regard to Great Britain until the signature of the agreement. ... Now that the agreement is signed, we shall do everything possible to prevent anything which might provoke hostile actions or propaganda against British interests. ...'. In a note to Lord Curzon dated 27 September 1921 after he had accused Russia of having, in breach of the agreement, continued anti-British propaganda in the East, Litvinov replied that the Russians had after the conclusion of the Anglo-Russian Agreement issued strict instructions 'ordering its representatives to abstain from any anti-British propaganda and to adapt their activities to the new relationship created between the Russian and British governments'. For the texts of the two notes, see Jane Degras (ed.), *Soviet Documents on Foreign Policy*, vol. 1: *1917–1924* (London, 1951), pp. 245–6 and 257–62. For the congress in Baku and the text of the appeal of the Comintern to the people of the East, see Degras (ed.), *The Communist International*, pp. 105–9.

Turkish Communist party.[1] A few days after the congress, a member of its presidium, Mustafa Subhi, organized a conference of members of the Turkish group in the Russian Communist party and including Communists from Turkey. As a student in Paris, Subhi had joined the French Socialist party and, after his return home, became the leader of the Turkish Socialist party, which had been founded in 1909 in Salonika. In 1913 he was arrested, but escaped in the following year and fled to Russia. There he joined the Bolsheviks and after the Russian Revolution became head of the Turkish department in the Central Bureau for the Peoples of the East in Stalin's office of the Commissioner for Nationalities. He edited the Turkish periodical *Yeni Düya* (New World)—published first in Moscow and later in Baku—translated the *Communist Manifesto* into Turkish, wrote a biography of Lenin among other things and returned to Turkey in November 1920.

Most recruits to Subhi's party were drawn from among Turkish prisoners of war whom he had trained in Communist propaganda. But independently, in 1919, a group of Turkish refugees returning from Germany after the war and calling themselves 'Spartakists' had formed Communist groups in Constantinople and Angora (as Ankara was formerly called). Earlier still the Angora Communist party had been formed—a rival to the Communist party, allied to Moscow—led by intellectuals, with a following among the peasantry and, above all, in the army. Their ideology was a curious mixture of pseudo-Marxist, pan-Turkish and pan-Islamic ideas—an 'adaption of Marxism to Turkish conditions' in the search for a 'Turkish road to Socialism'.

The Turkish Communist movement was, however, to be short-lived. Kemal Atatürk who, in 1919 as Commander of the Turkish Army in Anatolia, had overthrown the government of the Young Turks by insurrection and been proclaimed Head of State by the Turkish National Assembly in August 1920, had at first tolerated the Communists since he was seeking an alliance with Soviet Russia to help in resisting the victorious allies. But even while his negotiations with Moscow were still in progress he suppressed the Angora Communist party and liquidated the leadership of the other—Subhi's —Communist party. In the winter of 1920 the executive had decided to transfer its base to Turkey and in January 1921 seventeen of its leaders travelled by sea from Baku to Ankara. Upon landing at Trebizond they were arrested, Mustafa Subhi among them, to be drowned at sea on 28 January 1921—'the traditional Turkish method of secret execution', is Carr's comment on the ruthless action.[2]

But the event left Moscow's friendly relations with Kemal untroubled. In

---

1. The following description is based on Walter Z. Laqueur, *Communism and Nationalism in the Middle East* (London, 1956), p. 205–13; Edward Hallet Carr, *The Bolshevik Revolution 1917–1923* (London, 1953), vol. III, pp. 298–304.

2. ibid., p. 301.

its state of world isolation, an alliance with Turkey was of greater importance to the Soviet government than the Turkish Communist party. On 16 March 1921, within seven weeks of the Communists being murdered, a pact of friendship was signed between Soviet Russia and Turkey.[1]

The Turkish Communist party, deprived of its leadership, reconstituted itself in 1922 but was again prohibited after several months. Two years later, when the general political atmosphere had cooled down to some extent, it re-emerged from illegality. But a decree in March 1925, aimed at stabilizing the 'safety of the state', once again declared it illegal, and most of its leaders were arrested. This was the end of the Communist movement in Turkey—the only one in the Near East to have taken its impetus from the Baku congress.

1. For the ground-work for Soviet Russia's relationship with Turkey, see ibid., pp. 244–50, 294–8 and 301–4; Louis Fischer, *The Soviets in World Affairs* (Princeton, 1951), vol. I.

10 · Bolshevism and Social Democracy in India

In the event it was India which was to take up the key role in the Communist International's strategy for the revolution in Asia: 'If Russia is justly considered the citadel of the world revolution, then India may be described as the citadel of the revolution in the East,' wrote K. Troyanovsky in 1918.[1] The Communist International therefore strove above all in India for a breakthrough in its colonial policy. In 1920 it founded in Tashkent the Central Asian Bureau for the instruction of Indian Communists.

The pioneer figure in the Communist party of India (C.P.I.) was Manabendra Nath Roy (1886–1947), a revolutionary nationalist who in 1915 fled to Mexico to escape persecution by the British–Indian government and there turned to Communism. Invited to attend the Second Congress of the Communist International in Moscow in 1920, he made an impressive speech which ran counter to Lenin's theses on the colonial question, advancing the view that the conditions for a proletarian class struggle had already developed in India, and that the Communist party, as yet to be created, would become the standard-bearer of the revolutionary independence movement, not in alliance with the middle class but in the struggle against it. After the congress, he was dispatched with two consignments of arms, gold and Indian currency to Tashkent to head the Central Asian Bureau and organize an international brigade. This venture failed,[2] however, and from Tashkent he moved to Berlin where he founded in 1921 the English-language periodical *Vanguard of Indian Independence* (it later changed its title to *Masses of India*), to be smuggled into the country.

The first attempt at founding a Communist party in India was apparently undertaken in 1923; at all events, from February of that year *Vanguard* was

---

1. K. Troyanovsky, *Vostok i Revolyutsiya* (1918), p. 29, quoted in E. H. Carr, *Socialism in One Country, 1924–1926* (London, 1964), vol. III, Part 2, p. 658.
2. See Gene D. Overstreet and Marshall Windmiller, *Communism in India* (Berkeley and Los Angeles, 1959), pp. 35–6. This work is by far the most thorough history of the Communist movement in India.

issued with the sub-title, *Central Organ of the Communist Party of India*.[1] But two years later, when Percy E. Glading was dispatched to India as a representative of the British Communist party to examine the party situation there, he found that 'no Communist Party in fact existed'.[2]

In September 1925, Satya Bhakta founded an 'Indian Communist party'.[3] About eighteen months later, at the time when the English Communist, Philip Spratt, seconded from the British Communist party to the service of the Communist movement in India, arrived in Bombay early in 1927, it had 'fifteen or twenty members, four in Bombay'.[4] S. Tagore, leader of the Bengali Labour and Peasants' party, told Ossip Piatnitsky, general secretary of the central committee of the Communist International, in June 1927, in a conversation in Moscow, that the number of Communists in India was 'hardly more than a dozen', despite the fact that, as Piatnitsky implied, the Communist International had financed the movement with 'enormous sums of money'.[5]

The Communist party of India really only emerged at the conference which sat in Bombay in May 1927, and at which the various splinter groups, which had hitherto fought amongst themselves, agreed to elect a general secretary (S. Ghate) and a presidium (Muzaffar Ahmed, K. S. Iyengar and S. A. Dange). The party's organizational machine was, however, in the hands of Philip Spratt and Benjamin F. Bradley, another English Communist. These represented 'the *de facto* leaders of the Communist party of India. It was only under their leadership that the Communist movement received that impetus which the Indians were not able to convey.'[6] They organized the so-called Workers' and Peasants' party (W.P.P.) in the United Provinces, Delhi, Meerut, Bombay and several other towns.

But the ascendant of the young Communist movement was broken at one stroke in March 1929 when the government arrested thirty-one leaders.

1. See ibid., p. 49.
2. Quoted in Carr, *Socialism in One Country*, vol. III, Part 2, p. 667; see also Overstreet and Windmiller, *Communism in India*, p. 74. On the other hand, Zinoviev, as president of the Communist International, had reported to the Fourth Congress in November–December 1922 concerning Communist successes in India. 'We can,' he said, 'show valuable results for our work in India. I can tell the congress that during the last few months the work of our comrades has been crowned with success. Comrade Roy has, with a group of colleagues, founded a paper. . . . Our comrades have brought together Communist elements in India. . . . I believe this to represent a major step forward'—*Fourth Congress of the Communist International* (London, 1923), p. 291.
3. See Overstreet and Windmiller, *Communism in India*, pp. 77–80.
4. See Philip Spratt, *Blowing Up India. Reminiscences and Reflections of a Former Comintern Emissary* (Calcutta, 1955), p. 35.
5. For the conversation with Piatnitsky, see Overstreet and Windmiller, *Communism in India*, p. 97. The Indian government stated that the Communist International had placed at M. N. Roy's disposal the following amounts: £120,000 in July 1922, £120,000 in November 1922 and £2,000 in February 1923; see ibid., pp. 53 and 97. Roy reported in March 1924 that 'almost unlimited sums of money have been placed at our disposal'—ibid., p. 98.
6. ibid., p. 90.

In January 1930, having been found guilty at their trial in Meerut of a revolutionary conspiracy to overthrow the existing order they were sentenced to heavy terms of imprisonment.[1] Thus for four years the movement was deprived of its leaders, who were not released until the end of 1933.

Yet this trial—which stood among the most sensational of all political prosecutions, and which dragged on for almost three and a half years— became possibly the most effective instrument in assisting the spread of Communist ideas and aims in India. 'The revelation of our clandestine techniques,' Spratt reported, 'evoked admiration for us among the people: we had done what most of the young people hoped to do. . . . During the hearing we were able to make big speeches, which were published in the press; and what it was possible to say in favour of Communism was said.'[2] The case created martyrs and, in India especially, martyrs arouse warm sympathies. Furthermore, new leaders shortly took the places of the original imprisoned ones, among them B. T. Ranadive, who was to play a decisive role in the later history of the party.

Meanwhile a revolutionary situation had developed in the country. In 1930 and 1932, under the leadership of Mohandas Karamchand Gandhi (1869– 1948), the Indian National Congress called upon the masses to join the fight for national independence. And, for the first time in the history of the Indian continent, this diverse population of millions of peasants and workers had begun to move. The weapon used by Gandhi in the struggle was that of non-violent resistance to British rule. It took the form of an open denial of the law's status, of a refusal to co-operate in any way in public institutions, of a boycott of the authorities and of English goods, of a refusal by the peasants to pay taxes, and of mass demonstration by the workers in the face of official prohibition. The numbers of those arrested and imprisoned during the campaign were legion. What came into being was a formidable, non-violent revolution by an unarmed nation against the armed might of the British Empire.

Out of this revolutionary enthusiasm arose the first Socialist groups. In 1931, the Socialist party of Bihar, the Punjab Socialist party and the Labour

1. The accused were not sentenced for any concrete acts contrary to the law, but for illegal tendencies of the Communist International. The court stated in its findings that it had been proved that the Communist International was 'the head of all Communist organizations in the world', and that the 'setting-up of workers' republics in every country was its aim; that its policy was to incite to violent revolution'; that it was 'determined, particularly in India, to provoke a revolution whose immediate aim was to overthrow the sovereignty of the King–Emperor in British India'. The Communist party and the Workers' and Peasants' party were, therefore, as members of the Communist International, in the conspiracy to unleash revolution. For the text of the sentences, see M. R. Masani, *The Communist Party of India. A Short History* (London, 1954), pp. 37–8.

2. Spratt, *Blowing Up India*, pp. 51–2.

party of Bengal were formed, to be followed during the next two years by groups in Bombay, Uttar Pradesh and Delhi.[1]

The founders of these groups were, like the Communists, left-wing middle-class intellectuals who, inspired by a conviction that liberation from colonial rule was an essential prerequisite for the development of Socialism in India, had joined the fight for national independence. As members of the Indian National Congress, they stood in the front line during the stormy mass movement of 1932 and were arrested in great numbers. In the Nasik Prison, near Bombay, a meeting of the group leaders, among them Jayaprakash Narayan, M. R. Masani, S. M. Joshi, N. G. Goray and Asoka Mehta, resolved to found the Congress Socialist party as a focus for the left wing in the National Congress.

The Indian National Congress had been founded in 1885 by liberal nationalist intellectuals. During the early decades of its existence it had striven with emphatic loyalty to the British overlordship to win by constitutional means some participation in the existing system. Not until the early 1930s did the Congress develop, under Mahatma Gandhi's leadership, into a nation-wide revolutionary movement no longer satisfied with modest constitutional reforms but with its sights firmly set on attaining complete independence for India.[2]

The National Congress became divided over the question of tactics after the British government, under the pressure of the mass-movements of 1932, granted a degree of self-government through the channels of elected provincial parliaments. The Congress right wing, led by Sardar Patel, considered self-government in the provinces to be the first step in a gradual development which would have India's independence for its objective; it advocated calling off the revolutionary struggle and supporting the provincial elections. The left wing, on the other hand, under the leadership of Jawaharlal Nehru (1899–1964) and Subhas Chandra Bose (1897–1945), called for the struggle to continue until national independence had been realized, and so in effect rejected the offered constitutional reform and supported a boycott of the elections.

The National Congress had assembled in Patna on 17 May 1934, and, on the decision of its majority, proclaimed the cessation of hostilities and confirmed its participation in the elections. On the same day a conference of Socialists had assembled, also in Patna, under the chairmanship of Archarya Narenda Deva (1889–1950), to prepare for the founding of the Socialist party. It instituted a commission to sketch out the party constitution and

1. The following account of the history of the Socialist party of India is based on P. L. Lakhanpal, *History of the Congress Socialist Party*, with a Foreword by Prem Bhasin (Lahore, 1946); Hari Kishore Singh, *A History of the Praja Socialist Party* (Lucknow, 1959); *Praja Socialist Party. A Brief Introduction* (Bombay, 1956); and Saul Rose, *Socialism in Southern Asia* (London, 1959), pp. 14–58.

2. B. P. Sitaramayya, *The History of the Indian National Congress* (Bombay, 1947).

programme, nominated an organizational committee, with Deva as president and Narayan as general secretary, and fixed 21 October 1934 as the date of the founding congress in Bombay.

Over 150 delegates, representing thirty-one local Socialist groups, assembled for the inaugural congress, which also met under Deva's chairmanship. The party thus brought into being had been planned as a party within the National Congress, not as one in opposition. It recognized the National Congress—which had come to form a focal point for the forces of anti-imperialism and had won the trust of the broad masses in the nation—as a necessary instrument in the struggle for independence; and it had no wish to weaken it though, as the left centre in the Congress, it hoped to gain a leading position.

In his opening speech Narenda Deva analysed the historic situation which must govern the Socialists' attitude towards the National Congress. 'We should not forget,' he said, 'that the present stage of India's struggles is that of the bourgeois democratic revolution and therefore it would be a suicidal policy for us to cut ourselves off from the national movement that the National Congress undoubtedly represents. . . . Capitalist democracy is, in any event, preferable to serfdom under subjection to alien rule.'[1]

So the party took the title of Congress Socialist party (C.S.P.) to demonstrate its unity with the National Congress, and laid down in its statutes that only members of the National Congress could qualify as members of the C.S.P.[2]

The party's objective, the congress declared, was India's 'complete independence in the sense of separation from the British Empire and the constitution of a Socialist social order'. Its programme sought the nationalization of key industries, railways, mines and banks as the initial phase in the progressive nationalization of all the means of production, as well as the setting up of co-operative and credit societies for the private sectors of economic life; it also sought to dispossess without compensation the princes and big land-owners and to redistribute land and estates among the peasants by an agrarian reform.[3]

Jayaprakash Narayan (b. 1902) was elected as general secretary, while Ram Manohar Lohia (1910–67) was to be chief editor of the party organ, an English-language weekly appearing under the title *Congress Socialist*.

At its second congress, meeting in Meerut on 20 January 1936, the C.S.P. defined itself as a Marxist party. 'Only Marxism,' its declaration on the

1. Archarya Narenda Deva, *Socialism and National Revolution*, edited by Yusuf Meherally (Bombay, 1946), pp. 4–5.
2. The Kanpur Conference (February–March 1947) struck out this condition and dropped the word 'Congress' from the party's title.
3. For the text of the party constitution, its programme and other resolutions, see Lakhanpal, *History of the Congress Socialist Party*, pp. 37–8; Singh, *History of the Praja Socialist Party*, pp. 235–7.

character and tasks of the party stated, 'can lead the forces of anti-imperialism to their destiny. Therefore a knowledge of revolutionary technique, of the theory and practice of the class struggle, of the character and structure of a state moving towards being a Socialist society, is essential for party members.'[1]

In its origins, however, the Congress Socialist party was not simply a Marxist party in the tradition of the European Social Democratic parties, but rather a party of the Bolshevik version of Marxism. 'When the party was founded in 1934,' Jayaprakash Narayan said in a speech in 1952, 'we considered ourselves to be a Marxist party. Yet what did we, at that time, understand by Marxism? What did Marxism mean to the Socialists throughout the world? That was the time,' he said, 'when the Russian Revolution and the attempts by the Bolsheviks to construct Socialism were an inspiration to all Socialists. It may generally be said,' he declared, 'that, at that time, Marxism was, by us at least, largely identified with everything that Russia stood for.'[2]

Thus the Indian Socialists looked to Moscow for enlightenment rather than to Western Europe. It was one achievement of the 1917 Bolshevik Revolution to have rooted Marxism in India. 'The revolution in Russia is thought in India to be a triumph over depotism,' Lord Chelmsford, Viceroy of India, reported to Edwin Montagu, Secretary of State for India, in his Report on Indian Constitutional Reforms submitted to the British government.[3] Marxism had inspired the revolution in Russia which overthrew Tsarist depotism; now it became a source of inspiration for the Indian intellectuals who strove to overthrow British depotism in India. The revolution in Russia had apparently metamorphosed an established rigid social and economic order and had set in motion daring plans for the regeneration of society; and its example fired those who sought India's regeneration.[4]

1. For the text of the so-called 'Meerut Theses', see Lakhanpal, *History of the Congress Socialist Party*, pp. 142–4.

2. Report of the Special Convention of the Socialist Party, Pachmarhi (Madhya Pradesh) 1952 (Bombay, 1952), pp. 28–9. Narayan also described the disillusion which soon followed. 'We began', he said, 'as enlightened admirers of Soviet Russia. But the first shock came with the first "great purge" of 1936. During the first and second "purges" practically the entire old guard of the Bolshevik party, the men who had made the revolution, were annihilated. . . . Then came other shocks, the hardest being Stalin's pact with Hitler shortly before the outbreak of war in 1939, and then, when the war began, when Stalin divided Poland with Hitler . . .'—ibid., p. 29. See also Jayprakash Narayan, *Why Socialism* (Benares, 1936), pp. 55–6, 60 and 62.

3. Quoted in Masani, *The Communist Party of India*, p. 11.

4. Apart from its identification with the Communist régime, Marxism remained a seminal idea for Indian intellectuals. 'The appeal of Marxism,' the sociologist Edward Shils observed in his study of the Indian intellectual, 'which is very great indeed, and not just among Communists, rests on its claim to create a modern society, a modern India different from the India in which the Indian intellectuals are so enmeshed and by which they are so often abashed. Marxism . . . permits intellectuals who feel derogated to envisage a society in which their own ideas as to the good life will prevail. It promises the overthrow of the

'Russia,' said Narenda Deva, in his speech at the inaugural congress of the Congress Socialist party, 'is the only land without unemployment. . . . Factories, land, transport and credit systems have been socialized. . . . In place of anarchy we have planned guidance of economic development. . . . The first Five-Year Plan had a tremendous success. . . . The fact that the Soviet State is progressing rapidly despite the hostility of an antagonistic world, and even in the midst of widespread economic crisis, is in itself a proof positive that it has a message to give. . . .'[1] For Indian Socialists, Soviet Russia was the standard-bearer of the message of Socialism.

So it came about that India's Socialists, having adopted the Bolshevik version of Marxism, differed hardly at all from the Communists in their basic principles. 'The profound conflict which separates the Socialist from the Communist party did not exist in those days,' Madhu Limaye recollected from personal experience. 'Had the Communists adopted a friendly attitude towards nationalism and taken part in the struggle for independence, it is doubtful whether the Congress Socialist party would ever have seen the light of day.'[2]

The Communist party of India, however, remained implacably opposed to both the National Congress and the national independence movement under Gandhi's leadership. Its attitude was delineated by decisions taken by the Communist International. At its sixth congress, in August–September 1928, it had taken a sharp turn to the left in its tactics, had condemned the Social Democrats as 'Social Fascists', and had, contrary to Lenin's *Theses* of 1920, called on the Indian Communist party to oppose any alliance with the middle-class nationalist freedom movement. The resolution, passed in Moscow on 'Communist strategy in China and similar colonial countries', set the Communist party of India the task of 'freeing the masses from the influence of the national-reformist bourgeoisie . . . and rejecting the formation of any kind of block between the Communist party and the national-reformist opposition'. The duty of the Communist, it continued, was to 'unmask the national-reformism of the Indian National Congress and to fight the Gandhist phase of non-violent resistance'.[3]

hated and dazzling British and the Anglicized ruling groups who are guided by their ideas. It promises the liberation of coloured men from the white men who are equated with capitalists and foreigners. It permits India to deny the West, which it knows as a British West, and to do so on behalf of an ideal which is, at the same time, Western in content and origin'—Edward Shils, 'The Culture of the Indian Intellectual', in *Sewanee Review*, reprint April–July 1959, pp. 38–9. For Jawaharlal Nehru's avowal to Marxism, see his *Autobiography* (London, 1937), pp. 591–2.

 1. Deva, *Socialism and National Revolution*, p. 19.
 2. Madhu Limaye, *Evolution of Socialist Policy* (Hyderabad, 1952), p. 2. Limaye was a member of the C.S.P. executive.
 3. Quoted in Masani, *The Communist Party of India*, pp. 30–1 and 42–3.

In the spirit of the resolution, the Communist International published in 1930 its 'Platform of action for the Communist Party of India':

The greatest threat to the victory of the revolution in India is the fact that our people continue to harbour illusions regarding the National Congress, and have not understood how it is a class organization of capitalists, working against the fundamental interests of the working masses in our country.

Above all, this document denounced the left wing in the National Congress:

The most damning and dangerous hindrance to India's revolution is the agitation of leftist elements in the National Congress. . . . The exposure of the left-wing leaders of the National Congress. . . . The most ruthless fight against the 'left' national reformists are necessary conditions . . . for the mobilization of the workers and peasants under the Communist party banner.[1]

The formation of the Socialist party had, understandably, been a great inconvenience for the Communists. Throughout a decade, and without competition from any other Marxist party, they had controlled the whole area of Socialist propaganda. But now a Socialist party independent of the Communist International had arisen which also declared itself for Marxism and canvassed for supporters among the workers and peasants. The Communist party was itself divided into small cells and, despite a decade of propaganda, had remained isolated from mass opinion.[2] The Congress Socialist party, on the other hand, had succeeded in uniting Socialist groups scattered over the huge Indian continent into a common organization and had established itself as a champion of national independence in the eyes of the broad mass of people.

The Communist International, having decided at its sixth congress to turn the party line leftwards and to wage a 'most ruthless' fight against 'Social Fascists' (even while remaining unheedful of the triumph of Fascism in Germany), fought the Socialists as arch-enemies from 1928 until the beginning of 1935. Then, when Stalin's attempts to reach an understanding with Hitler had failed, it undertook to switch the party line back at its seventh congress in July–August 1935 and to support an anti-Fascist popular front with all democratic parties, and especially to promote a unity front with the Socialists.[3] Of 'Social Fascists' there could be no further mention, not even by Indian Communists.

1. Quoted in Masani, *The Communist Party of India*, pp. 42–3.
2. As Wang Ming informed the seventh congress of the Communist International in 1935 in his Report on the Revolutionary Movement in Colonial Countries, '. . . the Indian Communist has, until a short time since, been to a high degree isolated from the mass of the people and the anti-imperialist mass struggle. . . . The small, dispersed Communist cells were unable to combine themselves into an All-Indian Communist party'—quoted in ibid., p. 57.
3. See Braunthal, *History of the International, 1914–1943*, pp. 396–9 and 468–74.

Along with the new policies to which the Communist party was now committed, its attitude to the National Congress underwent a change; from being labelled a 'bourgeois party' it became 'a major anti-imperialist people's organization',[1] and the Congress Socialist party, from being despised as a 'camp-follower of the bourgeoisie', was now transformed into a Marxist sister-party. Communist policy was aimed at creating the 'unity of the whole left'. This task it allocated to the Congress Socialist party, which was to 'emerge as a powerful united party of the left welcoming with open arms all true and active anti-imperialists and all true Socialists and Communists into its ranks'.[2]

The initiative in creating a Socialist–Communist United Front had in fact been undertaken by the Congress Socialist party under Jayaprakash Narayan's leadership. From its very inception it had worked for a united Socialist party to include all Marxist factions, including the Communist party and the group led by M. N. Roy.[3] While this concept was strongly supported by Narayan, however, it did encounter a degree of opposition from several outstanding Social Democrats, among them Ram Manohar Lohia, M. R. Masani and Asoka Mehta. But a majority at the C.S.P.'s Meerut Congress in 1936 declared itself in favour of a United Front, and even for admitting individual Communists as C.S.P. members.

The Communist party naturally seized the chance of using the C.S.P. for its own purposes with enthusiasm. Having been driven underground by the ban since 1934 it had been seriously inhibited in its activities. As C.S.P. members, Communists could now work undeterred. Schooled in conspiratorial techniques, they were soon able to take over key positions in the party and its allied trade unions. Within a year of the Unity Front having been set up, the C.S.P. was thrown into chaos by conflicts between its Socialist and Communist members. But it was only in 1940 that the C.S.P. made the decision at its Ramgarh conference to expel the Communist party and dissolve the Unity Front.[4]

The Congress Socialist party had almost bled itself to death through its alliance with the Communists. Three of its biggest regional organizations in

1. *National Front*, 13 February 1938, quoted in Limaye, *Communist Party*, p. 32. The *National Front* was the official organ of the Communist party. In its zeal to form an anti-Fascist Popular Front, the Communist party even declared its support for the 'fight of Indian capitalists against the dominance of British capital'; and a resolution by its Polit-bureau in February 1937 demanded the additional inclusion of 'certain organizations of business people and industrialists'—*Communist*, March 1937, quoted in Overstreet and Windmiller, *Communism in India*, p. 164.

2. *National Front*, 13 March 1938, quoted in Limaye, *Communist Party*, pp. 32–3.

3. See Jayaprakash Narayan, *Socialist Unity and the Congress Socialist Party* (Bombay, 1941), p. 3.

4. For Communist tactics in infiltrating the C.S.P., see Masani, *Communist Party of India*, pp. 66–71; Limaye, *Communist Party*, pp. 33–9; M. R. Dandavate, *Three Decades of Indian Communism* (Bombay, 1959).

the states of Andhra, Tamilnad and Kerala had fallen under Communist rule, while in the other states it had lost many members; its foothold in the trade unions, the Peasants' Alliance and the Students' Federation had been preempted by the Communists.

The heavy losses of these five years were, however, to be recouped in the final struggle of the Indian independence movement.

When the Second World War broke out the British Viceroy proclaimed India a participant country. The National Congress at once demanded from the British government an assurance of India's independence as a condition of support for the war with Nazi Germany. This was refused. The Congress thereupon refused its collaboration, while abstaining, however, from any action that might have weakened the Allied war effort; as a symbolic protest it announced individual passive resistance. Yet not until after discussions between the British government and the National Congress on the future of India had broken down in the summer of 1942 did the Congress unleash, under the slogan of 'Quit India', a powerful subversive mass movement 'in which the Socialists played a magnificent role. All Socialist leaders who had escaped arrest went underground to organize the mass struggle against the British.'[1] Jayaprakash Narayan had been arrested in 1939, but escaped soon after the inception of the 'Quit India' movement to play, as the government recorded, 'an increasingly important role in the leadership of a movement which could no longer be differentiated from a revolutionary underground movement'.[2] The youth of the national freedom movement 'gathered in great numbers about the C.S.P. as the vanguard in the resistance movement against British rule in India'.[3]

The attitude of Indian Socialists to Britain's war with Hitler's Germany was clear. They wished to see the defeat of Fascist imperialism in Europe, but equally they wished to see an end to the rule of British imperialism in India. They could not advocate the Indian people's participation in the war so long as their country's freedom was not assured. 'How is an enslaved nation,' they argued, 'to fight with enthusiasm for the freedom of other countries?'

The attitude of Indian Communists towards the war was rather more complex. Up to the conclusion of the Stalin–Hitler pact of August 1939 they had, in company with Communists everywhere, been passionate advocates of a confrontation with Nazi Germany. The magic sea-change worked by the pact, however, made the war against Fascism, for which they had canvassed

---

1. *Praja Socialist Party, a Brief Introduction*, pp. 7–8; Masani, *Communist Party of India*, p. 82.
2. Quoted in Rose. *Socialism in Southern Asia*, p. 25.
3. *Praja Socialist Party*, p. 8.

so consistently, into a 'war of imperialism' and Britain and France were charged with being responsible for it.[1]

Moscow's version of the war, which condemned Britain as its creator, released the Indian Communists from any embarrassment of conscience in the crucial struggle of democracy against Fascism. Now, as Indian patriots and arch-enemies of imperialism, they could mobilize the masses in good conscience to fight the British. The National Congress, as we have seen, during the first phase of the war avoided mass actions which might have undermined the Allied position. The Communists, on the other hand, called on the masses to fight the British government, and organized protest strikes against the war—including one of 90,000 textile workers in Bombay in October 1939, among others—to try to paralyse Britain's war effort in India. They demanded that the National Congress should ratify a declaration put out under the title 'Proletarian Path', advocating 'the exploitation of the war crisis by the revolution'. The first step was to be a 'political general strike, together with a rent and tax strike', followed by a 'phase of armed uprising', including the 'storming of military and police posts in town and country districts, the destruction of government institutions and an actual offensive on the largest possible scale against the government armed forces'.[2] Gandhi and Nehru were branded as agents of imperialism, and the Socialists as Gandhi's lackeys.

Hitler's attack on the Soviet Union on 22 June 1941 overnight transformed Moscow's version of the 'imperialists' war' into a 'people's war of democracy against Fascism'. The rapid *volte-face* threw the Indian Communists into a considerable dilemma. Since the autumn of 1939, they had been attempting to sabotage Britain's war effort and had gained respect among the people as the most decisive pioneers of national liberty. But now Moscow expected them to ally themselves with Britain and her imperialist régime in India.

The Communist party hesitated for nearly six months. It only undertook to change its policy after Moscow had relayed strict instructions through the British Communist party in a letter signed by Harry Pollitt, the general secretary. Pollitt's letter was transmitted to the Indian Communist party by the British Minister for Home Affairs in the Indian government, Sir Reginald Maxwell.[3]

The Communist Politbureau thereupon issued a new proclamation condemning its earlier attitude to the war as a 'bourgeois nationalistic deviation' and declared its enthusiasm for Britain's fight against Germany in alliance with Russia. 'Today there burns in every Communist,' a C.P.I. circular

---

1. For the attitude of the Communist International towards the war, see Braunthal, *History of the International, 1914–1943*, pp. 504–14.
2. Quoted in Overstreet and Windmiller, *Communism in India*, p. 181.
3. See Masani, *Communist Party of India*, p. 80.

stated, 'irrespective of whether they are in prison, free, or in the underground, an intense desire to do everything they can to co-operate in the war effort, even under the present government'.[1] The British government then released all arrested Communists,[2] restored on 24 July 1942 the Communist party's legal status of which it had been deprived in 1934, and encouraged it to found a number of papers, including the English-language periodical, *The People's War*. Immediately afterwards, in August 1942, the government declared illegal the Congress Socialist party.

The Communist party had undertaken to change its attitude while the National Congress was still in conference with the British government over India's future. It had called for the acceptance of the British proposals and attacked Congress heavily for turning them down. When, following the breakdown of discussions, Congress called upon the Indian people to resist the British government under the 'Quit India' slogan, the Communist party threw itself into opposing the formidable and growing resistance movement. It defamed the Socialist parties active in the 'Quit India' movement as a Fascist 'fifth column', and called on the workers to support the war with all their strength. 'It is the workers' patriotic duty,' it stated, 'to take the initiative in organizing higher productivity and avoiding strikes. . . . The Communists fight openly and energetically against strikes which damage the country's defences.'[3]

As could have been anticipated, their attitude to the freedom movement discredited and isolated the Communists. To escape the odour of ostracism, the party changed tack once more after the end of the war, seeking contact with the nationalist camp and pleading for a 'united freedom front against the imperialist rulers of our fatherland', with whom it had co-operated while the war lasted. After India's independence had been proclaimed on 15 August 1947, the Communists, with reservations, declared their support for an Indian National Congress led by Nehru. A speech entitled 'A Stimulating Appeal to the People to Rally to Pandit Nehru' was given by the party general

1. Quoted in Overstreet and Windmiller, *Communism in India*, p. 205.

2. In an appeal to the British government to release Communist detainees, P. C. Joshi, general secretary of the Communist party, stated: 'Most of those arrested who are still imprisoned as Communists have, since the beginning of the year, categorically changed their attitude towards the war. Those Communists who are free have for several months given enthusiastic support to the war by speeches and in other ways. . . . Those still imprisoned are denied the freedom to support the war'—quoted in Masani, *Communist Party of India*, p. 278.

3. The congress of the Communist party of India, which assembled in Bombay on 23 May 1943, had stated in a resolution: 'The fifth column is being built by the "Forward Bloc", the party of the traitor Bose; from the Congress Socialist party which betrayed Socialism at the outset of the war . . . and has finished up in the camp of the Trotskyist traitors; and the Trotskyist group is a criminal band in the pay of the Fascists. . . . The Communist party declares that each of these three groups should be treated by any honourable Indian as the nation's worst enemy, and must be banned from political life and destroyed'—quoted in Limaye, *Communist Party*, pp. 48–9.

secretary, Puran Chand Joshi. In it he declared: 'All power to the government! It is threatened by reaction, and it is the duty of every one of us to rally in all sincerity to the government and assure it of our whole-hearted support.'[1]

Yet this tack to the right had to be changed again to the left after the founding of the Cominform in September 1947.[2]

The Cominform had called on the Communists of all countries to take up a revolutionary offensive. The Second Congress of the C.P.I., meeting in Calcutta at the end of February 1948, gave the new policy its inception. P. C. Joshi, having led the party as general secretary over twelve years and been responsible for its 'right' moderate policies, was ousted, to be replaced by B. T. Ranadive, his rival on the left wing. Ranadive was convinced, while also convincing a majority of his colleagues, that even as capitalist Europe 'was under the immediate threat of the revolution and stood on the brink of catastrophe', so was India ripe for the proletarian revolution. The congress resolution declared that 'a revolutionary upsurge' was in the making in India and the final phase of revolution, the phase of 'armed conflict', had already begun. It condemned the Indian Socialists, who 'preached the illusion that Socialism could be brought about by constitutional means'. It called on Communists to form 'a democratic front of all true revolutionaries'.[3]

Communist party policy was now directed at unleashing the revolution. It organized shock-troops[4] to attack railway stations, undertake bomb assaults and set buildings on fire. And, by a wave of general strikes, it attempted to paralyse the young state's administrative apparatus.[5]

The first mass strike planned for this purpose was a general strike of railwaymen scheduled to take place on 9 March 1948. Its specified task, laid down by a party circular of 23 February, was to set the revolution in motion. Party members were 'to prepare for clashes with the police . . . and to plan to capture key positions of the government. Not only the Socialist leaders,' it

1. *People's Age*, 19 October 1947, quoted in John H. Kautsky, *Moscow and the Communist Party of India. A Study in the Postwar Evolution of International Communist Strategy* (New York, 1956), pp. 19 and 23; Overstreet and Windmiller, *Communism in India*, pp. 260–4.

2. See pp. 144–5, 148–51.

3. Quoted in Overstreet and Windmiller, *Communism in India*, p. 273; Masani, *Communist Party of India*, p. 90.

4. A handbook was issued instructing the shock-troops in the use of weapons and hand-grenades and giving instructions for the formation of guerrilla forces with their instructions, tactics and tasks. These included, to quote at random, 'Attacks on police stations and the houses of the great landowners; ambushing police patrols, destroying them and seizing their weapons; sabotaging the enemy's lines of communication, the telegraph and telephone lines . . .'. The objective was, the handbook explained, 'to promote the mass movement which has developed in the country and to raise it to a higher level, when the whole country will take up arms'—quoted in Overstreet and Windmiller, *Communism in India*, p. 279.

5. For a review of these events, see Masani, *Communist Party of India*, pp. 90–6.

continued, 'but all of their followers who resist the strike are to be attacked.'[1]

During 1947–8 India had been involved in a terrible crisis. The proclamation of independence and the simultaneous constitution of Pakistan as a sovereign state had precipitated a devastating religious war involving mass-slaughter between Muslims and Hindus. Millions of Hindus, fleeing from Pakistan, had crowded out India's cities. A general strike by railwaymen, by preventing the transport of food, would have spread famine and paralysed the government machinery, creating chaos though hardly the required conditions for a Marxist proletarian revolution. But the All-Indian Railway Union, led by its president, Jayaprakash Narayan, came out against the strike, and the Communist action ended, as Joshi observed, in a 'complete fiasco'. Further attempts by the Communists to unleash general strikes similarly miscarried.[2]

The Communists met with more success, however, with their revolutionary tactic in the agrarian revolutionary situation which had developed in Telengana, a district of the Sultanate of Hyderabad in southern India. Early in 1946 the peasants had risen against a predominantly semi-feudal agrarian structure. Under Communist leadership, the movement developed towards the end of 1947 into a guerrilla war against the landowners. Within a few weeks 'soviets' had been set up in hundreds of villages, the landowners expelled and the land divided among the peasants. As Ranadive explained with some satisfaction to the party's second congress: 'Telengana is a major turning-point in the history of the battles taking place under our party's leadership.'[3] But when, in September 1948, the Indian army occupied the Sultanate to bring the country within the Republic of India, the Communist insurrection in Telengana collapsed.[4]

The course of action intended to unleash the revolution, adopted by the party at its Calcutta congress in February 1948, and which they continued to

1. Quoted in Limaye, *Communist Party*, p. 61.

2. 'We called for a general strike of the railwaymen on 9 March,' Joshi wrote; 'it was a complete fiasco. Not even our own comrades answered the call to strike. . . . In June we called for a general strike in Bengal to support a hunger strike by our comrades in prison. Again a fiasco, and Bengal is our best organized trade union province. In November 1949 we called on all jute workers to take part in a general strike; not a single factory came to a standstill. On 2 January 1950, we called all the textile workers in the country out on strike. Our press claimed that 75,000 had struck in Bombay; the semi-official agency reported 1,500 strikers. In no other textile centre was there a strike'—P. C. Joshi, 'Letter to Foreign Comrades' in *Views* (Calcutta), May 1950, quoted in Masani, *Communist Party of India*, pp. 284–5.

3. Quoted in Kautsky, *Moscow and the Communist Party of India*, p. 49. For the events in Telengana, see Overstreet and Windmiller, *Communism in India*, pp. 285–7 and 292; Masani, *Communist Party of India*, pp. 93–4, 292–3 and 300.

4. The Communists' activities in Telengana had in fact been criticized by leading Communists. In one analysis, a former member of the party's central committee reported: 'The guerrilla forces indiscriminately killed civilians in large numbers along with the big landowners and their agents. Their actions gave the party and the whole movement a bad name in the villages and cities'—quoted in Limaye, *Communist Party*, pp. 62–3.

pursue until 1951, had failed. The terrorist methods used, meant to stir the masses into revolutionary ferment, had in practice repelled the majority.[1] S. A. Dange, leader of the Communist trade unions, stated in a memorandum of September 1950 that, since the Calcutta congress of 1948, the Communist party had lost 80,000 out of about 100,000 members; that the Communist trade unions were in a 'totally paralysed and stagnant state'; that the peasants' organizations had 'practically been swept away'; and that the party had fallen prey to 'inertia and disintegration'.[2] The party itself admitted, in a circular of 16 September 1950, that it was 'on the verge of collapse and in a state of chaos, as a result of errors by the party leadership'.[3]

Total collapse was only to be avoided by a change of party policy. Accordingly a new programme was announced in April 1951. The concepts of revolution and Socialism as immediate practical solutions were now abandoned. On the contrary, it declared: '... The Communist party is not demanding the establishment of Socialism in our country. In view of the backwardness of the economic development of India and the weakness of the mass organizations of workers, peasants and toiling intelligentsia, our party does not find it possible at present to carry out Socialist transformations in our country.'[4]

The central committee elected as general secretary Ajoy Gosh, who with S. A. Dange and P. C. Joshi had headed the opposition within the party to the former 'adventurers' policy', and it revoked the call to terrorist action. 'No Communist,' it was now stated, 'can have anything to do with the tactics and methods of terrorism by individuals or guerrilla forces.'[5] The insurrection in Telengana, the party asserted, had not had the overthrow of government as its objective, but had been aimed solely at the feudal oppression which prevailed in the area. The party was ready to co-operate with the government in the peaceful dispersion of the guerrillas and by October their activities had ended.

Now it concentrated its attention on the parliamentary elections called

1. They also met opposition within their party. It said in a criticism of the Bengal party: 'Is it right to attack railway stations, to throw bombs at trams and buses, to set houses of Congress alight?'—quoted in ibid., p. 62.

2. S. A. Dange, Ajoy Gosh and S. V. Ghate, *A Note on the Roots of our Mistakes After Calcutta*, pp. 4–5, quoted in Overstreet and Windmiller, *Communism in India*, p. 302.

3. Quoted in Masani, *Communist Party of India*, p. 107. The following table of Communist party membership, based on official party sources, illustrates the effects of the policies of those years.

Year	Number of members
1948	89,000
1950	20,000
1952	30,000
1954	75,000

See Overstreet and Windmiller, *Communism in India*, p. 357.

4. Quoted in Kautsky, *Moscow and the Communist Party of India*, p. 135.

5. Quoted in ibid., p. 143.

for the winter of 1951–2. A manifesto of 1 May had already announced the setting up of the 'democratic people's front' to bring together not only Socialists and the masses of the workers and peasants, but also the bourgeois middle class and 'non-monopolistic capitalists'. In its election manifesto, published in August 1951, it set the front the objective of a 'democratic people's government', 'a government to represent the workers, peasants, middle classes and national bourgeoisie'. It would, the manifesto promised, 'work together with private industries and guarantee them their profits and interest' to encourage industrial development. Agrarian reform would similarly leave capitalist landowners enough land to operate profitable cultivation. . . . The revolution will not harm the rich peasants. They also, having suffered to some extent from feudal exploitation and usurers, will profit by the revolution.'[1]

The Socialist party, from its inception in 1934 and up to the constitution of India as a sovereign state in August 1947, had remained a loyal member of the Indian National Congress as its left wing. But while the Congress had been the instrument of the national freedom struggle, it could hardly be expected that, following the attainment of independence, it could be transformed into an instrument of Socialism. The Socialist party had, as it happened, succeeded, as Narayan said at the annual congress in Nasik in March 1948, in producing 'a climate of Socialism within the congress'. 'The fact,' he continued, 'that every congressman today is anxious to describe himself as a Socialist . . . is a tribute to the work of our party.'[2] And at its meeting in Karachi in 1931, the National Congress had indeed incorporated a Socialist element into its constitution by a resolution on 'fundamental rights' which declared: 'The state shall own or control the key industries, mines, railways, waterways, shipping and other means of public transport.'[3]

The National Congress, however, embraced followers of all classes and ideologies. As the organization of a national movement, it had fulfilled its aim with the attainment of independence. Now it decided to constitute itself as a political party. But the Socialist party felt that it would not then be able to represent effectively within the Congress the interests of peasants and workers. At its Kanpur conference in February 1947 it decided to break away from the Congress and, in the terms of its resolution, to 'march forward outside the Congress, carrying the triumphant standard of a Socialist state'.[4]

1. For the Communist election manifesto and an analysis, see Masani, *Communist Party of India*, pp. 139–51.
2. *Report of the Sixth Annual Conference of the Socialist Party*, Nasik, 1948, p. 68.
3. For the wording of the resolution, see Jawaharlal Nehru, *The Unity of India* (London, 1941), p. 406.
4. For the wording of the resolution, see Nasik Report, pp. 35–8. The party had, as already mentioned, removed the word 'Congress' from its title at the Kanpur congress in the previous year.

Within the Indian National Congress, the Socialist party had been a cadre party. At the time of the Nasik conference, in March 1948, it had numbered 5,139 active members and 3,671 candidates.[1] (Active members were pledged to devote fourteen hours a week to working for the party.) At the Patna congress, in March 1949, it decided to become a party seeking mass membership. The statutes were changed to end the two-tier system of membership, and a category of collective membership for individuals in the trade unions, peasants' federations and Socialist youth and student organizations was created.[2]

The party's growth was surprising. By the time of the Patna conference in 1949, it totalled 12,360 members; a year later, in June 1950, this had grown to 151,972 members, made up of 129,447 individual members and 22,525 collective members, mainly in the trade unions.[3]

The party's influence over the pre-war trade union movement had been dominant. During the war, with the Socialist leaders imprisoned, the Communists had been able to agitate unhindered and to seize the leadership of the trade union federation, the All-Indian Trade Union Congress (A.I.T.U.C.).[4] Shortly after the war, in May 1947, the National Congress founded a new trade union organization, the Indian National Trade Union Congress (I.N.T.U.C.), upon which, in December 1948, the Socialist party founded a Socialist trade union federation under the title *Hind Mazdoor Sabha* (H.M.S.). Its leaders were Jayaprakash Narayan and Asoka Mehta, with D. Desai as general secretary. At its inauguration, the trade union confederation embraced 427 trade unions with a total of 606,427 members; over the next two years its numbers increased to above 800,000.[5]

While the Socialist Party of India had from the beginning been a party orientated towards a Bolshevik version of Marxism,[6] Communism had lost much of its magic during the years of its tragic history. It had failed to

1. See Nasik Report, p. 104.
2. For the wording of the new statutes, see Report of the Eighth National Convention of the Socialist Party (Madras, 1950), pp. 203–12.
3. Madras Report, p. 154.
4. For the Communist infiltration of the A.I.T.U.C., see Overstreet and Windmiller, *Communism in India*, pp. 371–4.
5. At the end of 1952, the proportions of strength between the three trade union organizations, according to a report submitted to Parliament by the Minister of Labour, were as follows:

Indian National Trade Union Congress	1,548,568
Hind Mazdoor Sabha	804,337
All-Indian Trade Union Congress	758,314

See Oscar Ornati, 'Indian Trade Unions Since Independence', in *Far East Survey*, August 1954. I.N.T.U.C. and H.M.S. are members of the International Confederation of Free Trade Unions; the A.I.T.U.C. is a member of the Communist World Federation of Trade Unions.
6. See pp. 223–5.

emancipate the Russian proletariat. The dictatorship of the proletariat, set up by Lenin for the duration of society's transformation from a capitalist into a Socialist order, had degenerated into the dictatorship of a despotic bureaucracy, clamping the proletariat into new chains and, instead of building a Socialist society, had developed a system of state capitalism.

In the light of this experience, the realization grew in the ranks of the Socialist party that, as a method of achieving Socialism, Bolshevism had failed. This conclusion reached its expression in a new statement of principles adopted by the party's first post-war congress, held in March 1947 at Kanpur. This statement opted for democratic Socialism and 'the construction of a democratic Socialist society in India' and 'the eradication of imperialism, racialism, colonialism and other forms of national oppression and economic inequality among nations and the creation of a democratic Socialist world'.

The Kanpur conference was indeed, as the party's official survey stated, 'a landmark in the ideological evolution of Indian Socialism'. The policy statement which it adopted, 'for the first time in the history of the party, clearly distinguished democratic Socialism from totalitarian Communism and, while firmly rejecting the latter, emphatically asserted that there could be no Socialism without democracy'.[1] In the heated argument about the methods to be used in the struggle for Socialism, the party's general council decided that, under present conditions in India, not violence but the peaceful working of democracy was 'the only proper method' for bringing about a Socialist change of society.[2]

Thus, over sixteen years and 'by a slow and painful process', as Narayan described it at the 1950 party congress in Madras, the Socialist party evolved from the Bolshevik version of Marxism to a Marxist version of humanitarian democratic Socialism.[3]

This principle was further developed in an extensive programme of the Praja Socialist party, which emerged in September 1952 from the merger of the Socialist party with the *Kisan Mazdoor Praja* party. The programme, issued under the modest title of *Policy Statement*, is among the most fascinating documents of Asian Socialism—an outline for a Socialist order of society in India on the basis, explained at the outset, of 'a creative synthesis of the accumulated knowledge and experience of both Europe and India'.

In its conclusions it defines the conflict between democratic Socialism and Communism. Hierarchical concepts of the social order are rejected, as is 'the political and economic rule by a single person or a priviledged class by any kind of despotism, dictatorship, feudalism or capitalism'. It sought the rule of the working people over the social, economic and political forces of society by a system of self-government in every social, political and economic sphere,

1. *Praja Socialist Party*, p. 9.
2. *Statement of policy of the Socialist Party* (Bombay, 1951), p. 7.
3. For Jayaprakash Narayan's speech, see *Madras Report*, pp. 132–42.

as well as the democratic decentralization of power and responsibility. The people are considered as the source of authority, and the right to insurrection is recognized in the event of any single person or minority group or class attempting to seize control of the institutions of government or society.

Therefore democratic Socialism [the programme continued] is certainly opposed to Communism, which tends to be more totalitarian, authoritarian and dictatorial in character. In the Soviet Union—still considered to be their fatherland, by Indian Communists—Marxism has been transformed into bureaucratic Socialism, the proletarian revolution into a revolution of the bureaucracy, the dictatorship of the proletariat into a dictatorship by industry over the peasants and the dictatorship by a Communist party clique into a dictatorship over the whole of the population. . . . None of which equates with Socialism.[1]

The Socialist party had entered into the election campaign of 1951 with a manifesto based on a programme adopted by its Madras conference in 1950.[2] This developed plans for a far-reaching agrarian reform and Socialist legislation—reforms which would introduce 'light and hope into millions of homes darkened by poverty and ignorance'. But, at the same time, it declared that 'without a fundamental change in the social and economical structure of society, the problems of poverty and ignorance can never be surmounted'. 'As long as the present social order continues to rest on exploitation, inequality and privilege,' it continued, 'poverty cannot be banished.'

The party went into the campaign with high expectations. It had, during the course of a year, almost doubled its membership from 151,972 in 1950 to 295,554 in 1951,[3] and it had laid before the electorate its well-defined ideas for far-reaching reforms.[4] It could not, of course, hope to defeat the National Congress, the triumphant symbol of the national freedom struggle with its leader, Jawaharlal Nehru, the most popular figure in India. But its hope had been to emerge as the second strongest party, and so to win the recognized rights of an opposition party to the Congress government.

In the event the expectation was not fulfilled. While the Socialist party did indeed emerge as numerically the second strongest party according to the votes cast, the Communist party emerged as the second strongest party by parliamentary seats. The Socialist party vote was threefold that of the Communist party—11,216,000 to 3,484,000—but it gained only twelve seats

1. *Policy Statement*, adopted by the second national conference of the Praja Socialist Party, Gaya, December 1955 (New Delhi, 1956), pp. 6 and 93–4.

2. *Programme for the National Revival* in *Madras Report*, pp. 189–201. The manifesto appeared under the title *We Build for Socialism* (Bombay, 1951). For a review of the manifesto, see Singh, *History of the Praja Socialist Party*, pp. 137–49.

3. See Prem Bahsin's report in *Report of the Special Convention of the Socialist Party* (Pachmarhi, 1952) p. 120.

4. 'The Socialist party had issued the largest and best-written manifesto', W. Morris-Jones, 'The Indian Elections', in *Political Quarterly*, July–September, 1950, cited in Singh, *History of the Praja Socialist Party*, p. 137.

to the Communists' sixteen; furthermore, the Communists were in alliance with two parties which together had won 1,866,000 votes and ten seats in the *Lok Sabha*.

The Socialist party had not faced the Communist party alone in the election fight, but had had to compete for votes with ten other parties committed to a programme of Socialist change. Eight of them were splinter parties with revolutionary Marxist principles, of which two, with nearly seven million votes, could be considered ideologically close to the Social Democrat position. The strongest of these, the *Kisan Mazdoor Praja* party (K.M.P.P.), with more than six million votes and ten seats, merged shortly after the election with the Socialist party to become the Praja Socialist party (P.S.P.).

The fact that over a fifth of the electorate who went to the ballot box, or nearly twenty-four million electors,[1] voted for parties which stood for a Socialist transformation of society, reflects how the Socialist idea had developed in India following independence.

Even more indicative of the political mood, however, was the attitude which the National Congress party adopted during the campaign. To win the sympathies of the electorate it was also obliged to canvass in Socialist language, carefully taking on the appearance of a Socialist party; it obtained forty-seven million votes, or 45 per cent of those cast.

After the election, the Congress party allowed its Socialist colouring to emerge to an even greater extent. At a conference in Avadi, in 1955, it announced 'the establishment of a Socialist pattern of society' as the objective of the Congress. And two years later, in January 1957, the Congress amended its constitution, proclaiming as its aim 'the establishment in India of a Socialist Co-operative Commonwealth'. 'Essentially, this means,' the White Paper on India's Second Five-Year Plan explained, 'that the basic criterion for determining the lines of advance must not be private profit but social gain. . . . The benefits of economic development must accrue more and more to the relatively less privileged classes of society, and there should be progressive reduction of the concentration of incomes, wealth and economic power. . . . The public sector has to expand rapidly.' And the White Paper even declared that the First Five-Year Plan, which had ended in March 1956, had already laid the foundation on which to construct a society of a Socialist pattern.[2]

The Congress party's election manifesto in 1957 announced 'as its objective a society Socialist in character', in which, it explained, 'there would be

1. Over eleven million for the Socialist party, six million for the Communist party and its allies and eight million for the ten parties mentioned above. For an analysis of the election result and the characters of the parties, see Asoka Mehta, *The Political Mind of India* (Bombay, 1952).

2. Second Five-Year Plan (Delhi, 1956), VIII, 10.

no exploitation and no monopolies and where inequality of income would progressively be reduced'.[1]

The Socialist party thus came to stand in competition for votes both with the Congress party, confronting it in raiments of Socialism, and with the Communist party, which had meanwhile renounced any revolutionary aspirations and had taken on the mantle of a respectable, constitutional democratic opposition party, while trying to gain the trust of the masses as the representative of radical Socialism.

In its conflict with the Congress version of Socialism on the one hand and the unscrupulous opportunism of the Communists on the other, the Socialist party suffered a setback in the election campaign of April 1957. Certainly it won 11,640,000 votes, which were ostensibly 400,000 votes more than in the previous election, but since it had in the meantime amalgamated with the K.M.P.P. and both parties had together polled more than seventeen million votes in the earlier election, six million votes had actually been lost. The Communists and their associates won, by contrast, 11,400,000 votes, or six million more than previously.[2] They even won a small majority in the state of Kerala in southern India, and under the leadership of E. M. S. Namboodiripad, formed the first purely Communist government within a democratic state.

The Praja Socialist party had been enfeebled by a split which occurred a year and a half before the elections. In 1955, Ram Manohar Lohia, one of the party's most brilliant leaders, had broken away to form the Samyukta Socialist party (S.S.P.), which, in the elections of 1957, gained in its struggle with the P.S.P. over a million votes.

Differences rather in the cultural orientation of the party than in its fundamental principles had, in the last resort, destroyed its unity. The ideology and methods of the P.S.P. had been moulded on the Western European style of Social Democracy. Like the Congress party, it was orientated towards the West and sought to modernize India through the ideas, technology, institutions and democratic methods of Western Europe. Lohia, on the other hand, disdained westernization. In his search for an Indian road to Socialism, he stood for cultural nationalism, as was shown by his attitude to the complex problem of language in India whose many nations possess no common language. The second language which serves as a common language for the conglomerate of nations on the Indian sub-continent—for use in Parliament, the courts, the administration and universities—is English.

But in practice English serves only the educated middle class as a second

1. Quoted in *Fact and Fiction in the Congress Manifesto*, a Praja Socialist party publication (New Delhi, 1957), pp. 3 and 6–7.

2. In the earlier 1951–2 elections the Socialist party had won 11,216,000 and the K.M.P.P. 6,226,000 votes, equalling 17,442,000 votes together. The Communists won 3,484,000 and their associates 1,866,000 votes, amounting together to 5,350,000.

language. Lohia perceived the umbilical cord existing between India's privileged élite and their English education. Thus the English language in fact assumed the character of a class barrier, strengthening and sanctifying the exclusiveness and privileges of the educated middle class. Lohia therefore attacked the privileged position held by English as the second language, since in his view it was preventing the development of India's languages and culture. He demanded that it should be supplanted by Hindi, a language understood by a majority of the people.

The P.S.P. was not by any means opposed in principle to the substitution of Hindi for English as India's 'link language', but it saw the need for a longer transitional period than Lohia had visualized, and had declined to make the language question one of high priority, as Lohia had demanded.[1]

Lohia's alliance with cultural nationalism became a source of strength for the S.S.P. So did his party's association with the depressed classes—the *harijans*—for although the Constitution had abolished untouchability and made it an offence under the law, untouchability remained rampant in every town and village. In the elections of 1967, the S.S.P. outstripped the P.S.P. It polled 7,171,000 votes to the P.S.P.'s 4,456,000.

But far more fundamental were the dissensions within the Communist party. It split over differences of opinion over the methods and tactics to be used in its struggle for state power—whether this was to be achieved by armed insurrection or by parliamentary democracy, and whether it should pursue the Russian road to Socialism or an Indian road.

Following the collapse of the insurrection in Telengana and the fiasco of the revolutionary strikes of 1946–8, B. T. Ranadive, the leader of the party's left wing, as mentioned earlier,[2] had been overthrown as general secretary and replaced by Ajoy Gosh, leader of the party's right wing, who had opposed Ranadive's 'adventurist policy'. Under Gosh's leadership the party changed its tactics radically. It disclaimed force as a method in the political struggle and avowed its recognition of democratic constitutional methods as the instrument for the peaceful transformation of existing society into a Socialist commonwealth. It proclaimed an 'Indian road to Socialism' and stood with the leftists and centrists of the Congress party to support a 'national democratic front' as a milestone on the road to Socialism. The party's left wing, however, condemned this policy as both a betrayal of Marxism and 'parliamentary revisionalism'.[3]

China's invasion of India across the Himalayas in 1962 introduced a new element of dissension into the conflict within the party. While the right wing, now led by S. A. Dange (Ajoy Gosh died in 1962), supported the Nehru

1. For a brief survey of the controversy, see Sitanshu Das, *The Future of Indian Democracy* (London, 1970), pp. 33–4.
2. See page 231.
3. See Das, *The Future of Indian Democracy*, p. 21.

3 *Congress of the Socialist International in London, July 1955.*
On the platform (from left to right): Julius Braunthal, Edith Summerskill,
Morgan Phillips, Guy Mollet, Erich Ollenhauer

4 *Congress of the Socialist International in Vienna, July 1957*

government's armed resistance to the Chinese attack, the left wing, under the leadership of Namboodiripad, stood for the solidarity of the Indian Communists with Communist China. In an effort to preserve party unity, the C.P.I. national council, meeting in April 1962, divided its leadership between the left and right wings: Namboodiripad was elected general secretary and Dange chairman.

The party eventually split under the impact of the Moscow–Peking conflict[1] in July 1964, when the pro-Chinese left wing broke away to establish itself as the 'Communist party (Marxist)'. In the 1967 elections it polled 6,140,000 votes as against the 7,564,000 which went to the Moscow-recognized C.P.I. But the Communist party (Marxist) did become the strongest party in Kerala and West Bengal and in both states it was able to form governments in coalition with non-Socialist parties.[2]

Yet, in the event, the Communist party (Marxist) was also to be rent asunder by conflict over Peking's policy towards the India–Pakistan dispute over Kashmir. While the party supported India's claim to Kashmir, Peking supported Pakistan. Furthermore it recognized parliamentary democracy as the method for India's road to Socialism, while Peking despised this as a method. The policy of peaceful coexistence which it supported was rejected by Peking as a 'modern revisionism'. The press and radio of Peking relentlessly denounced the leaders of the Communist party (Marxist) as 'revisionists'. Ultimately its dissenting left wing split away in April 1969 to form, under the leadership of Charu Mazumdar and Kanu Sanyal, the 'Communist party (Marxist–Leninist)'.

As a revolutionary party, it adopted Mao Tse-tung's tactics of guerrilla warfare. In Naxalbari, in the northern regions of West Bengal, it established a base to promote a guerrilla war by the agricultural proletariat against the peasant landowners, taking over their land and killing not a few of them. The movement spread to Calcutta, subjecting the vast city to a rule of terror. By the end of 1969 well over 700 political murders had been reported.

The coalition government of West Bengal, led by the Communist party (Marxist), made an attempt to suppress the 'Naxalists' and arrested several of their leaders, but was unable to quell the movement. Under the impact of the violence which it had unleashed, the Communist coalition government foundered in March 1970.[3]

---

1. See page 475f.
2. The C.P.I. had become the strongest party in Kerala in the elections of 1957, ruling there as the leading force in a coalition government until 1959.
3. See Das, *The Future of Indian Democracy*, pp. 30–1.

11 · Hindu and Buddhist Socialism

1

Two thirds of India's electorate, numbering seventy-two million people, had, as we have seen, voted for the parties which had canvassed them in Socialist terms. In Burma, every party had pledged itself to some version of Marxism in competing for the votes of the electorate, however vaguely this was formulated. 'Marxist slogans', J. S. Thomson began an essay on Marxism in Burma, 'dominated the speeches in Burma's election battle of 1956. From the Prime Minister Nu, the leader of the Anti-Fascist People's Freedom League (A.F.P.F.L.), and Dr E. Maung, leader of the Communist-directed National United Front (N.U.F.), to U Tun Pe on the democratic right, the political leaders of Burma relied on a Marxist appeal to the electorate.'[1]

That Socialist ideas, let alone Marxist theories, could spread within a Hindu culture is a measure of the tremendous social and spiritual revolution which had been unchained by the struggle of the Asian peoples for national independence: for the concepts of Socialism are obviously in sharp contrast to the fundamentals of Hindu philosophy.

The Socialist ideas of a new economic order of human society and Socialism's concern with the material and social conditions of man contradict the Hindu belief in the vanity of human existence. According to the Hindu doctrine, Professor Prasad observed, 'the human being is on a pilgrimage to salvation. Material existence is a halting place on the way. Wealth, desire and the preservation of the individual are meaningless—illusory *maya*. Life is an endless cycle of desires and miseries. The individual's task is to free

1. John Seabury Thomson, 'Marxism in Burma', in Frank N. Trager (ed.), *Marxism in Southeast Asia* (Stanford, 1960), p. 15. Another study of Burma emphasized that, 'Marxism, although not Communism, was in fact the theory favoured in varying degrees by most of the political parties and organizations after the war, and so it has remained until the present day'—Malcolm D. Kennedy, *A Short History of Communism in Asia* (London, 1957), p. 442.

himself from this cycle: to renounce the world, scorn material things and ultimately annihilate the self by merging in the *Shunya*—the void or zero.'[1]

Thus Hinduism inculcates a complete detachment from the affairs of this life and complete indifference to social and economic suffering. The extinction of being is its noblest aim, non-existence being in its scale of values the highest ideal, the longing for non-existence being an expression of profound religious feeling. 'The Indian concept of life,' Jayaprakash Narayan, a leading contemporary Socialist, explained in one of his speeches, 'is that we live in order to achieve our deliverance—whether we call it *Nirvana* with the Buddhists or *Mokshe* with the Hindus—deliverance from the limitations of time and space, from the limitations of life and death, from bondage. This was regarded as the noblest effort, the noblest ideal for humankind to follow: deliverance. Every individual was expected to fight his own battle, not the state for him. Every individual had to struggle in order to free himself from the limitations that his *Karma* had imposed upon him.'[2] Thus Hinduism, rejecting the value of life, stands in contrast to Socialism, which sees life as the highest value.

Also completely incompatible with the religion of Hinduism is the premise of Socialism that all human beings are born equal, and that social and economic inequalities are caused by the social and economic structure of society. For Hinduism, human beings are by no means born equal, but are born into a hierarchy of castes—one into a higher, another into a lower caste, according to the merits and demerits of a being in past existences. The human individual is at the mercy of the inescapable round of rebirth and the soul's reincarnation, the infinite succession of life and death with the law of *Karma* being fulfilled—the inexorable law of retributive justice, according to which one is rewarded for good action and punished for evil, even if not in the present existence.[3] And each man has no choice except to be reconciled to his fate.

The very concept of social justice is therefore foreign to Hindu philosophy. According to the laws of Manu, each one of the four basic castes has been allotted by divine law a clearly defined social position in the hierarchy of Hindu society. Privileges go to the highest castes, and duties to the lowest—the caste of the *Sudras*, which, regarded as inferior by nature, is sentenced to

1. Narmadeshwar Prasad, 'Social Immobility in Asia', in Jayaprakash Narayan, *Cultural Freedom in Asia* (Tokyo, 1956) p. 144.

2. The speech quoted was given by Narayan at the Congress for Cultural Freedom in Rangoon in 1955; see ibid., p. 19.

3. The *Upanishads* teach that 'one can be reborn as a worm or a moth, or as a bird or as a tiger ... or as a human being ... according to one's *Karma*'—quoted in Edward J. Thomas, *The History of Buddhist Thought* (London 1933), p. 110. The *Rig Veda* universalize the concept of *Karma*. According to their teaching, all manifestations in the universe are subject to the law of *Karma*—from the course of the sun to the duties of every human being according to his caste; see ibid., p. 109.

servitude under the higher castes, and even more so the casteless, the so-called Untouchables rejected by Indian society.[1]

Within such a framework of a philosophy of life, social and economic disparities in human society can never be bridged by any social and economic change. For, in the Hindu's view, the hierarchical order is independent of any political, social or economic structure of society, and therefore remains untouched by social reform.[2] Like the movement of the heavenly bodies, it remains unchangeable.

Thus no human being is able to escape the fate imposed by the law of *Karma*, for merits and demerits in previous existences govern his present condition of life and his destiny in any future existence.[3] Within such a context, contemplating reforms with the object of setting up a social order of equals would naturally appear to be wanton interference with divine or cosmic laws. As one Indian Socialist lamented in despair: 'Hinduism militates against the spirit of modern Socialism. . . . The Gods in India tolerate indifference to the world, injustice to the suppressed, distinction for the dogmatist and agony for the social revolutionary.'[4]

Most of the young Indian intellectuals who had been inspired by Socialist and Marxist ideas in the 1920s and 1930s felt nevertheless that their roots still lay in the Hindu tradition; they did not, at any event, fundamentally challenge the Hindu concept of life. But they did seek a new interpretation of Hinduism.

The first real attempt to reconcile Socialism with the Hindu religious tradition was made by Mahatma Gandhi (1869–1948) during his later years. He had, he recorded, reached the conclusion from his studies of religious writings—even before reading *Das Kapital* and other works of Marx, Engels and Lenin during his imprisonment in the camp in the Aga Khan's palace—that 'Socialism was the only way to liberate mankind from its misery'. Yet he could only have reached this conviction by a fresh interpretation of the religious writings. As an orthodox Hindu, a *sanatani*, as he called himself, Gandhi held to the doctrine of a caste-order, the *varnashrama dharma*. 'I

1. *The Laws of Manu in the Sacred Books of the East*, vol. xxv, 1, pp. 88–91.

2. The Indian constitution has relieved the inequality under the law of the casteless pariah; but in practice the caste system has remained untouched by the political changes which have taken place in India since the struggle for independence began. See the excellent study by Narmadeshwar Prasad, *The Myth of the Caste System* (Patna, 1957).

3. 'The castes can exist side by side in embittered hatred only because each one has "earned" his fate, but this does not make the better fate of the other any more comforting for the socially injured. The ideas of revolution or aspiring to "progress" were unthinkable on this basis, as long and as far as the *Karman* teachings remained immovable'—Max Weber, *Gesammelte Aufsätze zur Religionssoziologie*, vol. ii: *Hinduismus und Buddhismus* (Tübingen, 1923), p. 122.

4. Birj Mohan Toofan, *The March of Science and Socialism and Indian Religious Society*, Paper of the Second Political Forum of the Asian Labour Institute (Friedrich Ebert Stiftung), Tokyo, October 1968.

believe,' he wrote, 'in the *varnashrama dharma,* but in the strictly vedic meaning, not in the present outward sense. . . . *Varnashrama* is inborn in human nature. . . . It is destined by birth. A person cannot change his *varna* [caste] according to free will. . . .'[1] But *varna* he interpreted as being 'the law of heritage' and the heritage of the professions. He rejected the hierarchical character of the caste-order as well as its scale of social and moral values;[2] just like every profession, so every caste was equal. And he rejected the overwhelming Hindu concept of the inherited inequality of the individual. 'I believe implictly,' he wrote, 'that all men are born equal.'[3]

He substantiated his profession of Socialism in a new selection of religious writings. 'As I have contended,' he wrote, 'Socialism, even Communism, is explicit in the first verse of the *Upanishads.*'[4] He rejected the principle of private ownership on the grounds of religious conviction, because, he said, it conflicted with the law of God's possession. 'Everything,' he stated, 'belongs to God and was from God. Therefore it was for his people as a whole, not for a particular individual.'[5]

But, with the idea of non-violence uppermost, he strove to abolish private property and to resolve economic conflict not by a class confrontation brought about by state legislation, but by friendly persuasion to convert the propertied classes to their duties as 'trustees' of society. As ownership came from God, and therefore possessions were given to the whole people, so, he concluded, 'when an individual had more than his proportionate portion he became a trustee of that portion for God's people.'[6]

'Non-violent Socialism,' as Gandhi envisaged it, had to rest on the principle of 'trusteeship'. 'Trusteeship,' he maintained, 'provides a means of transforming the present capitalist order of society into an egalitarian one. It

---

1. Mahatma Gandhi, *Jung-Indien. Aufsätze aus den Jahren 1919 bis 1922,* edited by Romain Rolland and Madeleine Rolland (Erlenbach and Zürich, 1924), pp. 345 and 347.

2. Gandhi passionately condemned the degradation of the untouchables as social outcasts. 'If we as Indians are the outcasts of the British Empire,' he wrote, 'then it is only a just reprisal meted out by a just God. Can we ask the English to wash their blood-stained hands before we wash our own? The principle of untouchability has lowered us, has reduced us to castelessness. As long as Indians consider untouchability to be a part of their religion, so long will freedom remain unattainable for us'—*Jung-Indien,* p. 278; see also pp. 221ff.

3. *Jung-Indien,* 29 September 1927, quoted in K. G. Mashruwala, *Gandhi and Marx,* with an Introduction by Vinoba Bhave (Ahmedabad, 1954), p. 75. Rabindranath Tagore not only rejected the hierarchical character of the caste-order, but the caste system in general. India's liberation from British rule would not be adequate, he wrote, if India could not free herself from the source of the main social evil—the caste-system. 'The narrow-mindedness which has made it possible for us to impose on a human majority [the *Sudras,* members of the lowest caste, and the casteless outcasts] the heavy yoke of inferiority, will support itself in a policy of tyranny. . . . The regeneration of the Indian people depends, in my view, immediately and perhaps only on the abolition of the caste-system'—quoted in Helmuth von Glasenapp, *Der Hinduismus* (Munich, 1922), p. 328.

4. M. K. Gandhi, *Towards Non-Violent Socialism,* edited by Bharatan Kumarappa (Ahmedabad, 1951), p. 132.

5. ibid., p. 135.   6. ibid., p. 135.

gives no quarter to capitalism, but gives the present owning class a chance to reform itself. . . . It does not recognize any right to the private ownership of property except in so far as it may be permitted by society for its own welfare. It does not exclude legislative regulation of the ownership and use of wealth. Thus under state-regulated trusteeship, an individual will not be free to hold or use his wealth for selfish satisfaction or in disregard of the interests of society. . . . The character of production will be determined by social necessity and not by personal whim or greed.'[1]

For the peaceful process of realizing Socialism by the method of trusteeship, Gandhi coined the expression '*sarvodaya*'—'all goods for all'. Vinoba Bhave later developed Gandhi's ideas, and attempted to realize them. Gandhi's technique of non-violent resistance to the ruling power of the state in India's struggle for independence had been a moral revolt, supported by a mass movement. By a similar technique of religious and moral appeal, Bhave attempted to achieve an agrarian revolution—a redistribution of land among the landless peasants by a mass movement of land donations—he called it the *bhoodan* movement—and the transfer of property rights to land to the common ownership of a village—called *gramdan*, 'common usufract' of the lands. In fact, since the beginning of the *bhoodan* movement in 1951, several hundred thousand square kilometres of land have been redistributed and thousands of villages been transformed into *gramdan* villages.[2] None of this has been effected by law or direct force, but solely by an appeal to religious and social conscience—an appeal which rests on the belief that all property is given by God for society at large and that the occupier is therefore not the owner, but only the administrator and trustee.

Like Marxist Socialism, *sarvodaya* strives to attain a classless order of society. But it rejects the Marxist road to Socialism: the class struggle, the fight for political power, the theory of state power as an instrument for changing a capitalist economy into a Socialist one as well as the role of force necessary to the process. It seeks to build a Socialist society, not by the state, but through the initiative of the masses; not by a class struggle, but through the harmonious co-operation of all classes; not by the overthrow of the ruling classes by a proletarian revolution, but through their conversion by moral and religious appeal.

In contrast to the Marxist's 'state Socialism', *sarvodaya* Socialism has been defined by Jayaprakash Narayan as a 'people's Socialism'. It seeks the

1. M. K. Gandhi, *Economic and Industrial Life and Relations*, edited by V. B. Kher, vol. I (Ahmedabad, 1957), p. 127. For a Marxist analysis of Gandhi's social ideas, see Buddhadeva Bhattacharyya, *Evolution of the Political Philosophy of Gandhi* (Calcutta, 1969). For a Marxist interpretation of Gandhi's historical role, see Julius Braunthal, '*Mahatma Gandhi und Indiens Revolution*', in *Der Kampf*, vol. XVII (1924).

2. For a survey of the successes as well as the setbacks of the *gramdan* movement, see Gene D. Overstreet, 'India', in James B. Christoph (ed.), *Cases in Comparative Politics* (Boston, 1965), pp. 486–95.

utmost decentralization of economic and political power, the highest degree of self-government and self-administration by the people, and the least degree of interference in economic and social life by the power of the state. It strives towards a 'non-party democracy', like that effected within the *bhoodan* movement by the co-operation of followers from different political parties who have common ideals and aims. And as an indispensable prerequisite for the realization of Socialism, it strives to develop social forms of life through a radical reassessment of the prevailing values and by a moral revolution.[1]

Gandhi's ethical and social ideals had exerted a deep influence on the Socialist party following its fusion with the K.M.P.P. under the leadership of Gandhi's disciple Acharja Kripalani. The 'Political Statement' adopted by the Gaya Conference in 1955 declared 'that Indian Socialists had recognized under Gandhi's impact the importance of non-violence in the struggle and the purity of his methods, like the decentralization of democracy and the economy'. For them also, it stated, 'the Socialist movement has never been exclusively an economic movement; it is also an ethical and cultural one. We have, therefore, worked for the moral and cultural as well as for the economic revolution.'

But, in variance with Gandhi's ideas, the declaration went on to say that 'class struggle is unavoidable in the social revolution' and that 'the party has never been deceived that moral appeals to justice might move the ruling classes voluntarily to liquidate their rule and exploitation'.

In affirming its Marxist concept of the class struggle, the conference declared: 'The class struggle must remain an insoluble symptom of the class society in its various forms so long as society is divided into classes. . . . No radical change in the economic order has ever taken place automatically. Even if the economic conditions were ripe for change, the ruling class would resist it. History knows of no single instance when a class has accepted the liquidation of its rule and privileges on a moral appeal and without a fight. And there is no reason to believe that India's capitalists would show themselves to be more human than their brothers in the rest of the world.'[2]

While the Praja Socialist party did not identify itself with the *bhoodan* movement, it gave it moral support.[3]

1. For the discussion of the differences between the Marxist concept of Socialism and *sarvodaya* Socialism, see Jayaprakash Narayan, *From Socialism to Sarvodaya* (Rajghat, 1958). For a profile of Vinoba Bhave, his teaching and action, see Suresh Ramabhai, *Vinoba and his Mission* (Sevagram, 1954). For a biographical essay on Narayan, see Herbert Passin, 'The Jeevan Dani: A Profile of Jayaprakash Narayan', in *Encounter*, June 1958, pp. 46–55.

2. Report of the Second National Conference of the Praja Socialist Party, Gaya, December 1955 (New Delhi, 1956), pp. 172 and 197. This 'political declaration', drawn up by Narenda Deva, is the most searching theoretical explanation of the party's ideology.

3. ibid., p. 182.

If there is any other Socialist party which is ideologically close to us [wrote one of its leaders], then it is the *bhoodan* movement. We cannot, however, in the present political and economic situation, accept the ideal of a 'non-party democracy' and a stateless society. But the general objectives and new values which the *bhoodan* movement is attempting to bring forth stem from our common rich past.[1]

2

In Burma, the national freedom movement had developed much later than in India. It received its initial impetus from a peasants' revolt in 1930–1. It was not until the 1930s that Marxist literature found its way into the country. When it did, the young nationalist intellectuals eagerly seized on Marxism as a source of enlightenment. It provided them with a theoretical basis and moral justification in their fight against British Imperialism as well as against the foreign capitalism whose exploitation had reduced their country to poverty. English capital was in possession of teak forests, petroleum sources and mineral mines, and had developed the production and export of rice to a high degree. Every village had its Indian, and often also its Chinese, moneylender, whose rates of interest were between 15 and 36 per cent. And when the price of rice dropped as a result of the rapid expansion in rice production, the Burmese peasant fell into debt and finally lost his land. 'The Indians, particularly the Chattyar moneylenders, came near to destroying the Burmese peasantry of Lower Burma.'[2] The peasants' reaction was the revolt of 1930.

About two thirds of the cultivated land in Burma had fallen into the hands of the Indian and Chinese moneylenders; Indian coolies, brought in from Bengal, had forced down the wages of the Burmese workers;[3] Indian and Chinese capitalists governed the rice-mills and the rice trade and, in Rangoon, the retail trade and most of the industrial factories. A capitalist middle class hardly existed among the indigenous Burmese. Rangoon, the capital of Burma, was more an Indian than a Burmese city. 'Almost all local-born nationalists belonged to the "suppressed" class, while the capitalist and imperialist, an almost complete stranger, belonged to the class of the "oppressor".'[4]

A social conflict—the peasants' revolt—had ignited the national struggle

---

1. Ishwarlal Desai, 'Need for a New Dimension', in *The New Socialist*, vol. I (1958).

2. Angus Maude, *South Asia* (London, 1960), p. 81; see also J. S. Furnivall, *Colonial Policy and Practice* (Cambridge, 1948), and *Introduction to the Political Economy of Burma* (Rangoon, 1957).

3. In December 1930 in Rangoon the situation came to a head in a riot by the Burmese dockers against the Indian immigrants, especially the Indian coolies. See D. G. E. Hall, *Burma* (London, 1950), p. 158.

4. Thomson, 'Marxism in Burma', in Trager ed., *Marxism in Southeast Asia*, p. 20. See also U Ba Swe, *The Burmese Revolution* (Information Department, Union Burma, 1952), pp. 10–11.

in Burma, and it became, unlike the national struggle in India, at the same time a fight against capitalism. It was a class struggle of the propertyless Burmese people against their exploitation by the property-owning classes of foreign nations. Marxism triumphed in Burma as an ideology because it offered the intellectual an understanding of the economic and social relationships in colonialism and showed him a way and an objective.

Yet, even as the oppressed in the religious age in Europe had over the centuries sought to justify their risings against oppression in religious concepts and by 'Holy writ',[1] so in Southern Asia Socialist ideas could only be formulated in religious language and concepts. Thus Gandhi deduced his version of Socialism from the holy scriptures of the *Rig Veda*, and the Islamic religious Socialists, as we shall see later, derived theirs from the *Koran*.

In Burma, a profoundly religious country, Marxism could only become the ideology of a mass movement by a symbiosis with Buddhism, which is deeply rooted in the country's religious, cultural and national traditions. Over many centuries of dynastic history it has come to govern overwhelmingly the emotions and thinking of the whole nation, and so Marxism had to be assimilated into Buddhist concepts and terminology.

The *Theravada* version of Buddhism found in Burma offers less resistance than Hinduism to the assimilation of Marxism. Buddhism is hardly touched by the Hindu concept of caste; the Buddhist monasteries include members of every caste as well as outcasts in their monastic communities. Buddhism entirely rejects the hierarchical structure of the caste-system.[2]

In contrast to the Hindu community, the modern Buddhists of Burma could draw upon ideas expressed centuries before the spread of Socialist and Marxist ideas and conclude from the teachings of Buddha 'that all men are born equal and that [social] differences are superficial and the work of men'.[3]

1. The classic documents which justify a social uprising by invoking the gospels are the Twelve Articles of the insurgent German peasants of 1525 in their fight for freedom from bondage. Bondage, the Articles stated, 'is most wretched seeing that Christ has released and bought us with his dearly shed blood, the shepherds as well as the illustrious, with no exceptions. Therefore it is shown by the gospel that we are free, and we wish to be so'. For economic and social motives in the early Church, see Karl Kautsky, *Ursprung des Christentums* (Stuttgart, 1908). For social-revolutionary elements in religious guise in the chiliastic movements of the Middle Ages, see Norman Cohn, *The Pursuit of the Millennium* (London, 1957); for a religious-Socialist undercurrent in the English revolution of the seventeenth century, see Eduard Bernstein, *Sozialismus und Demokratie in der englischen Revolution* (Stuttgart, 1908), and H. N. Brailsford, *The Levellers and the English Revolution* (London, 1961). The French Revolution of 1789 was the first political and social revolution to be free of religious undercurrents.

2. 'Not by birth does one become a Brahman, not by birth does one become casteless. . . . One becomes casteless by deeds, by deeds a Brahman,' the Buddhist writings stated; quoted in E. Sarkisyanz, *Buddhist Backgrounds of the Burmese Revolution*, with a Preface by Dr Paul Mus (The Hague, 1965) pp. 24–5. This work is the most thorough study of the social aspects of Buddhism so far undertaken.

3. *Maha Bodhi and the United Buddhist World*, vol. xv (August, 1907) cited in ibid., p. 121.

The Buddha gave the monastic order which he founded a democratic, republican constitution, which remained unweakened during two and a half millennia and which became, in the twentieth century, a source of inspiration for democratic ideologies.

Under the influence of Marxism, the teachings of Buddha were interpreted in their deepest social sense and were defined by some Buddhist thinkers as forerunners of Marxist ideas. As U Ba Yin, the minister for education, wrote, for example, Karl Marx must 'have been influenced directly or indirectly by Buddhism'. 'Buddhism is communistic,' he commented, 'because it rejects any form of rule and exploitation.'[1] Within the *Samgha*, the community of Buddhist monasteries, a 'Society of Marxist Monks' was formed, and these welcomed the beginning of Socialism in Burma as the dawn of an epoch which was to see the fulfilment of the Buddha's teaching.[2]

But above all it was U Ba Swe (b. 1915), in his attempt to harmonize Marxism with Buddhism, who impressed upon Burmese Socialism the peculiar character of a Buddhist–Marxist ideology. U Ba Swe stood among the outstanding leaders of the Burmese revolution and was one of the architects of the Burmese Republic; he had been general secretary of the Socialist party, president of the Trade Union Council and president of the Asian Socialist Conference.

U Ba Swe saw Buddhism, like Marxism, as a philosophy which strove to release mankind from suffering; Buddhist philosophy sought release from spiritual suffering, Marxist philosophy from economic suffering. Both philosophies pointed the way to *Nirvana*; Buddhism to a spiritual *Nirvana*— a spiritual state of the total release of human beings from passion and the demands of selfish greed; Marxism to a 'worldly *Nirvana*', the *Loka Nibban*, a 'state of peace and harmony'.[3]

Marxist theory, he stated in December 1951 at a conference of trade union leaders, 'is not antagonistic to Buddhist philosophy. The two are, frankly speaking, not merely similar. In fact, they are the same in concept. . . . Marxist theory deals with mundane affairs and seeks to satisfy material needs in life. Buddhist philosophy, however, deals with the solution of spiritual matters with a view to seeking spiritual satisfaction in this life and liberation from this mundane world.'

He then made a confession of faith. 'I declare,' he said, 'that I have implicit faith in Marxism, but at the same time I boldly assert that I am a true Buddhist. In the beginning, I was a Buddhist only by tradition. The more I study Marxism, however, the more I feel convinced in Buddhism.'

Yet, for the tasks which faced the Burmese revolution, only Marxism

1. Quoted in Sarkisyanz, *Buddhist Backgrounds of the Burmese Revolution*, pp. 192–3, 198.
2. See ibid., p. 199.   3. Quoted in ibid., pp. 169–70.

could provide it with an ideology. Marxism, he stated, 'is the guide to action in our revolutionary movement, in our establishment of a Socialist Burmese State for workers and peasants. Our revolution can only be achieved with Marxism as a guiding principle. Only Marxism can pave the way for the attainment of the goal to which we look forward. Our revolution is impossible without Marxism as a guide.'[1]

But, he hastened to add, the acceptance of Marxism as the guide to the revolutionary movement did not 'mean the adoption of Russian methods or Chinese methods or Yugoslavian methods. The Burmese revolution should be achieved by Burmese methods.'

Like U Ba Swe, so did U Nu (b. 1907) find his belief in Socialism mirrored in Buddhist philosophy. He was an ardent Buddhist, not merely by tradition, but through a deep study of Buddhist texts and he saw his destiny in the fulfilment of Buddhist teachings. To celebrate the 2,500th anniversary of Gautama Buddha's birth in 1954, he convened, as a Buddhist prime minister, the Sixth Grand Council in Rangoon to revive the purity of Buddha's original doctrines through a fresh scrutiny of the *Pali* canon. The expansion of Socialist ideology in Burma owed its success in no small degree to his conversion to Socialism. Together with Aung Saw and U Ba Swe, he stood in the forefront of the revolution; and after Aung Saw's assassination in July 1947,[2] he became its leader.

U Nu had received his impetus towards Socialism from Marxism after translating a selection from *Das Kapital* into Burmese, and Marxism had become the predominant influence in his view of social problems. Yet when he analysed them in his speeches and writings, he used the terminologies of Buddhism. When, for example, he defined the institution of private property as the cause of class division and class struggle, he was following in Marx's own footsteps. 'Since the inception of private property,' he said, paraphrasing the *Communist Manifesto*, 'the history of the world has become [a history of] class struggles.' In Marxist terms, he described how, through the institution of private property, humanity had been divided into the exploiting and the exploited, into oppressors and oppressed, and how the majority of people had become increasingly impoverished despite the abundance of natural resources. To justify the need to abolish private property, however, he turned to a 'correct' interpretation of Buddhist writings. Its abolition would, he said, 'not only end the bloody conflict between classes, but will also . . . eliminate class differences, overwork, theft, squabbling and fraud. . . . The world will rise to freedom out of this misery.'[3] But as he described the Socialist order of society in the picture he painted of the ideal future, it was as it had been promised in the Buddhist writings—a society without

1. U Ba Swe, *The Burmese Revolution* (Rangoon, 1952), pp. 7 and 4.
2. See page 261.
3. Quoted in Sarkisyanz, *Buddhist Backgrounds of the Burmese Revolution*, p. 215.

oppressors and oppressed, without capitalism, imperialism, or the bloodshed of wars and class struggles.[1]

While U Nu accepted the economic theories of Marxism, he rejected, however, its theory of the state, for he believed this might lead to a totalitarian system of government and the economic system of state capitalism, as it had in Russia. In a speech before the third congress of the A.F.P.F.L., the ruling party, in January 1958, he rejected Marxism as a philosophical-political ideology. But at the same time he confirmed his belief in the economic doctrine of Marxism and declared that 'the fundamental goal, which we must always keep in view, is the construction in the Union of Burma of a Socialist state in which capitalism plays no part'.[2]

Socialism he saw as an economic system, which would, in a sense, bring about the fulfilment of Buddha's teaching, at any rate as a way forward to the goal he had indicated; for the ending of greed, hate and passion at which Buddhism aims have their origins in the institution of private property. It was this attitude which won Socialism the support of the monks. When U Nu's Socialist programme for the February 1960 election was rejected by the so-called Buddhist Democratic party as being 'non-Buddhist', the abbots of the most respected monasteries declared themselves in favour of the programme and praised U Nu as the statesman who had come closest to the ideal of a Buddhist statesman in the tradition of the great King Ashoka.

The Socialist ideas advocated by U Nu and U Ba Swe had originally manifested themselves in the constitution defined by the constituent assembly on 24 September 1947. This had laid the foundations for a parliamentary democratic form of government as well as for a welfare state. The Two-Year Plan for Burma's Economic Development, which was also ratified by the constituent assembly, declared its aim to be 'the development of a fully Socialist economic constitution in Burma'.[3] Political and economic aims were explained in detail in an interim programme published by the government in December 1953, the introduction to which stated:

The ultimate objective of the government and the people of the Union of Burma, as embodied in the constitution, is to create a democratic Socialist state. We must never lose sight of the fact that the Socialist state which we wish to set up includes neither Communism nor state Socialism. The tyranny inborn to both systems must never be allowed to develop in the Socialist state as we wish to create it. . . . Socialism in Burma must be fully harmonized with the religious beliefs and cultural background and heritage of the people. . . . The new epoch is nothing less than the *Pyidawatha* state [welfare state], for whose creation we have pledged ourselves.[4]

The principles guiding the Burmese government in its setting up of a

1. See ibid., p. 223.   2. U Nu, *Towards a Socialist State* (Rangoon, 1958), p. 3.
3. U Mya, *The Two-Year Plan for Economic Development in Burma* (Rangoon, 1948), p. 40.
4. *Our Goal and Our Interim Programme* (Rangoon, 1953).

Socialist order of society were formulated in the 'Interim Programme' as follows:

(a) In the Socialist state that we shall create, commerce and industry must serve the interests of the *ludu* [masses], and the *ludu* must not serve the interest of commerce and industry. It must not be a system which will extract the maximum profit from the *ludu* without any regard for its welfare and interest.

(b) Ultimately, all trade and industry must be organized into public corporations and co-operatives controlled and managed by the representatives of the workers and consumers.

The programme stressed above all the necessity to realize the idea of equality and to develop a system of people's self-government in every sphere of political and economic life. The rights of equality and freedom were defined in Article II of the Union of Burma's constitution as 'basic rights', and democracy as 'our most treasured possession'.

To protect democracy the parliament passed the Democratic Administration Act, which delegated political power right down to the smallest village. 'Through this delegation of power', the 'Interim Programme' declared:

(a) the whole people of the Union will be pledged to take responsibility for the administration of their own affairs;

(b) by accepting this responsibility, the people will themselves become a bastion against the misuse of power by the government or power-hungry elements;

(c) the problems of *ludu* will [by self-administration] be solved far more carefully and more satisfactorily; ... and

(d) the execution of democratic rights and responsibilities in every village unit will lead to many people becoming educated to a strong belief in democracy and gaining the experience and knowledge necessary for democratic responsibility.[1]

The 'Interim Programme' embodied an important Socialist principle—the principle of solidarity in the struggle for human emancipation, unknown to Hinduism or Buddhism, which preaches indifference towards the world and its needs—an aspect particularly emphasized in the *Theravada* Buddhism which is predominant in Burma, Ceylon, Cambodia and Thailand. This defines the individual's liberation as an ultimate goal—not for humanity as a whole, but by a solitary quest along the Noble Eightfold Path by which the individual may achieve release from the recurrent cycle of worlds and existences.

Yet, even so, the people and government of a Buddhist country were able to pledge themselves constitutionally to establish a Socialist order of society, founded on the solidarity of the people. This phenomenon alone is a measure of the influence that Socialist ideas had in southern Asia on a religious reformation which had received its impetus from social and political upheaval.

1. *Interim Programme* pp. 6 and 1–3.

3

Socialism in Asia, as an idea and a movement, emanated from the nationalist revolution of its peoples. This shook the vast proletarian masses in the villages and towns out of the paralysing apathy into which they had subsided over the centuries. Hitherto they had accepted misery as an inescapable factor in that religious fatalism upon which the philosophies of Hinduism and Buddhism, as well as of Islam, rest. The national freedom movement had awakened their national consciousness. For the first time in their history they had entered into a conscious struggle to achieve specifically political aims.

Yet the nationalist revolution had also aroused their social consciousness. They had become aware of their own misery as no longer an inescapable fate, but as something which they could expect to be ameliorated by the state, which was now their state. They began to exert pressure to change the emphasis from a national to a social revolution—a revolution that would bring about the fulfilment of social justice.

However, Socialism in Asia received its impetus from economic as well as from nationalist imperatives. In the countries of southern Asia—pre-capitalist and industrially underdeveloped countries with small, embattled capitalist enclaves—the economic misery of the vast and fast expanding masses could only be relieved by the rapid development of the means of production; social justice could only follow upon an improved level of economic development.

The architects of the new independent states therefore faced the question of the method they would choose to bring about the rapid development of the means of production. The capitalist method, by which the agrarian countries of Europe and North America had been industrialized and which had increased their means of production a thousandfold, would have had the effect of subjecting the nations of Asia once more to the foreign rule from which the national revolution had liberated them. Yet since the rate of accumulation of indigenous capital would have been far too small to allow for rapid and extensive industrialization, the task, if left to foreign capital, would inevitably develop a system of a new colonialism. And if profit remained the sole motive behind industrialization, then only those branches of industry which could expect a relatively high return on capital would be developed, while immeasurable productive resources would remain unexploited. But, above all, capitalism hardly seemed an appropriate tool for constructing a society based on the principle of social justice which had inspired its national revolution.

The surprising expansion of Socialist ideas in southern Asia may thus be explained also by the fact that the governments of the newly independent states pursued economic progress by Socialist methods. They did not leave the development of the means of production to private capitalist enterprise working on an anarchical contest basis for the highest possible profit, but themselves took the initiative by creating a planned economy which, like India's Second Five-Year Plan, for example, saw its 'main task' as being 'to increase the income of the propertyless classes and to reduce the wealth and privileges of the propertied classes'.[1]

None of the new states of southern Asia planned a comprehensive socialization of the economy. They left one sector of industry to private enterprise and left the land in the hands of the peasants. But they secured the state's power over the economy by its control of key sectors. These, according to India's Second Five-Year Plan, were 'all industries of basic and strategic importance'—seventeen in all—which the government had developed as nationalized industries using Socialist methods. In a further group of twelve industries the state had taken the initiative for development while leaving private enterprise some room for manoeuvre, and the remaining industries were left entirely in the hands of private enterprise.[2]

Similar plans for economic reconstruction to those in India were followed by the governments of Burma, Ceylon and Indonesia. According to the varied conditions in those countries, they differed in details and degree. But a Socialist trend was general to them all.

1. See *Second Five-Year Plan 1956*, p. 17. 2. See ibid., pp. 13–16.

12 · Socialist and Communist Movements in Buddhist Countries

1. Burma

A Buddhist–Socialist ideology as the ideology of the Burmese nation had, as we have seen, developed in the course of the nationalist revolution. The group which was to become the spearhead of the revolution—*Dohbama Asiayone* (the 'We-Burmans Association')—was a nationalist organization founded in 1930 by students of the University of Rangoon. Their members referred to each other as *Thakin*, 'Master', taking the Burmese form of address to Europeans so as to demonstrate their objective: to make the Burmese masters in their own land.

But in the course of the 1930s under the influence of Marxist literature, many leaders of the Thakin party became either Socialists or Communists. In August 1939 the Socialists—Thakin Mya (1897–1947), U Ba Swe and Kyaw Nyein among them—founded a Socialist party under the title of the Burma Revolutionary party; and in 1943 the Communists, under the leadership of Thein Pe (alias Myint), Thakin Soe and Thakin Than Tun, founded the Burma Communist party.[1] Both parties were groups within the Thakin movement, which did not, however, declare itself for any Socialist ideology until the gaining of independence; it remained an exclusively nationalist movement.

The national movement, which until the uprising in Rangoon in July 1938 —an eruption of hatred between Burmese and Indians—was largely one of the intellectuals, provided the impetus for its transformation into a mass movement of workers and peasants; it accepted the leadership of the Socialist Thakins. In the wake of the uprising, U Ba Swe, together with Ba Hein,

1. See J. S. Thomson, 'Marxism in Burma', in Frank N. Trager (ed.), *Marxism in Southeast Asia* (Stanford, 1960), pp. 26–7, 29 and 306–7. This description is founded mainly on this essay, as well as on Malcolm D. Kennedy, *A Short History of Communism in Asia* (London, 1957); J. H. Brimmel, *Communism in South-East Asia. A Political Analysis* (London and New York, 1959); and Saul Rose, *Socialism in Southern Asia* (London, 1959), pp. 95–143.

organized a strike of the workers in the oil wells of Yenanyaung and Chank, and led them in a protest march from the wells to Rangoon. While the strike continued, the Thakins called for the first All-Burma Labour Conference to take place in July 1939. From this emerged the All-Burma Trades Union Congress (A.B.T.U.C.), founded on 30 January 1940. Several months later, in August, it announced its programme to include the setting up of a Socialist state, the nationalization of the means of production, minimum wages, social welfare, and equality under the law irrespective of race.[1]

Together with the striking oil workers, the peasants had massed to join the march to Rangoon. An All-Burma Peasants' Conference, organized by Thakin Mya, assembled under his chairmanship in the Shwe Dagon Pagoda and decided upon the formation of an All-Burma Peasants' Organization with the declared aims of national liberation for Burma, the raising of peasants' living standards, the revocation of rights to land tenure, the collectivization of land and oil, and the setting up of a Socialist state under worker and peasant leadership.[2]

The founding of the All-Burma Trades Union Congress and the All-Burma Peasants' Organization under the leadership of Socialist Thakin members were events of great historical significance. They alone had succeeded in arousing a national consciousness among the workers and peasants and in implanting Socialist ideas into the movement; and they, above all, had given the national and social revolution which they strove to achieve a mass base from which to work.

The Japanese occupation of Burma during the Second World War gave the Thakin movement its chance to organize a military force. Before the outbreak of war the Japanese government had offered military and financial aid to the Burmese in their struggle for independence. When, in 1931, Japan attacked China and occupied Manchuria and several of the northern provinces, it had set itself the objective not only of dominating the Chinese Empire, but also the whole of South-East Asia. To this end it tried to win the revolutionary independence movement in Burma as an ally. In view of the prevailing international situation, Japan was indeed the only foreign power which was in a position to assist the Burmese independence struggle. In secret negotiations, conducted by Aung San on behalf of the 'Burmese Revolutionary Group' with accredited representatives of the Japanese government, solemn pledges for the independence of Burma were demanded from and in fact given by the Japanese.

However, the Communists as well as some of the Socialists in the Thakin movement leadership declared themselves against any alliance with the Japanese: the Communists because the Soviet Union supported China

1. See Thomson, 'Marxism in Burma', in Trager (ed.), *Marxism in Southeast Asia*, p. 27.
2. See Rose, *Socialism in Southern Asia*, p. 97.

against Japan; the Socialists because Japan was a Fascist state. A majority of the Socialist Burma Revolutionary party as well as the revolutionary national-ists, on the other hand, advocated accepting the Japanese offer, because they did not believe that the fight against Great Britain for Burma's independence could be won without the support of a foreign power.

The agreement with the Japanese government was at length concluded early in 1940 by the 'Freedom Bloc'—a coalition formed after the outbreak of the war between the Thakin party and the Nationalist party, led by Ba Maw.

It was Bogyoke Aung San (1916–47) who was to emerge as the outstanding figure of the Burmese revolution. He finished his studies at the University of Rangoon in 1938, and shortly afterwards became general secretary of the Thakin party. To escape the threat of arrest he fled to China in 1940, and from there went to Japan, having already laid the foundation for the Burma Independence Army (B.I.A.) organized by Ne Win. The Japanese govern-ment had undertaken to give military training to the 'Thirty Heroes' re-cruited through the Socialist party, and to send them afterwards to Siam to liaise from there with the B.I.A. With the 'Thirty', Aung San returned to Burma in January 1942 in the wake of the Japanese invasion army as com-mander of the B.I.A.

The Japanese government had, as has been mentioned, given a solemn pledge that it would recognize Burma's independence, and the Japanese troops who marched into Burma were hailed as liberators by the population. The Japanese invasion had begun on 18 January 1942, and within five months, by the middle of May, the last British and Indian troops had either withdrawn from the country or been placed in prison camps. Burma was now in the hands of the Japanese.

But the Japanese government proved very reluctant to honour any of its promises. Over a year passed before, on 1 August 1943, when the fortunes of war had already turned against Japan, they would allow the independence of Burma to be declared and a government installed under the prime-ministership of Ba Maw. Thakin Mya became deputy prime minister, Aung San minister of defence, U Nu foreign minister, Than Tun minister of agriculture and Kyaw Nyein secretary of the cabinet and deputy minister for information.

But this government was only a façade; the country continued in practice to be ruled and plundered by the Japanese conquerors. It now became im-portant to organize a powerful resistance movement to expel the Japanese, and while the Communists and Socialists remained within the government, they began the dangerous game of mobilizing forces for a planned uprising against the army of occupation.

Aung San, as minister of defence and commander-in-chief, took the initiative. By November 1943 he had already established radio contact with the British government in India,[1] and in March 1944 the Burma Revolutionary party (it changed its name in September 1945 to the Socialist party) reached agreement with the Burma Communist party on the formation of a United Front to fight the Japanese occupation. The agreement was sealed on 1 August at a discussion between representatives of both parties (Thakin Mya, U Ba Swe and Kyaw Nyein for the Burma Revolutionary party, Thakin Soe and Than Tun for the Communists) and General Aung San in U Nu's apartment in Rangoon. On the same day that the United Front (it later took the title Anti-Fascist People's Freedom League—A.F.P.F.L.) entered into existence it issued a manifesto calling on the Burmese people to: 'Arise and chase out the Fascist Japanese bandits!' The army undertook the necessary clandestine printing and distribution.[2]

But the Socialist–Communist alliance did not survive for long. The A.F.P.F.L. leadership was divided between Aung San as president and Than Tun as general secretary; and Than Tun was, at the same time, president of the Communist party. The overwhelming majority of the A.F.P.F.L.'s membership of about 200,000, including army personnel, were in 1945 in the Revolutionary party's camp. The Communist party, differently and more strongly disciplined, tried to capture the leadership of the resistance movement. So that it would be clearly differentiated from the Communist party, the Burma Revolutionary party reconstituted itself in September 1945 as the Socialist party with Thakin Mya as president, U Ba Swe as general secretary and Kyaw Nyein as his deputy.

The latent conflict between the Socialists and Communists within the A.F.P.F.L. came to a head over the vital question of the tactics to be adopted after the re-entry into Burma of the British army. To assist the British invasion, the A.F.P.F.L. organized an armed uprising for 27 March 1945. The B.I.A., trained and armed by the Japanese, attacked the Japanese army on all fronts until the arrival of the British forces.[3]

But from the ruins of Japanese rule in Burma there arose not a free independent state, but once again a colonial country under the administration of a British governor. The utmost concession that Britain was willing to grant was to promise a transition from colonial to Dominion status over the course of six years; the independence for Burma demanded by the A.F.P.F.L. was categorically rejected.[4]

The Socialist party within the A.F.P.F.L. wanted to continue the fight by

1. See Thomson, 'Marxism in Burma', in Trager (ed.), *Marxism in Southeast Asia*, p. 29.
2. See Thomson, 'Marxism in Burma', in Trager (ed.), *Marxism in Southeast Asia*, pp. 29–30; Rose, *Socialism in Southern Asia*, pp. 102–3.
3. For the role played by the B.I.A. in these battles, see M. Collis, *First and Last in Burma* (London, 1946), pp. 232–7.
4. For a review of the development of the relationship between Britain and Burma in the years following the end of the war, see J. S. Furnivall, 'Twilight in Burma', in *Pacific Affairs*, March and June 1949, pp. 3–20 and 155–72.

revolutionary methods until Burma's independence had been gained. The armed forces of the national revolution were to be of decisive importance in this struggle. The B.I.A., or, as it later came to be called, the 'Burmese Patriotic Forces', had after the re-establishment of British rule largely been amalgamated into the Burmese army, under British command. But Aung San had organized those troops of the B.I.A. who escaped amalgamation into an armed 'People's Volunteer Organization' (P.V.O.) to constitute a fighting army of the A.F.P.F.L. in the coming ultimate struggle.

The Communists, however, rejected the revolutionary tactics adopted by the Socialists out of respect for the alliance between the Soviet Union and Great Britain. Like the Communists in India,[1] the Burmese Communists, in accordance with Moscow's policy, allied themselves with the British against the nation's struggle for independence. They betrayed the preparations for the uprising planned by the Socialists, and gave away the locations of their concealed arms depots.[2] Thus the treachery of the Communist party forced the A.F.P.F.L. to revert to a non-violent mass struggle.

Meanwhile, at the beginning of 1946, the Communist party, led by Than Tun, split into two. Its left wing, under the leadership of Thakin Soe, formed a new Communist party under the title 'Red Flags' to fight the original Communist party, now called 'White Flags', as well as the Socialist party and the A.F.P.F.L. The A.F.P.F.L. expelled it from its ranks. The 'Red Flags' aimed to seize state power by armed insurrection, taking Mao Tse-tung's method and strategy of guerrilla warfare as a model in their attempt to conquer the countryside.

The tussle for the leadership of the A.F.P.F.L.—between its Socialist and Communist members and between Aung San, its president, and Than Tun, its general secretary—became acute as the struggle for Burma's independence entered its last phase. In September 1946, Sir Hubert Rancer, the last British Governor of Burma, had, under pressure of a general strike, asked Aung San to form a provisional government. Aung San, wishing to secure for the A.F.P.F.L. a predominance on the ministerial council and to reduce Communist influence to a minimum, nominated among the nine council members six A.F.P.F.L. representatives, though these included only one Communist, passing over the party chairman, Than Tun, and nominating his rival, Thein Pe (alias Myint). The break-up of the Socialist–Communist coalition finally became inevitable when, the government having been formed, the question of the future policies in Burma's struggle for independence arose. Before its

1. See page 228.
2. For this accusation, see the testimony of the Socialist party, cited in Rose, *Socialism in Southern Asia*, p. 105; see also Thomson, 'Marxism in Burma', in Trager (ed.), *Marxism in Southeast Asia*, p. 32.

formation Aung San had pursued the technique of mass resistance by strikes and street demonstrations. Now he hoped the objective could be attained by negotiations.

In the meantime, however, the 'White Flag' Communist party had changed its policy course sharply to the left in line with the change of course made by the Soviet Union following the collapse of the alliance with the Western powers as a result of their differences about the countries of Eastern Europe and Germany. Britain was now to be treated as Russia's enemy. The Communist party condemned Aung San's new tactic as a betrayal of the revolution, and in October Thein Pe resigned from the ministerial council'[1] Upon this the Socialists suspended the 'White Flag' Communist party from A.F.P.F.L. membership.

The discussions which Aung San had initiated with Clement Attlee's Labour government on the independence of Burma were concluded, despite Communist resistance, in January 1947. The Attlee–Aung San Agreement guaranteed Burma 'full independence within one year' provided a clear majority of a constituent assembly, which was to be elected, declared its support. The Communist party condemned the agreement, accusing Aung San of having betrayed the country, and then attempted to set off national strikes in workshops, schools and universities.

In the event the elections to the constituent assembly in April 1947 saw them defeated; the predominantly Socialist A.F.P.F.L. gained 173 of the 220 seats and the Communist party only seven. On 17 October 1947, in fulfilment of the agreement, Attlee and U Nu signed the Treaty of Burma's Independence, to be proclaimed on 4 January 1948.

Aung San was not to live to see this triumphant conclusion to the struggle he had led. On 19 July 1947, when the government met under his chairmanship, nationalist fanatics invaded the conference room and murdered him together with six of his colleagues; among them was Thakin Mya, the founder and greatly esteemed leader of the Socialist party. The constituent assembly thereupon elected the president, U Nu, to succeed Aung San as prime minister.

Burma was now a free and sovereign state. In the Constitution, passed by Parliament on 24 September 1947, a month before the signing of the Attlee–U Nu Agreement, the setting up of a democratic Socialist order of society was proclaimed as the aim of the people and government of Burma. The prohibition of private monopolist undertakings was declared among the fundamental rights. The state was declared as the ultimate owner of all land, with the right to alter land tenures or to assume possession with a view to

1. Thein Pe was criticized by the Communist party for having accepted a post on the Council of Ministers, and he was expelled from the central committee and finally debarred from the party he had helped to found.

redistribution. Large landholdings were prohibited. For workers the state was to provide protective legislation designed to secure the right of association, limit hours of work, ensure annual holidays and improve working conditions.[1]

The 'White Flag' Communist party took up the position of a parliamentary opposition, but pledged its loyalty to the Constitution, for which it had voted. Very shortly afterwards, however, they found themselves having to decide whether to co-operate in the evolutionary process of setting up a young Socialist state, or whether, like their brothers of the 'Red Flag', they should attempt the revolutionary experiment of overthrowing the democratic Socialist régime to seize power by an armed insurrection. When the founding of the Cominform at the end of September 1947 finally confirmed the great gulf between the Soviet Union and the Western powers, it gave the signal for a radical leftward swing in the politics of Communist parties in all countries.[2] After an initial hesitation, the Burma Communist party decided to follow suit.

The new political course decided upon by the party became clear in an interview given by H. N. Goshal (alias Ba Tin) on 20 December 1947. Goshal, a member of his party's Politbureau, was Than Tun's closest adviser. He declared the Anglo-Burmese treaty to be a deception which 'virtually subjects Burma to permanent enslavement'. 'We Communists,' he said, 'regard this treaty as a treaty of national humiliation and permanent slavery. . . . Thakin Nu and his colleagues . . . have gone over to the imperialists and have become their willing tools.'[3] In a number of theses addressed 'to the present political situation in Burma and our tasks', he argued that the time to fight for power had arrived and that it was the duty of the Communist party to organize a national insurrection against the government of the A.F.P.F.L. The theses were ratified by the Communist party on 18 February 1948 and, at the end of the month, Than Tun declared in his opening address to the Calcutta congress of the Indian Communist party, to which he had led a delegation, that the Burmese party was determined to seize power—if possible without civil war but, if necessary, by a struggle during which the Communists would 'smash the feudal imperialist bourgeoisie'.[4] On 27 March he made a speech in Rangoon calling upon the masses to join a national insurrection against the A.F.P.F.L. government, and two days later the Communist rebellion began.

Burma now became for over two years the setting for a terrible civil war. In July and August 1948 the units of Communist troops in the P.V.O. and the army mutinied and joined the rebellion, and then in January 1949 the Karens—a national minority—also arose, demanding the establishment of an

1. See also pp. 252–3; Rose, *Socialism in Southern Asia*, p. 110.　2. See pp. 148–51.
3. Quoted in Thomson, 'Marxism in Burma', in Trager (ed.), *Marxism in Southeast Asia*, p. 38.
4. Quoted in Thomson, 'Marxism in Burma' in Trager (ed.), *Marxism in Southeast Asia*, pp. 38–9.

autonomous state within the framework of the Union of Burma. Within less than a year the Irrawaddy delta from north Rangoon to beyond Mandalay in the heart of the country was in the hands of the insurgents—the 'White Flag' and 'Red Flag' Communists, the P.V.O. and the Karens.

U Nu tried to reach an understanding with the Communist party. In June 1948 he put forward a 'programme for a united left', which formulated in fifteen points the aims of a joint government. Among them were the establishment of a political and economic relationship with the Soviet Union and the Communist countries of Eastern Europe similar to that which Burma maintained with Great Britain and America; the nationalization of monopolistic capitalist enterprises and foreign trade; the abolition of privately-owned large estates and their redistribution among the peasants; minimum wages and an eight-hour day; the right of association and the right to strike, to old-age pensions and other social benefits. Finally, in the fifteenth point, he proposed the formation of a 'League for the Propagation of Marxist Doctrine', 'to read, discuss and propagate the writings of Marx, Engels, Lenin, Stalin, Mao Tse-tung, Tito, Dimitrov and other apostles of Marxism'.[1]

The Communists rejected this programme, as well as the invitation to join the hated Socialists in a coalition government, with contempt. To deflect Communist enmity and make an understanding with them easier, the Socialists decided to surrender their position in the government; they resigned in April 1949 though without withdrawing their support from the government. Yet this attempt to call a halt to the bloodshed of the civil war also failed. The Communists were determined to carry their battle for power through to the bitter end—to the wrecking of democracy in Burma.

The insurrection was at length put down, but even so Communist guerrilla bands roaming the land succeeded in paralysing the administration of the republic for long afterwards. 'We can plan all we want to,' the government stated in desperation on 3 July 1956, eight years after the inception of the civil war, 'but so long as we have still not eliminated this cancer [the guerrillas] completely, we cannot hope to make economic and social advance. This unrestrained element has not only destroyed our attempts to raise productivity, but has also hindered our endeavours to export our products, with the result that the real income *per capita* in our country is now considerably lower than it was before the war.'[2] The Communist uprising had crippled the growth of the young Socialist republic, had paralysed its democratic processes and finally paved the way for a military dictatorship.

On U Nu's invitation, the Socialist party came back into the government in January 1950. Shortly afterwards an internal crisis finally split the party.

1. Thakin Nu, *Towards Peace and Democracy* (Rangoon, 1949), pp. 92–4. For the text of the fifteen points, see also Rose, *Socialism in Southern Asia*, p. 112.
2. *Burma Weekly Bulletin*, 12 July 1956, quoted in ibid., p. 130.

In the last analysis the party broke upon the rocks of ideological conflict. Its adherence to Marxism had never posed such a problem, despite the fact that the party contained a left wing, led by Thakin Lwin, which advocated a united front with the Communists, and a right wing, led by Kyaw Nyein, which rejected any form of Communist alliance. U Ba Swe represented the centre. Under his leadership the party had tried to reach an understanding with the Communists, and had even surrendered its position in the government to make room for the Communists. But he had failed.

Thakin Lwin, as president of the Trade Union Congress of Burma, formed with U Ba Swe and Kyaw Nyein the triumvirate of party leaders. At the beginning of 1950 he demanded the resumption of discussions with the Communists on the basis of a programme of 'Left Unity', and while this was welcomed by them, it was unacceptable to a party majority. In a speech to celebrate May Day, he vigorously attacked the party right wing and demanded that, for the sake of proletarian unity, the Trade Union Congress of Burma should become affiliated to the Communist-dominated World Federation of Trade Unions.[1] A division in the party had already shown itself over the question of a United Front with the Communists. It finally broke apart over attitudes to the Korean War.

The war in Korea presented the Socialist world with a question of conscience. It had begun with an attack by North Korea on South Korea when, on 25 June 1950, the North Korean army crossed the border between the two states along the 38th parallel.[2]

The North Korean state was, like the German Democratic Republic, one of Stalin's creations. Both areas had been occupied by the Soviet Union after the war—eastern Germany after it was conquered by the Red Army, North Korea after the victory of America and Great Britain against Japan. (Russia had remained neutral in the war of the Allies against Japan; it did not declare war until 8 August 1945, a week before the Japanese capitulation.)

At the Cairo Conference on 1 December 1943 and again on 26 June 1945 at the Potsdam Conference, the Allies had proclaimed the liberation of Korea from Japanese rule and the re-establishment of Korea as an independent sovereign state as being among their war aims. They had agreed that, after Japan's defeat, Soviet troops were to occupy Korea north of the

1. For the founding of the World Federation of Trade Unions, see pp. 11–14.
2. For detailed descriptions of the war in Korea and its background, see Max Beloff, *Soviet Policy in the Far East 1914–1951* (London, 1953), pp. 155–207: David J. Dallin, *Soviet Russia and the Far East* (New Haven, 1948), pp. 258–67 and 284–313. According to Communist historiography, Syngman Rhee, the president of South Korea, had planned the military seizure of North Korea with the help of American arms. 'When the United States finally gave the green light to Rhee to go ahead . . . and Rhee's army began the invasion of North Korea, its collapse was immediate and the North Korean People's Army met with universal welcome from the people of South Korea'—see R. Palme Dutt. *The International* (London, 1964), p. 305.

38th parallel and American troops the south until such time as the Korean people could, by free elections, install a government for the whole country.

In breach of the Potsdam Agreement, however, the Soviet government considered the military demarcation line to represent a political border, and the area occupied by them to be a Russian sphere of influence. It set up a military dictatorship in North Korea, organized a North Korean army, and installed a provisional government with Kim Il Sung, a Korean Communist who had lived many years in Russia, as president. They then sealed the country off from the South. When the United Nations ordered elections for Korea, the Soviet government declared the demand invalid and refused entry to a commission sent by the United Nations to supervise the elections. The elections therefore took place only in South Korea and the Republic of Korea was duly constituted—proclaimed on 15 August 1948 and recognized in December by the United Nations. A month later, on 9 September, the establishment of the Democratic Republic of Korea was declared in the North. Thus Korea was divided into two separate states.

The background to the history of the Korean War is necessary to our understanding of the discord between Socialists throughout the world—and not only in Burma—which it engendered at that time. It must also be remembered that the United Nations Security Council, which met within a few hours of the outbreak of the war, had demanded the immediate cessation of hostilities and the withdrawal of the North Korean Army to the 38th parallel, and that two days later it called upon members of the United Nations to support South Korea in resisting North Korea's attack. (As the Soviet Union had boycotted the Security Council since January it was unable to reverse these decisions by exercising its veto.)

Until this point the A.F.P.F.L. government of Burma had maintained neutrality towards the rivalry between the power blocs of the West and East. While India, Pakistan and Ceylon had stayed within the British Commonwealth Burma had left it so as to avoid the appearance of being in alliance with any one power of the Western bloc. It did, however, maintain good relations with the Western powers, though also equally good ones with the U.S.S.R., the Communist states of Eastern Europe and China; in December 1949 Burma had been the first Asian country to recognize the Communist government of China.

But now the Security Council resolution put Burma's neutral position in question; it could not evade expressing an opinion on the Korean War. Like the British Labour government and the Socialist coalition governments of Western Europe, after momentary hesitation it declared its unequivocal support for the decisions of the Security Council. It had been shown beyond doubt that North Korea had attacked the Republic of South Korea and had refused to cease hostilities and to withdraw its army in accordance with the Security Council's demand. With its support for the Security Council's resolution, the Burmese government had inevitably taken sides in the struggle of rivals.

Communists of all countries declared their solid support for North Korea; this war, they argued, was a national war of liberation—a war, they claimed, to liberate the people of South Korea, enslaved by American imperialism and subjected to a Fascist régime.

The Socialist International, on the other hand, had declared its solidarity with the United Nations' action against North Korea; while not directly charging the Soviet government (which had protested its innocence) with responsibility for the war, it did so accuse the Cominform, which had at its inaugural congress called on all Communist parties to direct their policies towards kindling revolutions in Europe and Asia. Until the outbreak of the Korean War, their methods for inciting revolutions had remained the mass-strike, as in France and Italy, or the armed uprising, as in India, Burma, Malaya and, as will be described later,[1] in Indonesia. Korea was the first occasion since the Russian invasion of Georgia in 1929[2] that direct warfare had been used by a Communist power as a means of gaining supremacy in a neighbouring country.[3] The Korean War was a 'danger signal', the Socialist International declared at its inaugural congress. 'It has shown that the Cominform does not shrink from using military aggression as a means of extending its power.'[4]

Many Socialists did, however, feel conscientious doubts over their attitude towards the war. They were under no illusions as to its origin; it had been planned by Stalin and Mao Tse-tung with the aim[5] of destroying the American strategic base in Korea which was aimed against the Soviet Union and China, as well as to set up the Communist régime in the southern half of the Korean peninsula. But while the war of South Korea against North Korea carried all the marks of a war by the United Nations to defend the independence of one of its member states, many Socialists saw it as a war for

1. See pp. 294–5.
2. See Braunthal, *History of the International, 1914–1943*, pp. 241–5.
3. The attempt to impose Communist domination by war in Korea, undertaken at the cost of terrible sacrifice, was a failure. After three years of war (June 1950 to July 1953) during which over two million people died in the fighting and almost three million from epidemics while North and South Korea were both devastated, it remained, as it had been at the outbreak, a country bisected by its previous frontiers—the North under a Communist dictatorship and the South under a military dictatorship.
4. Report of the First Congress of the Socialist International, Circular No. 100/51, Frankfurt (1951), 51, p. 137.
5. For this statement there is, of course, no documentary proof, since decisions of this kind are not retained on records by the Soviet authorities. But it seems unthinkable that the almost three months of discussion between Mao Tse-tung and Stalin in Moscow—which included among other things a military defence treaty (signed on 14 February 1950)—contained no reference to their common strategy for Korea. It appears equally unthinkable that the North Korean government could have been able, without the agreement of Stalin and Mao Tse-tung, to mount a military action such as to provoke the armed might of America.

retaining America's power position in the Far East, now threatened by Russia and China. And while they held no brief for the character of the Communist system of government to which the people of South Korea would be subjected in the event of a victory by the North, it seemed to them a lesser evil than the semi-Fascist dictatorship which General Syngman Rhee, the president of South Korea, had established.

In no country except Burma, however, did the discord generated by the attitudes of Socialist parties towards the war produce a fundamental split. Lwin left the party in protest and, with forty-three leading members of the Socialist party, the Trade Union Congress of Burma and the Peasants' Organization, formed the Burma Workers' and Peasants' Party (B.W.P.P.) on 8 December 1950.

In the declaration with which the B.W.P.P. tried to justify the split, it accused the Socialist party leadership of having deviated from its original purpose. 'The foundations of its original policy', it stated, which had been Marxism and Leninism, had been 'displaced by deviations and imitations . . . and the people's democratic revolution has been delayed'. The B.W.P.P., on the other hand, would never deviate from its Marxist–Leninist ideology and would, in the event of a Third World War, support those 'who support our people's democratic ideology'.[1]

The split dealt a crushing blow to the Socialist party. It was estimated that, following this event, party membership dropped from about 2,000 to no more than 200.[2]

U Ba Swe believed none the less, as he said, that the party had been strengthened and purged by the falling away of its left wing. It had undoubtedly been relieved of people who differed very little from the Communists in their ideology. The truth was, however, that it had not emerged in any way strengthened. It was in fact practically destroyed, and its leadership of the trade union movement had been lost to the Communists.

But it shortly recovered. The B.W.P.P. and the wing of the trade union movement affiliated to it were expelled from the A.F.P.F.L.; the Trade Union Congress, with U Ba Swe as president, was reorganized. At the elections in May 1951 the Socialist party emerged as the strongest individual party in the national front of A.F.P.F.L. and parliament. The A.F.P.F.L. had won about 80 per cent of the 375 seats to the two houses of parliament; three quarters of its representatives were members of the Socialist party.

The Socialist party was, however, no more than a cadre party; the number of its individual members was small—about 6,000 in its best period. Its strength lay in its dominant position in the A.F.P.F.L., which in 1956

---

1. Quoted in Thomson, 'Marxism in Burma', in Trager (ed.), *Marxism in Southeast Asia*, p. 44.
2. Rose, *Socialism in Southern Asia*, p. 44.

embraced about 435,000 individual and 625,000 collective members—the All-Burma Peasants' Organization, the Trade Union Congress, and the women's and students' organizations. The Socialist party had the majority on the executive committee, and thus a majority in the A.F.P.F.L. government—nine of the twelve seats on the Ministerial Council. U Nu, as president of the A.F.P.F.L. (he was affiliated to no party), became prime minister, and U Ba Swe, as general secretary of the Socialist party and vice-president of the A.F.P.F.L., deputy prime minister and minister of defence.

The A.F.P.F.L. emerged from the second parliamentary elections of April 1956 with its majority reduced, while the Communist-led opposition strengthened its position. In place of the 'White Flag' Communist party, which had won seven seats in the 1951 elections but had soon afterwards been made illegal and so had not canvassed in the 1956 elections, there was the left-wing Socialist B.W.P.P. which joined forces with a number of opposition parties to form a National Unity Front (N.U.F.), which won forty-five of the 248 seats.

Small as were the number of N.U.F. votes, they became of crucial significance during the government crisis which arose from a conflict between U Nu and Kyaw Nyein in April 1958. This developed into a bitterly fought struggle between U Nu and the Socialist party and caused the A.F.P.F.L. to split itself apart.[1]

The conflict, which tore the A.F.P.F.L. asunder, had its cause neither in ideological, political nor tactical disagreements within the government. It was a clash of personality: a struggle between U Nu and the Socialist party for the leadership of the A.F.P.F.L. and the government.

On 4 June 1958 the Socialists left the government to submit the conflict to the verdict of parliament, and on the following day, during an extraordinary meeting of the house, put forward a motion of no-confidence against U Nu as prime minister. A majority of A.F.P.F.L. delegates—ninety-seven to fifty-one—supported the motion. The decision thus rested with the N.U.F., which decided against the Socialists and in favour of U Nu. The Socialists, the N.U.F. declared, were bourgeois agents in the pay of capitalistic imperialism, while U Nu, on the other hand, 'is a nationalistic bourgeois and therefore the lesser of two evils'.[2] So they cast their votes into the balance against the motion of no-confidence and it was rejected by a majority of eight votes (127 to 119).

Three weeks later the split of the A.F.P.F.L. occurred. A majority on its general council—140 of the 260 members—expelled U Nu and his supporters and elected U Ba Swe as president. U Nu, however, refused to accept this

---

1. For a detailed history of this incident, see Sein Win, *The Split Story* (Rangoon 1959). Sein Win, chief editor of *The Guardian* (Rangoon), as a dispassionate observer, regarded U Nu as being responsible for the split. See also Frank N. Trager, 'The Political Split in Burma', in *Far East Survey*, vol. XXVII (October 1958).

2. See Sein Win, *The Split Story*, p. 68.

decision, the conference having been boycotted by his supporters, and with his following he constituted the 'pure A.F.P.F.L.'. In this way the original unity front broke into two mutually hostile camps.

The schism of the A.F.P.F.L. was an ill omen for the fate of democracy in Burma. It had formed the strongest front against the Communists; but now it was splintered. On its unity had rested the overwhelming government majority in parliament; but the government had been forced to rely on the support of the Communists and had had its majority reduced to eight votes.

U Nu now sought peace with the revolutionary Communists. Three weeks after the extraordinary meeting of parliament, he announced a proposal for a decree of total amnesty for all crimes committed during the uprising and of the legalization of those parties prepared to return to legality. The revolutionary Communists, however, demanded the incorporation of their guerrilla bands into the army before they would consent to a cessation of the armed struggle. For the army, which had fought a bitter eleven-year war against the Communist guerrillas, such a demand was unacceptable. The peace discussions broke down.

Unable to resolve the political crisis, U Nu resigned as prime minister at the end of October 1958, and passed power to General Ne Win (b. 1911), Chief of the General Staff. U Nu had urged that, whatever happened, the constitution should be preserved; he had proposed that the general should, with the sanction of parliament, form a caretaker government to run the country for a specified period during which Burma's political leaders could reorganize and prepare for a general election. Ne Win accepted these proposals.[1]

When the elections took place at the beginning of February 1960, the A.F.P.F.L. wing led by U Nu won a majority. But shortly after U Nu's return as prime minister, the Karens, backed by the Communist guerrilla bands, once again arose in armed conflict. General Ne Win, in order, he claimed, to save the country from disaster, now seized power by a *coup d'état* at dawn on 2 March 1962, arrested U Nu and all the cabinet members as well as the president and chief justice of the Union of Burma, abolished the constitution and the legislature, and set up a Revolutionary Council, consisting of about a dozen military officers, to rule by decree. On 30 April, in a manifesto, *The Burmese Way to Socialism*, he pledged himself to the full nationalization of economic life. This was a promise which, as an old Thakin and Socialist, he attempted to keep. The banks were nationalized and three quarters of trade and industrial businesses were placed under state control by a 'People's Bank' and a 'People's Civil Stores Corporation'.

Ne Win's *coup* marked the end of parliamentary democracy in Burma.

1. For the exchange of letters between U Nu and Ne Win regarding the handing over of power, see Sein Win, *The Split Story*, pp. 87–9.

He formed a party—the Burma Socialist Programme party—as the organ of his government and in March 1964 dissolved all other parties. Burma was now subjected to a total military dictatorship.

The revolution in Burma, having attained independence, now set itself the objective of building a democratic Socialist society. This was originally the common aim of both Communists and Socialists. The Communists had co-operated loyally with the Socialists to support the constitution as a base for social democracy. They had switched their policies only under the impact of decisions by the Cominform. Their aim had now become the destruction of democracy and the establishment of the Communist dictatorship—not by popular mass action, but, inspired by the triumphant tactics of Mao Tse-tung, through the actions of guerrilla bands. And indeed they did succeed in undermining democracy, paralysing the civil administration and dissolving constitutional order into chaos. But the dictatorship which arose from the ruins of democracy was not a Communist one, but an anti-Communist military dictatorship.

2. Ceylon

Ceylon's sovereignty as an independent state, proclaimed on 4 February 1948, had not been won by any dramatic national revolution, such as had occurred in India and Burma. By 1931 this British Crown Colony already possessed a considerable degree of national self-administration, and in 1946 it received by Privy Council decree full self-government on the basis of a parliamentary democratic constitution on the English model; only the country's defence and foreign policy remained under British control. Less than two years afterwards a British Act of Parliament granted the state full sovereignty—and, again, not under any pressure from a revolutionary mass movement, but in discussion with the indigenous aristocracy and middle class, organized in the Ceylon National Congress.[1] But because Ceylon's national freedom had not had to be fought for by the mass of the people, the transformation from crown colony to independent state, a transformation not accompanied by any social change, was not felt as a revolution in the consciousness of the masses.

The real revolution in Ceylon did not take place until 1956, when a Socialist party—the Sri Lanka Freedom party (S.L.F.P.)—gained an overwhelming victory in the elections and formed a coalition government with one of the country's three Marxist parties. It initiated a process which was to change feudal Ceylon into a social welfare state.

The S.L.F.P. was the youngest of the parties within the Socialist movement in Ceylon; it had been formed in 1951. A workers' party under the title

1. For Ceylon's constitutional development, see Sir Ivor Jennings, *The Constitution of Ceylon*, third edition (Bombay, 1954).

of Ceylon Workers' Congress had been founded as early as 1928, and in 1935 a Marxist party, the *Lanka Sama Samaya Party* (L.S.S.P.), had come into being.

The workers' party, under the leadership of A. E. Goonesiaha, was a small party consisting of several organized groups of industrial and agricultural workers. The L.S.S.P., on the other hand, was a party representing a broad mass of the urban proletariat as well as of intellectuals which, originally, like the Socialist party of India, had brought together Marxist Socialists of every alignment—Communists, Trotskyists and Social Democrats.

The founders of the L.S.S.P. were young intellectuals who had studied in England—N. M. Perera, Leslie Goonewardene and Colvin R. de Silva among them—and who, like a majority of members, were Trotskyists. The Communists, considering the Trotskyists to be the worst traitors to the cause of Socialism, had joined the L.S.S.P. to seize the party leadership and to change it into an orthodox Stalinist–Communist party affiliated to the Communist International. Thus almost from its inception the L.S.S.P. had fallen victim to a tussle between its Trotskyist and Communist factions until finally in 1940 the Trotskyist majority expelled the Communists from their ranks.

But the opportunity to found a Communist party did not arise until after Hitler's attack on the Soviet Union in 1941. Until then the Communists, as well as the Trotskyists, had condemned the war as a 'war of imperialism'. They had been persecuted by the government and their leaders arrested, and the L.S.S.P. had been declared illegal. Russia's alliance with the Western powers brought an end to the persecution of the Communists, but not to that of the Trotskyists. For while the Communists now proclaimed the war an 'anti-Fascist democratic war of freedom', which the workers were to support with all their strength, the Trotskyists continued to consider it as an 'imperialist' war.

Thus, so far as the government of Ceylon was concerned, nothing more stood in the way to the founding of a Communist party. This party also fulfilled all the expectations placed in it. It prevented, as far as it was able, the outbreak of strikes, called upon the workers to attain higher levels of production and defamed the anti-war Trotskyists in the underground movement as Japanese spies[1] (during the war Ceylon was threatened by a Japanese invasion).

The expulsion of the Communists from the L.S.S.P., however, by no means brought about internal unity. Shortly after the founding of the Communist party, a left group split away from the L.S.S.P. and formed another Trotskyist 'Bolshevist–Leninist Party'.

Until the formation of the S.L.F.P. in 1951, the Socialist movement in Ceylon was divided into four parties: two Trotskyist parties, one 'orthodox' Communist party and a workers' party. Their comparative strengths were

1. See Leslie Goonewardene, *The Difference Between Trotskyism and Stalinism*, with an Introduction by Colvin R. de Silva (Colombo, 1954), p. 2.

revealed in the elections of 1947. Of the ninety-five parliamentary seats, the L.S.S.P. won ten, the Bolshevist–Leninist party five, the Communist party three and the workers' party one. After the elections, the Bolshevist–Leninist party split in turn; one faction returned to the L.S.S.P. and the remainder joined with the Communist party to form a United Front.

The surprising phenomenon of the Socialist movement in Ceylon had been its predominantly Trotskyist complexion from the very outset.[1] With the exception of Spain, whose Trotskyist mass movement had been bloodily crushed by the Stalinists during the Spanish Civil War even before a triumphant Fascism exterminated all Socialist alignments,[2] Trotkyism had not been able to create an organized mass movement in any of those countries where it had won adherents—the United States, Mexico or France. Ceylon—a small, predominantly agrarian country with a population at the end of the war of hardly more than six and a half million—was the only country in which a Trotskyist mass party attracted hundreds of thousands of electors.

But since the Trotskyist party was at root a Communist party, though uncontaminated by Stalinism, it represented an obstacle to the development of a Communist party obedient to Moscow. What divided the Trotskyists from the Communists ideologically was their attitude towards the Soviet Union, which it charged with having betrayed the principles of the Bolshevik Revolution and with having changed Lenin's dictatorship of the proletariat into a bureaucratic system of despotism under Stalin's rule. Furthermore, the L.S.S.P. stood for a Communist ideology in the spirit of Trotsky's interpretation. This showed itself in the 'basic aims' of their programme, formulated at their party congress of 1950. (It is given here in some detail as a historic document of the only existing Trotskyist mass-party.) According to this the party strove to bring about:

1. The overthrow of the capitalist state, maintained in Ceylon through a political alliance between British imperialists and the Ceylonese bourgeoisie.
2. The seizing of political power by the working class at the head of the toiling masses and the establishment of a democratic Workers' and Peasants' (Soviet) government, i.e. the dictatorship of the proletariat supported by the urban and rural poor.
3. The achieving of real national independence. The severance of all political ties with the British Empire. The ending of all forms of colonial subjection to foreign capital.
4. The confiscation by the workers' state without compensation of all banks,

---

1. See George Jan Lerski, *Origins of Trotskyism in Ceylon. A Documentary History of Lanka Sama Samaya Party 1935–1942* (Stanford, 1968).
2. See Braunthal, *History of the International, 1914–1943*, pp. 486–9.

factories, plantations, big commercial concerns, means of transport, mines, etc., which will be run and developed as state-owned enterprises for the public benefit and not for private profit.

5. The nationalization of land. The transfer of all land (excluding large-scale modernized agricultural enterprises) for the use of the toiling peasants. The development of collective farms in peasant agriculture.

'These fundamental aims', the programme stated in conclusion, 'cannot be realized through bourgeois parliaments. The inevitable resistance of the bourgeoisie to their achievement necessarily calls for mass revolutionary action as the only means of realizing the will of the majority.'[1]

The Communist party was unable to compete with the radicalism of the L.S.S.P. programme. This contained all the characteristic features of Leninism: the role of the working class in its conquest of political power in alliance with the peasants; the dictatorship of the proletariat; the abolition of parliamentary democracy; the establishment of a Soviet system of government; the complete nationalization of the means of production; and revolutionary mass action as 'the only method' for winning the struggle for power.

By contrast, the Communist party, between its founding during the Second World War and until the end of 1947, avoided mentioning any of these principles even in its propaganda. It pursued a policy not of revolutionary mass action by the working class in a struggle against the aristocracy and bourgeoisie, but in accordance with the directives received from Moscow before the collapse of the Russian alliance with the Western powers, one of class co-operation with the 'anti-Fascist' wing of the bourgeoisie in the fight against the revolutionary L.S.S.P.[2]

Not until 1947, when Russia's alliance with the Western powers had broken down and the inaugural conference of the Cominform had made a transition to left-wing policies obligatory on all Communist parties, did it undertake a sudden switch of policy direction. Its propaganda declared that conditions for a Socialist revolution in Ceylon were now ripe and, until 1950, it tried to spark it off by promoting strikes and sabotage. This adventure foundered; not only on the prevailing power relations—a general strike in Colombo in 1947 had to be called off after a severe defeat—but also because the L.S.S.P., which was in fact at this stage the leading working-class party, refused to allow itself to be dragged into any such adventure. Thus the 'revolutionary period' in the history of Ceylon's Communist party came to an end.

The subsequent history of the Communist party may be chronicled briefly. It returned to a rightist course and allied itself in a United Front with

1. Quoted in Julius Braunthal, Report of the Bureau Meeting of the Asian Socialist Conference, Tokyo, November 1954, Circular No. 60/54, p. 7. For the theoretical basis of the programme, see Colvin R. de Silva, *Outline of the Permanent Revolution* (Colombo, 1955).
2. See Colvin R. de Silva, *Their Politics—and Ours* (Colombo, 1954), pp. 20–2.

the Bolshevist–Leninist party, which had splintered off from the L.S.S.P. and now called itself the *Viplavakari* ('Revolutionary') L.S.S.P. (V.L.S.S.P.) canvassing with it on a common list in the elections of May 1952.

Meanwhile, the S.L.F.P. had been formed and had laid its own Socialist programme before the electorate. In the election there were thus four parties within the Socialist movement facing each other. Their relative strengths showed themselves in the following results:

	Votes	*Seats*
S.L.F.P.	361,250	9
L.S.S.P.	305,133	9
Communist party (V.L.S.S.P.)	134,528	4
Workers' party	27,096	1

Following the elections, the Communist party at first sought a United Front with the L.S.S.P., but discussions broke down over the question of 'the right to criticize'—the right of the L.S.S.P. (disputed by the Communists) to criticize the Soviet Union or other Communist states. Subsequently it attempted to form an alliance with the S.L.F.P. by setting up a 'Democratic Front', but this the S.L.F.P. declined. Finally, in preparation for the 1956 elections, it sought to create a 'Grand Alliance of the People's Progressive Forces'. In a memorandum of the party programme, drawn up by the general secretary, Dr S. A. Wickremasinghe, the Communists declared: 'It is a present-day error to believe that the Communist party fights only on behalf of the workers and poor peasants. In our economic as well as our social programme, we fight for the genuine interests of the workers and peasants, the farmers and the unemployed, the intellectuals and the capitalist middle class'.[1]

'We have to be frank', the memorandum stressed. 'Today's Communist party does not demand Communism.'[2] 'The reorientation of the economy,' it stated, 'in no way seeks the usual solution for the agrarian problem by boldly confiscating feudal property. Immediate requirements do not, in fact, demand that we should take the property of present landowners, but that we should cultivate new, virgin land.' And as the Communist party guaranteed the retention of landed property by the aristocracy, so it also guaranteed the extension of capitalism during the process of Ceylon's industrialization. 'With the exception of key industries,' the programme stated, 'which will be organized by the state, the industrial sector will remain open to private enterprise by the people of the country. . . . Rapid industrialization can only be brought about with the participation of privately owned industries'.[3]

This, the programme stated in conclusion, was 'the new economic path of Ceylon's Communist party. . . . The people as a whole, apart from the

---

1. S. A. Wickremasinghe, *The Way Ahead. An Economic Policy for Ceylon* (Colombo, 1955), p. 84.
2. ibid., p. 83.   3.. ibid., p. 77.

imperialists and the capitalist middle men who work with them, will stand to gain. . . .'[1]

At the May 1952 elections the four parties within the Socialist movement between them won 828,000 of the 2,302,000 votes cast, or almost a third. The party, which had ruled Ceylon since 1947, the United National Party (U.N.P.), won 1,026,000 votes, however, and an absolute majority with fifty-four out of ninety-four seats.

Surprisingly the Sri Lanka Freedom party, founded on 2 September 1951, only nine months before the elections, emerged with its 361,000 votes as both stronger than the far older Socialist parties and as the second strongest party in the country. But the event which may be considered to have been the real revolution in Ceylon was its overwhelming victory in the next elections, in April 1956. Its number of votes increased from 361,000 to 1,046,000 and in alliance with the Trotskyist V.L.S.S.P. and two other groups, it gained a parliamentary majority with fifty-two seats.[2]

The Sri Lanka Freedom party was the creation of Solomon W. R. D. Bandaranaike (1899–1959). He was the son of a rich, landed aristocratic family, for whom loyalty to the British Crown had become a tradition; his father had received a knighthood from the British government. He had been brought up as Christian and was educated at Oxford, where he absorbed Social Democratic ideas, but at the same time developed a strong consciousness of Singhalese nationalism. After his returning to Ceylon in 1925, he abandoned Christianity to become a Buddhist, and exchanged his European style of dress for that of the simple traditional Singhalese national costume. He then formed a national movement—the *Sinhala Maha Sabha*—to promote Singhalese culture, religion and language.

The *Sinhala Maha Sabha* became a group within the United National party, which had been formed during the Second World War by a merger of several middle-class nationalist parties; the four parties within the Socialist movement were not affiliated. It was the left wing of the U.N.P. which pressed for social reforms, but evidently with little success. In July 1951 Bandaranaike withdrew his group from the U.N.P., of which he had been vice-president and in whose government he had been a minister, and in September founded the S.L.F.P. as a Socialist party.

Its ideals and objectives were formulated in a manifesto at the inaugural congress which declared:

The Sri Lanka Freedom party is a Social Democratic party. Economically, it believes that policy must be formed on the needs of the common man. In our country, where the great majority of people are living in poverty and problems of

1. ibid., p. 77.
2. The number of votes for the L.S.S.P. fell from 305,000 in 1952 to 274,000; and the Communist vote from 134,000 to 119,000.

unemployment and serious underemployment are growing in gravity, the approach to these problems on Socialist principles is the only effective method for their satisfactory solution. Politically it believes that the preservation and fostering of the democratic ideals and freedoms are essential for the true progress and happiness of our people, whose initiative and self-respect have been undermined by many years of servitude.

The Sri Lanka Freedom party aimed, the manifesto declared, at 'building a Social Democratic order of society by a government dependent upon the utmost participation by the people'. And it pledged itself to nationalize by stages the essential industries, the larger plantations, the transport system, the banks and insurance companies.

The realization of Ceylon's full national liberty and independence was also demanded. While Ceylon had indeed become a sovereign state, it had remained under the British Crown as a self-governing dominion within the British Commonwealth. The manifesto declared, however, 'the Government of Ceylon must be a free Republic, independent of the British Commonwealth and of all external control. . . . Therefore no bases can be permitted in our country for any foreign Power and all foreign troops must immediately be withdrawn from our country.'

But the factor which gave the party its particular attraction for the traditionally religious peasants as well as for the urban proletarian masses was, as the elections showed, its national religious character. Ceylon's ruling classes had become 'Westernized'; they had become Christians in considerable numbers, spoke English and dressed in European style. 'In culture and religion', the programme declared, 'our people can achieve the status of a truly free people only if the principles proclaimed go hand in hand with a revival of our cultures and the use of our national languages and the revival and stimulation of spiritual values, so that religion once again attains its rightful place as a vital force in the lives of our people.' Therefore, the manifesto demanded, the Singhalese language and Tamil, the language of the southern-Indian proletariat in Ceylon, should immediately be recognized as official languages, 'so that the people of this country may cease to be aliens in their own land; so that an end may be put to the iniquity of condemning those educated in Singhalese and Tamil to occupy the lowliest walk of life.'[1]

With this programme, the S.L.F.P. gained the position of being the second strongest party in the 1952 elections. For the 1956 elections it formed an alliance with the Trotskyist V.L.S.S.P. as well as with a Buddhist and a Singhalese nationalist group in a 'United People's Front'—the *Mahajama Eksath Peramuna* (M.E.P.)—on the basis of the programme outlined in the S.L.F.P.'s manifesto. It added two further demands: the eight-hour day and a guaranteed minimum wage. But it also intensified its stress on the Singhalese national character. The manifesto had demanded the recog-

1. *Manifesto and Constitution of the Sri Lanka Freedom Party* (Wellampitiya, 1951).

nition of Singhalese as well as Tamil—the language of the Indian minority of almost two million—as official languages. But in its election programme, the M.E.P. pledged itself to declare Singhalese as 'the only official language of the country', should it win.[1]

It was, however, this synthesis of Social Democratic, Buddhist, and nationalist elements in its programme that carried the M.E.P. to victory; its most passionate canvassers had been the Buddhist monks.

The government formed by Bandaranaike was a coalition of the S.L.F.P. and the V.L.S.S.P.; the other two groups had merged with the S.L.F.P. following the elections. The V.L.S.S.P. was represented in the government by its leaders, Philip Gunawardena and William de Silva.

The assassination of Bandaranaike—he was shot on 25 September 1959 by a fanatical monk—awoke deep sympathies throughout the country, above all among those who supported his party, for his widow, Sirima Ratwatte (b. 1916). She had been working in the social welfare movement, and had taken no active part in politics. The S.L.F.P. urged her to take up the party leadership in succession to her murdered husband. Under her leadership, and carried along by a wave of sympathy, the party once again achieved a brilliant victory in the elections of 1960. Thereupon she became prime minister—the first woman in the world to become a prime minister—and continued with the policy of reformist Socialism begun by her husband. From 1964 she governed in coalition with the parliamentary Trotskyist group, whose leader, Dr N. M. Perera—a brilliant politician who had become a highly respected Mayor of Colombo—was appointed to the government as Chancellor of the Exchequer.

From the elections of March 1965, the middle-class U.N.P. narrowly emerged with fifty seats as the strongest single party; but the S.L.F.P. retained forty-six seats and the three other Socialist parties held twenty-three seats between them.[2]

In the next elections, five years later, in May 1970, the coalition of the S.L.F.P. with the Trotskyists and neo-Moscow Communists gained an overwhelming majority of the seats: 115 out of 151, the S.L.F.P. holding ninety, the L.S.S.P. nineteen and the Communist party six. On this basis, Sirima Bandaranaike formed her second coalition government.

Thus these elections once more demonstrated the phenomenon of a

1. *Joint Programme of the M.E.P.* (Colombo, 1956). This concession, which Bandaranaike made to Singhalese nationalism in defiance of the Socialist principle of international solidarity, was to have tragic consequences. The law he introduced in parliament as prime minister declaring Singhalese to be an official language provoked, during May and June 1958, bloody confrontations between Indian and Singhalese in which, according to official estimates, 159 people were killed. The state of emergency then proclaimed was not lifted until the following March.

2. The L.S.S.P. won ten seats, as did the 'Marxist United People's Front', which had split away from the Trotskyists under Philip Gunawardena's leadership, and the Communists held three seats.

Socialist movement, deeply rooted in the Buddhist and Hindu masses of the country.

3. Nepal

In the history of the expansion of Socialist ideas in Asia, Nepal occupies a special position. This small country, almost entirely shut away from the outside world in the mountain ranges of the Himalayas, remained a feudal state into the 1950s. The aristocracy owned the land and the peasants who cultivated it were tied to the land by the ubiquitous agrarian system of *Birta*, and hence were the property of the landowner in a form of serfdom. Even as the estates of French aristocrats had been exempt from taxation until 1789, so, until only a few years ago, was the landed feudal property of Nepal. And like Japan under the *Shogunate*, Nepal, nominally an autocratic monarchy, had come to be ruled throughout the century from 1846 to 1951 by an aristocratic clan—the Rana family, whose head occupied the hereditary office of prime minister and enjoyed absolute power. The king had become to practical effect a prisoner in his own palace.

It is therefore all the more remarkable that this country, with its feudal economic, social and political structures, which had remained virtually untouched by changes in the modern world, should see the introduction of Socialist ideas, and that a Socialist party—the Nepali Congress—should take root and, in the first elections in Nepal's history, win an overwhelming majority and rule the country for a year and a half.

The predecessor of the Nepali Congress had been the Nepal National Congress, founded in Calcutta in January 1947. This was a national front uniting liberals and conservatives as well as Socialists in the common task of overthrowing the rule of the Rana clan, transforming Nepal's feudal autocracy into a constitutional monarchy and setting up a parliamentary democracy.

Among the founders of the National Congress had been Bishewar Prasad Koirala, who was to emerge as the outstanding personality of the Nepalese revolution. His father, a Brahman, had fled to India to escape political persecution, and when he returned after years of exile, had been placed in prison, where he died. His son was born in India, and after growing up there and completing his university studies, he joined the Congress Socialist party of India. Arrested in 1942 as an agitator of the revolutionary 'Quit India' movement, he spent the following two and a half years in prison at Patna. After his release in 1945, he canvassed for the idea of a Nepal National Congress along the lines of the Indian National Congress.

Shortly after the foundation of the Nepal National Congress in 1947, the first strike in Nepal's history occurred—a wage strike of cotton and jute workers in Biratnagar. It was brutally suppressed by the government, and many of the workers involved as well as their leaders were arrested, Koirala among them; he spent six months in prison. In the following year, after the National Congress, which had begun its struggle for constitutional reforms, was suppressed by a new wave of reaction, he was again arrested, but forced the authorities to release him after several months by a hunger strike lasting twenty-one days.

The National Congress hoped to lead the struggle for constitutional reform by Gandhi's method of non-violent resistance. Koirala, on the other hand, advocated the tactics of an armed rising for, he believed, only by the use of force could the rule of the Rana family be cast down.

This was obviously a conviction shared by King Tribhuvan, who could only gain his personal freedom through the defeat of the Rana clan. At all events, it was a member of the Nepalese royal family, Mahendra Bikram Shah, who, with a member of the Rana clan, Subarna Shamsher, formed early in 1949 an organization to bring about the fall of the Ranas by an armed rising. This was known as the Democratic Congress.

Koirala now tried to negotiate a fusion of the National Congress with the Democratic Congress, and he finally succeeded despite the opposition of one faction within his party. The fusion took place, after long discussions, in April 1950. Taking the title of Nepali Congress, the new organization had, according to its own estimates, 40,000 members at the time of its foundation, and rose to 100,000 half a year later.[1]

The Nepali Congress began to prepare for the rising without delay. It purchased arms, organized a para-military force, the *Raksha Dal*, and planned, with the king's agreement, to attack Kathmandu, the capital of Nepal, early in November 1950, to free the king and install him as constitutional monarch. This plan, however, came to the knowledge of the government. The force of 200 men dispatched to Kathmandu to carry out the *coup* was arrested, and the king fled to India.

The Nepali Congress did not, however, accept defeat, but called upon the country to rise. Under Subarna Shamsher's leadership the *Raksha Dal* attacked Birganj. The insurgents occupied the town, freed hundreds of political prisoners and repelled a counter-attack by government troops. From this strong-point the rising spread quickly throughout the country. It had become a revolution. 'The revolution,' recorded Bhola Chatterji, 'received incredibly strong support from all classes of the Nepalese people. Their repressed indignation at the ancient monstrous rule of the Ranas became a mighty flood in which the defenders of feudal barbarity were drowned. . . . It was only a matter of days before the army of the Nepali Congress marched in triumph into Kathmandu.'[2]

1. See Rose, *Socialism in Southern Asia*, p. 72.
2. Bhola Chatterji, 'Nepal Today', I: 'Emergence from Feudalism', in *Janata* (Bombay), 12 October 1958. For a review of subsequent events, see the three following articles in the issues for 19 October, 26 October and 2 November 1958.

The Rana government faced a desperate situation which it was incapable of mastering. The Rana prime minister, Mohan Shamsher, flew to Delhi to request the good offices of the Indian government in the role of adviser. A compromise was proposed by which the king was to return to Nepal as constitutional monarch, while a coalition government was to be installed with a Rana as prime minister and including five representatives of the Nepali Congress and four of the Rana clan; a constituent assembly was to be summoned. The compromise was accepted by a conference of congress and Rana representatives called in Delhi by King Tribhuvan in January 1951, and on the basis of the Delhi Pact the Nepali Congress ceased the armed struggle and the king returned to Kathmandu to announce the agreed coalition government, with Koirala as minister of the interior.

Democracy had now made its entrance into feudal Nepal. But it remained for the principles of democracy to be constructed into democratic institutions. The revolution had annulled the inherited right of the Ranas to lead the state, but it had not disarmed the Rana clan. It had installed the king as a constitutional monarch, but it had not safeguarded the constitution against a return to autocracy. This was the task which was to face the constituent assembly. But King Tribhuvan held back from issuing the writ to call the constituent assembly elections. Not until October 1957, two years after his death in March 1955, did his successor, King Mahendra, announce the issue of the writ; and the elections did not, in fact, take place until February 1959.

Several parties had emerged into the open following the outbreak of the revolution in Nepal: a Communist party under the leadership of Monmohan Adhikary; a United Democratic party under the leadership of K. I. Singh; a party with the title of *Praja Parishad*, formed by Tanka Prasad; and a party of the aristocracy, the *Gorkha Parishad*.

The Nepali Congress developed its ideology in competition with these parties. Under Koirala's leadership it had maintained a close connection with the Socialist party of India, but did not differ ideologically from other parties which had declared their loyalty to democracy. It was only in January 1956 at a conference in Birganj that the Nepali Congress proclaimed itself a Socialist party and became affiliated to the Asian Socialist Congress.

In its manifesto, which was to serve as a programme for the forthcoming elections, the Birganj conference declared the party's resolve 'to bring about a society based on the principles of social justice and on equality of opportunity, and of political, economic and social rights. In such a society there will be no privileges of birth and possession, nor exploitation of one another.'

The Nepali Congress believes [the manifesto continued] that such social objectives can only be achieved in a Socialist society, where the state owns or effectively controls the principal instruments and means of production and guarantees equitable distribution of wealth.

The manifesto categorically rejected the Communist methods of social change. 'The Communists claim,' it said, 'that the end justifies the means. Their strategy is the simple one of overthrowing the government of the day by revolutionary and violent means and of setting up their dictatorship. . . .'

The Nepali Congress [the manifesto declared] is opposed to methods that seek to achieve Socialism at the cost of democracy and spiritual values. It believes that it is not necessary to sacrifice democracy to achieve Socialism. In fact it believes that a true Socialist society can come into existence only when Socialism is wedded to democracy. The Nepali Congress therefore stands for the achievement of Socialism by peaceful and democratic methods.

The main part of the programme, which outlined the concrete economic reforms which the Nepali Congress intended to put into practice, was of course devoted to agriculture: the reform of land tenure and measures for the increase of agricultural production; placing a maximum limit on land-holdings; encouraging co-operative farming; the state farming of newly reclaimed lands; and the distribution of good seed and fertilizer.

As for the industrialization of that underdeveloped country, the programme proposed the establishment of the basic key industries—especially transport, energy and mining—by the state, which would own or control them. Meanwhile the development of medium-sized consumer-goods industries by private enterprise was to be encouraged, and cottage industries and small-scale industries were to be organized on a co-operative basis.[1]

The most powerful though not the most dangerous opponent of the Nepali Congress party was the Communist party. It was a comparatively small but well-organized party with a large following among students and intellectuals. Its standing rested on the prestige of the Chinese Communist party, which had seized power in that huge country by a glorious revolution. Its close alliance with its sister party in China lent it further weight. Nepal, embedded between the gigantic states of China and India, is dependent upon their goodwill. In any relationship between Nepal and China, the Communist party was a factor to be reckoned with.

It had taken no active part in the revolutionary struggle because, as its propaganda stated, it regarded it as an attempt of the bourgeoisie to place itself in power. The transformation of the Nepalese feudal state into a democracy appeared as obviously unwelcome to Peking as it did to Moscow. In any case, the party made no attempt to help in consolidating democracy. It concentrated its strength on the struggle against the Nepali Congress party, the sole power capable of building democracy.

By the Delhi Pact of 1951 the king, as we saw above, had pledged himself to

1. Nepali Congress, *Manifesto Adopted at Birganj* (Patna, 1956). For an analysis of the manifesto, see Rose, *Socialism in Southern Asia*, pp. 76–9.

summon a constituent assembly. But the election writ was only issued in time to allow elections to be held eight years later, in February 1959.

The elections represented an experiment in democracy in a country of high mountains, with no proper roads, with a population whose overwhelming majority was illiterate and who had, until very recently, known only centuries of despotic rule.

The result of this experiment was surprising. Of an eligible electorate of 4,121,000 men and women, 1,083,000, or 43 per cent, had gone to the polls. More surprising still was the election result. The Nepali Congress won an absolute majority of seats, with seventy-four out of 109.[1]

It was, therefore, a democratic Socialist government which the King of Nepal had to summon to be the first parliamentary government in the history of Nepal—a government of the Nepali Congress party under the leadership of Bishewar Prasad Koirala as prime minister and Subarna Shamsher as deputy prime minister.

Its life span was to be a year and a half. In December 1960 King Mahendra put an end to both the government and the experiment in democracy by a *coup d'état*. He dissolved parliament, suspended the constitution, arrested Koirala and other Congress party leaders and, in breach of the Delhi Pact, usurped the powers of government as an autocratic monarch. A few weeks later he suppressed all political parties by proclamation. Koirala, who had inspired and led the revolution of 1950 and overthrown the rule of the Rana clan to which the king had also been subjected, was only released after seven years of imprisonment.

1. Four parties and 267 independent candidates campaigned in the elections. The results were:

	Votes	Percentage of votes cast	Seats
Nepali Congress	660,000	38	74
Gorkha Parishad	305,000	17	19
United Democratic party	117,000	10	5
Communist party	130,000	7	4
Independents (collectively)	280,000	23	7

See *Asian Socialist Conference*, Information No. 4/1959. The system of representation on the English pattern which was used in the Nepalese elections favoured the strongest party. So the Congress party won its majority with barely two-fifths of the votes cast.

13 · Islamic Socialism and Marxism in Indonesia

'Among the many political parties in Indonesia today,' Soetan Sjahrir wrote in 1956, 'there is not a single party which would not declare its sympathies with a Socialist and collective order of society. . . . In Indonesia we are all Socialists, or at least leaning in the direction of Socialism, and this, too, is the spirit of our constitution.'[1]

In no other Asian country did Socialist ideas find such fertile ground as they did in Indonesia. As in Burma, no indigenous capitalism existed, no native bourgeoisie, hardly any urban middle class and only a thin scattering of aristocratic landowners. The big capitalist undertakings—plantations, petroleum industries, mines, shipping, banks and the big trading companies —were run by the Dutch; the retail trade and light industry by the Chinese.[2]

Indonesian nationalism was anti-capitalist, for the capitalism of Indonesia was not Indonesian, but a capitalism of the West. Indonesian intellectuals saw capitalism as a European economic system and colonialism as a political system to allow capitalism to exploit the people of Asia by subjecting them to European imperialism. They identified capitalism with both colonialism and imperialism. And since they hated colonialism and imperialism, they also hated capitalism. In Indonesia's struggle for national independence, they sought liberation from capitalism as much as from Dutch colonial rule.[3] The

1. Soetan Sjahrir, *Indonesian Socialism* (Rangoon, 1956), pp. 30–1. This account is based on this book and the classic work of George Mcturnan Kahin, *Nationalism and Revolution in Indonesia* (New York, 1952); Jeanne S. Mintz, *Mohammed, Marx and Marhaen. The Roots of Indonesian Socialism* (London, 1965); Arnold C. Brackman, *Indonesian Communism. A History* (New York, 1963); Donald Hindley, *The Communist Party of Indonesia 1951–1963* (Berkeley and Los Angeles, 1964); D. N. Aidit, *A Short History of the Communist Party of Indonesia* (New Delhi, 1955): Aidit was general secretary of the Communist party; Sjahrir was founder of the Indonesian Socialist party and prime minister in three governments.

2. See Hindley, *Communist Party of Indonesia*, pp. 14–15; Sjahrir, *Indonesian Socialism*, pp. 70–1.

3. See Kahin, *Nationalism and Revolution in Indonesia*, pp. 51–2, Sjahrir, *Indonesian Socialism*, p. 30.

concept of Socialism as the antithesis of capitalism was an important element in the conception of Indonesian nationalism. The Indonesian nationalist was also a Socialist and, in either instance, anti-capitalist.

Moreover, the economic factor in Socialist theory—the concept of common ownership in the form of primitive communism—had been familiar to the broad masses of the peasant population from ancient times. Until only one or two generations earlier, the idea of private ownership of the land had been alien to the overwhelming majority of Indonesians, almost 90 per cent of whom lived in villages. The land was the property of the village. Its sale was forbidden by an ancient prescriptive law (*adat*). And although rural village property had decreased during the course of the several decades preceding the revolution, the principle of common ownership had remained fundamental to the way they thought and felt.

Socialist ideas were also embodied in the political organization of the villages, which rested on three principles. First, the principle of democratic self-determination: all the affairs of the village were subjected to discussion among all members of the community—the *musjawarah*. Secondly, the principle of unanimous decision—the *mufakat*; the notion that the will of the majority is decisive and that the minority must bow to majority opinion was foreign to village tradition. Decisions were compromises of all the opinions represented in discussion and thus they embodied the collective will of the village community. From this stemmed the third principle of *gotong rojong*, the principle of joint responsibility for executing decisions, of solidarity and of mutual aid.[1]

A non-religious cultural movement among Indonesian intellectuals, the *Budi Utomo*, which sprang up in 1908, saw Marxist Socialism as a modern form of Indonesia's centuries-old system of *gotong rojong*, which embodied the Indonesian ideal of collectivism and rejected the socially destructive forces of liberalism and individualism in the capitalist West.[2]

The most important factor of all in the spread of Socialist ideas through Mohammedan Indonesia, however, was the Islamic reform movement known as the 'Modernists'. In contrast to the deeply ingrained individualism of Hinduism and Buddhism, Islam, like Judaism and Christianity, from which it originated, is a social religion teaching the brotherhood at least of all 'true believers' and their equality in the eyes of God,[3] and it carries

1. See Mintz, *Mohammad, Marx and Marhaen*, pp. 12–13.
2. See Sjahrir, *Indonesian Socialism*, p. 30.
3. Thus teaches the Koran: 'Believers are brothers, therefore make peace between your brothers and fear Allah, so that compassion may be bestowed.' Social and economic inequality, however, is defended as a social order instituted by God. Thus God pronounces through the Koran: 'We ourselves distribute your keep among you in your worldly existence, and We raise some of you in rank above others, so that the one may take the other into care.' Yet 'the Muslim tenet that all men are equal on account of their having been

within itself a nucleus of ideas of social justice. It had, however, become stultified by a ritual and dogma which taught the sanctity of traditional institutions.

The impetus in the Islamic reform movement had come from the Egyptian theologian, Mohammed Abduh (1849–1905). He had set out to purge religion of its accumulation of corrupt and superstitious influences and rituals and to develop it into a living and effective social force. 'His writings formed, and still form,' H. A. R. Gibb observed, 'a shield, a support and a weapon for the social and political reformers.'[1] He was the pioneer figure in the Islamic 'Modernist' movement which, before the First World War, spread its influence also to Indonesia, especially the aspiration to define the principles of the Islamic ethic by its social aspects—the principles of social and political justice.

In endeavouring to realize these principles, the 'Modernists' in Indonesia became the instruments of nationalism as well as the carriers of Socialist ideas. Some of them even discovered in the Koran traces of Socialism,[2] like Hadji Agus Salim, one of the Islamic popular leaders, who in a controversy with the Communists stated that twelve centuries before the birth of Karl Marx, Mohammed had preached Socialist economics.[3] The Islamic party *Masjumi* (*Madjelis Sjaro Moslimin Indonesia*), the largest single party in the country, embraced under Mohammed Votsir's leadership a faction of religious Socialists, who influenced the whole party with their concept of Socialism. In declaring its principles, the party stated its duty '. . . to lead the people on the road to Socialism and in the spirit of the teachings of Islam, to brotherhood and equality under a [republic] . . .'.[4]

This was the social and cultural soil in which the ideas of modern Socialism put down roots. An amplification of these ideas may be found in the constitution drawn up by parliament in August 1950 after the revolution. Article 31 stipulates:

created by the same Almighty God is dynamite under the foundations of the social structure'—C. A. O. van Nieuwenhuyze, *Aspects of Islam in Post-war Indonesia* (The Hague and Bandung, n.d.), p. 36.

1. H. A. R. Gibb, *Modern Trends in Islam* (Chicago, 1947), p. 42.

2. To take one example, the prohibition of usury—the charging of interest on loans.

3. Quoted in Kahin, *Nationalism and Revolution in Indonesia*, p. 76.

4. *Kepartaian dan Parlementaria di Indonesia* (Jakarta, 1954), p. 441, quoted in Mintz, *Mohammed, Marx and Marhaen*, p. 88. Under the influence of its Religious Socialist section, the *Masjumi* council declared as its principles (among others): 'Opposition to capitalism in principle, but acknowledgement of the necessity of its continuance for some time in certain sectors. A mixed political economy should be followed—co-operative, socialist and capitalist. Emphasis should be on the co-operative sector, with the state advancing credit to develop this. As the government acquires sufficient capital and administrative personnel, it should gradually nationalize transportation, communications, mining, oil production, large plantations and any large-scale industry whose nationalization will be in the country's best interests—quoted in Kahin, *Nationalism and Revolution in Indonesia*, p. 311.

1. The economy shall be organized on a co-operative basis.
2. Sectors of production which are important to the state and which affect the lives of most people shall be controlled by the state.
3. Land and water, nature's wealth, shall be controlled by the state and shall be exploited for the greatest welfare of the people.

As a 'fundamental principle', the constitution states, 'the right of property is a social function'.[1]

In accordance with the religious temperament of Indonesians, the constitution declares in Article 29: 'The state shall be based upon the belief in God of all mankind.'[2]

First among Indonesia's Socialist parties had been the Communist party— the *Partai Komunis Indonesia* (P.K.I.). It came into being two and a half decades before any other Socialist party, and was moreover the oldest Communist party in Asia and, until 1966, the largest Communist party in the world outside the Soviet bloc and China. It had been founded on 23 May 1920 in Semarang in Java and during its subsequent stormy history attracted over six million followers.

It had emerged from the *Indies Sociaal Democratic Vereeniging* (I.S.D.V.), the first Marxist organization in the history of southern Asia, founded in May 1914 in Semarang by the Dutch revolutionary Socialists, Hendricus M. Sneevliet,[3] H. W. Decker and P. Bergsma, and a group of Indonesian intellectuals. Its aim was to spread Socialist ideas to the broad masses of Indonesia. It started with 125 members and in October 1915 launched its periodical, *Het vrije woord*; seven years later this periodical was suppressed by the Dutch colonial government.[4]

The only Indonesian political mass organization which had developed at that time was the *Serakat Islam* party (S.I.), founded in 1912. Within four years it had won 300,000 members, and by 1919 its followers numbered two and a half million and it included twenty-two Indonesian trade unions with a collective membership of 77,000.[5]

The group organizations of peasants, workers and intellectuals formed

1. This article was officially interpreted by the Minister of Justice as follows: 'The social function of property is fundamental and must be interpreted so as to mean that property should not be used to harm society'—quoted in ibid., p. 462.
2. Quoted in ibid.
3. Sneevliet (1883–1942) had belonged to a left-wing group in the Dutch Social Democratic Workers party, which had split away in 1909 to form the Social Democratic party, from which was to emerge in 1918 the Dutch Communist party. Sneevliet, who arrived in Java in 1914, represented the P.K.I. at the second congress of the Communist International in 1920 under the alias of 'Mahring'. In 1918 he was arrested by the Dutch colonial government and expelled from Indonesia.
4. A. B. Belenki, 'La Gauche Social-Démocrate Indonésienne et la Révolution Russe', in Georges Haupt and Madelaine Reberioux (eds), *La Deuxième Internationale et l'Orient* (Paris, 1967), p. 320.
5. See Kahin, *Nationalism and Revolution in Indonesia*, pp. 65–6 and 75.

ideal targets for the Socialist propaganda of the I.S.D.V. In Semarang, with local *Serakat Islam* leaders, Semaon and Darsono, Sneevliet organized *Serakat Islam* groups within the I.S.D.V. and tried to bring their national aspirations into line with Socialist aims. *Serakat Islam* had originally been a national movement with no social objectives; it worked for self-government within the framework of the Dutch Empire. But by its second congress in October 1917, under the influence of its Socialist wing, it was demanding Indonesia's complete independence and calling for a fight against capitalism —admittedly only foreign 'sinful' capitalism, out of deference to the Indonesian businessmen who supported *Serakat Islam* with donations.

In the meantime most I.S.D.V. members had become Communists. At the second congress of the I.S.D.V. meeting on 23 May 1920 at the head-quarters of *Serakat Islam* in Semarang, it was decided by thirty-three votes to two to constitute the Communist party simply by changing the title of the organization. Semaon was elected president, Darsono vice-president and Bergsma secretary.[1]

Their active membership was small—1,140 in 1924. But the party enjoyed a predominant influence over the masses of the peasants, whom they had grouped into a new organization, *Serakat Rakjat*,[2] of 31,000 members within *Serakat Islam*, and also over the workers organized in the trade union council, founded by Semaon in 1922.

The Communist party, however, soon fell victim to that 'infantile disease of radicalism in Communism', about which Lenin could not give impressive enough warnings. It geared its policy to the assumption that the Communist revolution was imminent. At its fifth congress, in June–July 1924, the Communist International had asked all parties to concentrate their strength on capturing the trade union movement as an indispensable precondition for successful revolution. The mass following of the Indonesian party, however, was based not so much on the industrial workers as on the peasants, organized in *Serakat Rakjat*. Its conference of December 1924 decided to dissolve *Serakat Rakjat*—for the reason, the proposal said, that it included too many bourgeois nationalists who could not be relied upon in a revolution—and to replace this by a trade union base. And it proclaimed as its aim the setting up of a Soviet Indonesian Republic under a dictatorship of the proletariat.

This new party course, however, was not 'in line with Stalin's policy' at that time. In a speech made in May 1925 he accused the Indonesian Communists of 'leftist deviation' which 'overrates the revolutionary potentialities of the liberation movement and underrates the importance of an alliance between the working class and the revolutionary bourgeoisie against imperialism'. The Communists in Java, he said, 'who recently erroneously put forward

1. Sneevliet, expelled from Java in 1918, had emigrated to Moscow.
2. See Aidit, *A Short History of the Communist Party of Indonesia*, p. 6.

the slogan of a Soviet government for their country suffer, it seems, from this same deviation. That is a deviation to the left which threatens to isolate the Communist party from the masses and to transform it into a sect.'[1]

But Stalin's warning had been spoken to the winds. The party left wing, under the leadership of Alimin and Musso, gained control of the party. A conference of the party executive and trade union leaders in Prambanan in October 1925 decided to unleash a revolution by the Communist party to overthrow Dutch colonial rule and seize power. At this time the Communist party had no more than about 3,000 members, with a mass base of some 31,000 peasants and a somewhat smaller number of urban workers.[2] The date for the outbreak of the revolution was fixed for 18 June 1926 to allow time for the plan to be submitted to the executive of the Communist International for appraisal. Alimin and Musso went first to Manila, to discuss the plan with Tan Malaka,[3] the representative of the Communist International in South-East Asia, before going on to Moscow.

Moscow's reaction to the plans for the uprising has never been made public. It would seem unlikely, however, that after Stalin's condemnation of the party's leftward course the Communist International would have given its approval.[4] It was certainly rejected decisively by Tan Malaka. A revolution, he said, could only achieve its goal provided it had the support of the masses. And it was questionable whether the revolution which the party had planned could find the necessary mass support. A *coup* by the leaders without popular backing was doomed to fail. However, disregarding Tan Malaka's warning, the P.K.I. continued with its preparations for an armed uprising.

The Dutch colonial government, evidently deducing that the party was preparing for revolutionary action, withdrew its right to hold assemblies at the end of November 1925 and, after a strike by dock workers in Surabaya in December, it arrested many of the party's leaders. Yet not even then did the party relinquish its plan for revolution; it simply postponed the date.

The insurrection broke out in Java during the night of 12 November 1926, and was crushed by Dutch troops within a few days. In Sumatra, where it did not begin until early in the following January, it collapsed after a few weeks of guerrilla warfare. The P.K.I. had hoped to carry the masses of workers and peasants but its call to revolution did not meet with the expected response. 'The masses of the workers in the cities as well as on the

1. Joseph Stalin, *Marxism and the National and Colonial Question* (Moscow, 1940), p. 192; quoted in Kahin, *Nationalism and Revolution in Indonesia*, p. 79.

2. See ibid., p. 84.

3. Tan Malaka (1895–1949), one of the outstanding leaders of the Indonesian Communist party, had been arrested in 1922 and given the choice of imprisonment or exile; he chose exile, and had gone to Moscow.

4. See Kahin, *Nationalism and Revolution in Indonesia*, p. 83. Brackman, on the other hand, does not believe that Stalin rejected the plan; he trusted Musso until his death. See Brackman, *Indonesian Communism*, p. 16; see also Mintz, *Mohammed, Marx and Marhaen*, p. 40.

plantations,' Semaon reported, 'adopted an attitude of indifference towards the rebel movement.'[1]

The defeat was disastrous. Seven insurgents were hanged, 13,000 arrested, 5,000 sentenced to imprisonment and over 800 deported to the penal colony of Boven Digul in New Guinea. The party was declared illegal, and remained impotent for almost two decades.[2]

Several months after the defeat of the Communist party, on 4 June 1927, a Socialist party of a peculiarly Indonesian character came into being which was to emerge from the Indonesian revolution as the most powerful party in the country. This was the Nationalist party of Indonesia—*Partai Nasional Indonesia* (P.N.I.). Its founder, a young engineer from Java, was Achmed Sukarno (1901–70), whose eclectic Socialism intertwined threads of Marxism[3] and Islam to form a synthesis with Hindu-Buddhist mysticism. He called his synthesis '*Marhaenism*' ('Proletarianism'): 'A kind of Socialism . . . especially suited to the Indonesian community and its spirit', which rested in principle on the concept of *gotong rojong*, the system of mutual aid, which is one of the tendencies in the Indonesian mentality. *Marhaen*, he wrote in his *Manifesto of Marhaenism*, was 'the collective term for the small peasants, agricultural workers, factory workers and other employees in Indonesia . . . the 91 per cent of the population who live in desperate poverty'.[4] Sukarno was a fascinating personality and an inspiring orator who was able to develop his thoughts in the language of peasants and workers.

The aim of the party was to secure Indonesia's independence. It was not,

1. Semaon, *The Situation in Indonesia*, Co-Report before the 30th Session of the Comintern, *Inprecor*, 4 October 1928, quoted in Kahin, *Nationalism and Revolution in Indonesia*, p. 84; The Communist International declared itself solidly behind the uprising. Bukharin, its president, stated in a speech to a meeting of its executive: 'From this platform we welcome the workers and peasants of Indonesia, the broad masses of this Dutch colony, who lead in a bloody battle against capitalism. Our utmost support to the Indonesian people!' See *International Press Correspondence*, November 1926, p. 1429.

2. For the history of the uprising, see Kahin, *Nationalism and Revolution in Indonesia*, pp. 80–5; Brackman, *Indonesian Communism*, pp. 15–21; Mintz, *Mohammed, Marx and Marhaen*, pp. 31–3 and 38–42. For documentary material on the uprising, see Harry J. Benda and Ruth T. McVey (eds), *The Communist Uprising of 1926–1927 in Indonesia: Key Documents* (Ithaca, 1960). As an example of Communist historiography it mentions that, according to Aidit's statements, the uprising had not been decided, planned and executed by the party, but was a spontaneous reaction by the 'people' against 'provocations' by the Dutch Colonial government. It was only after the uprising began, he declared, that 'the Communist Party came forward to give it as good a leadership as possible . . .'—Aidit, *Short History of the Communist Party of Indonesia*, p. 8.

3. An example of Sukarno's wide reading in Marxist sources occurs in an important speech he made on 1 June 1945, in which he discussed Otto Bauer's definition of national character in his book *Die Nationälitatenfrage und die Sozialdemokratie* (Vienna, 1907). His knowledge of European Socialist literature—he quoted Jean Jaurès in the same speech—seems all the more noteworthy since he had studied not in Europe, like a majority of Indonesian intellectuals, but in Indonesia. See Kahin, *Nationalism and Revolution in Indonesia*, pp. 123 and 125.

4. *Manifesto of Marhaenism* (Djakarta, 1954), pp. 6–7.

as Sukarno often stressed, an Islamic party, for the independence it strove for was the simultaneous objective of Indonesian Christians as well as of Mohammedans. It would be pointless, he said, 'to await an aeroplane from Moscow or a caliphate from Istanbul' to come to support the struggle. Above all the party sought to organize the workers into trade unions, and it attracted many of the Communists whose organization and trade unions had been destroyed. Within two years the P.N.I. had attracted over 10,000 members.

The rapid growth of the P.N.I. and its anti-capitalist propaganda alarmed the Dutch colonial government. Sukarno, with seven other party leaders, was arrested at the end of December 1929, and after seven months of detention on remand was sentenced to three years' imprisonment, because, the verdict stated, he had 'by words' recommended the government's overthrow; at the same time the P.N.I. was declared illegal. Sukarno was, however, released in December 1931 before serving his full term, but after several months he was again arrested and following court proceedings was banished to an island. It was nine years before he was given his freedom in 1942 by the Japanese shortly after they began their invasion of Indonesia.

The same fate overtook Soetan Sjahrir (1909–66), an outstanding figure in the history of Indonesian Socialism and, with Achmed Sukarno and Mohammad Hatta (b. 1902), a member of the triumvirate which led the revolution and created the Republic of Indonesia. He had been brought up in Sumatra and had studied at Leiden University in Holland before returning to Indonesia in 1932. At the beginning of 1934 he was arrested as a result of his activities in nationalist organizations that had come into being after the suppression of the P.N.I. He was then imprisoned without trial for a year, and afterwards deported to the concentration camp in Boven Digul before finally being banished to the island of Banda Neira. He, too, was only able to return to Java after the Japanese occupation.[1]

The Japanese invasion began with the attack on Sumatra on 14 February 1942 and on 1 March on Java; eight days later the Dutch commander in charge of the Allied forces[2] capitulated. The Japanese, welcomed by the Indonesians as liberators from Dutch colonial rule, held out the promise of self-government so as to win the support of nationalist leaders, especially that of Sukarno and Hatta. For tactical reasons, both agreed to co-operate. Sukarno became president of an organization formed under Japanese auspices and representing all nationalist movements—the 'Centre of the People's

1. See Soetan Sjahrir, *Out of Exile*, with an Introduction by Charles Wolf, Jr (New York, 1949). This collection of Sjahrir's letters from prison is an important source for the history of the Indonesian freedom movement as well as a remarkable record of his personality.

2. Some 8,000 British and American soldiers were stationed in Java besides the Dutch troops.

Power' (*Poetera*), planned as an interim measure leading to self-government. Sjahrir, on the other hand, went underground to organize in Djakarta and other towns in Java a revolutionary movement which particularly attracted the student youth and developed into the most formidable underground movement to confront the Japanese.[1]

After Indonesia's declaration of independence on 17 August 1945, Sjahrir saw the time as being ripe to establish a Socialist party (*Partai Socialis*) designed to influence the character of the emerging state. The Socialist party was formed in Cheribon early in December 1945 by the fusion of two Socialist groups which had come to life independently in November; one was the group Sjahrir formed in Djakarta, the other one which Amir Sjarifuddin organized in Jogja. Sjahrir became chairman of the new party, and Sjarifuddin deputy chairman.[2]

The Socialist party rapidly developed into a party with a mass following. Members of Sjahrir's and Sjarifuddin's anti-Japanese underground movements, as well as young intellectuals, university students and many Communists, flocked to its ranks. Allied with the party, or affiliated to it, was the Socialist youth organization, *Permuda Socialis Indonesia* (*Pesindo*)—an alliance of seven militarily trained and armed youth organizations, 'the most dynamic and powerful of all youth organizations in the Republic';[3] the Labour party, *Partai Buruh Indonesia*, a foundation of trade union leaders; the largest peasant organization in the country—the *Barisan Tani Indonesia*—and, above all, the Indonesian Trade Union Council (S.O.B.S.I.), a federation of trade unions both of industrial workers in the towns and of plantation workers which included several hundred thousand members.[4]

In alliance with the sister organization, the Socialist party formed the left wing of the revolutionary camp. During the first years of the republic it was to be the dominant influence in both the government and the provisional parliament. Its leaders were to provide prime ministers for the young republic between November 1945 and February 1948: Sjahrir, from June 1945 to July 1947, and Sjarifuddin, from July 1947 to January 1948.

The promising development of the Socialist movement was, however, frustrated by the Communist party, which had re-emerged on 21 October 1945 after two decades of illegality. Re-organized under Mohammed Jusuf's leadership, it developed only slowly. Three years after its re-emergence it

1. See Kahin, *Nationalism and Revolution in Indonesia*, p. 112.
2. Amir Sjarifuddin, leader of a nationalist organization before the war, organized an underground movement with financial aid from the Dutch government. This was uncovered by the Japanese, and Sjarifuddin and several other leaders were arrested and sentenced to death. On Sukarno's intervention, Sjarifuddin's death sentence was commuted to life imprisonment; but four of its other leaders were hanged.
3. See Kahin, *Nationalism and Revolution in Indonesia*, p. 162.
4. See Sjahrir, *Indonesian Socialism*, p. 34. Kahin estimated the membership of the Trade Union Council as being at that time between 200,000 and 300,000—*Nationalism and Revolution in Indonesia*, p. 261.

counted, according to its reports, no more than 3,000 members against the 60,000 of the Socialist party.[1] It played no role in the first phase of the revolution. 'The weakness of the party in the political, ideological and organizational spheres,' Aidit recorded, 'made it incapable of giving [the revolution] a lead, even though the situation was objectively very favourable at that time.'[2] In the provisional parliament it was represented by only two members against the Socialist party's thirty-five.

The immediate task which it set itself was to gain the leadership of the Socialist mass organizations—the youth organization *Pesindo*, the Labour party and, above all, the Socialist party—by infiltrating undercover Communists. 'It is of importance to note,' Kahin stressed in his analysis, 'that a large number of Indonesian Stalinists, including some of the most important of them, did not join the Communist party. Instead they joined one or the other of the three chief non-Communist Marxist parties—the Socialist party, the Labour party or the *Pesindo*'.[3] Thus, for example, two leaders of the Socialist party, the deputy chairman, Amir Sjarifuddin, and the general secretary, Tan Ling Djie, who was also a member of the party executive, later openly admitted they had for a long period been clandestine Communist party members and had worked within the Socialist party only as Communist cells.

The key strategic position which the Communists had to occupy in their struggle for power was in effect the Socialist party, which, standing at the head of the group of Socialist organizations, exercised a predominant influence over both the provisional government and the provisional parliament. It was taken for granted that Sjahrir would be summoned as the first prime minister of the newly-formed republic; and following his resignation at the end of June 1947, that the deputy chairman of the Socialist party, Amir Sjarifuddin, should succeed him to the post.

Sjahrir had resigned as prime minister because the concealed Communist wing within the party, led by Sjarifuddin, had refused to support the negotiations with the Dutch government which were to lead to Indonesia's sovereignty under the Linggadjati Agreement.[4]

With Sjarifuddin's manoeuvre, the mounting crisis within the party, provoked by the Communists' tussle to gain its leadership, came into the open. He had, moreover, insisted on forming, in alliance with the Communists, a 'People's Democratic Front' (F.D.R.), which was in effect designed to serve as the instrument of Russia's power politics in Indonesia. A split had become inevitable.

1. Kahin, *Nationalism and Revolution in Indonesia*, pp. 257 and 277.
2. Aidit, *History of the Communist Party of Indonesia*, p. 23.
3. Kahin, *Nationalism and Revolution in Indonesia*, p. 159.
4. For Sjahrir's negotiations with the Dutch government, and Sjarifuddin's opposition, see Kahin, *Nationalism and Revolution in Indonesia*, pp. 206–8; Sjahrir, *Indonesian Socialism*, p. 36.

It occurred on 13 February 1948. Sjahrir, with twenty-five members of the executive, declared their separation and in the *Foundation Manifesto of the Partai Socialis Indonesia* (P.S.I.) announced the establishment of a new Socialist party. The manifesto claimed that Sjarifuddin's wing of the old party, by forming the F.D.R., would split 'the national force' of the Indonesian revolution. Yet 'the national struggle for Indonesia's independence', the manifesto declared, 'is a common cause for all the peoples of Indonesia'. It was a struggle of historical significance for Asia's future. The Second World War had created a vacuum in power politics. It was the task of the new Asian states to fill this and so to prevent either American capitalism or the Soviet Union entrenching themselves in Asia. 'The Republic of Indonesia,' the manifesto said, 'must, in a common endeavour with the other Asian countries, strive to achieve the unity of Asia as a third world power and must therefore refrain from any alignment towards the United States or the Soviet Union. . . . The P.S.I. regards it as its duty to pave the road for this new policy in Asia.'[1] The conference founding the new Socialist party elected a provisional executive with Sjahrir as chairman and Sumartojo as general secretary.

Yet the split became a triumph for the Communists. Despite the fact that a majority of party leaders—nineteen of its thirty-five representatives in the provisional parliament and four of the five members of the parliamentary working committee—followed Sjahrir's leadership, the great majority of the 60,000 rank-and-file members remained within the old party under Sjarifuddin.

Meanwhile the Communists had also managed to gain the leadership of the Socialist group of parties in parliament. Two weeks after the Socialist party had split away, on 26 February at a mass meeting at Surakarta, they formed the 'People's Democratic Front'—*Front Demokrasi Rakjat* (F.D.R.)—composed of the old Socialist party, the Communist party (P.K.I.), the Labour party and the youth organization *Pesindo*, in close alliance with the Indonesian Trade Union Council (S.O.B.S.I.).

Sjarifuddin, who had succeeded Sjahrir as prime minister on 3 July 1947, resigned on 28 January 1948 as a result of differences of opinion within the Cabinet. Sukarno as President of the Republic then appointed Mohammad Hatta, vice-president and leader of the Masjumi party, in his place. When Hatta invited the old Socialist party to join his coalition government they demanded the key ministries of defence and of the interior, which Sjarifuddin had combined with his office as prime minister; after Hatta rejected this demand the party went into opposition.

About three weeks after Sjarifuddin's resignation, on 17–21 February

---

1. *Foundation Manifesto of the Partai Socialis Indonesia,* one manuscript copy of which may be found in the Archives of the Socialist International in the International Institute for Social History, Amsterdam.

1948, leaders of the Communist parties in South-East Asia, including the delegates of the P.K.I., met at a conference in Calcutta to discuss Stalin's new policy as laid down at the founding conference of the Cominform at the end of the previous September.[1] Under the influence of Moscow's challenge, as the Calcutta conference stated, the Indonesian Communist party resolved to commence the struggle for power through revolutionary means. It was, in fact, in itself no more than a small party which, according to Suripno, a member of the P.K.I. Politbureau, had a membership of only 2,500 in Java and 500 in Sumatra.[2] But it did dominate the old Socialist party, the powerful youth organization, *Pesindo*, and, indeed, the F.D.R. itself.

In a detailed plan of action, put together by the leaders of the F.D.R., an attempt was to be made to invoke political pressure in the shape of a large-scale campaign of demonstrations by workers, peasants and soldiers, and ultimately by a general strike, to force the resignation of Hatta's government and its replacement by an F.D.R. government. Should the government fail to capitulate despite this pressure, the F.D.R. was to pursue 'the struggle through an insurrection or as a separate government'. Regular army units whose loyalty had been won for the F.D.R. and other armed elements within its organization had been assigned the role of shock troops in the action to follow.[3]

The military strength upon which the F.D.R. could call was far from negligible. While he was prime minister, Sjarifuddin had taken control of the ministry of defence and had infiltrated the officers' corps in the army with his followers; the F.D.R. could thus rely on some army units to support the rising. Furthermore, it could count on the militarily organized and armed Socialist youth organization, *Pesindo*, and several other para-military groups. And its predominant influence over the trade union leadership ensured support among the masses of the organized workers.

The country's situation now became critical. The Dutch government, refusing to grant Indonesia independence, blockaded the Republic, and a Dutch force of 145,000 stood by on Indonesian soil, ready to subjugate the country by force. (The second Dutch campaign against the Republic began in mid-December 1948.)

This was the situation when the F.D.R. began its action.

It organized mass demonstrations against the government [Sjahrir recorded], organized strikes and incited the peasants to redistribute the land. It tried to extend its influence in the army. The armed youth organization *Pesindo* developed into an independent force within the Republic, ruled by a spirit of hostility for the government. . . . There was a general fear that the actions of the *Front Demokrasi Rakjat* would finally escalate into an armed campaign with the aim of subjecting the state to its control. The number of clashes between the government forces and the armed

1. See pp. 179–80.
2. See Kahin, *Nationalism and Revolution in Indonesia*, p. 257.
3. For the text of the relevant documents, see ibid, pp. 270–1.

organizations of the *Front Demokrasi* increased day by day. . . . The tension between the *Front Demokrasi* and the government, supported by all non-Communist groups in the Republic, had [in August–September 1948] reached such a degree of intensity that an explosion was inevitable.[1]

The explosion occurred on 19 September, and ignited a civil war—the 'Madiun rebellion'—which ended after three months of fighting in a disastrous defeat for the Communists and the deaths of many thousands.[2]

In the last analysis, the Communist rising failed due to its inability to carry with it the broad mass of the people.

By far the most important factor which brought about our defeat [Suripno, a member of the party Politbureau, wrote], was the highly inadequate support received from the people. Outside the town of Madiun, where support by the people could be described as good, the support was very slender. In certain cases the inhabitants of a village assembled so as to take us prisoner. . . . The lesson which we learned—a highly valuable though bitter lesson—was that the people did not support us.[3]

There were whole provinces where not even the F.D.R. organizations gave their support. The parties in Sumatra and Bantam, affiliated to the F.D.R., declared themselves at the outset of the insurrection to be loyal to the government. In Java, a number of local organizations of F.D.R. parties, including even the local Communist party in the town of Bodjonegoro, refused to support the uprising, accusing its leaders of being 'Trotskyists'.[4]

Another factor in the Communist defeat had been the premature outbreak of the uprising. The central committee of the Communist party had, admittedly, pursued a policy in the summer of 1948 which took account of the eventuality of an imminent revolution. But as all evidence seemed to show, it had not unleashed the rising. At all events, it had not prepared for an immediate insurrection, but had been taken by surprise. It had, it is true, created a revolutionary tension. It was precipitated into the turmoil not by its own decision, but by the action of subordinate local leaders in the movement.[5] When the civil war began, however, it placed itself at the head of the rising as a matter of course.

This outbreak of the revolution was a belated echo of the call for revolutionary action which had been issued by the founding congress of the Cominform at the end of September 1947, and which had been taken up by the Calcutta Conference of the Asian Communist parties in February 1948. But

1. Sjahrir, *Indonesian Socialism*, pp. 38–9.
2. For an objective survey of these events, see Kahin, *Nationalism and Revolution in Indonesia*, pp. 288–300; see also the detailed description in Brackman, *Indonesian Communism*, pp. 91–9.
3. Suripno, *Why We Lost in Mutiara* (Djakarta, June 1949), quoted in Brackman, *Indonesian Communism*, p. 100.
4. See Kahin, *Nationalism and Revolution in Indonesia*, p. 301.
5. See the reasoning in ibid., pp. 284–6.

while the Communist parties of India and Burma lost no time in inciting uprisings and unrest in their own countries,[1] the Communist leadership in Indonesia had refrained from a radical change of policy until the summer of 1948.

One personal factor had also been important in the development of events. In the middle of August 1948, a month before the outbreak of the rising, Musso, the founder of the illegal Communist party of Indonesia in 1920, had unexpectedly arrived in Java after a twenty-two-year absence. After the failure of the rising of 1926, which he had planned and led jointly with Alimin, he had fled to Moscow and had there been working in the service of the Communist International. His return to Java was hailed jubilantly by the party, and he was at once elected general secretary.

It can only be assumed—for decisions of this kind never find their way into the documentary record—that in accordance with Moscow's offensive against the West, he had been sent to promote a Communist revolution in Indonesia like that already begun by the parties in India and Burma. He came, at any event, with a plan for the Communist seizure of power which he called the 'Gottwald Plan'. Even as in February 1948, Gottwald had forced the nomination of a government under Communist leadership as an alternative to civil war by massing armed workers in the streets of Prague, and then, having possessed himself of power, had established a Communist dictatorship in Czechoslovakia,[2] so, under pressure from the masses, with the F.D.R. at their head, was Indonesia to be forced to accept a new government, whose key political power positions would go to Communists. According to the 'Gottwald Plan' the armed rising was only to be considered in the event of the peaceful method failing.

Musso's plan did not differ fundamentally from the F.D.R.'s plan of action. But it seems that under his leadership the action was speeded up. An extraordinary Communist party conference decided a week after his return to amalgamate Sjarifuddin's old Socialist party and the Labour party 'into a single party of the working classes with the historic title of Communist Party of Indonesia',[3] and the leadership of each party accepted the decision unhesitatingly, the Labour party on 27 August, the Socialist party two days later, in the face of protests from many of their members.[4]

On 18 December 1948, a few weeks after the fighting between government troops and Communist guerrilla forces had ended, the Dutch government once again employed its army in Indonesia against the Republic. (The first Dutch military action against the Indonesian Republic had begun on 20 July 1947, finishing with a cease-fire at the beginning of December.) After

1. See pp. 231 and 262.   2. See page 178.
3. Quoted in Aidit, *History of the Communist Party of Indonesia*, p. 29.
4. See Kahin, *Nationalism and Revolution in Indonesia*, p. 277.

seven months of fighting the Indonesian people united in resistance, it capitulated: it agreed to a cease-fire and negotiations, and on 2 November 1949 an agreement was signed recognizing Indonesia's independence.[1] On 27 December 1949, the Republic of the United States of Indonesia (R.U.S.I.) came into existence as an independent, sovereign state. The national revolution had been triumphantly concluded.

Only now, when Indonesia had finally gained her sovereignty, did it become possible to think of rebuilding the Socialist parties destroyed by the civil war and the Dutch military action.

The Socialist party had to be reconstructed from scratch. Hundreds of its most active members had, as Sjahrir recorded, been killed in the front line of the battle against the Dutch. When the party executive assembled on 3 February 1950, two years after its formation, it showed 'that it could count only a few thousand members. . . . Its numbers were relatively so small that one could hardly speak of a party organization.'[2] And when, two years later, in February 1952, it met for its first congress in Bandung, it numbered within 150 local organizations no more than 17,529 members, and of these only 3,049 were full members.[3]

The party executive had drawn the appropriate lesson from the fate of the Socialist party. Before its split it had enjoyed a mass following, but then, infiltrated by Communists, it had become a tool of Communist policy and within six months of splitting had gone over to the Communist party lock, stock and barrel. The Communists had been successful in their manoeuvre because the genuinely convinced Socialists within the party had not been very numerous; the party brought together an amorphous mass which leant vaguely towards Socialist ideas but which was unable to distinguish between the democratic ideal of humanitarian Socialism and Communism's totalitarian concept.

The executive therefore decided first of all to build up a closed organization, an exclusive, cadre party of convinced Social Democrats, and only these were to be recognized as full members. Candidates for membership were to be proposed by two full members, and only admitted to full membership after a period of studying the party principles and its political attitude, and only if their manner of life matched Socialist principles. The party executive had assumed that the first congress would open the party door to

---

1. The agreement states in Article 1: 'The Kingdom of the Netherlands unconditionally and irrevocably transfers complete sovereignty over Indonesia to the Republic of the United States of Indonesia and thereby recognizes the said Republic of the United States of Indonesia as an independent and sovereign state. . . . The transfer of sovereignty shall take place at the latest on 30 December 1949'—quoted in Kahin, *Nationalism and Revolution in Indonesia*, p. 449. West Irian (West New Guinea), the western half of a jungle-clad island twelve times the size of Holland, but with a population of only 700,000, remained under Dutch rule; it was not transferred to Indonesia until August 1962.

2. Sjahrir, *Indonesian Socialism*, pp. 46 and 47.

3. *Partai Socialis Indonesia* (Djakarta, 1956), p. 5.

the masses, but the congress decided to retain the principle of a closed party. So its membership grew slowly.

The declaration of principles decided upon at the first congress particularly emphasized the democratic and humanitarian character of Socialism in sharp contrast to totalitarian Communism which denied rights of freedom to the individual.

> Socialism, as we understand it [the declaration said], is a Socialism resting on democracy, safeguarding human values and respecting the equality of all men. The realization of individualism shows itself through the treatment of the individual under the theory and practice of Socialism. Respect for the human individual is, in fact, the essence [of the ideas] of all the great architects of Socialism such as Marx and Engels. Socialism is, in fact, nothing more than the full realization of the democratic ideals, human liberty, and emancipation in the real meaning of the word.

This concept of Socialism, the declaration continued, separated the Socialist party from 'Socialism as it is understood by Moscow'.

> The Cominform differs from us in that it disassociates itself from our realization of human individualism. It looks upon individualism as no more than one abstract factor in the concept of a group or class, or only as a working force, a factor of production. It also differs in its spirit and spiritual attitude. Not only in theory, but also in practice, does it dispute the unity and equality of all mankind. In practice it considers and treats all those who do not obey the party's discipline and accept its teachings as enemies, who may be dealt with with no regard for moral consideration.

'Considering the Cominform's concept,' the declaration said, 'its theories are . . . a matter of secondary importance. Its spirit and mentality are, however, in irreconcilable conflict with Socialism as we understand it.'

A Socialist society, it continued, could only be evolved by a spiritually mature nation, fully conscious of its actions. It could never be fulfilled by people 'who remain slaves in character and attitude, unable to act or think without instructions'. Socialism could never be realized 'by force or the deception of the people through the exploitation of their ignorance'.

The declaration emphasized that the party's objective was revolutionary— 'nothing less than the changing and elimination of the old society and the setting up of a new, Socialistic order'. But the best and safest road to this goal was the democratic way.

If, however, 'a feudal absolutist state should arise', then there would be nothing left for the party to do except to turn to force—'if necessary by kindling an uprising in defence against tyranny and despotism'.[1]

Like the Socialist party, the Communist party also had to be completely reconstructed. During the insurrection it had suffered terrible losses, including both its leaders; Musso had fallen in a skirmish and Sjarifuddin had

1. *Partai Socialis Indonesia*, pp. 23–4 and 29–31.

been arrested and executed.[1] It had been declared illegal and charged with responsibility for the national catastrophe of the civil war.

Its first concern was therefore to clear itself of the blame for having instigated the bloodbath, and to shift the responsibility on to President Sukarno and Hatta, the prime minister. In its justification it affirmed that the uprising had been an act of self-defence 'by the people' in the face of 'provocation'. The civil war had been unleashed, it stated in a memorandum, by a speech made by President Sukarno on the night of 19 September in which he 'ordered a general attack [on the Communists] and the brutal slaying of all those whom he branded as agitators'. By this provocation, the Communist statement continued, the national anti-imperialist front, the F.D.R. 'which had been built up by the Communist party on the basis of a national programme', had been broken up. 'The anti-imperialist, national revolutionary forces had been destroyed, by, among other measures, the killing and arrest of 36,000 people who had formed the backbone of the revolution.'[2]

The party was destroyed. It seemed that its development had been thrown back by decades.

1. After the end of the civil war ten leading Communists were executed with Sjarifuddin in Socerakarta, and forty-one in Magelang—all without trial; see Brackman, *Indonesian Communism*, p. 109. The numbers of Communists killed and arrested during the civil war ran into thousands.

2. Quoted in Mintz, *Mohammed, Marx and Marhaen*, pp. 147 and 149. The chronology of events, however, contradicts this version. The uprising in Madiun began on 18 September at 3 a.m. The Communists captured the town by a surprise onslaught, raised the Red Flag over the town hall and installed a government which announced from the Madiun radio station: 'Madiun has risen! The revolution has begun! The people have disarmed the police and army. The workers and peasants have formed a new government. Our arms will not be laid down until the whole of Indonesia is liberated'—quoted in Brackman, *Indonesian Communism*, p. 93.

But Sukarno's 'provocation', which, according to the Communist statement, 'had forced the people and the soldiers to defend themselves' (see Mintz, *Mohammed, Marx and Marhaen*, p. 147), was given on 19 September at 10 o'clock in the evening, forty-three hours after the rising had commenced. In a radio speech from the station at Jogjakarta he declared: 'Yesterday morning Musso's Communist party undertook a sudden attack in Madiun, and has formed a Soviet government under Musso's leadership. It considers the seizure of power by force to be a step preluding the seizure of the whole government of Indonesia. . . . Support the government in the fight against the insurgents!'

Musso replied an hour and a half later in a radio speech from the Madiun station, declaring: 'On 18 September 1948 the citizens of Madiun took the power of state into their own hands. With this the citizens of Madiun have fulfilled their duty towards the national revolution, which must in fact be led by the people of Indonesia to choose between Sukarno and Musso! The people should reply: "Sukarno-Hatta, the slaves of the Japanese and Americans! Traitors must die!".'

Moscow radio reported on the same day that 'a people's government has been installed in Madiun and people's committees have formed themselves in other leading towns. This is a popular rising against the government of the Fascist Japanese Quislings, Sukarno and Hatta.' For the wording of Sukarno's and Musso's radio broadcasts and Radio Moscow's announcements, see Kahin, *Nationalism and Revolution in Indonesia*, pp. 292–4).

In Communist historiography, however, the myth of the 'Madiun provocation' lives on, as in the *Short History of the Communist Party of Indonesia*, published by the general secretary of the party in 1955. See Aidit, *History of the Communist Party of Indonesia*, p. 32.

This made the fantastic growth of the rejuvenated party all the more surprising. Its prohibition was lifted in September 1949 at the end of the Dutch
campaign, and it had begun again with a regrouping of its scattered followers
in 1950. According to its own account, in March 1954 it embraced 165,206
members and by the end of 1955 over a million. Besides this, it held a dominant influence over the Indonesian Trade Union Council, the *Sentral Organ-
isasi Buruh Seluruh Indonesia* (S.O.B.S.I.), which, in 1955, had two and a half
million members, as well as over the youth organization, *Permuda Rakjat*
(People's Youth), with 200,000 members, and the Indonesian peasants'
organization, *Barisan Tani Indonesia*, with 3,315,820 members.[1]

How is this rapid expansion of Communist influence to be explained in
Indonesia, almost without precedent in the history of those countries where
different parties have been able to canvass for followers in a free contest?
What forces drew such enormous numbers of workers, peasants and the
youth to the Communist party—a party which had, above all, been charged
with responsibility for the national catastrophe of civil war?

The civil war, we must remember, had been followed within a few weeks
by the Dutch military action, and when the party's renewed ascendant began
in 1951, memories of the civil war episode had already been eclipsed by the
even more profound impression made by the Dutch war campaign. During
the first days of their military action, the Dutch had promptly occupied all
the towns with overwhelmingly superior forces and Sukarno, Hatta and
Sjahrir, the leaders of the resistance, were arrested. The Dutch attempt to
bring the people of Indonesia to their knees had aroused a deep-felt patriotism. They had refused to capitulate and even though deprived of their
leaders, had defended themselves. By numerous hard-hitting guerrilla actions
they had paralysed Holland's ability to wage war until the government in
The Hague, in the train of seven months of angry fighting, came to reason
and saw that the Indonesian people could never be subjected by brute
force.

Shortly after the Dutch campaign began, the Indonesian government had
released from prison many thousands of Communists arrested during the
civil war; these swelled the ranks of the guerrilla fighters and were equal
patriots with the next man. Through their participation in the national war of
liberation they appeared to be rehabilitated.

After the end of the war with the Dutch, the Communists continued the
national fight. Peace discussions at The Hague had ended in compromise.
While Indonesia's sovereignty and independence had been recognized by
Holland, it had remained as a dominion within a Dutch–Indonesian Union;
thus Indonesia continued to be legally bound to Holland.[2] Neither had

1. See Hindley, *Communist Party of Indonesia*, pp. 65, 135, 189 and 165.
2. The Dutch-Indonesian Union was dissolved in discussions between both governments at The Hague in August 1954.

Holland renounced its claim to West Irian, a territory of the former Dutch colonial empire.

This compromise, which also placed a heavy financial burden upon the young republic, was opposed not only by the Indonesian Communists; the Socialists also opposed it. But the Communist party actively continued to campaign against The Hague agreement as an implacable anti-imperialist struggle. While the Socialists, to express their rejection, contented themselves with abstaining in the vote on the agreement in parliament on 10 December 1949, the Communists voted against it. Their propaganda declared that the agreement in no way meant liberation from Dutch colonial rule and that the country would remain enslaved by Dutch capitalism and imperialism.[1] This opposition to any political or economic union with Holland appeared as a genuine nationalist struggle and so won the Communists sympathy from the broad masses awakening to national consciousness.

The younger generation of Communist party leaders recognized that, if they were to develop into a party with a mass following, they had to transform its image from that of a revolutionary party of class rebellion and to portray themselves as a national patriotic people's party. However, when the party re-emerged in its new legality early in 1950, its leadership was in the hands of two of its veterans, Alimin and Tan Ling Djie. These were hardly the men to refurbish the party's image. Tan Ling Djie was later accused of being a 'liquidationist' and was disciplined by the party leadership, for he had advocated the liquidation of the Communist party and the founding of a Labour party in its place. Alimin, himself compromised by the failure of the 1926 uprising which he had led with Musso, did not wish to see the party's continuation except as a small party limited to conscientious revolutionary Communists.

The change of the party's image and its ascendant began when the leadership went to two young men: Dipa Nurantara Aidit (1923–65) and H. M. Lukman (1920–65). Aidit, the son of a forestry worker, had been a member of the central committee since 1947 as well as president of the parliamentary Communist group. Lukman had grown up in a Dutch internment camp in West Irian, where his father had been deported for taking part in the Communist rising of 1926. After being freed he had also occupied himself in the party secretariat. At the time of the Madiun revolt, Aidit and

1. The 'dissolution of Indonesia's semi-colonial status and its replacement by a system of people's democracy' was declared to be the party's aim in its programme adopted in March 1954 at its first congress since the civil war. In his report on the political situation, Aidit, the general secretary, explained that the Hague agreement had 'transformed an independent and sovereign Indonesia into a semi-colonial country, a country which apparently possesses a "right to self-government", but in which the real power, especially in the economic sphere, lay in the hands of the imperialists, the Dutch imperialists above all'—D. N. Aidit, *The Road to People's Democracy for Indonesia. Fifth National Congress of the Communist Party of Indonesia, March 1954* (Djakarta, 1955), p. 25.

Lukman had fled into exile, first to Vietnam and then to China, returning to Indonesia in July 1950. They gained the party leadership on the strength of their programme to transform it into a party of the masses. Within six months of their return, the veterans Alimin and Tan Ling Djie had been manoeuvred out of the leadership. Aidit's era had begun.

The new strategic plan which Aidit submitted to the conference in January 1952 was aimed at forming a 'United National Front' to include 'the national bourgeoisie'. The 'national bourgeoisie' was, in Aidit's definition, a capitalist class, but 'suppressed by foreign capitalism and local feudalism' and therefore 'anti-imperialist and anti-feudal and in this respect a revolutionary force'—in contrast to the 'comprador bourgeoisie', the 'grand bourgeoisie', serving the interests of the big foreign capitalist.

To pioneer a national front, the Communist party had to fulfil the role of a national, patriotic party. To this end Aidit announced in a speech in March 1952:

> For the Communists, work for the party is inseparable from work in the national interest, the interest of the homeland, the interest of the people. When a Communist fails to serve the interests of the nation . . . then he fails to serve the interests of the party and is not a good Communist. . . . Every Communist is a patriot, and for every patriot who is not a Communist the gates of the party stand open to receive him into membership.[1]

The party surpassed itself in the homage it paid to the symbols of Indonesian Nationalism: the national flag, the national anthem, national holidays, national heroes. In its basic principles it accepted without reservation the five principles of Indonesian nationalism formulated by Sukarno on 1 June 1945 during one of his famous speeches under the title *Panja Sila:* 'nationalism, internationalism, parliamentary government, wealth and belief in God Almighty', and it declared in its tactical guide-lines, 'in the fight for national interest we must hold to the principles of subordinating class and party interests to national interests, to placing national interests above the interests of class and party'.[2]

To win the allegiance of non-political workers, the S.O.B.S.I. trade union congress in January 1955 even deleted the terms 'Socialism', 'class struggle' and 'people's democracy' from its former constitution, for these 'emphasized the division between the S.O.B.S.I. trade unions and those trade unions which belonged to no trade union federation'. The former 1947 constitution of the S.O.B.S.I., the central committee stated in explanation, had hoped 'to mobilize the workers for the establishment of a Socialist society'. Such a revolution would, in any case, have failed under present conditions. It was therefore 'no longer the duty of Indonesian workers to fight capitalism and establish a Socialist society, but together with the peasants, middle classes

1. Quoted in Hindley, *Communist Party of Indonesia*, p. 123.
2. Quoted in ibid., p. 126.

and non-comprador bourgeoisie, to fight imperialism and establish the society of a people's democracy—as a first step . . . on the road to a Socialist society'.[1]

The party wished to appear not only as a national party, but also as a party of parliamentary democracy. In its declaration of October 1951 it laid claim to the description of 'a pioneer in defending respect for parliament', with the rider 'so we will always remain'.[2] Admittedly in its programme it advocated the setting up of a 'people's democracy' but, it emphasized, through the methods of parliamentary democracy, not by means of force. A peaceful transition to a people's democracy was, it stated, 'a possibility which we must aim to fulfil with all our strength. If this depends on us as Communists, so is this the best way, the ideal way for a transition to a people's system of democratic power . . . the peaceful road, the parliamentary road.'[3]

The main task which Aidit gave the party, however, was to win the sympathies of the broad mass of the peasants through a revolutionary agrarian policy.

By far the most important immediate task of the Indonesian Communists [he declared], is to develop an anti-feudal agrarian revolution, to confiscate the land of the big farmers and hand it over to the dispossessed and impoverished peasants as their personal property. The first step in our work among the peasants must be our support for them in their struggle for the realization of this immediate requirement and demand. . . . This is the foundation on which an alliance of workers and peasants is to be constructed. . . . The agrarian revolution is the essence of the people's democratic revolution in Indonesia. . . . Its slogan is: 'The land for the peasants!'[4]

Aidit had evolved this programme a year before the congress met, in an article on the future of the Indonesian peasants' movement in the party's theoretical monthly journal. 'Given these slogans,' he wrote, 'the peasants will not doubt the sincerity of our programme; they will even support it with all their strength. It is a guarantee for a genuine alliance between workers and peasants.'[5]

While from the beginning of 1951 the Communist party was striving to build a mass party and win a mass following among the peasants as well as the workers, the second congress of the Socialist party, which met in June 1955 in Djakarta, three months before the first elections for the parliament, showed no indication of considering any changes in the party's structure. The congress continued to insist on the principle of a closed organization of convinced Socialists, and considered the theoretical and political instruction of

1. Quoted in ibid., p. 144.   2. Quoted in ibid., p. 127.
3. Quoted in ibid., p. 131.
4. Aidit, *The Road to People's Democracy for Indonesia*, pp. 32–3.
5. D. N. Aidit, 'Haridepan Gerankan Tani Indonesia', in *Bintang Merah*, July 1953, quoted in Hindley, *Communist Party of Indonesia*, p. 161.

its members rather than propaganda among the masses to be its most important task. To match the Communist-dominated peasants' organization, the party had founded its own peasants' organization, the *Gerankan Tani Indonesia* (G.T.I.); and, to match the Communist-dominated trade union alliance, the S.O.B.S.I., it had formed the Indonesian Trades Union Congress (K.B.S.I.), while gaining the leadership of a number of trade unions (in particular those of the railwaymen, dockers, petroleum and plantation workers). But it was at pains not to jeopardize the autonomous character of these organizations through party propaganda. Moreover, 'many members of the party', as Sjahrir recorded, had 'taken on the manner of a political élite'. This was why 'the party disengaged itself more and more from the masses. Its opponents scorned it as a party of intellectual snobs.'[1]

The party had, in fact, attracted many intellectuals. But its activity was in general confined to the large towns, 'with the result that the peasants in thousands of villages were unaware of the Socialist party's existence'.[2] It had, admittedly, almost trebled its membership since its first congress in 1952, from 17,529 to 47,192, but the number of full members had increased only from 3,049 to 4,330.[3] Despite these facts the congress could not agree to any fundamental change of party structure; it stood firm on the principle of a cadre organization of trained Socialists.

This was how the situation stood when, three months before the elections, the congress decided, hesitantly, and against the opposition of one faction, to participate. To its surprise its meetings drew such large crowds that, as Sjahrir reported, 'some people in the party polled 20 per cent [of the votes]'. The same people forgot, however, 'that while they had addressed thousands at their meetings, there were millions in the villages who had never heard of the existence of the Socialist party'.[4]

The elections of 29 September 1955 ended in a crushing disappointment for the Socialists. They had hoped at least to emerge as one of the large parties in the country. But the party gained only two per cent of the 37,875,000 votes cast, and only five of the 257 seats in parliament. It had, admittedly, gone into the election battle as a cadre party and had begun its election campaign a mere three months before the election date, while the Communists, with the other parties, had opened their election campaign many months earlier. It was therefore genuinely surprising that even so they had managed to win 753,000 votes. But they had lost their position of a decisive influence in the state which they had until then occupied.

For the Communists, on the other hand, the election results were a triumph. They had polled 6,179,000 votes, or more than 16 per cent of those cast, and won thirty-nine seats. Seven years after their ruin in the terrible

1. Sjahrir, *Indonesian Socialism*, p. 51.   2. ibid., p. 55.
3. *Partai Socialis Indonesia*, p. 6.   4. Sjahrir, *Indonesian Socialism*, p. 57.

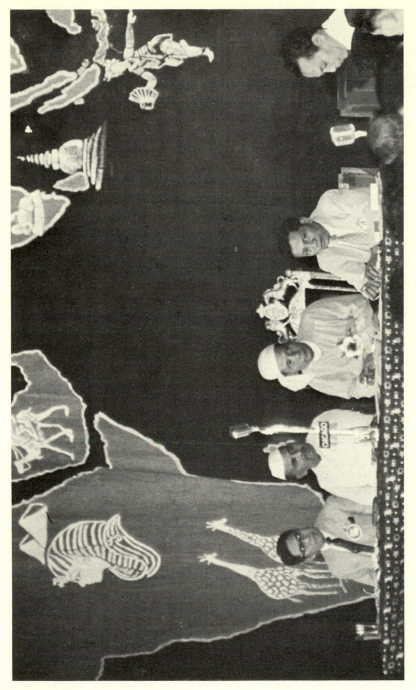

5 *The Chair at the Asian Socialist Conference.
(From left to right): U Hla Aung, Genda Sing, U Ba Swe,
Soerjokœsoemo Wijono*

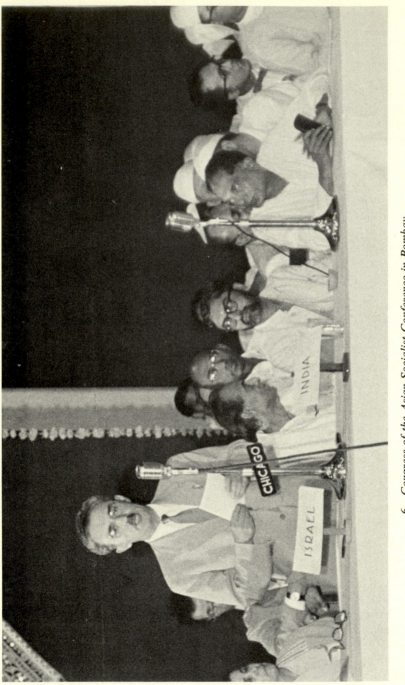

6 *Congress of the Asian Socialist Conference in Bombay.*
(From left to right): Moshe Sharett, J. B. Kripalani, Asoka Mehta,
Jayaprakash Narayan

defeat of the civil war, they had risen to rank as the fourth strongest party.[1] They had become a force to be reckoned with.

Despite its surprising success at the polls the Communist party could not expect to win at any time a majority of the electorate, and with it the power of the state by pure parliamentary methods. What it sought was to participate in state power, either through an alliance with one of the three leading parties within parliament, or in alliance with Sukarno, who now wished to consolidate his position as president of the republic by taking dictatorial powers through the suspension of parliamentary democracy.

What Sukarno had in mind was a change from the system of parliamentary democracy to a system of personal dictatorship under the name of a 'guided democracy'. In a speech of 28 October 1956, he stated that Indonesia 'was sick' of the party system; he asked that 'the people's leaders should mutually agree to bury all parties'.[2] A few months later, on 21 February 1957, he demonstrated in a speech how this 'guided democracy' should be constructed through a 'government of mutual aid', admittedly with party representatives in parliament, but with no opposition and with a 'national advisory council' consisting of representatives of the most 'functional groups', such as trade unions, peasants' organizations and other economic groupings.[3]

The Socialist party, like the *Masjumi* and most of the other parties, rejected Sukarno's concept of a 'guided democracy', fearing that it would destroy the most essential elements of democracy and concentrate power into Sukarno's hands.

1. The relative strengths of the parties are shown in the following table (the number of seats that each party had had in the provisional parliament appears in brackets):

Parties	Votes	Seats
Partai Nasional Indonesia (P.N.I.)	8,434,653	57 (42)
Masjumi	7,903,886	57 (44)
Nahdatul Ulama (N.U.)	6,955,141	45 (8)
Partai Komunis Indonesia (P.K.I.)	6,179,914	39 (17)
Partai Serakat Islam Indonesia (P.S.I.I.)	1,091,160	8 (4)
Partai Keristen Indonesia (P.K.I.)	1,003,325	8 (5)
Partai Katolik (P.K.)	770,740	6 (8)
Partai Socialis Indonesia (P.S.I.)	753,191	5 (14)

From H. Tinker and M. Walker, 'The First General Elections in India and Indonesia', in *Far East Survey*, July 1956, p. 108. In evaluating the influence of Socialist ideas in Indonesia, it must be remembered that, apart from the P.S.I. and the P.K.I., the two strongest parties—the nationalist (P.N.I.) as well as the Islamic party, *Masjumi*, with its predominant fraction of Christian Socialists—had canvassed on a Socialist programme, however vaguely formulated. These four parties had altogether won over two thirds of the votes cast (23,268,000 out of 37,875,000), and over two thirds of the seats in parliament (158 out of 257). Neither had the orthodox Islamic parties N.U. and P.S.I.I., nor the two Christian parties, P.K.I. and P.K., gone into the election campaign on any anti-Socialist platform.
2. Quoted in Mintz, *Mohammed, Marx and Marhaen*, p. 157.
3. For a detailed analysis of the doctrine of 'guided democracy', see ibid., pp. 165–92.

The Communist party, however, welcomed Sukarno's concept, for it opened out for them a possibility of attaining that participation in power which had hitherto been denied them, the parties represented in the government having rejected any coalition with the Communists. So now they turned against the system of parliamentary democracy. 'The Western system of democracy,' stated a declaration from its Politbureau, 'has harmed the development of the revolutionary and democratic movement in Indonesia'; it had shown itself incapable of solving the fundamental problems of society, and was used 'by foreign imperialists and their agents in the country' to play off party against party. Sukarno's concept, it continued, by no means threatened the party system or the parliamentary system; it even allowed for the development of democracy.[1] And to win mass support for the concept of 'guided democracy', it formed a non-party committee to organize meetings and street demonstrations. Within three days of Sukarno's speech, it set its propaganda campaign in motion with a grand opening in Djakarta: a mammoth gathering with a million in attendance.

Sukarno utilized a government crisis of 14 March 1957—brought about by an insurgent movement in Sumatra for autonomy in the provinces—to declare martial law throughout the country, and, in breach of the constitution, to nominate a 'business government'. The Communist party expressed its determined solidarity with the president and called 'on the whole people and the armed forces to support our President and Commander-in-Chief to the full'.[2]

It had placed itself absolutely behind Sukarno. During its meetings and through the speeches of its leaders it excelled in its praises of the president and in its attempts to identify the party with Sukarno. It justified its policies with quotations from his speeches and writings. It supported Sukarno in an action which to all intents would have legalized his dictatorship: the restoration of the 1945 constitution, which had granted the president unlimited powers. When parliament rejected the overthrow of the constitution which he put forward, Sukarno obtained what he wanted by decree in July 1959.

He now took over the trappings of power, installing a government of followers responsible not to parliament, but to him alone. In March 1960 he dissolved the elected parliament, replacing it with a parliament of his own nominees. By a series of decrees the press was brought to heel, and all political parties, apart from eight parties loyal to Sukarno, were suppressed.[3]

1. Quoted in Hindley, *Communist Party of Indonesia*, pp. 261–2.
2. Quoted in ibid., p. 263.
3. The Socialist party was prohibited in August 1960, and Sjahrir was arrested in January 1962. He became seriously ill in prison, and was released after three years to go to Switzerland for medical treatment. He died there in 1966. When his body was brought back to Java, it was interred in Djakarta with full honours in recognition of his services as one of the three leaders of the Indonesian revolution.

The parties recognized by the government were finally incorporated into a 'National Front' under Sukarno's leadership.

The Communist party had, if at times reluctantly, supported the eroding of the instruments of democracy through all its phases. To allay doubts within his own party, Aidit advanced the argument that, in the end, Sukarno's dictatorship could also find a road to Socialism. It was, he wrote, by no means inconsistent with Marxism that a man like Sukarno, though not a member of the working class, should become leader in a Socialist Indonesia.[1]

In acknowledging the value of his coalition with the Communist party, Sukarno nominated its representatives in considerable strength to serve in all branches of the administration: in the provinces and local communities, above all in parliament, in the advisory council to the government and in the National Front; and, in March 1960, he also summoned Aidit and Lukman to enter the government, if only as ministers without portfolio.

The Communist party's coalition with Sukarno had greatly enhanced its image in the country at large. In the local Javanese elections in 1957 it won 7,514,000 votes—an increase of 2,036,000 in this province alone over the 1955 elections. Its membership rose to over two million, and the mass organizations of trade unions, peasants, women and youth movements affiliated to it had a collective membership of twelve million.

Despite its massive strength, however, in the coalition the Communist party possessed hardly any degree of real political power. As Aidit told its congress in April 1962, any efforts by the party were, notwithstanding its participation in the government, sharply curtailed, for, he said, 'any proposal [by us] can be rejected by the government, and any action can be prohibited or obstructed by the authorities'. He and Lukman were ministers, it was true, but without possessing 'any power whatsoever'.[2]

So the Communist party had become a prisoner of its coalition with Sukarno, and there were no prospects for its escape. Moreover, since the Madiun revolt, the army had become a deadly enemy of the Communist party. Under the martial law decreed by Sukarno in 1957, which was to remain in force for three years, the army had gained tremendous power. During this period it had become the highest authority in the administrative apparatus of the state at large and in the provinces, and it was at pains to frustrate Communist activity. It had dissolved Communist local groups, suppressed Communist newspapers and arrested Communist shop stewards. It had even forbidden the party congress due to take place in August 1959; though it was allowed several weeks later through Sukarno's intervention, it was held only on the humiliating condition of supervision by military commissioners. It was, in

1. D. N. Aidit, *Peladjaran dari Sedjarah P.K.I.* (Djakarta, 1960), pp. 22–3, quoted in Hindley, *Communist Party of Indonesia*, p. 286.
2. Quoted in ibid., p. 297.

fact, only Sukarno's absolute authority which shielded the Communists from total suppression by the army. And Sukarno protected them because the great weight of political support which they carried represented a counter-balance to the army, which he felt to be a threat even to his own position.

Dissension against Sukarno among the higher officer ranks was prompted not so much by his having set up a dictatorial régime—the generals were by no means opponents of the system of 'guided democracy', declared by Sukarno to be an instrument for fulfilling the revolution in a 'Socialism à la Indonesia'—as by their hatred for the Communists. They felt themselves to be menaced by a growing Communist influence over Sukarno, and were obsessed with the fear that the Communists would one day seize power by a *coup d'état* and establish under their dictatorship an 'atheistic Socialism à la Moscow and Peking'.

It was on 1 October 1956 that upheaval finally gripped the country and a *coup d'état* actually occurred. Indonesia had become involved in a drastic economic crisis: galloping inflation had rapidly increased the cost of living for the urban population, and the devaluation of their wages had provoked mass strikes by the workers.

At midday on 1 October the peoples of Indonesia were unexpectedly informed by a newsflash over the radio that a so-called 'Movement of 30 September', unknown until then, had, under the command of Lieutenant-Colonel Untung, arrested a number of generals at Halim airport and installed an 'Indonesian Revolutionary Council' to take over the powers of state. This action had been taken, it continued, to forestall a *coup d'état* of a 'Council of Generals', planned for 5 October with secret American backing.[1]

The *coup* seemed to both their friends and enemies to be the work of the Communists. But in reality the 'Movement of 30 September' was a conspiracy of several high-ranking officers who with their troops had in the early-morning hours of 1 October murdered six of the generals they had arrested before attempting to occupy government buildings in Djakarta. Their aim was certainly not Sukarno's overthrow and the replacement of his dictator-ship by a dictatorship of the Communist party, or even by a military dictator-ship of the left, but simply, it appears, to eliminate those right-wing army generals who constituted a potential threat to Sukarno's régime.

The *coup* was put down within a few hours; it was not much more than an 'incident' in the history of the Indonesian revolution, which had hardly been starved of similar 'incidents'.

This single event, however, set in motion an immense avalanche of hatred and ruin to engulf the Communists. Generals had been murdered, and a list

1. For a lucid account of these events, see John Hughes, *The End of Sukarno* (London, 1968). Hughes describes the events as an eye-witness, having been correspondent in Indonesia for the *Christian Science Monitor* (Boston).

of generals came to light for whom the same fate had been intended. The surviving generals decided on a terrible revenge—the mass murder of Indonesia's Communists—the cruelty of which has in the annals of humanity's misdeeds been surpassed in our own time only by Hitler's holocaust of the Jews and Stalin's mass extermination of his opponents.

By orders of the generals, the Republic was to be 'purged' of Communists. Troops ranged the land, from village to village, and from town to town, systematically murdering all who came under suspicion of being Communist. In Central Java three quarters of the electorate had voted for the Communists; there were villages in which 100 per cent of the people were Communists. And in these cases the entire population, with the exception of small children, was butchered. In many villages officers spurred on the Communists' enemies to commit murder, surrendering arrested Communists to them for execution; these were slaughtered by the peasants with knives and scythes. The mass killing continued for over three months and the numbers of victims ran into hundreds of thousands.[1]

Yet the Communist party had had no responsibility for the officers' *coup* in Halim. They had neither planned it nor co-operated in its preparation.[2] But they did declare their solid support for it. The edition of the party's central organ, *Harian Rakjat*, which came out in the early hours of 2 October, contained a leader stating that the 'Movement of 30 September' had taken precautions to safeguard President Sukarno and the Republic of Indonesia 'against a *coup* by the so-called Council of Generals'; its action was 'patriotic and revolutionary. . . . We, the people', it continued, 'are convinced in our knowledge of the duties of the revolution, that the action of the Movement of 30 September is correct to safeguard the revolution and the people. The sympathies and support of the people undoubtedly turn to the Movement of 30 September.'[3]

This article was fateful. Surprisingly, it did not appear until after the revolt in Djakarta had been put down and must have been written during the afternoon of 1 October, when the editor obviously counted on the *coup*'s success. But by issuing this article the Communist party had affirmed its support for the *coup*, and by doing so played into the hands of the generals seeking revenge for the murder at Halim, presenting them with a document to justify their campaign to destroy the Communists: '. . . an act of

1. For the description of the mass murders, see ibid, pp. 141–61 and 173–83; for estimates of the numbers murdered, see ibid., pp. 184–9.

2. The Tokyo daily *Asahi Shimbun*, on the other hand, published an alleged 'confession' by Aidit in January 1967. He had been arrested on 22 November in a village in Central Java, and executed without trial within a few days. In his 'confession' he charged himself and the party leaders with full responsibility for planning the *coup*. For the wording of the evidence attributed to him, see Hughes, *The End of Sukarno*, pp. 168–72. The authenticity of this document is, however, questionable to the highest degree.

3. *Harian Rakjat* (Djakarta), 2 October 1965. For the text of the article, see Hughes, *The End of Sukarno*, p. 78.

unbelievable folly by the Communist party', Hughes comments, 'which set the seal on their fate'.[1]

That the Communist party wished to see the rising succeed—and with it the extermination of its enemies within the army—was only natural. But nothing was further from its motives than to overthrow Sukarno and seize power. Ever since its rejuvenation in 1951 under Aidit's leadership it had turned away from the path of conspiracy, had abandoned the class struggle against native capitalism and sought to harmonize class interests in a national front, following this rightward course with total consistency. It had firmly supported Sukarno's dictatorship in its guise of a 'guided democracy', and had identified itself with its objective—'Socialism à la Indonesia'. It had sought to win respect as a party of good patriots.

But its protestations of patriotism in no way convinced its enemies. To them, the Indonesian Communist party appeared as the party of Moscow and Peking whose systems glorified the Communist dictatorship. It affirmed the idea of a 'people's democracy'—and what this meant in practice had been revealed in those countries which had 'people's democracies'. It asserted its wish for a peaceful road to Socialism; but it had twice attempted to grasp state power by an armed rising.

It was in these historical experiences that mistrust of the Communists and a fear of Communist dictatorship was rooted; and it was this threat which fed the hatred against the Communists of Indonesia when it broke into the open in the terrible catastrophe of the autumn of 1965.

The suppression of the Communists was followed by the removal of Sukarno from power and the setting up of a military régime under General Suharto. It marked the end of the first period of Indonesia's national and social revolution.

1. Hughes, ibid., p. 77. For the question of the motives behind the *coup* and the responsibility of the Communist party, see ibid., pp. 103–15.

14 · Socialism and Communism in Japan

1

In India, Burma and Indonesia, Socialist ideas had permeated the broad mass of the people even before the industrial revolution had begun in those countries. In Japan, on the other hand, the industrial revolution was already well under way when, during the first decade of the century, the industrial workers organized themselves into a class. The Socialist movement in Japan was looking forward to a classless order of society before any other Asian country had even developed a capitalist class. Here, however, it was to encounter the resistance of a powerful capitalist class which could rely on the power of the state to support it in the class struggle. In the rest of Asia, Socialism was to receive its impetus from national revolutions kindled by the struggle against European imperialism and colonialism to which those countries were subjected. Socialism had represented the social content in the political struggle for national independence. But throughout its thousand-year history, Japan had never been subjected to foreign domination. Neither had the Japanese people ever risen in a revolutionary struggle to win their rights to freedom. The feudal system—the *Shogunate*—to which Japan had been subjected over six centuries was admittedly overthrown in 1868, though not, as in other Asian countries, by a people's revolution but by a dynastic revolution. This had not, of course, established the sovereignty of the people; it had 'restored' the position of the crown in the state—an absolute monarchy which rested on the Emperor's 'divinity'.[1]

1. The emperor's right to divinity, founded on the doctrine of his 'descent from the Sun goddess in unbroken line from time immemorial', was only retracted on 1 January 1946 by Emperor Hirohito's solemn proclamation. The constitution of 3 May 1947 declared the Emperor of Japan to be the 'symbol of the state and the unity of the nation, who derives his position from the will of the people, which is the basis of sovereign power'. This second revolution, which took power away from the emperor and established the people's sovereignty, did not, however, take place until after Japan's catastrophic defeat in the Second World War, when the country became democratized under the rule of the American forces of occupation.

The dynastic revolution began the process of dissolving the feudal structure of Japanese society and its transition towards a modern capitalist order. The development of capitalism in Japan, however, hardly changed the feudal character of its political structure. The feudal aristocracy remained in possession of material power. As before, they controlled the army and ruled the state bureaucracy; in addition, they monopolized industry concentrated in the hands of financial cliques known as *Zaibatsu*.

Under pressure from the upsurge of the middle class brought about by the process of industrialization, Japan finally, in 1899, became a constitutional monarchy after the Prussian model, as Bismarck had devised it, according to which actual power rested with the crown and the executive as representing the imperial will. By tax qualification, the electorate was limited to about 500,000. The constitution gave the middle class a strictly defined influence, but no power. And the working class remained excluded from any influence over politics. A year after the Constitution was promulgated, in 1900, a special police law was enacted against the working class to chain the trade unions, threaten incitement to strike with imprisonment, subject the press to an intensified censorship and to throttle the free formation of parties or the holding of assemblies. Not until a quarter of a century later, in 1925, did the working class become entitled to vote through the introduction of universal manhood suffrage, extending the franchise to about fourteen million people. At the same time, however, as anti-labour movement laws were intensified, Socialist propaganda against private ownership and the form of government which rested on the Emperor's 'divinity' (*Kokutai*) was threatened with the death penalty, and under the Peace Preservation laws of 1928, a special police corps was established to seek out 'dangerous thoughts'.

It was under these economic and political conditions—basically very different from those in any other Asian country—that the labour movement in Japan had to develop. Its pioneer was Sen Katayama (1858–1933), the son of a farmer, who had become a printer and emigrated to the United States to study at university while earning his keep as a day-labourer.[1] After obtaining his degree, he returned to Japan in 1895, and in July 1897 founded a Society for Promoting Trade Unions and, a few months later, the metalworkers' union; he became its secretary, and published the periodical *Rodo Sekai* (The Labour World), the first and only organ of the Japanese labour movement during these years.[2]

1. For a biography of Katayama, see Hyman Kublin, *Asian Revolutionary, The Life of Sen Katayama* (Princeton, N.J., 1964).

2. See Sen Katayama, *The Labor Movement in Japan* (Chicago, 1918), p. 38. See also Braunthal, *History of the International, 1864–1914*, pp. 240–2. The following account is based on: George Oakley Totten, *The Social Democratic Movement in Pre-war Japan* (New Haven, 1966); Allen B. Cole, George O. Totten and Cecil H. Uyehara, *Socialist Parties in Post-war Japan* (New Haven and London, 1966); and Robert A. Scalapino, *The Japanese Communist Movement 1920–1966* (Berkeley and Los Angeles, 1967). These three

The Social Democratic party (*Shakai Minshuto*) was established under the leadership of Sen Katayama, Isoo Abe (1865–1949) and Denjiro Kotoku Shusui with the co-operation of a number of trade unions at a conference on 22 May 1901. The manifesto issued by the conference declared its support for the nationalization of the means of production and for a fair distribution of the fruits of labour and of the land. It demanded political rights, particularly universal franchise, the abolition of the Upper House and the setting up of parliamentary democracy. It rejected anarchism, a concept advocated by some Socialists, as well as the use of force in the struggle for Socialism.

The Social Democratic party was, however, to be short-lived. The police confiscated the manifesto and dissolved the party within a few hours of its inauguration.

Soon afterwards, however, in 1903, Kotoku Shusui and Toshihiko Sakai (1870–1933) formed a Socialist propaganda society, which in the same year founded the periodical *Heimin Shimbun* (Commoners' Newspaper); it also published the first Japanese translation of the *Communist Manifesto*. But the life-span of this organization was also short: the society, together with its paper, was suppressed by the police in October 1905.

A few months later, in January 1906, the party reconstituted itself as the Socialist party (*Nihon Shakaito*). It won recognition as a legal party from the more liberal government which had taken office at the turn of the year, on condition that it represented a 'Socialism within the boundaries of the constitution'.[1] It was, at all events, a Social Democratic party in the spirit of the manifesto of May 1901 in its ideology and methods.

But a strong anarcho-syndicalist stream had come into being in the labour movement to challenge Social Democratic ideology. This anarchism was a reflection of the mood of a suppressed, impoverished and despairing working class. It had been excluded from parliament and in its battle for equality and the general right to vote it faced an extensive police apparatus ready to suppress any political movement among the workers. Parliamentary democracy seemed to be an unattainable goal, the fight for it to be a meaningless waste of working-class strength. On the other hand, the anarcho-syndicalist method of 'direct action'—the strike and the revolutionary general strike—seemed to present an irresistible weapon in the battle for working-class emancipation.

The pioneer of this stream within the party was Kotoku Shusui. He had travelled through the United States in 1906, and had returned to Japan

works are the most thorough studies extant of the Japanese labour movement. See also A. Rodger Swearingen and Paul F. Langer, *Red Flag in Japan: International Communism in Action, 1919–1951* (Cambridge, Mass., 1952); M. Beckman and Okubo Genji, *The Japanese Communist Party 1922–1945* (Stanford, 1969); Solomon B. Levine, *Industrial Relations in Post-war Japan* (Urbana, 1958); and E. S. Colbert, *The Left Wing in Japanese Politics* (New York, 1952).

1. Quoted in Totten, *Social Democratic Movement in Pre-war Japan*, p. 28.

deeply impressed by the concept of anarcho-syndicalism, put forward by Daniel de Leon in founding and leading the trade union council, the International Workers of the World (I.W.W.). In a speech to a party conference in February 1907, Kotoku attempted to convince it of the necessity for anarcho-syndicalist methods. The social revolution, he explained, could never be realized through the general right to vote and parliamentary methods, for parliament would always remain a weapon of the propertied classes. Socialism could only be attained through direct action by organized workers. He put forward a resolution demanding the implementation of direct action in the fight for Socialism. It was rejected by twenty-four to twenty-two votes, though a resolution in support of parliamentarianism and rejecting direct action received only two votes.[1] At all events, the government reacted to the conference with the immediate dissolution of the party.

The Socialist movement, having lost with the suppression of the party a common forum for all opinions, splintered into small groups of Socialists under Katayama's leadership, and of the Anarchists under Kotoku's leadership. Anarchist propaganda now took on the more serious form of sporadic strikes and industrial sabotage. During a counter-action by the government, the police 'discovered' an Anarchist conspiracy against the life of the Emperor Meiji. Numerous Anarchists were arrested, and after a sensational trial for high treason, staged in 1910–11, twelve Anarchists were hanged, Kotoku among them. The ruthless political persecution of Socialists as well as of Anarchists which now set in effectively stifled the Socialist movement. Katayama, his spirit broken, left Japan in 1914, never to return to his homeland.[2] More than a decade was to pass before the Socialist movement returned to life.

Its revival began gradually after the end of the First World War. In December 1920, the Socialist Party was once again reconstituted, this time under the title of Socialist Federation of Japan (*Nihon Shakaishugi Domei*). And the trade union movement, which had been non-political before the war, became one of the mainstays of the political labour movement.

Japan's industry had developed rapidly during the war, and the number of factory workers had doubled.[3] With this growth in the number of industrial workers the number of trade unions grew also: from forty in 1911 to 273 in

---

1. See Scalapino, *Japanese Communist Movement*, p. 3.
2. Katayama was sentenced to five months' imprisonment for leading a strike of tram-drivers in Tokyo in 1914, and after his release from prison was placed under police surveillance; he was thus unable to obtain work. He emigrated to the United States at the end of August 1914, and there met Trotsky, Bukharin and Kollontai, under whose influence he became a Communist. In 1921 he went to Moscow, and worked there in the service of the Communist International as a highly esteemed member of the presidium.
3. Their numbers rose from 853,000 in 1914 to 1,777,000 in 1919. See Totten, *Social Democratic Movement in Pre-war Japan*, p. 31.

1920.[1] Shortly after the war they came together in a trade union council, the General Federation of the Workers of Japan (*Nihon Rodo Kumiai Sodomei*). Rejecting the concept of harmony in class interests that had been prevalent among the trade unions before the war, the trade union council declared itself unequivocally for the necessity of class struggle. In its 1922 programme it stated:

> We shall, with boldness and through effective methods, fight to the finish against suppression and persecution by the capitalist class.
> We do not believe that the working and capitalist classes can co-exist peacefully.
> We shall, with the backing of the trade unions, struggle to win the full liberation of the working class and to set up a new society of liberty and equality with the pressure of the trade unions.[2]

After the war, a third force had further developed within the Socialist movement: the Union of Japanese Peasants (*Nihon Nomin Kumiai*), founded in April 1922. Most Japanese peasants held their land on lease. Wild inflation during the war had impoverished them through rent increases and the rapid price increase of their means of production. In 1918 they rose in a revolt which shook the country and unleashed an agrarian mass movement to fight for lower rents. The Union of Peasants had its origins in this movement; within four years of its founding it had 67,000 members.[3]

The Socialist Federation embraced Socialists of variegated tendencies: Anarchists as well as Social Democrats, and also a number of Marxist–Leninists. Marxism in Japan had not been taken up by intellectuals or students until after the outbreak of the Bolshevik Revolution in Russia, and then mainly in its Marxist–Leninist complexion.

A Communist party did, however, come into existence following the secret conference of a small group led by Kyuichi Tokuda (1894–1953), which met in Tokyo on 15 July 1922. This was, in fact, a creation of the Communist International. The founding of the party had been decided upon in Moscow in January 1922 at the First Congress of the Workers of the Far East. The congress, meeting under Katayama's chairmanship, was attended by a Japanese delegation headed by Tokudo and Mosaburo Suzuki (b. 1893). During detailed discussions with Katayama and the representatives of the International, the party programme was formulated and its foundation financed by the Communist International's Shanghai bureau.[4]

1. See ibid., p. 32.   2. Quoted in ibid., p. 40.   3. See ibid., p. 38.

4. 'The proof,' Scalapino declared in his study, 'that the Japanese Communist party originated as a creation of the Communist International and therefore of the Soviet Union, is overwhelming. In this respect the documentary material could not be more complete'— Scalapino, *Japanese Communist Movement*, p. 19. *The Official History of the J.C.P.* (Tokyo, 1932), in no way denies that the party was founded 'under the direct leadership and with the help of the Communist International'—quoted in Swearingen and Langer, *Red Flag in Japan*, p. 14.

For the Communist International, the establishing of a Communist party in Japan was a matter of high importance, for it considered Japan to be a revolutionary key position in the Far East. In the speech as president of the Communist International with which he opened the congress of the Workers of the Far East, Zinoviev stated:

If Marx had once said that without a revolution in England any revolution in Europe would be no more than an insignificant storm in a tea-cup, England being decisive in the history of the European revolution, then we must say that, without a revolution in Japan, any revolution in the Far East must remain only a local concern, a relatively unimportant storm in a relatively small tea-cup. . . . Not until there has been victory in Japan will the revolution in the Far East cease from being a storm in a tea-cup. Thus a very great responsibility rests on the young working class of Japan.[1]

At its first congress the Japanese Communist party did no more than constitute itself and vote in a central committee, under the chairmanship of the Socialist pioneer Toshihiko Sakai (1870–1933). It was only at its third congress, in December 1926, that it defined a programme of political demands: among them, the abolition of the imperial system of government and the confiscation, without compensation, of the estates of landed proprietors and religious foundations as well as of the emperor.

A party striving to overthrow the 'sacred' principles of the Japanese constitution, which rested on the emperor's divinity, could never, of course, attain legality. It remained illegal until after the end of the Second World War. From the outset it was a party of intellectuals, and its membership remained limited; even during its greatest expansion during the pre-war period, it had no more than 1,000 members.[2] But the spread of Marxism among intellectuals and students won it many potential followers in these circles, and the radical mood of the working class, oppressed by the state and by capitalism, formed fertile soil for its propaganda. It was only able to work under cover of disguise,[3] and could only gain influence through the tactical infiltration of existing organizations within the Socialist and proletarian movements.

Yet before the Communist party could penetrate the workers' movement, it was stopped in its tracks by a single blow from the police. In June 1923, during the course of one night, nearly all its leaders and stewards were

1. *Der Erste Kongress der Kommunistischen und revolutionären Organisationen im Fernen Osten*, published by the Communist International, 1922, p. 31. The English report appeared under the title: *Proceedings of the First Congress of the Toilers of the Far East* (Petrograd, 1922).

2. See Scalapino, *Japanese Communist Movement*, p. 67.

3. Its monthly journal, *Zenei* (Vanguard), issued in 1922 by Hitoshi Yamakawa (1880–1958), one of the party's founders, was able to appear, despite strict censorship, by the ploy of limiting itself to discussing theoretical Marxist problems and keeping its party character under cover.

arrested—about a hundred in all—on the basis, the press claimed, of a conspiracy uncovered by the police which had as its aim nothing less than the murder of the entire government and the setting up of a Communist dictatorship by *coup d'état*. This version remained the theme of a campaign by the press and various patriotic organizations, warning of the dangers of an insurrection, until two months later, on 1 September, an earthquake brought death and ruin to Tokyo. In the panic which the catastrophe precipitated, the police indiscriminately arrested radicals of every alignment in great numbers: Socialists, Communists, Anarchists and trade union leaders. Many were tortured in prison, and eight trade union leaders were murdered: Sakee Osugi, a leader of the Anarcho-Syndicalists, was throttled in prison with his wife and a small niece by a police commandant.

Most of those arrested were released during the spring of 1924. In discussing the future of their dispersed party, a majority among the freed Communist leaders opposed its reconstruction, a view advocated particularly strongly by Hitoshi Yamakawa. Conditions in Japan, he argued, were not yet ripe for the formation of a Communist party; first a base would have to be founded within the mass organizations—the trade unions, the peasants' organization and the Socialist student federations. Communists should concentrate on winning over these organizations to their cause. The existence of an illegal party would, moreover, divide the Communist camp, isolating it from the masses and inviting persecution to no purpose. In March 1924, a conference of leading Communists decided to dissolve the party.

Their decision naturally encountered angry resistance from Moscow. How could Communists ever entertain the idea of abandoning 'the one true party of the proletarian masses'! When, in 1925, Tokuda was dispatched with a small delegation to the Shanghai Bureau, Gregory Voitinsky, the Russian chief of the bureau, demanded that he should immediately reorganize the party, and he drew up guide-lines for their tactics (the 'January Theses'). The party leadership was instructed to win control over the existing workers, peasants' and students' organizations through the formation of cells within their leadership, and to bring them under the party's influence. But almost two years were to pass before, at the end of 1926, the party reconstituted itself completely.

Meanwhile the Socialists, whose federation was also dissolved by the government in May 1921, had attempted to organize a mass party based on the General Federation of Workers and the Peasants' Union. The impetus came from a Society for Political Studies (*Seiji Kenkyukai*), which had been founded in June 1924 by Socialist intellectuals of various stand-points; six months later it had about 4,000 members in fifty-three local groups. The initiative to form a 'proletarian party' was taken by the Peasants' Union of Japan (*Kumiai*), which convened a conference in June 1925, to which it invited the General Federation of Workers (*Sodomei*), the Council of Japanese Workers' Unions (*Hyogikai*), a Communist-controlled splinter group which had broken with the federation, the Society for Political Studies and a student organization which was under Communist influence.

The inaugural congress of the 'Proletarian party'—it took the title 'Peasants' and Workers' party' (*Nomin Rodoto*) met in Tokyo under police supervision on 1 December 1925. It formulated a programme representing a compromise between Socialist and Communist ideas, and it elected Motojiro Sugiyama, a Christian Socialist, to be its president, and Inejiro Asanuma (1897–1960), a Communist, to be its general secretary. (Asanuma soon left to become general secretary of the Social Democratic party.) Three hours after its inaugural meeting the party was dissolved by the police on the grounds that its programme contained Communist elements.

Shortly afterwards three new proletarian parties came into being in quick succession: on 5 March 1926, a Workers' and Peasants' party (*Rodo Nominto*), under mainly Communist influence; on 5 December 1926, a new Social Democratic party (*Shakai Minshuto*), with the backing of the General Federation of Workers; and on 9 December 1926, the Japanese Workers' and Peasants' party (*Nihon Ronoto*), a grouping of former Communists (including Mosaburo Suzuki, who after the war became leader of the Social Democratic party) and non-Communist Marxists; this latter party represented the centre in the Socialist spectrum. At about the same time, the Japanese Peasants' party (*Nihon Nominto*) organized itself as the right-wing faction within the Socialist movement.

Thus the Socialist movement in Japan came to be split between four legal parties and the Communist party. Its relative strength was to show itself during the first elections of 20 February 1928 to be held under the new electoral reform, forced through by the prime minister, Takaakira Kato, under pressure of public opinion and against the opposition of the Upper House. The right to vote was still, of course, restricted to males of over twenty-five years of age, and the candidature of the financially weak Socialist parties was considerably impeded, for the deposit required from every candidate was 2,000 Yen. Thus none of the four Socialist parties was able to put up candidates in every constituency. They had few candidates: seventeen for the Social Democratic party and forty for the Workers' and Peasants' party (*Rodo Nominto*) under the control of the illegal Communist party.

The elections produced the following results:

	Votes	Percentage of workers' votes	Seats
Social Democratic Party (*Shakai Minshuto*)	120,039	24·5	4
Workers' and Peasants' Party (*Rodo Nominto*)	193,047	39·4	2

Japanese Workers' and Peasants'			
party (*Nihon Ronoto*)	85,698	17·5	1
Japanese Peasants' Party (*Nihon*			
Nominto)	44,203	9·0	–
Local proletarian parties	46,766	9·5	1

The four Socialist parties received 489,000 votes between them, or 5 per cent of the total vote, against 9,376,000 votes for the middle-class parties.[1]

Within a few weeks of the elections, on 15 March 1928, the government prepared to deliver a devastating blow against the Communists. On this day the police arrested no less than 1,200 Communists, as well as Socialists and trade union leaders. Soon afterwards the government dissolved the Communist-controlled organizations: the Workers' and Peasants' party, the Council of Japanese Workers' Federations and the Proletarian Youth Federation.

> The Communist party of Japan [the government stated in justifying its action] seeks, as the Japanese branch of the world proletarian party, the Third International, to drag our Empire into the maelstrom of world revolution. It strives to change fundamentally the flawless, untarnished character of our nation, and to set up a workers' and peasants' dictatorship. . . . The theory and programme of the Communist party of Japan, which threaten our national foundation, are crimes worthy of death, and are not to be tolerated under any circumstances.[2]

Behind its façade of a constitutional monarchy with a constitution guaranteeing civil rights, Japan was a police state with formidable secret-police apparatus. The government was determined to use this weapon to bring about the physical destruction of the Communist party. It was only necessary to be suspected of Communist sympathies to become subject to police surveillance. The numbers of those arrested increased from year to year, and ran into thousands; according to the reports of the Ministry of Justice, there were 10,423 arrests in 1931, and 13,938 in 1932.[3] Many hundreds of those arrested were sentenced to heavy terms of imprisonment for having participated in illegal organizations which, according to the charges, set out to destroy private property and the existing form of government. Several of those accused received life sentences.

Following a second wave of arrests in 1929, the Communist party was deprived of almost all its leaders and officers. Their places were taken by new leaders, mostly young intellectuals, who tried to reconstruct the party; but these, too, shortly fell victim to the almost constantly recurring police raids. In 1932, the police found a list of all Communist party members, and most of them were arrested. The final attempt at rebuilding the party from its ruins

---

1. For statistics of the election results, see Scalapino, *Japanese Communist Movement*, p. 33; Totten, *Social Democratic Movement in Pre-war Japan*, p. 300.
2. Quoted in Swearingen, *Red Flag in Japan*, p. 31.   3. See ibid., p. 54.

was undertaken by Satomi Hakamada, a student, who had returned from Moscow in 1934; but he was arrested at the beginning of 1935. Hakamada's arrest confirmed the end of the Communist party as an organization. 'From this moment until 1946,' Scalapino closes his report on the party's pre-war history, 'Japanese Communism remained a concealed thought in the memories of a few "true believers", most of whom were in prison.'[1]

Japan had never been under any threat of a Communist dictatorship. But it did fall victim to a Fascist-military dictatorship, which involved the country in the adventure of an imperialist war which ended in a major national catastrophe.

Japanese Fascism was not, like its German counterpart, a populist movement, but a movement of the officer caste in the imperial army and navy, recruited in the main from the former *samurai* class and still imbued with the *samurai* tradition. It was because of the prestige attached to the *samurai* that the imperial army and navy enjoyed such a special position in the constitutional structure of the state. There were, it is true, reactionary, terrorist–nationalistic federations such as the 'Blood-sworn League' (*Ketsumeidan*), which fought against the modernization of Japan and Western ways and ideas, demanded the abolition of those meagre provisions for democracy laid down by the 1889 constitution—the parliament and the party system—loathed the Socialists as much as they did the Communists and worked for a return to the old-style pure Japanese absolutism. None of these leagues, however, developed into a Fascist mass movement.

A more serious programme for Japanese Fascism was worked out by Ikki Kita (1883–1937). He was both a Socialist and an ultra-nationalist. Like Motoyuki Takabatake, he had translated some of Marx's writings before embracing the concept of the *samurai* ideal, with which he shared a detestation of twentieth-century capitalism. He came to regard the imperial navy and army as the instrument which would carry out radical social reforms at home and realize Japan's bold national ambitions abroad. In his essay 'Sketch of a Plan for the Rebuilding of Japan', he demanded the revocation of the 1889 constitution and the installation of a revolutionary military

---

1. Scalapino, *Japanese Communist Movement*, pp. 43–4. Hakamada's arrest also put an end to the official organ of the Communist party, the illegal journal *Akahata* (Red Flag) which had appeared for the first time in February 1928. Moscow was not, however, very well informed of the scale of the catastrophe which had afflicted the Japanese Communist party. As late as February 1936, Sanzo Nozaka, one of their most esteemed leaders, who in 1931 had fled to Moscow to escape the threat of arrest, believed that the party was still operational. In a 'Letter to the Communists of Japan' he instructed them to concentrate their strength, in accordance with the rulings of the Seventh Congress of the Communist International of 1935, upon the formation of a people's front, to infiltrate the Social Democratic workers' and farmers' organizations with their members and to replace the phrase in their programme, 'the party strives for the overthrow of the imperial system', with 'the party strives for the overthrow of the military Fascist dictatorship'. Quoted in Totten, *Social Democratic Movement in Pre-war Japan*, p. 96.

government to nationalize the key industries, confiscate substantial wealth, abolish the 'barriers between nation and Emperor'—parliament and the parties—and arm itself for leadership in a revolutionary Asia.[1]

It was Kita's ideas which inspired the conspiracy to overthrow existing democratic institutions when, on 15 May 1932, naval and army officers bombarded the Bank of Japan, murdered the prime minister, Tsuyoshi Inukai, and demanded the nomination of a military government. This revolt was put down, but the ferment of Fascism spread throughout the armed forces. On 26 February 1936, a regiment rebelled, occupied several districts of Tokyo, the parliamentary offices, the Ministry of Defence and police headquarters, murdered the minister of finance, Tolka Korekiyo, Admiral Saito, and a large number of other outstanding statesmen, and vacated the city only after four days under the moral pressure of an appeal from the emperor. The leaders of the revolt, as well as its mentor, Kita, were hanged. But the army, encouraged by a Fascist mood among the peasants and middle classes, became a decisive power factor in the state. It set in motion the Fascist trend in Japan and the policy of harnessing the country's resources for equipping the armed forces to give Japan predominance in Asia. In October 1941, it forced through the nomination of General Hideki Tojo as prime minister to carry out its imperialistic programme.

But imperialist and Fascist ideas also found their way into the Social Democratic party and led to its splitting. The question of the Social Democrats' attitude to imperialism became critical when, on 18 September 1931, the Japanese army stationed on the Kwantung Peninsula to protect the South Manchurian Railway, on its own initiative occupied the Manchurian capital Mukden, and soon after, in 1932, occupied the entire Chinese province, which was proclaimed as the 'independent' state of Manchoukuo, but actually controlled by the Japanese army.

Such an act of imperialistic aggression by Fascist officers should have provoked the strongest protests from the party. But one faction, led by Katsumaro Akamatsu, actually declared itself solidly behind the military action. Akamatsu, a former Communist who had gone over to the Social Democrats, had participated at the party's inaugural assembly, becoming its general secretary in 1930; he was to finish his political career as a Fascist.

Akamatsu defended the rape of Manchuria by the theory of necessary 'living space' for the people. 'All nations,' he declared, 'are pledged to demand equality under the law for their existence. It is unthinkable that the Japanese should be confined merely to an island, and that they alone should

1. For Kita's concepts, see George M. Wilson, *Radical Nationalist in Japan: Ikki Kita, 1883–1937* (Harvard, 1970); for the history and ideology of Japanese Fascism, see Richard Storry, *The Double Patriots: A Study of Japanese Nationalism* (London, 1957); Ivan Morris (ed.), *Japan 1931–1945: Militarism, Fascism, Nationalism* (Boston, 1963).

be committed to sacrificing themselves in the cause of "World Peace".[1] Japan was overpopulated, Manchuria sparsely populated, and Manchuria offered 'living space' for millions of Japanese. It is true, he demanded 'the end of bourgeois rule in Manchuria, and its transformation into a National Socialist régime'. This, however, corresponded precisely with the demands of the military Fascists. They also demanded 'an end to the exploitation of Manchuria by finance capital'.[2]

In a resolution which he submitted in the name of his minority to the party's Sixth Annual Conference in January 1932, Akamatsu demanded a complete change of policy direction; a 'new campaign policy' in a national spirit. The party should be transformed into a nationalist party, emphasizing 'reverence for the national life of the community', and should formulate the national attitude of the Japanese proletariat in an antithesis of internationalism.[3] Akamatsu's suggestion that the Social Democratic party should be transformed into a party representing some kind of Fascism veiled as national socialism was rejected during the conference debate with much bitterness. Tetsu Katayama moved a resolution on behalf of the majority at the conference to reaffirm the three principles which had hitherto guided the party's policy and which also ought to guide it in the future: anti-capitalism, anti-Communism and anti-Fascism.

But the conference failed to reach any clear-cut decision out of fear of splitting the party. In the midst of an astounding ideological confusion, it passed both resolutions, despite the fact that they were clearly mutually contradictory.

Yet the split which the conference had tried to avoid by accepting both resolutions was bound to become unavoidable, for such an ambiguous attitude could not be maintained. At a meeting of the central committee on 15 April 1932 both resolutions were again put to the vote. The Social Demo-

1. Quoted in Totten, *Social Democratic Movement in Pre-war Japan*, p. 70.
2. Quoted in ibid., pp. 70–1.
3. The Social Democratic party of Japan had, in fact, been in loose contact with the Labour and Socialist International, but had not become affiliated because it feared that the government would take its alliance with an organization of foreign workers' parties as a pretext for its suppression. In a letter to Émile Vandervelde, the president of the International, who visited Japan in the summer of 1930 and brought up the question of its affiliation during talks with the party's National Council, Professor Isoo Abe informed him that after deliberating on the question, the party executive had reached the following conclusion:

'1. We are of the view that the Social Democratic party of Japan is, in its basic principles and political demands, in agreement with the Second International on its main points.
'2. But we do not believe that the time is yet ripe for us to affiliate ourselves to the Second International, because our party is not yet strong enough to partake in international action.'

For the text of the letter, see *Fourth Congress of the Labour and Socialist International 1931. Reports and Debate* (Zürich 1932), p. 417.

cratic resolution, proposed by Tetsu Katayama, was accepted by sixty-one to fifty-two votes, and Akamatsu at once left the conference with his followers, forming a few weeks later a Japanese State–Socialist party (*Nihon Kokka Shakaito*).

Like the Social Democratic party, the 'National Workers' and Peasants' Mass Party' (*Zenkoku Rono Taishuto*) had also shed its nationalist wing and, at a joint conference on 24 July 1932, the two parties decided to merge in the 'Socialist Mass Party' (*Shakai Taishuto*). Its programme still rejected Fascism, its proclaimed objectives being 'the overthrow of the decaying capitalist system' and the fight against Fascism and imperialist wars. The conference elected Isoo Abe (1865–1949), a university professor from Tokyo and a pioneer of Socialism in Japan, to be its chairman, with Hisashi Aso (1891–1940), a trade union leader, as general secretary;[1] and it founded the paper *Shakai Taishu Shimbun* (News of the Socialist Masses) as its official organ.

The Socialist Mass party itself finally succumbed to the growing Fascist trend throughout Japan. This had been strongly intensified by a sensational action by the army—a declaration of war against democracy. In October 1934, the Ministry of Defence issued a statement demanding the transformation of Japan's economic system into a totalitarian economy to serve as the basis for military rearmament. It proclaimed the army as the ultimate authority in the nation, and condemned the party system, which, it claimed, had undermined the nation's strength. Thus the army sought the subordination of national economic and political life to a totalitarian state power serving the preparations for a war which it planned to gain Japan's predominance in East Asia.

This concept revolted even the middle-class parties. But Aso, General Secretary of the Socialist Mass party, came to its defence. He denied that the army was trying to set up a Fascist system. 'Fascism,' he declared, 'considering the situation in Japan and the true character of the Japanese Army, is impossible.' The army was a socially progressive force, he maintained, and pleaded for 'a reasonable co-operation of the working classes with the army' as being necessary, 'if capitalism is to be overthrown by a social reformation'.[2] He believed that no social revolution in Japan could succeed through the masses alone: it also needed, as did the 'Meiji Restoration' of 1868, support from 'above', from the sources of power within the state.

Aso's view, supported by his right wing, was initially rejected by most members of the party, but the nationalist minority slowly grew to a majority. Japan's economic life had been hit hard by the international recession of the 1930s and, in the mood of desperation induced by mass unemployment, the ruin of the middle class and the bankruptcy of the peasants, the army

1. See Totten, *Social Democratic Movement in Pre-war Japan*, pp. 89–90.
2. Quoted in ibid., p. 92.

appeared as the saviour of the nation. The Socialist Mass party submitted to the current mood and, carried along by it, gained a surprising success in the elections of 30 April 1937. It won 928,934 votes and thirty-seven seats out of 466, to become the third strongest party in the lower house of parliament.[1]

The nationalist trend within the Socialist Mass party received a great impetus from the war psychosis which gripped Japan shortly after the elections. It must be kept in mind that the war in East Asia really began a full two years before the war in Europe—on 7 July 1937, when the Japanese army commenced its military campaign against China, conquered Nanking, Hankow and Canton and, in the north, Inner Mongolia and the provinces of Shansi and Shensi. The wave of hysterical nationalism invoked by every fresh report of a victory also overflowed into the party. Increasingly it came to identify itself with a state and government steering an open course towards Fascism. On the first anniversary of the outbreak of war, on 7 July 1938, the party proposed the formation of a 'National party' as an instrument of 'National unity'. Its purpose was to overcome class and party strife, to embody the 'national will', to 'reform' capitalism, to work to construct a 'New East Asia' and, at all events, to support with all its strength Japan's 'sacred war' against China.

During the next two years it tried to prompt the other parties into self-dissolution to help in building a 'new structure' of mass organization, and on 6 July 1940, it announced its own dissolution in every form. Several of its leading members, Tetsu Katayama and Isoo Abe among them, who had vainly opposed the party's surrender, had left even before this event occurred.

The middle-class parties followed the lead of the Socialist Mass party, and the totalitarian 'new structure'—a Fascist monopoly party—was founded under the title 'Society of the Imperial Rule Assistance' (*Taisie Yokusankai*) on 12 October 1940. This is the date of birth of the Fascist régime in Japan. At its head stood the prime minister, Prince Fumimaro Konoe. A number of leaders of the Socialist Mass party joined the government as the prime minister's nominees. Within fourteen months, on 7 December 1941, Japan's second fateful phase in its war for the conquest of Asia began with the attack on the United States fleet at Pearl Harbor.

2

On 2 September 1945, on the American warship *Missouri* in Tokyo Bay, the Japanese government signed the document of surrender imposed by the victorious Allies. Three days later, thirteen former Socialist members of

1. The Japanese Proletarian party, an alliance of Socialist parties, which, in contrast to the Socialist Mass party, persisted in its fight against Fascism and imperialism, won only 75,820 votes and one solitary seat in parliament. See ibid., p. 308.

parliament decided to form a new Social Democratic party and within two months, on 2 November 1945, its inaugural congress assembled. Constituted as the Social Democratic Party of Japan (*Nihon Shakaito*) it elected Tetsu Katayama (1887–1976) to be general secretary and, among others, Suehiro Nishio (b. 1891), a former trade union leader, and Chozuburo Mizutani (1897–1960), one of the leaders of the main peasants' alliance, as members of the party executive. Its manifesto proclaimed democracy, Socialism and peace to be the threefold aim of the party. 'Japan,' it announced, 'is in the act of witnessing a historic change.' It called on the 5,000 people assembled for the congress, as well as on the nation, 'to participate in the fulfilment of this historic effort. The doors of the Social Democratic party of Japan are open to everyone.'[1]

The political and social conditions for 'historic change' within the Japanese empire had been delivered at one blow. The empire had collapsed in a devastating catastrophe, and its collapse had simultaneously destroyed the myth of the emperor's divine rule which had supported the ideology of Japanese Fascism as well as the power of the army and the ruling classes. Its destiny had been a war to subject Asia to Japan's predominance, and its triumphs in China, Indonesia and Burma had been its justification. Yet what it had captured had been lost as quickly. Japan had been devastated, its cities reduced to ruins under the weight of American bombing, its forces of production destroyed. The futility of Fascism was revealed in the terrible heritage left by its collapse. The government, army and ruling classes, who had led the nation over the precipice, were finally discredited. The Social Democratic party, which had fought for decades under persecution against militarism, war and Fascism, now asserted its right to lead the nation in the process of 'historic change' on whose threshold Japan then stood.

The Communist party had meanwhile also reconstituted itself, and now, for the first time, became a legal party. Power was vested in the hands of the military chief of the victorious forces in the East—the Supreme Commander of the Allied Powers (S.C.A.P.), General Douglas MacArthur. Four weeks after the occupation of the country by American troops, on 4 October 1945, the Japanese government was directed to release immediately all political prisoners and, in accordance with the Potsdam Declaration, 'to revoke and suspend all laws, decrees, orders and instructions which restrict freedom of thought, religion, meetings and speech'.[2]

The Communists hastened to mobilize their forces in this new era of freedom. The first issue of their paper, *Akahata*, appeared as soon as 10 October, and, on 8 November, 300 Communists assembled in Tokyo for a 'consultative national conference preparatory to the First Party Congress'.

1. Quoted in Cole, *et al.*, *Socialist Parties in Post-War Japan*, p. 4.
2. Quoted in Swearingen, *Red Flag in Japan*, p. 88.

The congress met on 1 December 1945, as the Fourth Party Assembly. It elected Kyuichi Tokuda (1894–1953), who had founded and led the Communist party and was now released from eighteen years of imprisonment, to be general secretary.[1]

The party commenced its activities in the new period by declaring war on the Socialists. Even before the 'consultative national conference' had met to prepare the new party constitution and programme, the first issue of *Akahata* issued an 'Appeal to the Nation', edited by Tokuda and other released Communists, giving rough outlines of the declared aims of the party: among these was the overthrow of the 'imperial system' and the setting up of a 'people's democracy'. In its leader the paper stated that the 'pseudo-Socialists', having supported the 'imperial system', 'were unsuitable leaders for the nation'. Their party was a party of 'fermenting Fascism'—a 'social emperor party', which 'dreams' of rebuilding the collapsed 'imperial system'. Therefore the Communists could never form a united front with the Socialists. Instead they must try to organize, within the Socialist party, a wing opposed to its leaders and to unite themselves to the masses as a Socialist faction.[2]

But even in the Communist camp this vehement attack on the Socialists caused surprise and protests, as the minutes of the congress recorded. The critics of the policy had expected that the party would, like its European sister parties, work for a popular front with the Socialists and other democratic parties to bring about the democratic revolution. The Communist left wing, however, which dominated the party conference, remained adamant in its hostility to Social Democracy.

The situation did not last long. At the beginning of January 1946, Sanzo Nozaka (b. 1892) returned to Japan from fourteen years of exile—having spent the first nine in Moscow, and the next five in Yenan at Mao Tse-tung's headquarters. As a university student in London, he had been a founder member of the British Communist party, and had, like Tokuda, worked in the Communist party of Japan from its beginning. He had been arrested and imprisoned in 1928, but had escaped after three years to become a member of the presidium of the Communist International in Moscow.[3] The Japanese party therefore received him as the bearer of the political message of Moscow and Yenan. The party leadership set such store by his return that it summoned a new party congress (the fifth) for February 1946.

Nozaka set about changing party policy even before the party congress had assembled. In a declaration issued within a few days of his return, he advocated co-operating with the Social Democrats. The contention that Social Democracy sought to reinstate the 'imperial system', because it did

---

1. For a biographical sketch of Tokuda, see ibid., pp. 107–11.
2. See Scalapino, *Japanese Communist Movement*, pp. 48–9.
3. For a biographical sketch of Nozaka, see Swearingen, *Red Flag in Japan*, pp. 111–15.

not insist on the abolition of the monarchy, he rejected. The fact was, he declared, that all parties sought 'with one accord' to overthrow the 'imperial system', meaning the abolition of a constitution and its institutions which were vested in the power of the emperor. This was the essence of the matter, not the question of the emperor as a symbol of the nation.

The 'imperial system', Nozaka explained, could only be transformed into a democracy, serving the welfare of the masses, if all the democratic parties could work together in a united front. But this would have to be based on a programme common to all parties, though in no way demanding a uniformity of concepts and objectives.

In their 'Appeal to the Nation', in the immediate wake of Japan's capitulation, the Communists had welcomed 'with gratitude' the commencement of the 'democratic revolution' by the Allied forces of occupation and pledged their 'fervent support'. Nozaka reaffirmed this attitude. The American forces of occupation, he told the party congress, were to be seen as a liberating power, a power whose historic function was to sweep away feudal remnants and complete the middle-class, democratic revolution. In fulfilling this historic task, the Communist party must make up its mind to co-operate with the S.C.A.P.

The programme defined by the congress and based upon Nozaka's proposal, laid down the following aims for the 'middle-class, democratic revolution': the abolition of the 'imperial system'; a democratic constitution guaranteeing civic rights of freedom to all citizens; an agrarian reform; and a radical improvement in workers' living conditions.

The task which the party set itself following the completion of the middle-class, democratic revolution was to change Japan's capitalist order of society into a Socialist one. This change, Nozaka emphasized, could take place through a 'peaceful revolution' provided that the workers, peasants and 'progressive' bourgeoisie could 'come together under the leadership of the working class and its pioneers, the Communist party'. The Social Democratic party, Nozaka predicted, would then split in two, its right wing most probably developing into a middle-class party, and its left wing joining the Communists.[1]

This was the concept which Nozaka submitted to the congress; it formed the theoretical and tactical basis for the party's new policy.

The Communist party had still, however, to clarify its relationship with the Soviet Union. It was discredited before the war as a secret society of conspirators controlled from Moscow by the Communist International and which, as the tool of a foreign power, pursued its aims by force; this stigma still clung to it after the end of the war. It was an image which it naturally

1. For an analysis of Nozaka's concept, see Scalapino, *Japanese Communist Movement*, pp. 53–7.

wished to erase; hence the emphasis which the party congress placed on a peaceful revolution.

The party's ill-repute as Moscow's party became a particular disadvantage when the Soviet Union held back for years from repatriating Japanese prisoners-of-war, earning it special hatred.[1] Tokuda, however, tried to dissociate the party from Moscow. As early as the party congress of December 1945, he had announced a change of attitude towards the Soviet Union. 'Any direct link with the Soviet Union,' he said, 'would damage rather than benefit our movement.'[2] At the following party congress, in February 1946, he declared: 'We have at present no relationship with the Soviet Union. . . . And I would like to explain here that neither will our party have any relations with the Soviet Union in the future.'[3] And, on 4 April, the party issued the following statement:

Malicious propaganda by other parties has given the impression that our party remains allied to the Comintern or the Third International. As is known, this organization was dissolved in June [actually in May] 1943. It is therefore clear that our party does not today maintain any relations with any international organization.

We hereby declare that our party is a party of the Japanese people, dedicating itself to the liberation of the working masses in our country.[4]

From its new stance, the Communist party now sought a united front with the Socialists.

In the Social Democratic party, however, opinion was sharply divided on the desirability of a united front. Its left wing, led by Mosaburo Suzuki and Kanju Kato, both pioneers of the Socialist movement in Japan, advocated the front, but its right wing, under the leadership of Komakichi Matsuoka and Suehiro Nishio, rejected it; both had been involved in the most bitter struggle with the Communists in the trade unions during the pre-war period, and both were filled with the profoundest mistrust of their motives.

For the Social Democratic party, its relationship with the trade union movement, represented by Matsuoka, was of the utmost importance. The movement had expanded with fantastic speed when, following the instructions of the S.C.A.P., parliament issued a statute in December 1945 securing the right to strike and the signing of collective agreements with trade unions.[5] Within a year 17,000 trade union groups had emerged, embracing altogether nearly five million members.[6]

1. According to a news bulletin from Radio Moscow on 20 May 1949, the number of Japanese prisoners-of-war in Russia had totalled 594,000, of whom 70,880 were sent home during 1945, and the rest over the following four years—*Akahata*, 22 May 1949, quoted in Swearingen, *Red Flag in Japan*, p. 232.
2. Kyuichi Tokuda, *Naigai josei to Nippon kyosanto no nimmu* (Tokyo, 1949), p. 247, quoted in ibid., p. 230.
3. ibid., p. 236, quoted in ibid., p. 230.
4. *Akahata*, 7 April 1946, quoted in ibid., p. 231.
5. See Levine, *Industrial Relations in Post-war Japan*, pp. 24–5.
6. See ibid., p. 66.

The unions were partly under Socialist and partly under Communist leadership. The Communists wished to see a common central organization for all trade unions. But a majority of Socialists, familiar with the Communist tactic of cell formation in the trade unions during the pre-war movement, rejected any common organization for fear of reviving internal struggles.[1]

Thus, two separate trade union federations constituted themselves in August 1946: the Socialist-led 'General Federation of Workers' (*Nihon Rodo Kumiai Sodomei*) and the predominantly Communist 'Congress of Industrial Labour Organizations' (*Zen Nihon Sangyobetsu Rodo Kumiai Kaigi*, or *Sanbetsu*). According to their own records, *Sanbetsu* included twenty-one trade union federations with 1,600,000 members, and *Sodomei* twenty-four trade union federations with 850,000 members. *Sanbetsu* mainly had the unions in heavy industry, transport and public services; *Sodomei* the unions of the workers in textiles, light industry and the shipbuilding industry.[2]

When the question of a united front came up in 1946, it was true that the Communists had a greater influence over the trade union organization than the Socialists, but it seemed doubtful whether they could emerge from the impending elections as the strongest proletarian party. This consideration also contributed to the negative reaction of a majority of Socialist leaders to the idea of any alliance with the Communists. The elections, in which women were to vote for the first time, had been called for 10 April 1946, and these would reveal the proportionate strength of the two parties.

The election results were a triumph for the Socialists. They won four and a half times the Communist vote—9,858,406 to 2,135,757—and ninety-two seats to the Communists' five.[3]

But of far greater importance was the psychological effect of the elections. That the two Socialist parties, outlawed and persecuted under the old régime —the Communists more so than the Social Democrats—could win over twelve million votes between them was a measure of the extent of the change of spirit which had taken place in conservative Japan in under a year. The success of the Social Democratic party was not insignificant; as the third strongest party, it had become a power factor in the country. Yet perhaps even more surprising had been the number of votes gained by the Communist party, whose illegal organization the 'imperial system' had tried to throttle by imprisoning its leaders and officers.

In parliament, however, with five out of a total of 466 members, the

1. Such fears were not totally without foundation. A resolution passed by the central committee of the Communist party contained the following instruction on the formation of cells in trade unions and other organizations: 'Wherever there are three or more party members [in a trade union], they are to form a faction'—quoted in Swearingen, *Red Flag in Japan*, p. 153.
2. See Levine, *Industrial Relations in Post-war Japan*, pp. 70–1.
3. For a table of the Social Democratic votes in elections from 1946 to 1955, see *Yearbook of the International Socialist Labour Movement 1956–1957* (London, 1956), p. 337; for a table of the Communist votes, see Scalapino, *Japanese Communist Movement*, p. 314.

Communist group was of little importance. Also the Social Democratic party, with its ninety-two delegates, was powerless in the face of a tight-knit conservative majority. All key positions were held by the two leading conservative parties: the Liberal party, with 139 seats, and the Democratic party, with ninety-three.

Immediately after the elections the Communists, supported by the Social Democratic left wing, began a campaign of mass demonstrations for a democratic people's government. But in view of the relative strengths of the parliamentary parties, conditions were not propitious; the two large conservative parties had formed a coalition government under the prime minister, Shigeru Yoshida.

Under the impression that there existed a mass desire for a democratic people's front, the Socialist party suggested a Democratic League as a basis for joint action with the Communists and the trade unions. This attempt failed, however, as a result of objections by the Communists to the League's structure, which had been designed to block Communist infiltration. The Social Democratic party leadership therefore broke off the discussions, despite the objections of their left wing.

This episode confirmed the end to any hope of an alliance with the Social Democrats, which the Communists had sought. The Communists wished to create a United Front only under conditions enabling them to infiltrate the Social Democratic organizations and to transform them into a vehicle for their own policies. They did not conceal their intentions. They demanded that their party should take the lead in the democratic revolution.

But their demand stood in contradiction to the actual proportional strengths of the two parties. The first elections of the new era in April 1946 had already demonstrated the overwhelming strength of the Social Democrats in relation to that of the Communists; it appeared even more impressively in the second elections of April 1947. The Social Democrats gained 7,168,000 votes and 143 seats, while the Communist vote fell to 1,002,000, their representation to four seats.[1]

Following this Communist defeat, even the leaders of the Socialist left wing, Mosaburo Suzuki and Kanju Kato, who had hitherto fervently advocated an alliance with the Communists, reached the conclusion, in view of the incompatibility of the principles and tactics of the two parties, that a Socialist–Communist alliance would weaken rather than strengthen the

1. See *Yearbook*, p. 337; Scalapino, *Japanese Communist Movement*, p. 314. The election results were all the more surprising in view of the fact that membership of the Communist party was much stronger than that of the Socialist party. According to their own records the Communist party in 1947 numbered 70,000 members, but the Socialist party only 32,000. (For the Communist membership see Scalapino, op. cit., p. 67; for the Socialists, see *Yearbook*, p. 337.) Also the numbers of local Communist organizations were far greater than those of the Social Democrats; 5,625 to 1,336 in 1949—see Swearingen, *Red Flag in Japan*, p. 100.

Socialist movement. In a 'Manifesto of the Left', which they issued in May 1947, they drew the dividing line between their attitude and that of the Communists.

The Communists naturally persisted in their attempts to form an alliance with the Social Democrats, for they considered such an alliance to be the key to attaining power. But even though the question of Socialist–Communist unity cropped up in the Socialist camp during the years which followed— particularly after a split in the Social Democratic party during 1951—the Communists were denied any success in their endeavours; the political separation between Socialists and Communists continued to stand.[1]

The election victory of the Social Democratic party in 1947 placed it in something of a dilemma. With 143 seats, it had emerged as the strongest individual party in the lower house; it had won over a quarter (26·3 per cent) of the votes cast, and had therefore gained the right to lead in government. But the conservatives, split into two parties (the Liberals with 132 members, and the Democrats with 126), still represented a parliamentary majority. So the Social Democrats could only hope to form a government in coalition with one of the conservative parties. The question was whether, given these circumstances, the party should participate in government at all.

Its left wing warned against any such experiment. The country had become involved in a serious economic and social crisis; galloping inflation had pushed prices higher and higher and had devalued wages, a situation overflowing in a wave of strikes by impoverished workers. Any attempt to overcome the crisis by Socialist economic measures, the left reasoned, would inevitably founder on the resistance from the conservative coalition partners. A coalition with the conservatives would weigh down the party, and as a result would ruin the chances of any future Socialist government under more favourable conditions.

The right-wing Socialist majority, on the other hand, argued that the party could hardly desert the proletarian masses in the distress of a serious economic crisis and deliver them to the mercies of the conservatives alone. Besides, the new government would be faced with decisions of the utmost significance for the future of democracy in Japan: the country's constitution. Its destiny could not be left exclusively to a conservative government.

The party therefore decided to participate in the government. Tetsu Katayama, its chairman, became the first Socialist prime minister in Japan's history, presiding over a coalition of Social Democrats, the conservative Democratic party and the small People's Co-operative party.

But the life-span of Katayama's government was to be brief. It survived

---

1. For a comprehensive description of the Socialist attitude to the question of an alliance with the Communists, see Cole, *et al.*, *Socialist Parties in Post-war Japan*, pp. 110–20.

for only eight months, from June 1947 to February 1948. It met with no small success in constructing a democracy in Japan. But above all it failed, as had been anticipated, over the conflicts existing within the government between Socialist and capitalist ideology and between their different methods for overcoming the economic and social crisis.[1]

Yet Katayama's government was brought down not by a vote of no-confidence from the conservative opposition, but by an action of the left wing of the Social Democratic party. At its congress in January 1948, the left wing won the majority and while Katayama was again elected as party chairman, his position as prime minister was undermined. He resigned after the left-wing Socialists on the budget committee voted against the budget. Nevertheless the party decided to renew the coalition with the moderate conservative Democratic party, so as to prevent the right-wing conservative Liberal party from taking over power. Katayama even so declined to be recalled as prime minister. His place was taken by the chairman of the Democratic party, Hitoshi Ashida, with the leader of the Socialist right wing, Suehiro Nishio, as his deputy.

But this coalition government was also unable to survive its contradictions. It resigned in October 1948, eight months after taking office.

New elections were thereupon called for 24 January 1949, and ended with a catastrophic defeat for the Social Democratic party. It lost nearly half the votes it had won in 1947 (receiving only 4,129,000 votes compared to the earlier 7,168,000) and nearly two thirds of its seats; it won only forty-nine compared to its previous 143.[2]

The Communists, on the other hand, gained an unexpected victory. Their votes increased almost threefold over the election of 1947, rising from 1,002,000 to 2,984,000, and the seats they held rose from four to 35.[3]

The Communists' electoral success seemed to represent a triumphant vindication for the course of 'peaceful revolution' which, at Nozaka's prompting, the party inaugurated at the beginning of 1946. Nozaka had justified it theoretically with the argument that the bourgeois revolution had first to be completed in Japan before conditions became ripe for a Socialist revolution; that the guardian of the bourgeois revolution had, until now, basically been the American forces of occupation who had broken the rule of militarism,

1. For a history of Katayama's government, see ibid., pp. 16–22.
2. See *Yearbook*, p. 337.
3. See Scalapino, *Japanese Communist Movement*, p. 314. The Communists had not, however, only entered the election fight with a far stronger party organization than the Social Democrats, but also with a far greater financial effort. According to the records of both parties, the Communists spent 122,876,000 Yen, but the Social Democrats only 11,254,000 Yen; see Swearingen, *Red Flag in Japan*, p. 99. But it was above all the disappointment of the overwhelming expectations placed by the great mass of the electorate in the Katayama government as well as the dissension within the Social Democratic party which led to the defeat of the one and the success of the other.

feudalism and the 'imperial system' and were therefore to be considered as allies of the revolution; and that, to complete the bourgeois revolution, an alliance of the working class with the 'progressive' bourgeoisie as well as the peasants was essential and that, like the bourgeois revolution, so would the subsequent Socialist revolution take place peacefully.

This policy was in line with that followed by the Communist parties in France, Italy and Czechoslovakia, as well as in India, Burma and Indonesia, before the founding of the Cominform in September 1947; it had seemed until then also to be in line with the course of the foreign policy of the Soviet Union.

Meanwhile the relationship between the Soviet Union and the United States had collapsed and the shadow of the approaching Cold War was settling over the world. The founding of the Cominform had signalled for the Communist parties a change of course away from the tactics of 'peaceful revolution'. At its founding congress Andrei Zhdanov introduced the concept of the division of the world into two camps—the American-led imperialist-capitalist camp and the 'proletarian Socialist' camp led by the Soviet Union—and of an unrelenting struggle between the two.[1]

But the Communist party of Japan under Nozaka's leadership obviously did not feel bound by decisions of the Cominform. At all events, it undertook no change in its basic attitude at the party congress which assembled in December 1947, three months after the conference of the Cominform. And thus it remained until 1950.

Early in January 1950, however, the journal of the Cominform issued a sharp rebuke to Nozaka. He had, the paper declared, continued to justify his theory of a peaceful Socialist revolution even under the current conditions of an American occupation by stating that his concept rested on a Marxism–Leninism adapted to the special conditions in Japan—to its 'Japanization', its 'naturalization in Japanese soil'.

The Cominform, however, countered with the declaration that 'Nozaka's theory bore not the slightest resemblance to Marxism–Leninism'. It was 'a variation of the anti-Marxist and anti-Socialist theory of the amicable conquest of reaction by democracy and imperialism through Socialism'. Nozaka's theory of the historic role being played by the American forces of occupation in assisting the process of a peaceful development towards Socialism, the critic continued, was 'a theory of embellishment for the imperialistic occupation of Japan, a theory supporting American imperialism, and consequently a theory misleading to the masses in Japan ... an anti-democratic, anti-Socialist theory. It merely serves,' the Cominform declared, 'the imperialistic forces of occupation in Japan and the enemies of its independence, and it is therefore an anti-patriotic, anti-Japanese theory.'[2]

---

1. See pp. 148–51.
2. *For a Lasting Peace and for a People's Democracy*, 6 January 1950, quoted in Scalapino, *Japanese Communist Movement*, p. 61.

The dismayed party leadership rejected this attack by the Cominform. It did not deny that perhaps some tactical 'errors' might have been committed, but it affirmed its confidence in Nozaka. 'Comrade Nozaka,' the party's declaration stated, 'is the staunchest proletarian patriot, possessing the trust of the masses.'[1]

But hardly had their declaration appeared than the official organ of the Communist Party of China declared itself solidly behind the attack by the Cominform. Accusing Nozaka of 'important errors on points of principle', it condemned as entirely false his idea that, by exploiting the middle-class parliament through peaceful methods, the Communist party of Japan could gain the power of the state.

The Japanese Communist party now stood caught in the cross-fire between Moscow and Peking. As the central committee of the Communist party of the Soviet Union disclosed fourteen years later in a letter of the 18 April 1964 to the central committee of the Communist party of Japan, the attack by the Cominform had been undertaken 'on Stalin's personal initiative',[2] and had evidently been agreed with Mao Tse-tung when he arrived in December 1947 for a three-month visit to Moscow, as part of the framework for Communist strategy in Asia in the anti-American struggle.[3]

The immediate consequence of the Russo-Chinese attacks on the Japanese Communist party was internal disruption. Its left wing, under the leadership of Yoshio Shiga and Kenji Miyamoto, who as members of the central committee had both until now tried vainly to push the party leftwards, received a considerable impetus from the attacks. They formed within the party a faction of 'internationalists', accusing the majority in the party leadership of having 'Titoized' the party and demanding that it should bring its policies into line with those of the Cominform. The majority, on the other hand, tried to discredit the left as 'Trotskyists'.[4]

This bitter factional struggle, which shook the party to its roots, finally ended with the capitulation of Tokuda, general secretary, and Nozaka, its actual leader, under pressure from Moscow and Peking. The Politbureau submitted to Stalin a new programme entitled 'Basic Tasks of the Communist Party of Japan in the Approaching Revolution'—a document which, as the letter of the central committee of the C.P.S.U. of 18 April 1964 confirms, 'was supplied on Stalin's request and with the direct co-operation of the

---

1. Quoted in ibid., p. 63.
2. This letter emphasizes that the C.P.S.U. central committee 'not only condemns such criticism of fraternal parties, but also that the Twentieth Congress of the C.P.S.U. has strongly criticized Stalin's personality cult, which caused deviations from Lenin's rule of mutual relationships between fraternal parties'—quoted in ibid., p. 62.
3. For a detailed record of Russian and Chinese criticisms of the policy of the Communist Party of Japan, see ibid., pp. 57–67.
4. For a detailed report of this conflict, see Swearingen, *Red Flag in Japan*, pp. 222–9.

leaders of the Communist Party of Japan—Comrades Tokuda, Nozaka and others'.[1]

In these new theses, the American forces of occupation, which had until 1950 been welcomed by the Communist party as liberators from the ties of feudalism, militarism and the 'imperial system', were condemned as instruments of American imperialism, imposing on the people of Japan 'only chains and slavery'. There was no further talk of a 'bourgeois democratic revolution'; the phrase was replaced by the notion of a 'democratic revolution of national liberation' from domination by American imperialism. Neither was there any further mention of the concept of the 'peaceful revolution', which had, until 1950, been the basic policy of the party. 'It would be a serious error,' the new programme declared, 'to suppose that a new democratic government of national liberation could rise under its own will-power in a peaceful manner. . . . No, the peaceful road to liberation and democratic change in Japan is a fresh path of deceit.'[2]

These theses were based on the assumption that Japan stood at the threshold of an imminent national revolution which, under Communist leadership, would turn into a proletarian revolution.

The left course which the party now took was aimed at such a revolution; its destiny was to nurture it. The new direction showed itself in the party's identification with the Cominform's view of history—the close approach of a Third World War and the revolution which this would unleash; in its acknowledgement of force as an instrument of revolution; in strongly hostile propaganda against the United States and the occupation forces; in its declaration of solidarity with North Korea in the war against the South which had begun in June 1950; and, finally, in instigating acts of terrorism—sabotage in factories, the bombing of police stations, and violent attacks on policemen, soldiers and public officials.

Incited by Peking, the party conference of February 1951 debated the question of an armed struggle—the formation of military and para-military groups within the party, which were eventually to be developed into guerrilla formations and ultimately into a Japanese Red Army. The congress resolution emphasized the necessity for armed struggle against the instruments of state power.[3]

This radicalization of the Communist tactics offered the reactionary forces the chance they needed to open an offensive against the working class. Under pressure from the S.C.A.P., the freedom of public employees to organize was curtailed and thousands of workers suspected of being Communist were dismissed from factories and public works.

1. For the text of the letter, see Scalapino, *Japanese Communist Movement*, p. 81.
2. For the quotation, see ibid., pp. 81 and 82; for an analysis of the theses, see Swearingen, *Red Flag in Japan*, pp. 203–7.
3. See Scalapino, *Japanese Communist Movement*, p. 86.

The revolutionary tactics to which the party had switched also discredited it among the broad masses. From having gathered almost three million votes and thirty-five seats as well as attracting close on 10 per cent of the active electorate in the 1949 elections, in 1952 it lost over a third of its votes and all its parliamentary representatives.[1]

But of far greater consequence than losing the trust of a large section of the electorate had been the loss of the vast masses of workers in the trade unions. Several of the trade union organizations affiliated to the Communist-dominated trade union council, *Sanbetsu*, had even before 1950 organized themselves in opposition to the Communist leadership to form 'democratic leagues' (the *Mindo* Movement). This movement replaced the Communist leadership, disassociated itself from the *Sanbetsu* and under the leadership of Minoru Takano formed a new trade union federation, the General Council of Japanese Trade Unions (*Nihon Rodo Kumiai Sohyogikai*—abbreviated to *Sohyo*); it counted a membership of three million. *Sanbetsu* had had a million and a half members at its founding, and by the end of 1949 there were still 400,000; by the time *Sohyo* was established the figure had dropped to 47,000.[2]

Thus the revolutionary course taken by the Communist party ended in a heavy setback to the promising development anticipated after its brilliant election victory of 1949. Recognizing the reality of existing power ratios and the force of tradition in Japan, the party had attempted to achieve its aims on a 'Japanese road to Socialism'. The changes of policy undertaken a year later had arisen not from any recognition of changed conditions for a social revolution; they had been imposed by Moscow through the Cominform. The party had not of its own choice departed from the path of 'peaceful revolution'; it had been forced off it by Stalin, who, in his Cold War strategy against the Western powers, had attempted to spark off strong Communist insurrections in Japan as well as elsewhere.[3]

Most party leaders gradually came to realize how their 'adventurous ultra-left tactics' had foundered and badly shaken party unity. The 1955 party congress, however, formally reaffirmed the 'correctness' of the 1951 theses, but even so returned to the tactics of a 'right course'. It was not until after Khrushchev had made his historic speech to the Twentieth Congress of the Soviet Communist party in February 1956, seeking a détente with the Western powers and emphasizing the possibility of peaceful co-existence be-

1. The number of Communist votes fell from 2,984,780 in 1949 to 895,765 in 1952; and to 655,990 in the elections of 1953—see ibid., p. 314.

2. *Sanbetsu*'s membership fell again in 1952 to 27,000, and in the following year to 13,000; it was dissolved on 15 February 1958; see ibid., p. 331. For the founding and history of *Sohyo*, see Levine, *Industrial Relations in Post-war Japan*, pp. 74–88; for its structure, see ibid., pp. 89–98.

3. For the Communists' switch to revolutionary tactics under the Cominform influence in France, see page 153; in Italy, see page 66; in Czechoslovakia, see page 178; in India, see p. 231; in Burma, see p. 262; in Indonesia, see p. 294.

7 *Head of Stalin's statue in Budapest, pulled down in October 1956*

8 *Soviet tanks in Prague, August 1968*

tween nations of differing social and economic systems, that, in June 1956, a full meeting of the Japanese Communist party's central committee revised the theses on the necessity of revolution by force; they then returned to Nozaka's theory of a 'peaceful revolution'.

Now, once again, the party was slowly able to recoup its heavy losses. From having polled 655,000 votes in the 1955 elections, it took 1,012,000 votes in the 1958 elections. But even so they won only one seat, compared with the thirty-five they had held in 1949.

The Social Democratic party, on the other hand, had recovered surprisingly quickly from its heavy defeat in January 1949; a year and a half later, in the elections for the Upper House in June 1950, it had become the second strongest party with sixty-one out of 250 seats; and in local council elections, which were held simultaneously, it outstripped its gains at the polls in 1947.

But no sooner had the party regained its former strength than it became involved in an internal crisis. The dissension between left and right within the party was intensified by their respective attitudes to the peace treaty. The party had been unanimous in its insistence that Japan should be declared a neutral nation, neither concluding any military treaties with a foreign power nor granting any foreign military bases in Japan. Over and above this the left demanded, however, that the party should oppose the rearmament of Japan, for, it argued, Japan rearmed would risk its neutrality and might draw the country into foreign wars.[1] The Social Democrat right wing maintained, however, that it was impossible for Japan to remain completely defenceless in the face of a direct or indirect threat of attack from the Communist bloc; it had to rearm for self-defence.[2]

The contrasting attitudes between right and left were disputed passionately at the party congress of 1951. The rightist view was rejected by an overwhelming majority and its dominant position in the party undermined. The party's left wing gained fifteen seats on the executive to the ten of the right wing and the five of the centre; and its leader, Suzuki, was elected chairman.

The victory of the left did not end the conflict within the party. This in fact deepened when, on 4 September 1951, a security pact with the United

1. Following Japan's surrender, her armed forces had been entirely demobilized, and the Constitution of 3 March 1947, having, under Article IX, renounced war as a 'sovereign right of nations', gave a pledge that Japan's 'land, sea and air forces, as well as other war potential, will never be maintained'. But Article IX was compromised by S.C.A.P. when it decided to form a 'police reserve' of 75,000 men during the emergency created by the Korean War and which, later retitled 'self-defence', grew to number over 200,000. A nation-wide nationalist campaign, which had the backing of both the Liberal and Democratic parties, demanded during the negotiation of the San Francisco Treaty (which ultimately came into force in 1952) that Article IX should be amended to allow Japan to rearm.

2. See J. A. A. Stockwin, *The Japanese Socialist Party and Neutralism. A Study of a Political Party and its Foreign Policy* (London and New York, 1968).

States was signed in San Francisco together with the peace treaty. The peace treaty recognized Japan's right to self-defence but, in addition, the security pact gave the United States the right to maintain troops in the country until such time as Japan could 'take over responsibility for its own defence'.

The Socialist left, having conducted a stormy propaganda campaign against both pacts during the peace treaty discussions, demanded that the Socialist group in Parliament should vote against both treaties. The party split over this question during an extraordinary party congress on 23 October 1951.[1] The left-wing Socialists in parliament voted against both treaties; the right-wing Socialists only against the security pact.

The relative strengths of the two Social Democratic parties—each equally considering itself to be the 'true' party and clinging to its title—emerged in the elections of October 1952. The left party was supported by *Sohyo* and the teachers' and railwaymens' trade unions; the right by *Sodomei* and the remaining unions. The right won 4,012,000 votes, the left 3,493,000. Only at the elections of February 1955 was there a shift of power in favour of the left; it then won 5,642,000 votes compared to 5,071,000 for the right.[2]

Even though the two parties had entered the election contest of 1955 as rivals, the overall poll for the Social Democrats rose by three and a half million (from 7,168,000 to 10,713,000) and to 156 seats as compared with the 143 won in 1947.

The rank-and-file in both parties had, for a long time, been pushing for reunification. Under this pressure of opinion, both party executives set up a commission in August 1953 to clarify the problems of reunification, and commenced discussions between their presidents and general secretaries to try to arrive at a common parliamentary policy. In January 1955, the congresses of both parties met simultaneously and solemnly declared in favour of reunification after the February elections; they charged a joint commission with drafting a programme for a reunited party.

The 'Congress of the Reunification' met in Tokyo on 13 October 1955. Without debate it accepted the programme drafted by the joint commission and elected an executive on which both wings of the party were represented

1. At its meeting in Brussels on 14–16 December 1951, the General Council of the Socialist International had addressed an urgent appeal, 'in the fraternal spirit of International Socialism', to both Social Democratic parties to overcome their differences. 'The split in your party,' it stated, 'and the formation of two rival Socialist parties, would, we believe, be a disaster of the first magnitude for Japanese Socialism. It is our profoundest conviction, gained from experience of so many mistakes and defeats in the history of International Socialism, that no disputed question, however serious it may appear, can justify the damage which a split in the Socialist party must inevitably cause. Where a great Socialist party in a great country is pulled apart, the effects are felt throughout the entire international labour movement.' For the text of the appeal, see *Report on Activities (1951–1952) Submitted to the Second Congress of the Socialist International* (Milan, 1952), p. 30.

2. See *Yearbook*, p. 337.

in equal strength; Mosaburo Suzuki, of the left, became chairman, and Inejiro Asanuma, of the right, general secretary.

When the party had been founded ten years earlier, its manifesto merely asserted its threefold aim: democracy, Socialism and peace. Now, for the first time, the party formulated its basic principles and objectives into a programme. As its example it took the 'Frankfurt Declaration' of the Founding Congress of the Socialist International.[1]

The programme set out the task of achieving Socialism by peaceful revolution through parliamentary democratic methods. 'Socialism,' it stated, 'can be attained only through democracy, and democracy can be fully realized only through Socialism.' It therefore rejected Communism. 'Communism,' the programme declared, 'has trampled democracy underfoot. Denying individual freedom and the dignity of man, it has become irreconcilable with Socialism based on democracy.'

The precondition for a peaceful Socialist revolution, the programme explained, was the capture of political power by an 'absolute majority in the Diet'. Such a majority could be won by the party, provided it gathered to 'the working-class organizations as its core the organizations of farmers, medium and small enterprises, women, youth and others'.

The Social Democratic party of Japan [the programme continued] is necessarily a class party because of its stand for a Socialist revolution by democratic and peaceful means. . . . As the realization of Socialism is essentially the historic mission of the workers, it follows that they must form the core of our party, but farmers and fishermen, small traders and industrialists, intellectuals and others are also welcome in our midst as comrades who also suffer under capitalism. Herein lies the characteristic of our party as a class party of the masses.

The party, the programme explained, had also been set a national objective: achieving Japan's full independence. Japan had, in effect, lost its independence through the Security Treaty with the United States.

Japan [the programme states] is formally an independent state, as the conclusion of the Peace Treaty demonstrates, but, in fact, through the Security Treaty and the Administrative Agreement, [which allow for] the stationing of United States armed forces for an indefinite period and a network of innumerable military bases, her important key points are secured.

The programme demanded the renunciation of the Security Treaty, the withdrawal of all American troops from Japan, and the return of the Japanese Pacific island of Okinawa by an amendment to the peace treaty, which had transferred the sovereignty of the island to the United States.[2]

The fruits of the party's reunification were reaped in an impressive gain at the polls in the election of May 1958: the 13,093,000 votes polled represented

1. For the text of the Frankfurt declaration, see Appendix Two, page 531.
2. For the text of the programme, see *Yearbook*, pp. 338–48.

an advance of 2,380,000 over the 1955 elections when the two Social Democratic parties had faced one another in competition. And, for the first time, the party won 33 per cent of the entire poll; it increased its representation in parliament from 158 to 166 members. The gain in seats had naturally been inhibited by the tactics of the Communists, who had put up 114 candidates against the Social Democrats, thereby splitting the Socialist vote but still gaining only one seat.

However, within a bare eighteen months of this election victory, which seemed to hold out so much promise for its future, the Social Democratic party split afresh.

The programme worked out so painstakingly by the commission had been a compromise between the basic concepts of the Marxist left and the reformist right. It had not overcome the conflicts between the two factions over the party's character and their true intentions. For the left, led by Suzuki, the fight for Socialism against capitalism was the first priority, for, as the programme stated, the realization of Socialism was the 'historic mission' of the workers; the party's character as a workers' class party had to be preserved. Suehiro Nishio, leader of the Socialist extreme right, considered, on the other hand, that the struggle against Communism to defend democracy was the most urgent task. He advocated the party transformation into a democratic people's party.

This division of views also determined the differences of opinion over the Security Treaty and of attitudes towards the prevailing hostility between the Western powers and the Communist bloc. The left demanded the denouncing of the treaty, the withdrawal of American bases from Japan, Japan's neutrality in the Cold War and a détente with Communist China. Nishio, by contrast, pleaded for solidarity with the Western powers in their conflict with the Eastern bloc, arguing that, so long as international tension remained unresolved through the lack of an effective system of collective security, the security treaty would be necessary.

Over the years these conflicts, exacerbated by bitter struggles over the question of party tactics, intensified to an intolerable extent. At the extraordinary congress of September 1959, the left attempted to engineer Nishio's expulsion from the party. Thereupon in preparation for the founding of a new party in alliance with an anti-Communist trade union group, the 'Congress of the Trade Unions of Japan' (*Domeikaigi*), he organized a 'Society for the Reconstruction of the Party', which, as was explained, would seek the support of the 'whole nation, and not only workers' organizations and the peasants' alliances, for a new form of "democratic Socialism"'.

Nishio's new party came into being on 24 January 1960. It took the title 'Democratic Socialist party' (*Minshu Shakaito*). A blueprint for its programme was provided by the Godesberg Programme of the German Social

Democratic party. Its declared objective was the gradual development of Socialism by peaceful, lawful means, and opposition to any system of dictatorship, of the left as much as of the right. It rejected Marxism–Leninism as well as class-strife as methods for realizing Socialism. It sought to attain the image of a 'people's party' as against the image of the Social Democratic party as a 'class party'.[1]

Suehiro Nishio, a former metal-worker and trade union leader, had been a member of parliament since 1958 as well as a minister in Katayama's government and deputy prime minister in Ashida's government. His Socialist convictions were rooted not in Marxism, but in an idealistic humanism.

The splitting of the Social Democratic party undertaken by Nishio was deplored by the real leaders of the right, Inejiro Asanuma (1889–1960) and Jotaro Kawakami (1889–1965). Asanuma, a pioneer of the Japanese Labour movement, was elected party chairman shortly after the split; and, a few months later, on 12 October 1960, was murdered by a young nationalist fanatic. Kawakami succeeded him to the party chairmanship.

The two Socialist parties went into the election of November 1960 as unrelenting rivals, and the Social Democratic party came out of the elections by far the stronger of the two. It won 10,900,000 votes and 145 seats, while the Democratic Socialist party won 3,500,000 votes and seventeen seats.[2] Despite the internal strife in the Socialist camp, the total Socialist vote had increased by 1,300,000 over the 1958 elections, and the Socialist share of the poll had risen from 33 to 39 per cent.

It seems unlikely, however, that the two parties will remain separate in their advance into the future. The steady growth of a Socialist electorate, edging the Socialist movement ever closer to power, carries within itself a reunifying trend. The conflicts which split the party were disagreements over tactics—differences over relative values in the ideological justification of Socialism, and not conflicts over fundamental Socialist principles. Both parties have remained members of the Socialist International which embraces Socialists of every complexion—Marxists as well as reformists, religious as well as ethical humanists—in the spirit of basic principles and objectives which are common to all. It was a conflict of attitude to an actual political situation which broke the unity of the labour movement in Japan. Developments in the political situation may well pave the way to its reunification.

1. See Cole, *et al.*, *Socialist Parties in Post-war Japan*, pp. 74–5.
2. The election produced the following picture of the relative strengths of the three workers' parties:

	Votes	Percentage of votes cast	Seats
Social Democratic party	10,887,134	27.5	145
Democratic Socialist party	3,464,144	8.8	17
Communist party	1,156,722	2.9	3

15 · The Chinese Revolution

The strangest phenomenon in contemporary history has been the triumph of the Communist revolution in China: a leap from the fifteenth into the twentieth century. Marxism in its Leninist and Maoist version has, in only a few decades, become the ideology of a society whose thinking had been ruled for millennia by the teachings of Confucius.[1] A vast agrarian country, with hardly more than artisanal production for its goods, has become involved in a rapid process of change into a modern industrial state. China, for a century the helpless, humiliated victim of the rapacity of European and Japanese imperialism, is on a prodigious course to become the greatest world power in history.

The revolution in China took the Communist revolution in Russia as its example. But it differed from the Russian in both social character and technique. It was not, like the Russian, a revolution by the urban industrial proletariat, but a peasants' revolution, and its technique was not the armed uprising, as the Russian had been, but the guerrilla war.

But what distinguished it most from its Russian predecessor was its inevitability. The Communist revolution in Russia in October 1917 had not by any means been unavoidable; the Communist dictatorship which it set up had not been the only possibility for the regeneration of Russia. The alternatives had included a democracy under the dominant influence of the three Socialist parties—the Mensheviks, Bolsheviks and Social Revolutionaries—who together had won an overwhelming majority in the elections to the constituent national assembly.

In China, on the other hand, the Communist revolution had been the only hope for social regeneration. The middle-class revolution which preceded it had failed ingloriously. Its history, beginning in 1911 with the overthrow of

1. For the traditions of China, see H. G. Creel, *Chinese Thought from Confucius to Mao Tse-tung* (London, 1954); C. P. Fitzgerald, *China, a Short Cultural History* (London, 1935); Max Weber, *Gesammelte Aufsätze zur Religionssoziologie*, vol. I: *Konfuzianismus und Taoismus* (Tübingen, 1922).

the Manchu dynasty, had ended in 1949 with the fall of the impotent, soulless, corrupt and thoroughly autocratic dictatorship of Chiang Kai-shek. It had been a history of anarchy, civil war, economic decline and national humiliation during the Japanese invasion. The middle-class régime, fallen into general contempt, had failed totally; it could only be overthrown by a Communist revolution. There was no alternative; the revolution's victory was historically imperative.

The Chinese empire, which had been torn to shreds by the struggles between rival war lords and forty years of civil war, was united by the Communists. 'They gave China the strongest government which the land had known since the days of the great Manchu emperors of the seventeenth and eighteenth centuries. Some observers would go farther and call it the strongest that the Chinese had ever had.'[1]

The history of the Communist revolution in China in fact has no parallel in the history of Socialism.[2] The Communist party of China, formed in 1921 by a small group of intellectuals, differed during the first phase of its history in no way whatsoever from the Communist party of Russia by which it was, in fact, led until its devastating defeat in 1927. The Soviet Union had entered into an alliance with the Kuomintang, founded by Sun Yat-sen (1866–1925), the party of the national liberation movement which had formed a government in Canton and ruled the south of China. The Kuomintang was itself represented on the executive of the Communist International with the rights of an associate member. Moscow, therefore, instructed the Chinese Communist party to join the Kuomintang as the vehicle for the historically necessary bourgeois revolution.

But the main support of the Kuomintang, now led by General Chiang Kai-shek, came from the landowners and businessmen who felt their position to be threatened by the Communist party which, following an uprising in Shanghai in May 1925, had attracted a rapidly growing mass-following. Chiang Kai-shek, though he was an honorary member of the Communist International, decided to smash it. He arrested its army commissars and disarmed the Shanghai workers who, during the uprising, had opened the town gates to the advancing Kuomintang army. No sooner had he occupied the town, than he suppressed the Communist party in a terrible blood-bath.

Stalin, surprised by Chiang Kai-shek's change in political tactics, requested the Chinese Communists to adopt the technique of insurrection and sent Heinz Neumann, an agent of the Communist International, to organize an uprising in Canton. On 12 December 1927, units of the Fourth

1. Kenneth Scott Latourette, *A History of Modern China* (London, 1954), p. 208.
2. For an introduction to the history of the origins of the Communist Revolution and its development, see C. P. Fitzgerald, *Revolution in China* (London, 1954).

Army, under the command of Communist officers, occupied the town and proclaimed the 'Commune of Kanton'. Within a few days they were drowned in their own blood. It seemed as though the Chinese Communist party was finished.[1] Its central committee, led by Li Li-san, sought refuge in a foreign concession in Shanghai, but as a group deprived of leaders and followers it soon departed from the political scene.

The Chinese party was revived by Mao Tse-tung who after the catastrophe fled with a small guerrilla group to Chingkangshan in the wild mountain areas of Kiangsi province. There, under the command of Chu Teh, remnants of the Fourth Army which had escaped the massacre in Canton joined up with Mao Tse-tung's guerrilla group. They were to form the nucleus of the Red Army which by the beginning of 1929 consisted of about 10,000 men, and which, after a guerrilla war lasting twenty years, was to conquer the vast Chinese empire for the revolution.

Mao Tse-tung (1893–1976) was the son of a prosperous farmer in the central province of Hunan. He graduated from a college in Changsha, the capital of Hunan, in 1916, and went to Peking University, where, to earn a living, he became assistant librarian.[2] There he came under the influence of the two Marxist professors, Li Ta-chao and Ch'en Tu-hsiu, who founded the Communist party in China. Mao Tse-tung was among the twelve delegates at the Communist party's inaugural conference in his role as organizer of the revolutionary peasant movement in Hunan. He came to regard the 'hundreds of millions of peasants' rather than the industrial proletariat of the towns as providing the essential force for the revolution in China, as he wrote in a report on the peasant movement in Hunan for the fifth Communist party congress in April 1927.[3] Accordingly, he wrote, the party's strategy for the revolution, unlike that which had applied in Russia, would have to be based primarily on the peasantry, and it would have to be carried from the country-side into the town rather than vice versa. The party would have to attract the land-hungry peasant to the cause of the revolution by a programme of agrarian reform, aimed at redistributing the land, and by changes in the tenant system. Meanwhile the Red Army, composed of peasants, should pursue a guerrilla war to gain control of the rural districts, by-passing towns and setting up enclaves of soviets to serve as revolutionary bases.

This, however, was a view which contradicted Lenin's concept of the

1. For a brief description of these events, see Braunthal, *History of the International, 1914–1943*, pp. 320–9. For a detailed examination, see B. I. Schwartz, *Chinese Communism and the Rise of Mao* (Harvard, 1951); Conrad Brandt, John K. Fairbank and Benjamin Schwartz, *Documentary History of Chinese Communism* (Cambridge, Mass., and London, 1952); Harold K. Isaacs, *The Tragedy of the Chinese Revolution* (Stanford, 1951).

2. For a biography, see Stuart R. Schram, *Mao Tse-tung* (London, 1966).

3. See Malcolm D. Kennedy, *A Short History of Communism in Asia* (London, 1957), p. 76.

revolution. Lenin had also considered an alliance of the working class with the peasants as a necessary condition for the success of the revolution in agrarian Russia, but he saw the working class as providing its backbone. In his strategy, the towns had formed the revolutionary 'front' and the villages the revolution's 'hinterland'. Not until he had conquered Petrograd and Moscow did he spread the revolution into the villages.

But Mao Tse-tung, considering the village proletariat to be the social basis of the revolution in China, evolved a strategy in which the villages formed the revolutionary 'front' and the towns the revolution's 'hinterland'.[1]

During a decade of his leadership, from 1927 to 1937, the Communist movement in China developed from an industrial workers' party, led by theoretical Marxists, into an agrarian party of revolutionary peasants. In the soviets which the Communists organized in the districts they controlled, they created a new type of Communist régime based on the peasantry; it had the agrarian revolution as its immediate aim and the method of guerrilla war as tactics for the revolution. Thus, in adapting the Marxist–Leninist theory of revolution to the social conditions prevalent in China, Mao developed the concept of a dictatorship of the peasants rather than a dictatorship of the industrial proletariat.

The province of Kiangsi emerged as the first soviet republic in China. It was proclaimed by a congress of district soviets, meeting in Suichan, the capital of the province, on 7 November 1931. It elected a 'Provisional Central Government' under the leadership of Mao Tse-tung, with Chu Teh as commander of the Red Army and Chou En-lai as his deputy. It passed the basic laws of the republic, giving precedence to a law to redistribute the land among the poor peasants and the landless village proletariat.

Chiang Kai-shek regarded the destruction of the Soviet Republic of Kiangsi as his most urgent priority in consolidating the power of the Kuomintang. Between 1930 and 1934 he undertook five offensives against it, the fifth with an army of no less than 700,000 troops.[2] Though he failed to defeat the Red Army, he did succeed in paralysing the soviet republic with a blockade. Mao Tse-tung thereupon decided on a withdrawal which was to go down in China's history as a heroic epic: 130,000 soldiers and civilians left the Kiangsi republic in the autumn of 1934, broke through the blockade and, pursued by Chiang's troops and in continuous combat against local forces, marched for 12,000 kilometres through the barren wastes south-westwards along the Tibetan border through Kansu in the north of Shensi

---

1. 'The essential task of the Communist party,' Mao Tse-tung wrote in 1938, 'is not to start the armed struggle only after a long period of legal struggle, and not to attack first the big towns and then occupy the countryside afterwards, but to take them the other way round'—*Selected Works*, vol. II: *Problems of Warnda Strategy* (New York, 1954), p. 267.

2. For a description of this campaign, see O. Edmund Clubb, *Twentieth-Century China* (New York and London, 1964), pp. 194–202.

province on the edge of the Mongolian steppe to China's most remote area. The 'Long March', as it was to be known, took over a year.[1]

At the end of 1931, a Japanese army, stationed in Manchuria to safeguard the South Manchurian Railway, occupied the three eastern provinces of China which constituted Manchuria and, early in 1932, set up a Japanese satellite state which they called Manchukuo. This was the start of the Japanese invasion of China, aimed at subjecting the whole of that vast country to Japan's predominance.

Chiang Kai-shek, however, made no effort to resist the steady advance of the Japanese invasion, but instead concentrated his forces in attempting to wipe out the Communists. To press the battle against them, he directed an army under the command of Chang Hsueh-liang to attack the new Communist stronghold in the north-east, where, following the 'Long March', Mao Tse-tung had established a soviet republic with Yenan as its capital.

Then, in December, a sensational episode introduced a change into the relations between the Kuomintang and the Communist party. Chiang Kai-shek had gone to Hsian, to Chang Hsueh-liang's headquarters, to try to intensify the campaign against the Communists. Instead Chang Hsueh-liang seized him and forced him, under threat of assassination, to enter into negotiations with the Communists in response to their appeal to his troops to cease fighting their fellow Chinese and to join them in ejecting the Japanese. The negotiations which followed ended open fighting and resulted in a united front being presented to the Japanese.

Three months later, in an endeavour to consolidate the united front, Mao Tse-tung went even further. In February 1937, the central committee of the Chinese Communist party formally told the central executive committee of the Kuomintang that if the nation's strength were to be directed against external aggression, it would place its army under the direct strategic leadership of Chiang Kai-shek as generalissimo, and would make its government a part of that of the Republic of China, even ceasing to expropriate the holdings of landlords. It seemed that the Kuomintang and the Communists had reached a substantial measure of agreement, and civil war ceased.

Now, in the eyes of the nation, the Communist party appeared as the champion of national unity and as the main active force in the fight against the Japanese invader. It won the party the sympathies of a large majority of intellectuals and students, and an even larger number of peasants, who flocked to join its ranks. Its membership rose from 100,000 in 1937 to 1,200,000 in 1945.[2] 'In contrast with the exhausted Kuomintang,' Latourette

---

1. For a description of the 'Long March' and of the soviets, see Dick Wilson, *The Long March: 1935* (London, 1971); Edgar Snow, *Red Star Over China* (London, 1938).
2. See Latourette, *A History of Modern China*, p. 185.

observes, 'the Chinese Communist party came to the year 1945 with a tightly knit, disciplined membership, inured to hardship, equipped with armed forces which had been indoctrinated with its convictions, and with a philosophy of history and a programme held with unshakeable conviction and missionary fervour.' And, as he remarks later in his book, with leaders of 'tireless devotion and austerity' and an 'absence of corruption in Communist officialdom'.[1]

In the course of the guerrilla war against the Japanese, who had seized the towns and lines of communication but not the villages, the Communists brought the provinces of north and north-east China under their control. It was inevitable that, after Japan's capitulation in August 1945, the civil war should break out once again. 'Chiang Kai-shek,' General Stilwell, the commander of the American armed forces in China, recorded in his diary, 'hates the Communists. He intends to crush them . . . by occupying their territory as the Japs retire.'[2] In fact, Chiang Kai-shek issued an order to the Japanese that they were to defend whatever positions and towns they held in the Communist-controlled areas against attacks by Communists, and were to surrender only to the troops of the Kuomintang, who were flown in by the United States Air Force.

The astounding thing was, however, that Stalin, who had declared war on Japan eight days before its capitulation, issued identical instructions to the Soviet forces which had occupied Manchuria. Towns occupied by Russian troops were handed over not to the forces of Mao Tse-tung, but to those flown in by Chiang Kai-shek. During the Russian evacuation of Manchuria, the Communist forces in northern China had occupied the plains and taken possession of vast Japanese war supplies; in this the Russians had not hindered them. But the Russians did systematically dismantle Manchuria's industrial plant installations, removing machines, rolling stock and other movable goods to Russia as war booty. Had the Russians handed over this strongly developed industrial area to the Communists intact, the civil war would, in Fitzgerald's view, 'have been decided without further fighting', for once in possession of the Manchurian war potential, they would have been able 'to overthrow the Kuomintang whenever it suited them'.[3]

In the event, the civil war dragged on for almost another four years. The revolution finally triumphed not only on the battlefields, despite the numerical superiority of Chiang Kai-shek's American-equipped counter-revolutionary armies, but also in the villages and towns, for it embodied the hopes of a new order, while Chiang Kai-shek's régime had been discredited as impotent,

1. ibid., pp. 187 and 204.
2. Joseph M. Stilwell, *The Stilwell Papers*, edited by Theodore W. White (New York, 1948), p. 340.
3. See Fitzgerald, *Revolution in China*, p. 98.

corrupt, reactionary and devoid of ideas or inspiration.[1] The Communist revolution was victorious because it won to its cause not only the broad mass of the peasants, whom it freed from pressing burdens and raised from degradation, but also the intellectuals and the mass of the middle classes as well as the workers. It is a barely disputed verdict among historians of the Chinese revolution that it was carried to victory by an overwhelming majority of the Chinese people.

It was this social mass basis on which the construction of a Socialist order of society was to begin. There was, of course, no existing blueprint; the new society could only be developed through experimental processes.[2] Mao Tse-tung, its master builder, was well aware that Soviet Russian Communism could not serve as an example. 'The history of Russia,' he said on the eve of his triumphal entry into Peking on 3 February 1949, 'created the Russian system; the history of China will create the Chinese system.'[3]

Marxism had shaped the ideology of the Chinese Revolution, as it had for the Russian Revolution. But Mao Tse-tung did not believe that Chinese Communism could accept Marxism in its Russian or any other foreign version. While still in Yenan he had written in *China's New Democracy*, the book in which he set forth the ideals and programmes of the new order:

> In the past, China has suffered greatly by accepting foreign ideas simply because they were foreign. Chinese Communists should remember this in applying Marxism in China. We must effect a genuine synthesis between the universal truth of Marxism and the concrete practice of the Chinese Revolution. Only after we have found out our own national form of Marxism will it prove useful.[4]

Mao Tse-tung was resolved on seeking a 'Chinese road to Socialism'.

1. 'Chiang Kai-shek,' Stilwell noted, 'is bewildered by the spread of Communist influences. He can't see that the mass of the Chinese people welcome the Reds as being the only visible hope of relief from crushing taxation, the abuse of the army and Tai Li's Gestapo. Under Chiang Kai-shek they now begin to see what they may expect: greed, corruption, favouritism, more taxes, a ruined currency, terrible waste of life, callous disregard of all the rights of man. . . . I judge Kuomintang and the Communist party by what I saw: Kuomintang—corruption, neglect, chaos, a ruined economy, taxes, hoarding, black market, trading with the enemy. Communist programme—reduce taxes, rents, interest. Raise production and standard of living. Practise what they preach . . .'—Stilwell, *The Stilwell Papers*, pp. 317 and 318.

2. See Rostow, *The Prospects for Communist China* (New York and London, 1954), Parts 5 and 6 *passim*.

3. Quoted in Clubb, *Twentieth-Century China*, p. 302.

4. Mao Tse-tung, *China's New Democracy*, p. 61, quoted in Creel, *Chinese Thought from Confucius to Mao Tse-tung*, p. 266.

16 · Socialism in Israel

Socialism in Israel represents a unique historical phenomenon. The state of Israel came into existence as a result of Socialist initiative. Socialists have governed it since its foundation, realizing Socialist ideas in economic, social and cultural institutions, thereby imprinting Socialism more deeply into the character of the social order than in any other country that has a democratic system of government. The uniqueness of the Socialism which has developed in this country has its origin, like the state of Israel itself, in utopian concepts.[1] With the founding of the state of Israel a national utopia, and with the founding of the institution of the *kibbutz* a Socialist utopia, became reality.[2]

However, the cradle of Socialist Zionism stood not on the soil of Palestine where the new state was to arise, but in the vast ghettos of Tsarist Russia in which, at the turn of the century, nearly a third of world Jewry was living. Throughout Western and Central Europe, Jewish communities had been subjected to a gradual process of social and cultural assimilation into the nations where they lived. In Russia, on the other hand, as well as in Romania and the provinces of Galicia and Bukovina in the Habsburg Empire, they formed in effect a nation which was sharply distinct from all other nations—not only by their religion, but also as a separate cultural community jealously guarding its ancient traditions and customs and speaking its own language (Yiddish).

It was only in the last decade of the nineteenth century that a national self-awareness awoke among the Jewish people. From this there stemmed a national movement driven forward by a force working to bring the Jews together into an independent historical nation. With the awakening of this national self-consciousness there also came a class-consciousness to the Jewish proletariat of Tsarist Russia. 'The change in the attitudes of Jewish

1. See the essay by Isaiah Berlin, 'The Origins of Israel', in Walter Z. Laqueur (ed.), *The Middle East in Transition* (London, 1958), pp. 204–21.

2. The utopia of political Zionism was first outlined by Theodor Herzel in his book, *Der Judenstaat* (Vienna, 1896). The utopia of a Socialist Jewish state was developed by Moses Hess in *Rom und Jerusalem* (1862) and by Nachman Syrkin, *Die Judenfrage und der sozialistische Judenstaat* (Berne, 1898).

workers since the outbreak of the Russian Revolution [of 1905],' wrote Otto Bauer in 1907, 'is something which Europe has watched with amazement: from among the timid Jews of the ghetto there emerged the most heroic fighters of the great revolution.'[1]

Individual Socialist groups of Jewish workers had first emerged in Tsarist Russia in the 1890s. They came together under the leadership of Alexander Kremer, Noah Portnoy, Bronislav Grosser and Leon Fajner (who was to lead the Jewish underground movement against the Nazi occupation in Poland during the Second World War) at a conference in Vilna in September 1897, to form the General Jewish Workers' Union of Russia, Lithuania and Poland, a title which became abbreviated to the '*Bund*'.

The *Bund* was a Socialist, revolutionary and, indeed, a Marxist party. It led the Jewish workers in their struggle against the Polish and Russian as well as against the Jewish bourgeoisie, and, side by side with the Russian and Polish and Lithuanian Socialists, it led them in the underground battle against Tsarism. The central Socialist organization in the Russian Empire, embracing the Socialist parties of all the nations in the state, was the Russian Social Democratic Workers' party, founded in Vilna in 1898, which five years later was to split into Bolsheviks and Mensheviks. The *Bund* was one of its founder members, representing the Jewish proletariat among the Socialists of all other nationalities in Russia.

The *Bund* also pursued national objectives. It sought to awaken in the Jewish working class not only the awareness of their Socialist mission but also their national consciousness, so as to make them immune to assimilation with other nationalities and to keep alive and develop Jewish cultural values. It opposed the inequality under the law which Tsarism imposed on the Jewish people, and it fought for their recognition as equals among the other nationalities within the Russian empire.[2]

But shortly after its beginning the Jewish Labour movement was to split over conflicting attitudes towards Zionism. The purpose of Zionism was to win a homeland in Palestine for the Jewish people who had been deprived of their rights and subjected to persecution in certain countries, colonizing the area by the emigration of Jews from all over the world. The *Bund*, on the

---

1. Otto Bauer, *Die Nationalitätenfrage und die Sozialdemokratie* (Vienna, 1907), p. 372.

2. Ber Borochov, the pioneer of Socialist Zionism which developed out of opposition to the *Bund*, paid due respect in an essay he wrote in 1905–6, in which he discussed the *Bund*'s national programme in association with its historical role: 'The *Bund* has earned itself great praise from the Jewish proletariat. In the history of the Jewish Labour movement its name will stand in letters of gold, and future generations of Jewish workers will set up a splendid monument in Palestine. . . . It has done well in the development of class-consciousness among the Jewish workers, it has taught them to defend their interests by organized struggle, it has instilled in them the spirit of discipline and has developed the concept of democracy among them'—Ber Borochov, *Sozialismus und Zionismus. Eine Synthese*, edited by Mendel Singer (Vienna, 1932), p. 120.

other hand, rejected Zionism as a bourgeois, nationalist concept, seeing it moreover as an inappropriate solution to the 'Jewish question'. The situation of those millions of Jews concentrated in Russia would, it was argued, remain unaffected by the sparse numbers of Jewish emigrants which Palestine was capable of absorbing. The Russian Jewish working class could only attain national emancipation through the overthrow of Tsarism and social and economic emancipation through Socialism. The future of the Jewish proletariat was therefore inextricably linked to the future of the proletarian revolution in Russia. The *Bund* countered Zionism with the argument that it distracted the Jewish workers from their true historic task: the fight against Tsarism.[1]

But the concept of Zionism had meanwhile seized the imaginations of Jewish Socialists. In September 1900, three years after the *Bund*'s foundation, the first group of Socialist Zionists, consisting of about 150 workers and students, formed themselves into the movement known as *Poale Zion* (Workers of Zion) at a conference in Ekaterinoslav.[2] This group formed the nucleus of a movement which was to spread slowly throughout Russia and Russian Poland. At the inaugural conference of *Poale Zion* in Poltava in March 1906, thirty representatives (including Isaac Ben Zwi) from Warsaw, Lodz, Kiev and Odessa and other Russian towns together represented 16,000 members.[3]

It was Ber Borochov (1881–1917), the son of a Hebrew teacher in Poltava in the Ukraine, who was both the founder of *Poale Zion* and the progenitor of its ideology. As a high-school student, inspired by Marxism, he had been active in the illegal Russian Social Democratic party, but had become a Zionist through a Marxist analysis of the economic and social situation of the Jewish proletariat in Russia. In his writings he showed that the tragedy of the Jewish labour movement had its roots in the abnormal social and economic structure of the Jewish society; the Jewish people lived in economic isolation, excluded from the basic agrarian and modern industrial processes of production and restricted mainly to trading and light industry. This abnormal economic structure condemned the Jewish working class to impotence in the struggle for Socialism. But the normalization of Jewish society's economic and social structure could not be expected to emerge from the ruins of its present existence; nothing short of a national ideal could awaken the creative powers of the Jewish nation and only on the historic soil of Palestine could its renaissance be realized.[4]

For Borochov, the return of the Jewish people to nature, their establishing

1. See Raphael Abramovitch, '*Zionismus, Judenfrage und Sozialismus*', in *Der Kampf*, vol. XXII (1929), pp. 509–19.
2. See Borochov, *Sozialismus und Zionismus*, p. 331.
3. See ibid., p. 333; there is also a description of the conference by Ben Zwi in ibid., pp. 375–6.
4. For a biographical sketch of Borochov by Ben Zwi, see ibid., pp. 365–79; for a selection of his writings, see ibid., pp. 19–344.

a link with the soil as peasants, was the key precondition for the normalization of Jewish society.

> We have no land of our own [he wrote], and thus are of necessity separated from nature. Over the centuries the Jewish masses have blindly sought a path to take them back to the land. At last we have found it. The road is Zionism; it is the logical, natural consequence of an economic revolution in Jewish life. . . . It is the one movement capable of instilling reason, order and discipline, into Jewish life, the one solution to the economic and historical needs of the Jewish people.[1]

Borochov's vision was the prototype for Socialist Zionism, and for many years it was to remain a dream.

The inaugural conference of *Poale Zion* also decided to bring together the *Poale Zion* parties, formed in a number of other countries, into a 'World Federation of Socialist Zionist Parties' (*Ichud Olami*). This constituted itself at a conference in The Hague as the collective representative of the Socialist Zionist parties of Palestine, Russia, the United States, Great Britain, the Austro-Hungarian Empire and Romania.[2]

The Socialist Zionist World Federation naturally thought of itself as a part of the international labour movement, and hence sought affiliation to the Second International. But those parties in the International which were opposed to *Poale Zion* in their own countries—the Bundists, Mensheviks and Bolsheviks besides the Austrian Social Democrats—considered Zionism as a utopian, bourgeois-nationalist concept, and disputed its genuine Socialist character. And even those parties in the International which in no way doubted the genuineness of *Poale Zion*'s avowal of Socialism and accepted its proletarian character, saw it as at best a small sect of utopian Socialists of no significance to the international class struggle. The Zionist World Federation approached the Bureau of the Second International three times (in 1907, 1908 and 1911) with its application for membership; and it was rejected three times.

It was only during the First World War that recognition grew among Socialist parties of the historical peculiarity of the Jewish problem and with it an understanding of Zionism. In their peace manifesto of 10 October 1917, the Dutch–Scandinavian committee of the Second International declared: 'We recognize the international nature of the Jewish question and the need for it to be included in the peace treaty. . . . The promotion of the Jewish colonization of Palestine must have international protection.' In 1919 the Socialist Zionist World Federation was invited to attend the Berne conference of the Second International and, two years later, the founding conference of

1. Ber Borochov, *The Economic Development of the Jewish People* (New York, 1916), quoted in S. Levenberg, *The Jews and Palestine, A Study in Labour Zionism*, with a Preface by J. S. Middleton (London, 1945), p. 17.
2. See ibid., p. 111.

the Vienna International—an international of Socialist parties which had seceded from the Second International but which had also declined to join the Third International. And when the Second International and the Vienna International came together at the Hamburg conference of May 1923 to form the Labour and Socialist International, the recognition of *Poale Zion* as a member of the International was no longer in dispute.[1]

At the time of the founding of the Socialist Zionist World Federation, there had been in Palestine two small Labour parties: the *Poale Zion* party and the Zionist party of Labour Youth (*Hapoel Hatzair*). After a few years of slow growth, both groups were suppressed by the Turkish authorities during the First World War.

After the war, *Poale Zion* attempted to construct a common organization for the labour movement in Palestine. In 1919 it combined with the Farm Workers' Labour Union, founded in 1911, to form the Zionist Socialist Trade Union Federation of Palestine (*Achdut Ha'avoda*), and one year later, on 5 December 1920, at a conference in Haifa, a comprehensive organization for the Palestinian Labour movement was brought into being with the *Histadrut*, the General Federation of Jewish Labour in Israel. Among its pioneers were David Ben-Gurion (1886–1973), who, twenty-eight years later, was to proclaim Israel's independence and become its first prime minister, Isaac Ben Zwi (1886–1963), the future president of the republic, and Joseph Sprinzak (1885–1959), the future president of the *Knesset* (parliament). The conference defined the organization's structure and constitution, and elected Ben-Gurion to be general secretary.[2]

It attracted 4,433 members from among the 80,000 Jews who lived in Palestine at that time. But though it was a small organization, it set out to achieve nothing short of the construction of a Jewish Society of Labour in Israel. Its constitution declared:

> The General Federation of Jewish Labour, with a view to advancing all the social, economic and cultural interests of the working class and of building a Jewish Society of Labour in *Eretz Israel* [the land of Israel], organizes all workers who live by self-labour and do not exploit the labour of others.

Three years later a *Histadrut* congress supplemented the constitution with a concrete programme of tasks and objectives:

1. For the relationship of the Socialist International to *Poale Zion*, see ibid., pp. 113–19; for the Berne conference see Braunthal, *History of the International, 1914–1943*, pp. 150–9; for the inaugural conference of the Vienna International, see ibid., pp. 232–63; for the Hamburg Congress, see ibid., pp. 264–270.

2. For the history and development of the *Histadrut*, see W. Preuss, *The Labour Movement in Israel, Past and Present* (New York, 1963); N. Malkosh, *Histadrut in Israel. Its Aims and Achievements* (Tel Aviv, 1961); Levenberg, *The Jews and Palestine*, pp. 54–67; *Yearbook of the International Free Trade Union Movement 1957–1958* (London, 1957), pp. 299–303; Margaret Plunkett, 'The *Histadrut*. The General Federation of Jewish Labour in Israel', in *Industrial and Labour Relations Review*, vol. I, January 1958.

To organize workers in unions according to their trades; to establish and develop co-operative enterprises in all branches of industry and agriculture; to conduct the defensive struggle of the workers and improve their working conditions; to publish newspapers and literature; to promote comradely relations with Arab workers in the country and to foster links between the Jewish Labour movement and the international labour movement; to establish and develop mutual aid institutions, including a workers' sick fund.

To fulfil its tasks, the *Histadrut* developed a character without parallel in the history of the international labour movement. It became a central trade union organization, as it would have been in any other country. But it also became the largest industrial and commercial combine in the land; a combine of industrial enterprises working either on a co-operative basis or individually. It set up blast furnaces, brick-works, cement factories, steel, wood and glass industries and agricultural machine factories. It is by far the largest building contractor in the Near East. It is a federation of production, transport and sales co-operatives, but above all a federation incorporating nearly 1,000 collective and co-operative agricultural settlements. Nearly a fifth of all Israeli workers are employed in *Histadrut* enterprises.[1] It also controls the largest health service administration in the land, caring for three quarters of the entire population through its health insurance, *Kupat Holim*, and is the largest educational and cultural organization in the state. It is indeed, as it was planned from the outset, a federation 'of state builders and pioneers of a classless society of labour'.[2]

One of the leaders of the *Praja* Socialist Party of India, J. B. Kripalani, who has made a particular study of Israel's Socialist foundations, saw in them patterns which might be followed by the underdeveloped countries of Asia and Africa. They taught, he wrote, 'that revolutionary social construction on an egalitarian basis, free from exploitation, can be effected without recourse to violence and without dictatorship or impairing the freedom of the individual. It can be accomplished on the moral basis of justice, fair play and neighbourly co-operation.'[3]

1. The scale of *Histadrut*'s economic enterprises may best be illustrated by some figures: in 1965 the building federation, *Solel Boneh*, employed almost 30,000 workers with a turnover of I£400 million in Israel and a turnover of I£90 million for work in Africa, Asia and the Near East. Its agricultural co-operative society, *Tnuva*, absorbed two thirds of all agricultural products with a turnover of I£494 million, and the wholesale purchasing company which supplies the collective and co-operative settlements, *Hamashbir Hamerkazi*, had a turnover of I£450 million. The *Histadrut* altogether brings together over 270 productive and other co-operatives, and is part-owner of the national passenger and merchant fleet and airline. See *Facts about Israel 1968* (Ministry for Foreign Affairs, Jerusalem), p. 139.

2. *Programme of the MAPAI 1955*; see Julius Braunthal (ed.), *Yearbook of the International Socialist Labour Movement* (London, 1956), p. 310; for the full text of the programme, see ibid., pp. 301–14.

3. J. B. Kripalani, Preface to Julius Braunthal, *The Significance of Israeli Socialism and the Arab-Israeli Dispute* (London, 1958), p. 6.

It is true that the extraordinary historical and economic conditions under which the Jewish community had had to develop in Palestine were quite unique. They had enabled the working class to develop its powers of production by Socialist means. The problem facing the Socialists in Asia was to change an ancient, rigid, economic, social and political social structure. In Palestine, the Socialist pioneers had stepped into a social and economic vacuum. Until a few years before the founding of *Histadrut*, Palestine had been the southern part of the Syrian province of the Ottoman empire, becoming in 1922 a mandate of the League of Nations under British administration. Article 2 of the mandate pledged Britain to guarantee the 'setting up of a Jewish national Home'. But this Jewish national home had to be built from nothing; its economic and social basis had to be created. Palestine was an underdeveloped country, and the area set aside for the Jewish national home was a countryside of bare hills and swamps in Galilee in the north and of the Negev desert in the south. It could not be cultivated on a capitalist basis for, under existing conditions, no profit could be expected from invested capital. The draining of the swamps, the transformation of stony hills and sandy deserts into fertile soil, could only be undertaken by pioneers, fired in their work equally by a Socialist and a national ideal.

The Socialist pioneers were resolved from the beginning, at a time when a Jewish national home in Palestine was still not much beyond a utopian dream, that it should be built up as a Socialist venture on co-operative principles: in agriculture, in the form of the fully Socialist *kibbutz* or the semi-collective *moshav*; and in industry, by production co-operatives.

The unique economic and social creation which gave the country its characteristic stamp was the form of collective agricultural settlement, the *kibbutz*.

Translated, the Hebrew word *kibbutz* means 'group'. But this simple word has taken on a special meaning in Israel. It means a group of people who have joined together voluntarily into a community with no personal property or money economy to develop a Socialist form of communal life. When a similar ideal had been tried out by the early Socialists Robert Owen, Étienne Cabet and Charles Fourier almost a century before in America, it had failed.[1] In Palestine, this dream of a Socialist utopia was to become a living permanent reality. The Socialist Zionists in Russia who, their imaginations captured by this vision, planned to emigrate to Palestine, had only a vague idea of the task they had set themselves. As Joseph Baratz (1890–1968), one of the founders of the first *kibbutz*, recollected in his memoirs:

> What we wanted was to work ourselves, to be as self-supporting as we could and to do it not for wages but for the satisfaction of helping one another. . . . In our community we would do away with money altogether. We would have among us

1. For an account of the early Socialist colonies in America, see Mark Holloway, *Heavens on Earth. Utopian Communities in America 1680–1880* (London, 1951), pp. 101–58.

neither masters nor paid servants, but we would give ourselves freely to the soil and to another's need. . . . Neither lacking nor possessing anything, we hoped that in this way we would manage to live a just, peaceful and productive life.[1]

The *kibbutz* at Degania, which Baratz among others founded on the banks of the Jordan in 1909, became the pattern for the several hundred Socialist settlements subsequently created in Palestine: economic systems without money circulation, working systems without pay, a social grouping based on the common ownership of the means of production, a self-governing democratic community whose inhabitants participated in work and proceeds in the spirit of the Marxist's vision of Socialism: 'From each according to his abilities, to each according to his needs.'[2]

In 1919, the labour movement in Palestine entered the post-war era divided between three parties: the *Achduth Ha'avoda*, the *Hapoel Hatzai* and the Communist party. All three parties, as well as various splinter groups in the labour movement, were represented on the general council of the *Histadrut* according to the proportions of seats won at elections. (The eighty-seven members of the general council were, like parliamentary delegates, elected by universal, direct elections according to rules of proportional representation.)

On 6 January 1930, the two Socialist parties, the *Achduth Ha'avoda* and the *Hapoel Hatzai*, came together at a congress in Tel Aviv to form the Jewish Labour Party of Israel (*Mifleget Poale Eretz Israel*), known as M.A.P.A.I. for short. It began life with a membership of 6,000.[3] As its programme stated, it worked to create in Israel 'a social order, founded on Socialist and democratic principles'. It declared itself to be faithfully at one with the world labour movement in its fight to end class rule and all forms of social suppression. 'The party wishes to become a standard-bearer in fulfilling the [ideals] of the Zionist movement and a true member of the international Socialist labour movement.'[4]

The founders of the M.A.P.A.I. were men and women who were to go down in history as the architects of the state of Israel: David Ben-Gurion, Moshe Sharett (1894–1965), Joseph Sprinzack and Zalman Shazar, Ben Zwi's successor as president of the republic, to name only a few.

1. Joseph Baratz, *A Village by the Jordan. The Story of Degania* (London, 1954), pp. 44–5.

2. For the structure of the *kibbutz* and its internal life, see M. E. Spiro, *Kibbutz. Venture in Utopia* (New York, 1956); Murray Weingarten, *Life in a Kibbutz* (New York, 1955); see also Rushbrook Williams, *The State of Israel*, pp. 100–3; Levenberg, *The Jews in Palestine*, pp. 58–61; Julius Braunthal, *In Search of the Millennium* (London, 1945), pp. 307–9. Until 1967, 212 *kibbutzim*, with a total population of 82,000, had developed in Israel; there were also a further 295 semi-collective agricultural settlements of the *moshav* type with a total population of 115,000—see *Facts about Israel 1968*, p. 114.

3. See *Yearbook*, p. 297.

4. For an outline of the programme, see Preuss, *The Labour Movement in Israel*, pp. 100–102.

The party ideology was not based on any theoretical system, but on the belief, as it stated in its Declaration of Principles and Aims: 'that working-class unity in taking action, based on common ideals and on broadly agreed and honestly applied principles, is more important than theoretical uniformity'.

> M.A.P.A.I. is a party of deeds. . . . It believes in Socialism with individual liberty. When it says Socialism it means it. Its record of creative Socialism is written over the hills and valleys of this country, in the collective and co-operative villages, in socialized industries in town and country, in the great trade union and co-operative movement, and in the day-to-day struggle for the emancipation of the working class.[1]

Thus, the history of the party is largely the history of the economic, social and cultural achievements of the *Histadrut*. It is also inseparable from the history of the Republic of Israel which, as by far the strongest party, it has governed since its foundation and has shaped its entire social complexion. In its history, as Ben-Gurion describes it,

> the two motives of the Labour movement throughout the world—both social and national—found their most outstanding and special manifestation without parallel in any other country. It is in Palestine that it has become a pioneer movement in the truest and deepest sense of the word. As pioneers of the national renaissance and social deliverance of the Jewish people . . . they had to construct this new home upon the ruins of millennia—from the foundation to the roof.[2]

In 1944 a group within the M.A.P.A.I. broke away to merge in January 1948 with the *Hashomer Hatzai* (Young Guard) founded in 1927 to set up a left-wing Socialist Marxist party with the title *Mifleget Hapoalim Mameuhedet* (United Labour Party), or M.A.P.A.M. for short. Ideologically, it stood closer to Bolshevism than to Social Democracy. Its programme declared its 'identification with Marxism and Leninism', but emphasized its 'independence of any ideological and practical interpretation of questions of Marxism and Leninism by the Communist party congresses'.[3]

A Stalinist group within the party, however, led by Moshe Sneh (b. 1909), demanded its unqualified identification with Moscow's policies, even after Stalin had in 1952 set in motion a vast anti-Semitic campaign, to which, among others, M. Oren, a M.A.P.A.M. leader, had fallen victim; arrested in Prague while returning to Israel from Moscow, he had been sentenced as an 'Anglo-American spy' to a heavy term of imprisonment. Sneh and his

---

1. See 'Principles and Aims', in *Yearbook*, p. 299.
2. Ben-Gurion, in the Preface to Preuss, *The Labour Movement in Israel*, p. 11. For the history of the party, see Samuel Rolbant, *MAPAI. The Israel Labour Party* (Tel Aviv, 1956).
3. See Meir Yaari, *From Vision to Reality* (Tel Aviv, 1963) pp. 66–7. This book by M.A.P.A.M.'s general secretary is an outline thesis for its fourth congress, and is the best introduction to the party's ideology and policy. See also, by the same author, *What Faces Our Generation* (Tel Aviv, 1958).

followers were expelled from the party in 1953; he eventually joined the Communist party and became a member of its central committee.

In 1954 M.A.P.A.M.'s right wing also separated from it over the question of the party's attitude towards the Soviet Union, reconstituting itself as the *Achdut Ha'avoda* party. After this split, M.A.P.A.M. became mainly a party of the *kibbutz* movement, whose federation embraced about half the *kibbutzim*. In the elections of 1961, it won 7·5 per cent of the poll as against 34·7 per cent won by the M.A.P.A.I.[1]

The rival to these two Socialist parties is the Communist party of Israel (*Miflage Qimunistit Isre'elit*), or M.A.Q.I. for short. Founded at the beginning of 1921, its history is worth recounting in rather more detail, for it offers a classic example of a Communist party which is prepared, in its intellectual and political dependence upon Moscow, to sacrifice without question the vital interests of its own country, people and working class to the power policy of the Soviet Union.

It had emerged from the Socialist Labour party, a left-wing Socialist group which had been formed in 1919 under the impact of the Bolshevik Revolution in Russia, and was led by Yitzchak Meirson and Wolf Averbach.[2] After a bloody clash with the *Histadrut* at a May Day parade, it was banned by the British mandate government in Palestine and remained illegal until 1941, when the Soviet Union became an ally of Britain during the Second World War. The party was divided from the very beginning into two factions, and at that time it had between 200 and 300 members. In February 1924 it was accepted as a member of the Communist International.

As could be expected, Lenin having condemned Zionism as a reactionary movement, the party was a declared opponent of Zionism, stating its 'main duty' to be 'to fight Zionism in all its forms and to unmask the bankrupt Zionist swindle'.[3]

But in its fight against Zionism it could hardly expect to win the sympathies of the masses of proletarian Jews who had emigrated to Palestine from the ghettos of Europe in their search for a 'Jewish national home'. In the 1925 elections to the representative assembly of the Jews in Palestine (a kind of provisional government under the mandate), it won only 524 votes among the 50,436 cast.[4]

Moscow, which had doubtless recognized from the start that the Communist party of Palestine hardly had a brilliant future before it as a Jewish

1. See Preuss, *The Labour Movement in Israel*, p. 228.
2. The following description is based on an excellently documented study by Walter Z. Laqueur, *Communism and Nationalism in the Middle East* (London, 1956), pp. 73–119; Moshe M. Czudnowski and Jakob Landau, *The Israeli Communist Party* (Stanford, 1965), mimeographed MS.
3. Quoted in Laqueur, *Communism and Nationalism in the Middle East*, p. 77.
4. See Czudnowski and Landau, *The Israeli Communist Party*, p. 5.

party, instructed it through Karl Radek to 'Arabize' itself, to try to win the masses of the Arab proletariat by supporting the aims of Arab nationalism. The party installed an Arab, Ridwan al-Hilu, to be its general secretary and ceased publication of its Hebrew and Yiddish newspapers, replacing them with one in Arabic. (Only leaflets continued to appear in all three languages.)

But the attempt to organize the Arab workers was not very successful. Now the party tried to win 'the support of the feudal and nationalist elements . . . openly backing extreme Arab nationalism in Palestine and identifying itself with the extremist religious nationalist leader, the Grand Mufti of Jerusalem, Haji Amin al-Husaini, and the terrorists he had organized to oppose the British and the Jews'.[1]

The first insurrection promoted by the Grand Mufti occurred in August 1929. This was not a rising against the British mandate forces, like the later Arab rising of 1936–9, but a *pogrom* in which 133 Jews were killed and nearly 300 injured.[2]

The massacre in fact aroused the revulsion of the Communists. It brought into the open the whole question of whether the party's support for extreme Arab nationalism could be squared with Communist principles. The party leadership attempted to call a halt to the bloodshed. 'Enough of our brothers' blood has been shed in the cause of Jewish–Arabic co-operation,' their appeal to the Arabs stated.

But the executive of the Communist International considered the *pogrom* to have been an inevitable concomitant phenomenon of the start of a national Arab revolt against British imperialism and Zionism. It reproved the Communist party of Palestine for its pacific attitude and instructed it to support the Arab insurrection.[3]

A majority on the party central committee, which met in September, decided, despite strong protests from a minority, to accept the tactic commanded by Moscow. It now took the view that, 'in a country such as Palestine, a revolutionary movement without *pogroms* was impossible'.[4] A revolutionary movement, like that of the Arab proletariat, could neither be rejected by the Communists nor discouraged, its declaration stated, simply because it carried the risk of inciting *pogroms*. Had the Arab proletariat been strong enough, no *pogrom* would have taken place; it would not have been possible for the Grand Mufti to control the revolutionary movement. For this situation, the

1. ibid., p. 7.
2. See *Palestine Events 1929*, published by the Jewish Socialist Labour Party (*Poale Zion*) of England (London, 1929).
3. See J. Berger-Barseli, *Hatragedia shel Hamadafecha Hasovietit* (The Tragedy of the Soviet Revolution) (Tel Aviv, 1968), pp. 103–4. The author of these reminiscences was secretary of the Communist party of Palestine in the 1920s and later a member of the secretariat of the Communist International.
4. See *The Arab Revolutionary Movement and the Tasks of the Proletariat* (October 1929), quoted in Laqueur, *Communism and Nationalism in the Middle East*, p. 84.

central committee argued, 'the Social Fascists of the *Histadrut* were responsible'.[1]

The conflict between the opposition minority—belittled by Moscow as 'right-wing' and 'Bukharinist'[2]—and the majority was fought out at a conference in December 1929. The 'right-wing' minority was expelled from the party leadership and in a self-critical admission of guilt, it was stated that the party had lost itself in a swamp of opportunism and vague anti-imperialist slogans. The party, the resolution continued, 'has forgotten that the fellahin and bedouins are waiting for leadership and want to show what they can do with daggers and revolvers'.[3]

The Arab revolt came to life again in 1936 when, following Hitler's rise to power, many thousands of German and Austrian Jews emigrated to Palestine. The Communist party, like the Mufti, demanded the closure of Palestine to Jewish immigration. In Nazi Germany, the Communists argued, it was not only Jews who were being persecuted, but also non-Jewish workers; why should the Jews alone emigrate? The answer was obvious, the Communist propaganda asserted; it was because Britain planned to extend Palestine as a war base against the Soviet Union, and considered the Jewish immigrants to be potential soldiers of the 'Zionist-imperialist-Fascist army'.[4]

Thus the Communist party justified its opposition to Jewish immigration into Palestine as a fight against British imperialism in solidarity with the Soviet Union. In its preparations for a rising planned by Arab nationalists in the spring of 1936, the party's executive committee reached agreement with Husaini, the Grand Mufti, on the following strategy: 'The Arab Communists are to participate actively [in the fight] to destroy Zionism and imperialism, while the Jewish members [of the Communist party] are to weaken Jewish community life from the inside.' To co-ordinate the actions of Arab nationalists with those of the Communist party, two leading Arab Communist party members, Nimr 'Uda and Fuad Nasin, were seconded to the Arab general staff as liaison officers.

The insurrection commenced in May 1936 with a general strike by the Arabs which lasted for six months, accompanied by heavy fighting which constantly renewed itself over the course of the following three years.[5]

But the uprising was to be the ruin of the Communist party. It lost not

1. Quoted in ibid., p. 84.

2. In 1929 Nicolai Bukharin was removed from the presidency of the Communist International as a 'right deviationist' following his dispute with Stalin; he was executed in 1938.

3. *Forward*, 25 December 1929, quoted in Laqueur, *Communism and Nationalism in the Middle East*, p. 85. *Forward* was the Yiddish monthly of the Communist party; it ceased publication in 1931, while its Arabic monthly, '*Ala'l Amam*, continued to be published.

4. Leaflet of the Communist party, 22 May 1934, quoted in Laqueur, *Communism and Nationalism in the Middle East*, p. 93.

5. See John Marlowe, *Rebellion in Palestine* (London, 1946).

only most of its Arab members, but also most of its Jewish ones. The profound devotion to the cause of Communism and the Soviet Union demanded a degree of self-denial in their idealism which, for most of them, proved intolerable. Thus they fell away from the party. 'In the year 1939 there existed a party executive, but no followers.' A mere 300 Jewish members remained inside the party at that time.[1]

Meanwhile the danger of Hitler waging a war which threatened the Soviet Union had moved closer. Instructed by Moscow, the Communist parties of all countries called on the workers to form an anti-Fascist united front to resist Hitler. Accordingly, the executive committee of the Communist party of Palestine issued an alarm call on 1 August 1939: 'International Fascism wishes to occupy the Near East and Palestine. But all patriots will defend their homeland. . . . Neutrality means support for Fascism.'[2]

A few weeks later, however, Stalin first concluded his non-aggression pact and shortly afterwards his Treaty of Friendship with Hitler's Germany and sealed it 'in blood'.[3] This abrupt change in Moscow's policy was, to say the least, embarrassing for the Jewish Communists in Palestine. They tried to explain why it was now Chamberlain and no longer Hitler who had to be fought, why the working class was no longer to resist Nazi Germany but was rather to resist Great Britain in her war against Nazi Germany. Thus, in its statement of October 1939, the executive committee of the Communist party declared:

This Hitler, against whom Chamberlain is now fighting, is no longer the same one who intended to fight against the Soviet Union. He has ceased to be Chamberlain's policeman and now has to do as Moscow tells him.[4]

The words 'Hitler' and 'Fascism' suddenly disappeared from Communist propaganda. When Jewish soldiers who had volunteered for war service were shipped by the British High Command to the war zone as a Jewish battalion, the Communist party addressed an appeal to them to realize that they would be used as imperialistic 'cannon fodder' in the service of the 'international finance oligarchy' to fight not against Hitler, but against the Soviet Union.[5]

And, after France had fallen and Great Britain stood alone in the war against Nazi Germany, the Communist party executive issued the following appeal to the Jewish workers of Palestine:

1. See Laqueur, *Communism and Nationalism in the Middle East*, pp. 100 and 104.
2. Leaflet of the Communist party, quoted in ibid., p. 104.
3. See Braunthal, *History of the International, 1914–1943*, pp. 493ff. and 504ff.
4. Leaflet of the Communist party, October 1939, quoted in Laqueur, *Communism and Nationalism in the Middle East*, p. 105.
5. *Kol Ha'am*, June 1940, quoted in ibid. *Kol Ha'am* is an Arab monthly of the Communist party.

Not a single soldier, not a single penny for imperialism! The Communist party declares in this critical hour that a Jewish army under the command of the traitorous Zionist gangsters and British imperialism stands in sharp antagonism with the essential interests of the Jewish masses in this country. . . . Show your opposition to supporting the war in every possible way![1]

But when Hitler finally attacked the Soviet Union in June 1941, the Communist party called on the Jewish workers to report for war service in the British army, now 'brothers-in-arms' of the 'heroic Red Army'. The party was again legalized and organized itself under the leadership of Meir Vilner (b. 1918) as president and Shmu'el Miqunis (b. 1903) as general secretary of the Jewish section, while Taufio Tubi (b. 1922) and Emil Habibi led the Arab section.

After the war, the question of Palestine's future became essential to the hundreds of thousands of Europe's Jews who had escaped extermination in the gas chambers of Hitler's concentration camps and now hoped for a home in Palestine. The question referred to the United Nations for decision was whether or not Palestine should be set up as an undivided Arab–Jewish state, or whether the country should be divided into two independent states of Arabs and Jews. The M.A.P.A.I. under Ben-Gurion's leadership rejected the idea of a joint state in which the Jews would inevitably be subjected to the rule of the Arab majority; it demanded the partition of Palestine and the setting up of a Jewish state. As the Arab nationalists protested vehemently against the idea of partition, so the Communist party advocated an undivided Arab–Jewish state.

To the surprise of the Communist party, however, the Soviet Union did not reject out of hand the idea of partitioning Palestine and setting up a Jewish state. When the U.N. General Assembly debated the question of Palestine's future on 15 May 1947, Andrei Gromyko, the Soviet delegate, pointed to the fact 'that no single state of Western Europe has been able to defend the elementary rights of the Jewish people and to protect them against the henchmen of Fascism'. Six million Jews had been murdered, he said, 'and hundreds of thousands of Jews are now wandering through Europe in search of a home'. It would be unreasonable, he declared, 'to deny the Jewish people the fulfilment of their endeavours to set up their own state'. A joint Jewish–Arab state would be desirable, but in view of the hostility existing between Arabs and Jews, which could not be expected to lead to peaceful co-existence, the partition of Palestine into two independent states— one Jewish and one Arab—would be the best solution.[2] Thus when, on 29 November 1947, the General Assembly of the United Nations finally resolved the question of Palestine's future the Soviet Union voted for the

1. Leaflet of the Communist party, July 1940, quoted in ibid., p. 106.
2. For the text of Gromyko's speech, see *Zionist Review*, 23 May 1947.

partition of Palestine and the setting up of a Jewish state. The Soviet Union was also the first government to recognize Israel *de jure* on 26 May 1948. (The United States had admittedly recognized it a few days earlier, but only *de facto*.)

'The recognition of Israel by the Soviet Union was a blow for the Communists, who had, from the foundation of their party, fought against Zionism.'[1] But without hesitation the party now changed its policy to harmonize with the Moscow 'line'; it had become a Zionist party. When on 15 May 1948 the British mandate forces withdrew from Palestine and the armies of Egypt, Jordan, Syria, Lebanon and Iraq attacked the state of Israel proclaimed the previous day, the party called on its members to participate actively in the Jewish war of defence. After the republic had consolidated its position, it took up the constitutional role of a Jewish–Arab party in opposition.

Its following among the workers organized in trade unions and *kibbutzim* remained relatively small. In the elections to the general assembly of the *Histadrut* in 1960, it received only 2·8 per cent of the votes cast compared to 86·3 per cent obtained by the three anti-Communist Socialist parties.[2]

Its share of workers' votes was greater in the general election to the *Knesset*. In the 1961 election it polled 4·1 per cent of the votes—a growth which can be explained by the Communists' position as the party representing Arab nationalism in Israel.

The Communist party has consistently tried to serve not only as an instrument of economic and social protest [for the Arabs], but also, and mainly, as the organ of protest against the real and imagined oppressions of this minority. . . . The Arab nationalists to a high degree see the Communist party as an organization which is able to support its feelings and hopes, and they are prepared to ignore the social and economic theories of Communism. This attitude has been influenced and encouraged by the penetration of the Near East by the Soviet Union.[3]

In the purely Arab districts, the Communists won 40 per cent of the votes.[4]

1. Czudnowski and Landau, *The Israeli Communist Party*, p. 8.
2. The M.A.P.A.I. received 55·4 per cent of the votes, the M.A.P.A.M., 7·6, and the *Achdut Ha'avoda*, 66 per cent; see Preuss, *The Labour Movement in Israel*, p. 228.
3. Czudnowski and Landau, *The Israeli Communist Party*, pp. 90–1. For the changes in Soviet policy and the policy of the Communist party of Palestine, see Scott D. Johnston, 'Communist Party Politics in Israel', in Robert K. Sakai (ed.), *Studies in Asia 1964* (Lincoln, 1964), pp. 105–20.
4. See Czudnowski and Landau, *The Israeli Communist Party*, p. 43. In the 1965 elections seven Arab delegates were elected by a poll of over 85 per cent of the Arab electorate: two each for the two Arab parties, the Co-operation and Fraternity party and the Progress and Development party. These four Arab delegates were allied to the Labour party in the *Knesset*. In the Communist group of four delegates, the Arabs had two representatives, and in the M.A.P.A.M. group of eight members, one delegate. The proportionate strength between non-Communist and Communist (Arab) members of the *Knesset* was five to two.

In 1967, however, the Communist party split over the Soviet Union's attitude to the Arab–Israeli war in June of that year. Its hostile policy towards Israel had begun to worry the consciences of some Communists before the war's outbreak. For how could a genuine Communist advocate with a clear conscience the policy of a Socialist state which had allied itself with the pseudo-Socialist but, in reality, military Fascist dictatorships of Egypt, Syria and Iraq against a genuine Social Democratic state; a policy which, moreover, rather than trying to seek a peaceful solution to the tragic conflict between the Arab states and Israel, incited the Arabs to wage war against the Jews, and also armed them to promote a war which had the objective, as the Arab leaders openly proclaimed, of destroying Israel and its Jewish population in a monstrous *pogrom*.

Even so, up to the outbreak of the war, the Israeli Communists continued to support Moscow's Arab policy with the arguments that it was frustrating the Western powers' imperialist plans for the Near East; that by arming the Arab states it intended nothing beyond establishing a balance of armed forces between the Arab states and Israel; and that since it wished to avoid war, its influence over the Arab countries would secure peace.

But the Arab leaders did not feel themselves in any way inhibited in their war plans by Moscow's policy; on the contrary, they felt themselves encouraged. And when in May 1967 President Nasser of Egypt blockaded the Straits of Tiran against Israeli shipping and concentrated 100,000 troops and 3,000 Russian tanks in the Sinai ready to attack Israel, what choice (and the Communists themselves threw up this question) was left to Israel in the face of this immediate threat to its existence as a state and to the lives of its population, except to defend itself by a counter-offensive? Moscow, however, condemned Israel in the Security Council of the United Nations as the aggressor.

This verdict was intolerable for a number of Israeli Communists. But still a majority of the party central committee identified itself with Moscow's attitude. In its resolution it condemned Israel's war as having the character of 'the continuation of the policy of the imperialistic powers (mainly, and above all, that of the United States of America)', a war of 'Israel's rulers against the anti-imperialist Arab states . . . to expand its territory and to force a settlement which would dissolve the rights of the people of Palestine'.[1]

This interpretation of the war's 'character' was rejected by a group in the party led by its general secretary, Shmu'el Miqunis, and Moshe Sneh. Following a bitter quarrel with the group led by Vilner and Tubi, they separated to form their own Communist party. It was subsequently branded

1. See Meir Vilner, 'The 16th Congress of the Communist Party of Israel', in *World Marxist Review*, May 1969, No. 3, p. 17. The congress, which met at the end of January 1969 in Tel Aviv, endorsed the central committee's resolution.

by the Moscow-orientated party as a 'nationalistic, anti-Communist group in the pay of a pro-imperialist, aggressive government policy'.[1]

While the unity of the Communist movement fell apart, the split in the Socialist movement in Israel was healed on 21 January 1968 at an extraordinary congress in Jerusalem in the presence of 2,500 delegates, the president of the Socialist International and representatives of Socialist parties in fourteen countries. Three parties—the M.A.P.A.I., *Achdut Ha'avoda* and the R.A.F.I. (*Reshimat Poale Israel*), a group which had splintered off from M.A.P.A.I. in 1965—combined together into the Labour party of Israel (*Mifleget Ha'avoda Hayisraelit*). The congress declared this event to be 'a turning point not only in the history of the Israeli Labour movement, but also in the annals of the Republic of Israel'.[2] The congress elected three general secretaries: Golda Meir of M.A.P.A.I. (she was succeeded by Pinhas Sapir), Israel Gatili of *Achdut Ha'avoda* and Shimon Peres of R.A.F.I.

The process of unifying the Socialist labour movement was completed a year later, on 19 January 1969, with the signing of an agreement of close alliance between the Labour party and the M.A.P.A.M.; the two parties reached accord on the basis of a joint programme with common lists for the electoral campaign and agreed to form a joint representation in the *Knesset*.

In the 1965 parliament the Labour party had been represented by fifty-three delegates out of 120—the M.A.P.A.M. by eight. By their alliance, the two parties together won an absolute majority in the *Knesset* with sixty-one delegates. Previously the M.A.P.A.I. had always been by far the strongest party in the *Knesset*. In none of the six parliamentary elections since the foundation of the Republic had it held less than forty seats out of 120 (in the 1959 elections it had won forty-seven). But as it had never held a majority, it had to work until then in coalition with the middle-class parties. The unification of the splintered Socialist movement had laid the foundation for a truly Socialist government in Israel.

1. See ibid.
2. See *Socialist International Information*, 10 February 1968; see the same issue for the 'Charter of the Labour Party of Israel', which formed the basis for unity.

17 · The Asian Socialist Conference

The emergence of Socialist parties in South and South-East Asia after the Second World War posed the question of establishing an international organization to serve as their common forum. Their rivals, the Communist parties—founded by and directed from Moscow, as earlier chapters have shown—were integrated within the Communist world movement with Moscow at its centre.

The Socialist parties in Asia, however, had not been created by the Socialist International, but had arisen out of their peoples' struggle for national freedom and independence against their domination by the European colonial powers. They had come into being through the initiative of individual Socialists and had developed in isolation both from their brother parties in Europe and from the Socialist International.

But the need for a common organization of the Asian parties had become critical. Some, such as the Socialist parties of Japan and India and the M.A.P.A.I. of Israel, did join the Socialist International. Yet, in the light of the particular problems confronting Asian Socialism, they all felt the necessity for a separate international organization, independent of the Socialist International though closely associated with it.

Such an organization was founded during a conference assembled in the town hall of the Burmese capital of Rangoon on 6–15 January 1953. It took as its title the Asian Socialist Conference.

The Socialist International, as its secretary recorded in his report to the third congress, considered this conference to be

the most momentous event in the contemporary history of international Socialism. It was the first time that representatives of Socialist parties from all parts of the vast Asian continent had met and, in spite of the great differences in their cultural and political background and traditions, they united in a common fraternity, based on common principles and a common approach to the great problems of policy.[1]

1. Julius Braunthal, *Report on Activities (1952–1953)*, submitted to the Third Congress of the Socialist International, Circular No. 90/53, p. 14.

The conference was attended by 177 delegates representing the Socialist parties of ten Asian countries. From India there were seventy-seven delegates, led by Jayaprakash Narayan and Asoka Mehta; from Japan thirty delegates, led by Suzuki and Matsuoka; from Indonesia a delegation of twenty-six, led by Soetan Sjahrir; and from Israel a smaller delegation, led by the foreign minister, Moshe Sharett, and the trade union leader, Reuven Barkatt. The Burmese Socialist party, which received the congress as its guest, was represented by a delegation of fifteen members led by the minister for defence, U Ba Swe, and the minister for industry, U Kyaw Nyein. Delegations were also sent by the Socialist party of Pakistan, the Pan-Malaysian Labour party and the Progressive Socialist party of the Lebanon. Present as observers were delegates from the Tunisian Neo-Destour party, the Algerian Nationalist party, the Nepali Congress, the African Congress of Uganda and the People's Congress against Imperialism. Guest delegates were sent by the Communist League of Yugoslavia led by the deputy prime minister, Milovan Djilas, and the deputy foreign secretary Alés Behler, as well as by the International Union of Socialist Youth and the Socialist International. The importance which the International attached to this congress was shown by the status of its delegates: Clement Attlee, leader of the British Labour party, who had as prime minister made such a historic contribution by granting independence to Burma as well as to India, Pakistan and Ceylon (he was received in Rangoon with special honours as the guest of the Burmese president), Guy Mollet, leader of the French Socialist party, and Kay Björk, international secretary of the Swedish Social Democratic party.

The founding of such an international organization had been a suggestion of the Socialist Party of India. Its general council had decided in August 1947 to take the initiative in calling a congress of Asian Socialist parties. In its declaration it stated:

The world Socialist movement has, until now, been an exclusively Western European movement. In this form its main aim has been the abolition of capitalism.

But if Democratic Socialism is to participate decisively in opposing totalitarian Communism by the creation of a Socialist order of society, it must attach no less importance to another task, namely the battle for the development of political power in the underdeveloped countries.[1]

The general secretary briefed Shrimati Kamaladevi and Ram Manohar Lohia to do the preliminary work before calling a world Socialist conference to take place in Bombay. But nearly five years were to pass before, in March 1952, a conference of the Socialist parties of India, Burma and Indonesia set up a committee to summon the congress, and a further six months went by before it met in Rangoon.

Meanwhile the Socialist International was endeavouring to achieve the

1. Socialist Party of India, *Report of the Sixth Annual Conference, Nasik 1948* (Bombay, 1948), p. 115.

closest possible relationship with the Socialist parties of Asia. Two of these parties—the Social Democratic party of Japan and the M.A.P.A.I. of Israel—were already full members, and the Socialist party of India was an advisory member of the Socialist International.

At first the Socialist International had sought to formulate an ideological basis for a world-wide International. Its founding congress in Frankfurt in 1951, at which the Socialist parties of Japan and India were represented, had, as already described, defined a declaration of the principles of democratic Socialism. The basic ideas of these were incorporated into a declaration of principles by the congress of the Socialist parties of Asia.[1] Its subsequent congress in Milan in 1952, at which the Socialist parties of Burma, India, Indonesia, Israel and Japan had been represented, formulated a declaration of principles for Socialist policy towards underdeveloped countries.[2] This congress had also included in its debate a memorandum on the relationship of the Socialist International towards the Socialist movement outside Europe submitted by Morgan Phillips, president of the International. This stated at the beginning:

> The Socialist International must avoid the danger of becoming merely a 'Western' or 'White' International. All the parties at present members of or associated with the Socialist International are European or of European derivation, with the exception of the Japanese Socialist Democratic party and the Indian Socialist party.

The memorandum proposed that the International should:

> (a) encourage and assist the development of democratic Socialist organizations in countries where they do not exist;
> (b) draw into the International as many of the existing parties as are eligible.[3]

The congress raised the places on the bureau of the International from ten to twelve, elected Japan, Israel and Canada to represent non-European parties and reserved one seat on the bureau for a further Asian party.

The organization which emerged from the conference in Rangoon—the Asian Socialist Conference (A.S.C.)—was, as its president, U Ba Swe, stated in his opening speech, not intended in any sense to be an Asian International. 'While it has never been the intention of the sponsors of this conference to establish a rival International,' he said, 'they feel that there should be a machinery for closer contact and co-operation among Asian parties and also for executing some of the resolutions that might be passed by this conference.'[4]

1. For the debate of the declaration of principles at the Frankfurt Congress, see page 199; for its text, see Appendix Two, page 531.
2. For the discussion of this declaration, see page 210; for its text, see Appendix Four, page 538.
3. Braunthal, *Report on Activities 1952–53*, Socialist International, Circular No. 90/53, p. 17.
4. Quoted in ibid., p. 20.

The inaugural document of the A.S.C. stated:

1. The organization of Asian socialist parties will be a democratic and voluntary association of Socialist parties which seek to establish Socialism as formulated in the 'Principles and Objectives of Socialism'.
2. The purpose of the organization will be:
   (a) to strengthen relations between the Asian Socialist parties;
   (b) to co-ordinate their political attitudes by consent;
   (c) to establish closer relations with the Socialist parties all over the world; and
   (d) to establish liaison with the Socialist International.[1]

During the debate at the founding congress of the A.S.C. about its relations with the Socialist International, two points were given special emphasis: first, its independence of the Socialist International, but secondly, the closest possible co-operation between the two organizations.

The points were dealt with through an agreement by which both organizations assumed the right of representation at one another's congresses, conferences and meetings of their bureaux with a view to the close co-ordination of one another's political actions.

The Rangoon conference elected U Ba Swe as chairman, Soerjokoesoemo Wijono (Indonesia) as general secretary, Madhav Gokhale (India), Roo Watanabe (Japan) and U Hla Aung (Burma) as secretaries, and chose Rangoon to be the seat of the Secretariat.

The main achievement of the congress during its nine days of deliberations was to formulate the basic principles and objectives of the Socialist parties of Asia as well as laying down guide-lines for agrarian policy and policy for economic and political development in its member countries—a document nineteen pages long. It is one of the key documents in the intellectual history of Socialism, since for the first time it developed the basic ideas of a Socialist ideology in nations that were in a semi-feudal pre-capitalist stage of society and in transition towards more highly developed social forms.

The declaration of principles outlines briefly the origins of modern Socialism as a protest against capitalism and the capitalist order of society and the split of the Socialist movement in two—Communism and democratic Socialism. It differentiates sharply between democratic Socialism and Communism.

The essence of democratic Socialism [it declared] is the striving to attain greater happiness, justice and dignity, and the fullest possible chance of self-expression for the human being. In seeking to abolish exploitation of class by class and of man by man, Socialism recognizes man both as an integral part of a class or group and as a single human individual. It therefore avoids totalitarian forms of government and methods of coercion.

1. For the structure of the organization, see *Resolutions of the First Asian Socialist Conference, Rangoon 1953* (Rangoon, 1954), pp. 1–2.

Therefore the declaration rejected Communism.

Communism, as practised today in its totalitarian form in the Soviet Union and its satellites, has degenerated into a régime which [allows] the complete subordination of the individual and the group to the centralized power of the leadership of the ruling party. Under the Soviet system, state power imposes absolute domination and exacts blind obedience; man is expected to give up his freedom and individuality, degrading himself to an abstract part of an all-powerful state in which only one will prevails.

Communism therefore stands for the negation of all the concepts of freedom, individual self-expression and genuine mass-responsibility which are the breath of democratic Socialism.

Like the Frankfurt declaration of the Socialist International, the declaration by the Asian Socialist Conference represents Socialism as a social and economic as well as a humanitarian concept.

While striving to build a new society on higher economic productivity and social justice, Socialism is dedicated to the creation of a new and richer culture and the shaping of a new and better form of life. Social and economic progress have a significance only to the extent that they make for greater human happiness. Hence it is the ambition of Socialism to provide a higher satisfaction of man's spiritual needs.

Socialism opposes feudalism and capitalism, whether conservative or liberal, because they are contrary to human justice; it opposes totalitarianism, whether Fascist or Communist, because it is degrading. Socialism strives to secure the sharing of each individual in the cultural heritage and spiritual progress of mankind.[1]

In all the Asian countries subjected to European rule, the Socialist parties, as earlier chapters have shown, fought in alliance with the nationalist parties for the independence of their countries; they were the standard-bearers of the national idea. The declaration of principles by the A.S.C. stressed this attitude. 'Nationalism in the colonial and so-called underdeveloped countries,' it states, 'has, in common with Socialism, a passionate devotion to the cause of freedom and justice. Although the paths of these two movements may diverge after the gaining of independence, Socialist and Nationalists remain brothers-at-arms as long as the struggle for independence lasts.'

But how may nationalism be brought into line with the concept of internationalism, which is one of the fundamental principles of Socialism? This question was put to the debate during a seminar at the congress addressed by Soetan Sjahrir.

Sjahrir justified the nationalism of Asian Socialists as an ideology in the struggle for their people's liberation from suppression and exploitation by foreign countries. And as this struggle represented a struggle against the rule of foreign capital, it was also a class struggle. The struggle to achieve national self-determination, which derived its justification from the theory of human

1. For the full text of the declaration, see *Resolutions of the First Asian Socialist Conference*, pp. 3–21, and Appendix Five, page 543.

rights and the sovereignty of the people, revealed Asian nationalism as a struggle for democracy. The struggle against the rule of foreign capital had been led by Asian nationalism with the tenets of anti-capitalism and anti-imperialism—'in other words', Sjahrir said, 'with the weapons of Socialism'.

Therefore, Sjahrir explained, Asian nationalism carried 'within itself the seeds of social renaissance, for it opposes the conditions under which people live under colonial rule—feudalism and colonial autocracy'.[1]

The nationalism of the Asian Socialists was, therefore, compatible with the principles of Socialist internationalism so long as it served as a weapon in the struggle for the political and social emancipation of the Asian peoples. But after the attainment of freedom in Asia, Sjahrir emphasized, nationalism will run the danger of turning into an ideological weapon of political and social reaction, of degenerating into chauvinism—national egotism, self-glorification and intolerance—as had been the case with many European countries.

The A.S.C. showed its avowal of Socialist internationalism by a specific declaration of solidarity with the freedom struggles of colonial peoples. 'Socialists,' its declaration stated, 'share with all fighters for national liberty the passionate desire for the assertion of human rights and for personal and collective freedom; they therefore associate themselves with the struggle against colonial, as any other, oppression'.

To co-ordinate the actions of individual parties against colonialism, the bureau of the A.S.C. set up an Anti-Colonial Bureau at its meeting in Hyderabad in August 1953, electing U Kyaw Nyein as chairman and Jim Markham, a representative of the Convention People's party of the Gold Coast, as secretary. It sent U Hla Aung to Central Africa, Kenya and Uganda on a mission to prepare an All-African Conference and in July 1953 a delegation, led by its general secretary, S. Wijono, to the Stockholm congress of the Socialist International, on whose initiative was passed a resolution on the current problems of colonialism.[2]

The second congress of the A.S.C. assembled in Bombay under the chairmanship of U Ba Swe—who had, meanwhile, become prime minister of Burma —at the beginning of November 1956. The number of affiliated parties had increased since the first congress. It now embraced the following parties:

1. Soetan Sjahrir, *Nationalism and Internationalism* (Rangoon, 1953), p. 5. This booklet, published by the A.S.C., is a transcript of Sjahrir's address to the seminar of the A.S.C. and the debate which followed.

2. For the resolution, see *Report of the Third Congress of the Socialist International, Stockholm 1953*, Circular No. 115/53, p. 138. For an account of A.S.C. activity, see *Three Years of the Asian Socialist Conference* (Bombay, 1956).

Socialist Party of Burma
Praja Socialist Party of India
Partai Socialis Indonesia
Social Democratic Party of Japan
Malayan Labour Party
Vietnam Socialist Party
Sri Lanka Freedom Party
Pakistan Socialist Party
Nepali Congress
Israel Socialist Labour Party (M.A.P.A.I.)
Progressive Socialist Party of Lebanon.

And the following 'fraternal organizations':

The Socialist International
The International Union of Socialist Youth
The Socialist Alliance of the Working People of Yugoslavia.

The congress met during an international crisis. A few days before it assembled, on 2 November, Britain and France undertook their military intervention in Egypt to occupy the Suez Canal which had been nationalized by Nasser's government in July in breach of the agreement concerning the canal's administration. Simultaneously, Israeli troops had entered Sinai to counter the attacks by Egyptian guerrillas (*fedayeen*) by destroying their military positions. On 23 October the revolution against the Soviet dictatorship broke out in Hungary, to be put down by an invasion of the Russian army on 4 November.[1]

These events dominated the congress. It condemned the 'cynical intervention' of Britain and France in Egypt as well as their attempt to seize the Suez Canal. It recognized the right of the Egyptian government to nationalize the Suez Canal, but it demanded that the canal, which Egypt had blockaded against Israeli shipping, should remain open 'as an international waterway for all nations without exception'.

But opinion in the A.S.C. was not so unanimous towards the intervention of Israeli troops in Sinai. Mobarak Sagher in the name of the Pakistani delegation, and Vladimir Bakarić in the name of the Yugoslav delegation, demanded that a sharp, uncompromising condemnation of Israel should be delivered, even though the action had been undertaken by a Socialist government led by M.A.P.A.I. The Pakistanis were prompted in their feelings by an Islamic solidarity with the Arabs, and the Yugoslavs wanted to show their solidarity with the Soviet Union which supported Egypt's position against Israel. During the debate Moshe Sharett, the leader of the Israeli delegation, justified Israel's action on the grounds that the perpetual armed

1. See page 418.

raids of the *fedayeen* into Israel had been backed by the Egyptian government and that it now blockaded the Suez Canal and the Straits of Tiran to Israeli shipping.

As it happened, the resolution passed by the congress omitted 'to condemn' Israel, but it did show its disapproval of the Israeli action, 'despite the events that had led up to the occupation of Egyptian territory by Israeli troops'; it appealed to the government of Israel to withdraw its forces.[1]

The congress was, however, unanimous in its condemnation of the Russian invasion against the revolution in Hungary. It acclaimed 'the heroic rising' of the Hungarian people in their fight for freedom, and stated:

The congress is deeply concerned by the armed intervention of Soviet forces against Hungary's freedom. It demands the withdrawal of these troops and appeals to the United Nations to make its authority felt against this armed intervention.

Under the impact of the international crisis, which dominated the debate in congress, the A.S.C. reaffirmed its attitude towards the United Nations as an indispensable instrument for averting the danger of a new war. This view had been formulated in its declaration of the principles and objectives of Socialism adopted by the inaugural congress in Rangoon, which stated:

The Socialists of Asia look upon the principles of the United Nations Charter as holding out the best hope for the maintenance of peace in the world and as capable of providing a basis for peace as firm as is possible in the present stage of the development of mankind.

The Bombay congress renewed its declaration of support for the United Nations. It stated in its resolution:

The A.S.C. affirms the principles of the United Nations and its declaration of universal human rights. . . . It emphasizes firmly its confidence in a friendly solution to conflicts between nations and on questions of territorial integrity and the independence of states.

The resolution further demanded China's admittance into the United

---

1. For the wording of the resolution, see *Socialist International Information*, 17 November 1956. The General Council of the Socialist International, meeting at the end of November 1956 in Copenhagen, declared in its resolution that 'while recognizing the provocation suffered by Israel . . . [it] deeply regrets the recent resort to armed force in the Middle East, and in particular the invasion of Egypt by Great Britain and France in breach of the Charter of the United Nations'. The resolution demanded, among other things, 'the unconditional withdrawal of British, French and Israeli forces from Egyptian territories'; it appealed to the United Nations to prevent Arab attacks and guerrilla battles in the border districts of Egypt and Israel by using its emergency troops and to 'press if possible, through direct negotiations, for a Middle East settlement which will cover the ending of the state of war [of the Arab States against Israel] and the economic blockade of Israel; mutually agreed frontier adjustments; the solution of the problem of Arab refugees'. The resolution demanded 'free passage for Israeli ships both through the Suez Canal and the Gulf of Aqaba and effective guarantees both for Israel and the Arab states against aggression from any quarter'. For the text of the resolution, see *Socialist International Information*, 8 December 1956.

Nations, and stated its support for the reunification of Korea on the basis of free elections and for the reunification of Vietnam by friendly methods'.[1]

The congress confirmed that Rangoon was to be the seat of the A.S.C. secretariat, and that U Ba Swe was to be chairman. It also elected Prem Bhasin, a representative of the *Praja* Socialist party of India, to be general secretary, with U Hla Aung as his deputy.

But the congress was in fact to be the last in the history of the Asian Socialist Conference.[2] The organization was never formally dissolved, but it became paralysed by internal crises in a number of its member parties, and, as has been described in earlier chapters, by the suppression of others; its activities ceased early in 1960.

Its importance in the history of the International had been its inspiration of young, budding parties, often existing in still pre-capitalist, semi-feudal countries and preoccupied with vaguely Socialist and Communist views, by the ideology of democratic Socialism; and by awakening them to the awareness of the brotherly solidarity which unites them with Socialists throughout the rest of the world.

1. For the text of the resolution, see *Socialist International Information*, 22 December 1956.
2. The last conference of the bureau of the A.S.C. met at the end of March 1958 in Kathmandu, Nepal. The Socialist International was represented by Reuven Barkatt.

PART FOUR

The Moral Crisis of Communism

18 · Yugoslavia's Revolt against Moscow's Hegemony

Stalin had founded the Cominform as one of his instruments to secure the hegemony of the Soviet Union over the states which had fallen under its sphere of influence. The role of the Russian Communist party in leading the international Communist movement had itself seemed to be undisputed even before the founding of the Cominform. It was based on the same axiom that Dimitrov reformulated in December 1948:

> All Communist parties throughout the world must form a single front under the direction of the most powerful and experienced Communist party, that of Lenin and Stalin. All Communist parties have a universally recognized leader and teacher—Comrade Stalin.[1]

Yet after the dissolution of the Communist International[2] in May 1943 there was no longer any international organization by which Moscow could bring to bear its direct authority over the leadership of foreign Communist parties. Such an organization was, however, created in September 1947 in the Cominform. One of the motives behind its foundation, as soon became clear, was to bring back under control one party in particular, the Communist party of Yugoslavia, whose leader, while publicly affirming his loyalty to Stalin, had in practice come into conflict with him.

Moscow's right to control those states which fell within the Russian sphere of influence was, for Stalin, beyond question. He regarded them not as sovereign countries, simply allied to the Soviet Union by formal agreements, but as Russian satellite states under direct Kremlin rule; and he saw the Communist leaders who were in control, not as representatives of their country and party, but merely as governors. He had been responsible for installing them in each country—with the exception of Yugoslavia—and dismissing them if they failed in their allotted role.

1. Quoted in the declaration of the COMISCO Secretariat of 20 December 1949. This document is without a circular number; it is preserved in the Archives of the Socialist International in the International Institute for Social History, Amsterdam.
2. See Braunthal, *History of the International, 1914–1943*, pp. 528–30.

As Gomulka remarked after Stalin's death, 'In the bloc of Socialist states [he had stood] at the summit of a hierarchy of flattery. All those under him bowed their heads before him. It was not only leading personalities in the Communist Party of Russia and the Soviet Union who scraped and bowed, but also the Communist party leaders in the other countries of the Socialist camp.'[1]

Thus Stalin believed that he would have no problem in dethroning Tito, leader of the Communist party of Yugoslavia, marshal and prime minister, when he declined to submit to his leadership. 'One hint with the little finger,' he remarked to Khrushchev, 'and there will be no Tito. He will fall.'[2]

Josip Broz Tito (b. 1892), son of a Croatian peasant, had, until his break with Stalin, been unquestionably loyal to him as a strict and orthodox Communist. In 1920 he had returned from Russia, where he had been taken as a prisoner-of-war after fighting as a soldier of the Austro–Hungarian army, as a convinced Communist, and his work in the Communist party thereafter filled his life. When, in 1928, he was accused of disseminating Communist propaganda, he made a challenging speech in defence of his party's principles and its loyalty to Moscow; he received a sentence of five years in prison. After his release in 1934, he was sent to Moscow to the Secretariat of the Communist International and on his return to Yugoslavia in 1937 he became general secretary of the party, which was then shattered by internal strife and government persecution.[3]

Tito had led his party in strict compliance with Moscow's instructions. Those were the days of the 'Great Purge' of real or imaginary anti-Stalinists in the Communist movement. Its victims in Russia in 1937–8, according to Tito himself, included 'over a hundred' Yugoslav Communist émigrés; they had disappeared into the prisons never to be seen again.[4] After his return, Tito's most urgent duty under orders from the Communist International had been a 'thorough purging' of the Yugoslavian party. As he later admitted, he had devoted himself to this work with complete devotion. His 'total occupation' during 1938–9 had been, as he recorded, 'purging the party of suspicious elements—of a good few provocateurs infiltrated into the Com-

1. Speech at the Eighth Party Congress of the Central Committee of the Communist Party of Poland (United Workers' party) in Paul E. Zinner (ed.), *National Communism and Popular Revolt in Eastern Europe. A Selection of Documents on Events in Poland and Hungary, February–November 1956* (New York, 1956), p. 228.
2. See Khrushchev's speech to the Twentieth Congress of the Communist Party of the Soviet Union on 25 February 1956, in *The Dethronement of Stalin* (London, 1956), p. 25.
3. For the history of the rise and development of the party up till the outbreak of the Second World War, see Ivan Avakumovic, *History of the Communist Party of Yugoslavia* (Aberdeen, 1964) vol. I; for Tito's rise, see Vladimir Dedijer, *Tito Speaks. His Self-Portrait and Struggle with Stalin* (London, 1953), pp. 36–128; Phyllis Auty, *Tito: A Biography* (London, 1970).
4. See Avakumovic, *History of the Communist Party of Yugoslavia*, p. 127.

munist party of Yugoslavia by the police'; the standard accusation used to remove anti-Stalinists from the Communist movement. Tito had proved his reliability in Stalin's service.

And he continued to do so throughout the first phase of the war. He did not hesitate for a moment to call off the fight against Hitler, in which he had led an anti-Fascist people's front up till the signing of the Hitler–Stalin pact. The pact was hailed by him as an instrument for peace, and the Russian invasion of Poland as an act of 'the liberation of comrades' by Russia, while the 'British and French imperialists' were accused of having attacked Germany so as 'to safeguard their world rule and the exploitation of the colonial and semi-colonial nations without competition by other imperialist states'. It was now, the Yugoslav Communists declared, 'the English financial oligarchy, supported by the Social Democratic traitors, Attlee, Citrine and Co., which is forcing the British people to continue a bloody war for the sole purpose of safeguarding the suppression and exploitation of colonial peoples'.[1]

Tito came into conflict with Stalin only in the course of the guerrilla war which he led against the German forces of occupation in Yugoslavia. The history of this war, which became a national epic, is touched on here only as it relates to the conflict between Stalin and Tito.[2]

It began with the German invasion of Yugoslavia on 6 April 1941, ten weeks before Hitler's attack on the Soviet Union. Belgrade was bombarded, the Yugoslav army routed by the German troops entering from Hungary, Bulgaria and Romania. King Peter II and his administration fled, leaving the country to be dismembered. Parts of Slovenia were annexed by Hitler, Dalmatia by Mussolini; Croatia, with Bosnia and Herzegovina, fell under the régime of the Croatian Fascist *Ustaši* leader, Ante Pavelić, and was declared to be an independent state; Serbia was subjected to the rule of the German occupation force.

Already by the middle of May, the *Chetniks*, or Serbian Home guards, had risen against the Germans under the leadership of Colonel Draža Mihailović and within a few weeks had gained control of the Serbian country-side, with the exception of the larger towns and the main roads. It was not until after Hitler attacked Russia that Tito entered the fight against the German occupation forces,[3] organizing guerrilla bands and co-operating with Mihailović.

1. *Communist*, 6 April 1940, quoted in ibid., pp. 175–6.
2. For the history of the guerrilla war, see F. W. D. Deakin, *The Embattled Mountain* Oxford, 1971); Stephen Clissold, *Whirlwind, An Account of Marshal Tito's Rise to Power* (London, 1949); Dedijer, *Tito Speaks*, pp. 129–246; Mosa Pijade, *La Fable de l'aide soviétique à l'insurrection nationale yougoslave* (Paris, 1950); Fitzroy Maclean, *Eastern Approaches* (London, 1949).
3. 'We cannot stand idly by,' the party's manifesto stated, 'while the precious blood of the heroic peoples of Soviet Russia is being spilt'—quoted in Clissold, *Whirlwind*, p. 31.

But the alliance between the two men was to break apart on their ideological and organizational conflicts after only a few months. When in November the Germans began their counter-offensive against the guerrillas and in a terrible carnage destroyed the Serbian resistance movement, Tito withdrew his partisans by a 'long march', fighting the Germans and Italians as they went, through Montenegro and Eastern Bosnia into the mountain districts of North Bosnia, there to reorganize his battle forces. In the summer of 1942 he had hardly more than 7,000 men.[1]

There now existed two resistance movements: the official one of the *Chetniks*, recognized by the Allies and commanded by Draža Mihailović, who had in January 1942 been promoted by the Yugoslav government-in-exile in London to the rank of general and made minister of war; and the Communist partisans under Tito. Mihailović, a Serbian nationalist like his *Chetniks*, who were largely drawn from the conservative farmer class, considered the Communists to be a greater threat to Serbia than the Germans. After the defeat of the resistance movement at the end of 1941, he called off his fight against the Germans and shortly afterwards *Chetnik* detachments began to operate side by side with German and Italian troops against the Communist partisans. Mihailović had transformed Yugoslavia's national fight for freedom into a civil war between the *Chetniks* and the Communist partisans. Tito denounced Mihailović and his *Chetniks*, not without reason, as national traitors, and his appeal to patriotism swelled the ranks of the partisans.[2]

Of even more importance to the rapid growth of the partisan movement was the religious-national civil war which broke out between Croatian and Serbian nationalists even before the civil war erupted between the Communists and their enemies. What divided these two peoples was not language —the common language was Serbo-Croatian—but religion. The Croats were Catholics, the Serbs Greek Orthodox Christians or Mohammedans. After being set up by Hitler as dictator of a Croatia enlarged by Bosnia and Herzegovina, Pavelić was determined either to change the Greek Orthodox and Mohammedan Serbs of Bosnia and Herzegovina into Croats by 'converting' them to Roman Catholicism, or else to exterminate them. *Ustaši* detachments appeared in Serbian villages in Bosnia and Herzegovina, assembled their inhabitants in the church and demanded their immediate conversion to the Roman faith. If they refused—as they almost always did—

1. See R. V. Burks, *Die Dynamik des Kommunismus in Osteuropa* (Hanover, 1969), p. 155.
2. 'It is clear from information received by the War Office,' the British General Staff reported on 6 June 1943, 'that the *Chetniks* are hopelessly compromised by their relationship with the Axis forces in Herzegovina and Montenegro. In recent battles in this district it has been the well-organized Partisans [of Tito] and not the *Chetniks* who have held down the Axis forces'—quoted in Winston S. Churchill, *The Second World War*, vol. v: *Closing the Ring* (London, 1952), p. 410.

the church doors were locked and the building with the people inside, men, women and children, was burnt down.

Immediately these massacres began in north-west Bosnia, the Serbs rose against the Croats in a desperate war of vengeance, while thousands of Serbian peasants, out of fear of the *Ustaŝhi*, on the one hand, and Croatian peasants, out of fear of the *Chetniks*, on the other, fled from their villages to join the Communist partisans in the mountains.

The Communist partisans fought against the *Chetniks'* Serbian nationalism as well as against the *Ustaŝhi's* Croatian separatist movement. While the *Chetniks* fought to win control of a future Yugoslavia, and the *Ustaŝhi*, in alliance with the Germans and Italians, were defending the Great Croatian state proclaimed by Hitler and Mussolini, it was the Communist partisans who sought a united Yugoslavia on the basis of the equality of all its peoples. They therefore became the true bearers of Yugoslav nationalism.

It was Tito's historical achievement to place the idea of a united Yugoslavia on a supra-national basis as the war's objective. On 26 November 1942, an assembly of partisan divisional commanders which he had summoned to Bihać, his headquarters in Western Bosnia, founded an 'Anti-Fascist National Council for the Liberation of Yugoslavia' (*Antifaŝisticko Vjeĉe Narodnog Oslobodjenja Jugoslavije*, abbreviated to A.V.N.O.J.), which at its second meeting, at Jajce on 29 November 1943, constituted itself as the provisional government and proclaimed Yugoslavia's unity on a supra-national basis:

1. The people of Yugoslavia do not recognize and have never recognized the partition of Yugoslavia by the Fascist imperialists, but have shown in their mutual fight their determination to remain united within Yugoslavia.
2. In order to achieve the principle of sovereignty for the Yugoslav nation, and in order that Yugoslavia should become a genuine home for all its peoples and no longer an arena for the machinations of reactionary influences, Yugoslavia will be founded upon federal principles, safeguarding equality for all the nations of Serbia, Croatia, Slovenia, Montenegro, Bosnia, and Herzegovina.[1]

The concept of overcoming separation and the mutual hatred among the various populations by a Yugoslavian nationalism gave the resistance movement an ideology which inspired the great mass of the people, especially the student youth, who flocked to enter the partisan camp. 'The force which swung the balance in favour of the Partisans, was the mobilization of the people on a supra-ethnical basis . . .'.[2] The partisan army, which, as we have seen, numbered barely 7,000 in the summer of 1942, could by September 1943,

---

1. Quoted in Burks, *Die Dynamik des Kommunismus in Osteuropa* (Hanover, 1969), p. 133.
2. Chalmers A. Johnson, *Peasant Nationalism and Communist Power: The Emergence of the Revolutionary China 1937–1945* (Stanford, 1962), p. 171. This study of the Communist guerrilla movement in China makes a comparison with the guerrilla campaign of the Communists in Yugoslavia. See also Burks, *Die Dynamik des Kommunismus in Osteuropa*, pp. 230–2.

according to Churchill's statement, count on 200,000 men, who 'had within a few weeks disarmed six Italian divisions'.[1]

And a few months later, on 22 February 1944, he reported in a speech to the House of Commons that Tito's partisans had undertaken 'offensives on a large scale against the Germans and had inflicted heavy losses on the enemy'. 'The partisan movement,' he continued, 'has quickly overtaken the fighting forces of General Mihailović in its numbers . . . and Marshal Tito has at present assembled about him over a quarter of a million men . . . organized into several divisions and corps.'[2]

But Tito had already clashed with Stalin over the very question of setting up an official resistance movement independent of the *Chetniks*. Like Britain, the Soviet Union was allied to the Yugoslav government-in-exile and had therefore recognized Mihailović's *Chetniks* as the only Allied army. Stalin had raised no objections to the formation of Communist partisan groups, but had insisted that they should be integrated with the *Chetniks* under Mihailović's command. Since Tito rejected this condition, Stalin denied the partisans the moral and material support of the Soviet Union, even though Tito had kept him fully informed of the fact that, by the end of 1941, the *Chetniks* had not only ceased to fight the Germans and Italians but were actually in league with them in fighting the Communist partisans. Mihailović, who had betrayed the Allied cause, was celebrated in the Soviet press as a national hero,[3] while Tito's partisan army received no mention whatsoever. Furthermore, in November 1942, the Soviet government declared its readiness to supply the *Chetniks* with arms, as well as to dispatch a military mission to Draža Mihailović.[4]

In the desperate position in which the partisans found themselves, Tito had sent repeated pleas for help to Moscow. The first appeal had gone out on 17 February 1942. After six weeks of silence, instead of arms he received a telegram advising him to collect arms from the enemy, for, it stated, the 'technical difficulty' in dropping arms from the air was so 'formidable', that 'it could not be anticipated that this difficulty would be overcome in the near future'. And when, two months later, on 23 April, Tito again asked Moscow by telegram whether he could now 'soon hope for arms', Stalin replied that 'you can, unfortunately, expect neither ammunition nor automatic arms from us shortly'.[5]

In April 1943, Tito's partisan army had fought its way southwards through Croatia and across the Neretva river in Herzegovina. The Germans now mounted a major offensive against it in an attempt to encircle and finally destroy it once and for all. Three German divisions, which included battle-

---

1. Churchill, *Closing the Ring*, p. 412.   2. ibid., pp. 420–1.
3. See Dedijer, *Tito Speaks*, pp. 170–1.   4. See ibid., pp. 179–80.
5. For the text of these telegrams, see ibid., pp. 175–7.

hardened alpine troops, attacked the partisan force from the north, and another German division from the east; and three Italian divisions with *Chetnik* and *Ustaši* units attacked them from the west.

There were under Tito's command no more than three ill-equipped and hungry divisions to resist the major assault—and these were hampered by having to care for about 3,000 sick and wounded from earlier battles. The position of the partisans had indeed become critical. Against the overwhelming strength of their enemies, they put up a desperate struggle to break through the ring of steel, subjected to continual bombardment from the air and having to fight their way by night through terrain that appeared impassable. Yet, in the nick of time and during one of the most heroic battles of the war, they succeeded in breaking out of the ring by forcing the gorge of the Sutjeska river with two divisions, while the greater part of the rear-guard division perished together with most of the wounded in its care.[1]

In this desperate situation, Tito once more appealed to Stalin for help. 'I must again ask you,' his telegram said, 'whether it is really impossible to send us any kind of support. Hundreds of thousands of refugees are threatened by starvation. Is it really impossible to help us after twenty months without the slightest material help from any source?'

Moscow's reply was: 'Unfortunately we have, until now, been unable to find a satisfactory solution to the problems raised by insurmountable technical difficulties.'[2]

It was only after the Tehran Conference at the end of November 1943 when the Allies—on the prompting of Churchill, not of Stalin—recognized the partisan army, which had meanwhile been retitled the 'National Liberation Army' by A.V.N.O.J. in recognition of its military achievement as an allied army—that it was supported by the Soviet Union as well as by Britain.

Yet hardly had this conflict between Tito and Stalin been healed, than another broke out. While the Tehran Conference was in progress, A.V.N.O.J. had, as we saw, met in Jajce to constitute itself as the provisional government, with the 'sole authority to represent the Yugoslav nation', revoking the rights of the government-in-exile and forbidding King Peter II to return to Yugoslavia.

Tito had not told Stalin of this plan, obviously fearing that he would raise objections. Stalin was taken by surprise. The reaction from Moscow was, as Tito recorded in his memoirs, 'furious; the action was condemned as "a knife in the back of the Soviet Union"'.[3] It placed Stalin as much as Churchill in a position of no small embarrassment, for the Yugoslav

1. For a most impressive eyewitness account of this battle, see Deakin, *The Embattled Mountain*. The author, then a captain in the British army, leader of the first British military mission to Tito, was parachuted into the mountains of Herzegovina in the middle of the battle in May 1943.
2. For the texts of these telegrams, see Dedijer, *Tito Speaks*, pp. 190–1.
3. Quoted in ibid., p. 266.

government-in-exile of King Peter was recognized as an ally by the governments of Britain and the Soviet Union. And Churchill, to whom Stalin had granted a 50 per cent influence in Yugoslavia,[1] disliked the idea of sacrificing the king and even more the prospect of Yugoslavia under Communist rule. Even as later in Greece he supported the king and his right-wing partisans to prevent a Communist ascendancy in that country, so he supported Mihailović's partisans to prevent the ascendancy of the Communists in Yugoslavia. In Greece, Churchill was to be able to decide the course of the struggle between the anti-Communist royalists and the Communist republicans by the deployment of British troops.[2] But no British military intervention was feasible in Yugoslavia, simply because British troops could not be landed there. And since Britain could not dispatch an army to Yugoslavia, the defeat of the strong German and Italian forces in that country could only be expected from the Communist partisans.

Churchill did indeed become convinced by the reports he received from the British mission dispatched to Mihailović and Tito that the king could not be retained, and even the British Embassy in the residence of Peter II in Cairo had telegraphed to London as early as 25 December 1943: '. . . The partisans will be the rulers of Yugoslavia. They are for us of such military value that we, subordinating political to military considerations, must give them our fullest support. It is highly doubtful whether we can continue to consider the monarchy as a unifying element.'[3]

Thus, under pressure from Churchill, King Peter was forced to dismiss Mihailović as his minister of war and Božidar Purić as his prime minister, and to nominate Ivan Subasić, who had been governor of Croatia before the German occupation, as a prime minister for the provisional government acceptable to Tito.

While both conflicts were finally resolved and the Soviet Union as well as Britain came to support the partisan army with arms deliveries, Stalin never forgot that Tito had dared to disobey him. When Tito visited Stalin in Moscow in September 1944 for the first meeting he had with him, his reception was, he recorded in his memoirs, 'very cold'. When Stalin had reproved him for forming a provisional government, he had then replied simply by telegram: 'If you cannot send us support, at least do not hinder us!'[4] This was not the manner expected by Stalin from Communists, even from those in the highest positions.[5]

When Tito met Stalin in Moscow, the Red Army, having occupied Bulgaria,[6] was already standing on the borders of Yugoslavia during its

1. See page 93.   2. See page 108.
3. Quoted in Churchill, *Closing the Ring*, p. 414.
4. Quoted in Dedijer, *Tito Speaks*, p. 233.
5. In a later conversation with Tito, Dimitrov described to him how Stalin, when he received Tito's telegram, had 'stamped his feet in rage'—quoted in ibid.
6. See page 117.

advance into Hungary. Tito was determined to prevent any occupation of Yugoslavia. Through the Soviet High Command Stalin had requested, 'in the interests of joint action against German and Hungarian troops in Hungary', as TASS reported on 29 September 1944, 'to allow the temporary passage of Soviet troops across Yugoslav territory at the borders with Hungary'. Tito granted this request only on condition that the Soviet troops should 'leave the civil administration of A.V.N.O.J. alone' and 'that they withdraw after the fulfilment of their tasks'.[1]

On 7 December 1944 the Red Army, under the command of Marshal Malinovsky, crossed the Danube. And, on the following day, the partisan army was already advancing against Belgrade. In the battle for the city, which dragged on for days, as well as in the subsequent fighting in Croatia, the partisan army received the support of Soviet troops. But it was only with a general offensive by the Yugoslav army, starting on 20 March 1945 and ending in victory on 15 May, that Yugoslavia was finally liberated.[2]

This victory was of the utmost importance for Tito's position *vis-à-vis* Moscow. All the countries of Eastern Europe under German rule had been captured and occupied by the Soviet army. Yugoslavia was the one Eastern European state to have liberated itself from German rule by its own forces— the forces of the partisan army. This achievement made Tito the only Eastern European Communist leader who possessed the authority to ward off the threat of occupation by the Red Army[3] and to follow a policy independent of Moscow which must inevitably meet with Stalin's disapproval.

The military success of the partisans had ensured political success for the Communist party in the elections to the constituent assembly called for 11 November 1945. The party had canvassed on a unity-list in the 'National Front', which it controlled but on which all anti-Fascist parties were represented; and it won an overwhelming majority[4] —not through a régime of terror, like the Communists in Poland and Romania, or through a large-scale electoral fraud, as in Hungary[5]—but because a majority of the people

1. Quoted in Dedijer, *Tito Speaks*, pp. 232–3.
2. In this battle 30,000 Yugoslavs and nearly 100,000 Germans fell; the number of German prisoners of war was 209,000, among them the commander of the German army, Colonel-General Alexander von Löhr. Yugoslavia's casualties were terrible. Out of a population of less than 20 million, 1,700,000 had been killed in battle or had died in German concentration camps; see ibid., p. 244.
3. When Tito visited Stalin in March 1945 for the second time, the withdrawal of those Russian troops still in Yugoslavia was agreed.
4. The National Front polled 90·48 per cent of votes cast. Admittedly only those parties represented in the National Front could put up candidates, and even though the elections were free in the unanimous opinion of foreign observers, it must be assumed that some administrative pressure by the authorities under Communist control must have had some effect on the results in towns and villages. But even if doubts may be cast on the size of the Communist election victory, it is certain that a great majority of electors voted for the National Front of their own free will.
5. See pp. 101, 116, 203.

recognized that their country had been liberated by the Communist guerrillas and not by foreign armies, and because the Communist party appeared as the guardian of Yugoslav nationalism, by which it was hoped to overcome mutual hatreds between nations within the state.

The power which the Communists won in the elections was consolidated by setting up a dictatorship of the party on the Soviet Russian pattern, proclaimed not as a 'dictatorship of the proletariat', but as a 'people's democracy', a style of title which was later to be generally adopted for the system of government in Communist dictatorships. Even so, in its early years it was a régime marked by no less cruelty and doctrinaire excesses than the régime in Moscow.

The dictatorship by the Communist party of Yugoslavia differed, however, from the Communist dictatorships in the Russian satellite states in its origins, which were a decisive factor in its relationship with the Soviet Union. It had not been established by force by the occupying Red Army, or by leaders nominated from Moscow to be representatives of the Soviet government, but by the leaders of the partisan army who, celebrated as the liberators of their country, had had power invested in them by the broad mass of the people. And, although the Communist party's loyalty to the Soviet Union was beyond question, Stalin could not expect that under Tito's leadership, especially in the light of their war-time experiences, it would willingly serve the cause of the Soviet Union.

In fact Tito had left him in no doubt whatever concerning this issue. In a speech made in Ljubljana in May 1945, immediately after the war, he had stated bluntly: 'We demand that everybody should be master in his own house. We have no wish to be used as pawns in international haggling. We have no wish to become involved in any sphere of influence.' These comments concerned Trieste, the annexation of which to Yugoslavia Tito had demanded in contradiction to Stalin's agreements with the Allies.

Tito was at once called to heel. The Yugoslav government was informed by the Soviet Ambassador in Belgrade that the Soviet government 'considers Tito's speech to be an unfriendly attack upon the Soviet Union' and threatened that 'if he permits himself one more such attack against the Soviet Union, he will be openly criticized and disowned in the [Soviet] Press'.[1]

The Communist dictatorship under Tito's leadership did not therefore fulfil the function intended by Stalin for the Communist dictatorships in the Russian satellite countries. For him their purpose was not simply the expansion of Communism, but predominantly to obtain Soviet control of

---

1. See the letter from the central committee of the Communist Party of the Soviet Union to the Communist Party of Yugoslavia of 4 May 1948 in *The Soviet-Yugoslav Dispute* (London, 1948), pp. 35 and 36. This letter, as Dedijer mentions in *Tito Speaks*, was signed by both Stalin and Molotov.

their war potential. This conception was based on the primary condition of Moscow's absolute hegemony over these countries and therefore on the rule of Communist party dictatorships whose leaders were dependent upon Moscow.

But Tito was by no means dependent upon Moscow. His prestige in his country was founded on his military triumph as marshal during the war, and his position in the party was established as the admired leader of the Communist revolution. And, as long as he controlled the party machine, his position was unassailable. Stalin's threats would have no effect on Tito's decision to remain 'master in his own house' and to pursue independently of Moscow a 'Yugoslav road to Socialism'.

Moscow tried to undermine Tito's position by infiltrating the party and state machine with agents of the Russian secret service, the N.K.V.D.[1] And another means by which Stalin tried to secure Tito's subjection to Moscow's authority was the Cominform. He had settled on Belgrade as the seat of its secretariat[2] so as to bring its influence to bear immediately, and when he finally broke with Tito, he tried to overthrow him by his expulsion from the Cominform.[3]

Stalin's break with Tito became apparent in the middle of March 1948, when the Yugoslav government was unexpectedly notified by the Soviet government that it was withdrawing its military and technical advisers from Yugoslavia forthwith.

The complaints by which Stalin justified his action in the exchange of letters he had with Tito[4] do not, on the face of it, seem very weighty; they include, for example, a remark made by Milovan Djilas, one of the Yugoslav Communist leaders, about the not very satisfactory behaviour of Russian troops in Yugoslavia, but which Stalin took as an insult to the Soviet army; or Tito's request that the considerable salaries of Soviet advisers which Yugoslavia had to pay—they were four times the incomes of Yugoslav army commanders and three times those of Yugoslav ministers—should be somewhat reduced. And as if Tito were responsible to him for the administration of the Yugoslavian state, Stalin complained that the Yugoslav state and party machine remained 'full of the friends and relatives of the German Quislings and the murderers of General Nedić', while high-ranking Yugoslav officials are in the service of British espionage'. Referring to the teachings

---

1. The N.K.V.D., the People's Commissariat of Internal Affairs, had been founded in 1934 as the successor of the O.G.P.U., or State Political Administration, which had in 1922 succeeded the *Cheka*, or 'Extraordinary Commission for Combating Counter-Revolution, Sabotage and Speculation', set up in 1917. In 1946 the N.K.V.D. became the Ministry of Internal Affairs (M.V.D.).
2. See page 150.
3. See Adam B. Ulam, *Titoism and the Cominform* (Cambridge, Mass., 1952).
4. For the texts of the letters, see *The Soviet-Yugoslav Dispute*.

of Marxism–Leninism on party structure, Stalin also admonished the Yugoslav party for its absence of internal democracy, its hesitant policy towards the collectivization of agriculture and its hasty nationalization of industry.

But what Stalin was complaining about in reality was Tito's refusal to surrender his position as 'master' in Yugoslavia. This seemed to Stalin to represent no small disloyalty, as the tone of his letters made clear—the haughty tone of an uncouth superior towards his subordinates, disregarding the fact that Tito was the leader of a foreign Communist party and the ruling head of a sovereign state; a tone of voice obviously meant to refresh Tito's memory concerning Stalin's standing among Communist parties and governments.

Even so, Tito remained anxious to try to make up his quarrel with Stalin.[1] In reply he answered every single point and suggested that a delegation from the Communist party of the Soviet Union should be sent to Belgrade to examine points of disagreement on the spot.

Stalin's concern, however, was not to settle differences but to overthrow Tito. He saw him as the obstacle to the establishment of Moscow's predominance in Yugoslavia and he feared that, if he remained in power, leaders in other Russian satellite states might also free themselves from the Kremlin's hold. Tito's overthrow was to serve as a warning.

He had intended that the Cominform should execute the plan. It was called to Bucharest in the middle of June 1948 and Tito was summoned to attend. The Yugoslav party central committee, however, rejected the invitation.[2]

In its resolution the Cominform conference accused the leaders of the Communist party of Yugoslavia of having pursued an 'unfriendly policy towards the Soviet Union'; of having 'slandered' it with arguments taken 'from the arsenal of counter-revolutionary Trotskyism'; of having 'brutally suppressed the elementary rights of party members' under a 'shameful, genuinely Turkish régime of terror'; and of having with 'unbounded ambition, arrogance and vanity' refused to acknowledge their errors.

As a result of their attitude and their refusal to appear at the conference the Yugoslav party leaders had, the resolution stated, 'placed themselves outside the community of the brotherhood of Communist parties and the united Communist front, and thus outside the Cominform'. 'They have

1. For a very informative debate by the executive of the Communist party of Yugoslavia on Stalin's letters, see Dedijer, *Tito Speaks*, pp. 335–64.
2. 'It was clear,' Dedijer commented on this decision, 'that there was no guarantee that Tito would return alive from this conference.' He recollects the fate of the Politbureau members of the Ukrainian Communist party who, after resisting Stalin's Great Russia policy, were invited by him for a discussion to Moscow and were arrested by the N.K.V.D. on entering the Kremlin and later shot—*Tito Speaks*, p. 366.

broken with the international tradition of the party and have taken the road to nationalism.'[1]

The resolution closed with a barely concealed call to Yugoslav party members to rise in revolt against Tito and overthrow him. The Cominform, it stated, did not doubt that,

there exists within the Communist party of Yugoslavia sufficiently sound elements, who are loyal to Marxism–Leninism, to the international tradition of the party and to the united Socialist front.

It is their duty to force their present leaders to confess publicly to their errors and to correct them. Should the present leaders of the Communist party of Yugoslavia show themselves incapable of doing this, it is the duty [of the 'sound' elements] to remove them and to install a new international party leadership.[2]

It was unthinkable to Stalin that, faced with choosing between him and Tito, the Yugoslav Communists would do anything except decide in his favour as the 'greatest Socialist after Marx and Lenin, the glorious leader of the Soviet Union and of the proletariat of the world'—as he was glorified also in Yugoslavia.

But he was mistaken. Undaunted, Tito faced his party's court of justice. On the day following the publication of the Cominform resolution in *Pravda* on 29 June 1948, the central committee assembled for a plenary session, rejected the accusations of the Cominform point by point and decided to publish at once the Cominform resolution in full with their own explanations in the party organ *Borba*, and to summon the fifth congress to Belgrade for 21 July.

The congress was attended by 2,344 delegates representing 468,175 party members. The hall was decorated with Stalin's bust, as well as with one each for Marx, Engels and Lenin, and with a portrait of Tito. The congress lasted for six days. Its discussions, including Tito's own report on the conflict, which took no less than eight hours, as well as the debate which followed, were broadcast in full by the Yugoslav broadcasting service, and at the end Tito was re-elected as party chairman by 2,318 votes to five.[3]

There is no question that an overwhelming majority of the party did, in fact, rally to Tito's side, and it can hardly be doubted that the secret police also played their part in ensuring that no opposition to him emerged.

For Stalin, the failure of his action against Tito was possibly the greatest disappointment of his life. He reacted by an outbreak of insane acts of

1. Dedijer says that Andrei Zhdanov, who, with Georgi Malenkov and Mikhail Suslov, represented the Soviet Union, had told the conference: 'We are in possession of information that Tito is an imperialist spy'—ibid., p. 370.

2. For the text of the resolution, see *Soviet-Yugoslav Dispute*, pp. 61–70.

3. For a description of the congress, see Dedijer, *Tito Speaks*, pp. 377–381; see also Vladimir Dedijer's further book on Yugoslavia's conflict with Moscow, *The Battle Stalin Lost: Memoirs of Yugoslavia, 1948–1953* (New York, 1971).

persecution. Above all he feared the infection of the Russian satellite countries with the bacillus of 'Titoism'. Until Stalin's break with Tito, the leaders of individual 'people's democracies' had continued to seek their own road to Socialism according to the special conditions in their countries—a path which deviated from the 'Russian road to Socialism'. Now that Tito had been outlawed as a 'Fascist' and an 'imperialist spy', any thought even of a 'special road' to Socialism was branded as 'Titoism' and persecuted as a crime.[1] Any heads suspected of such a notion rolled under the axe of the dictator in the Kremlin. Thus Traichko Kostov, deputy prime minister of Bulgaria, Koci Xote, secretary of the Communist party of Albania, Laszlo Rajk, foreign minister of Hungary with seven of his associates, Rudolf Slansky, general secretary of the Communist party of Czechoslovakia, and the foreign secretary, Vlado Clementis, with nine of their associates, were executed on charges of having 'conspired against the state', of 'Titoism', 'cosmopolitanism' and 'Zionism'. And those who escaped Stalin's henchmen, such as Wladislaw Gomulka, general secretary of the Communist party of Poland, were imprisoned.

Stalin now saw himself surrounded by enemies even in the Soviet Union, his régime, and even his life, threatened. At the beginning of 1948 he unleashed a new wave of purges to 'cleanse' the Communist party and the country of 'anti-Stalinists', purges even more terrible than those of the 1930s, which threw hundreds of thousands into concentration camps[2] and only ceased with his death in March 1953. During this period the totalitarian system in the Soviet Union reached completion. Every branch of intellectual and cultural life—art as well as science, music as well as biology[3]—became subject to Stalin's dictatorship.

Tito reacted to Stalin's outlawing of Yugoslavia with a criticism of Stalinism as a monstrous debasement of Communist ideas, and of Soviet

---

1. Now, for example, the Communist party of the German Democratic Republic (S.E.D.), under Walter Ulbricht's leadership, hurriedly refuted the 'particular German road' to Socialism, which had been intensively discussed, inside the party as well as in the Communist press, and which had been stimulated by one of the most prominent leaders of the party, Anton Ackermann. 'The party executive has ascertained,' it was stated in explanation in September 1948, 'that there are also in the S.E.D. false theories on a "particular German road" to Socialism. . . . The attempt to construct such a special German road to Socialism would lead to it disregarding the great Soviet example'—quoted in Wolfgang Leonhard, *Die Revolution entlässt ihre Kinder* (Cologne and Berlin, 1955), p. 516.

2. Following a debate on the reappearance of concentration camps, the meeting of the International Socialist Conference in Copenhagen in June 1950 drew 'the attention of the free world to the fact, that only five years after the end of the Second World War, after the destruction of Hitlerism and the condemnation of the cruelties of the concentration camps by the civilised world', once again 'millions of people suffer in concentration and forced labour camps'—Report of the International Socialist Conference, Copenhagen, June 1950, Circular No. 155/50, p. 108.

3. For the most bizarre example of the coercion of science by Stalin's dictatorship and its disastrous consequences, see David Joravsky, *The Lysenko Affair* (London, 1971); see also Zhores Medvedev, *The Rise and Fall of T. D. Lysenko* (London, 1969).

imperialism as a rejection of the fundamental principles of Socialism.[1] Until the break with Stalin, the Yugoslav system of government had hardly differed from the Stalinist system. There is no doubt that this criticism of Stalinism simultaneously called into question the Yugoslav system of Communist rule.[2]

In 1950, a process of liberalizing the dictatorship did in fact begin in Yugoslavia with the development of an ideology of 'pure' Leninism in contrast to its degeneration under Stalin's rule and in changes in the economic structure of Yugoslav Communism.[3] The significance of the revolt by Yugoslavia's Communists against Moscow's hegemony can hardly be underestimated. It represented a landmark in the history of the international Communist movement. It initiated the world-historical process of the emancipation of Communist parties from the domination of Moscow—a process of possibly not less importance than the Reformation by which the Protestant Christian churches had gained their emancipation from Rome. It also created the first condition for the process of transforming despotic Communism into Socialist democracy.[4]

Yugoslavia's revolt against Moscow's hegemony and the change of her political and economic structure towards a liberalization of the Communist dictatorship, which culminated in the adoption of a new constitution in 1953,[5]

1. Milovan Djilas, at that time the most prominent leader of the Yugoslav Communist party after Tito, raised the whole question of how Soviet imperialism differed from that of the old capitalist monopolies. 'All that is new here,' he said, 'is the fact that the state which all, or nearly all, believe to be Socialist, has through its own internal state capitalist development, turned into an imperialist power of the first order, but as for the actual forms, through the relatively poor development of its forces of production, what characterizes this new state-capitalist imperialism is precisely that it has the old colonial-conquest imperialist forms, accompanied, albeit, in Socialist uniforms, by the old political relations: the export of capital is accompanied by a semi-military occupation, by the rule of an official caste and the police, by the strangling of any democratic tendencies, by the establishment of obedient governments, by the most extensive corruption and by unscrupulous deception of the working people'—*Borba*, 26 November 1950, quoted in John Strachey, 'Task and Achievement of British Labour', in R. H. S. Crossman (ed.), *New Fabian Essays* (London, 1952), p. 206.

2. See Milovan Djilas, *The New Class. An Analysis of the Communist System* (New York, 1957).

3. For an excellent assessment of Yugoslavia's economic system as it developed after the break with Moscow and the liberalization of the dictatorship, see Carl Landauer, *Contemporary Economic Systems. A Comparative Analysis* (Philadelphia and New York, 1964), pp. 433–87.

4. The treatment of this event in Communist historiography is itself not uninteresting. In William Z. Foster's *History of the Three Internationals* (New York, 1955), published before Khrushchev's penitent visit to Belgrade, Tito is considered, according to convention, as a 'Fascist'. In R. Palme Dutt's *The International* (London, 1964), which appeared after the reconciliation between Moscow and Belgrade, the reader may seek in vain for even the name Tito: this event, which shook the world Communist movement, goes unmentioned.

5. Yugoslavia's constitution of 1946, which had been copied from Stalin's Soviet constitution of 1936, was replaced in 1953 by a new constitution based on the principle of a kind of 'direct economic democracy'.

had raised the question of relations between the Yugoslav Communist party and the Socialist International. This was debated at the meeting of its general council in October 1952, on the basis of memoranda submitted to the bureau by the affiliated parties.

A sympathetic attitude towards Yugoslavia on the part of the International was advocated above all by the British Labour party. In the autumn of 1952 it sent a delegation to Yugoslavia which communicated its impressions in a memorandum circulated to the parties of the International. 'There can be no doubt,' this emphasized, 'that Yugoslavia's recent development since the break with Moscow—and particularly since the recent constitutional changes—represents a bold and important experiment. It is essential to look at it realistically.

We must [the memorandum continues] accept the fact of a strong, one-party, national government in Yugoslavia. After the political and social experience of the inter-war years, and particularly the desperate struggle for independence, such a government was inevitable; just as it was inevitable that the new leadership should come from the partisan element. We could not expect the hard-won political power to be frittered away or national unity to be jeopardized in the face of very real threats from Yugoslavia's Stalinist neighbours.

Yugoslavia, the memorandum emphasized, was no parliamentary democracy 'as we understand it in Britain, and it probably never will be. . . . Its social and economic conditions may not be a suitable basis for such a form of government.' Nor was Yugoslavia, the memorandum asserted, 'a Communist state on the Soviet pattern any longer, though it retains many Soviet features'.

'Clearly therefore, neither Western-type parliamentary democracy nor Russian-type Communism is acceptable to the Yugoslavs or workable in their country. The vital question is whether their revolution is leading them towards a new form of Socialism which will bring them nearer in spirit and in practice to our form of Social Democracy.'

The success or failure of the Yugoslav experiment [the memorandum concluded] has an importance far beyond the gaining of an ally for the Western powers. It is of vital importance to the Yugoslav peoples, who have suffered misgovernment and occupation for decades. And if it succeeds in evolving a workable political formula, it could become an example to other countries with analogous conditions, countries which are both unsuited to Western parliamentarianism and hostile to Stalinism.[1]

Likewise the Norwegian Labour party, which had established contact with the Yugoslav organization, greeted the social and economic reforms in Yugoslavia as a 'daring political experiment which will be of importance to the international Socialist movement'. This development, it declared, 'has a right to our support and should be observed by the whole Socialist movement with sympathy'.[2]

1. Circular No. 19/53.   2. Circular No. 47/53.

The M.A.P.A.I. of Israel, which had, like the Social Democratic party of Switzerland, established contact with the Communist party of Yugoslavia, 'in principle' advocated developing 'existing contacts so as to establish a closer co-operation which may later lead to its affiliation into the Socialist world'.[1]

Although no Socialist party came out against unofficial contacts with the Communist party of Yugoslavia, the general council considered any formal connection with the Socialist International hardly to be possible, so long as it declined to show, as the Labour party of Sweden stated by invoking the Frankfurt declaration, 'its readiness to recognize, theoretically or practically, the principle of an organized opposition to the régime'. For although Yugoslavia is attempting to realize a new form of Socialism, her régime remains one that is based on a one-party system, and while she has established a mass political organization which accepts non-Communists as members—the 'Socialist Alliance of the Working People of Yugoslavia'—no right to form political parties apart from the Communist party is recognized. And since the Socialist International is founded on the principles of democracy, it cannot accept the Yugoslav Communist party as a member. Any attempt to do so, the Swedish Labour party warned, would 'most probably precipitate an acute crisis'.[2]

On the basis of the parties' memoranda, the general council of the Socialist International decided to establish no official contact with the Communist Party of Yugoslavia, but to leave it to individual parties to regulate their relationship according to their discretion.

The quarrel between Yugoslavia and the Soviet Union was mended by Khrushchev's visit to Belgrade on 26 May 1955. He appeared at the head of a delegation of the Communist party of the Soviet Union, and declared on arrival: 'We sincerely regret what has happened. . . .'

A year later the Cominform, which Stalin had used as a weapon against Tito, also ended. After the break with Yugoslavia its seat had been moved from Belgrade to Bucharest, and it had met only once, in November 1949 in Budapest, but merely to denounce, once again, 'the murderers and spies of Belgrade' and to call upon the 'loyal Communists' of Yugoslavia finally to chase the 'Tito band' from office.[3] This was the third and final conference of the Cominform. On 17 April 1956 it ceased its activities by a decision of its central committee.[4]

1. Circular No. 45/53.
2. Circular No. 3/53. For the memoranda of other parties of the International, see Circulars No. 12/53, 13/53, 14/53, 15/53, 16/53, 18/53, 21/53, 22/53, 23/53, 25/53, 26/53, 41/53, 49/53. These may be found in the Archives of the Socialist International in the International Institute for Social History, Amsterdam.
3. *For a Lasting Peace and for a People's Democracy*, 29 November 1949.
4. See Zinner (ed.), *National Communism and Popular Revolt in Eastern Europe*, pp. 9–15.

19 · The Insurrection in East Berlin

The uprising of workers in the German Democratic Republic, which broke out on 16 June 1953, was completely different in character and origin from the revolt against Moscow by the Communists in Yugoslavia.

On that morning several hundred building workers at a block of flats in the *Stalin-Allee* in the Soviet Zone of Berlin stopped work in protest against the raising of the work norm, decreed by the government a few weeks earlier. They then marched to the government building on the *Wilhelmsplatz* to demand the revocation of the order.

This gesture of protest against the deterioration of working conditions set in motion an avalanche of feeling against the political system. As the building workers marched from their construction site through the city centre and the working-class district around the *Alexanderplatz*, thousands of men and women joined them, and, as news of the demonstration spread, workers from other factories also went on strike and began marching to the seat of government. Before long an angry crowd of tens of thousands was encircling the government buildings.

On the following day, 17 June, the workers in most of the bigger industrial centres of East Germany came out in support of a general strike; in Halle, Leipzig, Dresden, Jena, Rostock, Chemnitz and Gorlitz. In East Berlin a huge crowd filled the wide *Unter den Linden* and the *Lustgarten*. At one o'clock the radio declared a state of emergency: demonstrations, meetings, assemblies and other groupings of 'more than three persons' as well as walking in the streets between nine o'clock at night and five o'clock in the morning were forbidden. Then, hardly an hour later, formations of Russian tanks, infantry and police force attacked the demonstrators. In the clashes which followed seventeen died and hundreds were injured.[1]

---

1. For a description of these events, see Arno Scholz, Werner Nieke and Gottfried Vetter, *Panzer am Potsdamer Platz* (Berlin–Grunewald, 1954); see also Rainer Hildebrandt, *Als die Fesseln fielen. . . .* (Berlin–Grunewald, 1956); Hermann Weber, *Von der S.B.Z. zur D.D.R. 1945–1958* (Hanover, 1966), pp. 79–92, and, for an eye-witness account by a Com-

The demonstrations had not been the work of any conspiracy. Nobody had planned them, nobody had foreseen them. They had surprised the workers themselves as much as they had surprised the government, the Communist party and the trade unions. It had been a spontaneous outburst of resentment among the working class, a fundamental demonstration against the system of government erected by Moscow in East Germany.

The suppression of the rising with the backing of Russian tanks was followed by a reckoning. Max Fechner, one of the old guard of the Social Democratic party, who had, in 1945, advocated the party's union with the Communist party and been made minister of justice, was at once relieved of his office when he stated in a press interview: 'The right to strike is guaranteed by the Constitution. The strike leaders will not be punished for their actions as members of the strike committee.' He was replaced by Dr Hilde Benjamin, who introduced a new 'policy of retribution'. The state of emergency remained in force until 21 June, and between then and early December 427 demonstrators were sentenced by the ordinary German courts to a total of 1,457 years hard labour or imprisonment, while two were sentenced to death and four to imprisonment for life; moreover, sixteen others were sentenced to death by Soviet summary courts and executed.[1]

The uprising precipitated a crisis within the party; its leaders were consternated. The central committee of the party, when it met on 21 June, four days after the rising, stated, as one would expect, that the revolt was a well-prepared 'Fascist provocation' against the state, and it called the demonstrating workers 'bandits acting at the instigation of Adenauer, Ollenhauer, Kaiser and Reuter'.[2] But the total number of these 'bandits' who actually went on to the streets to demonstrate against the government, according to available estimates, came to between 300,000 and 372,000, while the main support for the rising came from the workers in the big industrial plants: from Leuna, with a work-force of 28,000, Buna with 18,000, Wolfen with 12,000, Henningsdorf with 12,000 as well as the other large factories who joined the demonstration in serried ranks.[3]

This was not a revolt by groups of dissatisfied intellectuals or former Social Democrats. The whole proletariat had risen against the party's leadership, Communists as well as Social Democrats. The Communist experiment of the Socialist Unity Party of Germany (S.E.D.), as the Communist party had been renamed after its merger with the Social Democrats of the S.P.D., had failed on ideological grounds. Otto Grotewohl, the S.P.D. leader in the

munist official, ibid., pp. 299–301. See further Stefan Brant, *Der Aufstand. Geschichte und Deutung des 17. Juni 1953* (Stuttgart, 1954); Eugen Stamm, *Juni 1953. Der Volksaufstand vom 17. Juni 1953* (Bonn, 1961).

1. For a list of sentences, see Scholz, Nieke and Vetter, *Panzer am Potsdamer Platz*, pp. 200–5.

2. Quoted in Weber, *Von der S.B.Z. zur D.D.R.*, p. 85. 3. See ibid., p. 83.

Soviet Zone, had hesitantly agreed to the merger with the Communist party expecting confidently that the democratic traditions of Social Democracy would permeate the united Socialist Party.[1]

Now the uprising had demonstrated that the Social Democratic tradition had indeed filtered through to the mass following of the S.E.D. Communists and Social Democrats had struck, had marched and demonstrated together against the system of the dictatorship of the party and government. The ideological basis of the party had been called in question—the dogma of the 'democratic centralism' of its structure, upon which the dictatorship of the hierarchy over the party was founded, as well as the dogma of its role as leader, upon which the dictatorship of the state rested.

Moscow, however, could never allow these principles to be questioned, for their abandonment would inevitably emasculate the Communist leadership of the party. It would, moreover, threaten the Soviet Union's predominance in East Germany, which could only be secured by a firm Communist dictatorship. So the Soviet armed forces intervened and, once the rising had been put down, the party was 'purged' of its Social Democratic elements. The tragedy of the uprising had set the seal of failure on Grotewohl's illusions. Now, as prime minister, it fell to him to purge the party of the democratic tradition which he had hoped would permeate the S.E.D.

The first victim of the purge, as already mentioned, was Max Fechner, who, after being deprived of his office as minister of justice, was expelled 'as an enemy of the party and the state from the ranks of the S.E.D.'. Wilhelm Zaisser was dismissed as minister for state security and, together with Rudolf Herrnstadt, chief editor of the S.E.D. central organ, *Neues Deutschland*, was suspended from the party's central committee as the leader of a 'faction hostile to the party, with a defeatist line aimed against the party's unity'. 'The political-ideological content of the Zaisser-Herrnstadt faction aimed against the party,' the central committee stated in justification of the expulsion, 'rests on their essentially Social Democratic concept of the role of the party, on their idolization of spontaneity among the disorganized masses and their policy of capitulation which is ultimately aimed at re-establishing capitalist rule in the German Democratic Republic.'[2]

Among other victims of the 'purge' there also fell Anton Ackermann, the theoretician of a 'German Road to Socialism'; he was dismissed as director of the Marx-Engels-Lenin-Stalin Institute and as secretary of state in the Foreign Office. The same fate overtook Elsa Zaisser, chief of the Ministry of Adult Education, and Elli Schmidt, chief of the State Commission for Trade and Supply and chairman of the Democratic Guild of Women; as well as the complete central executive committees of the metalworkers' and woodworkers' trade unions together with many thousands of 'wavering and

1. See pp. 78–9.
2. Quoted in Scholz, Nieke and Vetter, *Panzer am Potsdamer Platz*, p. 183.

capitulating elements'. In the iron grip of Walter Ulbricht, whose instrument Grotewohl had become, the S.E.D. became the most Stalinist of all Communist parties, and the German Democratic Republic the most servile of all the Russian satellite states.

The uprising evoked the most profound sympathies throughout the Socialist world. The congress of the Socialist International, meeting in Stockholm one month after the events in Berlin, sent fraternal greetings to the workers in the Soviet Zone of Germany. 'They dared,' the resolution stated, 'to rise against a totalitarian régime. They demonstrated before the whole world that the urge for liberty cannot be repressed. They gave a magnificient example to all the peoples in all countries under despotic domination.'[1]

1. Report of the Third Congress of the Socialist International, Stockholm, 15–18 July 1953, Circular No. 115/53, p. 140.

20 · The Dethronement of Stalin

The event which shook the world Communist movement most profoundly was the posthumous dethronement of Stalin which took place at the Twentieth Congress of the Communist Party of the Soviet Union in February 1956.

Through his glorification by the Communist world press, Stalin had become a legendary figure for innumerable Communists during his lifetime: a symbol of the myth of the Soviet Union and of its ideals for which they were prepared to sacrifice themselves. 'We know,' said Togliatti, 'how many Communists in our country have died with his name on their lips. . . . We know that whole armies of our partisans went into battle carrying this name.'[1] He had been elevated to rank with Marx, Engels and Lenin as one of the four greatest Socialists of all time and, after his death on 5 March 1953, he had been interred at Lenin's side in the mausoleum at the Kremlin walls.

Barely short of three years later, on 25 February 1956, his immense stature was shattered by the speech Khrushchev made to the Twentieth

1. Quoted in Donald L. M. Blackmer, *Unity in Diversity. Italian Communism and the Communist World* (Cambridge, Mass., 1968), p. 26. In Russia Stalin was blatantly idolized by Soviet propaganda. The following extract from an 'Ode to Stalin' was published in *Pravda*:

> O Great Stalin, O Leader of the Peoples,
> Thou who didst give birth to man,
> Thou who dost rejuvenate the centuries,
> Thou who givest blossom to the spring,
> Thou who movest the chords of harmony;
> Thou splendour of my spring, O Thou
> Sun reflected in a million hearts.

—*Pravda*, 28 August 1936, quoted in Edward Rogers, *A Commentary on Communism* (London, 1951). And, as late as two months before Stalin's dethronement, *Izvestia* could still declare in an article entitled 'The Great Continuer of Lenin's Work': 'In observing the 76th anniversary of the birth of J. V. Stalin, the Soviet people remember with great gratitude the services to the party and the Fatherland of this true pupil and continuer of the great work of Lenin. Stalin served our people honourably and earned the universal respect of the workers. He was an indefatigable organizer, a very great theoretician and propagandist of Marxism–Leninism, an ardent fighter for the happiness of the workers and for peace and friendship among the nations'—*Izvestia*, 21 December 1955, quoted in Panas Fedenko, *Khrushchev's New History of the Soviet Communist Party* (Munich, 1963), p. 126.

Congress. He described to the amazed delegates how Stalin had secured his power over the party and state by setting up a personal despotism, purging the Bolshevik old guard and sending thousands upon thousands of active Communists to their deaths as spies and enemies of the state.[1] And he showed how Stalin had foisted the cult of his own personality on to the party, so that his glorification by party and government officials had more or less come to be a test of their degree of loyalty. Stalin's personality, as Khrushchev characterized it in his speech, bore the stamp of a cruel tyrant, drunk with power, who had trodden over mountains of his comrades' dead bodies to become the sole ruler of the Russian empire.[2]

Khrushchev's disclosures spread consternation throughout the ranks of the Communist parties and especially amongst their intellectual leaders. It had been admiration for the Soviet Union—'the myth of October' as the historian of the Communist party of Italy had called it[3]—which had moved countless intellectuals to join the Communists as the party standing closest to

1. For an investigation of Stalin's crimes, see Robert Conquest, *The Great Terror. Stalin's Purge of the Thirties* (London, 1968). According to his calculations, at least 6,500,000 lives were destroyed over the decade 1930–40. Approximately one million were actually executed between 1933 and 1938 (p. 529), at least two million more perished in concentration camps in the same period (p. 532); and at least three and a half million died during the enforced collectivization. According to Sakharov, 'at least ten to fifteen million people perished in the torture chambers of the N.K.V.D. from torture and execution, in camps for exiled kulaks and so-called semi-kulaks and members of their families and in camps "without the right of correspondence" which were in fact the prototypes of the Fascist death-camps where, for example, thousands of prisoners were machine-gunned because of "overcrowding" or as a result of "special orders".' He asserts that 'in 1936–39 alone more than 1·2 million party members, half of the total membership, were arrested. Only 50,000 regained freedom; the others were tortured during interrogation or were shot (600,000) or died in camps'—Andrei D. Sakharov, *Progress, Coexistence and Intellectual Freedom*, with an Introduction by Harrison E. Salisbury (London, 1968), pp. 52 and 55. Alexander Solzhenitsyn, the famous Soviet author, himself a prison-camp victim who made an intimate study of the system, arrived at quite similar estimates.

2. For the full text, see *The Dethronement of Stalin* (London, 1956). The speech was given at a secret meeting of the Twentieth Congress on 25 February 1956, to which only delegates of the Communist party of the Soviet Union were admitted, and no delegates from fraternal parties. The stenographer's minutes of the congress did not record the speech, but only reference to a closed session at which Khrushchev gave a report entitled 'The Cult Personality and its Consequences'—see Fedenko, *Khrushchev's New History*, p. 128. The text of the speech had, however, been reproduced in a document for the information of foreign Communist parties, a copy of which came into the hands of the United States government and which was published in the *New York Times* on 4 June 1956. As soon as Khrushchev's secret speech was published in the world's press, he disowned it as a fabrication by foreign intelligence agencies. But, although never published in the Soviet Union, it was discussed at Communist party conferences. The official *History of the C.P.S.U.* (Moscow, 1959) recorded: 'On the basis of decisions taken at the Twentieth Congress, the Central Committee fully revealed Stalin's great mistakes, the instances of gross infringement of Socialist legality, abuse of power, arbitrary acts and the repression of many honest people, including prominent figures in the party and government' (p. 727)—quoted in Fedenko, *Khrushchev's New History*, p. 180.

3. Giorgio Galli, *Storia del Partito communista italiano* (Milan, 1958), pp. 258–9, quoted in Blackmer, *Unity in Diversity*, pp. 28–9.

Communist Russia. But now the aura which had veiled the Soviet Union had fallen away and a gruesome reality been brought to light. 'I saw in the face of my dearest friend,' Fabrizio Onofri, a member of the central committee of the Communist party of Italy, was one to describe this disturbing event, 'the rising pallor of despair—a profound, intensive and unquenchable despair, with no escape. And thus I felt the same pallor rising in my face, day by day. We all felt in the centre of our being that we were struck by death. It was as if an abyss had opened beneath us, had opened within ourselves.'[1]

The Communists were now faced with the painful question of how it could come about that one single person could so monopolize power in party, state and society, and how Lenin's creation, the Soviet Union, could degenerate under the leadership of his successor into a barbaric caricature of Socialism.

In no Communist party was this question discussed so passionately as in the Italian party,[2] for Italy was the only country where a great Socialist party, the P.S.I. under Nenni's leadership, was associated with the Communist party by a pact[3] and had therefore until now felt as close to the Soviet Union as did the Communist party. Hence the Communists were all the more impressed by criticism from the Socialists, especially that of Nenni, which called in doubt even the Soviet system itself. 'The question here,' he explained in an article in *Mondo Operaio*, 'is not the legality of the Revolution [in Russia], but that of the institutions—the party, the Soviets—which have been forged by the revolution in the fire of its experience. Instead of these institutions,' he continued, 'developing forms in which the free political will of the individual citizen as well as the masses might have been expressed to a growing extent, they were continually emptied of their democratic content; their power has been made barren and their function stifled.[4] In a letter to Mikhail Suslov, one of the secretaries of the Soviet Communist party, to whom he sent the quoted article, he went even further in his criticism. He referred to the degeneration of the Soviet state; to the suppression of democratic life in the party and in the state; to the transformation of the dictatorship of the proletariat into a dictatorship of the party and ultimately into the dictatorship of Stalin. The Soviet system, like the party, he continued, had been suffocated in a crisis.[5]

Togliatti, as the leader of the Italian Communist party, formulated his position *vis-à-vis* the crisis of the Soviet régime only hesitantly. He had been a loyal follower of Stalin during the long years of his Moscow exile. He had

1. Fabrizio Onofri, *Classe operaia e partito* (Bari, 1957), p. 107, quoted in Blackmer, *Unity in Diversity*, p. 42.

2. By far the best analysis of this discussion, on which this account is based, is to be found in Blackmer, pp. 22–58.

3. See page 51.

4. Pietro Nenni, '*I vergognosi fatte del rapporto segreto di Krusciov*', in *Mondo Operaio*, June 1956, quoted in ibid., p. 47.

5. See ibid., p. 48.

kept silent during the bloody excesses of Stalin's 'great purge', had consented to Tito's expulsion from the Cominform and condemned the uprising of workers in the Soviet Zone in Germany as an 'imperialist counter-revolution'.

He therefore tried to salvage what he could of Stalin's reputation. 'It is impossible,' he declared at a party conference, 'to deny Stalin's greatness, or his achievements, or to destroy them.'[1] Moreover, Stalin alone could hardly have been responsible for the 'mistakes', as the monstrosities which had occurred were later euphemistically termed. In a detailed account in *Nuovi argomenti*, he pointed to the 'collective responsibility of the whole group of political leaders for [Stalin's] errors, including those comrades who have taken the initiative in condemning them'. The basis for these events, he continued, could not be explained merely by Stalin's 'cult of personality'. 'The explanation of the events,' he argued, 'can only be found by a careful study of how the system characterized by Stalin's mistakes came into being in the first place. Only then will it become possible to understand how these mistakes were not of a personal nature alone, but had deeply penetrated the reality of the Soviet way of life.'[2]

He did not, however, examine the 'reality of the Soviet way of life' which Stalin had developed, because this would undoubtedly have put in question Lenin's concept of the Communist party in Russia: the principle of the 'leading role of the party within the state' (the euphemism for dictatorship of the party in the the state) and the principle of 'democratic centralism' (i.e. the dictatorship of the leadership over the party). These were the concepts which had made it possible for the strongest personality within the leading group to seize power by the control of the party machine, and to establish a personal dictatorship.

Togliatti stated, however, that 'Stalin, despite the mistakes he had committed, had had the support of the greater part of the country . . . and above all of the leading [party] cadres'. But Stalin had been able to secure this 'support' only by his control of the party machine, and through it of the state, which had given him the power to eliminate anyone who came under even a vague suspicion of not supporting him.[3]

Even so, Togliatti, as was to be expected, defended the system of Communist dictatorship in the Soviet Union simply as the basis for genuine

1. *L'Unità*, 23 March 1956, quoted in ibid., p. 38.
2. *Nuovi argomenti*, No. 20 (May-June 1956), quoted in ibid., p. 51.
3. Where the party machine was concerned, Khrushchev commented in his speech: 'Stalin acted not through persuasion, explanation, and patient co-operation with people, but by imposing his concepts and demanding absolute submission to his concept. Whoever opposed this concept and tried to prove his viewpoint, as well as the correctness of his position, was doomed to be removed from the collective leadership and to subsequent moral and physical annihilation.' Thus, as Khrushchev recorded, ninety-eight of the 139 central committee members of the party, i.e. 70 per cent, were arrested and shot (mostly in 1937-8), as well as 1,108 out of 1,966 delegates to the Seventeenth Party Congress. See *The Dethronement of Stalin* (London, 1956), pp. 6 and 10.

democracy. The institutional guarantees against the misuse of personal authority of the kind that existed in the western democracies—the multi-party system and the independence of the courts—were, he said, unnecessary to the Soviet Union, damaging and even impracticable. But he pleaded for reforms so as to create 'genuinely effective guarantees against mistakes similar to those made by Stalin'.[1]

Thus, as Blackmer sums up his analysis, Togliatti had managed to maintain his own detachment and that of the Communist party of Italy from the system of Stalinism by emphasizing the necessity for reforms while, at the same time, keeping his faith as a Marxist–Leninist.[2]

The essence of Togliatti's article for the internal history of the international Communist movement lay, however, in the revelations it contained on the relationship between Moscow and the Communist parties. This was not, as it has been interpreted, a straight declaration of independence by the Italian Communists aimed at the Soviet Union, but a barely concealed criticism of control from Moscow. Hitherto Togliatti had submitted himself to Moscow's control. In the conflict with the Yugoslav Communists, he had acknowledged the leading role of the Russian Communist party in the international Communist movement, he had recognized the principle of Moscow's control and condemned 'Yugoslavia's road to Socialism' as a heresy.

But now he fundamentally disavowed this concept. He demanded that Moscow should respect the autonomy of individual Communist parties and recognize their right to pursue a different road to Socialism. The Cominform's lack of respect for the independence of parties had, he continued,[3] been a 'grave mistake'. The Russian pattern, he emphasized, was no longer binding, either in countries governed by Communists, or in those where the Communists did not represent the leading party. 'The experience of constructing a Socialist society in the Soviet Union,' he explained, 'cannot provide guidelines for the solving of questions which we and the Communist parties in other countries are facing today.' And since various roads to Socialism were possible and necessary, there would also spring up various centres of the international Communist movement to form a 'poly-central system' in accordance with 'new situations, changes in the structure of the world and the structure of the workers' movement itself'.[4] According to the logic of

1. Quoted in Blackmer, *Unity in Diversity*, p. 54.
2. ibid., pp. 54–5.
3. Togliatti disclosed that the Communist party of Italy had declared itself to be against forming the Cominform, and that he had rejected a proposal by Stalin in January 1951 that he should give up the leadership of the party and take on the office of general secretary of the Cominform; see Blackmer, *Unity in Diversity*, p. 61. This episode gives another indication of the importance of the role Stalin intended for the Cominform, for Togliatti was one of the most prominent figures in the international movement, and the party which he led was the largest Communist party outside the Soviet Union and China.
4. *L'Unità*, 26 June 1956, quoted in Blackmer, *Unity in Diversity*, p. 61.

these arguments, therefore, the Communist party of the Soviet Union had played out its role both as the centre of the international Communist movement and as its leading party.

It had been the Twentieth Congress of the Soviet party which had broken the bonds by which the international Communist movement had been fettered. In this fact lay the significance of the congress as a corner-stone of its history. Before the Twentieth Congress, any challenge to Moscow's predominant position in the international Communist movement had been a dangerous venture. Tito, having dared to reject Moscow's demands for hegemony, had been expelled from the Communist world federation and condemned as a Fascist, while the leaders of other Communist parties who came under suspicion of Titoism had paid for it with their lives. Their fate had served as a warning.

But now the Twentieth Congress had repudiated the expulsion of the Communist party of Yugoslavia as having been a 'mistake' by Stalin, and it had moreover recognized the right of individual Communist parties to autonomy. The Cominform had condemned the 'Yugoslav road to Socialism' as a nationalist road, and under Stalin's orders any Communist party leaders who became suspected of the crime of taking a 'special road to Socialism'—Kostov in Bulgaria, Rajik in Hungary, Slansky in Czechoslovakia—had been executed or, like Gomulka in Poland, imprisoned. The Twentieth Congress had, however, admitted the feasibility of 'various roads to Socialism'.

Only a few years earlier, the Cominform had rejected the method of parliamentary democracy in the fight for Socialism, propagating revolutionary insurrection as the only possible method in the struggle for power. But the resolution of the Twentieth Congress had stated that 'radical changes in the historical situation'—the growing strength of Socialism and democracy throughout the world—had made it possible for the working class in a number of capitalist countries to 'win a stable majority in parliament' and to create the conditions 'to secure fundamental social change'.

The most acute diversion from the spirit of the Cominform which the congress undertook was in the Soviet Union's foreign policy. The Cominform had seen the world as split into two camps—'imperialist' and Communist—and conflict between the two had been declared inevitable.[1] The congress, however, renounced the Leninist precept that 'wars are inevitable so long as imperialism exists', and proclaimed the possibility of and desirability for 'peaceful co-existence' between states of different social systems.[2] With this it initiated a policy directed at a détente between the Soviet Union and the Western powers.

Like the Seventh Congress of the Communist International of 1935, the Soviet congress of 1956, in giving a new direction to Soviet foreign policy,

1. See Appendix Seven, pp. 549–550.
2. For Mao Tse-tung's opposition to this concept, see page 479.

suggested a united front with Social Democrats and their parties previously slandered by the Cominform as 'auxiliaries to the imperialist camp'. The congress, however, stated that 'today many Social Democrats stand for active struggle against the war danger, for *rapprochement* with the Socialist countries, for unity of the labour movement'. It was the unequivocal wish of the congress to pave the way for friendly relations with the Social Democrats. 'We sincerely greet these Social Democrats,' the declaration further stated, 'and are willing to do everything necessary to unite our efforts in the struggle for the noble cause of peace and in the interests of the working people.'[1]

The general council of the Socialist International, meeting in Zürich on 24 March, a month after the congress, now had to define its attitude to the Communist offer of collaboration. The change in Soviet foreign policy and Communist attitudes towards Social Democracy had been preceded by a change in Soviet internal policy. In fact, shortly after Stalin's death, a 'thaw' had begun to loose the ice-hard grip of dictatorship. Many thousands of political prisoners had been released from concentration camps, the uncompromising harshness of the régime softened and the leaden weight which had hung over the country's spiritual life eased. Reforms were announced by the congress which seemed to promise the beginning of an era of democratization of the Soviet system.

But in fact no idea was more remote from the intentions of the congress than to change the institution of the Communist party dictatorship into a Social Democracy. It did, admittedly, decide 'to create firm guarantees that henceforth a similar situation [to that brought about by the 'personality cult' under Stalin] can never again arise, either in the party or the state, to ensure that the party leadership be organized on the collective principle, on a correct Marxist–Leninist policy, with the active participation of the working millions'.[2] But the reforms the congress planned were intended only to prevent the re-emergence of a dictatorship by a single personality over the collective Politbureau. They did not therefore attempt to change the system of dictatorship, but only to 'de-Stalinize' it.[3]

1. Quoted in R. Palme Dutt, *The International* (London, 1964), p. 333.
2. *History of the C.P.S.U.*, p. 643, quoted in Fedenko, *Khrushchev's New History*, p. 128.
3. This was made quite clear by a resolution of the central committee of the Soviet party (of 30 June 1956) 'Regarding the overcoming of the personality cult and its consequences'. It attacked Communist critics who, like Togliatti, 'tried to explain by some kind of degeneration' in the Soviet system how this terrible thing could have happened which had been condemned by the Twentieth Congress under the heading 'Stalin's Mistakes,' and who therefore advocated reforms to the system to create effective safeguards against a return to a despotic régime. The resolution of the central committee rejected such an idea in no uncertain terms. The personality cult, it declared, should be put down to the special historical conditions of the Soviet Union's development and to Stalin's aberrations, but not to any degeneration of the Soviet system. 'It would be a serious mistake,' it stated, 'to conclude from the past that the social system of the Soviet Union had changed in any way or that the character of the Soviet social system should be seen as the source of such a personality cult'—*Pravda*, 2 July 1956, quoted in Blackmer, *Unity in Diversity*, p. 71.

At all events, the general council of the Socialist International could see in the decisions of the Moscow congress no more than 'changes of tactics', not providing 'adequate proof' of a genuine change in the principles and policies of the Communist dictatorship and therefore 'providing no grounds for departing from the position taken up by democratic Socialism which firmly rejects any united front or any other form of political co-operation with the parties of dictatorship'.

'The general council of the Socialist International,' the statement declared at its close, 'considers the minimum pre-condition, even the possibility of talks on an international basis, to be the re-establishment of genuinely free democratic Labour movements in all the countries where they existed before and have been suppressed or eliminated by the Communist dictatorship.'[1]

1. *Socialist International Information*, 10 March 1956.

21 · Poland's October

The revelation of Stalin's system of terror at the Twentieth Congress of the Communist Party of the Soviet Union had been particularly disturbing for Poland, a country placed under a similar system. The effect, as Edward Ochab, general secretary of the Polish Communist party,[1] wrote two months later, was 'prodigious'.[2] The accumulations of resentment against the rule of Moscow felt by a majority of Poland's workers and intellectuals during the years since 1945 burst out in a sudden flood of criticism at their own régime.

Polish nationalism had never, in its pride, come to terms with Russian predominance. The younger generation of Polish Communists, having fought as partisans during the war against the German occupation forces, had sought, under Wladislaw Gomulka's leadership, to find a 'Polish road to Socialism'. But in 1948 such a road was condemned by Moscow as an 'opportunist and nationalistic deviation', Gomulka was overthrown and Boleslaw Bierut (1892–1956) and Jakub Berman (b. 1906), who had both been appointed by Stalin and had returned from the Soviet Union to Poland in the wake of the Red Army, took care that the Polish revolution would follow the 'Russian road'.

Now the Twentieth Congress had openly displayed the degeneration of the Russian revolution and discredited the Soviet Union as an example to the

---

1. The correct title of the party when it merged with the Polish Socialist Party (P.P.S.) in mid-December 1948 was 'Polish United Labour Party' (*Polska Zjednoczona Partia Robotnicza* or P.Z.P.R.); see p. 102.

2. See Oscar Halecki, 'Poland', in Stephen D. Kertesz (ed.), *Eastern Central Europe and the World: Developments in the Post-Stalin Era* (Notre Dame, Indiana, 1962), p. 47. The dismay among the old guard of Polish Communists was all the more profound as a result of the congress's disclosure that the dissolution of the Polish Communist party in 1938 (see Braunthal, *History of the International, 1914–1943*, pp. 338–9) had been ordered by Stalin 'without cause'; almost all the members of its central committee, having been ordered to Moscow, were arrested and executed as 'Trotskyist traitors'. Gomulka had escaped this fate, because at the time of the party's dissolution he was still serving a long term of imprisonment, to which he had been sentenced following his arrest in 1936.

Polish revolution. It had, moreover, heralded the end of Stalinism as a system of government, initiated a new direction in the Soviet Union's internal and foreign policies and opened new paths to the Communist world movement. To many Communists, the congress had seemed, as Jerzy Moravski, one of its secretaries, said a month later, to be 'a turning point between two eras'.[1]

The ferment which the congress evoked among the mass of the workers broke out in a grass-roots insurrection on 28 June 1956 in Poznan, one of Poland's largest industrial cities. The impetus came from a strike of workers in a large locomotive works, after their complaints against wage reductions were rejected by the government. This strike rapidly grew into a general strike which developed into a political strike and an open revolt. With fierce cries of 'Bread and freedom!', a demonstration of 50,000 demanded free elections and the withdrawal of the Russians. Police headquarters and the prison were stormed by the demonstrators, one policeman being lynched, and the party headquarters, broadcasting house and local offices were occupied. Supported by tanks, troops put down the revolt after two days of street fighting. According to official statements, fifty-three people were killed and over 300 wounded.

The insurrection was a heavy blow for the régime. It demonstrated that it had lost the confidence and support of the working class. The government, which sent a delegation to Poznan under the leadership of the prime minister, Jozef Cyrankiewicz (b. 1911), as soon as the uprising had been suppressed, attributed these events to 'provocation by imperialist agents' and the 'reactionary underground movement'.[2]

The party leadership was, however, divided in its attitudes to events. The Moscow-dominated Stalinist faction, having denounced the revolt as a rising by the counter-revolution, demanded the tightening-up of censorship and the throttling of the freedom movement; the 'revisionist' faction, which had seen the uprising as a spontaneous outbreak of deep dissatisfaction with the régime, insisted on liberalization. A middle-of-the-road position was taken by Cyrankiewicz as well as by Edward Ochab, who had become general secretary after Bierut's death in March 1956. The conflicts between these factions were fought out during the Seventh Plenary Conference of the central committee when it met in Warsaw from 18–28 July 1956 in the presence of N. A. Bulganin and Georgi K. Zhukov of the presidium of the Communist party of the Soviet Union.

1. *Trybuna Ludu*, 27 March 1956, quoted in Paul E. Zinner, *National Communism and Popular Revolt in Eastern Europe* (New York, 1956), p. 55.
2. See Halecki, 'Poland', in Kertesz (ed.), *Eastern Central Europe and the World*, p. 49. The Moscow edition of *Pravda*, on 2 July 1956, stated that the revolt had been financed by the United States government.

The central committee naturally recognized that 'events in Poznan could not be treated in isolation from the situation applying throughout the country', and it recommended measures to raise workers' living standards, to extend 'workers' democracy' in the factories as well as in the party, in the 'people's council committees' and in parliament, and to ensure strict observance of 'Socialist legality' and legal procedure and finally the rehabilitation of political prisoners unjustly accused and sentenced.[1]

The central committee's decisions did not, however, satisfy the wing of the party which was asking for a fundamental liberalization of the system by institutional reform, nor did it quieten the profoundly excited mass of the workers, and above all the intellectuals, who were awaiting the opening of a new epoch.

A strong current of anti-Russian feeling, fed by the Poles' traditional hatred of the Russians, ran through the Polish wish for independence. The central committee, however, avoided stating any views on the problem of the Soviet Union's predominance in Poland, apparently legalized by the signing of the Warsaw Pact[2] on 14 May 1955. This document had placed Poland within the Eastern bloc under the leadership of the Soviet Union and the Polish army, like the armies of other states in the bloc, had been placed under the command of a Soviet marshal, Ivan Koniev. It might therefore have seemed all the more important to issue some word of protest against the intervention of the Soviet Union in Poland's internal affairs. But the central committee simply reaffirmed its unconditional loyalty to the Soviet Union 'in Poland's national interest'. 'The ties of solidarity with the Communist party of the Soviet Union,' the resolution declared, were 'an infallible guarantee . . . of the peace and victory of Socialism'. Yet it was this very predominance of the Soviet Union that had provoked the revolution of the mass of workers and intellectuals against Russia's powerful influence over every sphere of public life in Poland—political and economic as well as intellectual—which had descended over the country like a nightmare.

Trust in the party leadership had been severely shaken throughout its ranks, and the central committee decisions had done nothing to restore it. The recall of Gomulka, who had come to symbolize the renaissance of Polish national Communism, was no longer in question. He appeared to be the man of the hour.

Wladislaw Gomulka (b. 1905), a fitter by trade, had served the movement with devotion from his earliest youth. At seventeen he formed a youth group,

1. For the text of the resolution, see Zinner (ed.), *National Communism and Popular Revolt in Eastern Europe*, pp. 145–86.
2. The Warsaw Pact, set up by Moscow to oppose the NATO treaty, was a twenty-year alliance of friendship and mutual aid between Poland, Czechoslovakia, Hungary, Romania, Bulgaria, Albania and the German Democratic Republic under the military leadership of the Soviet Union.

and a few years later joined the illegal Communist party, suffering repeated arrests and sentences; altogether he spent five years in prison under Pilsudski's régime and that of his successor (and later a further four years under the Communist régime). When the German army overran Poland in 1939, he managed to escape from prison in the confusion. After Hitler's attack on the Soviet Union, he organized the underground Communist movement and in 1943 became general secretary of the newly founded Communist party. When, after its liberation, Poland began to follow a 'Polish road to Socialism', he was removed from his post as general secretary by Moscow in September 1948 and expelled from the party a few months later. He was arrested in 1951, to be released only two years after Stalin's death.[1] Now since the party, or at least its majority, had decided upon taking up once more a 'Polish road to Socialism', it had to recall Gomulka. Already by July 1956 the central committee had decided to rehabilitate him; one week later the politbureau restored him to party membership and immediately elected him as member of the central committee.[2]

The Soviet government was disturbed by the way the situation was developing after the insurrection in Poland. It was apprehensive lest Gomulka's return to the party leadership might shake the unity of the Soviet bloc. Its influence had been directed at strengthening the position of the Stalinists in the tussle between the party leaders faithful to Moscow and the 'revisionists', and it had tried to block Gomulka's rise to power.[3] When the politbureau summoned the central committee to its eighth plenary meeting for 19 October 1956 and Gomulka's election as general secretary seemed a virtual certainty, it decided to intervene.

The discussions of the central committee had already begun on the morning of 19 October, when an aeroplane arrived unexpectedly in Warsaw with, as its passengers, the presidium of the Communist party of the Soviet Union—Khrushchev, Molotov, Kaganovitch and Mikoyan, accompanied by Marshal Koniev; they demanded an immediate account of the situation from the Polish party leaders. 'As the reason for their sudden arrival,' the President of State, Aleksander Zawadzki, told the plenum of the central committee, 'our Soviet comrades gave the deep disquiet of the presidiums of the central committee of the C.P.S.U. on the course of events in Poland . . ., particularly those concerning various kinds of anti-Soviet propaganda, against which no,

1. For a biography of Gomulka, with a detailed description of the origins and early history of the Communist party, see Nicolas Bethell, *Gomulka: His Poland and His Communism* (London, 1969).

2. See Zinner (ed.), *National Communism and Popular Revolt in Eastern Europe*, p. 187.

3. For a description of Moscow's influence over the internal party conflict in favour of the Stalinist faction, see Zbigniew K. Brzezinski, *The Soviet Bloc: Unity and Conflict* (Cambridge, Mass., 1967), pp. 248–67.

or at least insufficient, action had been taken by us. . . . As proof, they indicated examples in a number of our newspapers.'[1]

In the meantime a Soviet division stationed in Silesia had been moved in the direction of Warsaw, on the pretext of autumn manoeuvres, and units of the Polish army under Marshal Constantin Rokossovsky, who was Moscow's man, had also advanced towards the city.

The news of the Russian leaders' arrival and of the Russian troop movements evoked a fearful agitation throughout the whole country, especially in Warsaw. The Communist party organization in Warsaw, which had flocked to support Gomulka, mobilized the workers in the factories, while General Waclav Komar, commandant of the Polish security forces—who had been arrested with Gomulka in 1951 and only released after four years—placed his troops in key strategic positions throughout the city. Workers and students demonstrated in the streets and called for arms.[2]

In the talks with the politbureau the deputation from Moscow held out the threat of military force in the event of Poland withdrawing from its alliance with the Soviet Union and the Warsaw Pact. As guarantee for the continuation of the existing relationship between the two states, they insisted on the retention of Russia's men of confidence—above all Marshal Rokossovsky, whom Stalin had installed as chief of staff of the Polish army—in their positions of power in both party and government.

Breaking with Moscow or dissociating Poland from the Warsaw Pact had at no point been in the minds either of the central committee or of Gomulka himself. The pact was seen as much by the Polish nationalists as by the Communists to be indispensable for the protection of Poland against Germany. What had been called in question was the *de facto* recognition of the principles of equality and independence in the relationship existing between the two states. The politbureau declared that it was prepared to send a delegation to Moscow to clarify this question or, as the official bulletin put it, to discuss the problems 'of strengthening political and economic co-operation between the Polish People's Republic and the Soviet Union'. But it left the Soviet delegation in no doubt whatever that the party, under Gomulka's leadership, was determined to follow a fresh course in its internal policies. It refused to give the personal guarantees for the inviolability of Russia's

1. *Nowe drogi*, No. 10 (1956); see *Ost-Probleme*, 8 February 1957.
2. The possibility of military intervention by the Soviet Union had been deeply disturbing to the party rank and file before the arrival of the Soviet delegation. 'I was confronted by a phenomenon,' Ochab reported to the plenum of the central committee, 'that was really a problem on its own. At innumerable meetings of students and workers all over Poland, resolutions and speeches declared that the central committee would be defended against troops—in other words, against the Soviet army, which allegedly posed a threat. Who,' he added, 'would ever have dreamt that one might find oneself in a situation where party members, people with a radiant faith in the victory of the Communist cause, would be forced to the desperate realization that they could be threatened by the troops of their friends?'—*Nowe drogi*, No. 10; see *Ost-Probleme*, 8 February 1957.

alliance with Poland that had been demanded under the threat of intervention by the Red Army. Moreover, the mood within the party, as Ochab described it, and especially the military mobilization of Warsaw in particular, were signs that Poland would never capitulate without a fight. Since in the end the party affirmed its support for continuing the alliance, the Soviet delegation dropped their insistence on personal guarantees and returned to Moscow on 20 October.[1]

On the next day Gomulka was elected general secretary of the party by an overwhelming majority, while Rokossovsky was dropped from the central committee and the politbureau before being dismissed as minister of defence three weeks later. The central committee had made clear the party's decision to pursue in the future an internal policy independent of Moscow.

The party programme for this new direction in internal policy had been unfolded by Gomulka in the speech he made to the central committee the day before his election. In giving his reasons, he rejected Moscow's version of the insurrection as a counter-revolutionary assault against the foundation of Socialism in Poland. 'The workers of Poznan,' he said, 'went into the streets to protest not against Socialism, but against the rot which had spread so far and wide within our social system . . . against the distortion of fundamental Socialist principles. . . . The clumsy attempt to show the hurtful tragedy of Poznan as the work of imperialist agents and provocateurs is politically naïve.' He then referred to the roots of the crisis. 'The reason for the Poznan tragedy and the deep dissatisfaction of the whole working class,' he declared, 'must be sought within ourselves, in the leadership of the party, in the government.'[2]

The central committee's resolution announced a 'renewal of Leninist principles in the workers' movement' and freedom to criticize within the party. 'The party organs,' it declared, 'should not use disciplinary methods to force party members to renounce deviating viewpoints.'[3]

Several reforms were then put through in quick succession. The sphere of operations of the secret police was restricted, an end made to police terrorism, political prisoners were released, many among them being rehabilitated, and press censorship was moderated considerably. Above all the Polish parliament, or *Sejm*, was acknowledged as 'the highest organ of state power' and its legislative function was recognized. It seemed as though October 1956 had ushered in a revolution, as though the process of change from a system of

1. For a discussion of Moscow's policy during the Polish crisis, see Adam B. Ulam, *Expansion and Co-Existence. The History of Soviet Foreign Policy 1917–1967* (London, 1968), pp. 581–2, 590–4.

2. See Zinner, (ed.), *National Communism and Popular Revolt in Eastern Europe*, pp. 207–8.

3. ibid., pp. 243 and 244.

Communist dictatorship to one of Social Democracy had begun, as though Poland stood on the road to freedom.[1]

Poland did indeed experience a period of freedom, though it was not to last for long. The 'revisionists' had admittedly won the day; but their victory had been incomplete. The Stalinists had merely been forced back, not put to flight. The struggle between revisionists and Stalinists for power over party and state had lost none of its intensity.

Gomulka was certainly able to reinforce his position against the Stalinist faction over the course of the next two years. He held back, however, from the full implications of revisionism. His main objective had been the reform of a Stalinist economic policy. He had decentralized the state's industrial apparatus, had abolished the compulsory collectivization of agriculture, had dissolved a majority of collective farms (*Kolchos*) and had handed over the land to the farmers to be privately worked.

He had also redefined the position of the Soviet Union in relation to Poland. In line with the decision of the politbureau, he had visited Moscow on 18 November, a month after the October revolution in Poland, in company with President Zawadzki and the prime minister, Cyrankiewicz. Their discussion with the Soviet government on Poland's position within the alliance had resulted in a declaration recognizing the principle of equality between the two states and respect for their 'territorial integrity, national independence and sovereignty'; furthermore, the Soviet Union had given assurances that it would not in future interfere in Poland's internal affairs.

Gomulka, for his part, opposed any internal political reforms which could have jeopardized the predominance of the Communist party. The logical consequences of revisionism, which aimed at realizing intellectual and political freedom, seemed, he feared, to threaten its position. He was convinced that Socialism in Poland—a mainly agrarian country, whose farming communities were dominated by the reactionary power of the Catholic church—could only be achieved by the Communist party retaining its domination. Within two years of the changes of October, at the eleventh plenary session of the central committee in December 1958, he was defining 'the fight against the poison of revisionism' as the party's main task.[2]

On this slippery slope under Gomulka's rule Poland slid more and more deeply into a system of neo-Stalinism. The revisionist faction within the party was gradually eliminated, party control over the workers' movement was intensified, the process of its democratization was ended, the country's intellectual life was shackled and finally even anti-Semitism came to be used

1. For this aspect of the October revolution, see Richard Hiscocks, *Poland: Bridge for the Abyss? An Interpretation of Developments in Post-War Poland* (Oxford, 1963).
2. See Halecki, 'Poland', in Kertesz (ed.), *Eastern Central Europe and the World*, p. 56.

as a weapon against revisionism. Gomulka did not even hold back from displaying the lowest depths in tragic self-humiliation when, in August 1968, Polish troops marched into the sovereign Socialist Republic of Czechoslovakia together with the Russian army to put down a movement which had the support of the whole country, and which, like Poland under his own leadership, had sought a road to Socialism independent of the Soviet Union.[1]

1. For an investigation of the neo-Stalinist reaction in Poland under Gomulka's régime, see Jacek Kuroń and Karol Modzelewski, *Monopolsozialismus. Offener Brief an die Polnische Vereinigte Arbeiterpartei*, edited by Helmut Wagner (Hamburg, 1969). The authors of this analytical programmatic study were both lecturers at the university in Warsaw and members of the Communist party who were arrested in November 1964, and, in July 1965, sentenced to three years' imprisonment for the 'dissemination of material dangerous to the state'. See also Adam Ciolkosz, '"Anti-Zionism" in Polish Party Politics', in the *Vienna Library Bulletin*, 1968.

leadership . . .

Warsaw and members of the Communist party, who were arrested in November 1964, and,

22 · The Tragedy of the Hungarian Revolution

In Hungary, the Twentieth Congress of the Communist Party of the Soviet Union, which had so profoundly shaken the intellectuals and workers as well as the Communist party of Poland, evoked hardly a response. There was nothing in the attitudes of the working class during the next seven months to indicate an impending crisis, nor was there anything revealing a change of policy in the attitude of the Communist party leadership.[1]

It is true that 'a new course' had been initiated several months after Stalin's death. But this had stemmed not from any decision by the leadership of the Hungarian Communist party, but from direct orders given by the central committee of the Soviet Communist party. It had sprung from a realization that Hungary 'stood on the brink of a catastrophe' which could drag down the Communist party with it. Mátyás Rákosi, prime minister and general secretary of the party, together with two of his closest colleagues, Mihaly Fárkás and Ernö Gerö, as well as Imre Nagy, one of the most respected members of the party central committee but who stood in opposi-tion to Rákosi's policies, were summoned to Moscow in June 1953. They were told to undertake an immediate change of direction and to install Nagy as prime minister.

Within a few days the party central committee met in Budapest and appointed Nagy as prime minister in accordance with Moscow's instructions. He began in office on 4 July with a speech in parliament criticizing Rákosi's agricultural policies, condemning police terrorism under Rákosi's régime and announcing the closure of the concentration camps. Imprisonment in concen-

1. See Paul E. Zinner, *Revolution in Hungary* (New York and London, 1962), pp. 196–202. This book, on which this description of events is based, is a classic. For a detailed bibliography of literature about the revolution, see ibid., pp. 364–70. For the documents of the revolution, see Paul E. Zinner (ed.), *National Communism and Popular Revolt in Eastern Europe* (New York, 1956). For a review of events, see Stephen D. Kertesz, *Eastern Central Europe and the World: Developments in the Post-Stalin Era* (Notre Dame, Indiana, 1962), pp. 120–55; see also Ference A. Váli, *Rift and Revolt in Hungary* (Cambridge, Mass., 1961). For a Communist version, see Herbert Aptheker, *The Truth about Hungary* (New York, 1957).

tration camps was genuinely stopped, political prisoners were released, farmers were allowed to leave collectives and the production of consumer goods was increased at the expense of heavy industry.

This was a course which Rákosi could hardly wish to see. He was determined to block it, and to destroy his rival. He still held Moscow's trust and, as general secretary, controlled the party. First he suppressed any reference in the press to the central committee's appointment of Nagy as prime minister or to his reform programme, so as to 'diminish the importance of the person as well as the programme of the new prime minister through silence'.[1] His next move was to isolate Nagy in the party by reorganizing the politbureau and surrounding him with enemies in the government. Ernö Gerö became minister of the interior to undermine Nagy's internal reforms, and Andreas Hegedüs became minister of agriculture to do likewise for the agrarian reforms. But what Rákosi feared most was Nagy's rehabilitation of those Communists who, in 1949, had been sent to their deaths or placed in prison. For, as Zinner remarks, should 'the truth about Kádár, Kállai, Losonczy and Szakasits, quite apart from Rajk, have been disclosed, his own fate would have been sealed'.[2]

But Nagy, having been installed by Moscow, could only be deposed by Moscow. So, in the autumn of 1954, Rákosi went to Moscow and, master of intrigue that he was, convinced the Soviet leaders that Nagy's reforms would endanger the foundation of the Communist régime. Nagy was thereupon summoned to Moscow in January 1955 and informed that he no longer enjoyed Russia's trust. In February, Rákosi told the country that, owing to a heart ailment, Nagy was no longer able to exercise his duties as prime minister, and in the following month M. A. Suslov appeared as an envoy of the Communist party of the Soviet Union to attend a meeting of the central committee which passed a resolution condemning Nagy's reforms as 'opportunist deviation'. Six weeks later, on 18 April 1955, Nagy was dismissed as prime minister. In justification of its decision the central committee's resolution had explained that,

Comrade Imre Nagy, as a member of the politbureau and chairman of the Council of Ministers, represented political views which were in the strongest conflict with the general policy of the party and hostile to the interests of the working class, the working farmer and the people's democracy. . . . These anti-Marxist, anti-Leninist attitudes of Comrade Nagy represent a comprehensive system.[3]

This was the end of the 'new course'. Rákosi was once again restored to the possession of full power over party and state. He installed Hegedüs as prime minister, reorganized the politbureau anew, deprived Nagy of all party

1. See Zinner, *Revolution in Hungary*, p. 164.
2. ibid., p. 171. Janos Kádár, minister of the interior, Gyula Kállai, foreign minister, Geza Losonczy, a member of the party's central committee, and Árpád Szakasits, its president, had all been overthrown by Rákosi in 1951, arrested and expelled from the party.
3. Quoted in ibid., p. 174.

functions as member of both the politbureau and the central committee, and finally, in November 1955, achieved his expulsion from the party. Nagy, who had become a Bolshevik as a prisoner of war in Russia in 1918 before the formation of the Communist party in Hungary, and who had served the Communist movement faithfully over nearly four decades, ceased to be a 'comrade'.[1]

Nagy's overthrow, however, did nothing to shake the working class out of the paralysing apathy by which it had been affected ever since the setting up of the régime of terror. Not even in the ranks of the Communist party was there any movement to oppose Rákosi's return to power; until a few weeks before the outbreak of the revolution, no organized opposition group existed within the party or its leadership.

It was three years after the Twentieth Congress that the first signs of an opposition to the régime became apparent, and then only in the intellectual camp—among groups of writers and journalists, especially in the Petöfi circle, which was formed in March 1956.[2] This was a Communist discussion club of professional people—university professors, artists, writers and students. It organized public debates on Marxist themes, in which the ruling régime was also subjected to critical analysis in the light of Marxism. Thus, for example, the Marxist philosopher, György Lukács, opened one such debate with a statement on the 'bankruptcy of Marxism in Hungary'.[3] These debates attracted many hundreds of listeners and its last, on 27 July, even many thousands. On this occasion a discussion took place between old and young Communists from seven o'clock in the evening until three o'clock the following morning in what was already a mood of insurrection. Many speakers demanded press freedom and Rákosi's resignation and any who tried to defend the régime were shouted down. The central committee at once issued an unambiguous warning and the Petöfi circle ceased its activities.

Yet short as its work had been, the criticisms of the régime aired in its debates had undoubtedly set in motion a fermentation—but still only within intellectual circles. The Petöfi circle had no contact with the workers.

Rákosi remained as unruffled by the mood among the intellectuals as he had been by the Twentieth Congress, at which he had been present as a delegate of the Communist party of Hungary. After his return from Moscow there was nothing in his attitude to imply any shaking of his confidence in the Stalinist course to which he was committed. He acted as though nothing out of the ordinary had occurred in Moscow or, at any event, nothing which

1. For an account of Nagy's personality and political career, see Miklos Molnar and Laszlo Nagy, *Imre Nagy: Réformateur ou Révolutionnaire* (Geneva, 1959).
2. Sandor Petöfi, a famous Hungarian poet, whose freedom verses had incited Hungary's revolt against the Habsburgs in 1848; the choice of his name for the club showed its tendencies.
3. See Zinner, *Revolution in Hungary*, p. 209.

would make certain reforms of the régime in Hungary desirable. In his report on the congress to the central committee, he made only a brief reference to Khrushchev's criticism of the system which had led to Stalin's misdeeds, and to which a generation of Communists in the Soviet Union had fallen victims, for this might well have invoked criticisms of his own system for suppressing opponents. So the burning question of rehabilitating innocently sentenced Communists and Social Democrats, raised as a result of Khrushchev's criticism, was left untouched.

But the rehabilitation of Rákosi's victims of oppression was the question which now ate into the body of the Communist party like a festering wound; it had become a weapon for the anti-Stalinists to use within the party against Rákosi. He now appeared to be burdened with the murders of innumerable comrades, and it was in particular upon the demand for the rehabilitation of Rajk, who had come to stand for the victims of Rákosi's system of terror, that the opposition within the party focused.

Rákosi at length came to believe that he could disarm the opposition by making a frank confession of his complicity in Rajk's judicial murder. He finally did so in May 1956 in a speech to a meeting of Budapest party stewards. But he did not, as might have been expected, resign as a consequence. Furthermore, in the same speech Rákosi attacked the anti-Stalinists who were striving for the liberalization of the régime. The class struggle, he declared, was by no means ended, and so the party must not grow weak in the struggle against the enemy. Instead of liberalization, a new wave of persecutions was in the air. Rumours began to circulate in Budapest that Rákosi was contemplating an increase of police terror and planning the arrest of several hundred opponents, leading intellectuals among them. The situation had now become intolerable. The conflict in the party organization between Stalinists and anti-Stalinists threatened the leadership with collapse. But there was not an organized force within the party which might have overthrown Rákosi; the opposition was disorganized and had no leaders.

It was in this atmosphere of tension that a change of scenario came about in classic Moscow style. On 18 July 1956, when the central committee was assembled in Budapest for a meeting, suddenly and unexpectedly there appeared Anastas T. Mikoyan, a member of the presidium of the Communist Party of the Soviet Union and deputy prime minister, to inform Rákosi that he was no longer general secretary of the party. Rákosi, more than a little surprised, protested and asked Khrushchev for an explanation over the telephone. Khrushchev confirmed the decision of the Soviet leaders.[1]

1. About the motives for this decision, taken by the inner circle of Soviet leaders, it is only possible to conjecture. The overthrow of Rákosi, who had heaped abuse on Tito after his break with Stalin, might be interpreted as a gesture of appeasement by Moscow towards

Rákosi was now powerless. He offered his resignation to the central committee, confessed his responsibility 'for the errors which have seriously damaged our Socialist development . . ., have reduced the attraction of our party and hindered the development of Leninist standards in party life'. It had, he admitted, also been his fault that the process of rehabilitating the innocent victims of persecution had taken place so awkwardly and with so many setbacks.[1] With these words Rákosi departed from the Hungarian political scene.

But what had taken place was simply a change of scenario, not of régime. Moscow had picked Ernö Gerö to be Rákosi's successor, and Gerö was Rákosi's *alter ego*, like him an out-and-out Stalinist. Hegedüs also remained as prime minister. As concessions to the opposition, however, General Mihaly Fárkás, commander of the security police, having been responsible for brutal infringements of 'Socialist legality', was demoted, expelled from the party and later arrested; and Laszlo Rajk, General György Palffy, Tibor Szonyi and Andreas Szalai, all of them hanged in 1949, were rehabilitated by the central committee on 3 October 1956. It also decided to re-bury the victims of the terror at a state funeral, so that, the resolution declared, 'we may pay our final respects to these honourable fighters and revolutionaries . . ., comrades who were sentenced and executed as a result of political processes in days gone by'.[2]

The ceremony of reburial was set to take place on 6 October 1956. This day was to be the prelude to the Hungarian revolution. For the first time since the setting up of the Communist dictatorship, the people marched in the streets in hundreds of thousands to demonstrate their objection to the régime. 'The silent demonstration of hundreds of thousands of mourners,' the central organ of the party wrote on the following day, 'represented a vow that we shall not only remember the four dead leaders with clarity, but that we should also remind ourselves of the dark workings of tyranny, of unlawfulness, slander and the deceit of the people.'[3]

The political paralysis which had seized the country was at last dissolving. The opposition dared to emerge into the open. On 17 October the Association of Writers, a Communist trade union, demanded that a party congress should be summoned to elect a new party leadership. 'The unanimous condemnation by the people of the crimes and the errors,' the resolution declared, had

Yugoslavia. Khrushchev was at this time seeking a reconciliation; it might then follow that the Soviet leaders, informed of the crisis within the Hungarian party, had decided to bring about the necessary change of general secretary which the central committee was incompetent to achieve as their solution to the crisis. For a discussion of this question, see Zinner, *Revolution in Hungary*, pp. 215–17.

1. For the text of Rákosi's farewell speech, see Zinner (ed.), *National Communism and Popular Revolt in Eastern Europe*, pp. 341–2.
2. For the text of the resolution, see ibid., p. 385.
3. *Szabad Nép*, 7 October 1956; for the wording, see ibid.

'consequences which only a new and democratically elected party leadership was capable of fulfilling'.[1]

A few days later news of events in Warsaw reached Hungary. This had an intoxicating effect upon the students. 'Meeting is followed by meeting in our universities in Budapest, Pecs, Szeged,' the party central organ reported on 23 October. 'They meet in a passionate and stormy atmosphere, like a raging river that is overflowing its banks. . . . They recall the tremendous excitement in the Hungarian universities and among students immediately following the liberation.'[2]

At a number of students' meetings on 22 October it was agreed that on the following day they should march to the Petöfi monument in Budapest to demonstrate the Hungarian people's solidarity with the people of Poland. The resolution accepted by these meetings had demanded that the party central committee should assemble to take measures 'to safeguard the development of a Socialist democracy'; to summon Imre Nagy and other comrades who had fought for Socialist democracy and for Leninist principles to lead the party and government; to eject Rákosi from the party central committee and to finish 'current attempts to bring about a Stalinist and Rákosi-ist restoration'.[3]

These were most certainly not revolutionary demands; there had been no talk of reforming the institution of dictatorship; nobody at that time was thinking in terms of revolution. The party's central organ, which printed the resolution on the next day, stated:

. . . our student youth has made known its political attitude before a wide public. We welcome the standpoint which student youth has taken. We share their view that those who have sullied Socialist humanism ought to be publicly judged. We agree with their view that the veteran fighters of the labour movement should find a role in leading the party and country. We share their view that no room exists in the party leadership for those not consistently willing to advance along the road which the Twentieth Congress . . . has described.[4]

The student demonstration began, as announced, on 23 October with a rally before the Petöfi monument. An actor recited one of Petöfi's poems that had inspired the revolution of 1848: 'Arise, Hungary, the Fatherland is calling. Now or never!' And this was followed by the oath: 'We are no longer willing to be slaves.' Then the demonstration marched to Kossuth Square before the parliament building; the square was filled with a huge crowd.[5] 'The calm and orderly behaviour of the demonstrators was impressive,'

1. *Trodalmi Ujsag*, 20 October 1956, quoted in Zinner, *Revolution in Hungary*, p. 229.
2. *Szabad Nép*, 23 October 1956, quoted in ibid., p. 232.
3. For the text of the resolution, see ibid., pp. 230–1.
4. *Szabad Nép*, 23 October 1956; for the complete text, see ibid., p. 393.
5. The numbers were estimated at between 150,000 and 200,000—*Szabad Nép*, 28 October 1956; see Zinner (ed.), *National Communism and Popular Revolt in Eastern Europe*, p. 425.

Charles Coutts, an English Communist, reported back from Budapest to the *Daily Worker*.[1] The crowd then awaited a speech by Ernö Gerö, which had been announced for eight o'clock in the evening.

In the meantime groups of students had marched to the radio building and had asked that their resolution should be put out over the air. After this request had been turned down and the crowd repeated its demand more and more threateningly, detachments of the secret police, with fixed bayonets, stormed from the building and opened up on the crowd with rifle fire.

This act of violence was the spark which ignited the revolution. Throughout the night Budapest echoed with small-arms fire in exchanges between demonstrators and troops. In the early hours of the next morning, students and workers stormed the radio building and the printing works and editorial offices of the party paper, *Szabad Nép*, and besieged government buildings.

That night, in the panic which seized the party leadership, Gerö called upon the Soviet troops garrisoned near the capital for help.[2] In the early hours of 24 October the first Russian tanks rolled into Budapest.

The Communist party central committee assembled during the evening of 23 October and sat through to the early hours of 24 October. It decided to declare martial law, to change the politbureau and to recall Imre Nagy as prime minister.

On the next day, despite the enforcement of martial law, thousands of demonstrators again assembled before the parliament building. Russian tanks had taken up positions, but did nothing to disperse the crowds. Suddenly Hungarian security police troops, who had occupied the roofs of surrounding houses to protect the near-by party headquarters, opened fire on the crowds, killing and wounding not only demonstrators, but also members of the tank crews. The Russian troops returned fire, and in the panic also fired on the crowds. The numbers of dead and wounded ran into hundreds.

The turmoil unleashed by the massacre in Budapest was phenomenal. Workers left their places of work, set up barricades and armed themselves with rifles, revolvers and ammunition taken from armament factories, and even from the police and Hungarian troops themselves, who, led by Colonel

1. Quoted in Peter Fryer, *Hungarian Tragedy* (London, 1956), p. 44. This book is a description of events during the revolution. Fryer, a member of the British Communist party and for many years one of the editors of its daily newspaper, the *Daily Worker*, arrived in Budapest, where he was sent by his paper, only during the last stages of the revolution. His reports on earlier events were based on information from Hungarian Communists as well as from Charles Coutts, who lived in Budapest at that time and edited the Communist periodical, *World Youth*.

2. Up until the signing of the treaty with Austria on 15 May 1955, Russian troops had remained in Hungary on the pretext of safeguarding the Soviet Union's communications with Austria, whose Eastern Zone they occupied. Subsequently, the Soviet Union derived its right to station Russian troops on Hungarian soil from the terms of the Warsaw Pact of 14 May 1955.

Pál Maléter, had joined the revolution. The rising, having begun as a protest movement against the Stalinist régime in Hungary, now also became a powerful protest movement against the presence of Soviet troops in the country.

Meanwhile Mikoyan, accompanied by Mikhail A. Suslov, arrived in Budapest from Moscow. They saw that to recall Nagy as prime minister was not enough to silence the insurrection, and that a new party leader was essential. Mikoyan had overthrown Rákosi four months before; now he overthrew Gerö, whom the central committee had allowed to stay on as general secretary while the politbureau was changed, and in his place put János Kádár. He had been one of the party leaders since its revival in 1945; he had become minister of the interior in 1948 to succeed Rajk, but in 1951 had been deposed by Rákosi as a potential rival, arrested, expelled from the party and not rehabilitated until 1955.

The leadership of the revolution was now in the hands of Imre Nagy as prime minister and János Kádár as general secretary of the party.

Nagy, a professor of agriculture, possessed neither a revolutionary temperament nor a leader's strength of decision. He had criticized Rákosi's policies of over-centralizing the economy and forcing through the collectivization of agriculture, but he had never fought for power within the party; he had proved incapable of attracting about him the opposition to Rákosi. In 1953, he had been placed in power by the Soviet leaders, not by the revisionist faction within the party and, after his overthrow in 1955, abandoned by friends and comrades, he had withdrawn from active politics.

During the revolutionary ferment which gripped the masses in October 1956, he had come to represent a symbol for the ideas behind the freedom movement although nothing was further from his intentions than to stand as its figurehead. His name was on the lips of all those who had gathered in front of the parliament building on 24 October but he resisted pressure from his friends to seize the leadership of this leaderless movement. After making a short address to the crowds calling out for him in front of the parliament building, he went to the party secretariat, where the central committee was assembled, and remained there until 26 October, the day after his nomination as prime minister. Not even then did he feel himself to be the leader of the revolution; it was a role that had been forced on him by events.

Meanwhile the revolution had spread from Budapest across the entire country. Workers and students formed 'revolutionary councils', or, as in Debrecen, 'Socialist revolutionary councils', and took over public offices. With a few exceptions, this takeover of power occurred without any use of force.

On 26 October the central committee, having sat in permanent session since the 23rd, issued a proclamation. It announced the *i*mpending formation of a new government on the 'broadest national basis' so as to regularize the relationship between Hungary and the Soviet Union on the basis of independence, complete equality and mutual non-interference, and promised 'the return of Soviet troops to their garrisons after order had been re-established'; it also announced an amnesty 'for all those who have taken part in armed combat and who have laid down their arms by ten o'clock this evening'; but for any who continued the fight, it threatened 'destruction without mercy'. Yet the clashes in Budapest were halted only two days later, after Nagy had changed the government and had announced on the radio the dissolution of the hated secret police and the cease-fire order to the troops. His speech, and the announcement of the composition of the new government, which included György Lukacs, the Marxist philosopher, as well as Zoltán Tildy, the former leader of the Small Peasants' party and president of the republic from 1946 to 1948, seemed to signal the victory of the revolution.

The decisive shift in the revolution occurred on 30 October. Over the radio Nagy announced 'the abrogation of the one-party system and the formation of a government based on the democratic co-operation among the coalition parties of 1945'. This was nothing less than the end of the rule of dictatorship and the beginning of a rule of democracy. Moreover, he declared, the government had decided to commence 'negotiations with the Soviet government about the withdrawal of Soviet troops from Hungary' and not from Budapest alone. And he appealed to the Soviet Government, as a first step, to withdraw Soviet troops from Budapest without delay.[1]

Nagy's exciting announcement was followed on the radio by one no less sensational from Kádár, which stated basically that the Communist party had placed itself in liquidation. This colossal organization of 900,000 members had in fact fallen into ruin during the initial impetus of the revolution. The party, Kádár said, which had once 'inspired our people and country with the noble idealism of Socialism', had 'degenerated through the blind and criminal policies of Rákosi's Stalinist gang into an instrument of despotism and national enslavement'. He announced that, 'in accordance with the wishes of many true patriots and Socialists who have fought against Rákosi's despotism', a new party would be formed to come into being on 1 November. This would 'once and for all purge itself of the crimes of the past' and would develop democracy and Socialism 'not in slavish imitations of foreign examples, but in the spirit of Marxist–Leninist teachings, free from Stalinism, along a road which matches our country's economic and historical character'.[2]

1. For the text of the declaration, see Zinner, *Revolution in Hungary*, pp. 453–4.
2. Quoted in ibid., p. 464. The nominated party leaders were János Kádár, Imre Nagy, Sandor Kopacsi, Geza Losonczy, György Lukács, Zoltán Szanto and Ference Donath. Nagy, Donath, Kopacsi and Losonczy were arrested during the Soviet counter-revolution; Nagy was executed and the others sentenced to between twelve and fifteen years' hard labour. Losonczy died in prison.

The coalition government which Nagy had announced was formed on 1 November. It incorporated the Communist party, represented by Nagy, Kádár and Losonczy, the Social Democratic Party, represented by Anna Kéthly, Gyula Kelemen and Jozsef Fischer and representatives of the Small Peasants' party and the National Farmers' party (which retitled itself the Petöfi party); one other member of the government was Colonel Pál Maléter, who had joined the revolution together with the troops under his command, to represent the revolutionary committees, which in the meantime had been set up in towns and villages throughout the country.

The question overshadowing all others, even before the new government took up office, was the withdrawal of Soviet troops from Hungary and the settling of the legal relationship between Hungary and the Soviet Union. The political revolution, soon after it began, had been transformed into a passionate national revolution, inflamed by the massacre committed by the Russian tank troops in Budapest on 24 October. Hungary's national pride had revolted against the predominance of Moscow in Hungary which had shown itself with so much provocation in the streets of Budapest. The national independence of Hungary, her separation from the Warsaw Pact and the declaration of her neutrality had become the slogans of the revolution.

It appeared at first as though the Soviet government had recognized the strength of the national current in the Hungarian revolution, and was seeking a compromise solution of the conflict. Once again it sent Mikoyan and Suslov, who had returned to Moscow on 26 October, to Budapest on the 30th, declaring at the same time that, 'in view of the fact that the presence of Soviet military units in Hungary could serve as a pretext for any deterioration in the situation, the military commandant has been ordered to withdraw the Soviet military units from the city of Budapest as soon as this is considered to be necessary by the Hungarian government'.

It went on to state that the Soviet government was prepared 'to enter into appropriate discussions with the government of the Hungarian People's Republic and the other members of the Warsaw Pact over the question of the presence of Soviet troops in Hungarian territory'.[1]

On the 30th, Russian troops did, in fact, vacate the capital. But already on the following day fresh Soviet armoured divisions, stationed in Romania, were pouring back into the country to occupy airports and railway stations and to take up strategic positions. On the morning of 1 November, Nagy summoned the Soviet Ambassador, Y. V. Andropov, to his office—Mikoyan and Suslov having returned to Moscow the previous night—to protest against the Soviet troop movements, which were in breach of the Warsaw Pact. He demanded an authoritative statement on whether the Soviet Union still stood by its declaration of 30 October. Having referred the matter back to Moscow,

1. *Pravda*, 31 October 1956, quoted in ibid., p. 488.

the ambassador reassured Nagy that the Soviet Union considered its declaration still to be in force and that it proposed to set up commissions to discuss the Warsaw Pact and the military and technical questions concerning a withdrawal from Hungary.

Thereupon Nagy called together nine leading personalities of the Communist party, including Kádár, Lukács and Szanto, to ask their advice over Hungary's future relations with the Soviet Union. Seven of them advocated Hungary's withdrawal from the Warsaw Pact and the declaration of her neutrality, though Lukács and Szanto were undecided. The cabinet, meeting afterwards, stated its solid support for the decision taken by the conference of the Communist party leaders. Within a few hours, Nagy, in the presence of members of the government, informed the Soviet Ambassador of their decision and cabled it at once to the secretary general of the United Nations, Dag Hammarskjöld. He also asked that 'the question of Hungary's neutrality and its defence by the four Great Powers' should immediately be placed on the agenda of the United Nations General Assembly.

In the night of 1 November the Soviet Ambassador visited Nagy with a proposal by the Soviet government that he should withdraw the Hungarian government's appeal to the United Nations, and that thereupon Soviet troops would be withdrawn from Hungary. Nagy accepted. On the next day he was told by the Soviet Ambassador that the Soviet government had taken note of Hungary's withdrawal from the Warsaw Pact and requested an early meeting of the commission, which was to discuss the future relationship between the two states, as well as of the technical and military commission.[1]

The Hungarian-Soviet commission for technical and military questions met on 3 November in the Russian headquarters on Tokol, an island in the Danube. After several hours, four members of the Hungarian delegation, including the minister of defence, Colonel Pál Maléter, were arrested by the chief of the Russian secret police, General Ivan Serov; they were never seen again.

Unsuspectingly, Nagy remained through the night of 3 November in the parliament building awaiting the return of his military delegation. Meanwhile Russian troops had surrounded Budapest, and in the dawn of 4 November they opened fire. By using the discussions as a stratagem, the Soviet government had lulled the Hungarian government into a false sense of security. Nothing had been done to prepare for defence, the Hungarian army had not been placed on the alert, the nation had remained unwarned about the immediate danger of military intervention. The Russian attack came as a total surprise. At five o'clock on that morning the Hungarian nation was startled by Nagy's declaration over the wireless:

1. For a detailed description of Nagy's negotiations with the Soviet Ambassador, see Zinner, *Revolution in Hungary*, pp. 326–31 and 334–5.

Today in the early hours of the morning, Soviet troops have begun an attack on the capital with the undoubted intention of overthrowing the legal democratic government of Hungary. Our troops are fighting. The government is at its post.

Yet within barely an hour of this declaration, Communist members of the Nagy government, Kádár among them, issued a statement transmitted by a radio station in east Hungary—an area already occupied by Russian troops—that they had in fact dissolved their connection with the government on 1 November, having realized that Nagy had fallen victim to reactionary influences and that 'our people's republic, the strength of the workers and peasants, and our social achievements are being threatened with destruction by the growing strength of the counter-revolutionary threat'. They had therefore taken the initiative in forming a counter-government—a 'Hungarian revolutionary workers' and peasants' government'. Then Kádár stepped up to the microphone to announce the composition of the government he had formed. He announced reforms and promised, with particular emphasis, that 'workers who have taken part in these most recent events will under no circumstances be persecuted'.[1]

There had been nothing in Kádár's behaviour on 1 November to indicate any impending break-off of his loyalty to Nagy's government which he had helped to form. At the conference of the nine Communist leaders on 1 November, he had advocated the denouncing of the Warsaw Pact and the declaration of Hungary's neutrality, and when the Soviet Ambassador had been informed of this decision in the presence of the government, it was Kádár who had told him that he would, if necessary, 'fight with rifle in hand' against the Russians in the streets.[2] On the same day he had announced over the radio the setting up of a new Communist party planned for 1 November, and had celebrated the revolution, which 'had overthrown the Rákosi régime [and had] . . . won freedom for the people and independence for the country, without which there can be no Socialism'.

In this broadcast Kádár had also given a warning of the dangers of a counter-revolution.[3] 'The people's revolt,' he said, 'had arrived at a crossroads. Should the democratic parties fail to show the necessary strength to consolidate the achievements of the revolution, they will find themselves facing a counter-revolution.' But, he stated, 'the blood of the youth of

---

1. Quoted in ibid., pp. 337–8.   2. See ibid., pp. 325 and 329.

3. The struggle against the dangers of a counter-revolution was in these days as much a slogan for the Social Democrats as for the Communists. Anna Kéthly, in an article on re-establishing the Social Democratic party, had also written on 1 November in *Népszava*, the Social Democratic daily, appearing for the first time since its suppression in 1947: 'The Social Democratic party . . . has won potential life from a régime which termed itself a people's democracy, but which was no democracy either in form or appearance. . . . Liberated from a prison, we need to watch that our country does not become another prison in another colour, that the factories, mines and the land remain in the possession of the people'—quoted in Fryer, *Hungarian Tragedy*, pp. 74–5.

Hungary, our soldiers, workers and peasants, has not been spilt to replace Rákosi's despotism with the rule of a counter-revolution. . . . We must,' he declaimed, 'destroy the hiding-place of counter-revolution and reaction. . . . We must ultimately safeguard our democratic society.' And he appealed to the 'newly formed democratic parties to overcome the danger of the threatening counter-revolution and of foreign intervention by consolidating the government'.

The 'danger of foreign intervention', to which Kádár had referred, had however been threatened only by the Soviet Union; the only way to ward it off was by the withdrawal of Russian troops from Hungary. 'The people,' he said, 'had proved by their spilt blood that they decisively support the efforts of the government to achieve a total withdrawal of Soviet troops. We have no wish,' he declared, 'to be dependent any longer. We do not wish our country to become a battlefield.'[1]

This speech, as we have seen, was broadcast on 1 November, at ten o'clock in the evening to be precise. After making it, Kádár mysteriously disappeared from Budapest. He had fled, and only returned in the wake of the Russian armoured divisions to head the counter-revolution.

The death struggle of the revolution lasted for four days. The guns of the Soviet artillery laid Budapest in ruins.[2] The numbers of dead and wounded totalled thousands, and over 100,000 fled to Austria and Yugoslavia. Nagy himself sought refuge in the Yugoslav Embassy. When he left it on 22 November, equipped with a letter of safe-conduct signed by Kádár, he was arrested in the street by the Soviet police and abducted to Romania. In 1958, with three of his fellow Communists, including Pál Maléter, he was accused of high treason, sentenced to death by a secret court and executed. The anonymous revolutionary fighters were dispersed and broken, many of them being deported to Russia[3] or imprisoned by Hungarian special courts. It was not until an amnesty in March 1963 that about 3,000 political prisoners were set free.

The Soviet action in Hungary had evoked the most profound concern

1. Quoted in Zinner, *Revolution in Hungary*, p. 364.

2. Peter Fryer, correspondent of the London *Daily Worker*, who left Budapest on 11 November, sent his paper the following eye-witness account: 'Vast areas of the city, above all the workers' districts, are in ruins. Budapest has for four days and nights been under continual bombardment. Dead lie in the streets—streets ploughed up by tanks and sown with the ruins of a bloody war. . . . I saw this city, once so beautiful, shot to pieces, destroyed and subjected to attrition. It was heart-breaking for one who loves the Soviet Union as much as he does the Hungarian people'—Fryer, *Hungarian Tragedy*, pp. 83 and 84. The report did not, of course, appear in the paper, and Fryer, who resigned as editor as a consequence, was suspended from the British Communist party.

3. György Lukács had also been arrested as a member of the Nagy government, and deported to Romania. The Communist party did not hesitate from excluding from its ranks even this brilliant Marxist thinker. He was, however, allowed to return to Hungary after a time, but it was only in 1962 that he was again accepted as a party member.

throughout the world; what had occurred seemed unbelievable. In deepest peace a great power had suddenly overnight attacked by force of arms a sovereign state, had overthrown its legal government and in a bloody fight had cast down the masses who rose to defend their country. The General Assembly of the United Nations, convened for an extraordinary meeting on 4 November, demanded that the Soviet Union should 'cease immediately its armed attack on the people of Hungary'.

The general council of the Socialist International, at its meeting in Copenhagen on 30 November 1956, issued a resolution stating:

The Socialist International is following the events in Hungary with the deepest sympathy for the Hungarian people. It is profoundly shocked by the suppression of the freedom movement by the Russian military forces and full of admiration for the continued resistance of the Hungarian workers.

In the name of freedom-loving Socialism, we solemnly protest against the Russian war against the Hungarian people. The action of the Soviet government is a brutal negation of the humanitarian and democratic principles of Socialism. . . . The desire for freedom . . . must not be drowned in blood by Russian tanks.

The resolution demanded that the right of every nation to self-determination should be recognized—'a right which formerly was also proclaimed by the Soviet Union'. And it demanded the immediate implementation of the resolution of the United Nations requesting the withdrawal of Russian troops and the granting of access to U.N. observers.[1]

Communists now found themselves in a state of utter confusion. For how were they to square Soviet action with fundamental Socialist principles—'the elementary principle,' as Lenin said, 'to which Marx was always true, namely, that no nation can be free which suppresses other nations'? The Soviet action was all the more confusing as only a few days before these events, the Soviet government had itself proclaimed anew the principle of the equality of all Socialist nations.

Five days before invading Hungary, in its declaration of 30 October, the Soviet government had, in fact, stated its willingness to withdraw its forces from Hungary and had laid down the principles which it regarded as forming the basis for relations between Socialist countries:

The countries in the broad community of Socialist countries, united by common ideals to construct a Socialist society and by the principles of proletarian internationalism, can only set up their mutual relationship on a basis of complete equality, respect of territorial integrity, national independence and sovereignty and mutual non-interference in internal affairs.[2]

1. For the text of the resolution, see *Socialist International Information*, vol. VI, 10 December 1956. The general council had also elected a delegation to examine the situation in Hungary on the spot, 'so as to speak, as the representatives of twelve million democratic Socialists, with the Hungarian workers'. The Hungarian government, however, refused entry to the delegation of the International, as well as to the commission set up by the United Nations.

2. *Pravda*, 31 October 1956. For the text of the declaration, see Zinner (ed.), *National Communism and Popular Revolt in Eastern Europe*, pp. 485–9.

Without doubt Hungary was for the Communists a Socialist country. How then was an action of the Soviet government against a Socialist country to be morally justified, an action which was no different from the naked use of force employed by imperialist governments and which, above all, so blatantly transgressed against the sacred principles which they had themselves proclaimed?

Moscow's propaganda resolved any contradiction between principles and the action of the Soviet government by the well-tried method of 'dialectics', by which they had, for example, condemned Britain's war with Germany as an imperialist war of capitalistic high finance and then, the moment Hitler attacked the Soviet Union, by the magic of dialectics had transformed it into a people's war of independence. In the same way they explained the Soviet Union's war against Hungary as an act of Socialist solidarity, intended to save a Socialist country from the seizure of power by a counter-revolutionary reaction.[1]

From the very beginning Moscow had in fact denounced the revolution in Hungary as a 'counter-revolutionary conspiracy'. The rising of the people after the demonstrations in front of the parliament building on 24 October, which had been broken up by fire from the Russian tanks, had, wrote *Pravda*, been 'provoked by the British and American imperialists'—it was an 'adventure aimed against the people', but one which had 'collapsed'.[2]

The central organ of the Hungarian Communist party, however, at once rejected this concept as an 'error'. 'What has occurred in Budapest,' wrote *Szabad Nép*, 'was neither aimed against the people nor was it an adventure. Above all, it did not collapse. . . . What collapsed was the rule of the Rákosi gang. . . . We may state with certitude that the accusations by *Pravda* that the revolt was incited by British and American imperialists has deeply offended and insulted the million and a half inhabitants of Budapest.' It was not imperialist intrigues, said *Szabad Nép*, which had unleashed this 'bloody, tragic but enlightening struggle', but 'the errors and crimes' of those Hungarian leaders who had been overthrown by the insurrection,

1. This was the version of events which came to be accepted by all Communist parties. Thus, for example, the Communist party of Italy, the largest Communist party outside the Soviet bloc, declared: 'It is essential to decide either to defend the Socialist revolution or to support the white counter-revolution—the old, Fascist and reactionary Hungary. . . . No third camp exists'—*L'Unità*, 25 October 1956, quoted in Blackmer, *Unity in Diversity*, p. 82.

2. *Pravda*, 28 October 1956. For the text of this article, see Zinner (ed.), *National Communism and Popular Revolt in Eastern Europe*, pp. 435–40. The Soviet delegate, V. Kuznetsov, declared to the General Assembly of the United Nations on 13 November that the uprising in Hungary, led by Fascists, had been a 'bloodthirsty orgy' organized by counter-revolutionary forces. The Communist press surpassed itself with descriptions of the murders of Communists under the rule of a 'white terror'. Fryer confirms that in Budapest several members of the dreaded and hated secret police were lynched. In this act of vengeance, he remarked, some Communists may also have fallen victim. But he denies emphatically that such murders had amounted to a mass symptom under the 'rule of a white terror'—Fryer, *Hungarian Tragedy*, pp. 79–81.

and above all by their failure to safeguard 'the sacred flame of national independence'.[1]

'By no means can we agree with those,' *Szabad Nép* had written on the previous day, 'who characterize the events of the last few days as counter-revolutionary attempts at a *coup d'état*. The movement began with a demonstration by the student youth expressing a deep-seated emotion, a noble and glowing passion, shared by the entire nation. . . .' From this movement, 'a great national democracy has developed in our country, embracing all the people and welding them together, a movement that was forced underground by past tyranny but which, touched by the first breath of freedom, has begun to burn in high flames'.[2]

How could the statement by Moscow by which it had tried to justify the Russian invasion of Hungary—that the revolution had been a 'counter-revolutionary conspiracy'—be reconciled to the fact that at its head had stood the senior and most prominent of Hungarian Communists—Imre Nagy, Zoltán Szanto, György Lukács—and that it had been the works councils in the factories which had organized the working class to oppose the Russian invasion?

If the Soviet intervention really was necessary to put down a counter-revolution [Fryer wrote on 11 November in his report to the *Daily Worker*], then how can it be explained that it was in the workers' districts of Újpest to the north of Budapest and Csepel to the south—both Communist strongholds—that Soviet troops encountered the strongest resistance? Or how is it to be explained why the workers in the famous steel town of Stalinváros declared that they would defend their Socialist town—built with their own hands—against the Soviet invasion?

'I saw for myself,' Fryer described his own experience of the invasion, 'how the Soviet troops, thrown into battle against the "counter-revolution", fought not Fascists or reactionaries, but the people of Hungary: workers, peasants, students and soldiers.'[3]

That the revolution had genuinely been a people's movement against the tyrannical rule of Rákosi's régime can be denied as little as the fact that it was the proletarian masses who were defending the liberty won in the revolution against Russian troops.

The question must now be examined why the Soviet Union should have undertaken such an action which discredited it throughout the world and shook the faith of innumerable Communists who fervently considered it to be a Socialist, anti-imperialist power. Initially, it seemed, the Soviet Union had hesitated. There are no indications that the Soviet government planned any military action before 30 October. Its declaration of that date showed

---

1. *Szabad Nép*, 29 October 1956. For the text of the article, see Zinner (ed.), *National Communism and Popular Revolt in Eastern Europe*, pp. 449–51.
2. *Szabad Nép*, 28 October 1956. For the text, see ibid., p. 425.
3. Fryer, *Hungarian Tragedy*, pp. 78–9.

its readiness to solve the question of the Russian troops in Hungary by negotiations with the Hungarian government.

But the same day, Nagy had announced the transformation of the Communist régime into a democracy by the repeal of the one-party system on which it had been based. In this act Moscow saw a threat to the cohesion of the Soviet bloc, since the guarantee of its unity remained the power position in the bloc's member states of Communist parties loyal to the Soviet Union. It was not to be expected that Hungary would feel itself linked to the Soviet Union by any special loyalty under a democratic régime. For Hungary, moreover—which was under no threat from any of its neighbouring states—the most effective guarantee of its security was obviously its position as a neutral state, and not an alliance with Russia, which carried the risk of Hungary becoming once again, as Kádár said, 'a battlefield' in a war between East and West. For these reasons, Kádár himself, at the conference of Communist leaders on 1 November as well as afterwards in the discussion with the Soviet Ambassador, had supported a declaration of Hungarian neutrality.[1]

The Soviet government apparently decided for military action only after 30 October when Nagy had announced the changing of the Communist dictatorship into a democracy, and Russia became convinced that Hungary would, under a democratic régime, leave the Soviet bloc. Thus when on 1 November Nagy did indeed renounce the Warsaw Pact, the Soviet government began to move the Soviet army against Hungary.

The action of the Soviet Union against Hungary provides a classic example of imperialist power policy—the subjection by military force of a small, helpless country to the predominance of a great power, and the safeguarding of this predominance by an imposed government. But it also provides a classic example of a reactionary counter-revolution—the overthrow of a government brought to power by a revolution and the destruction of the liberty which the revolution had won.

The Soviet action, like the Hitler–Stalin pact, proved a watershed in the history of the Communist movement. Under its ideological pretence, the Soviet invasion had been presented as an episode in the world-wide struggle between the forces of Socialism and capitalism, and many Communists salved the resulting conflict of conscience with this interpretation. But for many others the Soviet action seemed to be what it really was—a brutal violation of a fundamental principle of Socialism—and they parted from a movement which, in the service of the great-power interests of the Soviet Union, had betrayed its ideals.

1. What actually took place when Kádár disappeared from Budapest after his radio speech, to return at the head of a Russian-nominated government in the wake of the invading Soviet troops, is a carefully guarded official secret, though the inferences of the event are obvious.

23 · 'The Spring of Prague'

The 'Spring of Prague'—the revolution which took place in Czechoslovakia in the spring of 1968—is among the most momentous events in the history of the Communist movement. A Communist party in full possession of state power had revoked the Communist system of government and had decided to change the institutions of society, on which rested the dictatorship of the party, and to create a 'new model of Socialist democracy'.

The action of the Communist party in Czechoslovakia in the spring of 1968 had not, like those of the Communist parties in Yugoslavia and Hungary, stemmed from a revolt against Moscow's predominance; the friendly relationship between Czechoslovakia and the Soviet Union was not in question at the time of these events. The action was the first attempt by a ruling Communist party, undertaken with a full awareness of its significance —and it was this awareness which gave it its historical importance—to realize, by changing the political structure of the Communist state, the idea of freedom and the self-determination of the people in a Socialist society.

This action did not contradict Lenin's concept of the struggle for Socialism. He had proclaimed the 'dictatorship of the proletariat' (as the dictatorship of the Communist party was euphemistically termed) as the proletarian type of régime for the period of transition from the capitalist to a Socialist order of society—a type of régime which, he assumed, would 'die away' after the resistance of the capitalist classes to the construction of Socialism was broken.[1]

The Czech Communists had now felt that it was this stage of development which had been reached in their country. The material foundation for a Socialist order of society had been laid, the means of production had become common property and the resistance of the capitalist classes to Socialist change had indeed been broken. 'Since the end of the 1950s,' the 'Action

1. V. I. Lenin, *Staat und Revolution: Ausgewählte Werke* (Moscow, 1947), vol. II, pp. 225–7.

Programme of the Party' explained in justifying the reforms that were destined to transform the régime of dictatorship into a Socialist democracy, 'our society has entered upon a new stage of development. . . . The characteristic of the present stage is that already there no longer exists any antagonism between classes'; and that the 'dictatorship of the working class has [in our country] fulfilled its most important historical mission'.[1]

And thus there grew among the Czech Communists the perception that the system of dictatorship, resting on the principle of the denial of freedom of autonomy, had turned into fetters hindering the development of Socialism, because Socialism means, in Marx's interpretation, the realization of the highest degree of individual freedom and of the people's autonomy. They now began to seek the means to overcome the system of dictatorship by a system of Socialist democracy.

1

The dictatorship of the Communist Party in Czechoslovakia had, as soon as it was established in February 1948 by a *coup d'état*,[2] degenerated under Klement Gottwald's rule into a soulless, bureaucratic despotism; under Antonin Novotný (1904–1975), Gottwald's successor as the party's general secretary after his death in 1953 who four years later became president of the republic, it had stultified into barrenness.

The impetus for the spiritual revolt against the system, as in Poland and Hungary, came from the Communist intellectuals, who awoke within the party a consciousness of the contradiction between the ideals of Socialism and the reality of the dictatorial régime. Thus Eduard Goldstücker, professor of German literature (and later Rector) at the Karlova University in Prague, who began the process of criticizing the régime, wrote in 1963: 'If the history of our time has shown something beyond any shadow of doubt, it is the misfortune of believing that a new, higher, social order may be reached without humanity or justice, and that while great human achievements may

1. See K. Paul Hensel, *et al.*, *Die sozialistische Marktwirtschaft in der Tschechoslowakei* (Stuttgart, 1968), pp. 289 and 300. The 'Action Programme of the Communist Party of Czechoslovakia', which carried the sub-title 'The Czechoslovakian Road to Socialism', had been decided by a plenary session of the central committee on 5 April 1968. This comprehensive document, which will be examined in the pages which follow, appeared as a supplement to the party's central organ, *Rudé Právo*, on 8 April 1968. For the full text, see Hensel *et al.*, pp. 286–337. For the most detailed description of the events, on which this presentation has been based, see Harry Schwartz, *Prague's 200 days. The Struggle for Democracy in Czechoslovakia* (London, 1969); see also Philip Windsor and Adam Roberts, *Czechoslovakia 1968. Reform, Repression and Resistance* (London, 1969); Robert Rhodes James (ed.), *The Czechoslovak Crisis 1968* (London, 1969); Z. A. B. Zeman, *Prague Spring. A Report on Czechoslovakia* (London, 1969); Wolfgang Horlacher, *Zwischen Prag und Moskau* (Stuttgart, 1968); and Robin Alison Remington (ed.), *Winter in Prague. Documents on Czechoslovak Communism in Crisis* (London, 1969).

2. See page 178.

be represented in theory, they can in practice be trampled on.'[1] It was with this appeal to the party to make a personal appraisal of its destiny that the struggle for a 'Socialism with a human face' began.

But under Antonin Novotný's rule no basic reforms were to be expected. It was true that, following the Twentieth Congress of the Communist party of the Soviet Union, the severity of the régime in Czechoslovakia had gradually been eased, and in 1960 many political prisoners were released by amnesty. But none of the régime's institutions had been 'de-Stalinized'. Novotný had risen to power under the Stalinist system and he had reinforced it by infiltrating the party machine with his trusted followers. He feared reforms, not simply because they conflicted with his concept of the road to Socialism, but also because they threatened his position in power. The path to reforms could only be opened by a complete change of leadership—from the top right down to the local organizations. The fight for reforms began with a bid by the reformists to liberate the party from its Stalinist leadership.

The reformists began their fight against the party leadership by demanding the rehabilitation of the innocent victims of Gottwald's and Novotný's reign of terror. Seventy thousand Communists and non-Communists considered to be non-conformist by the régime had been imprisoned, and eleven Communists occupying the most eminent positions in party and state—including Rudolf Slánský, general secretary of the party and deputy prime minister, and Vladimir Clementis, leader of the Communist party of Slovakia and foreign secretary—had been sentenced to death at a show trial in November 1952 as 'Trotskyist, Titoist and Zionist conspirators' and hanged.[2] In the same year, fifteen writers were given sentences totalling 220 years.

While the régime persecuted suspected Czech Communists on the charge of 'Trotskyist and Titoist deviation', it persecuted suspected Slovak Communists who demanded national autonomy for their country for 'bourgeois nationalist deviations'. Among the numerous victims of these persecutions by Gottwald and Novotný had been the Slovak leaders, among them Clementis, executed in 1952 following the Slánský trial, Gustav Husák and Ladislav Novomcsky, both sentenced during a show trial in 1954 to life imprisonment, and only released by the 1960 amnesty but not rehabilitated until 1963.

In the eyes of Slovak Communists, Clementis, Husák and Novomcsky were national martyrs, while Novotný, who had unleashed the wave of persecution against the Slovaks in 1952, was the arch-enemy of their national

1. *Literárni Noviny*, February 1963, quoted in Schwartz, *Prague's 200 Days*, p. 20. Goldstücker, one of the most outstanding leaders of the revolt of the intellectuals, was sentenced to life imprisonment in 1954 and pardoned in 1960.

2. For the history of this monstrous trial, see Eugen Löbl and Dusan Pokorný, *Die Revolution rehabilitiert ihre Kinder. Hinter den Kulissen des Slánský-Prozesses* (Vienna, 1969). Löbl, deputy minister of foreign trade, had been arrested in 1949 and was only amnestied in 1960. He had been one of the defendants in the Slánský trial.

aspirations. They urged the rehabilitation of the victims of these persecutions, not only out of an injured sense of justice, but also as a tactical device in their struggle against Novotný and his régime.

Under the pressure of this movement, a commission of investigation into the political trials of the 1950s was set up by the Twelfth Congress of the Communist party of Czechoslovakia at the request of the Slovak Communists, supported by the Czech reformists. Novotný sacrificed as scapegoats three of the most hated representatives of the rule of terror: the minister of police, Karol Bacilek, the President of the High Court, Josef Urvalek, who as attorney-general in the Slánský trial had asked for the death sentence to be passed on the eleven accused, and the prime minister, Villiam Siroký, who, although a Slovak, had been responsible for the proceedings against the Slovakian leaders. Bacilek was dismissed as minister of police and expelled from the presidium of the party, Urvalek was relieved of his post and in September 1963 Siroký was dismissed as prime minister.

With Bacilek's overthrow began the rise of Alexander Dubček, who, five years later, was to be carried to power by a revolutionary upsurge. Bacilek had at the same time been general secretary of the Communist party of Slovakia as well as its representative in the presidium of the central organization of the Czechoslovak party. In April 1963 a congress of the Slovak party relieved him of both functions and elected Alexander Dubček, one of a group of younger local party leaders who were unsullied by the régime's Stalinist misdeeds, to be his successor.

Following their success at the Twelfth Congress on the issue of rehabilitation, the reformists took as target for their criticism the stagnation of economic life which had set in at the beginning of the 1960s and made fundamental reforms of the economic system their immediate objective. A severe economic crisis in 1963 had shown the inefficiency of the centralized planned economy which had been set up on the pattern of the Soviet Union. It had become, as the Czech Marxist economist Ota Sik, director of the Economic Institute in the Academy of Science, had shown in his analysis, an obstacle to economic growth. He developed a programme for the reorganization of the economy through comprehensive decentralization, based on the autonomy of management and workers' participation.[1]

This programme, which was discussed within the party for a year and a half (though not published until October 1964) was approved finally in January 1965 by the central committee and placed before the Thirteenth Congress for approval in June 1966. But the programme for economic reforms also had political significance. 'It represented,' Ota Sik said in his

---

1. The most thorough documentary examination of the programme for economic reforms may be found in Hensel, *The Social Market Economy in Czechoslovakia*; see also J. F. Brown, *The New East Europe* (London, 1966), pp. 96–100.

speech to the congress, 'a large step along the road to democratizing our society.' This was, however, only a beginning: 'The whole problem of democratizing the party's internal relations' had to be thoroughly studied, and it was necessary to prepare true institutional and constitutional changes throughout the whole political sphere and administration'.[1]

The Stalinist wing of the party, still in control of the central committee, watered down the programme and, when it was finally accepted by the congress, its execution was delayed and sabotaged. Novotný was determined to prevent any weakening of the government's authority that could result from democratic reforms. A new press law, which came into force on 1 January 1967, was intended once again to tighten up the shackles on the press, which had been relaxed somewhat since 1963. By this new law, the press was placed under direct control of the Ministry of Culture, the right to edit papers was granted only to organizations, not to individuals; and the ministry could refuse to register a paper or periodical (and without registration they could not appear legally) unless they guaranteed to 'fulfil their social mission'. For the first time in the history of the Czechoslovak Republic, the press became subjected to pre-censorship and its attitudes prescribed by ideological and political 'guide-lines' laid down by the Communist party.

The press law provoked a revolt among writers and journalists; it broke out at the congress of the Union of the Czechoslovak Writers which met at the end of June 1967. The congress became, in effect, a court of justice for airing charges against a political régime that was crippling the nation's intellectual life and degrading its writers and journalists to the status of party hacks.

The key-note was struck by the opening speech given by Milan Kundara, a member of the presidium of the union. 'The period between the two world wars,' he said, 'was a period of the greatest flowering in the history of Czech civilization.' Its development was interrupted by the Nazi occupation and later by Stalinism, and these had, he explained, 'isolated our country from the outside world and reduced our literature to naked propaganda'. This, he said, was 'a tragedy which threatens the Czech nation with removal to the farthest limits of European civilization'.

Under the prevailing system, the Czech novelist Ludvik Vaculik, who was also a veteran Communist party member, explained in another speech, fear penetrated all the pores of society. 'We have fallen,' he said, 'into political indifference and a state of resignation, worrying over petty details and dependent upon petty authorities, into a slavery of a new and unusual kind. . . .'

I do not believe [he said], that independent citizens can exist in our country. . . . I do not myself feel safe as a citizen. I see no guarantees for my safety. . . . But do the authorities, the government and its members, themselves hold guarantees for their

1. *Rudé Právo*, 5 June 1966, quoted in James, (ed.), *The Czechoslovak Crisis*, p. 6.

personal safety, and without which creative work, including that of politics, remains impossible? Our society faces the bankruptcy of its expectations and hopes. Throughout these twenty years [of the Communist régime] no single human problem has been solved in our country—neither that of fulfilling such basic necessities as apartments, schools and economic prosperity, nor that of satisfying life's cultural requirements, and which no undemocratic system can satisfy: a full sense of social values, and the subordination of political decisions to ethical criteria.

The resolution of the congress protested against the introduction of censorship as well as the party's influence over literature and the press. In a concluding address, the chairman, Jan Procházka, a deputy member of the party's central committee, stated his agreement with the criticisms that had been voiced by various speakers and with 'all who fight oppression, persecution and the venom of anti-Semitism'.

The question of anti-Semitism, raised during the congress, had become urgent in Czechoslovakia in the wake of the Arab–Israeli war of June 1967. When the war began, the Czechoslovak government had broken off diplomatic relations with Israel, as had the Soviet Union, and, like the Soviet Union, had condemned Israel as the aggressor, while Communist propaganda, with anti-Semitic undertones, had identified Zionism with Nazism. But this political line had turned out to be in marked contrast to the enthusiasm with which Israel's victory over its enemies, many times its superior in manpower and armaments, was greeted by many Czechs. In his speech to the congress, which met a few days after the war, the playwright Pavel Kohout, who had formerly been the party's most effective propagandist but who had developed into a rebel, had defended Israel's 'right to fire the first shot', even, he said, as it had been Czechoslovakia's right in 1938 to defend itself against the threatened Nazi invasion by a strategy appropriate to the situation. Also, as a Communist, he could not forget Israel's achievements. 'In Israel,' he said, 'they have transformed the desert into a garden. . . . Almost the entire system of agriculture is organized along Socialist and Communist lines.'[1]

Israel's victory also proved to be Novotný's defeat. His régime had supplied Egypt with Czech arms and, after their defeat, he promised the Arab states full support in rearming. Also, as general secretary of the party, he had led the anti-Israel propaganda campaign.

The criticisms of his anti-Israel policies at the writers' congress irritated Novotný considerably as it placed the odium of anti-Semitism on his shoulders. This was sensationally amplified by an unusual act taken by one of Czechoslovakia's most popular writers, Ladislav Mnacko, who had been decorated with the highest literary medal and whose books enjoyed sales of over a million copies. Shortly after the congress he travelled to Israel so as

1. For extracts from the speeches at the congress, see Zeman, *Prague Spring*, pp. 56–65; Schwartz, *Prague's 200 Days*, pp. 42–8.

to protest, he said, in a broadcast which was transmitted to Czechoslovakia over foreign radio stations, against the Czech government's policy, for, he said, 'in Czechoslovakia one is prevented from speaking about the crisis in the Near East'. It had become impossible for him, he continued, 'even by silence to support a policy which could lead to the extermination of an entire nation and the destruction of a complete state. . . .' For an explanation of this policy, which he found incomprehensible, he referred to the wave of anti-Semitism which had swept the country after the Slánský trial, and against which so far no action had been taken. 'But if,' he said, 'we wish to remain a healthy, Socialist humanitarian country, the system in Czechoslovakia has to be completely changed.'[1]

Novotný reacted to the writers' criticisms with suppressive measures. A few days after the congress the young novelist Jan Beneš, who had been held in detention since September 1966, was sentenced to five years' hard labour, and Pavel Tigrid, the editor of a Czech periodical in Paris, was sentenced in absentia to fifteen years' hard labour for 'mutinous activity and espionage'. Vaculik and two other writers who had criticized the régime at the congress were expelled from the party; Procházka was expelled from the central committee; and the Union of Writers was deprived of its organ, Literárni Noviny, the reason being given that it had become a 'platform for disseminating liberal tendencies' and 'political opposition'; the periodical was placed under the control of the Ministry of Culture. Mnacko was stripped of his literary decoration, deprived of his Czech nationality and expelled from the party. And in a speech at the beginning of September Novotný issued a warning to the rebel intellectuals; the party, he said, had until now tolerated differences of opinions. But democracy and freedom had their limits. The Communist party ruled the country and was determined to assert itself by any means necessary. It was not, of course, a warning meant to win him the trust of the intellectuals.

It would perhaps have been possible for Novotný to ignore the criticism of the intellectuals had it not become obvious that he had simultaneously lost the trust of the wide circles within the party—above all, that of the Slovak Communists. The crisis in the party leadership came into the open on 30 October 1967 at a conference of 110 members and forty-six candidates of the central committee, summoned to discuss the 'position and role of the party during the present stage of the Socialist society'.

The campaign against Novotný's régime was opened by Dubček. He demanded changes in the party structure, a transition to new methods and, above all, a change in its relationship to the state: the separation of the party from the state, and especially of the function of party general secretary

1. Quoted in Schwartz, Prague's 200 Days, p. 50.

from that of the president of the republic. With this latter demand Dubček placed on the agenda the resignation of President Novotný as general secretary of the party.

Novotný was taken by surprise by this turn of events, and to gain time to organize a counter-attack, his supporters pressed for a postponement of the conference before it could take any decisions. But the subsequent conference of the central committee, assembled on 19 December, was also unable to reach any decisions. The presidium was prevented from laying before it a resolution concerning the general secretary, since no majority could be found to support any of its proposals. This question revealed it as being split down the middle; the party leadership was paralysed. During a three-day debate, the pent-up hatred, accumulated over the years, discharged itself in bitter criticism of the presidium. Ota Sik openly declared its bankruptcy, pointing to the catastrophic economic situation in the country and the urgent need for drastic action to avert a crisis. He demanded not only the election of a new presidium, but also forms of democracy within the party which would uproot Stalinism: an end to the ban on organized opposition groups within the party and their legalization.

Novotný defended himself to the best of his ability. He pleaded guilty to certain errors and promised that concessions would be made to meet the desires of the Slovaks. But the course which the debate took made it clear that his overthrow was imminent. To prevent any decision being taken in this climate, Novotný's supporters forced a further postponement until the beginning of January.[1]

The conference curtailment was followed by an intensive round of meetings of Novotný's opponents. His supporters, on the other hand, were trying to gain not only the support of party officials, but also that of the Soviet Ambassador in Prague, Stepan Czervonenko, whom they tried to convince that any liberal régime following Novotný's overthrow would be to the disadvantage of the Soviet Union. And rumours were circulated that the Soviet Union would intervene should the party go over to a 'revisionist course'. At the same time, the head of the security department on the central committee, Miroslav Mamula, mobilized the army. On his instructions, Major-General Jan Sejna canvassed senior army officers for declarations of loyalty to Novotný and prepared a military insurrection. Dubček, informed of this threat by General Vaclav Prchlik, revealed the plans for an army insurrection at a meeting of the presidium. Novotný protested that he had no knowledge of them and issued orders to stop the uprising.[2]

This was the last phase in the power struggle between the conservative and revolutionary forces in the party. On 5 January 1968, the Czech broadcasting service announced the resignation of Antonin Novotný as general secretary of the Communist party and Alexander Dubček's election as his successor.

1. See ibid., pp. 58–9 and 63–6.   2. See ibid., pp. 66–7 and 105–6.

The fall of Novotný, which ended nearly fifteen years of his control over party and state, happened at a meeting of the central committee, on 3 January. With Novotný the old, Stalinist régime had also gone down. The way was now open to the reform and regeneration of Communism.

2

Alexander Dubček (b. 1921), whose leadership was expected to bring about the needed reforms, conceived them as a means of realizing true Marxist–Leninist principles, which ought, in his opinion, to guide the party in the construction of Socialism but which had become distorted under Novotný's régime. Thus, in the first statement issued after his election as general secretary, Dubček reaffirmed his belief in Lenin's fundamental principles, as well as his 'loyalty to Marxism–Leninism'.[1]

The social and party reforms which he sought to achieve were certainly in the spirit of Marxism, though they were not compatible with the Leninist concept of the Communist party's role in state and society, at least not as it had developed under Stalin to become the tradition of Soviet Communism.

The issue of the 'Action Programme of the Communist Party of Czechoslovakia' provided a blueprint for reform devised by Ota Sik, Pavel Auersperg and Radovan Richta, with Dubček's co-operation. The ideas it contained had been discussed at numerous party meetings and in articles in the party press, and it was finally accepted as the official programme on 5 April 1968 at a plenary session of the central committee.

The Action Programme rejected the doctrine of the leading role of the party in state and society as it had prevailed until now and reinterpreted it in a new spirit. 'The leading role' of the Communist party had in the past, it declared, often been 'understood as a monopoly, as a concentration of power in the hands of the party organization. This has stemmed from the false doctrine that the party is the instrument for the dictatorship of the proletariat.'

This damaging concept [it stated] has weakened the initiative and responsibility of national and social institutions, damaged the party's authority and made it impossible for it to fulfil its own functions.

The aim of the party is not to become an overall 'administrator' of society, binding all organizations and every step in life by its directives.[2]

The party should of course endeavour to maintain the leading role in state and society which it possessed—though not through the force of dictatorship, but through the 'people's voluntary support'. 'It cannot realize its leading role by dominating society,' the programme explained, 'but only

1. Quoted in James (ed.), *The Czechoslovak Crisis*, p. 10.
2. See Hensel, *Die sozialistische Marktwirtschaft* . . . , p. 297.

by faithfully serving free, progressive Socialist developments. It cannot gain authority by force, but must always win it anew by its action. Its policies cannot be put in motion by decrees, but only through the efforts of its members and the integrity of its ideals.'[1]

The system of dictatorship into which the party had degenerated under the previous régime was condemned as a 'bureaucratic system'. 'In the internal life of the republic' it had shown 'sectarianism, the suppression of democratic rights and personal freedom', while 'breaches of legality, and elements of caprice and the misuse of power' had come to light. The consequences had been 'stagnation in standards of living . . . catastrophic housing conditions . . . an inefficient system of public transport, a low standard of goods and services and a lack of culture. . . . It is understandable that fears for Socialism, for its humanist message and human face, should have arisen.'[2]

. . . We wish [the Action Programme declared] to develop in our country a progressive Socialist society, free of all class antagonism . . . [a society] offering through the richness of its resources a decent human existence . . . and which makes room for the development of the human personality.

We wish to advance towards the construction of a new model of a Socialist society, profoundly democratic and suited to the Czech situation. [But] our personal experience as well as scientific Marxism have led us to the unanimous conclusion that these objectives can never be achieved on the old lines and by using rude means which have outlived their usefulness and continuously hold us back.

We take full responsibility for declaring that our society has entered a difficult period in which we can no longer rely on traditional methods. We can no longer force life into moulds. . . .

The task now before us is to pave the way, in unknown circumstances, to experiment, to give Socialist development a new character, by which we seek support from the creative ideas of Marxism and from international recognition.[3]

Further, the Action Programme maintained:

We are not undertaking these measures so as to surrender any of our ideals—even less to begin a retreat before our opponents. On the contrary: we are convinced that these measures will help us to free ourselves from the burden which has given our opponents the advantage for so many years, and by means of which they have blunted and prevented the effectiveness of Socialist ideas and negated the attraction of the Socialist example.[4]

In the Soviet Communist tradition, the working class constitutes the object of Communist party policy as the 'vanguard of the proletariat', and the party itself the object of the policies of its leadership group, the politbureau. On this system was founded the dictatorship of the leadership group over the party, and of the party over the proletariat. The leadership group alone made the decisions, with no participation by the party's rank and file, whose role was to act as 'transmission belt' for the decisions passed down by the

1. See ibid., p. 297.　　2. See ibid., pp. 288 and 291.
3. ibid., pp. 335-6.　　4. ibid., p. 336.

politbureau. And since it possessed a monopoly in the dissemination of thought and opinion, the leadership group alone decided what the people should and should not be allowed to know.

It was this tradition, on which the Communist system had rested hitherto, with which the Action Programme now broke. 'Socialism,' it stated, 'cannot mean only the liberation of the working people from the predominant exploitation of class relationships, but must also, more than in any other democracy, make it possible to bring the individual personality to full development.'

The working class, no longer dictated to by an exploiting class, is not to be instructed by arbitrary interpretations of power about what it is and what it is not allowed to be informed about, when it is allowed to express its public view and when it is not.[1]

Neither should it be allowed to suppress opinions under the pretext of being 'anti-social'. Every restriction upon freedom of opinion, the programme said, should be based on a law defining what was anti-social. It was possible that the ideological enemies of Socialism might try to misuse the democratic process. But, 'in our present stage of development, the principle remains valid that in the conditions prevalent in our country it is possible to confront bourgeois ideology only by a public confrontation of ideas'.[2]

Under no circumstances, the programme declared, should the use of the state secret police be permitted as an instrument to suppress freedom of opinion. Their task was 'to protect the state against the activities of hostile enemy agencies'.

Every citizen not guilty in this respect must live assured that his political convictions, ideas, personal faith and affirmations will not become a matter of attention to the security police organization.

The party states categorically that the use of this machine must never be allowed in solving internal political questions and conflicts in a Socialist society.

The party's policies [the programme continued] must never lead to a situation where non-Communist citizens feel that the party is restricting their freedom and rights, but rather that they should perceive in the party's activities a guarantee of their rights, freedom and interests.[3]

The sharpest contrast with traditional Soviet Communism was the part of the programme which postulated freedom of opinion for Communist party members. This was a right which had never been questioned under Lenin.[4] It had been annihilated only by Stalin, whose régime had condemned,

1. ibid., p. 303.   2. ibid., p. 304.   3. ibid., pp. 310 and 289.
4. During the terrible economic crisis in the Soviet Union in 1921, the Tenth Congress of the Communist party had accepted a motion put forward by Lenin forbidding the formation of opposition groups within the party, but it had not in any way restricted freedom of opinion for its members. But this decision, which Lenin had probably seen as no more than a temporary emergency measure, laid the foundation stone for the monolithic totalitarian structure of the Communist party as it was developed by Stalin.

suppressed and often cruelly persecuted every opinion of party members which was in conflict with the opinion of the dominating leadership group. It was this destruction of the freedom of opinion of party members which had made the dictatorship of the leadership group over the party possible, and which had led to its degeneration into the despotic rule of one man over party, state and society which had come to be termed the 'cult of personality'.

The Action Programme secured for party members not only unrestricted freedom of opinion, but further deduced from this right the duty to realize it in serving the party.

Each party member and party organization [the programme declared] has not only the right, but also the duty, to take the initiative in coming forward according to the best of their knowledge and belief with criticisms or views on debated questions which deviate from the official one. . . .

It is not acceptable that Communists should have this right restricted, or that an atmosphere of mistrust and suspicion should be created against those who come forward with different views. The use of reprisals against minorities under whatever pretext, as has occurred in the past, is not acceptable. . . .[1]

A few months later the draft of this concept was incorporated by the central committee into the new party statutes submitted to the Fourteenth Congress, summoned to take place on 9 September 1968.[2] The minority, the new statutes stated, 'has the right to stand up for its views (even if these have been rejected by the majority), and to ask that they be reconsidered in the light of new knowledge and experience'. And, to ensure freedom of expression, the statutes declared that minority representatives should be 'exposed only to ideological influences'; hence they could represent their views without fear of reprisal.

As a further measure in democratizing the party, the draft statutes provided for secret ballots for party officials and restricted their periods in office to prevent the creation of a party bureaucracy. Moreover they decreed the separation of state from party functions; party leaders were no longer to be allowed to hold high state office at the same time.[3]

The demand for the separation of party from state function had already been emphasized in the Action Programme. In the Soviet Communist tradition which Czechoslovakia had inherited, the Communist party *was* the state. But the power monopoly which gave it this position in the state was incompatible with democracy, which rested on the principle of active self-government by the people, as well as irreconcilable with the right to these freedoms without which democracy, and particularly a social democracy, was unthinkable—the freedoms of thought, speech, assembly and organization.

1. Hensel, *Die sozialistische Marktwirtschaft* . . . , p. 299.
2. The draft statutes were published in *Rudé Právo* on 10 August 1968; see Windsor, *Czechoslovakia 1968*, p. 60.
3. See James (ed.), *The Czechoslovak Crisis*, p. 28.

The programme had stated consistently: 'The power of the Socialist state cannot be monopolized by any single party or a coalition of political parties; it must be available to all political organizations.'[1]

But it had, on the other hand, evaded the question of any return to the pluralist system of political parties existing before the Communists had seized power. Yet this was inseparable from the logic of the democratizing process. 'A democracy,' Vaclav Havel reasoned in *Literárni Listy*, 'can only be taken seriously provided the people have the opportunity freely to elect those who are to govern them. This, in turn, presupposes the existence of at least two genuine alternatives, which means two equally independent forces standing an equal chance to become the leading power in the state should the people so decide.'

Thus, it seemed to Havel that the 'only consequential and effective method in our situation . . . is a revival of the two-party system, adapted to a Socialist structure of society. And since this will naturally not involve any parties which are based upon class principles, and therefore have varying and contradictory ideas dictated by class interests on the country's agrarian and social development, their interrelationship might be based on a historically new type of coalition co-operative. . . .'[2]

Havel's second party could only, of course, be the Social Democratic party which, in breach of its constitution, had been merged with the Communist party in 1948.[3] The majority of Social Democrats had not in fact joined the Communist party, and many of them, stimulated by the sense of freedom which now ran through the country, began to demand the revival of the old party. In May, five of its veteran officials, who had been cruelly persecuted by the Communist régime (including Zdenek Bechyne, who had been imprisoned for fourteen years) issued a public declaration announcing the party's re-establishment. 'Only now,' it stated, 'in this time of democratic Socialism, has it become possible to renew the party's real work in the spirit of our ninety-year-old Socialist and democratic tradition. . . . The renewed activity of Social Democracy will not dissipate the forces of the working people, but, on the contrary, will reactivate the democratic, Socialist and freedom-loving masses, who have so far stood aside.' And the declaration issued a reminder of the 'historical fact' that, 'wherever in Europe Social Democracy has disappeared from political life, citizens' rights to freedom and democracy have disappeared with it'.

This declaration awoke a strong response among the ranks of veteran Social Democrats, above all in the working population, as well as among

1. Quoted in Zeman, *Prague Spring*, p. 123.
2. *Literárni Listy*, No. 6, 1968, quoted in Horlacher, *Zwischen Prag und Moskau*, pp. 65–6.
3. See page 179.

students. Within a few weeks, fifty-four Social Democratic organizations had come to life in Prague, Brno and other towns, and nearly 500 workers' and students' groups had been formed.[1]

It was only to be expected, however, that Moscow should consider the revival of a Social Democratic party in a Communist state as an intolerable provocation of Soviet Communism. A letter from the Communist parties of the five Warsaw Pact powers which later invaded Czechoslovakia underlined the danger that Social Democracy represented to the Communist régime:

> The Social Democrats persist in demanding the establishment of their party; they organize illegal committees, and strive to split the Czechoslovak labour movement and take the country's leadership into their hands so as to re-create a bourgeois social order.[2]

For the leaders of the Czech Communist party, the demand for the revival of the Social Democratic party was certainly an embarrassment. Accused by Moscow of allowing the activity of 'anti-Socialist forces', they were unable at this stage to legalize the Social Democratic party, which Moscow had denounced as being among the most dangerous. They therefore rejected the Social Democrats' demand on the grounds that 'any step which splits the unity of the Marxist party will weaken the difficult struggle for new policies in the construction of Socialism'. Restoring the system of the old political parties would run contrary to the spirit of the Action Programme.[3]

But the Action Programme had not by any means been advocating a one-party system to support the Communist power monopoly, but a system, however undefined as yet, which would assure different political streams of a participation in power through their organizations.

The programme's main significance in this respect was defined by Gustav Husák, leader of the Slovak government from 1946–50, a few months before it was drawn up. His views are particularly interesting as symptoms of the mood of the 'Prague Spring', since as a politician he was a pragmatist rather than a revolutionary and had within barely a year become the main instrument of Russia's counter-revolution. A few weeks after Dubček's election as party general secretary early in January 1968, Husák had written in the periodical *Kúlturný Zivot*:

> The citizen wants guarantees that he may freely exercise his right to vote [between various trends], to be in control and [a position of] responsibility. This is a problem for the progressive democratization of the social order, which embodies the liberation and development of all the creative forces dormant in the people, their physical and intellectual potentialities and duties. The problem is to find institutions that warrant the co-operation of millions of hands and brains.[4]

1. Vilem Bernard, *Report to the Eleventh Congress of the Socialist International in Eastbourne, June 1969*; *Socialist International Information*, vol. xix, 4 October 1968.
2. For the text of the Warsaw Pact letter, see Horlacher, *Zwischen Prag und Moskau*, pp. 139–46.
3. *Rudé Právo*, 8 June 1968.   4. Quoted in Schwartz, *Prague's 200 Days*, p. 81.

The leverage to bring about the fundamental transformation of a society based on dictatorship into a Socialist democracy was to be provided by the structural reforms in the means of production, planned by the Action Programme. These, like the political reforms, were based on a system of balance between necessity and freedom, between the autonomy of the producers in the production process and the needs of the community at large within the state.

The Action Programme in fact provided a full outline for the building of a Socialist order of society in a highly developed industrial state. It was not a utopian programme. It was based on concrete measures destined to realize the idea of freedom in Socialism under prevailing economic and social conditions. It was a programme for the final phase of a social revolution which had begun after the liberation of Czechoslovakia in May 1945.

The Communist revolution in Czechoslovakia, like the Communist revolution in Russia, had destroyed the class rule of capitalism based on the private ownership of the means of production; it had, as the Action Programme stated, 'freed the working people from the rule of an exploitative class relationship'. The essential means of production had become the property of the nation; they had been nationalized. The social relationship of the working class to the means of production was no longer that of a class relationship between proletariat and bourgeoisie, but a relationship between the working class and the state as the monopoly owner of the means of production.

But, at the same time, taking Stalin's Soviet Communism as its model, it had destroyed the historic achievements of the bourgeois revolution which contained the seeds of the essentials of Socialism: civil liberties and political democracy. For Socialism, as seen within the movement since its inception a century ago—and as it was most certainly seen by Karl Marx—is a concept intended to realize the highest degree of individual freedom and the fullest participation of the masses of the people in their own destiny. Since the Communist revolution was based on dictatorial coercion, the superstructure of society (in the Marxist meaning of the term) which it developed—the political and social institutions, the law and judiciary, the theories and ideologies—necessarily became subjected to the system of a totalitarian dictatorship.

There have been not a few Communists—above all Lenin himself—who were (and still are) aware of the tragic contradiction of the Soviet Communist reality as against the essential idea and ideal of Socialism. The Communist revolution in Russia, a socially and culturally backward and predominantly agrarian country which was only in the early stages of modern industrial development, was faced with the tremendous problem of achieving rapid industrialization. This could only be achieved by the brutal force of dictatorship through a sequence of experiments which had the ultimate objective of realizing a truly Socialist society as their inspiration. These were Lenin's New Economic Policy (N.E.P.), which followed the period of 'war Communism'; then, after the failure of the N.E.P., the Five-Year Plans; then the first attempts to overcome the despotism of Stalinism by introducing the principle of the 'collective leadership' of the party; and finally Khrushchev's experiment of 'liberalizing' the dictatorship.

Yet none of these experiments had brought forth in Russia an essentially Socialist society. They had failed, because they did not attempt to overcome the system of dictatorship as it had developed under the pressure of the process of industrialization. They were, in fact, seeking to consolidate it, even after the process of industrialization was completed. The object of economic liberalization was merely to loosen the fetters of dictatorship over the productive apparatus, and which hindered productive growth. And the object of liberalizing the political system was to eliminate the brutal despotic features introduced by Stalin's rule of terror, since these had in any case become superfluous, and were hardly appropriate for winning the sympathy of the people.

The Czechoslovakian experiment, however, sought not merely to liberalize the dictatorship, but nothing short of its total dissolution by introducing a 'Socialism with a human face', in Dubček's gripping phrase. It sought to set up a 'new, vigorous democratic model of a Socialist society', as the programme said, not in the remote future, but without delay.

The importance of the Czech Communists' Action Programme cannot easily be overestimated. Philip Windsor has praised it as 'among the most outstanding political achievements of modern history'.[1]

It was an experiment which, had it not been strangled at birth by the Soviet invasion of the country, could have become a 'new model of Socialist society' of immeasurable significance as a pattern for a crisis-free transition from dictatorship to Socialist democracy.[2] It could also have enriched the methods of democratic Socialism, and could, above all, have paved the way to overcoming the conflicts which have split the international labour movement.

1. Philip Windsor, 'Czechoslovakia, Eastern Europe and Détente', in *Czechoslovakia 1968*, p. 10.

2. A. D. Sacharov, the most respected nuclear scientist in the Soviet Union, hailed the Czech experiment in an article, widely read in the Soviet Union, under the title: 'As I Imagine the Future': 'We are convinced that Communists throughout the world equally oppose all attempts to revive Stalinism in our country. After all, the power of Communist ideas to attract would thereby be drastically reduced. Today the key to a new progressive order of the system of government lies in intellectual liberty alone. This the Czechs have understood particularly, and there is no doubt that we should support their daring initiative, so important to the future of Socialism and all humanity'—*The Times*, 9 August 1968.

3

One of the most astonishing phenomena about the Czech revolution was the way in which it developed. It had begun with a palace revolution in the central committee of the Communist party, the instrument of state power. An alliance between the Czech 'revisionists', demanding political and economic reforms, and the Slovak Communists, demanding national autonomy, had overthrown the political *status quo*. Antonin Novotný, embodying in his person the *ancien régime*, had been forced to resign as party general secretary and Alexander Dubček, a symbol, as it were, of the new régime, had been elected in his place.

The party rank and file had remained indifferent to the change in the central committee and the shift in the balance of power between reformists and conservatives which had brought it about; they had begun to play their part only after the palace revolution on 5 January 1968. Novotný himself had given the impetus. He was not prepared to accept his overthrow; he carried his fight to retain power into the party organizations, an apparatus which he controlled.

But the struggle for leadership between reformists and conservatives had become a struggle over principles. The problems of regenerating the party and society, until then discussed only in small groups of intellectuals or in the conclave of the central committee, became a subject for open and passionate discussion at party meetings. And criticism of the previous régime, until then voiced only in secrecy at small party committees and in private conversation, now became a public issue.

It grew into a scandal which opened the gates to a deluge of criticism of Novotný's former rule. On 1 March 1968, the country was startled by the news that Major-General Jan Sejna, who, it was publicly revealed, had been under investigation for the misappropriation of a vast sum of money, had used his diplomatic passport to escape to the United States. Sejna had been secretary of the politbureau in the Ministry of Defence, a member of parliament and a protégé of Novotný, who, in the face of objections from the officers' circles in the army, had promoted him to the rank of general in 1960 when he was still only thirty-three. When his escape became known, General Prchlik, who had secretly informed Dubček in December of the planned military *coup* to save Novtoný, also publicly disclosed that Sejna, together with General Vladimir Janko, the deputy minister for defence, had issued marching orders to an armoured division stationed in Western Bohemia for the *coup* against Prague in March. Janko shot himself a few days before he was due to appear before a government commission to be examined about the military conspiracy.

The nation's excitement, aroused by the disclosure of the *coup* as well as by Sejna's escape and Janko's suicide, which could be interpreted only as a confession of guilt, was considerably intensified when it also became known that Sejna together with Novotný's son, the head of the International Printing Corporation in Prague, had been involved in several sordid incidents of corruption. In fact the corruption which had permeated Novotný's régime seemed to become personified in these two men, and Novotný was himself compromised. A flood of petitions and resolutions implored the government and party to investigate Sejna's case in all its shabbiness, to clean up political life and to purge the offices and positions of influence of all people who were soiled by corruption. A huge meeting of students in the Congress Palace in Prague on 20 March, at which, among others, Sik and Goldstücker had spoken, sent a message to the National Assembly demanding Novotný's resignation as president of the republic. Two days later, on 22 March, he resigned as head of state, and on 30 May he was expelled from the central committee and had his party membership suspended.

With Novotný toppled from his last position of power, the party apparatus on which his rule had rested also collapsed. His followers, who had controlled the local party organizations, were overthrown, and the party, from having been the instrument of Novotný's conservative régime, became the powerful standard-bearer of the revolution.

The Russian intervention, however, was shortly to unite the whole Czech nation in a testimony to the revolution. It began shortly after the plenary session of the central committee on 5 January which had elected Dubček as general secretary. Dubček's life history left no doubt of his loyalty to the Soviet Union. He had grown up in the Soviet Union from the age of four, when his father, a veteran Communist, had emigrated there. After returning to Czechoslovakia in 1939, he had fought in the illegal Communist movement in Slovakia and been twice wounded in combat against the German forces of occupation. Four years later he had risen to be secretary of a local organization and, to prepare him for higher party functions, he had been sent by his party to attend the training college in Moscow from 1950 to 1958. Shortly after his return he became a member of the central committee of the Slovak party and, in 1963, its general secretary.

It seemed that while the Soviet leaders did not mistrust Dubček himself and were not really worried over his election, they were alarmed by the 'revisionist' trend which had carried him to power. Three weeks after his election they summoned him to Moscow and warned him, as *Pravda* reported, about the development in Czechoslovakia of situations which might lead to a 'weakening of the Czech Communist party and to a strengthening of dangerous attitudes among certain circles in Czech society that were vulnerable to middle-class ideological influences and imperialist propaganda'. There was taking place in Czechoslovakia, the Soviet leaders claimed, a 'revival of rightist, revisionist elements, who could exploit the complicated situation which has developed in the country for their own aims, which are remote from the interests of Socialism'.[1]

This report did not appear in *Pravda*, however, until seven months after Dubček's visit and a few days after the invasion of Czechoslovakia by half a million Russian troops. This somewhat belated information of the conversation which the Soviet leaders had had with Dubček was no doubt intended to show how Moscow had warned him that it would not tolerate any extension of 'revisionism' in Czechoslovakia.

The rank and file of the Czechoslovak Communist party were, however, never informed of Moscow's warning. But even if they had been they would not, given their prevailing mood, have been deeply impressed. The warning could not have held back the basic flood of 'revisionism' already under way.

Moscow now applied more pressure. On 23 March, the day after Novotný's dethronement from the presidency, the Soviet leaders called together the leaders of the Warsaw Pact countries (with the exception of Romania) in Dresden for a meeting to warn Dubček and his delegation in the name, as it were, of the pact countries about a development which, they declared, 'could lead to a counter-revolutionary *coup*'. 'Anti-socialist elements', the report in *Pravda* (which did not appear until after the invasion) said, had wrested control of the broadcasting system and press from the party and had consolidated their position. To prevent the 'counter-revolutionary danger', the Communist parties of the Warsaw Pact were ready 'to help their Czech comrades to repel the increasingly impudent anti-Socialist elements and to strengthen the position of Socialism in Czechoslovakia'.[2]

It seems, however, that the Soviet leaders failed to convince the Czechoslovak delegation at Dresden either that their country was threatened by a counter-revolution or that the reforms planned by the party could lead to a 'counter-revolutionary *coup*', any more than that the supporters of the reform movement were in truth 'impudent anti-Socialist elements'. For hardly two weeks after the meeting, on 5 April 1968, a plenary session of the central committee of the Czechoslovak party took the historic decision to accept the Action Programme which would, it announced, engender a renaissance of Socialism in Czechoslovakia.

However, in any case, the Action Programme contained no grounds for concern that the relationship between Czechoslovakia and the Soviet Union as well as the other Warsaw Pact countries might be changed. It placed full emphasis on the loyalty of the Czechoslovak Republic to the Soviet Union and its Warsaw Pact allies.

The fundamental direction of Czechoslovakia's foreign policy [the programme declared] emerged and proved itself during the national freedom struggle as well as

1. *Pravda*, 22 August 1968; quoted in Schwartz, *Prague's 200 Days*, pp. 76–7.
2. Quoted in ibid., 118–19.

during the processes of Socialist change in our country. It was based on the alliance and co-operation with the Soviet Union and the other Socialist states. . . .

It will remain our endeavour to deepen our friendly relations with our allies—the states of the Socialist world community—on the basis of mutual esteem, sovereignty and equality, mutual respect and international solidarity.[1]

So far as Russia was concerned, these words were not empty assertions. Czechoslovakia was, in fact, the only country in the Soviet bloc on whose genuine friendship the Soviet Union could depend. The peoples of the other member states of the Soviet bloc (with the exception of Bulgaria) despised and hated the Russians. The Czechs had, however, since the birth of Czech nationalism over a century before, felt a bond of kinship with their Slav brothers. And since the Second World War, after which Czechoslovakia had expelled three million Germans from her territory, an alliance with Russia had become an essential element in her security, for who but the Soviet Union could protect her against a German revenge, by which the Czechs, rightly or wrongly, felt themselves to be threatened? Germany was, for the Czechs, the arch-enemy. Most of them loathed the Germans who, during the Habsburg Monarchy, had treated them as helots following the battle of the White Mountain in 1620, and who in 1938 had again subjected them to their rule. And it was the Soviet army which in 1945 had liberated them from this brutal alien régime. Like the Czech hatred of Germany, Czech friendship for Russia had its roots in the nation's history. The Action Programme had re-emphasized this friendship.

But this fact did not allay Moscow's anxieties. It had no need to fear that Czechoslovakia might dissolve its alliance with the Warsaw Pact powers and declare its independence, like Hungary in 1956. But the democratization of the Communist party and the state, for which the Action Programme had paved the way by restoring freedom of thought and opinion as well as the emancipation of the press and radio from the shackles of censorship, appeared to threaten the rule of Stalinism which remained the system of government for the Communist parties in the Soviet Union, Poland and East Germany. For should such a 'new, vigorous democratic model of a Socialist society' emerge as a result of the reforms and demonstrate that it was indeed possible to realize Socialism without suppressing freedom, then no moral justification remained for the system of dictatorship in these countries. In any case, the Czech example would certainly strengthen those forces which were seeking to transform the system.[2]

1. See Hensel, *Die sozialistische Marktwirtschaft*, pp. 333–4.
2. It was Walter Ulbricht, dictator of East Germany, who was most appalled by the prospect of the Czech virus of liberty infecting his own country. In a memorandum circulated as early as May to the top leaders of the East German Communist party, the situation in Czechoslovakia was described as catastrophic: 'The counter-revolution is on the brink of victory. . . . A return to the pre-war bourgeois régime is in principle proposed by the Action Programme of the Czechoslovak Communist party, directed implicitly against the found-

The Soviet leaders had made up their minds to put an end to this experiment, either by diplomatic pressure, or, if necessary, by military intervention. They invited Dubček to Moscow for a fresh discussion on 4 May together with the prime minister, Oldrich Černik, the chairman of the National Assembly, Josef Smrkovský and the general secretary of the Slovak Communist party, Vasil Bilak, to demand their approval for manoeuvres in Czechoslovakia by the Warsaw Pact armies, and for the permanent stationing of Russian troops in the country. Dubček sanctioned the proposed manoeuvres, for, he feared, otherwise Russian troops would enter the country as an invasion force, but he rejected the garrisoning of Russian troops on Czechoslovakian soil.

The manoeuvres began on 20 June. Tens of thousands of Russian, Polish, East German, Hungarian and Bulgarian troops, supported by hundreds of tanks, marched into Czechoslovakia. This display of men and armament was intended to intimidate the 'revisionists'.

But they did not allow themselves to be frightened. A week later, on the 27th, four Prague daily papers printed a manifesto under the title 'Two Thousand Words', describing in moderate terms the degeneration of the old Communist régime and calling on the party and nation to continue the process of regeneration begun by the Action Programme, and to 'complete the work of the humanization of the régime'. Written by the distinguished writer, Ludvik Vaculik, the article carried the signatures of about seventy scholars, writers and artists—almost all of whom, including Vaculik, were Communist party members.

Moscow took the article as its cue to sound a warning roll of thunder in the direction of Prague. *Pravda* denounced it as 'an open call to battle against the Communist party of Czechoslovakia and against the constitutional power'; and Dubček was put under pressure from Moscow by telephone to undertake 'decisive measures'.

What exacerbated Moscow's especial wrath was evidently a passage at the end of the article:

The possibility [it said] that foreign troops might interfere in our development has led to considerable unrest. In view of the powerful superiority of the forces with which they are able to confront us, there is nothing to do except to remain steadfast and polite and not begin [the fight] ourselves. We can demonstrate to our

ation of Socialism . . . the assurances of friendship towards the U.S.S.R. and its Socialist allies . . . are worthless, since those who offer them can no longer guide the developments of their own country and no longer hold any power. . . . Class enemies and imperialist agents are infiltrating Czechoslovak territory without difficulty. . . . Things have reached the point where the situation has ceased to be an internal problem for Czechoslovakia. . . . The Czechoslovak government is thus violating its treaty obligations and is guilty of treason against its allies'—*Literárni Listy*, 30 May 1968, quoted in François Fetjo, 'Moscow and its Allies', in *Problems of Communism*, November–December 1968.

government that we stand behind them, with arms should this be necessary. And we can reassure our allies that we shall fulfil our alliances, friendship and trade agreements.[1]

A few days later, Leonid Brezhnev, leader of the Russian Communist party, hinted during a speech in Moscow that the Soviet Union would not tolerate any development in Czechoslovakia which, in his words, might upset the 'national pattern' of the Communist system and weaken the 'comradely alliance between Socialist countries'. The Soviet Union, he declared, 'cannot and will not remain indifferent to the fate of Socialist construction in other countries'.[2]

Thus it was announced to the whole world that the Soviet Union claimed the right to interfere in the development of other states under Communist party rule which deviated from the system of Soviet Communism—a doctrine which was to become known as the 'Brezhnev doctrine'.

Immediately after Brezhnev's speech, Dubček was asked to appear before the Warsaw Pact leaders so that measures could be decided against the threat to Communist power in Czechoslovakia. Such an obvious interference in their internal affairs was, however, rejected by the party presidium; it politely turned the invitation down. Moscow thereupon summoned the leaders of the pact forces which were participating in the manoeuvres to a conference in Warsaw on 14 July. And in an article entitled 'Attack on Basic Socialist Foundations in Czechoslovakia', *Pravda* branded all those who had supported the manifesto of 'Two Thousand Words' as 'counter-revolutionaries in the service of foreign imperialists'.[3]

The numbers of Czechs and Slovaks who declared their solidarity with the manifesto were legion. Their ranks were swelled as a result of the embitterment felt at Moscow's hostile attitude towards the reforms they strove for. And if the manifesto had, for Moscow, become the symbol of the 'counter-revolutionaries', for the Czechs it became the rallying-point for their protest against the Soviet Union's interference in their country's internal affairs. The flood of resolutions declaring support for the manifesto grew, as Schwartz has shown, into a kind of plebiscite rejecting Moscow's interference.[4]

The crisis came to a peak on 15 July with a letter from the five-power conference in Warsaw to the Czech Communist party. The development in Czechoslovakia, it stated—'the rise of the forces of reaction supported by imperialism'—had pushed the country away from the Socialist path, 'and therefore threatens the interests of the whole Socialist system'. The danger referred to was that of Czechoslovakia 'separating itself from the Socialist community'.

1. An English translation of the full text appeared in *The Times Literary Supplement*, 18 July 1968.
2. Quoted in Schwartz, *Prague's 200 Days*, pp. 174–5.
3. See ibid., pp. 178–90.   4. See ibid., p. 179.

This, the letter declared, 'is no longer a question for the Czech Communist party alone. It is a question involving all Communist parties and states united in alliance. . . .' The victory over Nazi-Fascism had advanced the borders of the Socialist world into the heart of Europe as far as the Elbe and the Bohemian forests. 'We will never accept,' the letter stated, 'that this historic achievement of Socialism . . . might be endangered . . ., that imperialism, from outside or from within, might breach the Socialist system and change the balance of power to its advantage.'

On the basis of this right, which the Soviet Union had hereby usurped, the conference instructed the Czech Communist party to undertake measures to fight the 'danger of counter-revolution' and of the 'separation of Czechoslovakia from the Warsaw bloc'. It specifically demanded 'a decisive and courageous attack on the right wing [of the party] and anti-Socialist forces; the suppression of any political parties which oppose Socialism'; and the re-introduction of censorship in the press, broadcasting and television.[1] (The censorship had been abolished on 26 June 1968.)

The party presidium at once published the Warsaw letter together with its reply. It emphatically rejected any assertion of a 'counter-revolutionary danger' in Czechoslovakia as completely unfounded. It admitted that 'the strong current of healthy Socialist action is accompanied by extremist trends, with which the remnants of anti-Socialist forces in our society are trying to swim'.

We do, however, see no real reasons [the presidium continued] to allow our present situation to be described as counter-revolutionary and to issue statements about an immediate danger to the basis of the Socialist system or that Czechoslovakia is preparing to change the direction of its Socialist foreign policies.

'Our alliance with and friendship for the Soviet Union,' the presidium declared, 'is deeply rooted in our social system, in the historical tradition and experience of our people, their interests as well as their thoughts and feelings.'

Considering our bitter historical experience of German imperialism and militarism [the presidium emphasized], it is inconceivable that any Czechoslovak government might ignore these experiences and foolishly endanger the fate of our country, even if it were not Socialist. We categorically reject any suspicion in this respect.

The presidium as decisively rejected the suppressive measures demanded by the Five-Power Conference.

Any sign of a return to these methods [it stated], would provoke the resistance of an overwhelming majority of party members, as well as of the working classes—workers, peasants in co-operatives and intellectuals. By such a step the party would endanger its leading role and create a situation in which a conflict of power could well arise. This would indeed endanger the people's Socialist achievements as well as our mutual interests in the anti-imperialist front put up by Socialist society.

1. For the text of the Warsaw letter, see Horlacher, *Zwischen Prag und Moskau*, pp. 139–46.

The Communist party, declared the presidium, was

dependent upon the voluntary support of the people. It does not fulfil its leading role by the fact that it rules society, but by the fact that it serves a free, progressive Socialist development. It cannot impose its authority, but must all the time earn it by its actions. It cannot enforce its policies by decrees, but only through the work of its members and the credibility of its ideals.

In particular, the presidium once again rejected the demand of the conference that it should place the press and broadcasting back under censorship.

An overwhelming majority of all classes and ranks in our society supports the abolition of censorship and is in favour of freedom of opinion. The Communist party of Czechoslovakia has tried to show that it is capable of a political leadership and administration distinct from the discredited bureaucratic-police methods.

Finally the presidium turned against the interference by the Warsaw conference parties in the country's internal affairs. 'We do not believe,' they stated, 'that the common cause of Socialism can be promoted by holding conferences where the policies and activities of a fraternal party are judged without their representatives being present.' And it reminded the conference of the declaration by the Soviet government of 30 October 1956, which had affirmed the principles of mutual relations between Socialist countries: complete equality, respect for territorial integrity as well as for national independence and sovereignty and mutual non-interference.[1]

The answer from Prague was clear. But to dispel any doubts in his own country, Dubček, in a broadcast speech of 18 July, affirmed the Communist party's determination to carry through the Action Programme and 'not to abandon even one of its principles—principles of a Socialism which has not lost its human face'.

'After many years,' he said, 'an atmosphere has now been created in our country where everyone may openly and with dignity voice his opinion, so demonstrating the fact that the cause of our country and the cause of Socialism is a common cause for us all.'

---

1. For the Soviet declaration, see page 425; for the text of the Czechoslovakian reply to the Warsaw letter, see Horlacher, *Zwischen Prag und Moskau*, pp. 149–62. Over a year after the Soviet declaration of 30 October 1956, the right to autonomy and sovereignty of Communist-ruled countries was more explicitly confirmed by a meeting of twelve parties in Moscow, on 14 November 1957, who stated in their declaration: 'The Socialist countries base their relations on principles of complete equality, respect for territorial integrity, state independence and sovereignty and non-interference in one another's affairs. These are vital principles'—*Soviet News* (London), 22 November 1957. And in March 1965, only three years before the invasion of Czechoslovakia, these same principles had been reaffirmed by a conference of nineteen Communist parties, again held in Moscow: 'Each Communist party is entirely independent and autonomous. Only decisions which have been made by the party itself are binding on the party'—*Pravda*, 12 March 1965.

We therefore declare, openly, quietly, but firmly, that we are aware what it is all about. There is no other way for our people apart from the most profound democratic and Socialist transformation in our country.[1]

On the next day, the 19th, it became known that the Soviet leaders wished for a meeting between the Soviet politbureau and the Czechoslovak presidium, to take place on 22 or 23 July in either Moscow, Kiev or Lvov. But just as Tito during his conflict with Stalin had declined an invitation to Moscow in view of doubts whether he would ever come back,[2] so the presidium declined to meet the Soviet leaders in the Soviet Union; it insisted on a meeting on Czechoslovakian territory. The meeting took place in the little town on Cierna-nad-Tisoû in eastern Slovakia on the Russian border.

To set the scene for the conference, *Pravda* 'disclosed' that a box containing American arms had been found in Czechoslovakia close to the German border—unmistakable proof, it asserted, of plans for a *coup* by American imperialists in Czechoslovakia—and that NATO and F.B.I. documents which had come into the possession of the Soviet government had revealed the actual plans. It also announced that reservists in the Soviet Union had been called up to take part in manoeuvres on the western borders of the Soviet Union near the Czech frontier. And at thousands of meetings the Russian people were being warned of the imperialist threat to Czechoslovakia. The campaign against Czechoslovakia in the Soviet press had reached a pitch which anticipated an imminent Soviet military action.

It was in this tense atmosphere that the Soviet–Czechoslovakian conference assembled at Cierna-nad-Tisoû.

Three days before, a special issue of *Liternárni Listy* had published an appeal drafted by the dramatist Pavel Kohout to the party presidium to remain steadfast in Cierna and not to capitulate. It reminded them of the enslavement of the Czech people over the centuries. 'With the exception of two brief interim periods,' it stated, 'we have been condemned to create our national existence in secrecy. In fact, we have been repeatedly on the brink of destruction.'

[But now] the moment has come, when, after centuries, our country has again become a cradle of hope . . . , a moment in which we can prove that Socialism is the one true alternative for the whole of civilized humanity.

We had expected that in particular all the members of the Socialist camp would greet this fact with sympathy. But instead we have been accused of treason. We are accused of a crime which we have not committed and are suspected of dark motives which we have never entertained.

The threat of an unjust sentence hangs over us. And whatever form this may take it will leave a tragic stain on the idea of Socialism throughout the whole world in future years.

1. For the text of Dubček's speech, see Windsor and Roberts, *Czechoslovakia 1968*, pp. 169–73.
2. See page 386.

'Comrades!' the appeal to the presidium said in closing, 'it is your historic duty to avert this danger. . . . Defend the path which we have begun to traverse. . . . In our name write a fateful page in the history of Czechoslovakia.'[1]

Feverishly circulated as a petition, this appeal had been signed within a few days by a million Czechs and Slovaks.

The conference at Cierna was stormy and almost broke off several times. The Czechs demanded the evacuation of the Russian troops, who had remained in the country even though the manoeuvres had terminated on 30 June. The Soviet leaders, on the other hand, demanded the 'normalization' of the political conditions in Czechoslovakia in the Stalinist tradition: the reversion to a system of totalitarian dictatorship by the Communist party, and, especially, the reintroduction of censorship and the suppression of all freedom movements. And as a guarantee of 'normalization', they demanded the right to impose a military occupation on Czechoslovakia.

At length, however, it seemed as though the conflict had been resolved. The Czech delegation evidently reaffirmed Czechoslovakia's loyalty to the Soviet Union and the Warsaw Pact, pledging itself to retain the Communist party's leading role in the state in the spirit of Marxism–Leninism. These concessions were not, however, made public, though in a broadcast on 2 August Dubček declared that the Communist party 'would persist in the path it has taken since January. There is no alternative for our nation or the working people of our Czechoslovak fatherland.'[2]

The threat to Czechoslovakia's sovereignty, which had been the most hotly disputed contention at the conference, seemed to have been averted. On 3 August, the last Russian troop units moved back over the border. The Soviet press ceased its attacks on Czechoslovakia, and on the same day the delegates met in Bratislava, in the hall of mirrors in the old town hall, to sign the document resulting from the Cierna discussions. It renewed affirmations of the principles 'of equality, respect for the sovereignty, national independence and territorial integrity of the powers of the Warsaw Pact'.

4

Seventeen days after the signing of the peace of Bratislava,[3] on 20 August at eleven o'clock at night, a Russian army, half a million strong and with

1. Quoted in Schwartz, *Prague's 200 Days*, pp. 190–1.   2. ibid., pp. 195–6.
3. For the question whether the discussions in Cierna and the signing of peace in Bratislava had been a manoeuvre of deception—'the most complicated political and diplomatic fraud in history', as Schwartz calls it—see *Prague's 200 Days*, p. 203. See also Heinz Brahm, *Die Intervention in der C.S.S.R.*, *Berichte des Bundesinstituts für Ostwissenschaftliche und Internationale Studien*, 15/1969. For a detailed investigation of this question, see James,

thousands of tanks, invaded Czechoslovakia from the east, north and south with the support of East German, Polish, Hungarian and Bulgarian troops. By three o'clock the next morning, parachutists dropped from Russian war planes had occupied the presidium building of the government in Prague and arrested the prime minister, Oldrich Černik, while armoured troops had surrounded the Hradschin Castle, the residence of the president, as well as the secretariat of the central committee. Two hours later, the following report was broadcast by 'Vltava', the Soviet Union's illegal radio station:

> TASS [the official Soviet news agency] is authorized to state that the leaders of the party and government of the Czechoslovak Socialist Republic have requested the Soviet Union and other allied nations to come urgently to the aid of the fraternal nation of Czechoslovakia with armed forces.
> This request was made as a result of the threat to the Socialist system in Czechoslovakia by counter-revolutionary forces who had conspired with foreign hostile forces.[1]

The Soviet government's action, like their action in Hungary in November 1956, had been planned as a combined invasion and *coup d'état*. In Hungary, as Soviet troops were crossing the border, Kádár, a member of Nagy's constituted government, announced over the radio the formation of a new government.[2] In the same way, as Soviet troops were entering Czechoslovakia, Dubček was to be overthrown as general secretary and Černik as prime minister, and a pro-Soviet government was to be proclaimed, with the task of calling at once on the Soviet Union to provide armed help against the 'counter-revolution'. The Soviet government was so certain of the success of its plan, that it instructed its delegate at the United Nations to declare to the Security Council on the evening of 21 August:

> Armed units from the Socialist countries have, as is known, entered the territory of the Czechoslovak Socialist Republic in response to a request from the government of that state, which has turned to its allied governments for aid with armed forces.[3]

The scheme, however, misfired. In their quest for a Czech Kádár, the Soviet leaders conspired with Alois Indra, one of the secretaries of the Communist party central committee, who, together with Vasil Bilak and Drahomir Kolder, did in fact try to depose Dubček at a meeting of the presidium during the night of 20 August, two hours before the invasion began. Černik branded the attempt as treason and the unsuspecting presidium,

---

'Invasion and Resistance', in *Czechoslovakia 1968*, pp. 102–5; for the development of the events preceding the invasion in the complex of the inner-political problems of the Soviet Union, see the excellent examination in Windsor, 'Eastern Europe and Détente', pp. 55–79.

1. *Pravda*, 21 August 1968. For the text of the radio broadcast, see Robert Littell (ed.), *The Czech Black Book* (New York, Washington and London, 1969), pp. 23–4. The Czech original of this book—a collection of diary entries and documents—was issued by the Historical Institute of the Czechoslovakian Academy of Science, and printed and distributed in Prague in the autumn of 1968.

2. See page 422.   3. Quoted in Schwartz, *Prague's 200 Days*, p. 215.

surprised by news of the invasion, at one o'clock in the morning of the 21st issued a proclamation 'To the people of the Czechoslovak Socialist Republic'. The armies of the Soviet Union and four other powers, it stated, had 'two hours ago crossed our borders without the knowledge of the president of the republic, the presidium of the National Assembly or the first secretary of the Communist party'. This action, it declared, was 'in conflict with the fundamental principles governing relationships between Socialist states and a denial of the basic standards of international law'. It called on the citizens of the Republic 'not to resist the invading armies, since defence of our borders is impossible'. It requested the party stewards to remain at their posts and announced the assembly of the central committee.[1]

In Hungary, Soviet troops within a few days had arrested all the members of the government they could get their hands on, and so had stifled any possibility of constitutional protest. Certainly in Prague the prime minister, Černik, had been arrested at once, with, a few hours later, Josef Smrkovský, president of the National Assembly, and Dubček, general secretary of the party, and all three taken, handcuffed, in an aircraft to the Soviet Union.

The Soviet leaders held back, however, from arresting General Ludvik Svoboda (b. 1896), Novotný's successor as president of the republic. He had fought for Russia in two world wars; in the first in the Czech Legion, and in the second as commander of the Czechoslovak Army Corps; and he had been decorated as a 'Hero of the Soviet Union' and a 'Hero of the Czechoslovak Socialist Republic'. They evidently hoped that this old and ailing man would, under pressure, sanction the invasion as Beneš had sanctioned the *coup d'état* of February 1948. In the early hours of 21 August, General I. Pavlovsky, supreme commander of the invasion forces, appeared in the Hradschin in the company of Indra and J. Lenárt, both members of the party presidium, to ask Svoboda to appoint a new government. He rejected this request as unreasonable.[2]

In Hungary, the Soviet army had entered the country as an army at war; it had bombarded Budapest so as physically to destroy the possibility of organized resistance. Moscow's policy in Czechoslovakia was to occupy the country without bloodshed if possible and by sheer weight of its huge invasion force to suppress any possible attempts at resistance at the outset, while at the same time staging a *coup d'état* by the Stalinist group within the party. For the Soviet leadership, it was inconceivable that they might not gather a sufficient number of Communist party officials ready to stage the necessary *coup* for the sake of their deep-rooted loyalty to the Soviet Union.

It was here that the policy failed. Unperturbed by the arrest of their prime

1. For a description of the meeting at which the Presidium occupied itself with preparations for the Fourteenth Congress, called for 9 September 1968, see *The Czech Black Book*, pp. 12–18; for the text of the proclamation, see ibid., pp. 10–11.

2. See Brahm, *Die Intervention in der C.S.S.R.*, p. 23.

minister, the Czechoslovak government had already by seven o'clock in the morning of 21 August issued a proclamation which stated:

Against the will of the government, the National Assembly, the leaders of the Communist party and people, Czechoslovakia was today occupied by troops of the five Warsaw Pact powers.

Thus, for the first time in the history of the international Communist movement, an act of aggression has been undertaken by the allied armies of Socialist countries against a state led by a Communist party.

The proclamation then demanded the evacuation from the country of the troops of the five Warsaw Pact powers, that they should respect the Warsaw Pact and acknowledge Czechoslovakia's sovereignty, and appealed to the citizens of the country not to tolerate any government that was not elected under free and democratic conditions.[1]

On the same morning, the National Assembly met in an extraordinary session attended by 162 members and issued a proclamation declaring:

The National Assembly of the Czechoslovakian Socialist Republic, elected by the Czechoslovakian people as the highest organ of the power of state and called together by the President of the Republic . . . declares, that no constitutional organ of the Czechoslovakian Socialist Republic has been empowered to discuss [the entry of foreign troops into our country], nor has it sanctioned such discussions or invited the occupation troops of the five Warsaw Pact countries.

Moreover, the president of the National Assembly, Joseph Smrkovsky, testified that 'shortly after 21 August 1968, the presidium of the National Assembly asked all members of parliament to submit sworn statements in writing saying whether any of them had invited the troops. All 296 deputies (that is, the number who were in parliament at that time) submitted to the presidium their written statements that they had not invited anybody or any troops into Czechoslovakia.

The National Assembly categorically demanded 'urgent information from one of the responsible leaders of the five Warsaw Pact states so as to explain the illegal action authoritatively to the highest organ of state power in Czechoslovakia'.[2]

Thus the statement by the Soviet government, that it had been 'urgently requested' by the leaders of the Czech government to send armed troops into the country, was unmasked as a lie by the government as well as by the National Assembly.

TASS was authorized by the Soviet government to state that leaders of the Communist party of Czechoslovakia had requested the entry of the Warsaw Pact troops. This statement was also rejected within twenty-four hours by a remarkable announcement.

1. For the text of the proclamation, see *The Czech Black Book*, pp. 56–8.
2. ibid., pp. 74–5.

The central committee of the Communist party had, on 31 May 1968, decided that an extraordinary fourteenth congress should convene on 9 September, to discuss the Action Programme, debate the new party statutes and elect a new central committee. Delegates to the congress were elected during June and July at party meetings of local, district and regional organizations.

In the face of the invasion, the leaders of the central committee quickly took the decision to convoke the Fourteenth Congress at once. On the morning of 21 August, while Soviet troops were pouring into the country, the central committee used a clandestine radio station to summon the delegates to the conference. They were to assemble in the strictest secrecy on the following day, 22 August, in a huge factory block in the Prague suburb of Vyscocany. So as not to awake the suspicions of Soviet patrols, delegates arrived in working clothing and mingled with other workers going into the factory.

Under these extraordinary circumstances, 1,192 of 1,543 elected delegates arrived for the congress. 'It was indeed an historic congress. Each delegate risked his life. Again and again the reports came: occupation troops are moving closer to us. . . .',[1] General Svoboda described the event.

The congress elected a new central committee which included Dubček, Černik, and Smrkovský, who were absent in prison, as well as Svoboda, Husák, Goldstücker and Ota Sik, and then issued a proclamation to the 'Comrades and Citizens of the Czechoslovakian Socialist Republic':

Czechoslovakia is a sovereign and free Socialist state, founded on the free will and support of its people. Its sovereignty, however, was violated on 21 August 1968, when it was occupied by troops of the Soviet Union, Poland, the German Democratic Republic, Bulgaria and Hungary.
This action is being justified on the grounds that Socialism was endangered and that the intervention was requested by some leading officials.

However, the proclamation continued, it had been ascertained with absolute clarity, through statements made by the president of the republic, the National Assembly, the presidium of the government and the central committee, that no constitutional authority and no authorized representative of the Communist party had requested the foreign intervention.

Nor was Moscow's moral justification for the invasion in any sense true.

There is no counter-revolution in Czechoslovakia [the proclamation declared], and Socialist development is not in danger. As has been demonstrated by the tremendous confidence shown in the new leadership of the party by Comrade Dubček, the people and the party are fully capable of solving by themselves the problems that have arisen.
Indeed, action is being taken that is leading towards the realization of the fundamental ideas of Marx and Lenin on the development of Socialist democracy.

1. For Svoboda's description, see ibid., pp. 83–5.

Czechoslovakia had loyally fulfilled its commitments to the Warsaw Pact, the proclamation continued. But by contrast, 'the sovereignty of Czechoslovakia, the bond of the Warsaw Pact and the agreements of Cierna and Bratislava have been trampled underfoot'. Then the congress solemnly stated:

A Socialist Czechoslovakia will never accept either a government of a military occupation administration nor a domestic collaborationist régime dependent on the forces of occupation.

The congress demanded the immediate withdrawal of foreign troops. If discussions between the Soviet representatives and the free constitutional representatives of the government and party had not opened within twenty-four hours, the entire working population of the country would be called upon to demonstrate its protest against the invasion by a one-hour general strike on 23 August.[1]

This proclamation by the Fourteenth Congress of the Communist party was followed by one from the presidium of the Trade Union Council. In the name of the trade union movement, it declared 'full support for the president of the republic, the government of Černik, the National Assembly and the central committee of the Communist party under Dubček's leadership' and, 'in this serious hour for our nation', it appealed to the chairman of the Trade Union Council of the Soviet Union, Alexander Shelepin, as well as to the workers in Russia, to demand the immediate withdrawal of the occupation armies from the territory of the Czechoslovak Socialist Republic.

The invasion had taken place, the appeal said, 'at a time when our people strongly believed in the assurances given by the statesmen of the Soviet Union at Cierna and Bratislava that the sovereignty of our Socialist state was guaranteed unconditionally'. But now a 'tragic error' had occurred 'which can have unforeseeable consequences for the international workers' movement and the Socialist and Communist world'.[2]

As all these documents show, there was no constitutional state organ—the president of the republic, the government or the National Assembly as well as the constitutional representatives of the working class, the Communist party and the Trade Union Council—which did not categorically reject Moscow's claim that the Soviet Union had sent its forces into Czechoslovakia in response to a request from 'leaders of the party and government'. No party or government leader had been authorized to summon foreign troops, and no one could be found to substantiate Moscow's statement; the Soviet government was itself unable to name these leaders. There can therefore be no doubt

1. *Rudé Právo*, 22 August 1968. For the text of the proclamation see *The Czech Black Book*, pp. 80–1; see also Appendix Eight, p. 551. For the proceedings of the congress, which were tape-recorded, and other relevant documents, see Jiří Pelikán (ed.), *The Secret Vyscocany Congress* (London, 1969).
2. For the text of the proclamation, see *The Czech Black Book*, pp. 149–50.

that the invasion of Czechoslovakia was initiated by the Soviet government alone.

5

The attempt was made by Moscow to justify this monstrous rape committed by a Communist government against a state governed by Communists as a life-saving operation for Socialism. 'Counter-revolutionary forces', the Kremlin stated, had threatened the foundations of Socialism in Czechoslovakia. 'The objective of the counter-revolution,' a publication prepared in Moscow for distribution in Czechoslovakia said, 'was to rob the Czechoslovak Communist party of its leading role, to snatch power from the workers and peasants, to destroy the state and the public corporations founded by the people . . . and to guide Czechoslovakia into the road to the re-establishment of capitalism.'[1]

This claim, as the documents quoted show, was also decisively rejected as false by all the organs of the state and society. 'The claim that there was a threat of, or actual, counter-revolution in the country,' Joseph Smrkovsky declared, 'is a propaganda invention. There was no force in the country which could have removed the Communist party from power or overthrown the social system. At any time, the vast majority of the citizens spontaneously supported the then policy of the Czechoslovak Communist party.' When, a year after he had been overthrown, Dubček was summoned to a plenary session of the now Stalinist central committee, held on 26 September 1969, he was able to state without encountering any contradiction:

There has never been any proof that a centre of counter-revolutionary forces existed. Neither our secret service nor a foreign secret service has discovered any proof of this nature.[2]

According to Moscow's theory, however, the counter-revolution was not amenable to proof; it was, *Pravda* wrote, 'a new historical phenomenon'— the phenomenon of a counter-revolution which, while it existed, was not perceptible, or was, in Moscow's words, 'a peaceful counter-revolution'.[3]

This phenomenon of a 'peaceful counter-revolution' against Socialism was all the more strange, S. Kovalev explained in *Pravda*, for having been undertaken by a group within the Communist party.

What the anti-Socialist forces of the right wing [of the Communist party] in Czechoslovakia tried to bring about [he wrote], was not the development of Socialism in its original form or the adaptation of Marxist–Leninist principles to the

1. Quoted in Robert Littell's Introduction to *The Czech Black Book*, p. ix. This publication, entitled *On the Events in Czechoslovakia*, was distributed in many thousands of copies by Soviet troops in Czechslovakia during the autumn of 1968.

2. *Guardian*, 8 November 1969.

3. *Pravda*, 11 September 1968, quoted in *The Czech Black Book*, p. viii.

special conditions in the country, but the truncation of the foundation of Socialism and of the fundamental principles of Marxism–Leninism. . . . Under a cloak of 'democratization', these elements had step by step shaken the Socialist state. . . . They gradually prepared a counter-revolutionary *coup d'état*.[1]

It had, of course, to be admitted that Moscow had repeatedly and emphatically warned the Communist party of Czechoslovakia against the democratization of the Socialist régime; the freedoms of thought, speech and press were, in its eyes, anathema to the Socialist system.

The Czech Communists, however, saw the path to Socialist democracy as the one road possible for the regeneration of the Socialist system. And even if that road was mistaken in the opinion of the Soviet leaders, in the opinion of the Czech Communist leaders it was the correct one for their country. It was one which they had chosen after careful consideration and with full constitutional sanctions. And it had seemed at Cierna and Bratislava as though the Soviet leaders had accepted this fact and had assured the Czech delegates that they had no need to fear any restriction of Czechoslovakia's sovereignty.

To Prague it had seemed unthinkable that the country's sovereignty could be placed in question. Mutual respect for sovereignty between Socialist states and the principle of mutual non-intervention in internal affairs clearly formed the basis of their interrelations. Not only had these principles been reaffirmed in the Soviet Union's declaration of 30 October 1956,[2] but they were already contractually incorporated in Article 8 of the Warsaw Pact.

The signatory powers state that they will act in the spirit of friendship . . . guided by principles of mutual respect; they will not interfere in one another's internal affairs.

And Article 1 of the Warsaw Pact specifies that no conflict arising between individual countries must be settled by force:

The leading parties to the contract pledge themselves in accordance with the covenant of the United Nations to refrain in international relations from threats of force or the use of force and to solve international conflicts by peaceful means.[3]

The Czech Communist leaders therefore considered an invasion by the Soviet Union to be beyond imagining. They saw the Warsaw Pact as providing adequate protection against the use of force for them as for their allies. The stark notion that a Socialist government could breach the Socialist principles of the people's right to independence and self-determination and unexpectedly attack another Socialist country by force of arms was not to be entertained. The possibility of a Russian invasion had not been considered for a moment

1. *Pravda*, 26 September 1968; for the text of the article, see *Current Digest of the Soviet Press*, vol. xx, No. 39.
2. See page 425.
3. For the text of the Warsaw Pact, see James (ed.), *The Czechoslovak Crisis 1968*, pp. 161–5. For an examination of the role of the Warsaw Pact in the Russo-Czech conflict, see ibid., pp. 31–55.

by Communist party and government leaders; in fact, neither party nor government, which had at their command over eighteen divisions of one of the best-trained and best-equipped armies in Eastern Europe, had made any sort of defence preparation.

6

So how did the Soviet leaders justify this invasion which contradicted the Socialist principles of sovereignty and self-determination to which they ostensibly subscribed?

The theoretical solution for this contradiction was developed by S. Kovalev in the article in *Pravda* which has already been quoted. He admitted that 'the action by the five Socialist countries [against Czechoslovakia] contradicted the Marxist–Leninist principles of sovereignty and the right to self-determination of nations'—but this was only an 'abstract sovereignty' and only an 'abstract right of a people's self-determination'. 'Marxistic dialectics,' on the other hand, 'reject one-sided explanations for historical phenomena.' The sovereignty of Socialist states, he wrote, 'was not to be interpreted in the spirit of the Marxist concept of legal criteria, valid also for relations between Socialist countries, in a formal sense, and divorced from its connection with the class struggle'.[1] Sovereignty and the right to self-determination were not for Socialist countries absolute, unlimited rights, since 'they must not be allowed to contradict the interests of world Socialism' in executing these rights. Decisions taken by Communist parties in Socialist countries over the path their development was to take 'must damage neither Socialism in their own country nor the fundamental interests of other Socialist countries'. 'World Socialism is a social system "indivisible",' he declared, 'and its defence is a common cause for all Communists.'

The development in Czechoslovakia, he stated, had threatened the country's Socialist foundations. 'The Communists in its fraternal countries could not, of course, remain inactive for the sake of an abstract sovereignty while the country was endangered by an anti-Socialist degeneration. . . . Formal respect for the freedom of self-determination in the special situation pertaining in Czechoslovakia,' he wrote, 'would have meant self-determination not for the working people, but for their enemies.'[2]

A few weeks later, on 12 November 1968, this theory was proclaimed as an official doctrine by the general secretary of the Communist Party of the Soviet Union, Leonid I. Brezhnev, at the Fifth Congress of the Polish Communist party in Warsaw.

---

1. Marx, it may be recalled, considered it to be 'one of the duties of the working classes' —as he proclaimed in his *Inaugural Address*—'to vindicate the simple laws of morality and justice which ought to govern the relations of private individuals as the rules paramount in the intercourse of nations'.
2. *Pravda*, 26 September 1968.

In his opening speech he said:

The Socialist states stand for the strict respect of the sovereignty of all countries. They decisively oppose any interference in the affairs of all states and any violation of their sovereignty.

This general principle, however, was not unconditionally valid for Socialist states, as Brezhnev pointed out. For, he continued,

if internal or foreign forces hostile to Socialism should attempt to turn the development of any one Socialist country towards the restoration of the capitalist order, if a danger to Socialism develops in that country, then it becomes not only the problem for the country in question, but a general problem which is a matter of concern for all the Socialist countries.[1]

How the doctrine was to be interpreted was shown by the Soviet leaders during their conflict with Czechoslovakia. They considered the action initiated by the Communist party of developing a Socialist democracy as an attempt by 'internal and foreign enemies of Socialism' to restore capitalism and so, according to the views of the Soviet leaders, 'endanger the common interests of the Socialist camp'. And since the Czechoslovakian Communists had persisted in their path, pointing to their rights to self-determination and their country's sovereignty, the country had been occupied by the Soviet Union 'in the mutual interest of the Socialist camp'.

An earlier example of the practical application of this doctrine had already been given by the Soviet leaders in their invasion of Hungary in 1956. The Hungarian situation, however, had been more complicated. The revolution in Hungary had been aimed not only at the transformation of a Communist society into a Social Democratic one but the state also broke away from the Warsaw Pact and declared Hungary to be neutral. It thus challenged the Soviet Union's interests as an imperialist power.

For Czechoslovakia, on the other hand, the Warsaw Pact was, as we have seen, a binding condition for its security, which no government in the country could have avoided. It was not therefore Czechoslovakia's foreign policy which had been called in doubt, but its internal development: the process of transforming a Communist dictatorship into a Socialist democracy. The Soviet leaders' fear was that the Czech experiment might offer an impetus to similar developments in other states of the Soviet bloc, and ultimately in the Soviet Union itself. So to vitiate the experiment, they lashed out. The Brezhnev doctrine was therefore intended not merely to justify Soviet action against Czechoslovakia, but also to serve as a warning to any other countries in the Soviet bloc which might attempt to democratize their system.

The basic implication of its message was that the Communist parties of Socialist countries were not by any means free to develop their political

1. *Neues Deutschland*, 13 November 1968.

system in accordance with their own wishes. Their sovereignty and right to self-determination was, in practice, limited. Should in the view of the Soviet leadership any of their decisions 'endanger the common interests of the Socialist camp', then the Soviet Union is justified to intervene. This was particularly applicable to any decision to democratize the Communist system, which would, according to the theory of the Soviet leaders, inevitably lead to the restoration of capitalism. Therefore any attempt by states in the Soviet bloc to change the system of Soviet dictatorship into a system of Socialist democracy would be suppressed by the Soviet Union with force of arms.

7

The action that the Soviet Union had taken against Czechoslovakia aroused an outcry of indignation in the democratic Socialist world and precipitated a profound crisis in the Communist movement. The general council of the Socialist International, meeting in Copenhagen on 21 August, the day of the invasion, passed a resolution declaring:

> The Socialist International condemns the invasion as an act of naked aggression which lays bare the imperialist character of the relationship which the Soviet Union seeks to impose upon her Warsaw Pact allies. . . .
> This act of imperialism, reminiscent of Hitler's invasion of Czechoslovakia, outrages the sovereign right of the Czechoslovak people to determine without foreign interference their own way of life. . . .
> The Soviet Union and her accomplices in this act have revealed to the world once again their long abuse of the terms 'Socialism' and 'Democracy'.[1]

The Communist world was profoundly dismayed. 'The international labour movement,' wrote Ernst Fischer, who was then a member of the politbureau of the Austrian Communist party, 'has been hit by the greatest intellectual crisis in its history.' He asked that the Communist party of Austria should break off relations with the Communist party in Moscow. The invasion, declared Roger Garaudy, a leading Marxist philosopher who was a member of the politbureau of the French Communist party, had been 'a crime against hope, a crime against Socialism, a crime against the future'.[2] He demanded the resignation of the Soviet leaders. The leader of the Swedish Communist party, Carl-Henrik Hermanson, requested the severing of relations between Sweden and the Soviet Union. With the exception of the five Communist parties whose governments had undertaken the invasion, the Soviet action was criticized by nearly all the European Communist parties. But reactions to the event were not unanimous throughout the whole of the world Communist movement, nor even within the European parties them-

1. *Socialist International Information*, vol. XVIII, 21 September 1968.
2. Roger Garaudy, *La Liberté en sursis-Prague 1968* (Paris, 1969), p. 24.

selves.[1] In the conflict of conscience between their avowed principles on the one hand and their loyalty to the Soviet Union as the supreme bulwark of the world Communist movement on the other, many Communists chose to sacrifice Socialist principles to the duty of Communist solidarity.

To Socialists of all tendencies it seemed inconceivable that a Communist government could undertake an act of warfare against a fraternal Socialist country. Communists could only perceive these events as a tragedy. The idea which raised Socialism to a universal ideal was its concept of universal peace. For the century from the birth of the modern Socialist movement, this had been one of its dominant ideas. Socialism held out a promise for world peace. In a world that was torn by nationalist and imperialist conflicts, war had seemed unavoidable, and warfare between capitalist and Communist states well within the bounds of possibility. Wars between Socialist states had seemed unimaginable.

It was an ideal which had been shattered earlier by the war of the Soviet Union against Socialist Hungary in 1956. But at that time the Soviet leadership had been able to convince the astounded world that it had taken up arms to defend Socialism against a brazen imperialistic assault. Under Nagy's leadership, they asserted the Hungarian Communist party had lost control of the country, and the capitalist counter-revolution had arisen openly. What occurred in Hungary, the Kremlin insisted, had been a war between Socialism and capitalism.

But in Czechoslovakia the Communist party had not lost its authority. When its conflict with Moscow broke out, the whole nation flocked to its side, making it stronger and mightier than ever before. Unlike agrarian Hungary, which only two decades earlier had emerged from a semi-feudal society, the foundations of the Communist party had not been laid on sand to fall apart at the first impact of the crisis. The party in Czechoslovakia was solid and established, with its roots in the soil of a highly developed industrial nation and with a million and a half members; already in the days of the First Republic it had been one of the largest parties in the country.

Even Moscow had been unable to prove that there had been any acute danger of a capitalist counter-revolution in Czechoslovakia. What had actually occurred was a peaceful change in the leadership of the party—the Stalinists being replaced by 'revisionists'—and the beginning of a process of democratization of the Communist régime—a process admittedly stimulated by the ideas of Socialist intellectuals, but which had received the powerful support of the Communist party. Moscow's war against Czechoslovakia had

1. For an analysis of the reactions of individual Communist parties to Moscow's armed intervention, see Heinz Brahm, *Der Kreml und die C.S.S.R. 1968–1969* (Stuttgart, 1970); see also Kevin Devlin, 'The New Crisis in European Communism', in *Problems of Communism*, November–December 1968.

not been a war between Socialism and capitalism, but a war between the Soviet Union and 'revisionism', a war against a 'new model of Socialism'.[1]

The Soviet action against Czechoslovakia threw up two fundamental questions for Communists: that of the autonomy of Communist parties and that of the true character of 'revisionism'.

The 'Brezhnev doctrine', by which the Soviet action had been justified, disputes the unconditional right to autonomy of individual Communist parties in Socialist countries; they were not free to pursue a policy which might threaten the Socialist foundations in their countries and therefore damage the interests of other Socialist countries.

The principle of international solidarity is certainly unchallengeable. But who is the international moral authority in the Communist world entitled to judge the policy of individual Communist parties? While the Communist International, and later the Cominform, remained in existence, they were recognized by the Communist parties as the supreme moral authority. But since both these international bodies have been dissolved, there has been no international Communist court of justice to which Communist parties are accountable. Neither are they to be bound by criticisms made by individual fraternal parties. The principle of mutual respect of sovereignty—proclaimed by both the Moscow declaration of 1956 and the Warsaw Pact of 1956—safeguards their right to follow a course of policy which, in the light of their own knowledge and conscience, does not contradict the spirit of international solidarity.[2]

After the dissolution of the Cominform, the Soviet leaders had taken upon themselves the prerogative of an international Communist court of justice which could, so to speak, give its verdict in the name of 'Socialism' on the policies of Communist parties in Socialist countries. The sanction that the Communist International and the Cominform had employed against parties that did not submit to their verdict had been expulsion—as, for

1. The armed intervention by the Soviet Union and its allies had, of course, been a war, but not one involving mass slaughter (though the Soviet Union had been quite prepared for this), because unlike the Hungarians, the Czechoslovak Communists had, on the advice of their party leaders, offered no resistance to the overwhelmingly superior forces of the invading armies.

2. This was reaffirmed in a declaration at the conference in Moscow in November 1960 which was attended by eighty-one Communist parties. A French Communist, André Wurmser, referred to it in supporting the protests of the French Communist party against the Russian invasion. 'In truth,' he said, 'the tragic decision of this month of August is wrong, not only according to our opinion but according to our law, the law of the Communist parties of the whole world. . . . Who took the responsibility for the intervention? Not the Communist parties, since the French Communist party, the Italian Communist party, and the very great majority of the eighty-one parties that signed the 1960 declaration, were opposed to it, but only some Communist parties, which set themselves up on their own authority to be judges without appeal'. André Wurmser, '*Le Mois tragique*', in *France Nouvelle*, 4 September 1968.

example, the expulsion of the Swedish and Norwegian parties from the International,[1] and the Yugoslav party from the Cominform.[2] The sanction that the Soviet leaders employed against parties in Socialist countries which did not bow down before their verdict was war—war against Hungary in 1956, and against Czechoslovakia in 1968.

The crime which Czechoslovakia had committed, and for which it was invaded and occupied, was, in the view of the Soviet leaders, 'revisionism'. For, according to the Soviet theory, 'revisionism' is a heretical deviation from Marxism–Leninism, as corrupting for Socialism as 'social-democracy', which, if it took root in countries under Communist rule, would endanger their Socialist foundations and pave the way for the restoration of capitalism.

But what, in fact, is 'revisionism'? It is a concept of Communist policy which aims to develop Socialism beyond the stage of dictatorship towards a new type of Socialist society, radically different from the Russian type.

Yet, for Lenin, it was self-evident that each country, according to its peculiar conditions, would develop a 'particular originality' of Socialism on a particular road. In an article which he wrote in October 1916 he said:

> All nations will attain Socialism; this is inevitable. But they will attain it not quite on the same road. Different forms of democracy, variations of the dictatorship of the proletariat, and differences in the pace of the transformation of society will impart a peculiar originality to Socialism.[3]

Stalin, however, saw any deviation from Moscow's type of Socialism as a crime, like the 'crime' of 'Titoism', and he delivered any leaders of a ruling Communist party whom he suspected of it to the executioner. And Stalin's heirs in the Kremlin, regardless of their criticism of his 'cult of personality', have in practice remained Stalinists. They no longer call the pursuit of a type of Socialism different from the Russian type 'Titoism', since they crave Tito's friendship, but they do call it 'revisionism'. Like Stalin, as Roger Garaudy wrote when protesting against the invasion of Czechoslovakia, 'they tend to confuse Stalinism with the historical form which it has happened to take in their country. Anything which contradicts this form is, for them, in conflict with Socialism.'

The essence of the conflict between Moscow and Prague was in reality the doctrine that Soviet Communism as it had developed under the particular historical and economic conditions in Russia—a system of Socialism without freedom—was the only conceivable form of Socialism and that the synthesis of freedom and Socialism as envisaged by Karl Marx was a utopia.

But the historical conditions under which Socialism could be developed in

1. See Braunthal, *History of the International, 1914–1943*, pp. 311–13.
2. See pp. 386–7.
3. V. I. Lenin, *Sämtliche Werke*, vol. xix, p. 281.

Czechoslovakia were entirely different from the conditions under which Socialism had developed in the Soviet Union. In the Soviet Union it had been necessary for the agrarian society to be transformed into an industrial society to serve as a basis for a Socialist society and the Czechoslovak Communists did not dispute the need for a totalitarian dictatorship to enforce this process.

Czechoslovakia, on the other hand, was an industrial society, even before the Communists seized power in the country and, following its liberation in 1945, the means of production had been progressively transferred from capitalist to public ownership. Capitalism had by this stage been abolished, the capitalist class dissolved and the material and social foundations for a Socialist society created.

Such an achievement could have been possible in Czechoslovakia, even without invoking the force of a dictatorship, and a Czechoslovakian road to Socialism would have been feasible there since Socialism was the acknowledged creed of a great majority of the people. It had been Moscow which had enforced the 'Russian road to Socialism' on the country.

The Czechoslovakian Communists had come to lose any confidence in the 'Russian road to Socialism', in the need for force as an instrument to achieve Socialism; and all the more so after the economy had stagnated and the intellectual life of the nation become sterile under the system of bureaucratic dictatorship on the Russian model. They no longer accepted that the Russian type of Socialism was the only possible structure. They were seeking for a new model.

They therefore took the decision to complete the revolution of the material conditions of Socialism by revolutionizing its 'superstructure' and to enter a new phase of Socialist development—in Friedrich Engels's words, the phase of transition 'from the realm of necessity to the realm of freedom'. The reforms proposed in their Action Programme—new statutes to change the party structure and, above all, the restitution of freedom of opinion, of press and radio—were designed to be the means of this transition.

It was the concept of a new type of Socialism against which the Soviet leaders inveighed, condemning it as a 'revisionist' concept which contradicted Marxism–Leninism. It was the abolition of the censorship which had, above all, aroused their profoundest displeasure. Just as Metternich had enforced his infamous 'Karlsbad Decisions' in September 1819, committing the German federal states to the suppression of freedom of thought, press and learning, so, 150 years later, the Soviet leaders had in their negotiations with the Czechoslovakian leaders insisted on the reimposition of censorship over press and radio—in the name of 'Marxism–Leninism'.

The Czechoslovak Communists would have had very little difficulty in demonstrating convincingly that their concept was based not only on the tenets of Marxism, but that it was also in harmony with Lenin's theory of transition from a proletarian dictatorship to a system of freedom.[1] And so far as Marx was concerned, he regarded the freedom of the press as such a valuable element, both for civic government and human dignity, that he devoted an essay of no less than fifty pages to making his point.[2] But the Czechoslovak Communists chose not to engage in a theoretical discussion over interpretations of Marxism–Leninism, but simply insisted on their right to autonomy—their right to decide their own road to Socialism.

The Soviet leaders, however, saw the establishing of freedom of thought, press and radio in a Communist-ruled country as the most basic manifestation of 'revisionism'. In their opinion, it was damaging to the interests of the other Communist-ruled countries and since the Czechoslovak leaders had refused Soviet demands to reimpose censorship and abandon 'revisionism', they had, in Moscow's view and according to the Brezhnev doctrine, forfeited their party's right to autonomy and their country's right to sovereignty.

8

The frustration by the Soviet Union of the Czechoslovak experiment of creating a 'new model of Socialism' was the heaviest blow which Socialism had ever suffered—a blow of even more importance historically than that which had struck it through Fascism. For while Facism had been able physically to suppress the Socialist parties, it had not been able to kill their spirit; this continued to live on in the masses as was manifested by the rapid reconstruction of the parties once Fascism had collapsed.

Moscow's struggle against 'revisionism' is, on the other hand, a crusade against the very spirit of Socialism. It is an attempt to exterminate the very ideas without which the regeneration of Socialism in Communist-ruled countries would be impossible. The destruction of 'revisionism' in Czechoslovakia, the nipping in the bud of all new forms of Communist régime, which,

1. '. . . if the resistance of the capitalists has finally been broken, if the capitalists have disappeared, if there are no longer any classes (i.e. no differences between the members of society as they relate to the co-operative means of production)—only then . . . can there be talk of freedom. Only then will a genuine comprehensive democracy, in truth without exception, become possible and be realized,' wrote Lenin in *Staat und Revolution*, pp. 225–6.

2. This essay appeared in the *Rheinischer Zeitung* in 1843 under the title: '*Debatten über Pressefreiheit und Publikationen der landständigen Verhandlungen*'; it is reprinted in Franz Mehring (ed.), *Gesammelte Schriften von Karl Marx und Friedrich Engels 1841–1850*, vol. I (Stuttgart, 1913), pp. 208–58. One would search in vain for this text in the four volumes of selected works by Marx and Engels issued by the Foreign Languages Publishing House in Moscow in a popular edition for the Marx, Engels and Lenin Institute in 1950, and which were issued by the Communist S.E.D. in Berlin in 1953. Considering the state of the press in the Soviet Union and East Germany at that time, the republication of Marx's views would hardly have been appropriate.

had they been allowed to mature, would have eroded the despotic character of Soviet Communism, the reimposition of a system which suppressed the elementary rights of freedom through the Soviet Union's military might, shattered the faith in a gradual transformation of that Russian autocracy which had made the Soviet Union into one of the great reactionary forces of the present age.

It was the belief of many Socialists—Otto Bauer, the leading theoretician of Austrian Marxism, among them—that the system of the Communist dictatorship under which Russia has been industrialized would, through its own internal pressures, develop into a system of Socialist democracy. For, it was assumed, the industrial revolution, by creating the material conditions for a Socialist order of society, would necessarily be accompanied by a cultural revolution, which in turn would create the intellectual conditions for the establishment of Socialism. Given both conditions in the realization of Socialism, the system of dictatorship would lose its historical function: it would become superfluous and, as Otto Bauer expected, would wither away. The craving for freedom of the masses awakened to self-consciousness by the cultural revolution would, with the demands of modern technology, form an irresistible force for liberating the spirit from the shackles of dictatorship.[1]

Such an optimistic perspective had seemed to be justified when, after Stalin's death in 1953, the harshness of his régime was softened and it appeared that the measures of liberalization then taken were heralding the reform of the system. It proved an illusion. So far no real signs of any change have been seen in the totalitarian system. And the action of the Soviet leaders against Czechoslovakia's 'revisionism' had once again demonstrated their iron determination to see that their system remained immutable. The liberalization of the Stalinist régime had, it is true, moderated its most barbaric excesses.[2] But the system itself remained untouched by the aspirations of liberalization; the optimistic expectation that it would necessarily change during the process of the economic and technical development into a democratic system remained unfulfilled.

Yet how are we to understand this incredible paradox, that a Communist party, inspired by the Marxist concept of the emancipation of humanity, and creating over half a century of its rule one of the greatest industrial states of

1. See Otto Bauer, *Zwischen zwei Weltkriegen?* (Bratislava, 1936), pp. 165–8, 207, 208.
2. Thus, for example, the writers Andrei Sinyavski and Yuri Daniel were not eliminated by a bullet in the back of the neck for the over-explicit social criticism in their work, as would most probably have happened to them under the Stalinist régime. In strict observance of 'Socialist legality', they were sentenced respectively to no more than seven and five years' hard labour in Siberian concentration camps. For the conditions in the Siberian labour camps to which political prisoners were sent, see Alexander Solzhenitsyn, *One Day in the Life of Ivan Denisovich* (London, 1963), and Anatoli Marschenko, *My Testimony* (London, 1969). Solzhenitsyn was a prisoner in these camps from 1945 to 1953, Marschenko from 1960 to 1966.

the world, whose means of production are exclusively state property and in which the capitalist classes no longer exist and capitalist class rule has been completely eliminated, should continue to maintain a régime denying liberty? And how are we to explain why it is that these leaders of state and party should, like Metternich a century and a half before them, fear freedom of thought like the plague and hence maintain all the instruments of free thought —press, radio, literature and film—under subjection to an air-tight system of censorship?

The fear of freedom of thought has always been synonymous with the fear of the ruling classes of the rebellion of the ruled; the struggle of the subjected classes for freedom of thought was inseparable from their struggle for economic and social emancipation. So if the Soviet Union is indeed a classless society, how can the phenomenon of the suppression of freedom of thought be explained? If in the history of class struggles class-ridden societies had indeed suppressed it because it threatened the existing class structure, what institution could freedom of thought possibly endanger in a classless Socialist society?

The very institution of the Socialist foundation on which such a society is based—the institution of the common ownership of the means of production —makes the restoration of capitalism in the Soviet Union not only completely unthinkable (and, in fact, wished for by none) but also the material pre-conditions for the development of a new capitalist class are completely absent.

If, then, freedom of thought is not a threat to the existing order, what purpose is served by its suppression? Together with all other civic rights, freedom of thought was suppressed in the Soviet Union at a time when the revolution was threatened by the class enemies of Socialism and, later on, when it had to face the immense problems of industrializing the country. Freedom of thought was suppressed to protect the Bolshevik Revolution. In the meantime, the class enemies of Socialism have been destroyed and the problems of industrialization solved.[1] The period of transition from a class-divided to a homogeneous, classless society, and from an essentially pre-capitalist economy to a new, industrialized and highly developed state-owned economic order, has long been concluded.

1. More than thirty years ago, at the Eighteenth Congress of the Communist party of the Soviet Union, in March 1939, Stalin had declared: 'We have destroyed the exploiting classes; in our country there are no longer classes of enemies.' So what purpose continued to be served by the system of dictatorship based on a formidable secret police machine which had, at the time of the 'Great Purge', executed thousands of Soviet citizens and sent tens of thousands to the concentration camps? In his view, the rule of terror was still necessary, because, he explained, the Soviet Union was encircled by capitalist states which 'infiltrate our country with spies and murderers'—as, he asserted, the trials of Trotsky and Bukharin had revealed. 'So long,' he said, 'as the capitalist encirclement is not replaced by a Socialist encirclement, so long must the power of the state, the army and the secret police remain strong'—*Problems of Leninism* (Moscow, 1947), pp. 632 and 634.

What other purpose then continues to be served by the suppression of the freedom of thought in the Soviet Union? Clearly only the protection and perpetuation of an absolutist system of bureaucratic state power, as this has developed out of the Soviet state under Stalin's rule—a totalitarian system based on the bureaucratic apparatus of a centralized monolithic party and a state monopoly of ideology and all the instruments for the formation of public opinion.[1]

The Soviet action against Czechoslovakia was an act in defence of the system of absolutism in Russia. Freedom of thought in Czechoslovakia had to be suppressed, the democratization of the Communist régime in that country thwarted, since the spread of freedom and democracy in any Communist-ruled country could have aroused a movement of freedom and democracy in the Soviet Union itself, so threatening the system of Soviet Communism. This is the historical significance of the Soviet action. It became a tragedy for Socialism.

9

The tail-piece to the history of the subjection of Czechoslovakia to Moscow's predominance may be briefly told. On 24 August 1968, three days after the invasion began, a delegation of the presidium of the Czechoslovak Communist party was informed by the Soviet leaders in Moscow that Czechoslovakia was to be occupied by the Russian army until the state and its institutions had been 'normalized'.

This was followed by a classic example of the re-Stalinization of a de-Stalinized state and society. The passive resistance put up by the Czechoslovakian nation, in particular by its working class, was unique in history. The process of 'normalization' had therefore only been able to proceed step by step. Dubček was overthrown as general secretary and Gustav Husák installed as his successor. Gradually the 'revisionists' were forced out of the positions they held in the party—from the top down to the local organizations —and replaced by Stalinists. The 'purge' was then extended to the press and radio, the trade unions, the administrations of state and public institutions and the universities and schools. During the first two and a half years following the occupation, nearly half a million party members were either expelled or left of their own accord.[2]

But now the Soviet government had to face the more intricate problem of

1. For an interesting investigation into this phenomenon, and, in particular, into the position of the bureaucracy in Soviet society, see Bertram D. Wolfe, *An Ideology in Power. Reflections on the Russian Revolution* (New York, 1969).

2. As Husák reported to the central committee of the party in December 1970, 259,670 members had been expelled and another 150,000 had left since August 1968—*Guardian*, 16 December 1970.

how to remove the stigma of having invaded a fraternal state—the Socialist Republic of Czechoslovakia—with which it was marked by the proclamations of the Czechoslovak government, the National Assembly and, above all, by the Fourteenth Congress of the Communist party.

To rewrite history so as to reinterpret the historical fact of the invasion as a generous act of international Socialist solidarity in response to an appeal by the Czechoslovak leaders for help against the threat of an imminent counter-revolution proved a complex task. It took more than a year of the re-Stalinization of the party before its central committee felt in any position to repudiate the party's original attitude to the invasion. At its plenary session on 26 September 1969, it revoked the proclamation of the Fourteenth Congress, which had indicted the Soviet Union of the crime of invasion, by the simple expedient of declaring the congress illegal and its decision null and void. Still a further year was to pass before the central committee had the courage to offer their official version of the events of August 1968, which blatantly contradicted the experience of the nation. A statement issued on 14 January 1971 under the title 'Lessons drawn from the Critical Developments in the Party and Society after the 13th Party Congress' declared:

In August 1968 . . . our country was on the verge of civil war. It was necessary to decide whether to wait until the counter-revolution had provoked a fratricidal fight in which thousands would die and to grant international assistance only afterwards, or whether to arrive in time to prevent a bloody tragedy. . . . The entry of the allied troops . . . prevented such bloodshed and was therefore the requisite and only correct solution.

Yet, the crucial question remained, 'who in Czechoslovakia had considered the country to be on the verge of civil war', and, above all, who had decided on allowing 'the entry of allied troops' into the sovereign Socialist Republic of Czechoslovakia? In answer, the statement asserted:

Thousands of Communists, individual citizens, and entire collectives of working people, representatives of all the strata of the people and of diverse organizations, including members of the party central committee and the central committee of the Slovak National Council . . . began to turn to the leadership of the fraternal parties and also the governments of our allies, begging them, in this historically grave moment, to grant international assistance to the Czechoslovak people in the defence of Socialism.[1]

And, three months later, Gustav Husák declared in Moscow as the head of a fraternal delegation of the Czechoslovak Communist party to the Twenty-Fourth Congress of the Communist party of the Soviet Union:

On behalf of our delegation, we want to express from the rostrum of this congress our sincere thanks to the Communist party of the Soviet Union, to the

1. *Pravda* (Bratislava), 14 January 1971, quoted in the *Guardian*, 14 January 1971, and in *Problems of Communism*, May–June 1971.

Soviet government and the Soviet people, for having understood the anxieties of the Czechoslovak Communists regarding Socialism and their appeals for help.[1]

It was this farce which constituted the final act to the great tragedy of the spring of Prague.

1. Radio Moscow, 1 April 1971, quoted in *Problems of Communism*, May–June 1971. It may be recalled that Husák, having a few days after the invasion returned with other leaders of the Czechoslovak Communist party from Moscow, where they had been told that the Russian troops would stay in their country, said in a statement: 'The question poses itself, who invited these armies? . . . The question was never discussed to the end: it has not been resolved. No names have been published. When the matter was discussed in Bratislava, Prague and Moscow with our leaders, all members of the leadership of the federal and Slovak parties without exception gave their word of honour that they were not involved in the *démarche* and had no knowledge of it. I know of no leading personality in Czech or Slovak political life of whom it could be said with certainty that he had taken this step'— *Pravda* (Bratislava), 28 August 1968, quoted in *Problems of Communism*, May–June 1971.

24 · Peking's Break with Moscow

The position of central authority which the Communist party of the Soviet Union held in the Communist world movement had been called in question by the revolt in Yugoslavia, the revolution in Hungary and the reformist movements of Poland and Czechoslovakia. Peking's break with Moscow shattered it.

The conflict between China and the Soviet Union grew out of a disagreement over the ideology and strategy to be adopted in the struggle to attain Communist predominance in the world.[1] These questions had originally been thrown into relief by the Twentieth Congress of the C.P.S.U. in February 1956. This, as we saw,[2] toppled Stalin from his plinth; recognized 'different roads' to Socialism; declared in favour of peaceful methods to bring about the Socialist revolution; and, above all, proclaimed the principle of peaceful co-existence between Communist and capitalist states as a guiding principle in the foreign policy of Communist countries.

Mao Tse-tung to all intents stated his firm agreement with the decisions of the Twentieth Congress when, in November 1957, as head of the Chinese delegation, he took part in the conference of sixty-four Communist parties assembled in Moscow to celebrate the fortieth anniversary of the Bolshevik Revolution. The conference declaration, drafted by representatives from twelve ruling Communist parties, contained an appreciation of the 'immense importance' of the 'historic decisions' of the Twentieth Congress as 'the start of a new phase in the world Communist movement'. Three years later, in November 1960, a conference of eighty-one Communist parties, attended by

1. The following description is based on: John Gittings, *Survey of the Sino-Soviet Dispute. A Commentary and Extracts from Recent Polemics 1963–1967* (London and New York, 1968); Alexander Dallin (ed.), *Diversity in International Communism. A Documentary Record, 1961–1963* (New York and London, 1963); Heinz Brahm, *Pekings Griff nach der Vormacht. Der chinesisch-sowjetische Konflikt vom Juli 1963 bis März 1965* (Cologne, 1966); and Richard Löwenthal, *World Communism. The Disintegration of a Secular Faith* (New York, 1964).
2. See pp. 396–7.

Chou En-lai as leader of the Chinese delegation, unanimously affirmed the decisions of the Twentieth Congress and the declaration of November 1957.[1]

The change in Peking's and Moscow's relationship did not become publicly obvious until the Twenty-Second Congress of the Communist party of the Soviet Union was held in October 1961. In their speeches Khrushchev and Mikoyan strongly attacked the leaders of the Albanian Communist party, Enver Hoxha and Mehmet Shehu, who had refused to de-Stalinize the party and rehabilitate its victims of Stalinism. Chou En-lai, present at the congress as head of Peking's delegation, rejected their attack in his opening speech. 'This public one-sided condemnation of a fraternal party,' he declared, 'does not encourage unity'; China, he warned, would not sanction Albania's expulsion from the Communist camp. And without waiting for further debate, he demonstratively left the congress to lay a wreath on Stalin's grave with the inscription: 'To the greatest Marxist-Leninist, J. Stalin'.[2]

In the public challenge to Moscow conveyed by Chou En-lai, a long-fermenting resentment at the Soviet Union's attitude to China had come to the surface. Stalin, whom Peking now once again glorified, had hardly shown himself to be a genuine friend of the Chinese revolution, or, in particular, of Mao Tse-tung. He had treated him with superciliousness, never uttering a word of appreciation for his achievements. When Soviet troops occupied Manchuria after Japan's surrender, they behaved as though they had conquered an enemy country, not part of China; the many factories and plants which they dismantled were shipped as booty to the Soviet Union. Stalin had been contemptuous of Mao Tse-tung's partisans, sceptical of Communism's chances in China, and distrustful of a revolution asserting itself without his advice or approval. He had based his policies on an anticipated victory by the nationalist government of Chiang Kai-shek. He did not believe that Mao Tse-tung would be able to crown the revolution by triumphantly unifying the country. He had 'categorically' informed Harry L. Hopkins, when he was sent to Moscow by President Truman in May 1945, that,

he would do everything he could to promote the unification of China under the leadership of Chiang Kai-shek. He further stated that this leadership should continue after the war, because no one else was strong enough. He specifically stated that no Communist leader was strong enough to unify China. In spite of the

1. For the text of the 1957 declaration, see Gittings, *Survey of the Sino-Soviet Dispute*, pp. 310–20; for the text of the 1960 declaration, see *World Marxist Review*, December 1960.

2. For Khrushchev's criticism, see Dallin (ed.) *Diversity in International Communism*, p. 29; for Mikoyan's criticism, see ibid., pp. 60–3; for Chou En-lai's rejection of their criticism, see ibid., p. 51; for the complexity of the problem as it relates to Albania, see William E. Griffith, *Albania and the Sino-Soviet Rift* (Cambridge, Mass., 1963). Disregarding Chou En-lai's demonstration of homage to Stalin, the congress agreed that his coffin should be removed from Lenin's mausoleum at the Kremlin.

reservations he expressed about him [Chiang Kai-shek], he proposed to back the generalissimo.[1]

Stalin had certainly subordinated the interests of the Chinese revolution to the Soviet Union's power-political interests. As the price for recognizing Chiang Kai-shek's government after the war he had, at the Yalta Conference in February 1945, secured Russia's predominance in Outer Mongolia, the lease of Port Arthur and 'rights of precedence' on the China–East Manchuria railway, administered jointly with China. After Japan's capitulation in August 1945, he instructed Mao Tse-tung to call off his struggle with Chiang Kai-shek, to enter into talks with him about the setting up of a coalition government and to amalgamate the Red Army with the forces of the Kuomintang. Mao Tse-tung revealed in a speech at the Tenth Plenum of the Chinese Communist party in September 1962:

> In 1945, Stalin refused to permit China to carry out a revolution, He said to us: 'Do not have a civil war with Chiang Kai-shek, otherwise the republic of China will collapse.' However, we did not obey him and the revolution succeeded.[2]

Over the next three years the Red Army captured all of northern China except for Peking and Tientsin.

In the summer of 1948 Mao Tse-tung was planning his ultimate offensive against the Kuomintang forces. A defeat for the army of the Kuomintang did not at that time, however, have any place in Stalin's strategy for the Cold War. He therefore tried to dissuade Mao Tse-tung from seeing the plan through.[3] But Mao Tse-tung again rejected his advice, and when the Communist offensive began in September it swept away the last Nationalist stronghold in north China.

Mao Tse-tung's refusal to submit to Stalin's leadership had hardly kindled the Russian leader's sympathies for the Chinese revolution. After his experience with Yugoslavia, he was also worried, with reason, that a Communist China might not unquestioningly accept Moscow's authority but would pursue an independent policy. 'Even after the success of the revolution,' Mao Tse-tung recollected during a speech in March 1967 at the twelfth plenary meeting of the Chinese Communist party, 'Stalin feared that China

---

1. Robert E. Sherwood, *The White House Papers of Harry L. Hopkins*, vol. II (London, 1948), pp. 891–2. Soon after Hopkins's talk with Stalin, on 4 June 1945, Truman passed on Stalin's comments to T. V. Soong, Chiang Kai-shek's brother-in-law and prime minister. See Kenneth Scott Latourette, *A History of Modern China* (London, 1954), p. 190.

2. *Mainichi*, 9 March 1967, quoted in Gittings, *Survey of the Sino-Soviet Dispute*, p. 12. See also Vladimir Dedijer, *Tito Speaks* (London, 1953).

3. 'Stalin insisted through Lio Shao-ch'i [who had returned from talks with him in Moscow] that the Chinese Communists should continue with the guerrilla war and not commence the *coup de grâce*. The Berlin crisis, he argued, which was then at its climax, would not lead to world war; it was therefore important to continue to force America to waste its forces through useless assistance to the Kuomintang.' See C. P. Fitzgerald, *Revolution in China* (London, 1954), p. 108.

would degenerate into another Yugoslavia and that I might become a second Tito. I later went to Moscow and concluded the Sino-Soviet Treaty of Alliance. This was also the result of struggles. Stalin did not wish to sign the treaty; he finally signed it after two months of negotiations.'[1]

This agreement was not in itself particularly generous. The Soviet Union did no more than surrender to China its rights over the Manchurian railway and promise to evacuate Russian troops from Port Arthur (they were only withdrawn as late as May 1955), but retaining control of the strategically important port of Dairen and of Manchuria's lines of communication. Although Russia did grant China a loan, this was for only $300 million over five years—far less than United States aid to South Korea alone—and only in the shape of Russian machines and technical advisers. China was to make repayments in raw materials, tea, gold and American dollars.

It also seems possible that, in his talks with Stalin, Mao Tse-tung brought up the question of the agreements signed under the Tsars by which a helpless China had been forced to surrender to Russia vast areas north of the River Amur and east of the Russian Ussuri as well as a part of Chinese Turkestan (Sinkiang). In its first decree of 9 November 1917 the Soviet government had 'denounced absolutely and immediately' all treaties designed 'to retain or increase the territories of Greater Russia'.[2] And, in its declaration to the Chinese people of 25 July 1919, it had promised 'to return to the Chinese people everything that was taken from them by the Tsarist government'.[3] It is quite probable that Mao Tse-tung reminded Stalin of these promises, and so provoked his refusal even to vacate Port Arthur.

Khrushchev, who followed Stalin to power, was equally unwilling to return a single square mile of the areas annexed by the Tsarist government. During his visit to Peking in July 1954, when Mao Tse-tung raised the question of Outer Mongolia, he refused even to speak about it.[4] Mao Tse-tung was obviously not satisfied with this rejection. 'We have yet to submit the bill,' he said.[5]

But it was not only the unresolved question of revising the Tsarist treaties but

1. *Mainichi*, 9 March 1967, quoted in Gittings, *Survey of the Sino-Soviet Dispute*, p. 15. Mao Tse-tung had arrived in Moscow at the beginning of December 1949. The agreement was signed on 14 February 1950.

2. See Jane Degras (ed.), *Soviet Documents on Foreign Policy*, vol. I: *1917–1924* (London, 1951), p. 2.

3. ibid., p. 159. This promise was established in Article I of the draft agreement which the Soviet government submitted to the Chinese government on 27 September 1920. This read: 'The government of the Russian Federated Soviet Republics declares as void all treaties concluded by the former government of Russia with China, renounces all the annexations of Chinese territory . . . and returns to China free of charge, and for ever, all that was ravenously taken from her by the Tsarist government'—see ibid., p. 214.

4. *Pravda*, 2 September 1964: 'Mao Tse-tung's Discussions with Japanese Socialists'; for the text, see Brahm, *Pekings Griff nach der Vormacht*, pp. 202–5.

5. ibid., p. 205.

also the Soviet Union's foreign policy which became a source of Chinese resentment towards Moscow's attitude. Afraid of the possible outbreak of a new world war, Khrushchev sought an understanding with the United States. Mao Tse-tung, however, saw in the United States the arch-enemy of Communist China. It had armed the Kuomintang during the civil war and had withheld its recognition of the government of the People's Republic of China after the victory of the revolution. It had blocked China's nomination to the United Nations while securing for Chiang Kai-shek's government in the island of Formosa, whither it had fled with the remnants of its army after its defeat, a permanent seat on the Security Council. Moreover, by stationing the Seventh Fleet in Chinese territorial waters, it had prevented the reincorporation of Formosa into the Chinese state.

Mao Tse-tung had attempted to solve the Formosan question peacefully in talks with the United States held in the summer of 1955. He had appealed to Chiang Kai-shek to return to his fatherland and to erase the memory of past conflicts. But the talks, which dragged on until the end of 1957, were frustrated by the conditions imposed by America. Mao Tse-tung was unable to visualize the United States as being anything but an unrelenting enemy to Communist China.

In the same year, 1957, the Soviet Union had launched the first satellite into orbit round the earth and had exploded its first atomic bomb. Mao Tse-tung believed that the Soviet Union had already overtaken the United States in rearmament. 'The East wind has gained the upper hand over the West wind,' he declared on his arrival in Moscow in November 1957. And, at the conference of the representatives of the twelve ruling Communist parties, he criticized the principle of peaceful co-existence, as was later to become known from a report submitted by the secretary of the Central Committee of the Communist party of the Soviet Union, Mikhail Suslov.[1]

Khrushchev did not, however, allow himself to be pushed off course in his foreign policy, which was aimed at an understanding with the United States. The conference declaration reaffirmed the resolutions of the Twentieth Congress, including the principle of peaceful co-existence between Communist and capitalist states to form a 'sound basis of the foreign policy of the Socialist countries and the dependable pillar of peace and friendship among the peoples'.

Only three years later, during the second Communist world conference in Moscow in 1960, where Chou En-lai represented the Chinese party, did Peking's opposition to Moscow's foreign policy emerge in a battle over the conference's principles, precipitated by a challenge through a resolution put forward by the Chinese delegation. In his attempts to attain an easing of

1. *Pravda*, 3 April 1964. For the text of Suslov's report, see Brahm, *Pekings Griff nach der Vormacht*, pp. 65–134.

international tensions, Khrushchev had visited the President of the United States, Dwight D. Eisenhower, in September 1959 at his farm at Camp David, and had reached an understanding with him over paving the way to peaceful international relations by a joint declaration rejecting war as a method for settling conflict between nations.

Mao Tse-tung, on the other hand, did not wish to see any easing of hostility between Communists and imperialists, or between the Soviet Union and the United States. And so, at the conference, Chou En-lai asked that the United States should be condemned as 'the outstanding force of war and aggression', under whose leadership 'the imperialists form their politics— military-political alliances to fight in common against the Socialist camp and to strangle the national liberation, working-class and Socialist movements', as the resolution stated in the final form adopted by the conference.

In fact the conference had wrangled over the draft of the resolution, which threw doubt on the actual success of Khrushchev's discussions with Eisenhower, for almost three weeks. The outcome was a compromise which sought to screen Peking's opposition to Moscow's foreign policy.[1] While the resolution certainly declared that the 'aggressive nature of imperialism has not changed', it also stated that 'a definite section of the bourgeoisie' in capitalist countries favoured the policy of peaceful co-existence, taking a 'sober view' of the dire consequences of a modern war. And the conference finally gave sanction to the principle of peaceful co-existence. 'Peaceful co-existence of countries with different systems or destructive war—that is the alternative today. There is no other choice . . . ,' the resolution declared.

The disputed question of the position which the Communist party of the Soviet Union occupied in the Communist world movement, which Chou En-lai had also evidently raised, was similarly solved by a compromise. Hitherto Moscow had insisted on recognition for its party's 'leading role'. The new formula read:

The Communist and Workers' parties unanimously declare that the Communist party of the Soviet Union has been, and remains, the universally recognized vanguard of the world Communist movement. . . .

This compromise had been evolved because neither Khrushchev nor Mao Tse-tung wished to disrupt Sino-Soviet relations further. These had been

1. That the formula for the 1960 declaration had been a compromise was confirmed by a letter dated 28 July 1964 from the central committee of the Communist party of China to the central committee of the Soviet Communist party. 'You are perfectly well aware,' it stated, 'that the Communist party of China has always been against this formulation. At the two discussions between our fraternal parties, you repeatedly asked us to accept this formulation unconditionally, since otherwise you would get into great difficulties. It was only out of respect for your difficulties that we agreed to a compromise.'—see ibid., p. 187.

disturbed since 1958 above all by the Soviet Union's refusal, in contravention of a secret agreement of 1957, to place the plans for the atomic bomb and the technical details of its manufacture at China's disposal. Moscow did not wish to see China's rise to become the Soviet Union's equal in power. To Peking's criticism of Moscow's attitude, Khrushchev reacted by recalling Russia's technical advisers in the summer of 1960.[1]

The rift between Peking and Moscow did not, however, emerge publicly until the Twenty-Second Congress of the Communist party of the Soviet Union in October 1961. The three-week debate over the drafting of the resolution at the Communist world conference of 1960 had been conducted behind closed doors. While it is true that various indications, such as the recall of the Russian experts from China, had given rise to assumptions that the harmony between the two great Communist powers was not undisturbed, the depths of the conflicts which divided them and the animosity which these evoked had remained concealed from the eyes of the world.

But, at its Twenty-Second Congress, the Communist party of the Soviet Union received a public challenge from Peking. By the attitude Chou En-lai showed in his speech to the congress—his condemnation of Khrushchev's criticism of the Communist party of Albania, his powerful attack on the President of the United States, John Fitzgerald Kennedy,[2] with whom Khrushchev was currently holding talks about the limitation of nuclear armaments and, above all, by his homage to Stalin—he indicated that the Communist party of China was no longer inclined to recognize the leading role of the Communist party of the Soviet Union as the central authority of the Communist world movement. China declared herself to be solidly behind the Albanian party in its conflict with Moscow, and when on 25 November 1961 the Soviet Union broke off diplomatic relations with Albania, simultaneously expelling the Albanian party from the Communist camp, Peking refused to sanction its decision and paid tribute to the

1. 'You have cast overboard the standards of international relations,' a letter of 29 February 1964 from the central committee of the Communist party of China to the central committee of the Communist party of the Soviet Union complained, 'and within the short period of one month have unscrupulously withdrawn 1,390 Soviet specialists working in China, torn up 343 contracts as well as supplementary contracts for the employment of specialists, and have cancelled 257 projects for scientific and technical co-operation. . . . Thus many of our important projects and scientific research programmes have had to be broken off half completed. . . . Your breaking of your word has disrupted our basic political economy and inflicted heavy losses in the Socialist reconstruction of China. You have taken advantage of the opportunity presented by China being inflicted with heavy natural catastrophes to take these far-reaching steps'—*Seven Letters. Correspondence between the Central Committee of the Communist Party of China and the Central Committee of the Communist Party of the Soviet Union* (Peking, 1964). For the text, see Brahm, *Pekings Griff nach der Vormacht*, pp. 144–55; for the quoted extracts, see ibid., pp. 147–8.

2. For Chou En-lai's speech, see Dallin (ed.), *Diversity in International Communism*, pp. 48–9.

Albanian party as 'a militant Marxist–Leninist party, steeled in revolutionary struggles'.[1]

One may well ask why Mao Tse-tung did not raise the question of the Soviet Union's leading role prior to the first Communist world conference of November 1957. This conference had in fact been confronted by Moscow with a *fait accompli*: Stalin's degradation; the far-reaching changes in the Communist ideology as announced by the Twentieth Congress of February 1956; the Soviet intervention in Poland; and the invasion of Hungary by Soviet forces eight months later. These actions, which were of vital significance for the whole Communist movement, had been undertaken by the Communist party of the Soviet Union as the leading party in the Communist world movement from its own position of absolute power.

As we shall see, Mao Tse-tung had even then entertained strong fundamental doubts about the ideological changes undertaken by the Twentieth Congress of the C.P.S.U. and the new foreign policy which it had initiated. Moreover, he felt that his own self-esteem was hurt as a result of Moscow's autocratic method. In his own party he was regarded as the Lenin of China. The Chinese Communists looked up to him as an outstanding innovator of revolutionary strategy, the architect of China's unity and as a leader and theoretician of genius.[2] He was indeed the leader of the greatest revolution in Asia's history. The revolutionary strategy which he had evolved in contradiction to Stalin's had conquered a huge empire. His thoughts had enriched Marxism–Leninism. He felt himself to be the heir to the Marxist–Leninist heritage. He claimed the rank in the hierarchy of the world Communist movement which, after Lenin's death, Stalin had assumed for himself.

But the leaders of the Communist Party of the Soviet Union were not prepared to concede him any such rank; they did not even accept him as an equal partner in the leadership of the world Communist movement. They did not consult him about the far-reaching decisions which the Twentieth Congress was going to take nor was he informed about the intention to degrade Stalin's reputation in the Communist world. In common with the leaders of all the other Communist parties at the conference, Mao Tse-tung had been taken by surprise by Khrushchev's secret speech.

If Mao Tse-tung did not raise the whole question of the position of the

1. For the Soviet notes about the rupture of diplomatic relations with Albania, see ibid., pp. 145–50; for the message of tribute from the Chinese central committee to the Albanian party, see ibid., pp. 202–3.

2. Liu Shao-ch'i, for example, writing with the authority of a leading theoretician, in his report to the Seventh Congress of the Communist party of China in April 1945 had praised Mao as 'China's greatest theoretician and scientist', and described his thought as an 'admirable example of the rationalization of Marxism'. In a later speech (1949), he claimed that the thought of Mao was applicable not only to the Chinese revolution, but to the struggle for emancipation throughout the world. Quoted in Stuart R. Schram, *Mao Tse-tung* (London, 1966), pp. 332–4.

Communist party of the Soviet Union as the supreme authority in the Communist world movement at the council of the leading Communist parties in November 1957 (at all events, the 1957 declaration contains no reference to it) this is most probably to be explained by China's dependence on economic support from the U.S.S.R.

In the three years between the first and second Communist world conferences, however, relations between Peking and Moscow deteriorated and the Soviet Union went back on its commitments of support for China by its recall of Russian technical advisers in the summer of 1960. Only now did Mao Tse-tung feel able to commence the fight against Moscow's hegemony. He did this by declaring his solidarity with the Albanian party, then in revolt against Moscow.

Mao's initial gesture of opposition to Moscow was followed by open attacks revealing the depth of the ideological and strategic conflicts which had developed between the Chinese and Soviet Communist parties—conflicts concerning both the prospects of Socialism and the methods and tactics to be used in the fight against the forces of capitalism and imperialism as well as the attitude to the overwhelming question of the actual danger of a third world war.

In a number of declarations Mao Tse-tung condemned the new policy inaugurated by the Twentieth Congress as a 'revision' of Marxism–Leninism, and the course towards an international easing of tension and a *détente* with the United States pursued by Khrushchev as a betrayal of the world revolution. He maintained that Khrushchev's theory of the conquest of capitalism by the example of the superiority of a Socialist economy, as he had developed it at the Twentieth Congress, degraded the struggle between capitalism and Socialism to economic competition between the capitalist and Socialist camps. Rather than a policy of international class struggle, he was pursuing a policy of international class-collaboration; and rather than an international crusade against imperialism, he was promoting an understanding with the United States about the division of world rule.

These accusations were based on the fact that the new policy inaugurated by Moscow was indeed no longer inspired by Lenin's concept of world revolution. As far as possible, it sought to change the capitalist order into a Socialist one by peaceful means, by the very methods of parliamentary democracy which Lenin had rejected. In 1947, by creating the Cominform, Stalin had attempted to revive the revolutionary tradition in the Communist movement, which had evaporated during the war in the period of the alliance between the Soviet Union and the Western Allies. But the revolutionary strategy to which the Communist parties had switched in the spirit of the Cominform manifesto had proved unavailing in both Europe and Asia.

Khrushchev had liquidated the Cominform, and with it the revolutionary prospects of Socialist development. In contrast to Lenin's interpretation of parliamentary democracy as an instrument of bourgeois rule and his strategy to seize power by the armed rising of the working class and the establishment of the dictatorship of the proletariat as an instrument of Socialist revolution, the Twentieth Congress stated in its resolution that a 'real opportunity' could arise for the 'working class in a number of capitalist countries' to 'win a stable majority in parliament and transform the latter from an organ of bourgeois democracy into a genuine instrument of the people's will'. The declaration adopted by the conference of 1957 was even more explicit:

> Today in a number of capitalist countries the working class, headed by its vanguard, has the opportunity, given a united working class and popular front or other workable forms of agreement and political co-operation between the different parties and public organizations, to unite a majority of the people, win state power without civil war and ensure the transfer of the basic means of production to the hands of the people.

This formulation of the possibility of a peaceful transition to Socialism was reiterated in the statement issued by the conference in 1960.

And also in contradiction to Lenin's theory that wars are inseparable from imperialism and that therefore, as the Cominform manifesto declared, the outbreak of a fresh world war between the 'imperialist and Socialist camps' seemed inevitable,[1] the Twentieth Congress firmly held the view that wars *are* avoidable, that the dangers of a new world war could be avoided by a policy aiming at a state of peaceful co-existence and the international reduction of tension. Khrushchev even saw a 'real possibility' that the rapid growth of the forces of Socialism and peace might create conditions which, the 1960 declaration stated, 'would eliminate world war from the life of society even before Socialism achieves complete victory on earth with capitalism still existing in a part of the world'.

The new policy which Khrushchev introduced at the Twentieth Congress and its ideological justification—an adaptation of Leninism to modern economic and social conditions—was based on the expectation of a peaceful development of Socialism without world revolution.

As was later disclosed, Mao Tse-tung expressed his doubts on the changes to ideology and policy decided upon by the Twentieth Congress[2] to the conclave of the leaders of the twelve ruling Communist parties when it assembled in

1. To the end of his days Stalin held the view that wars were inevitable so long as imperialism existed. To refute the opinion of certain prominent Communists that wars might be avoided, he wrote in 1952: 'To eliminate the inevitability it is necessary to destroy imperialism'—*Economic Problems of Socialism in the U.S.S.R.* (New York, 1952), p. 30.

2. Mao Tse-tung's objections, submitted in a memorandum to the central committee of the Communist Party of the Soviet Union, were later published by the Chinese in *The Origin and Development of the Differences between the Leadership of the C.P.S.U. and Ourselves* (Peking, 1963), pp. 58–62.

November 1957. He did not, as he explained, believe in the possibility of a peaceful Socialist transformation of capitalist society; history offered no examples of a successful revolution without force. Forceful revolution, he declared, was 'a universal law of the proletarian revolution'.[1]

He also doubted the possibility of preserving peace so long as imperialism was not completely destroyed. As against the theses of the Twentieth Congress that a new world war was by no means inevitable and that international peace and co-existence offered the most favourable conditions for the world triumph of Socialism, he stood by Lenin's thesis that war was inborn in imperialism, and that a new world war, regardless of its cost in human lives, would by no means be a catastrophe, as Khrushchev had said in justifying the policy of co-existence. 'Can one foresee,' he explained, and as Suslov recorded, 'how many human sacrifices a future war might demand?'

Perhaps it will be one third of the world population of 2·7 billion, or, in other words, no more than 900 million people. . . . Even if half the human population was destroyed, the other half would remain, but at this cost imperialism would be completely destroyed and there would only be Socialism in the entire world, while in half or one century the population would again increase, probably by more than half.[2]

Mao Tse-tung did not demand that the Soviet Union should pursue a foreign policy aimed at provoking world war. But he did insist that its policy should be directed towards a world revolution, regardless of the dangers of a new world war; that with its full weight it ought to promote the national and social revolutions of Asia, Africa and Latin America, for, as a declaration of the central committee of the Communist party of China stated on 14 June 1963: 'the wide spaces of Asia, Africa and Latin America are the most important areas of attack for the world revolution'.[3] 'The revolution for national liberation in Asia, Africa and Latin America,' Mao declared, 'appears today to be the most important force aiming a blow directly against imperialism.'[4] But a policy which sought to lessen international tension by a

1. On 31 March 1964, the Communist party of China publicly declared its disagreement with the view that a peaceful transition to Socialism was possible and demanded that the 1960 statement should be revised. See R. Palme Dutt, *The International* (London, 1964), p. 339. As early as 1938, Mao Tse-tung had made plain his views on the role that force was to play in the struggle for power. 'Political power,' he wrote, 'grows from the barrel of a gun. From the barrel of a gun anything can grow. . . . With the help of guns the Russian Communists have produced Socialism. . . . The experience of class war in the age of imperialism has taught us that the working class can defeat the armed bourgeoisie and landlords only by the force of the gun. In this sense, we may say that only by the gun can the entire world be transformed'—*Selected Works*, vol. II: *Problems of War and Strategy* (New York, 1954), pp. 272 and 273.

2. *Pravda*, 3 April 1961; for the text, see Brahm, *Pekings Griff nach der Vormacht*, p. 79.

3. Quoted in Suslov's report; for the text, see ibid., p. 70.

4. *Jen-min Jih-pao*, 22 October 1963, quoted in Suslov's report; for the text, see ibid., pp. 70-1. *Jen-min Jih-pao* (The People's Newspaper) is the daily paper of the central committee of the Communist party of China. The article also appeared in the party's bi-monthly theoretical journal *Hung ch'i*, and was without doubt inspired by Mao Tse-tung.

détente with imperialist America was incompatible with the revolutionary struggle against imperialism. The central committee of the Communist party of China told the central committee of the Communist party of the Soviet Union in a letter of 28 July 1964:

> If you unilaterally reduce the foreign policy of the Socialist countries to 'keeping the peace' and 'peaceful co-existence', it follows that they must forgo any advance against imperialism or support for the revolution of the suppressed and enslaved nations.[1]

Even after his overthrow in October 1964, Khrushchev continued to be criticized in the Chinese press in the strongest terms for having pursued a policy aimed at 'co-operating with the reactionaries of all countries to confront the national liberation movements and revolutions of the masses of the people'.[2] And his successors to the Soviet Union's leadership were told, 'You aim the points of your battle spears not against U.S. imperialism and its lackeys, but against the revolutionary peoples of all countries who are fighting imperialism and its lackeys.'[3]

The accusation that the Soviet Union was working for an alliance with the United States in the struggle to dominate the world became the corner-stone of Mao Tse-tung's anti-Moscow propaganda. He supported it with a theory that the world, as he remarked in a conversation with a group of Japanese Socialists in September 1964, was divided into two 'zones': one zone embraced Asia, Africa and Latin America, and the other was the Soviet-American zone. In other words: one zone contained the nations which were suppressed by imperialism and were fighting for their freedom, and the other was the zone of the imperialist United States, with which the Soviet Union was striving to become allied. The Soviet Union, he continued, had 'hatched a plot with the United States of America in the struggle for world rule'.[4] 'With every fragment of their being they [the leaders of the Soviet Union] strive for an alliance with American imperialism.'[5] 'In the present-day world,' said Mao Tse-tung, 'two great powers, namely the United States of America and the Soviet Union, wish to dominate the whole world in a state of mutual accord'.[6]

Yet it was not only ideological conflicts such as those concerning the prospects of Socialism and strategy in the world revolution which had brought about

1. For the text of the letter, see Brahm, *Pekings Griff nach der Vormacht*, p. 187.

2. *Hung ch'i*. 21 November 1964; for the text, see ibid., p. 229.

3. *Jen-min Jih-pao*, 23 March 1965; for the text, see ibid., p. 249.

4. Quoted in *Pravda*, 2 September 1964, in the report on Mao Tse-tung's talk with the Japanese Socialists; for the text, see Brahm, *Pekings Griff nach der Vormacht*, p. 206.

5. Quoted in a letter of 15 June 1964 from the central committee of the Communist party of the Soviet Union to the central committee of the Communist party of China; for the text of the letter, see ibid., p. 179.

6. Quoted in John Paasche, '*Mao Tse-tungs Theorie von den Zwischenzonen*', in *Ost-europa*, Nos. 1–2, p. 35.

the rift between the two great Communist powers, but also conflicts of national interest between China and the Soviet Union.

Out of their own resources, with no help from Moscow and under unimaginable difficulties, the Chinese Communists had after more than two decades of civil war won the government of the world's largest state. As one of the most illustrious and strongest of the world's Communist parties, they had worked for and hoped to be granted a share of the leadership in the Communist world movement, seeking in particular Moscow's recognition of Peking's leading role among the Communist parties of Asia. But the Communist party of the Soviet Union had not been prepared to abdicate its position as the supreme authority in the world Communist movement, or even to share it, for its predominance over the Communist parties in every other country was a significant element in the power which the Soviet Union wielded. Every diminution of its influence over the international Communist movement would diminish its political power status in the world at large.

Now, however, the Soviet Union had to defend its position in the world, not only in its conflict of interests with capitalist America, but also in a conflict of interests with Communist China—a conflict between Russia's policies as a great power and the national aspirations of the Socialist People's Republic of China. Having endured a century of national humiliation, China now strove to restore the former greatness of the Chinese Empire—to regain the territories snatched from China by the imperialist powers and to recover its sphere of influence over those countries which had recognized the supreme overlordship of the Chinese imperial state. But not all its endeavours matched the interests of the Soviet Union. When, for example, following its conquest of Tibet in 1950–1, China also tried in its expansionist drive to seize the Indian border territory of Ladakh in the Himalayas during the Indo-Chinese war of 1962, it entered into conflict with the power political interests of the Soviet Union, anxious to maintain its friendly relations with India. So as not to place these in jeopardy, the Soviet Union denied its Communist allies any diplomatic or moral support and demonstratively stressed its friendship for India.

A conflict of far greater significance developed between Peking and Moscow after Mao Tse-tung, as he had promised he would in his talks with the Japanese Socialists, 'presented the bill' to the Soviet Union for the list of Chinese territories annexed by the Tsarist government through 'unequal treaties': he requested the return of over a million and a half square kilometres of border territories and raised the question of China's relation with Outer Mongolia, which until a few decades ago had been a part of China until, Mao said, it had been 'subjected' by Russia 'to its rule'.

Moscow's answer was not unexpected. 'We have before us a bare-faced expansionist programme of far-reaching demands,' *Pravda* declared, rejecting the request unconditionally. 'The present Sino-Soviet border', it explained, had been 'created historically' and 'firmly secured by life itself'; 'the agree-ments regarding the borders' created a foundation 'which certainly must be taken into account'. Any revision of the agreements was therefore out of the question. It would represent a breach in the right to self-determination for the peoples of these territories, for, reasoned *Pravda*, 'If the borders of Tsarist Russia were established through the policies of imperialist conquerors, the borders of the Soviet Union were created by the free expression of the will of the people on the foundation of a free right to national self-determination.' And, *Pravda* warned: 'The peoples who belong to the Soviet Union will never allow anybody to interfere with their right to decide their own destiny for themselves.'[1] This warning was followed by a concentration of Soviet troops along the Sino-Soviet border.

Thus the conflicts between Peking and Moscow about the question of Communist ideology and strategy came to be transformed into conflicts over territorial rights, and the theoretical dispute, which had developed into a struggle between rivals for the leadership of the Communist world movement, was expressed in war-like actions. On the Ussuri River, Chinese and Russian troops clashed in armed conflicts, and across the 7,000 kilometres of the Sino-Soviet borders the armies of the two great Communist powers faced one another in readiness for war.

That two states ruled by Communists could arm against one another in preparation for a war would have seemed fantastic had the world not already witnessed the military actions by the Soviet Union against other fraternal parties. Whenever a Communist state had entered into conflict with the great-power interests of the Soviet Union, its leaders had never hesitated to crush it by military force. The moral justification which they had offered to an alarmed Communist world for their actions was based on the notion that the great-power interests of the Soviet Union and the interests of Socialism were identical. Thus any encroachment upon the Soviet Union's power status by fraternal Communist parties could accordingly be defamed as counter-revolutionary.

This was the concept which had been questioned by Yugoslavia, East Germany, Hungary, Poland and Czechoslovakia in their revolts against Moscow's hegemony. But now it was being fought out against the largest of the Communist states—a state in the ascendant, becoming a great military power. The Soviet Union does not see its security as being endangered by China's irrelevant territorial demands: it does, however, fear China's rival claim to a leading role in the 'Socialist world system' and its status as one of the great powers. To defend its own position, the Soviet Union today threatens China with its immensely superior armed might.

It is a symptom of the moral confusion in the leadership of the Com-

---

1. *Pravda*, 2 September 1964; see Brahm, *Pekings Griff nach der Vormacht*, pp. 209 and 211.

munist movement that ideological and even territorial conflicts between Peking and Moscow are able to degenerate into a deadly hostility where a war by the Soviet Union against China seems actually on the horizon. But such a situation, which ought to be morally inconceivable in Socialism, has occurred repeatedly throughout the history of the Communist movement. Time and again Soviet armoured divisions have invaded Communist countries. As a result, a war by the Soviet Union against China seems by no means to be beyond the grounds of possibility. Such an event would indeed represent both the greatest moral catastrophe in the history of Communism and a fateful tragedy for the world at large.

The First Hundred Years

25 · Destiny of a Vision

The three books which comprise the *History of the International* represent an attempt to describe the history of the first century of the modern Socialist movement at least in its outlines. If this has been a daring enough venture, an assessment of the role which the movement has played in the processes of the century's social and intellectual history must be considered rash. This is a task which must be left for future historians, who will have the advantage of a viewpoint from which to place the phenomenon of Socialism in a total perspective of the century's historical development. What the contemporary historian can achieve at best is try to draw up some kind of interim statement of the triumphs and tragedies in the mainstream of the Socialist movement, of its successes and reversals, its expectations and disappointments—as they have been described in the pages of the whole work—and to assess these against the achievements which appear to him to be lasting and therefore of historical significance.

The most amazing phenomenon in the history of the modern Socialist movement has indeed been the unprecedented spread of Socialist ideas across the world. The First International, which gave it its initial impetus, seemed to the London *Times* to be 'a great idea in a small body'. In the course of a single century, this great idea in a small body has inspired a world movement, for which no social movement in the history of mankind can offer a parallel, for none of the social movements of the past possessed a universal character. Neither does history offer any example of an intellectual or religious movement that caught the imagination of all humanity, of all races and cultures. There is no philosophy or ideology which ever became the common intellectual property of all peoples, and none of the great religions ever became a world religion, embracing all mankind.

The Socialist idea, however, has permeated all cultural fields, has inspired the thinking of all races, has become the fundamental principle for nations containing a third of humanity. It acts as the social dynamic in the process of change of the highly developed capitalist social order of Europe as much as of the pre-capitalist one of the peoples of Asia and Africa now freed from colonial rule. With Socialism, for the first time in history, a spiritual and social movement has come into being to embrace the whole world.

However, we immediately face the question of what it is that nations of such a variety of cultures and representing so many stages of economic and social development understand by Socialism, and what Socialism really means.

For a definition of Socialism, there always have been and there are today a number of theories. But each of these holds the basic concept in common: the idea of a classless society, of equal and free men and women—a society emancipated from every form of economic and political enslavement. This concept had been the fundamental meaning of Socialism from its inception, and it has remained so—a concept to guide the Socialist movement in every country, whatever variations there may have been in ideology or methods of realization. It remains the common goal of the British as much as of the Russian Socialist movements, of the Chinese as much as of the Scandinavian, of the Indian as much as of the German, however profound their theoretical and political differences.

In the last resort, these are differences of ideology and method between the old Socialist movements which developed under the economic, social and political conditions of capitalist countries, and the young Socialist movements which arose under entirely different conditions in the semi-feudal pre-capitalist countries; differences between the European character of the Socialist movement which evolved in an atmosphere of democratic tradition, and its Oriental character, emerging from traditionally autocratic societies.

1

That the Socialist movement could spread throughout the pre-capitalist countries, take power and effect what have been the most considerable social and political changes in the history of our times is a paradox of Socialist theory—at all events, as it was developed by Marx. As he demonstrated clearly in his historical-philosophical writings, a Socialist society can only emerge from a capitalist society, for only capitalism can bring about the economic social and cultural conditions for the development of Socialism.[1]

1. 'No social order ever disappears,' he wrote in 1859 in his Preface to *The Critique of Political Economy*. 'until all the productive powers for which there is room within it have been developed; and new, higher relations of production never make their appearance until the material conditions of their existence have been developed in the womb of the old society.' A society, he wrote a decade later in the Foreword to *Capital*, can 'neither jump nor decree away the natural phases of development'. Marx's entire life's work was directed at justifying the idea of the natural evolution of Socialism out of capitalism—the proof 'of the developing of the formation of society as a natural historical process'.

The notion of the possible transition of a pre-capitalist into a Socialist society would have been unthinkable to him. Socialism, according to his theory, could evolve only from the 'womb' of capitalism, and force—an act of the revolutionary seizure of power by the working class—in his view merely performed the function of the 'midwife of history'.

Under the impact of the February revolution in Russia in 1917, Lenin revised Marx's theory of the evolution of Socialism. According to Marx's view of history, a revolution in semi-feudal agricultural Russia could only be a bourgeois revolution, a revolution to burst the chains of feudal autocracy so as to develop productive forces on a capitalist basis. Economically and culturally backward, Russia was still only at the outset of its capitalist phase, and not yet ripe for a Socialist revolution.

Yet, Lenin believed that it was possible to transform the bourgeois revolution immediately into a Socialist revolution. The workers, he insisted, had to seize power, set up a 'dictatorship of the proletariat' in alliance with the peasants and industrialize the country themselves.[1] Thus could Russia simultaneously 'skip' the bourgeois capitalist phase of development and construct a Socialist order of society during the processes of industrialization.

As he saw it, the instrument of Socialist revolution could only be the Communist party: a hierarchical, strictly centralized party subject to military-type discipline and led by an élite of professional revolutionaries.[2] His theory governing its structure, its leading role in the state as the true organ of the 'dictatorship of the proletariat' as well as the nature of the dictatorship itself[3]—defined by his successors as 'Leninism'—was the cornerstone for his concept of the proletarian revolution.

However, this theory was also a revision of the Marxist theory of the Socialist revolution.[4] Marx conceived the proletarian revolution as a conscious act by the working class—the 'immense majority', as he termed it—

1. 'Let us workers,' Lenin suggested, 'ourselves organize large-scale production, proceeding from what capitalism has created so far, on the basis of our experience as workers and with the aid of the strictest iron discipline, maintained by the state power of the armed workers'—V. I. Lenin, *Ausgewählte Werke*, vol. II: *Staat und Revolution* (Moscow, 1947), p. 159. This book, which Lenin wrote in the summer of 1917, a few weeks before he seized power, outlines his theory of the proletarian revolution and its problems.

2. See Braunthal, *History of the International, 1914–1943*, pp. 74–9.

3. 'Dictatorship,' he explained, 'means nothing other than power backed by direct force and restricted by nothing—no laws or regulations'—V. I. Lenin, *Sämtliche Werke*, vol. xxv: *Geschichtliches zur Frage der Diktatur*, p. 549.

4. Stalin agreed that there was a 'grain of truth' in the definition of Leninism as 'the application of Marxism to the particular conditions of the situation in Russia'; but, he went on to say, this was inadequate, for it represented Leninism as a peculiarly Russian phenomenon. He asserted that Lenin had developed Marxism further 'under the new conditions of capitalism and of the struggle of the proletariat. . . . Leninism is the Marxism of the era of imperialism and the proletarian revolution'—J. V. Stalin, *Problems of Leninism* (Moscow, 1947), pp. 13–14.

and not the work of a conspiratorial 'advance guard of the proletariat', as Lenin called the Communist party. And he regarded the dictatorship of the proletariat as the most highly developed form of direct democracy by the whole working class, and not, like Lenin, as an instrument for the dictatorship of an exclusive party over the working class. Nor did Marx consider the dictatorship of the proletariat to be the antithesis of democracy; democracy's antithesis was, for him, the 'dictatorship of the bourgeoisie' which, while concealed by formally democratic political institutions, dominated society as the owners of the means of production.[1]

The tremendous experiment which Lenin attempted in contradiction to Marxist theory triumphed. The Soviet Union, which was his creation, was the first pre-capitalist state to be transferred into a modern industrial state not by a bourgeois-capitalist revolution, but by a proletarian-Socialist revolution. As it became one of the world's largest industrial countries, it was the first where the means of production had been developed not by the initiative of private enterprise, but by national planning, and the first state committed to building a classless society.

Even so, the experiment failed to fulfil its essential destiny. While it certainly created the material conditions for the existence of Socialism, it did not produce the Socialist order of society which Lenin had himself envisaged; a 'higher type of democracy', with no bureaucracy, no police, and no standing army; a commonwealth of free men and equals where the state, as 'the organized and systematic use of force against human beings', as he defined it, had 'withered away'.[2]

But what grew out of the process of this experiment to use the power of

1. Marx regarded the Paris Commune of 1871 as the model for the dictatorship of the proletariat. 'The Commune,' he wrote, 'has been formed by the deputies of the districts of Paris, elected by universal suffrage. . . . It was not a parliamentary body, but a working agency combining the legislative and executive functions.' Thus the Commune was based on the support of a majority of the people, expressing its will by universal suffrage and, above all, by the right of each constituency to recall any representative it might have chosen. 'Nothing could be more foreign to the spirit of the Commune,' Marx wrote, 'than to supersede universal suffrage by hierarchic investiture'—Karl Marx, *Der Bürgerkrieg in Frankreich (1871)* (Berlin, 1952), pp. 70–2.

2. 'Democracy means equality,' he wrote. '. . . It means the formal recognition of equality between citizens, the equal rights of everyone to define the constitution and administer the state.' The essence of democracy—the principle of equality—would, he explained, be realized only once 'all were participating in the administration of the state'. 'From that moment when all members of society, or at least the overwhelming majority, have learned to govern the state themselves, to take the government of the state into their own hands . . . , the necessity for any government whatsoever begins to fade. . . . The more democratic the "state" . . . the more quickly the state [as an organized systematic force to be used against human beings] will begin to wither away.' Lenin's concept was based on the assumption that 'all citizens will become employee and worker in a state syndicate, embracing the whole nation'; and '*all* will have learned independently to guide social production, and they will, in fact, guide it'—*Staat und Revolution*, pp. 234–7. The emphases in the text are Lenin's own.

the state to graft a Socialist society on to a pre-capitalistic one was not in fact 'an association in which the free development of each is the condition for the free development of all' as proclaimed by Marx and Engels in the *Communist Manifesto*; nor was it even Lenin's stateless society, without bureaucracy, police or army. The state became a leviathan, a monster state, which by means of an all-powerful bureaucratic apparatus of state and economy, the police and, above all, the secret state police, the standing army and the monopoly of power over thought and spirit, dominated the people. In the Soviet Union, the state became indeed an 'organized and systematic use of force against humanity', attaining unlimited power in the process of industrialization and infiltrating every pore of society.

It was an inevitable development due to the inherent nature of dictatorship. Rosa Luxemburg, one of the foremost Marxists of her day, had warned against the experiment of attempting to impose Socialism by force.

The Socialist system of society [she wrote] must be and can only be a historical product, born from its own school of experience at the critical hour and out of the fact of living history. . . . Yet if this is so, then it becomes clear that Socialism cannot by its own nature be imposed by decrees. . . . The entire mass of the people must participate. . . . Otherwise Socialism will be commanded from the baize table of a dozen intellectuals.[1]

Yet this is exactly how it happened. A 'dozen intellectuals' decreed the pace for an industrialization calculated so as 'to catch up and overtake' the highly industrialized countries of the West within a few years. Since the bourgeois-capitalist phase still had to be reproduced in state capitalist form, the capital to support such rapid industrialization had to be accumulated by state coercion—by extracting the maximum amount of work for the minimum consumption. Thus the 'dictatorship of the proletariat', originally set up by Lenin as no more than an instrument to suppress the capitalist classes, inevitably became a dictatorship over the proletariat by the bureaucracy of the Communist party, since it was only by state coercion that the workers and peasants could be forced to carry the immense burden which had been laid on their shoulders by the process of industrialization. And in dealing with the incalculable difficulties imposed by the development of the means of production, the dictatorship became increasingly hardened and far-reaching, degenerating under Stalin's rule into a system of totalitarian despotism.

It was a process which simultaneously transformed the classless character of Soviet society. The propertied classes had been exterminated during the Communist revolution. The Soviet Union became a country without a capitalist class. But it did develop a new social stratum which had all the

---

1. '*Die russische Revolution*', in *Rosa Luxemburg, Politische Schriften*, edited by Ossip Flechtheim, vol. III (Frankfurt, 1968), p. 135.

characteristics of a privileged élite. As Christian Rakovsky wrote as early as 1930:

> We are developing from a proletarian state with bureaucratic distortions— Lenin's description of the political form of our state—into a bureaucratic state with some surviving proletarian-Communist features. Before our eyes there has arisen— and continues to arise—a high class of rulers, subdivided internally on an increasing scale, spreading by means of self-interested co-option and by direct and indirect appointment (bureaucratic promotion, sham election). This new type of class takes its stand on a type of private ownership which is also new—the possession of the power of the state. Bureaucracy 'possesses the state as its private property', wrote Marx in his critique of Hegel.[1]

This process of economic and social differentiation began with the first Five-Year Plan of 1928, when Stalin contemptuously rejected the principle of equality of income and standard of living which Lenin had advocated[2] as a 'petit bourgeois' illusion. But, as G. D. H. Cole observed in discussing some of the problems raised by Socialism, 'evidently a society does not become Socialist merely by turning men and women into public employees, if they continue to be paid and graded much as they would be under a capitalist system. Such a society would be not Socialist, but only state capitalist—a very different thing.'[3]

The Communist revolution, inspired by the shining vision of Socialism— 'a realm of freedom', in Engels's words—had in fact by force of circumstance created an empire of universal servitude.[4] What has developed during the first half-century of the Communist system of dictatorship is a complete managerial state with the social superstructure of a welfare state, which since Stalin's death has admittedly shed some of the more barbaric features of its terroristic character, but whose political system comes closer to the spirit of 'enlightened absolutism' in the Asiatic sense—a form of society still in every

1. Quoted in David Rousset, 'The Class Nature of Stalinism', in *Saturn*, vol. III, No. 1, January–February 1957. 'An anti-Leninist pseudosocialism,' observed A. D. Sakharov, 'led to the formation in the Soviet Union of a distinct class—a bureaucratic élite from which all key positions are filled and which is rewarded for its work through open and concealed privileges'—*Progress, Coexistence and Intellectual Freedom* (London, 1968), p. 56. For the emergence of the rule of bureaucracy, see L. Trotsky, *The Revolution Betrayed* (New York, 1937).

2. In his blueprint for the construction of a Communist society, Lenin had envisaged the following development: '*All* citizens will become paid employees of the state' who '. . . work in the same way, keep strictly to the norm of their work and receive equal pay. . . . The whole of society will become *one* office and *one* factory, with equal work and equal pay'— *Staat und Revolution*, p. 236. The emphases in the text are Lenin's own.

3. G. D. H. Cole, *World Socialism Restated* (London, 1956), p. 31.

4. What occurred in Russia was a harsh fulfilment of the 'irony of history' to which Friedrich Engels pointed in a letter he wrote to Vera Zasulich on 23 April 1885 about the future of revolutions. 'The people who boasted that they had "made" a revolution have always on the following day seen that they had no idea what they were doing, that the revolution they have made does not in the least resemble the one they would have liked to have made. This is what Hegel called the irony of history'—quoted in Gustav Mayer, *Friedrich Engels. Eine Biographie* (The Hague, 1934), vol. II, p. 424.

respect, ethically and spiritually, branded by the 'birth-marks of the old society' out of whose 'womb' it came forth.[1]

One of the 'birth-marks of the old society' which continues to defile the Soviet Union is anti-Semitism. Tsarist Russia was truly the classic country of modern anti-Semitism, nursing a sense of hatred, which became deeply ingrained in the emotions of the broad mass of the people and incited by government and the hierarchy of the Eastern Orthodox Church. The millions of Jews in the Russian empire were denied equal rights, confined within ghettos (the Pale of Settlement) and made victims of ever-recurrent and bloody pogroms.

The Communist party of Russia, under Lenin's leadership, naturally saw the effacement of this ugly 'birth-mark' of Tsarist Russia—a phenomenon which Socialists of every shade of opinion and in every country abhorred and fought against as an ideological weapon of reaction and counter-revolution— as one of the tasks of the construction of a Socialist society. Anti-Semitism was made a criminal offence and all trace of discrimination against Jews in public life was erased. Jews were numbered among the most devoted members of the Communist party, attaining high positions in its leadership and, indeed, in every sphere of political, economic and intellectual life of Soviet society, out of all proportion to their numerical strength in the population.

Yet, within a few years of Lenin's death, a number of symptoms indicating a recurrence of anti-Semitism had become apparent. Stalin, as his daughter Svetlana has testified,[2] became violently anti-Semitic during the course of his struggle for power in the party against his rival Trotsky and, later, against the leaders of the internal opposition within the party, Zinoviev, Kamenev and Radek, who were all of Jewish origin. At their trials in 1936–8, they were defined as 'people without a fatherland', devoid of any Russian national feeling. Jews were dismissed in great numbers from responsible positions in the party organization, the state administration and scientific institutions.

In April 1942, during the Second World War, a Jewish Anti-Fascist Committee was formed with Stalin's authority to mobilize the opinion of world Jewry on behalf of the Soviet Union. But, at the same time, the Soviet press kept silent about the massacres of Jews behind the enemy lines. The death-camps of Auschwitz and Majdanek received hardly a mention, and even after the war no monument was permitted to the 50,000 Jews who were slaughtered by the Germans in the ravine of Babi Yar on the outskirts of Kiev. When Yevgeni Yevtushenko published his famous poem, which begins with

1. Thus, in his *Critique of the Gotha Programme* (1875), Marx had described certain characteristics of a society which had 'not *developed* itself on its own basis, but the other way round, just as it *emerged* from capitalist society'—in the case of the Soviet Union, from Tsarist society. See Karl Marx and Friedrich Engels, *Ausgewählte Schriften*, vol. II (Berlin, 1953), p. 13. The emphases in the text are Marx's own.
2. Svetlana Alliluyeva, *Only One Year* (London, 1969), pp. 131–76.

the line 'There is no memorial at Babi Yar', in 1961, he at once encountered fierce official criticism; and when Shostakovitch took the poem as the theme for his thirteenth symphony, he was forced to withdraw it after the first performance in December 1962, though it was later reissued with the 'controversial' parts revised.

The record of the Jews of the Soviet Union during the war had been unimpeachable. More than fifty of them had served as generals, and not a few Jewish soldiers were awarded the highest Soviet order. But, within hardly three years of the war ending, a new anti-Semitic campaign was unleashed, prompted by the enthusiastic response of the Jews in the Soviet Union to the founding of the state of Israel in 1947. Before this, the Soviet Union had pleaded in the United Nations for the recognition of Israel as a move against Britain, but now the Soviet press began to denounce the state of Israel as 'a tool of Western imperialism', while Soviet Jews who showed their sympathy with Israel were treated as suspected 'enemies', as 'rootless cosmopolitans' and men of 'uncertain loyalty'.[1] The Jews were deprived of their rights as a nationality, which they had hitherto enjoyed within the U.S.S.R.; Jewish theatres, periodicals and publishing houses were closed down, their personnel purged. All the leaders of the war-time Anti-Fascist Committee, with the exception of Ilya Ehrenburg, were liquidated, among them Lozovsky, former head of the International of Red Trade Unions and later vice-minister for foreign affairs and the popular Yiddish writers and poets, David Bergelson, Itzik Pfeffer and Peretz Markish. The co-founders of the Jewish Anti-Fascist Committee, Henryk Erlich and Victor Alter, leaders of the Bund and members of the executive of the Socialist International, had been executed as 'Nazi agents' as early as 1942.[2]

The persecution of Russia's Jews culminated in 1953 in the affair of the 'doctors' plot'. On 13 January, *Pravda* and *Izvestia* officially announced that

1. Alexander Solzhenitsyn, in his novel *The First Circle*, describes the shock felt by one of his characters, Adam Roitman, at the recrudescence of anti-Semitic propaganda in the party press. Roitman, an old and devoted Bolshevik and a holder of the Stalin Prize, is yet as a Jew denounced as a 'cosmopolitan'. '. . . This noble word [cosmopolitan] formerly used to denote the unity of the whole world, this proud title given only to the most universal geniuses, such as Goethe, Dante and Byron, suddenly became mean, crabbed and vicious, and hissed from the pages of the newspapers in the sense of "Yid". . . . Perhaps his memory deceived him, but hadn't he been right in thinking that during the Revolution, and for a long time afterwards, Jews were regarded as more reliable than Russians? In those days, the authorities always probed more deeply into the antecedents of a Russian, demanding to know who his parents were and what the sources of his income were before 1917. No such checks had to be made on Jews: they had all been on the side of the Revolution which delivered them from pogroms and the Pale of the Settlement'—*The First Circle* (London, 1970), pp. 510–11.
2. See Isaac Deutscher, *Stalin* (London, 1966), pp. 589–93. For a detailed survey, especially of the persecution of Jewish intellectuals in the Soviet Union, see Yehoshua Gilboa, *The Black Years of Soviet Jewry* (New York, 1971); for a general survey of the Jewish question in the Soviet Union, see Lionel Kochan (ed.), *The Jews in Soviet Russia since 1917* (London, 1970).

nine Jewish doctors who attended the ruling group in the Kremlin had been arrested as agents of the United States and British secret services. Acting under orders, the official account asserted, they had murdered two party leaders, Andrei A. Zhdanov and Alexander S. Scherbekov, and had conspired to poison a number of Soviet marshals.[1] Stalin, as Khrushchev revealed in his secret speech to the Twentieth Congress of the Communist party of the Soviet Union, had personally ordered the use of torture in interrogating the arrested doctors.[2] Two of them, Professor M. B. Kogan and Professor Y. G. Etinger, died under the interrogation.

After Stalin's death, anti-Semitic propaganda in the Soviet press was stopped, the survivors among the arrested doctors were released and indiscrimate terror against the Jews ceased. But then, when the Soviet Union endeavoured to incorporate the Arab countries of the Middle East into its sphere of influence, anti-Semitism made its reappearance in the guise of anti-Zionism. The destruction of Israel—a Socialist oasis in the Middle East—would deprive the Socialist world of one of the most promising and, indeed, fascinating experiments in Socialist reconstruction. Yet its destruction was the well-publicized objective of Egypt, Syria, Iraq and Jordan at the time when the Soviet Union began to provide these countries with a gigantic arsenal of bombers and tanks as well as with thousands of military advisers in preparation for the final battle. And when, in June 1967, the battle ended after six days with an inglorious defeat for the Arab countries, the Soviet Union condemned Israel as the 'aggressor', broke off diplomatic relations and poured a vast quantity of new bombers and tanks into Egypt for a further battle.[3] Exactly as in the last months of Stalin's life, anti-Semitic propaganda in Russia reached a high pitch of fury. Zionism was to be identified with Judaism, according to the official line, and Judaism with capitalism and

1. See Deutscher, *Stalin*, pp. 603–6.

2. 'Stalin,' Khrushchev recorded in his speech to the congress, 'personally issued advice on the conduct of the investigation. . . . He said that Academician Vinogradov should be put in chains, that another one should be beaten. Present at this congress is the former minister of state security, Comrade Ignatiev. Stalin told him curtly: "If you do not obtain confessions from the doctors we will shorten you by a head." Stalin personally called the investigating judge, gave him instructions, advised him on which investigative methods should be used; these methods were simply—beat, beat, and once more beat'—*The Dethronement of Stalin* (London, 1956), p. 25.

3. Andrei Sakharov, the distinguished academician, considers that a 'direct responsibility' for the tragic situation in the Middle East lies with the Soviet Union. '. . . There was,' he writes, 'an irresponsible encouragement of so-called Arab unity, which in no way had a Socialist character—look at Jordan—but which was purely nationalist and anti-Israeli. . . . The preventive six-day war in face of threats of destruction by merciless, numerically vastly superior forces of the Arab coalition, would have been justified. . . . The breaking of relations with Israel appears a mistake, complicating a peaceful settlement in this region and complicating a necessary diplomatic recognition of Israel by the Arab governments'—*Progress, Coexistence and Intellectual Freedom*, with an Introduction by Harrison E. Salisbury (London, 1968), p. 39.

imperialism, particularly with the capitalism and imperialism of the United States. To take one example, *Pravda* stated:

Zionism encompasses 70 per cent of American lawyers, 60 per cent of physicists (including those who are concerned with the mass production of secret weapons) and more than 45 per cent of American industrialists.[1]

Thus anti-Semitism, which Lenin had sought to eradicate from Russia, once more became a characteristic of Soviet society.

The paradoxical character of the Soviet Union—a state formed by a Socialist revolution in the spirit of Socialist principles but which has developed an ultimate form of absolutist government—is revealed dramatically in its foreign policy. Lenin had called it into being as an outpost of the Socialist world revolution. Under Stalin's leadership, it became the cynical accomplice of world Fascism. Stalin perpetuated and consolidated the schism in the international workers' movement, as the second volume of the present history described. He frustrated its need for a common defence against the threat posed by Hitler's rise to power and sealed a pact of friendship with the hangman of thousands of Communists and Socialists. During the war, in the struggle to death between democracy and Fascism in Europe, he had not remained neutral but supported the Fascist powers. He had charged the democracies of Britain and France with the responsibility for the war unleashed by Hitler; he congratulated Hitler on his victory over France; he justified Hitler's invasion of Belgium, Holland, Denmark and Norway; and, by disseminating propaganda through the individual Communist parties, he tried to wear down the forces of moral resistance in Britain and France in the war against Hitler.[2]

Stalin's foreign policy was guided by Machiavellianism on a world scale. He paved Hitler's road to power, since he hoped for the destruction of Social Democracy, which he considered to be an invincible obstacle to the Communist party's rise to power in a democracy. The Nazi régime, he believed, would ultimately collapse, and the Communist party would then inherit its power. And faced with a decision for war, he believed he could reach agreement with Hitler over a division of the world between Fascism and Communism, as he had reached agreement with him over the division of Poland.

The Soviet Union, emerging from the war as one of the world's two great powers, had also become one of the strongest imperialist states. As the present volume has witnessed, it incorporated the countries which it captured during the war into the Russian orbit and afterwards kept them in

1. *Pravda*, 4 October 1967, quoted in Zev Katz, 'After the Six-Day War', in L. Kochan (ed.), *The Jews in Soviet Russia since 1917* (London, 1970), p. 336.

2. For Stalin's policy during the war, see Braunthal, *History of the International, 1914–1943*, pp. 493–530.

vassalage, crushing by force their impulses towards national independence.[1]

Soviet imperialism stemmed from a dual impulse: first, obtaining strategic security for the Soviet Union's western frontiers by a buffer formed by its satellite states and secondly, achieving the extension of Communism within these countries. By exploiting its identification with the cause of Communism, the Soviet Union morally sought to justify both facets of its imperialism.

But Moscow's hegemony, established in the vassal states by the Stalinist system of government, frustrated any development of the system of dictatorship into a system of Socialist democracy. The régime of the bureaucratic hierarchy in the Soviet Union, threatened by the establishment of Socialist democracy, and therefore suppressing any freedom movements in its own country, was not prepared to tolerate the development of democracy in its subject states; wherever a revolution pinned its colours to democracy, as it did in Hungary and Czechoslovakia, it was put down in an armed counter-revolution by the Soviet Union.[2]

The transmutation of the Soviet Union's historical role in Eastern Europe is a paradox: from having been the spearhead of the social revolution in these countries, she became a force of reaction, suppressing their aspirations to attain a social order at a higher level.[3]

The contradiction between ideal and reality in the Soviet Union, between its

1. Milovan Djilas, once the most prominent leader of the Yugoslavian Communist party after Tito, discussed the whole question of the way in which Soviet imperialism differed from capitalist imperialism. 'All that is new here,' he said, 'is the fact that a state which all, or nearly all, believed to be Socialist has, through its own internal state-capitalism development, turned into an imperialist power of the first order. But as for the actual forms, what characterizes this new state-capitalist imperialism is precisely that it has the old colonial-conquest imperialist forms accompanied, albeit, in "Socialist" uniforms, by the old political relations: the export of capital is accompanied by a semi-military occupation, by the rule of an official caste and the police, by the strangling of any democratic tendencies, by the establishment of obedient governments, by the most extensive corruption and by an unscrupulous deception of the working people'—*Borba*, 26 November 1950, quoted in John Strachey, 'Tasks and Achievements of British Labour', in R. H. S. Crossman (ed.), *New Fabian Essays* (London, 1952), p. 206. *Borba* is the central organ of the Yugoslav Communist party.

2. A historical parallel to the Soviet Union's counter-revolutionary intervention in Hungary and Czechoslovakia may be found in Tsarist Russia's counter-revolutionary intervention against the revolutions in Austria and Hungary in 1848. When they broke out, Tsar Nicholas concentrated a strong force on the German frontier and informed Count Thun, the Austrian emperor's special emissary in St Petersburg, that the granting of constitutions to Galicia and Hungary would be intolerable to Russia. 'I could not allow a centre of insurrection on my doorstep. . . . If constitutions are granted in those areas, or if revolution begins in Galicia and is not vigorously suppressed, I shall be forced against my will to cross the Austrian frontier and restore order in the name of Emperor Ferdinand'— quoted in L. B. Namier, *1848: The Revolution of the Intellectuals* (London, 1946), p. 94. The Russian army actually crossed into Austria and put down the revolution in Hungary.

3. For a Marxist criticism of Soviet Communism, see Roger Garaudy, *Le Grand Tournant du Socialisme* (Paris, 1969). Garaudy, a professor of philosophy, was one of the oldest members of the central committee of the French Communist party, its representative in the presidium of parliament and head of its Institute for Marxist Studies. He was expelled from the politbureau and the central committee at the party congress of February 1970.

revolutionary origins and its counter-revolutionary function, and above all, between its dynamic in the process of transforming its economic and social basis and the rigidity of its political superstructure, must eventually demand a solution, as the revolution in Czechoslovakia has shown. It was economic stagnation, the stagnation of the standard of living of the working people, which became the last straw in the revolution in Czechoslovakia. The dominant system of dictatorship was seen to be shackling economic development and a new model of Socialism was sought. As has been shown, the inspiration for the revolution originated within the leadership of the Communist party; its support came from an overwhelming majority of the hundreds of thousands of Communist party members, and the whole nation rallied jubilantly to their side.

The Soviet Union can scarcely evade the democratic phase of development indefinitely. The system of dictatorship, as it has ossified under the conditions of an industrial revolution achieved by the instrument of the power of the state, must, as it fetters intellectual freedom and individual initiative, become an increasing hindrance to development in the technological revolution which the industrial world is witnessing today. It can only become more and more intolerable, and must, therefore, as in Czechoslovakia, engender economic and political crises which will in the end enforce reforms. If the history of the first fifty years of the Russian revolution has been a history of experiments in the transformation of an agrarian country into an industrial state based on Socialist principles, then a period of experiments during the transformation of its political structure may be anticipated, which would ultimately complete the revolution.

2

The Socialist movement in the industrially developed countries of the European tradition had rejected from the start the Communist version of Socialism because it was based on the negation of a principle which, prior to the Communist revolution in Russia in 1917, had been recognized by all Socialist parties of the world—including Lenin's Bolshevik party—as self-evident and fundamental: the principle of political democracy as the expression of the idea of universal equality, the right to self-determination of the people and, above all, the idea of the freedom of the spirit as the well-spring of democracy.[1] These were the achievements of many centuries of battle: for freedom

1. Otto Bauer, perhaps the most prominent figure of the left in the Labour and Socialist International, regarded 'individual and intellectual freedom as the most precious achievement of the struggle of mankind for freedom through the centuries. . . . We are not willing,' he declared in his speech to the Fourth Congress of the International, 'for the sake of Socialism, to surrender the rights to freedom, the guarantees of individual and intellectual freedom, for which the best of mankind have died at the stake of the Counter-reformation, in the

of religion and conscience in the era of the reformation, for freedom of opinion in the era of enlightenment, for political freedom and democracy in the era of the bourgeois revolution. By realizing these ideas, the European peoples achieved their political emancipation. 'While it is not admittedly the ultimate stage of human emancipation,' Marx had observed, 'it is the final stage of human emancipation within the hitherto existing world order.'[1]

The objective which the Socialist movement had set itself from the very beginning had been the political emancipation of the working class within the 'present world order', as well as its economic emancipation in a future world order. The achievement of political democracy was seen as its immediate task.

When the International was formed in 1864, the principle of political equality for the working class on a democratic basis had by no means been recognized in a majority of European states. The working classes had as yet gained no measure of political emancipation. While it is true that, to a certain extent, they had a share in the achievements of bourgeois democracy and its hard-won area of freedom—freedom of thought, of conscience and civic rights—they were allowed no participation in governmental power; excluded from the franchise, they were subjected to the political régime of the property-owning classes. The struggle for the universal right to vote as a means of liberating the working classes from the political rule of the middle class had been one of the leading objectives in the fight of the Socialist parties during the period of the First and Second Internationals. Parliamentary democracy, founded on universal suffrage and today accepted unquestioningly as a standard requirement for any political system, indeed represents one of the achievements of the Socialist movement.

The Russian system of dictatorship by the Communist party, as Lenin established it, rejects democracy. It recognizes no rights to personal freedom as these developed during the processes of 'human emancipation' in the countries of Europe. It is founded on naked force. It is, as Lenin defined it, 'a power, based immediately on force, unrestricted by any laws or regulations.'[2] For countries with a tradition of freedom, the Russian system may be equated to a system of reaction.

The tradition of freedom as it grew in Europe in the struggle against absolutism was, indeed, foreign to Russia. It had never known the phenomenon of human emancipation in European nations—an age neither of reformation nor of enlightenment nor of bourgeois revolutions. The tradition in Russia was one of autocracy, and Lenin in fact perpetuated this tradition

dungeons of absolutism, and on the barricades of countless revolutions'—*Vierter Kongress der Sozialistischen Arbeiter-Internationale, Wien, 1931* (Zürich, 1932), pp. 529–30.

1. Karl Marx, '*Zur Judenfrage*', in Franz Mehring (ed.), *Gesammelte Schriften von Karl Marx und Friedrich Engels* (Stuttgart, 1913), p. 409.

2. See page 493.

when he replaced the fallen Tsarist autocracy with the autocracy of the Communist party.

Under the conditions pertaining in Russia in the days of the Bolshevik revolution, a system of dictatorship seemed to be the only conceivable direct road to Socialism. But, Lenin believed, this system was likewise the only conceivable road to Socialism in the democracies. Democracy, he admitted, was 'of immense importance' in the freedom struggle of the working class, but it was only a 'stage' in the history of their struggles.[1] In the revolutionary situation, as it had developed in the backwash of the First World War, democracy would be an obstacle on the road of the working class to power and Socialism. He called on the workers of every country to emulate the Bolshevik revolution in Russia and seize state power by armed uprising; to destroy democracy, set up dictatorships of the proletariat and introduce government by the working class for the period of transition to Socialism. He founded the Communist International as an instrument for the Communist world revolution.

Lenin's doctrine had devastating consequences.[2] It wrecked the unity of the international workers' movement, dividing it into two mutually hostile camps, paralysed its dynamism and, in Italy and Germany, paved the way for Fascism. It retarded the development of the Socialist movement for decades.

3

When, following the Second World War, the European Socialist movement revived after its suppression by Fascism, the question facing it was no longer the one of dictatorship *versus* democracy on which the international Socialist movement had split after the First World War. The Communist parties of Western Europe and the Americas swore their undying loyalty to the cause of parliamentary democracy, while, in the countries of Eastern Europe, where, as in East Germany and Czechoslovakia, the parties had *de facto* established their dictatorships, the dictatorships were restyled as 'people's democracies'. Lenin's formulation of the 'dictatorship of the proletariat' disappeared from Communist vocabulary; even to mention it had become an embarrassment.

Similarly there was no further talk of Lenin's doctrine of the armed uprising among the European Communist parties; it remained valid only for the underdeveloped countries of Asia. When revolutionary situations arose in France and Italy immediately after the war, the Communist parties in no way attempted to seize power, but on the contrary made every effort to restrain the

1. 'Democracy,' he had said, 'is of immense importance in the freedom struggle of the working class against the capitalists. Democracy is by no means, however, a boundary which cannot be crossed, but only a stage on the road from feudalism to capitalism and from capitalism to Communism'—*Staat und Revolution*, p. 234.

2. These were described in Braunthal, *History of the International, 1914–1943*.

workers from a struggle for power. They combined with the Socialist and liberal parties of the middle classes to consolidate these two dislocated capitalist parliamentary democracies.[1] After being expelled from government in 1947, they did, it was true, inspire mass strikes, partly in protest against economic stringencies, partly as a tactical manoeuvre to force their readmittance to government, but not as any prelude to a revolutionary uprising to gain power.[2] There was never any question of this.

It was also never in question for the Communist party; not even in the revolutionary situation which developed in France under the shock of a severe economic crisis in May 1968. Here was a genuine revolutionary situation—a spontaneous outbreak of revolutionary ferment among the mass of intellectuals and workers and even within the middle class. Students, numbering tens of thousands, rose to occupy the universities, throwing up barricades in the streets; ten million workers came out in a general strike— the largest strike movement in the country's history—occupying factories throughout France and marching through Paris in mass demonstrations side by side with the students. For the first time since the resistance movement ended with the liberation, intellectuals and workers were joined in a common cause. However varied their motives may have been, their common objective was to overthrow the despised presidential régime of General de Gaulle and to set up a new order of society. Power lay about them in the streets; they had only to pick it up.

In this revolutionary situation, the attitude of the Communist party was decisive. It was the largest party by far of the working class in France and it controlled the strongest of the three trade union confederations, the *Confédération Générale du Travail*. But the party, surprised by the revolutionary outbreak, faced it helplessly; it deflected any idea of a revolutionary struggle for power. It scaled down the revolutionary movement into a wages movement, and in discussions with the government of de Gaulle put an end to it.

Since the end of the war the Communist parties of Western Europe, especially those of France and Italy, had become reformist. They no longer sought to change the capitalist order of society through revolutionary methods, but, like the Social Democrats, through parliamentary democracy. They strove to take over the power of the state as an instrument for social change, not through a revolutionary uprising, but through democratic methods—to gain a majority of votes in parliamentary elections.[3]

1. See pp. 33, 52.   2. See pp. 42, 65.

3. 'The working class and its advance guard—the Marxist–Leninist party,' a conference of sixty-four Communist parties declared in Moscow in 1957, 'seek to achieve the Socialist revolution by peaceful means.' In a number of capitalist countries, it further stated, it was today possible for the working class, by forming a proletarian united front or a people's front in co-ordination with various parties, 'to unite a majority of the people, win state power without civil war, and ensure the transfer of the basic means of production into the hands of the people'. For the full text of the resolution, see *Current Digest of the Soviet Press*, 1 January 1958.

Here is no answer to the question whether Communist parties have changed in their basic attitude to the problems of the struggle for Socialism, or only in their tactics; whether their avowals of democracy are genuine or well-planned deceptive manoeuvres; or whether, having once seized power by democratic methods, they would in any way change democracy, based on the right to freedom, into a system of dictatorship, based on a 'people's democracy'. It is only being established as a historical fact that since the end of the war the Communist parties of Western Europe have advocated the principles of parliamentary democracy and have, in co-operation with the left-wing parties of the middle class as well as the Socialists, sought a share in governmental power.

Their ideology has, however, remained undisturbed by any change in political attitude. Lenin's interpretation of Marxism has remained unchallenged during the half-century since the founding of the Communist International in 1919, regardless of the considerable changes that have occurred in the structure of capitalism, in the social power relationships and the programmatic basis of the Communist movement. Marxism–Leninism had ossified into a dogma.

4

The democratic Socialist movement, on the other hand, has experienced a total retreat from Marxism since the end of the Second World War. Marxism had been the predominant ideology of the Second International. Practically all its affiliated parties (the British Labour party was a notable exception) programmatically acknowledged the Marxist theory of irreconcilable antagonism to the capitalist state, proclaiming the revolutionary change of the capitalist order of society as their aim, and shared the millennial vision of the *Communist Manifesto*—the vision of the inevitable collapse of the capitalist world and of the triumph of Socialism as 'an iron law of history'.

But every Socialist party contained its reformist wing, which, in contrast with the concept of revolutionary Socialism, represented a concept of evolutionary Socialism—a theory of the gradual evolution through social and political reforms of the capitalist society into a Socialist form of society, of capitalism 'growing into' Socialism.[1] This theory, the reformists said, was based on a recognition of the ability of capitalism to change, a recognition

1. Engels believed with Marx that, in countries which had fully developed parliamentary democracies, such a change was possible without a revolution by force. 'One may imagine,' wrote Engels, 'that the old society might peacefully develop into the new society in countries where the representation of the people focuses power to itself, where, constitutionally, one may do what one pleases once a majority of the people has given its support—in democratic republics such as France and America, or in monarchies such as England where the dynasty is helpless against the will of the people'—'*Zur Kritik des sozialdemokratischen Programmentwurfs 1891*', in *Die Neue Zeit*, Year xx, vol. i (1901–2).

that, as Marx had written, 'present society is not a solid crystal, but an alterable organism constantly in process of change'.[1] And even as the main emphasis in the struggle by the Socialist parties had been towards social, political and economic reforms, so the reformists asked for a theoretical and, above all, a tactical alignment of Socialist parties to a process of social change by reform: a positive attitude towards the state, a readiness to enter into alliances with the progressive groupings within the middle class and a readiness to form coalitions with left-wing middle-class parties.[2]

The conflict between Marxism and reformism was hammered out in vehement debate at the congresses of the Second International. A majority emerged to support the Marxist version of the class struggle; of irreconcilable conflicts between the proletariat and the bourgeoisie as well as the bourgeois-capitalist state; and they therefore declared themselves against the participation of Socialist parties in bourgeois governments. They did, however, recognize a right to national defence, but pledged the parties, in the event of their being unable to prevent the outbreak of war, 'to utilize the economic and political crisis created by war to rouse the masses and thereby to hasten the downfall of capitalist class rule'[3]—in other words, to unleash a social revolution.

However, as the crisis of the First World War unexpectedly revealed, the Marxist ideology of the Socialist parties stood in marked contrast to the basically reformist attitude of the vast proletarian masses. During the days of peace they had been ready to fight the capitalist state, but as soon as a war threatened its existence, they rallied to its side as their fatherland. In peace they had cherished the international solidarity of the working class as a fundamental tenet; but as soon as war broke out, they surrendered themselves to a burst of patriotism and nationalism. In every belligerent nation—with the exceptions of Russia and Serbia—they unhesitatingly declared themselves in favour of their country's defence in August 1914, granted their capitalist-imperialist governments the credits needed to conduct the war and placed themselves at their service.[4]

This tragic abandonment of the tradition of the Socialist International in the conflict of interest between national survival and the concept of international proletarian solidarity was a moral defeat for the Socialist movement

---

1. Marx, in his Foreword to the first edition of *Capital* (1867).
2. For the conflict between Marxists and reformists in the Second International, see Braunthal, *History of the International, 1864–1914*, pp. 255–84. For a detailed description of the currents within the parties, see G. D. H. Cole, *A History of Socialist Thought*, vol. III: *The Second International 1889–1914* (London, 1956); for the theoretical basis of the discussion, see George Lichtheim, *Marxism. An Historical and Critical Study* (London, 1961).
3. This final draft of the resolution on the attitude of the International towards war, submitted by Lenin, Luxemburg and Martov, was voted upon at the Stuttgart congress of 1907. For the full text of the resolution, see Braunthal, *History of the International, 1864–1914*, pp. 361–3. For the congress debate over the war question, see ibid., pp. 320–56.
4. See ibid., pp. 1–35.

from which it never recovered; it formed a traumatic experience for a whole generation of Socialists. The crisis which it unleashed paralysed the International. During the war, internal struggles divided the parties between their patriotic, reformist wings and the left wings of internationalists and Marxists. After the war, it grew into the most serious crisis in the history of Socialism when Lenin, with his programme of world revolution, formed the Communist International and split the international workers' movement. Its internal history during the period between the two world wars was one of internecine strife over the problem of dictatorship *versus* democracy, which was only ended with the common wreck of the Socialist and Communist movements throughout almost the whole of Europe under the blows of Fascism.

After the Second World War, the ideal of freedom assumed first place in the scale of values acknowledged in the ideology of the European Socialist parties. The Socialist movement had, from the start, been a freedom movement—indeed, the vanguard of the people's struggle for civic rights, freedom and democracy.[1] In the light of the experience of totalitarian Communism—ostensibly a Socialist system, yet lacking the elements of freedom—the Socialist movement became increasingly aware of the problems posed by freedom in the struggle for Socialism. In the programmes which the parties formulated after the war, the emphasis was placed on freedom and democracy as foundations for the Socialist form of society to which they aspired. Thus, when the Socialist International was revived after the war, it gave these points precedence in its programme:

1. Socialists work by democratic methods to bring about a new society in freedom.
2. There is no Socialism without freedom. Socialism can only be realized through democracy, democracy can only be fulfilled through Socialism.[2]

But the use of democratic methods, unless there is a period of social crisis, precludes any dramatic, revolutionary transformation of capitalist society. For 'under the conditions of universal suffrage, electorates do not vote for revolutions—unless the revolutions have already happened', as G. D. H. Cole remarked when considering the question of how it was that a Socialist government in Britain—that of the British Labour party following its landslide victory in 1945—while attempting to reform the capitalist system, had not radically transformed its structure.[3] In a democracy, the nature and extent of Socialist reforms carried out by a Socialist government must depend on the

1. For a study of the role of freedom in the working-class struggle for power, see Susanne Miller, *Das Problem der Freiheit im Sozialismus* (Frankfurt, 1964).
2. For the debate on the declaration made at the International's inaugural congress, see page 201; for the full text, see Appendix Two.
3. G. D. H. Cole, *Is this Socialism?* (London, 1954), p. 6. For a discussion of the contemporary problems of Socialism, see Crossman, (ed.), *New Fabian Essays*.

level of development of a Socialist consciousness in the broad mass of the people. Otherwise it would simply be overthrown in the next elections, should its reform activities be seen by a majority of the electorate as an infringement of their material interests. Socialism can develop in a democracy only if a Socialist ethos exists within that society. It can become a living reality only in an atmosphere of dedicated self-sacrifice, solidarity, social discipline and a voluntary subordination of group interests to the common social interest for the sake of the Socialist cause.

Such an idealism among the broad mass of workers and middle-class intellectuals has not infrequently emerged in the history of Socialism. In the count of its martyrs—those who have been executed, tortured, condemned to imprisonment or the concentration camps—Socialism does not lag behind any religious or social movement of the past. But idealism is not to be awakened merely by an appeal to exclusively material interests. Socialism originated as a workers' protest movement, not only against the system of capitalist exploitation to which they were subjected, but also against the social injustice which the system embodied and the notorious spirit of ruthless greed by which it was governed.[1] It was the ethos of Socialism—its promise of a world of social justice and human solidarity—which had aroused the enthusiasm within the movement.

The achievements of the Socialist movement have, indeed, been considerable. Its struggle for social justice has brought about a change in social conscience regarding the social function of the state. At the time when the International was formed, the state's active role, as Lasalle characterized it, was seen as confined to that of 'night watchman': it was only asked that it should protect property, and administer law and order; it was not to interfere in 'the free play of economic forces' or the relationship between capital and labour, and certainly not to protect the workers against exploitation; the capitalist's freedom to exploit his labour was not to be hindered by law. Neither the state nor society at large felt any responsibility for the fate of the workers, vegetating at that time in utter misery.[2] The liberal-capitalist principle of *laissez-faire*, which then governed the attitude of the state to social problems, excluded any influence by the forces of the state over the living conditions of the workers. *Laissez-faire* was breached for the first time in England by the Ten Hours Act of 1847—a 'great act', as Marx hailed it in his *Inaugural*

1. 'Socialists,' the declaration of the founding congress of the International states, 'oppose capitalism not only because it is economically wasteful and because it keeps the masses from their material rights, but above all because it revolts their sense of justice'—see page 203.

2. For a description of the situation of the English working class during the first half of the nineteenth century, see the classic work by J. L. and Barbara Hammond, *The Bleak Age* (London, 1934). For their situation as it still was at the end of the nineteenth and the beginning of the twentieth century, see E. Royston Pike, *Human Documents of the Age of the Forsytes* (London, 1969).

Address to the founding congress of the First International, not only because of the 'immense physical, moral and intellectual benefits' which greater leisure brought to the factory workers, but also 'as the victory of a principle; it was for the first time that in broad daylight the political economy of the middle class succumbed to the political economy of the working class'.

During the eight decades after the founding of the International and up to the end of the Second World War, the Socialist movement managed by hard struggle to wring from the ruling classes one or another social reform. It was only after the Second World War, when Socialist parties formed majority governments, as in Britain and Sweden, or participated as leading parties in coalition governments, as in other European countries, that they became a predominant power and that 'the political economy of the working class' began to develop. It was only then that a basic process of change began from a *laissez-faire* capitalist state to a Welfare State. This had become possible through a change in social awareness: the responsibility of society and the state for the social welfare of the broad mass of its people had now been unquestioningly accepted.[1] What the Socialist movement had in fact achieved was the social recognition of the new rights of the working class: the rights to health, housing, education, economic security in old age and during times of unemployment, and, especially, the right to work. The state had been placed under an obligation to secure through its economic and financial policies the highest possible employment.[2]

Every measure taken to realize these rights represents an interference by the state in capitalist rights: 'a victory of the political economy of labour over the political economy of capital'.

The 'political economy of the working class' has revolutionized the function of the state. It has become a regulator with enormous power, controlling the life of the economy at its roots. The destiny of the economy and the living standards of the working class are no longer, as they were before the war, at the mercy of an anarchic 'free play of economic forces'. The calculated intervention of the state represents a decisive control over the economic life of a country.

While the Welfare State evidently realized certain basic Socialist ideas, it by no means succeeded in changing the class structure of the capitalist state; it still fell a long way short of an egalitarian classless society. While structural

1. The scale of social welfare may be illustrated from the Budget estimate presented by the British Labour government in year 1969–70. Out of a total expenditure of £20,067 million, over two fifths, or £8,771 million, was directed towards state welfare institutions, i.e. £1,853 million to the National Health Service, £1,073 million to the construction of homes, £2,300 million to the education services and £3,545 million to old-age and unemployment welfare—*Guardian*, 5 December 1969.

2. During the period between the two world wars there was in Britain, for example, an average of 14 per cent of workers unemployed; since the end of the war, the average has been 2 to 3 per cent.

changes within capitalism have often made the individual owner of the means of production into a share-holder, and while the state as a regulator of the political economy has broken the absolute control of capital over the productive processes, the class character of society has remained untouched, with both economic and political power concentrated in the hands of large capitalist combines.

The state's welfare service and the policy of progressive taxation adopted by Socialist governments have, it is true, brought about a new distribution of the nation's wealth. The proportion of the working-class participation in the general well-being of society has, indeed, been enlarged, its living standard increased. But the rich have not got poorer and their numbers have not been reduced. And while poverty in terms of destitution, which had been a mass phenomenon before the war, has virtually disappeared, there continues to exist in the affluent society many considerable enclaves of harsh deprivation.[1]

5

The Welfare State is an achievement of the Socialist movement's century-long struggle for social justice. The question, however, remains of whether it is a phase in the process of the development of a Socialist society, or only a phase in the process of humanizing capitalism.

A Socialist order of society can only develop out of a Welfare State provided it eliminates the economic foundations of the class structure of that society. From the very outset it was a tenet of the Socialist movement that the class structure of the capitalist society, and with it the associated dominance of capital over labour and of the property-owning over the deprived classes, could only be overcome by bringing the means of production into public ownership. The nationalization of the means of production was, in fact, the fundamental socio-economic objective which the Socialist parties set themselves.

In the post-war period, however, there were changes in the view of Socialists on the priorities of Socialist reconstruction.[2] Certainly, in several countries, a considerable sector of the economy was nationalized by the Socialist party in power. In Britain, for example, mines, railways and the steel industry, gas and electricity, civil aviation and the key position in the British national economy, the Bank of England, were all nationalized. Much the same occurred in varying degrees in France, Italy and Austria. In Israel,

1. See Peter Townsend, *Poverty, Socialism and Labour* (London, 1966).
2. For an account of these changes, see Albert Lauterbach, *Kapitalismus und Sozialismus in neuer Sicht* (Reinbeck, 1963). See also Fritz Klenner, *Das Unbehagen in der Demokratie. Ein Beitrag zu Gegenwartsproblemen der Arbeiterbewegung* (Vienna, 1956). See also Ralph Miliband, *Parliamentary Socialism* (London, 1960); Anthony Crosland, *The Future of Socialism* (London, 1956); and Douglas Jay, *Socialism in the New Age* (London, 1962).

where nearly two-thirds of the means of production are socialized, the sector consisting of the co-operative and trade union collective ownership of the means of production is larger than that owned by the state.

But the transfer of the means of production into public ownership as a lever for transforming the class structure of capitalist society is no longer the supreme objective of Socialist parties.[1] Nationalization has, in their view at all events, lost its former priority. What they now seek essentially is, as the declaration of the Socialist International stated, 'effective democratic control of the economy'. The various forms of public ownership which might be developed, the declaration stated, 'should be regarded not as ends in themselves but as means of controlling basic industries and services on which the economic life and welfare of the community depends, of rationalizing inefficient industries or of preventing private monopolies and cartels from exploiting the public'.

But not even the most effective democratic control over the economy which remains essentially rooted in a capitalistic system of production will be incapable of bringing forth a classless society and realizing the original and genuine ideals of Socialism.

It was the experience of Russian Communism which raised the whole question of the role played by the nationalization of the means of production, the speed and extent necessary for the development of a Socialist form of society. In Russia, the nationalization of the whole means of production has transformed private capitalism into state capitalism, developing not a classless society, but a totalitarian society with new classes and class privileges.

The need to submit to public control the basic industries on which the life and well-being in a community depend is, of course, recognized as a principle by every Socialist party. But, in considering the Russian experience, the Socialist parties have been forced to ask themselves whether the collectivization of *the whole* means of production is, in fact, necessary to overturn the capitalist economic order or whether state control over the 'commanding heights' of the economy would be sufficient to ensure effective control of the economy. Indeed, they had had to ask themselves whether a concentration of

1. One of the largest parties in the Socialist International, the Social Democratic Party of Germany, has abandoned this objective completely. In their 'Basic Programme' decided on at an extraordinary party conference in Godesberg in November 1959, it stated that 'free competition and free initiative for the employer' were 'important elements in Social Democratic economic policy'. The co-operative ownership of the productive means of production is, however, recognized in their programme as 'a legitimate form of public control'. The programme, however, by no means strove to overcome the capitalist economic system. 'The private ownership of the means of production,' it declared, 'has a claim to be protected and promoted, so long as it does not hinder the setting up of a just social order'—*Programme der deutschen Sozialdemokratie* (Bonn), pp. 192 and 193. For a detailed analysis of the programme, see Willi Eichler, 'Die politische Rolle des Programms', in *Geist und Tat*, Nr. IV (1969) pp. 193–210. Eichler was chairman of the programme commission. See also Harold Kent Schellenger, *The S.P.D. in the Bonn Republic: A Socialist Party Modernizes* (The Hague, 1960).

the economic power in the hands of the state does not by itself imply a threat to freedom.

In debating the whole question of nationalizing the means of production, the Socialist parties have reduced it to a matter of economic and political expediency, while the problem of humanizing the present social order has been given precedence in Socialist objectives. Thus the declaration of the Socialist International stated:

> Socialism means far more than a new economic and social system. Economic and social progress have moral value to the extent that they serve to liberate and develop the human personality.[1]

But the advances which the Socialist parties have striven for in their policies are nevertheless reforms only of the existing economic order: to raise the material living standards and cultural levels of the workers and to allow them to lead a dignified human existence within capitalism. The Socialist policy of reform admittedly alleviates class conflicts in a capitalist society, but it does not remove them. It tames the greedy impulses of capitalism but does not eliminate them. As long as the economic basis of capitalism remains intact, reforms cannot by themselves create a form of society which would provide for all—and not merely for an *élite*—the pre-conditions for 'liberating and developing the personality'.

6

The promise held out by Socialism was the creation of a new world. The movement inspired by this vision regarded itself as the standard-bearer of a historic mission for humanity, as an instrument to bring about a new civilization and to realize its humanistic ideals within the context of an industrial society. And its unshakeable confidence in the ultimate triumph of the 'iron law of history', as Marx perceived it, had fired the idealism of the movement.

This vision of a new world has gradually faded in the Socialist movement. What it promises today is a continual growth of workers' participation in society's wealth through a more equitable distribution of income and a more rational and civilized ordering of the existing society.

But if idealism is to be reawakened, a vision of a new world is essential; for without idealism, no new world can be created. All the great turning-points in human history—the one of early Christianity, kindled by the Messianic hopes of the Old Testament prophets, the age of the Reformation, the age of the Enlightenment, of the English and French revolutions—were inspired by visions of a new world. The capitalist world, governed by greed for material values and quickly-won gratification, lacks any inspiring social ideal; the

1. See p. 203.

drive to increase production and mass consumption engenders no impulse towards a higher and nobler form of society. The more rapidly the material wealth of the capitalist world accumulates, the more glaring appears its bankruptcy of ideas and hopes for mankind's regeneration. In Marx's words, it leaves man 'depraved by the whole structure of our society, lost in himself, alienated and dominated by inhuman conditions and forces'.[1]

The gulf between the material affluence of society created by highly developed capitalism and its lack of social inspiration for a meaningful future of mankind becomes intolerably wide. The revolt of students in the world's richest countries—in the United States as well as in France, Britain, Germany, the Netherlands and Japan—is a symptom of a profound discontent with a society satiated with material goods. Over and above the students' concrete demands for reforms of their academic institutions—however confused the ideas behind their protest against the political and social *status quo* may have been—these disturbances revealed a basic dissatisfaction with a society which knows no higher aim than to achieve ever-increasing wealth; which wallows in its riches while in vast areas of the world millions upon millions live out their lives in the most extreme poverty and uncertainty; which, after two world wars, feverishly rearms in preparation for a third world war that can only end with the destruction of half the human race because it appears incapable of creating the foundations for a lasting peace.

For Socialists, the development of Soviet Communism is more depressing still. Like the capitalist society, the Soviet Communist society pursues as its main objective an increase in production and military rearmament. Yet democracy in capitalist society secures for its members at least no small degree of political and intellectual freedom; the political power of the property-owning class is balanced by the political power of the working class, the power of capital by that of the trade unions, and there are no restrictions on the freedom of thought. Further, in the democratic contest for governmental power, the balance of strength between classes may well shift in favour of the working class and capitalist governments be replaced by Socialist governments.

Yet, in the Communist society, the people remain dumb grist for the mills of the ruling bureaucracy; intellectual freedom is suppressed and spiritual bleakness has become its trademark.

The contrast between this 'crude Communism', as Marx defined it in his treatise *Nationalökonomie und Philosophie* in 1844,[2] and Socialist ideals becomes as intolerable as the contrast between the material wealth of the capitalist world and its vacuum of social ideals. It was because 'crude Communism' had become intolerable that the Czechoslovak Communists shook

---

1. Karl Marx, *Zur Judenfrage*, p. 414.
2. S. Landshut and J. P. Mayer (eds.), *Der Historische Materialismus. Die Frühschriften* (Leipzig, 1932), vol. I, pp. 292–4.

themselves free of it in their search for Socialism with a human face. Their revolution of 1968 was of historical importance for having demonstrated the possibility of reforming the existing political institutions in a Communist society and, above all, of reforming it by an impulse from within. Thus the victory of the Russian counter-revolution over the Czechoslovak revolution seems, in a historical perspective, to be merely an episode in the struggle for freedom. And however long the rule of the Russian reaction may last in Czechoslovakia, it cannot exterminate the currents of freedom and must eventually be overturned. This, at all events, has been the experience of revolution and counter-revolution throughout the history of the European peoples.

7

The conclusion of the history of the first century of the International, as narrated in the three volumes that constitute this book, suggests some reflections on the future of Socialism. These would not, of course, be expected from a historian; it is not his professional duty to project the future. Perhaps they will, on the other hand, be expected from an author who has experienced six of the ten decades of the history of the international Socialist movement as one of its active members.

It has been an experience of tremendous political and social change: of the overthrow of three monarchs in Europe and of an age-old empire in Asia; of the Russian and Chinese revolutions; of the emancipation of the under-developed nations of Asia and Africa from imperialist and colonial rule. And it has been an experience of the elevation of the working class from being politically oppressed, socially degraded, vegetating in poverty and culturally deprived, to a human existence and the heights of political power.

It has been an experience of revolution and counter-revolution. The impetus for revolution has come from the people's impulse for emancipation from political servitude and material poverty and, deep down, from the ancient chiliastic yearning for a new world—a world of peace and freedom, equality and brotherhood.[1]

The political and social changes of the past fifty years have realized several ideas of the Socialist revolution: they have changed the face of the world and raised humanity to a higher level of civilization. But despite the wonders of its technology and science, which have theoretically provided the means to end poverty, the human race has until now been unable to find a social solution to the problem; the vast majority of mankind continues to

1. Thus, in the declaration made at its inaugural congress, the Socialist International defined as the objectives of international Socialism: 'Socialists work for a world of peace and freedom, for a world in which the exploitation and enslavement of men by men and of peoples by peoples is unknown, for a world in which the development of the individual personality is the basis for the fruitful development of mankind' (see page 203).

experience the most desperate want. Two great powers, the United States and the Soviet Union, have become determinant for the world; their only answer to the danger of atomic war, however, consists in accumulating more and more frightening nuclear weapons in a balance of terror; and, as yet, the overwhelming majority of mankind remains subjected to despotic régimes.

No particular prophetic gift is required to see that a world which is unable to solve the basic problems of its human society is moving towards a most serious crisis; or that, at all events, the era of political and social change which began half a century ago is as yet unfinished.

No changes in a political system, whatever these may be, could have greater importance for the future of Socialism and for mankind than the transformation of the Soviet Union's system of totalitarian dictatorship into a system of Socialist democracy. But is such a change to be anticipated? And, if so, in what forms and by what social forces? A rising among the masses could only provoke a tragedy. It would without doubt be wrecked on the vast apparatus of power on which the system of dictatorship in the Soviet Union rests. The reaction against it would be terrible. A Stalinistic régime of terror would be reconstituted, possibly under a military dictatorship.

Yet a non-violent change of the system is only conceivable by a 'revolution from above', like that which took place in Czechoslovakia when a palace revolution by leading freedom-conscious Communists overthrew the conservative régime in search of a 'new model of Socialism'. It was a revolution which had developed spontaneously out of a ferment of protest against the system of bureaucratic dictatorship which had held the Communist party itself and, above all, the broad mass of the people in its clutches. The revolution had become inevitable because of the people's urge for freedom. The non-violent 'revolution from above' prevented the outbreak of a violent 'revolution from below'. It was only under the pressure of ferment within the party and among the mass of the people that it became feasible for the ruling group voluntarily to embark on a process of reform which would inevitably erode its power and privileges.

The Soviet Union, however, shows no perceptible signs of any fermenting protest against the dictatorial system. The protests made by intellectuals have aroused no response in the country at large. However, if the régime is apathetically accepted by the mass of the people, no revolution, either from 'above' or 'below', is to be anticipated.

There are many Socialists who hold this view. They question whether the urge to freedom is, in fact, inborn in mankind, whether the emancipation from political servitude is an inexorable law and whether the peoples of the Soviet Union's Communist empire are necessarily subject, like those of Western Europe, to the process of historical development towards a higher level of civilization. The precious gift of freedom was won by a century of struggle by the peoples of Western Europe, while an overwhelming majority of mankind has for millennia been subjected to slavery and despotism as if it were an established law of nature. But if, as the experience of history seems to show, the urge to freedom is not fundamental, then there seems to be no reason why the masses in the Soviet Union should revolt against a system of government which, while it admittedly denies them freedom, satisfies their material requirements in life.

Apart from anything else, however, the theory which states that the urge to freedom is an exclusive characteristic of the peoples of Western Europe and not a universal human experience is, at any rate, in direct contradiction with the history of the Russian people. Twice in our own century did the Russian workers rise against the Tsarist absolutism, shaking its hold in their first revolution and overthrowing it in their second; they then defended their revolution through the years of unimaginable sacrifice and privation. The Russian people have been the most revolutionary people of the twentieth century. It does not therefore seem all too fantastic to anticipate that, in the course of a future moral or political crisis—against which the Soviet Union will be as little immune as the United States—the Russian people's latent urge to freedom might once again engender a movement powerful enough to enforce fundamental changes of the system of dictatorship towards a Socialist democracy.

Such an event would be of the utmost importance for the future of Socialism. It would offer the Socialist movement throughout the world a new inspiration and would reunite the divided international labour movement. Socialism has been discredited by the ugly face of Stalinism; a Socialism with a human face in the Soviet Union, which such a revolution could set in motion, would revive a spirit of enthusiasm and idealism within the world Socialist movement.

The victory of the Bolshevik revolution in Russia in October 1917, and its subsequent experiments in economic and social reorganization in the spirit of Marxist theories, gave the world-wide expansion of Socialist concepts a powerful impetus. Until that moment the Anglo-American world, for example, had taken hardly any note of either Socialism or Marxism. The phenomenon of a European great power which acknowledged Marxism as the ideology of the state, and which was attempting to construct a Socialist order of society, enthralled workers throughout the world—in 1918 the British Labour party, founded in 1905, declared itself in its programme to be a Socialist party—and a rapid growth of literature discussing the problems of Marxism and Socialism revolutionized the traditions of social thought. Above all, the revolution imparted a powerful inspiration to the workers' movements of the democracies of Western Europe and America.

Yet of even greater importance was the impact of the Russian Revolution on Asia. During the period between the two world wars, it stimulated the formation of Communist and Socialist parties in China, Japan, India and Indonesia—catalysts for a Socialist ethos in the society which developed in southern Asia after the Second World War and which, in the Far East, produced the People's Republic of China.

The Russian revolution did in fact set in motion a Socialist world revolution—not, however, quite in the way that Lenin had imagined. The system of a Communist dictatorship was of relevance for the social revolution only in pre-industrialized, semi-feudal countries with their traditions of autocracy. In the industrially developed countries, with their traditions of parliamentary democracy, the social revolution could only take place through a process of infiltrating Socialist elements into the institutions and economic structure of the capitalist society.

The transition of an old to a new form of society is a crucial process taking up a complete era in human history and continuously interrupted by severe setbacks. The change in Europe from a feudal-aristocratic to a capitalist-bourgeois social order was the history of several centuries. The course of the Socialist world revolution is probably being subjected to a similar measure of time since it began with the Russian revolution half a century ago. Its achievements up to date still fall far short of realizing the ideal by which it was inspired. The Communist revolution remains incomplete since the essentials of Socialism remain unfulfilled. And the Social Democratic revolution in the Western nations—the gradual transformation of capitalist into social welfare states—is no more than a preliminary phase in the development of a Socialist society.

But the forms of society which have emerged from this revolution—the Communist society as much as capitalist society transformed by reformist social democracy—are not set forever like hard crystals. Through the dynamic of the idea from which the revolution stemmed, they are undergoing a continuous process of social change to bring about its realization.

Such an optimistic perspective of Socialist development may, however, seem bold in the light of the crisis which grips Socialism at present, the spiritual lack of direction in which mankind now seems imprisoned and the prevailing pessimism of a world living under the threat of nuclear war. And, indeed, the impetus to exorcize man's currently prevalent spiritual depression cannot be expected to emerge until the danger of the destruction of civilization in a third world war has been averted.

However, reflections on the future of Socialism can only be based on the optimistic assumption that humanity has a future, that it can escape the threatened catastrophe of self-destruction in a new world war and that, freed from this nightmare, it can set itself a new purpose. But this new purpose can be none other than a restructuring of human society into a Socialist world community—the realization of the Socialist vision.

The prognosis may seem daring. But, for Marxist Socialists, it is the logical consequence of their view of the world historical process.

Socialism is an optimistic faith, a faith in mankind's ability to attain self-regeneration, in its capacity to reach even higher levels of civilization; and it is in Marxism that this belief has found its theoretical foundation.

But the Socialist vision is not utopian. It grew out of social and economic necessities. And, for half a century, it has been in process of materialization; in one third of the world under the Communist system of government; in a further third under the system of Social Democracy. Socialism is the predominant trend in the development of a new age of mankind.

Appendices

SOCIALISM AS A WORLD MOVEMENT

An Attempt at a Numerical Assessment

Socialism as a world movement in the years 1968–1969 comprised—as shown in the tables—an estimated number of 207 parties with a total of more than 60 million members and 369 million voters.

An exact survey of the members and voters of democratic socialist parties can, however, be given only for the member parties of the Socialist International, as shown in Table I. The survey for the strength of Communist parties in Table II is incomplete. The number of Communist votes in several countries, such as China, Cuba, North Korea, was not available or in other countries under Communist rule officially announced as almost 100 per cent.

Even less complete is the list in Table III showing the membership of the parties which are neither affiliated to the Socialist International nor consider themselves as Communist parties. They are left-wing Socialist parties or Maoist or Trotskyist parties, as well as those which claim to be Socialist but which are not rooted in the Socialist tradition; finally there are democratic, revolutionary, nationalistic parties with Socialist tendencies whose Socialist character is questionable. An example of this is the Indian National Congress, a democratic party with Socialist aims whose leadership is however dominated by representatives of bourgeois-capitalist interests; or the 'Arab Socialist' parties of Egypt, Syria and Iraq under the rule of a nationalistic, militaristic-Fascist dictatorship which, however, like the left wing of the Indian National Congress, attempt to win the support of the masses by using Socialist rhetoric. These parties figure on the list not as genuine Socialist parties but as parties of a potentially Socialist movement.

For none of these parties was it possible to discover its membership, but for several, the number of votes they obtained in elections before December 1969 was available.

The figures in Tables I, II and III show approximately the comparative survey of tendencies in the world Socialist movement at the end of 1969:

	Number of parties	Members	Votes last election
Socialist International	54	15,360,977	76,206,588
Communist parties	87	45,568,607	246,889,482
Parties with Socialist tendencies	66	—	45,461,848
	207	60,929,604	368,557,918

TABLE I

THE PARTIES OF THE SOCIALIST INTERNATIONAL

(Source: *Socialist International Information*, vol. xx, No. 1, January 1970)

This table shows the strength of the parties affiliated to the Socialist International. In December 1969 it comprised a total of approximately 15,360,000 members and more than 76 million voters. In 1969, Socialist parties were in government in the following countries:

Belgium	Madagascar
Federal Republic of Germany	Mauritius
West Berlin	Norway (since March 1971)
Finland	San Marino
Great Britain	Singapore
Iceland	Sweden
Israel	Switzerland
Italy	

Parties	Members	Votes last election	Per cent
†Aden—People's Socialist Party	30,000	—	
Argentine Socialist Party	21,000	179,855[1]	1·9
Australian Labor Party	2,000,000	2,750,000[2]	47·0
Austrian Socialist Party	702,926	1,928,922	42·5
Belgian Socialist Party††	216,500	1,449,315	28·0
†Bermuda—Progressive Labor Party	1,000	12,930	34·3
*Bulgarian Socialist Party in exile			
Canadian New Democratic Party	325,000	1,360,330	17·3
†Chile—Radical Party	27,500	307,126	13·4
†Costa Rica—National Liberation Party	75,000	225,530	49·5
*Czech Social Democratic Party in exile			
Danish Social Democratic Party	225,046	975,058	34·2

Parties	Members	Votes last election	Per cent
*Estonian Social Democratic Party in exile	—	—	—
Finnish Social Democratic Party††	100,000	664,919	27·7
French Socialist Party	100,000	3,654,003	16·5
German Social Democratic Party††	749,632	14,074,455	42·7
Berlin, West—Social Democratic Party††	—	829,955[3]	56·9
Great Britain—Labour Party††	6,086,625	13,064,951	47·9
*Hungarian Socialist Party in exile	—	—	—
Icelandic Social Democratic Party††	3,000	15,061	15·7
*All-India *Praja* Socialist Party	213,001	4,456,487	3·1
International Jewish Labor *Bund*	21,000	—	—
Ireland—Labour Party	10,000	223,282	17·0
Israel Labour Party††	286,000	632,035[4]	46·2
World Union of Socialist Zionists	150,000	—	—
Italian Socialist Party (P.S.I.)	350,000 ⎫	4,604,329[5]	14·5
Italian Unitarian Socialist Party (P.S.U.)	135,000 ⎭		
Jamaica—People's National Party	125,000	217,173	49·2
Japan Socialist Party	46,202	10,074,099	21·4
Japan Democratic Socialist Party	51,500	3,636,891	7·7
Korea (South)—United Socialist Party	17,500	104,975	0·9
*Latvian Social Democratic Party in exile	—	—	—
*Lithuanian Social Democratic Party in exile	—	—	—
Luxembourg Socialist Workers' Party	4,000	46,733	32·3
Madagascar Social Democratic Party††	1,110,000	1,943,623	93·6
Malaysian Democratic Action Party	10,000	259,000	12·5
Malta Labour Party	7,600	61,774	42·7
Mauritius—Labour Party††	30,000	220,000	56·0
Netherlands—Labour Party	116,922	1,619,694	23·6
New Zealand Labour Party	40,000	534,327	44·3
Norwegian Labour Party	200,000	992,524	46·7
†Paraguay—Revolutionary *Febrerisita* Party	3,500	16,741	2·6
†Peru—*Aprista* Party	55,000	623,501	34·3
*Polish Socialist Party in exile	—	—	—
*Romanian Social Democratic Party in exile	—	—	—
San Marino—Social Democratic Party††	816	2,328	17·9
Singapore—People's Action Party††	10,000	65,812[6]	84·4
Spanish Socialist Workers' Party in exile	9,000	—	—
Swedish Social Democratic Labour Party††	940,000	2,420,242	50·1
Swiss Social Democratic Party††	55,728	233,873	23·5
United States Socialist Party	3,000	—	—
†Venezuela—Democratic Action (A.D.)	450,000	939,935	25·6

Parties	Members	Votes last election	Per cent
†Venezuela—Popular Electoral Movement (M.E.P.)	250,000	475,909	13·0
*Vietnam (South)—Socialist Party	7,000	—	—
*Yugoslav Socialist Party in exile	—	—	—
Totals	15,370,998	76,997,197	—

* Consultative Member	1. last election, July 7, 1963	4. cast for Labour Alignment
† Observer Member	2. estimate of first votes	5. parties united at election
†† Party in government	3. SPD votes in West Berlin elections	6. only 7 seats contested

TABLE II

THE COMMUNIST PARTIES

(Source: *World strength of the Communist Party Organizations*, Department of State, Washington, 1969)

The Communist world movement, which since the dissolution of the Communist International in 1943 has no central organization, is split into two groups: the parties recognized by the Soviet Communist party and the parties gathered around the Communist party of China. The table lists the parties of both groups. Communist parties rule the following countries (situation March 1971):

Albania	Mongolia
Bulgaria	North Korea
China	North Vietnam
Cuba	Poland
Czechoslovakia	Romania
German Democratic Republic	Soviet Union
Hungary	Yugoslavia

In 1968, the parties of the Communist world movement grouped approximately 45,500,000 members, as follows:

	Members	Percentage of Communist world movement
In countries under Communist governments	42,500,000	94·5
Of which in the Soviet Union and China	30,500,000	71·6
Total in Western Europe	1,959,000	3·1
Total in all other countries	1,100,000	2·1

Of the combined total of 1,959,000 members of Communist parties in Western Europe, the Italian Communist party had about 1,500,000 and the French Communist party about 275,000 members. The total for the Communist parties in the other countries of Western Europe came to 184,000.

Countries	Parties	Members	Votes last election before Dec. 1968	Per cent
Afghanistan	Communist Party	400	—	
Albania	Workers' Party	66,327	978,114	100·0
Algeria	Communist Party		—	
Argentina	Communist Party	60,000	—	
Australia	Communist Party	4,750	23,056	0·1
Austria	Communist Party	27,500	18,638	0·4
Belgium	Communist Party	12,500	170,686	3·3
Bolivia	National Liberation Front	6,000	33,075	3·0
Brazil	Communist Party	15,750	—	
Bulgaria	Communist Party	613,393	5,744,072	99·8
Burma	Communist Party	5,000	—	
Cambodia	Revolutionary People's Party	100	—	
Canada	Communist Party	2,500	4,344	0·1
Ceylon	Communist Party	2,300	109,684	2·4
Chile	Communist Party	45,000	286,367	12·2
China	Communist Party	17,000,000	—	
Colombia	Communist Party	9,000	51,000	21·0
Costa Rica	Popular Leading Party	600	—	
Cuba	United Socialist Revolutionary Party	60,000	—	
Cyprus	Reform Party of the Working People	13,000	—	
Czechoslovakia	Communist Party	1,700,000	9,412,309	99·9
Denmark	Communist Party	6,600	29,824	1·0
Dominican Republic	Communist Party	1,100	4,829	0·4
Ecuador	Communist Party	1,650	16,990	2·0
El Salvador	Communist Party	200	—	
Finland	Communist Party	49,000	502,812	21·2
France	Communist Party	275,000	4,435,357	20·0
German Democratic Republic	Socialist Unity Party	1,769,912	11,196,961	99·9
German Federal Republic	Communist Party	13,000	222,504	0·6
Great Britain	Communist Party	32,562	62,112	0·2
Greece	Communist Party	37,000	540,687	12·0
Guatemala	Workers' Party	750	—	
Guyana	Leading Party of the Working People	100	—	
Honduras	Communist Party	11,000	—	
Hungary	Communist Party	600,000	7,105,709	99·7

Countries	Parties	Members	Votes last election before Dec. 1968	Per cent
Iceland	Workers' Alliance	1,000	16,923	17·6
India	Communist Party (pro-Moscow)	55,000	7,564,180	5·2
	Communist Party (Marxist)	70,000	6,140,738	4·2
Indonesia	Communist Party	5,000	—	—
Iran	Mass Party	1,000	—	—
Iraq	Communist Party	2,000	—	—
Ireland	Communist Party	125	183	0·01
Israel	MAKI (pro-Israel)	1,000	15,712	1·6
	RAKACH (pro-Arab)	1,000	38,827	2·8
Italy	Communist Party	1,500,000	8,555,477	26·9
Japan	Communist Party	250,000	2,190,563	4·8
Jordan	Communist Party	700	—	—
Korea (North)	Communist Party	1,600,000	—	—
Laos	People's Party	50,000	—	—
Lebanon	Communist Party	6,000	—	—
Luxembourg	Communist Party	500	25,000	15·5
Malaysia	Communist Party	2,000	—	—
Mexico	Communist Party	5,250	225,000	2·3
Mongolia	Revolutionary People's Party	48,570	—	—
Morocco	Party of Freedom and Socialism	600	—	—
Nepal	Communist Party	8,000	—	—
Netherlands	Communist Party	11,500	248,808	3·6
New Zealand	Communist Party	400	1,207	0·1
Nicaragua	Socialist Party	200	—	—
Nigeria	Communist Party	1,000	—	—
Norway	Communist Party	2,500	22,270	1·0
Pakistan	Communist Party	1,450	—	—
Panama	People's Party	250	—	—
Paraguay	Communist Party	5,000	—	—
Peru	Communist Party	5,000	—	—
Philippines	Communist Party	2,000	—	—
Poland	United Workers' Party	2,030,068	18,982,316	98·7
Portugal	Communist Party	2,000	—	—
Romania	Communist Party	1,800,000	12,388,786	99·8
Singapore	Communist Party	200	—	—
South Africa	Communist Party	500	—	—
Spain	Communist Party	5,000	—	—
Sudan	Communist Party	7,500	—	—
Sweden	Communist Party	29,000	145,172	3·0
Switzerland	Workers' Party	4,000	28,723	2·9
Syria	Communist Party	3,000	—	—
Thailand	Communist Party	2,500	—	—
Tunisia	Communist Party	100	—	—

Countries	Parties	Members	Votes last election before Dec. 1968	Per cent
Turkey	Communist Party	1,500	—	—
Uruguay	Communist Party	21,000	69,750	5·7
USA	Communist Party	14,000	—	—
USSR	Communist Party	13,500,000	143,570,976	99·8
Venezuela	Communist Party	5,000	103,368	2·8
Vietnam (North)	Workers' Party	766,000	—	—
Vietnam (South)	Communist Party	284,000	—	—
Yugoslavia	Communist League	1,013,500	5,606,373	89·1
		45,568,907	246,889,482	

TABLE III

PARTIES WITH SOCIALIST TENDENCIES

(compiled by Alan Day, staff member of the Socialist International)

1. *Left-wing Socialist parties in Europe*

The following list comprises left-wing Socialist groups which have split off from social-democratic parties and have constituted independent parties. They are not affiliated to the Socialist International.

Countries	Parties	Votes in last elections before Dec. 1969	Per cent
Denmark	Socialist People's Party	174,506	6·1
	Left Socialists	57,182	2·0
Finland	League of Workers and Small Farmers	61,830	2·6
France	Unified Socialist Party (PSU)	874,212	4·0
Greece	Social Democratic Union in exile	—	—
Italy	Socialist Party and Proletarian Union	1,414,043	4·5
Netherlands	Pacifistic Socialist Party	197,051	2·9
Norway	Socialist People's Party	121,900	3·5
		2,900,724	

2. *Socialist tendencies in Asia*

A number of parties listed below were members of the Asian Socialist Conference, namely the Anti-Fascist Freedom League of Burma, the *Sri Lanka*

Freedom Party in Ceylon and the National Congress Party in Nepal (see also pp. 256, 270, 278). The *Samyukta* Socialist Party in India is a splinter party of the *Praja* Socialist Party; the other two Indian parties listed are left-wing Socialist parties.

The party of the Indian National Congress, which in 1955 at its Congress in Avadi had proclaimed the construction of a Socialistic type of society as its aim (see p. 238), despite the fact that it also comprised a strong anti-Socialist wing consisting of representatives of capitalistic landowners, merchants and industrialists, split in 1970 into the Ruling Congress Party, supported by the *Praja* Socialist Party, and the anti-Socialist Opposition Congress Party. In the last election before the split, in 1967, the Party obtained more than 59,000,000 votes (40 per cent of the votes cast). It has to be assumed that the Ruling Congress Party, which is listed among the parties with Socialist tendencies, represented approximately half of those who voted for the party in 1967.[1]

The *Lanka Sama Samaj* Party in Ceylon is a Trotskyist party, the only existing mass party of that tendency. The Socialist Party of Indonesia, a founding member organization of the Socialist Asian Conference was dissolved by President Sukarno in 1960 (see p. 306). The Socialist Community Party of Cambodia was founded by Prince Norodom Sihanouk who became its President and ruled the country in its name.

Countries	Parties	Votes in last election before Dec. 1969	Per cent
Burma	Anti-Fascist Freedom League	—	—
Cambodia	Socialist Community Party	—	—
Ceylon	*Sri Lanka* Freedom Party	1,216,526	30·0
	Lanka Sama Samaj Party	317,006	7·8
	Sri Lanka Socialist Party	130,874	3·2
India	*Samyukta* Socialist Party	7,171,627	4·9
	Peasants' and Workers' Party	1,028,755	0·7
	Forward Bloc	627,910	0·4
	National Congress Party (ruling)	28,500,000	20·0
Indonesia	Socialist Party (1955 election)	753,191	2·0
Korea (South)	Mass Party	249,561	2·3
Malaysia	Workers' Party	330,898	16·0
Nepal	National Congress Party (1959 election)	660,000	38·0
		40,986,348	

1. In the 1971 election, it won, however, two thirds of the seats in Parliament instead of the 20 per cent given in the table.

3. *Parties in the Middle East*

This list includes two questionable Socialist parties, the *Al Baath* Socialist parties in Iraq and Syria, which by their name 'All-Arab Socialist Renaissance' and by their slogan 'Unity, Freedom, Socialism' proclaim themselves as Socialist. At present they are, however, nationalistic parties of army officers without mass support which in the two countries took power by *coup d'état*, established a military dictatorship and have struck down all opposition, in Iraq by a terrible massacre, especially of the Communists.[1] In Israel, the left-wing Socialist Marxist party M.A.P.A.M. (see p. 357) has been allied since 1969 with the Labour Party M.A.P.A.I. In the 1969 election it presented its candidates jointly with the Labour Party on the same lists and became a member of the governmental coalition. It is not affiliated to the Socialist International. The Progressive Socialist Party of Lebanon was founded by Kemal Jumblatt, chief of a mountain clan, and joined the Lebanon coalition government.

Countries	Parties	Votes in the last election	Per cent
Iraq	*Al Baath* Socialist Party	—	
Israel	M.A.P.A.M. (1965 election)	79,985	6·7
Lebanon	Progressive Socialist Party	—	
Syria	*Al Baath* Socialist Party	—	
Turkey	Labour Party	276,101	3·0
		356,086	

4. *Parties in Africa*

Most parties in this list are ruling parties which proclaim Socialism as their programme. They range from 'Arab Socialism' in Algeria, Egypt and Tunisia, to 'African Socialism' in Guinea, Kenya, Zambia, Senegal and Tanzania, and include 'Islamic Socialism' in feudal Morocco. They are nationalistic parties consisting of embryonic left-wing as well as right-wing reformist tendencies, some, as the Arab Socialist Union in Egypt, with Fascist tendencies. In nearly all these countries, they are the only party admitted by law.

Countries	Parties
Algeria	*Front de Libération Nationale* (F.L.N.)
Angola	*Movimento Popular de Libertação de Angola* (M.P.L.A.)
Chad	*Parti Progressiste Tchadien* (P.P.T.)

1. 'The oppression of thousands of Communists and democrats in Iraq,' stated a protest in the official Communist publication *World Marxist View*, vol. XIII, of August 1970, '. . . continues unabated. . . . In the last two years since the present régime came to power many Communists, democrats and left-wing nationalists have been killed, including Sattar Khadair, member of the central committee of the Iraqi Communist party.'

Countries	Parties
Cameroun	*Union Nationale*
Congo-Brazzaville	*Parti des Ouvriers Congolais*
Egypt	Arab Socialist Union
Gambia	People's Progressive Party (P.P.P.)
Gabon	*Parti Démocratique*
Ghana	Progress Party
	National Alliance of Liberals
Guinea	*Parti Démocratique*
Kenya	African National Union (KANU)
Mali	*Comité National de Défense de la Révolution* (C.N.D.R.)
Morocco	*Union Nationale des Forces Populaires* (U.N.F.P.)
Mauritius	*Parti du Peuple Mauricien* (P.P.M.)
Mozambique	Frente de Libertação de Mocambique (FRELIMO)
Niger	*Parti Progressiste Nigérien*
Senegal	*Union Progressiste Sénégalaise* (U.P.S.)
Sierra Leone	All People's Congress Party
South Africa	Coloured Labour Party
Tanzania	African National Union (TANU)
Tunisia	*Parti Socialiste Destourien*
Uganda	People's Congress
Zambia	United National Independence Party
Zimbabwe	African People's Union (ZAPU)
	African National Union (ZANU)

5. *Parties in Central and South America*

Some of the parties mentioned in this list, such as the Social Democratic party of Argentina and the Socialist parties of Chile and Uruguay, are parties with Socialist traditions but not affiliated to the Socialist International. The other parties are democratic revolutionary parties with Socialist tendencies.

Countries	Parties	Votes in the last elections before Dec. 1969	Per cent
Argentina	*Partido Socialista Democrático*	—	—
	Movimiento Nacionalista Revolucionario (M.N.R.)	88,171	8·0
Bolivia	*Movimiento Revolucionario Pazestenssorista*	61,309	5·5
Chile	*Partido Socialista*	240,069	12·8

Countries	Parties	*Votes in the last elections before Dec. 1969*	*Per cent*
Dominican Republic	*Partido Revolucionario Dominicano* (P.R.D.)	494,570	36·8
Ecuador	*Partido Socialista* (P.S.E.)	—	—
	Movimiento Democrático Revolucionario	—	—
El Salvador	*Movimiento Nacionalista Revolucionario*	17,462	4·0
Guatemala	*Partido Revolucionario*	192,523	37·0
Guyana	People's Progressive Party	113,027	36·9
Mexico	*Partido Revolucionario Independente*	—	—
Puerto Rico	*Partido Popular*	—	—
Uruguay	*Partido Socialista*	11,559	0·9
	Battlista 515		
		1,218,690	

APPENDIX TWO

AIMS AND TASKS OF DEMOCRATIC SOCIALISM

Declaration of the Socialist International adopted at its First Congress held in Frankfurt-am-Main on 30 June—3 July 1951

PREAMBLE

1. From the nineteenth century onwards, capitalism has developed immense productive forces. It has done so at the cost of excluding the great majority of citizens from influence over production. It put the rights of ownership before the rights of man. It created a new class of wage-earners without property or social rights. It sharpened the struggle between the classes.

Although the world contains resources which could be made to provide a decent life for everyone, capitalism has been incapable of satisfying the elementary needs of the world's population. It proved unable to function without devastating crises and mass unemployment. It produced social insecurity and glaring contrasts between rich and poor. It resorted to imperialist expansion and colonial exploitation, thus making conflicts between nations and races more bitter. In some countries powerful capitalist groups helped the barbarism of the past to raise its head again in the form of Fascism and Nazism.

2. Socialism was born in Europe as a movement of protest against the diseases inherent in capitalist society. Because the wage-earners suffered most

from capitalism, Socialism first developed as a movement of the wage-earners. Since then more and more citizens—professional and clerical workers, farmers and fishermen, craftsmen and retailers, artists and scientists are coming to understand that Socialism holds the key to their future. Socialism appeals to all men who believe that the exploitation of man by man must be abolished.

3. Socialism aims to liberate the peoples from dependence on a minority which owns or controls the means of production. It aims to put economic power in the hands of the people as a whole, and to create a community in which free men work together as equals.

4. Socialism has become a major force in world affairs. It has passed from propaganda into practice. In some countries the foundations of a Socialist society have already been laid. Here the evils of capitalism are disappearing and the community has developed new vigour. The principles of Socialism are proving their worth in action.

5. In many countries uncontrolled capitalism is giving place to an economy in which state intervention and collective ownership limit the scope of private capitalists. More people are coming to recognize the need for planning. Social security, free trade unionism and industrial democracy are winning ground. This development is largely a result of long years of struggle by Socialists and trade unionists. Wherever Socialism is strong, important steps have been taken towards the creation of a new social order.

6. In recent years the peoples in the underdeveloped areas of the world have been finding Socialism a valuable aid in the struggle for national freedom and higher standards of life. Here different forms of democratic Socialism are evolving under the pressure of different circumstances. The main enemies of Socialism in these areas are parasitical exploitation by indigenous financial oligarchies and colonial exploitation by foreign capitalists. The Socialists fight for political economic democracy, they seek to raise the standard of living for the masses through land reform and industrialization, the extension of public ownership and the development of producers' and consumers' co-operatives.

7. Meanwhile, as Socialism advances throughout the world, new forces have arisen to threaten the movement towards freedom and social justice. Since the Bolshevik Revolution in Russia, Communism has split the international labour movement and has set back the realization of Socialism in many countries for decades.

8. Communism falsely claims a share in the Socialist tradition. In fact it has distorted that tradition beyond recognition. It has built up a rigid theology which is incompatible with the critical spirit of Marxism.

9. Where Socialists aim to achieve freedom and justice by removing the exploitation which divides men under capitalism, Communists seek to sharpen those class divisions only in order to establish the dictatorship of a single party.

10. International Communism is the instrument of a new imperialism. Wherever it has achieved power it has destroyed freedom or the chance of gaining freedom. It is based on a militarist bureaucracy and a terrorist police. By producing glaring contrasts of wealth and privilege it has created a new class society. Forced labour plays an important part in its economic organization.

11. Socialism is an international movement which does not demand a rigid uniformity of approach. Whether Socialists build their faith on Marxist or other methods of analysing society, whether they are inspired by religious or humanitarian principles, they all strive for the same goal—a system of social justice, better living, freedom and world peace.

12. The progress of science and technical skill has given man increased power either to improve his lot or to destroy himself. For this reason production cannot be left to the play of economic liberalism but must be planned systematically for human needs. Such planning must respect the rights of the individual personality. Socialism stands for freedom and planning in both national and international affairs.

13. The achievement of Socialism is not inevitable. It demands a personal contribution from all its followers. Unlike the totalitarian way it does not impose on the people a passive role. On the contrary, it cannot succeed without thorough-going and active participation by the people. It is democracy in its highest form.

I. POLITICAL DEMOCRACY

1. Socialists strive to build a new society in freedom and by democratic means.

2. Without freedom there can be no Socialism. Socialism can be achieved only through democracy. Democracy can be fully realized only through Socialism.

3. Democracy is government of the people, by the people, for the people. It must secure:

a. The right of every human being to a private life, protected from arbitrary invasion by the state.

b. Political liberties, like freedom of thought, expression, education, organization and religion.

c. The representation of the people through free elections, under universal, equal and secret franchise.

d. Government by the majority and respect for the rights of the minority.

e. The equality before the law of all citizens, whatever their birth, sex, language, creed and colour.

f. Right to cultural autonomy for groups with their own language.

g. An independent judiciary system: every man must have the right to a public trial before an impartial tribunal by due process of law.

4. Socialists have always fought for the rights of man. The Universal Declaration of the Rights of Man which has been adopted by the General Assembly of the United Nations must be made effective in every country.

5. Democracy requires the right of more than one party to exist and the right of opposition. But democracy has the right and duty to protect itself against those who exploit its opportunities only in order to destroy it. The defence of political democracy is a vital interest of the people. Its preservation is a condition of realizing economic and social democracy.

6. Policies based on the protection of capitalist interests cannot develop the strength and unity needed to defend democracy from totalitarian attack. Democracy can only be defended with the active help of the workers, whose fate depends on its survival.

7. Socialists express their solidarity with all peoples suffering under dictatorship, whether Fascist or Communist, in their efforts to win freedom.

8. Every dictatorship, wherever it may be, is a danger to the freedom of all nations and thereby to the peace of the world. Wherever there is unrestrained exploitation of forced labour, whether under private profit or under political dictatorship, there is a danger to the living and moral standards of all the peoples.

II. ECONOMIC DEMOCRACY

1. Socialism seeks to replace capitalism by a system in which the public interest takes precedence over the interest of private profit. The immediate economic aims of Socialist policy are full employment, higher production, a rising standard of life, social security and a fair distribution of incomes and property.

2. In order to achieve these ends production must be planned in the interest of the people as a whole.

Such planning is incompatible with the concentration of economic power in the hands of a few. It requires effective democratic control of the economy.

Democratic Socialism therefore stands in sharp contradiction both to capitalist planning and to every form of totalitarian planning; these exclude public control of production and a fair distribution of its results.

3. Socialist planning can be achieved by various means. The structure of the country concerned must decide the extent of public ownership and the forms of planning to apply.

4. Public ownership can take the form of the nationalization of existing private concerns or the creation of new public concerns, municipal or regional enterprise, consumers' or producers' co-operatives.

These various forms of public ownership should be regarded not as ends in themselves but as means of controlling basic industries and services on which the economic life and welfare of the community depend, of rationalizing inefficient industries or of preventing private monopolies and cartels from exploiting the public.

5. Socialist planning does not presuppose public ownership of all the means of production. It is compatible with the existence of private ownership in important fields, for instance in agriculture, handicraft, retail trade and small and middle-sized industries. The state must prevent private owners from abusing their powers. It can and should assist them to contribute towards increased production and well-being within the framework of a planned economy.

6. Trade unions and organizations of producers and consumers are necessary elements in a democratic society; they should never be allowed to degenerate into the tools of a central bureaucracy or into a rigid corporative system. Such economic organizations should participate in shaping general economic policy without usurping the constitutional prerogatives of parliament.

7. Specialist planning does not mean that all economic decisions are placed in the hands of the Government or central authorities. Economic power should be decentralized wherever this is compatible with the aims of planning.

8. All citizens should prevent the development of bureaucracy in public and private industry by taking part in the process of production through their organizations or by individual initiative. The workers must be associated democratically with the direction of their industry.

9. Democratic Socialism aims at extending individual freedom on the basis of economic and social security and an increasing prosperity.

III. SOCIAL DEMOCRACY AND CULTURAL PROGRESS

1. While the guiding principle of capitalism is private profit the guiding principle of Socialism is the satisfaction of human needs.

2. Basic human needs must make the first claim on the distribution of the fruits of production: this need not deprive the individual of the incentive to work according to his capacity. Socialists accept as self-evident the individual's right to be rewarded according to his efforts. But they believe that there are other incentives, like pride in work well done, solidarity and team spirit which can be strengthened when men work for the common interest.

3. Socialism stands not only for basic political rights but also for economic and social rights. Among these rights are:

the right to work;
the right to medical and maternity benefits;
the right to leisure;
the right to economic security for citizens unable to work because of old age, incapacity or unemployment;

*the right of children to welfare and of the youth to education in accordance with
their abilities;*
the right to adequate housing.

4. Socialists strive to abolish all legal, economic and political discriminations between the sexes, between social groups, between town and countryside, between regional and between racial groups.

5. Socialism means far more than a new economic and social system. Economic and social progress have moral value to the extent that they serve to liberate and develop the human personality.

6. Socialists oppose capitalism not only because it is economically wasteful and because it keeps the masses from their material rights, but above all because it revolts their sense of justice. They oppose totalitarianism in every form because it outrages human dignity.

7. Socialism fights to liberate men from the fears and anxieties from which all forms of political and economic insecurity are inseparable. This liberation will open the way to the spiritual development of men conscious of their responsibilities and to the cultural evolution of complete personalities. Socialism is a powerful factor in promoting this cultural development.

8. Socialism seeks to give men all the means to raise their cultural standards and foster the creative aspirations of the human spirit. The treasures of art and science must be made available to all men.

IV. INTERNATIONAL DEMOCRACY

1. The Socialist movement has been an international movement from the beginning.

2. Democratic Socialism is international because it aims at liberating all men from every form of economic, spiritual and political bondage.

3. Democratic Socialism is international because it recognizes that no nation can solve all its economic and social problems in isolation.

4. Absolute national sovereignty must be transcended.

5. The new world society for which Socialists strive can develop fruitfully in peace only if it is based on voluntary co-operation between nations. Democracy must, therefore, be established on an international scale under an international rule of law which guarantees national freedom and the rights of man.

6. Democratic Socialism regards the establishment of the United Nations as an important step towards an international community; it demands the strict implementation of the principles of its Charter.

7. Democratic Socialism rejects every form of imperialism. It fights the oppression or exploitation of any people.

8. A negative anti-imperialism is not enough. Vast areas of the world suffer from extreme poverty, illiteracy and disease. Poverty in one part of the world is a threat to prosperity in other parts. Poverty is an obstacle to the

development of democracy. Democracy, prosperity and peace require a redistribution of the world's wealth and an increase in the productivity of the underdeveloped areas. All people have an interest in raising the material and cultural standards in those areas. Democratic Socialism must inspire the economic, social and cultural development of those areas unless they are to fall victim to new forms of oppression.

9. Democratic Socialists recognize the maintenance of world peace as the supreme task in our time. Peace can be secured only by a system of collective security. This will create the conditions for international disarmament.

10. The struggle for the preservation of peace is inseparably bound up with the struggle for freedom. It is the threat to the independence of free peoples which is directly responsible for the danger of war in our time.

Socialists work for a world of peace and freedom, for a world in which the exploitation and enslavement of men by men and peoples by peoples is unknown, for a world in which the development of the individual personality is the basis for the fruitful development of mankind. They appeal to the solidarity of all working men in the struggle for this great aim.

APPENDIX THREE

STATEMENT ON SOCIALISM AND RELIGION

Resolution of a Special Conference of the Socialist International

Bentveld, 9–11 March 1953

1. Socialism is a moral protest against the debasement of man in modern society. It proclaims human dignity and the right of every man and woman to equality of opportunity, to spiritual, intellectual, political and economic freedom, and to the exercise of responsibility in decisions affecting work and life.
2. Socialism seeks to create a new social order, based on these principles, by transforming property and social relations. Socialist policy, therefore, is the practical working-out of an ethic which may be derived either from religious or from non-religious sources.
3. The ethical principles on which Socialist ideals and policies are based are associated with the finest traditions of creative culture. Socialism, which uplifts those who have been deprived of their human rights, is becoming a world-wide force for the enriching of life.
4. Socialism recognizes the part played both by religion and by humanism in the shaping of the civilizations and ethical systems of the world. It

especially recognizes that in Europe the Christian Gospel is one of the spiritual and ethical sources of Socialist thought. It welcomes the growing awareness among Christians of the social implications of that Gospel.

5. Socialism is in itself neither religious nor anti-religious; it is a political movement for the transformation of society. There should be no denominational political parties.

APPENDIX FOUR

SOCIALIST POLICY FOR THE UNDERDEVELOPED TERRITORIES

A Declaration of Principles adopted by the Second Congress of the Socialist International

Milan, 17–22 October 1952

PREAMBLE

1. The Socialist International aims at the liberation of all men from economic, spiritual and political bondage and the creation of a world society based on the rule of law and voluntary co-operation between free peoples.

2. To this end it seeks to establish in every country equal citizenship and democratic institutions through which to maintain and expand the political freedom and economic well-being of all the people. It rejects every form of racial discrimination.

3. It seeks to create between countries relationships which express the fundamental unity of all mankind and which recognize the just aspirations of all peoples to a full and free life. It recognizes the value of different cultures and seeks to promote human dignity in all lands.

4. The Socialist International therefore rejects without reservation capitalist imperialism which binds peoples in the chains of political domination and economic exploitation and which creates the disastrous myth of racial superiority.

5. It rejects too the international tyranny which Communist imperialism seeks to impose upon the peoples of the world. The oppression and exploitation of any people, whatever ideological justification may be sought for it, is diametrically opposed to the principles of democratic Socialism.

6. The Socialist International recognizes the upsurge of national consciousness as a stage in the emancipation of nations. Communist propaganda attempts to divide the free world by exploiting nationalist fervour for its own ends. Socialists condemn chauvinistic nationalism which denies international solidarity. They are convinced that genuine national aspirations can only be realized through democratic Socialism.

7. The Socialist International strives for equality as a guiding principle in the relations between individuals and between communities. Vast areas of the world still suffer from extreme poverty, illiteracy and disease. The people eke out a meagre existence at the margin of subsistence and lack the material basis for a full and free life. Socialists work to end misery which saps the energy of men, destroys their hopes, breaks their spirits, and makes impossible the attainment of full human dignity.

8. Such inhuman conditions are grave obstacles to the development of democracy and to the evolution of a free world society in which all peoples have equal opportunity and equal respect. They are a moral and economic danger to advanced countries. They are a threat to peace. They are a challenge to Socialists.

9. Where peoples are unable immediately to sustain modern systems of democratic government and are politically dependent on another country, democratic Socialists support the creation as rapidly as possible of the conditions in which full self-government can be achieved. The interests of the people of the dependent territory are for Socialists the paramount interests: they seek to eradicate economic backwardness, not to exploit it; to remove all forms of subjection and not to profit by dependent status.

10. Socialists endeavour to create between sovereign states and dependent territories a vital partnership, the objects of which are to make possible the peaceful and rapid transition to genuine democratic self-government and to expand the area of international co-operation between free peoples.

11. Democracy, prosperity and peace require the fullest utilization of natural resources, an increase in the productivity of the underdeveloped areas and the redistribution of the world's income in order to close the gap between living standards in the different parts of the world. All peoples have a vital interest in raising material and cultural levels in the underdeveloped areas. Democratic Socialism must inspire the economic, social and cultural development of these territories.

12. The Socialist International works therefore for the acceptance by the free peoples of the world of a World Plan for Mutual Aid which would make an all-out attack on poverty everywhere and which would express in action the international solidarity of working people the world over.

I. SOCIALIST TASKS IN THE UNDERDEVELOPED REGIONS

1. The peoples of the underdeveloped regions are becoming increasingly conscious of their poverty, yet too many of the inhabitants of most of these territories still have an attitude of resignation towards it and, in ignorance, sometimes resist the new ideas and techniques which would raise their living standards. Socialists seek to create the psychological atmosphere in which economic development can go forward and to win

the confidence of the masses for the new attitudes, relationships and techniques which are necessary to this end.

2. Progress occurs only where people are inspired by the confidence that man can by conscious effort enlarge his possibilities. Without such an attitude the necessary changes in material techniques and social institutions will not be freely accepted. Socialists therefore demand the spread of education which encourages such an attitude.

3. For economic development to go forward people must not only desire progress; their social, economic, legal and political institutions must be favourable to it. Fundamental adjustments will be necessary. Old ideas have to be scrapped to make way for universally accepted new. Customs and traditions which hamper production have to be replaced. Economic relationships which rob the individual of the fruits of his labour have to be broken. Bonds of caste have to be burst. Legal and political systems which concentrate power in the hands of a small class intent on maintaining its own wealth and privileges have to be reformed. Under reactionary, selfish or corrupt leaders, the masses will remain apathetic and dispirited or their misery may become fertile ground for any ideology which will hold out to them promise, however false, of means towards a better life. Given vigorous and honest leadership, the masses can be inspired with an enthusiasm for human progress. Socialists in the underdeveloped territories aim at providing that creative leadership.

4. Full economic development which will raise the living standards of the depressed masses cannot be achieved by the development of any form of capitalism, indigenous or other, but only by Socialist planning. Policies based on the principles of Socialism are of the essence of the task.

5. Socialists in the underdeveloped territories strive to establish governments which will grant to the toilers on the soil land reforms which will abolish agrarian feudalism and which will assure a sufficient share of the increased yield of his labour to induce him to invest in new ventures, to adopt improved techniques, to put forth intensive effort to increase production, and so to raise his standard of living.

6. They seek action which will provide the cultivator with facilities for borrowing the funds necessary to enable him to start operations with adequate equipment and without a heavy debt burden, to organize the agricultural unit which will maximize output and to establish co-operative organizations wherever suitable.

7. They work for development programmes which will bring to domestic industry in peasant economies better appliances and improved techniques both of production and of organization, and which will build up, where appropriate, secondary industries under planned direction. They support action which will assist the necessary flow of capital to their countries, provided there is full protection against imperialism in any form.

8. Socialists seek to create efficient and reliable administrations, capable of undertaking effective economic planning and to strengthen Socialist parties, free trade unions and peasant organizations, essential in a society inspired by the principles of democratic Socialism.

9. They aim at a balanced economy adjusted to the needs of their own peoples and to the demands of an expanding world economy, which will gradually produce prosperity for the working people everywhere.

II. THE TASK OF SOCIALISTS IN THE DEVELOPED COUNTRIES

1. Socialists in the developed countries recognize that the eradication of extreme poverty throughout the world is as much the moral responsibility of the peoples of the technically advanced countries as it is of those who live in underdeveloped areas.

2. They recognize that it is vital to the cause of freedom and humanity throughout the world that the vast economic and social changes which are necessary to create decent living standards for the depressed millions should be undertaken in co-operation with the more advanced nations of the free world. Financial assistance from these countries is needed because the rate of capital accumulation in the underdeveloped territories is quite insufficient to support rapid economic development and social progress.

3. The underdeveloped territories require investment to raise the level of health and education and to improve the administrative techniques of their governments. They need schools, technical colleges and vocational training centres. They need hospitals, dispensaries and improved housing. Investment is necessary, too, in scientific research and to provide the statistical and other services without which planned development cannot take place. Investment of this kind will earn no direct return and will have to be met either from the general revenues of the countries concerned or from external assistance in the form of grants.

4. They require investment in basic equipment—for transport and communications, to develop electric power, for irrigation schemes, for soil conservation and a multitude of similar public works. Quite often the return on such investment would be sufficient not only to cover running costs but to amortize the initial outlay. It is the easiest type of investment to finance by means of loans, but long amortization periods and low interest rates are necessary. In special circumstances there will not be enough return to amortize the loans, and grants may be necessary.

5. They require investment in the productive sector: in agriculture and fisheries, in mineral resources and in new prime and manufacturing industries. In these fields investment both from public and private sources will be needed.

6. Such development cannot be achieved without a great increase in competent administrators, devoted to the public interest, of managerial staffs and of technicians at all levels.

7. Socialists in the advanced countries seek to promote governmental action to help meet these pressing needs of the underdeveloped territories by extending to them technical aid and financial assistance. They press for international co-operation in any field where international action is desirable.

8. Socialists reject plans which serve only the narrow short-term interests of industrial nations and which conflict with the fundamental principle of equality in relations between different peoples. They reject attitudes of superiority towards less fortunate peoples and seek to build up a wholly new relationship based on mutual respect and co-operation to meet common economic needs. That is why they promote the transformation of existing colonial economic systems.

9. Aid should be given immediately to meet recurring problems like famines. Long-term aid for investment should be supported to secure for the underdeveloped countries a steady increase in the average standard of living, a fairer distribution of national income, greater security for the poorest inhabitants, the greatest possible stabilization of the economy, an increase in productivity and progress in political emancipation.

10. It is the primary task of Socialists in the more advanced nations to create a public opinion favourable to active participation in a programme of assistance to underdeveloped countries and a willingness on the part of the more fortunate peoples to play their vital role in this world effort, even if it should entail temporary sacrifices.

III. THE WORLD PLAN FOR MUTUAL AID

1. The Socialist International appeals to democratic Socialists the world over to unite in whole-hearted support for a World Plan for Mutual Aid.

2. The world development plan should provide for programmes at three levels—a general world programme, regional programmes and bi-lateral programmes.

3. Bi-lateral programmes would cover assistance from metropolitan countries to their associated overseas territories. Where political relations are good and partnership in economic and political advancement is accepted, both giving and receiving countries will doubtless continue with this sort of programme.

4. Regional programmes would be used to provide funds for investment both in social development and production where a number of supplying countries co-operate in assisting an area consisting of several receiving countries. The main participants would be the countries being developed and the supplying countries with political associations with them.

5. The general world programme would be a co-operative effort for supplying relief and assistance out of a general pool, and for creating a general development fund. First aid supplies of food, medicine and other equipment should be organized in this general programme, since it is only by estimating supplies and requirements for many countries that supplies can be shared more fairly and the most urgent needs met first. Social development, such as health and educational services, and assistance in technical matters should be organized in the general programme as far as possible, in order to economize the efforts of the available experts, and to make the most use of the results of research of all kinds. All countries should be invited to join in this programme of relief, assistance and development. The contributions from the developed countries should be assessed on an agreed basis which takes into account their resources and their contributions to other programmes.

6. To make the plans as efficient as possible, to avoid overlapping and to fix the right priorities in respect to the urgency of each item, the three types of programme will have to be co-ordinated within the framework of the World Plan for Mutual Aid.

7. To devise and to carry out these programmes, executive agencies will be required. Existing Agencies like the International Bank for Reconstruction and Development, the Technical Assistance Administration, the International Labour Organization and other Specialized Agencies of the United Nations, will render useful services and new agencies may have to be created.

8. By an all-out effort at all three levels freedom from want can be achieved for peoples now living in grim poverty in the underdeveloped regions of the world. A new era of international co-operation and good will can be initiated. Democracy will be strengthened and expanded throughout the world and mankind will be brought a stage nearer the co-operative commonwealth of free and equal peoples which is the goal of Socialist endeavour.

APPENDIX FIVE

PRINCIPLES AND OBJECTIVES OF SOCIALISM IN ASIA

Declaration of the Founding Congress of the Asian Socialist Conference

Rangoon, 6–15 January 1953

1. Modern Socialism and the Socialist movement arose in Western Europe as a reaction to the evils of capitalism. The capitalist order broke down feudalism, dissolved its hierarchy and abolished serfdom. It ushered in the machine age and quickened the pace of life and progress. It also brought

in its wake insecurity of livelihood, unemployment and periodic economic crises. The wage labourer became an immediate victim of capitalism. He conceived capitalist society as a class society in which the capitalists subjugate and exploit the workers as a class. A labour movement came into being which developed into a movement against capitalism and eventually into a movement for the establishment of a new social order, the Socialist society.

2. The growth of capitalism was accompanied by the expansion of its orbit of power and of its impact upon human society. Each national capitalist class was no longer content with profits within its own country or from its own people. There developed an urge towards ever-widening spheres of activity and power. The process led to the spread of colonial imperialism, i.e. the subjugation of backward and underdeveloped countries and their economic dependency through the imposition of foreign control upon important sources of their existence.

At the same time, capitalism brought about a speedy progress of the technology of production. It resulted in the creation of great material wealth and stimulated the progress of science and the expansion of the abilities and skills of man. The wealth created, however, was distributed with gross inequality among the men and countries which participated in its creation. In each country the capitalists appropriated the larger part, leaving the smaller to other groups, including the working class. Moreover, although directly or indirectly colonies made a major contribution to this development, they received a much smaller share of the world's produce for distribution among their own people than was acquired by countries on a high level of capitalistic development in industry and commerce.

This process led to the existence side by side of super-developed and underdeveloped countries in the world. It created a situation which was felt by the colonies to be one of exploitation of one people by another. Antagonism and tensions between these categories of peoples ensued.

3. The growth of the labour and Socialist movements proceeded concurrently with the development of capitalism. Within the highly industrialized capitalist countries, the organized workers and the Socialist parties gained an increasing influence in the affairs of the State. This influence was used to expand and defend the democratic, political and social rights of the workers and of the common people in general. The legal and economic position of the workers consequently improved. The progressive intervention of the State in economic life was used to secure a more equitable distribution of the national income. Political democracy hence became more meaningful and precious for the broad masses of the people and for the workers in particular. For these reasons, class antagonism in some countries decreased in sharpness. In other countries, under the impact of war and economic depression, capitalist democracy degenerated into Fascism which led to the violent suppression of the working class.

While such were the trends in the capitalist states of the West, evolution in the colonies and the underdeveloped countries proceeded along entirely different lines. Here capitalism stood out as a system of naked exploitation of man by man, i.e. the native worker by the foreign and indigenous capitalist. The revulsion of feeling against foreign rule was further exacerbated by the consciousness of the entire colony being exploited by the metropolis. Class antagonism was aggravated by racial animosity.

4. The reaction against capitalism and capitalist society assumed different forms. The Socialist movement split in two—Communism and democratic Socialism. At the same time, national freedom movements took up the struggle against imperialism and the colonial régime.

The essence of democratic Socialism is the striving to attain greater happiness, justice and dignity, and the fullest possible chance of self-expression for the human being. In seeking to abolish exploitation of class by class and of man by man, Socialism recognizes man both as an integral part of a class or group and as a human individual. It therefore avoids totalitarian forms of government and methods of mass coercion.

Communism, on the other hand, as practised today in its totalitarian form in the Soviet Union and its satellites, has degenerated into a régime of the complete subordination of the individual and the group to the centralized power of the leadership of the ruling party. Under the Soviet system state power imposes absolute domination and exacts blind obedience; man is expected to give up his freedom and individuality, obliterating himself as an abstract part of an all-powerful state in which only one will prevails. Communism, therefore, stands for the negation of all concepts of freedom, individual self-expression and genuine mass responsibility which are the very breath of democratic Socialism.

Nationalism in the colonial and the so-called backward countries shares with Socialism a sense of passionate dedication to freedom and justice. While after the advent of independence the paths of these two movements may diverge, as long as the struggle for independence continues, Socialists and Nationalists are comrades in arms; they also often uphold the same appreciation of the democratic rights of man.

In view of these convictions, we, the Socialist parties in Asia, declare our rejection of Communism and express our determination to continue our struggle to supersede capitalism and feudalism by democratic Socialism.

5. To this end, we, the Socialist parties of Asia, in this first Asian Socialist Conference assembled, have agreed upon and do hereby proclaim the following aims and principles:

(a) Socialism strives for the creation of a social order free from the exploitation of man by his fellow man. It envisages a society of free and equal people co-operating together for common happiness and common progress.

(b) The economic aim of Socialism is to provide security for everyone's livelihood, to eliminate unemployment, to increase wealth, to expand production, and to bring about an equitable distribution of national income and national wealth.

(c) To achieve this objective, production must be directed towards the satisfaction of the needs of society as a whole and not to the profit and advantage of a few. This is only possible if production is properly planned.

(d) The purpose of Socialist planning is to raise productivity, to abolish methods of production which are unsuitable because of their obsolete, irrational and inefficient character, to improve the technique of production in all fields, and to secure a rational utilization of natural resources.

(e) Socialist planning and the attainment of the high aims of Socialism require that the whole people should actively and responsibly participate in the process of production, as far as possible according to each producer's own volition and initiative, so as to prevent an excessive growth of bureaucracy, either official or non-official. The participation of labour, skilled and unskilled, as well as of the consuming public, in guiding production without diminishing its efficiency is an essential condition of ensuring a democratic control of economic and social life.

(f) The exact forms of planning to be applied and the extent of public ownership should depend on the economic and social structure of the country concerned, but the central aim should be to foster a continued expansion of the nationalized and co-operative sectors of the country's economy.

(g) Socialism in Asia and in other underdeveloped countries must concentrate its special attention on the lot and future of the peasant, whose urge towards improvement and progress is just as powerful as that of the worker, if not more so. The fact that most Asian countries are predominantly agricultural and that the peasant class forms an overwhelming proportion of their population must affect the entire character and trend of Asian Socialism.

(h) It is the fundamental principle of Socialism that land should be distributed among those who till it. Socialism considers the peasant entitled to public and State support. The improvement of the methods and tools of production and the general raising of the levels of village life call for active attention and have a special bearing on the development of the technology of the small enterprise.

(i) Socialism can only flourish in freedom; in a democratic society it can only be realized in a democratic way, including peaceful methods of mass struggle. On the other hand, full and creative democracy is only possible in a Socialist society. Socialism, therefore, upholds the democratic rights of the people, namely freedom of speech, of organization, of assembly, of faith and conscience, of election of representative bodies. These rights must be granted to all. They imply the right of opposition parties to exist and operate. But the Socialist state, as well as Socialist parties, have also the right, in fact are duty-bound, to defend democracy. Socialism upholds full equality of rights of all men and women regardless of race or creed. It is pledged to remove any inferiority of caste. It has to be the vehicle of ensuring to women full equality of rights and dignity of position.

(j) Socialism does not rest content with a guarantee of political rights. It seeks to safeguard basic economic and social rights which include: the right to work; the right to leisure, including leave with full pay; the right to free medical care in case of illness or pregnancy; the right to economic security, including state support for the aged, sick and unemployed; the right to family allowances; the right of children and the young to good care, education and training according to their abilities; the right to decent housing.

(k) Whilst striving to build a new society based on high economic productivity and social justice, Socialism is dedicated to the creation of a new and richer culture and the shaping of a new and better form of life. Social and economic progress have a significance only to the extent that they make for greater human happiness. Hence it is the ambition of Socialism to provide a higher satisfaction of man's spiritual needs. Socialism opposes feudalism and capitalism, whether conservative or liberal, because they are contrary to human justice; it opposes totalitarianism, whether Fascist or Communist, because it is degrading. Socialism strives to secure the sharing of each individual in the cultural heritage and spiritual progress of mankind.

(l) Socialism believes in international collaboration and in the reign of peace. It considers the attainment of both to be based on the equality of rights between individuals and states alike, and on the right of each people to national self-determination.

(m) The world Socialist movement has a common goal. Yet in different countries Socialism develops in different forms and in different ways, because of different national and historic conditions. In view of this diversity, as well as in the light of the common ultimate objective, equality of status and mutual collaboration between the Socialist movements of various countries are indispensable.

(n) Socialism envisages the world safe, prosperous, free and peaceful—a world where man enjoys all material and spiritual benefits as provided by a full life and by highly developed science and technique, free from fear of unemployment and starvation, of illness and old age, of insecurity and persecution. It believes in the Universal Declaration of Human Rights. It believes in the unity of mankind.

APPENDIX SIX

DECLARATION ON COLONIALISM

Joint Declaration, adopted by the Fourth Congress of the Socialist International and the Asian Socialist Conference

London, 12–16 July 1955

1. The Universal Declaration of Human Rights, to be respected by all peoples in the world, recognizes the dignity of man and his inalienable right to choose his own way of life provided that he does not infringe this right for his fellow men.

2. The right of peoples to self-determination, again provided that it does not infringe the same right for other peoples, and that it does not prejudice their freedom or the peace of the world, is a basic principle of the democratic system of society. The Charter of the United Nations recognizes this right.

3. Self-determination, hitherto regarded by imperialist nations as a privilege, must be exercised as a right by colonial and dependent peoples and satellite countries.

4. Colonial and dependent peoples aim towards the realization of this right to self-determination and of their own dignity.

5. The colonial rulers and imperialist powers still cling to their 'sacred mission', whether in its old or new interpretations, only to justify their self-interest and for safeguarding their domination as long as possible.

6. As long as there are colonial powers and dependent peoples there will always be a continuous and persistent struggle for freedom and against economic enslavement.

7. The struggle against colonial rule is in essence the human protest against poverty, misery, degradation and indignity, which any form of imperialism necessarily entails for the peoples under it.

8. But national freedom is only a means to human freedom. The struggle against colonialism should aim at the emancipation from any form of exploitation of man by man and at social and economic equality of the suffering masses and the establishment of a democratic Socialist society.

9. The continuation of colonialism and imperialism, besides economic disequilibrium and the politics of spheres of influence, is one of the main sources of international unrest and serves as a constant threat to the peace of the world.

10. All genuine democrats fully share with these fighters their passionate desire for human rights and freedom, and therefore associate themselves with the struggle against colonial and any other form of oppression

and for a world order free from slavery, hunger, political terror and war.

11. We solemnly resolve that all nations and peoples of the world shall be free and dedicate ourselves to that endeavour with all the strength that we command.

12. The Asian Socialist Conference and the Socialist International appeal to the Socialist parties all over the world to observe Dependent Peoples' Freedom Day in the spirit of this declaration.

APPENDIX SEVEN

MANIFESTO OF THE COMINFORM

Adopted at the Founding Conference

Szklaraska Poreba, 21–27 September 1947

During the war the states allied against Germany and Japan marched together and constituted one camp. Differences, however, existed in the Allied camp both in the determination of war aims and in the tasks of the post-war peace settlement. The Soviet Union and the democratic countries considered as the basic war aims: the restoration and consolidation of the democratic order in Europe; the elimination of Fascism and the prevention of the possibility of a new aggression by Germany; and the establishment of close and durable co-operation among the European nations. The United States, and in agreement with her Britain, had other war aims: the getting rid of market competitors —Germany and Japan—and the consolidation of their dominant position.

As a result of the second world war and the post-war period, substantial changes have occurred in the international situation. These changes are characterized by a new distribution of the basic political forces in the international arena, by changed relations between the victor states, and by their regrouping. Two opposite political lines took shape. At one extreme the policy of the U.S.S.R. and the democratic countries, aimed at the disruption of imperialism and the consolidation of democracy; at the other, the policy of the U.S.A. and Britain, aimed at strengthening imperialism and strangling democracy.

Since the U.S.S.R. and the countries of the new democracy have become a hindrance to the realization of the imperialist plans of world domination, a campaign was proclaimed against those countries, reinforced by threats of a new war on the part of the most zealous imperialist politicians in the U.S.A. and Britain. Thus two camps came into being: the imperialist anti-democratic camp with the basic aim of establishing the world domination of American imperialism and the routing of democracy, and the anti-imperialist democratic camp with the basic aim of disrupting imperialism, strengthening democracy, and eliminating the remnants of Fascism. The struggle between the two camps is taking place in an atmosphere of the intensification of the general crisis of capitalism, the weakening of the forces of capitalism, and the strengthening of the forces of Socialism and democracy.

The Marshall plan is only the European part of a general plan of world expansion being carried out by the U.S.A. The plan for the economic and political enslavement of Europe is being complemented by plans for the enslavement of China, Indonesia, and the South American countries. Yesterday's aggressors, the capitalist magnates of Germany and Japan, are being prepared by the U.S.A. for a new role—that of becoming a weapon of U.S. imperialist policy in Europe and Asia. The tactical methods used by the imperialistic camp are most varied: we find a combination of threats of force, blackmail, extortion, various political and economic pressures, bribery, and the utilization of internal strife for strengthening its position.

A special feature in the tactical methods of the imperialists is the utilization of the treacherous policy of right-wing Socialists of the type of Ramadier and Blum in France, Attlee and Bevin in England, Schumacher in Germany, Renner and Schärf in Austria, and Saragat in Italy, who strive to conceal the true predatory essence of the imperialistic policy under the mask of democracy and Socialist phraseology, but who in fact remain in all respects loyal supporters of the imperialists, bringing disintegration into the ranks of the working class and poisoning their outlook. It is no accident that the foreign policy of British imperialism found in the person of Bevin its most consistent and zealous executor.

Under these conditions it is essential for the anti-imperialist democratic camp to unite, work out a co-ordinated programme of action, and evolve its own tactics against American imperialism and its British and French allies, and against right-wing Socialists, in the first place those of Britain and France. To counter this front of imperialists and nationalists there is an imperative necessity for all democratic countries to oppose to them a united front. There is a great task awaiting the Communist parties, that of preserving freedom and peace. The new American policy, supported by the British, is nothing but the policy of the pre-Munich days of 1938.

There must be the closest collaboration by Communist parties in the official policy of the nations, in their economic and social policy, and in all other spheres of social life. The chief danger for the working class at the present moment is that of under-estimating its own forces and over-estimating the forces of the imperalist front. Every concession to the U.S. line makes the backers of that line more aggressive. That is why the Communists will form the spearhead of the resistance against plans for imperialist expansion in the political, economic, and ideological fields, and will rally all the democratic and patriotic forces of the nations to which they belong. The forces for peace are so important and so great that, if only they will be strong in the defence of peace, the plans of the aggressors will suffer a complete collapse.[1]

APPENDIX EIGHT

DECLARATION OF THE EXTRAORDINARY FOURTEENTH CONGRESS OF THE CZECHOSLOVAK COMMUNIST PARTY

Adopted in Prague on 22 August 1968, one day after the invasion, and addressed to the Citizens of the Czechoslovak Socialist Republic

Comrades, citizens of the Czechoslovak Socialist Republic:

Czechoslovakia is a sovereign and free Socialist state founded on the free will and support of its people. Its sovereignty, however, was violated on August 21, 1968, when it was occupied by troops of the Soviet Union, Poland, the German Democratic Republic, Bulgaria, and Hungary.

This action is being justified on the grounds that Socialism was endangered and that the intervention was requested by some leading Czechoslovak officials. However, yesterday's Central Committee proclamation, the second radio broadcast of the President of the Republic, the proclamations of the National Assembly and the Government of the Republic, and the statement of the Presidium of the Central Committee of the National Front make it clear that no competent Party or constitutional authority has requested such an intervention.

There was no counter-revolution in Czechoslovakia, and Socialist development was not endangered. As was demonstrated by the tremendous confidence shown in the new leadership of the Party by Comrade Dubček, the people and the Party were fully capable of solving by themselves the problems that have arisen. Indeed, action was being taken that was leading toward the realization of the fundamental ideas of Marx and Lenin on the development of Socialist democracy. At the same time, Czechoslovakia has not breached its treaty commitments and obligations; it has not shown the slightest interest in living in future enmity with the other Socialist states and their peoples. These obligations, however, were violated by the troops of the occupying countries.

Czechoslovakia's sovereignty, the bonds of alliance, the Warsaw Pact, and the agreements of Cierna and Bratislava were trampled underfoot. Several leaders of the state and Party were unlawfully arrested, isolated from the people, and deprived of the opportunity to carry out their functions. A number of establishments of the central authorities have been occupied. Grave injustices have thus been committed.

1. *Keesing's Contemporary Archives*, 4–11 October 1947.

The Congress resolutely demands that normal conditions for the functioning of all constitutional and political authority be immediately created and that all detained officials be released forthwith so that they can assume their posts.

The situation that was created in our country on August 21 cannot be permanent. Socialist Czechoslovakia will never accept either a military occupation administration or a domestic collaborationist régime dependent on the forces of the occupiers.

Our basic demand is, of course, the departure of foreign troops. If the stated demands are not complied with, particularly if, within twenty-four hours, negotiations are not begun with our free constitutional and Party leaders for the departure of foreign troops and if Comrade Dubček does not make a timely statement to the nation on this matter, the Congress requests all working people to stage a one-hour protest strike on Friday, August 23 at 12 noon. The Congress has also decided that, if its demands are not accepted, it will undertake further necessary measures.[1]

APPENDIX NINE

THE WORLD TODAY: THE SOCIALIST PERSPECTIVE

Declaration of the Socialist International endorsed at the Council Conference held in Oslo on 2–4 June, 1962

The Socialist International reaffirms the principles of the Frankfurt Declaration of 1951 on the 'Aims and Tasks of Democratic Socialism'.

In the 'fifties, it became apparent that the many new scientific discoveries, if applied for peaceful purposes, made possible for the first time in history the elimination of hunger and poverty from the face of the earth. The same discoveries, used for military purposes, could cause the end of our civilization.

There are few decades in history which have produced such vast and varied changes. The work which Socialist governments began of responding to the urge for independence among colonial peoples was carried forward. By 1960, most countries of Asia and Africa had won their independence and joined the concert of free nations. Thus, for the first time in history, peoples of all continents meet together freed from alien domination. The Socialist International greets the thousand million people of the new states and welcomes their participation in the common quest for justice, equality and peace for all mankind.

Nevertheless, colonization still survives. It is significantly entrenched in countries where no Socialist movement has been allowed to exist and where

1. From *Rudé Právo*, 22 August 1968, quoted in *The Czech Black Book*, pp. 80–1.

democracy itself has been suppressed. The Socialist International finds no moral justification for the continued existence of colonialism and condemns it in all its forms.

In many democratic countries in the past decade, economic expansion enabled striking progress to be made towards the welfare society, and consequently the age-old insecurities of their citizens were substantially reduced. Yet at the same time, the gap in the standard of living between rich and poor nations has widened still further. Hundreds of millions still suffer from hunger and poverty.

In the 'fifties, the will of the human spirit for freedom and dignity was repeatedly asserted. In many countries of Latin America, dictatorships were overthrown. In some parts of the Communist world, the iron grip of Stalinism was weakened. Stalin himself was condemned. The proclamation of destalinization was prompted by popular pressure to break with the detested past and to initiate new policies. But the brutal repression of freedom in the Communist world and the ceaseless efforts of Communism to extend its sphere of influence continue.

In the decade that is over, the world faced many crises. In some parts of the world, armed conflict broke out. However, the deep-seated hostility to war that characterizes peoples everywhere helped to avert world war.

SOCIALISM AND INDUSTRIALIZED COUNTRIES

The most dynamic impulse towards social change has come in countries where democratic Socialist parties have been able to exert effective influence. History has not confirmed the doctrine of the increasing misery of the proletariat. The worst excesses of capitalism have been corrected through the constant activity of the Socialist parties, the trade unions, and the co-operative societies. New forms of ownership and control of production have emerged. Mass unemployment has been eliminated, social security extended, working hours have been reduced and educational and vocational opportunities widened.

Even where democratic Socialists have been in opposition, their opponents have often been obliged by public opinion to adopt essentially Socialist solutions for the problems of full employment and social welfare. Likewise, in the United States of America, pressures of trade unions and other progressive social forces have made their influence felt.

Despite these improvements, serious problems continue to plague industrialized societies. We believe that they cannot be solved without the application of the principles of democratic Socialism.

Permanent control by the state and public institutions over the economy undoubtedly diminishes the danger of the recurrence of economic crises. Nevertheless, recessions, which interrupt steady economic expansion, still continue.

The increasing concentration of economic power and the growth of monopoly when not controlled also create serious problems. The increasing size of industrial undertakings has brought into being a new class of managers, who enjoy great power without being responsible to the community for the manner in which they exercise it. A task facing Socialism is to make this group aware of its social responsibilities.

In many countries, the level of investment, though higher than it was, is still far below what could be achieved in a properly planned economy. Investment is, moreover, frequently wasteful. Too often, it is directed towards immediate capitalist profit, instead of strengthening in a planned fashion the basis of the economy or meeting urgent social and cultural needs.

Notwithstanding the considerable improvement in the standard of living of the mass of the people, gross inequalities in the distribution of wealth and income remain. The greater part of the privately-owned wealth is still in the hands of very few. Tax evasion and the immense appreciation of capital values perpetuate this evil. Society is still divided into social classes with differences in status and living standards, based on the accident of birth and inheritance, and resulting in differences in opportunities for education and training. Exaggerated emphasis on purely materialist aims is increased by modern business advertising and by the commercialization of cultural activity, imposing a trend towards drab conformity.

Democratic Socialism has achieved much, but greater tasks still lie ahead. There is no single method to remedy the evils of present-day society. To achieve a fair distribution of wealth, we require an extension of public ownership and control and other legislation to curb private monopolies, to effect a radical reform of the tax system and to protect consumers.

State action, authorized by democratic decisions, is essential to provide for a rapid rate of economic expansion, a sufficiently high level of investment and the swift application of modern scientific techniques. This involves economic and social planning as a central government responsibility.

In democracy, a framework must be created within which the workers can effectively influence decisions and conditions in industry and the economy generally.

The democracies must improve and extend the techniques which will enable them to direct their economic resources so as to serve the long-term interests of the people and to facilitate a more substantial contribution to world economic development. They have yet to establish sufficiently close cooperation with one another to assist the steady development of international trade, unimpeded by high tariff barriers and undisturbed by exchange and currency crises. Economic planning outgrows the borders of national states. The establishment of regional economic organizations is a recognition of this fact.

The free development of the human personality can be ensured only by a reform of the existing social and economic structure. For those still living in poverty, improvement of conditions must be realized by a system of fair wages and of effective social security and family allowances and individual care and help. A basic requirement is the provision of a general system of education with a truly democratic character and ensuring genuine equality of opportunity for all. Education in citizenship, vital to democracy, should be promoted both by the state, and by voluntary organizations, such as political parties, trade unions, co-operatives and educational associations.

Democracy can hope for survival only if it can base itself on the keen interest and active participation of citizens in its functioning. The democratic process can be extended and deepened through territorial decentralization and industrial democracy. Press, radio and television, free from undemocratic controls and pressures, should provide ample opportunities for free, responsible debates on political issues.

The challenge of the generation that inherited the changed society of the 'sixties is to find the ways and means of completing the task begun. To meet this challenge, this generation must direct its ingenuity and energy to the world as a whole.

SOCIALISM AND EMERGENT NATIONS

The emergent nations, with their hundreds of millions of people, have a heavy burden of poverty to overcome. Their difficult task is an exciting one because independence has released great reservoirs of vitality. There should be available to the new states the whole stock of science, technology and political experience that has been accumulated by the developed countries.

These new states have the opportunity of escaping the evils of capitalism and Communism alike. The capitalist methods of ruthless exploitation of the workers, involving the uprooting of the peasants and driving them into urban slums, are not only obnoxious, but also unnecessary. The Communist method is equally obsolete, consisting as it does of abstracting surplus value through terror and undertaking break-neck industrialization by the sacrifice of the needs of the people and more particularly at the cost of agricultural development.

The future belongs no more to Communism than to capitalism. Communism and capitalism point back to an age where human beings were treated as raw materials and not as the source and objective of all efforts. The Socialist International greets with satisfaction the fact that so many of the new states, striving to plan their economic future, are inspired by the ideas of democracy and Socialism.

The new states have the opportunity to plan their economy, combining agriculture with industry, reviving agriculture through improved peasant farming and co-operative organization. Better distribution of industries and decentralization of the productive process can obviate the growth of new urban conglomerations. The new states, which began their industrial journey not with steam power but with electricity, have greater freedom to plan their development.

The emergent nations, with the co-operation of the developed countries, can avoid many conflicts such as those between urban and rural populations. The new nations suffer from stagnant economic conditions and an ossified social structure. Balanced development depends on releasing and co-ordinating the forces of individual and economic initiative, without allowing private enterprise to reap the profits for the enrichment of a small minority. Fair play and fair shares must now become the basis of their policy.

These possibilities can be fully realized only if the new states pay due attention to the spread of education, for children as well as adults, to the diffusion of skills and general knowledge among the people and to helping families to plan their growth.

The future of emergent nations in this age of transition depends on the efforts of Socialists and other democratic progressive forces in new nations and on aid from the developed countries. The need is greatest in training, in the provision of skilled technicians and in the accumulation of investment capital. Industrialized countries should provide at least 1 per cent of their national income for grant aid programmes. It should be the consistent policy of the Socialist International to unite the Socialist forces of all countries in the great endeavour of accelerating the progress of the new states.

The Socialist International recognizes the right of all nations to self-determination. Nationalism has often been a liberating and uplifting force, but when it is taken to extremes, it can threaten human freedom and progress. The dangers of nationalistic excesses, where the welfare of the people is sacrificed to the claims of the state, can be averted if, on the one hand, the Socialists in the richer countries succeed in raising the sights of their people above their national needs, and, on the other hand, Socialists in the new countries develop their economy in such a way that the yardstick is human welfare and not national prestige.

There is the danger that the people of new states will be lured by the false perspectives of authoritarianism. Recent experiences in Europe, in Asia, in Africa, in Latin America show how barren this repudiation of democracy can be.

The countries of Latin America, although long free from colonial rule, share some of the problems of emergent nations. Here, scores of millions of people also present democratic Socialism with the insistent problems of hunger, illiteracy and disease.

The developing countries face a tremendous task of transformation involving basic reorientation of the rhythms of life and work of their people. The Socialist International recognizes that these far-ranging changes in patterns of thought and behaviour among hundreds of millions of people cannot be brought about unless the developed countries also undertake some fundamental adjustments in their patterns of thought and action. To that pioneering task of social innovation and adjustment, the Socialist International will dedicate its main efforts.

SOCIALISM AND THE COMMUNIST COUNTRIES

Substantial economic expansion in the Soviet Union has led to improved living standards but, above all, to greater military potential. In China, industrialization is advancing. The fact that the formidable power of a state containing 600 million people is subject to totalitarian rule and severe discipline cannot be ignored. It presents a threat to other Asian countries. Industrialization and modernization at the tempo at which they are realized in the Communist sphere are maintained only at the cost either of preventing the essential freedoms from developing or destroying them where they are already in existence.

In the case of Russia this was accompanied, especially in the earlier part of the decade, by ruthless exploitation of the countries of Eastern Europe. The risings of the people in East Germany, Poland and Hungary, who showed such dauntless courage against overwhelming odds, were in part provoked by these policies. Although the revolts were suppressed, they forced the Soviet leaders to make concessions. However, the Soviet Union strives to retain political control over the countries of Eastern Europe. The ban on the activities of the Socialist parties in these countries has continued, though their ideals and traditions have been kept alive in the minds and hearts of countless supporters.

The Communist world is no longer led from one centre of power. The Russian and Chinese leaders differ on essential issues of policy. Their divergent interests lead to a clash of ideology. This is the most important open breach so far in the structure of the Communist bloc.

Despite opposition from the Chinese Communists, the Soviet leaders abandoned the theory of an inevitable war between capitalism and Communism. As a consequence, they now claim to base their foreign policy on the principle of peaceful co-existence. In practice, however, this is only a change of tactics, and the struggle against the non-Communist world is continued in a different form. The Communists admit that the conflict is not diminished, but the emphasis merely shifted from the purely political to the economic, social and ideological fields.

Communism is not merely a social, political and economic system, but a set of doctrines which its advocates claim to be infallible and which they strive to extend all over the world.

Rivalries in the Communist sphere between different centres of Communist power and currents of opinion concerning Communism, make it manifest that Communist pretensions to totalitarian control over the individual, the nation and the development of society, are incompatible with the nature of man, the role of the nation and the evolution of human society.

For Communists, the end justifies the means, and there is a permanent contradiction between what they say and do.

Although the Communist countries claim to be peace-loving, the way in which they have used their military power has aggravated tension in the world. Although they encourage the non-aligned countries when they can exploit the attitude of the latter in their own favour, they condemn them when they cannot.

Although the Communist countries use the strongest anti-colonial language, they have enslaved scores of millions of people.

Misusing the word Socialism, their one-party dictatorships represent in fact tyranny, denying those freedoms of speech, religion, criticism, voluntary organization and contacts with the outside world which are the essence of a democratic society.

SOCIALISM AND WORLD PEACE

The ultimate objective of the parties of the Socialist International is nothing less than world government. As a first step towards it, they seek to strengthen the United Nations so that it may become more and more effective as an instrument for maintaining peace. Nations should settle their disputes peacefully, without resort to force. The Charter of the United Nations and the decisions based on it should be respected by all. Its constitution and structure must reflect the increasingly important role which the new countries play on the world scene. Membership of the United Nations must be made universal, so that all nations, including China, may be represented by their governments in power.

We deny that the world is forever destined to be polarized into blocs. Our constant endeavour is to put an end to the Cold War. East–West rivalry has largely been imposed upon an unwilling world by the Communist leaders. In Asia tensions have been aggravated by Chinese actions in North India and elsewhere, but also by some aspects of American policy. This rivalry is dangerous. It diverts energies from constructive tasks. To democratic Socialists co-existence is not enough. International co-operation is the need for our time.

The Socialist International stands for complete disarmament both in nuclear and conventional weapons, including all countries and subject to truly effective controls. We shall never give up the patient search for practical solutions to outstanding disputes between nations.

Democratic Socialists seek nothing but lasting peace, but they will firmly defend their liberties. They therefore reject the idea that democracies should disarm unilaterally. The power of defence in the event of attack must therefore be preserved as a deterrent to aggression.

The United Nations has often helped to resolve disputes between nations. However, it is, in its present form, not in the position to grant protection to a country which is the victim of aggression and to guarantee the security of every country. In these circumstances, each nation must accept responsibility for its own security. Some consider that a non-alignment foreign policy serves the security and the political stability in their own area in the best way. The International respects the desire of nations to be free to pursue their destiny without commitment in power relations of the world. Most of the Western democracies have joined to form the NATO Alliance. The democratic Socialist parties in the countries of the Alliance consider this a powerful bulwark of peace and declare their firm determination to uphold it.

While it is vital that the uncommitted countries should not fall under Communist control, no attempt should be made to draw them against their will into the Western alliance. Nor must the opposition to Communism be allowed to develop into support for Fascist, reactionary and feudal régimes. On the contrary, pressure should be continually maintained for the restoration of liberties and for social and economic reforms.

FUTURE PROSPECTS

In 1951, we declared in Frankfurt:

'*Socialists work for a world peace and freedom, for a world in which the exploitation and enslavement of men by men and peoples by peoples is unknown, for a world in which the development of the individual personality is the basis for the fruitful development of mankind.*'

These words sum up our faith.

We now stand at a great divide in history. Man, through his mastery over nature and the maturing of feeling for justice and equality, is struggling to shed the old moulds of work and thought.

We democratic Socialists proclaim our conviction that the ultimate aim of political activity is the fullest development of every human personality, that liberty and democratic self-government are precious rights which must not be surrendered; that every individual is entitled to equal status, consideration and opportunity; that discrimination on grounds of race, colour, nationality, creed or sex must be opposed; that the community must ensure that material resources are used for the common good rather than the enrichment of the few; above all, that freedom and equality and prosperity are not alternatives between which the people must choose but ideals which can be achieved and enjoyed together.

We are determined to build peace not by conquest but by understanding.

We repudiate alike the soulless tyranny of Communism and the wasteful injustice of capitalism.

To us, both freedom and equality are precious and essential to human happiness. They are the twin pillars upon which the ideal of human brotherhood rests.

In proclaiming once again our faith in that ideal, we know that we speak for humanity everywhere.

The Socialist International calls upon the people of the world, and youth in particular, to seize the opportunities that the efforts of earlier generations have at long last opened up for all, and to continue the struggle for a better world.

APPENDIX TEN

A. TABLE OF PRESIDENTS AND SECRETARIES
1864–1964

First International

PRESIDENT:	George Odger
TREASURER:	George W. Wheeler
SECRETARY FOR GERMANY:	Karl Marx
SECRETARY FOR FRANCE:	Victor Le Lubez
SECRETARY FOR ITALY:	Giuseppe P. Fontana
SECRETARY FOR POLAND:	J. E. Holtorp
SECRETARY FOR SWITZERLAND:	Hermann F. Jung
GENERAL SECRETARIES:	Johann Georg Eccarius
	William R. Cremer

Second International

PRESIDENT:	1900–1923	Emile Vandervelde
SECRETARIES:	1900–1905	Victor Serwy
	1905–1920	Camille Huysmans

Vienna International

SECRETARY:	1921–1923	Friedrich Adler

Labour and Socialist International

PRESIDENTS:	1923–1924	Arthur Henderson
	1924–1925	T. C. Cramp
	1925–1929	Arthur Henderson
	1929–1936	Emile Vandervelde
	1936–1939	Louis de Brouckère
	1939	J. W. Albarda
	1940	Camille Huysmans
SECRETARIES:	1923–1940	Friedrich Adler
	1923–1925	Tom Shaw

Socialist International (precursor: COMISCO)

PRESIDENTS:	1948–1957	Morgan Phillips
	1957–1963	Alsing Andersen
	1963	Erich Ollenhauer
	1964–	Bruno Pittermann
VICE-PRESIDENTS:	1951–1952	Louis Lévy
	1951–1963	Erich Ollenhauer
	1952–1969	Guy Mollet
	1957–1963	Hugh Gaitskell
	1963–	Tage Erlander
	1963–	Harold Wilson
	1966–	Willy Brandt
	1969–	Pietro Nenni
SECRETARIES:	1949–1956	Julius Braunthal
	1956–1957	Bjarne Braatoy
	1957–1969	Albert E. Carthy
	1969–	Hans Janitschek

Communist International

PRESIDENTS:	1919–1926	Grigori Zinoviev
	1926–1929	Nicolai Bukharin
	1929–1931	V. M. Molotov
SECRETARIES:	1919	Angelica Balabanoff
	1919–1920	Karl Radek
	1921–1922	M. Kobiecky
	1922–1931	Otto Kuusinen
		Ossip Piatnitski
		Walter Stöcker
		Mátyás Rákosi
	1931–1939	Dimitri Manuilsky
	1939–1943	Georgy Dimitrov

B. TABLE OF CONGRESSES AND CONFERENCES
1864–1964

First International

Foundation meeting:	London	28 September 1864
Conference:	London	25–29 September 1865
First Congress:	Geneva	3–8 September 1866
Second Congress:	Lausanne	2–8 September 1867

Third Congress:	Brussels	6–13 September 1868
Fourth Congress:	Basle	5–6 September 1869
Conference:	London	17–23 September 1870
Fifth Congress:	The Hague	2–7 September 1872
Sixth Congress:	Geneva	4–8 September 1873
Conference:	Philadelphia	15 July 1876

Anti-authoritarian International

First Congress:	Geneva	1873
Second Congress:	Brussels	1874
Third Congress:	Berne	1876
Fourth Congress:	Verviers	1877

World Socialist Congress

First Congress:	Gent	1877
Second Congress:	Chur	1881

Anarchist International

First Congress:	London	1881
Conference:	Paris	1889
Conference:	Chicago	1893
Conference:	Zurich	1896
Second Congress:	Amsterdam	1907

Second International

First Congress:	Paris	14–19 July 1889
Second Congress:	Brussels	3–7 August 1891
Third Congress:	Zurich	9–13 August 1893
Fourth Congress:	London	26–31 July 1896
Fifth Congress:	Paris	23–27 September 1900
Sixth Congress:	Amsterdam	14–20 August 1904
Seventh Congress:	Stuttgart	18–24 August 1907
Eighth Congress:	Copenhagen	28 August–3 Sept. 1910
Ninth Congress:	Basle	24–25 November 1912
Extraordinary session of the Bureau:	Brussels	29–30 July 1914
Tenth Congress:	Berne	3–8 February 1919
Conference:	Lucerne	1–9 August 1919
Eleventh Congress:	Geneva	31 July–4 August 1920

Socialist Parties of Neutral Countries

Conference:	Copenhagen	17–18 January 1915

Zimmerwald Movement

First Conference:	Zimmerwald	5–8 September 1915
Second Conference:	Kienthal	24–30 April 1916
Third Conference:	Stockholm	5–12 September 1917

Inter-Allied Socialist Parties

First Conference:	London	14 February 1915
Second Conference:	London	28–29 August 1917
Third Conference:	London	20–24 February 1918
Fourth Conference:	London	15 September 1918

Central European Socialist Parties

Conference:	Vienna	12–13 April 1915

Vienna International

Conference:	Vienna	22–27 February 1921

Executive Committee of the Three Internationals

First Conference:	Berlin	2–5 April 1922
Second Conference:	Berlin	23 May 1922

Labour and Socialist International

First Congress:	Hamburg	21–25 May 1923
Second Congress:	Marseilles	22–27 August 1925
Third Congress:	Brussels	5–11 August 1928
Fourth Congress:	Vienna	25 July–1 August 1931
Conference:	Paris	21–25 August 1933

Socialist International (precursor: COMISCO)

Preparatory Conference:	London	5 March 1945
First Conference:	Clacton	2–5 May 1946
Second Conference:	Bournemouth	3–8 November 1946
Third Conference:	Zurich	6–9 June 1947
Fourth Conference:	Antwerp	29–30 November 1947
Fifth Conference:	London	20–23 March 1948
Sixth Conference:	Vienna	4–7 June 1948
Seventh Conference:	Baarn	14–17 May 1949
Eighth Conference:	Paris	10–11 December 1949
Ninth Conference:	Hastings	18–19 May 1950
Tenth Conference:	Copenhagen	1–3 June 1950
First Congress:	Frankfurt	30 June–3 July 1951

Second Congress:	Milan	17–21 October 1952
Third Congress:	Stockholm	15–18 July 1953
Fourth Congress:	London	12–16 July 1955
Fifth Congress:	Vienna	2–6 July 1957
Sixth Congress:	Hamburg	14–17 July 1959
Seventh Congress:	Rome	23–27 October 1961
Eighth Congress:	Amsterdam	9–12 September 1963
Ninth Congress:	Brussels	5–6 September 1964

Communist International

First Congress:	Moscow	2–6 March 1919
Second Congress:	Moscow–Petrograd	19 July–7 August 1920
Third Congress:	Moscow	22 June–12 Aug. 1921
Fourth Congress:	Moscow	5 Nov.–5 Dec. 1922
Fifth Congress:	Moscow	17 June–8 July 1924
Sixth Congress:	Moscow	17 July–1 Sept. 1928
Seventh Congress:	Moscow	25 June–20 Aug. 1935

Communist Information Bureau (*Cominform*)

Founding Conference:	Szklaraska Poreba	21–27 September 1947
Second Conference:	Bucharest	June 1948
Third Conference:	Budapest	November 1949

World Conferences of Communist Parties

| First Conference: | Moscow | 16–19 November 1957 |
| Second Conference: | Moscow | 30 Nov.–4 Dec. 1960 |

Bibliography

PREFACE

Original sources:

Socialist International Information.

Literature:

Bach, I. A., W. E. Kunina and B. G. Tartatovsk, in: *Voprosi Istoriki* (Moscow).
Brügel, Dr J. W., *Tschechen und Deutsche 1918–1939.*
Guttsman, W. L., *The British Political Élite.*
Lorwin, Val R., in: *The Annals of the American Academy.*
Schwarz, Max, MdR, *Biographisches Handbuch der deutschen Reichstage* (Hanover, 1965).
Sturmthal, Adolf, in: *The American Political Science Review.*

PART ONE: THE DESTINY OF SOCIALISM

INTRODUCTION

Literature:

Braunthal, Julius, *History of the International, 1914–1943* (London, 1967).
Drachkovitch, Milorad M., ed., *The Revolutionary Internationals 1864–1943* (Stanford, 1966.)

1 THE BRITISH LABOUR INITIATIVE

Original sources:

Report of the Forty-Second Annual Conference of the Labour Party (London, 1943).
Report of the Forty-Fifth Annual Conference of the Labour Party (London, 1946).
Report of the 18th Congress of the Communist Party of Great Britain (London, 1945).
Report of the 73rd Annual Trades Union Congress (Edinburgh, 1941).
Report of the World Trade Union Conference (London, 1945).

Report of the World Trade Union Congress (Paris, 1945).
Report of the Proceedings of the 2nd World Trade Union Congress (Milan, 1949).
Yearbook of the International Socialist Labour Movement, Julius Braunthal, ed., 2 vols. (London 1956–1960).
Yearbook of the International Free Trade Union Movement, Julius Braunthal and A. J. Forrest, eds., 2 vols. (London, 1957–1962).

Literature:

Braunthal, Julius, *History of the International 1914–1943* (London, 1967).
Deakin, Arthur, *et. al., Free Trades Unions leave the World Federation of Trade Unions* (London, 1949).
Gottfurcht, Hans, *Die Internationale Gewerkschaftsbewegung im Weltgeschehen* (Cologne, 1962).
Sherwood, Robert E., *Roosevelt and Hopkins* (New York, 1948).

2 SOCIALISTS AND COMMUNISTS IN FRANCE

Original sources:

Bulletin intérieur, February–March 1946.
C.G.T. Congrès, 1946.

Literature:

Bloch, Jean-Pierre, *Mes jours heureux* (Paris, 1946).
Blum, Léon, *A l'Échelle humaine* (Paris, 1946).
    Le Problème de l'unité (Paris, 1945).
Bonté, Florimond, *Le Chemin de l'honneur* (Paris, 1949).
Borkenau, Franz, *Der europäische Kommunismus. Seine Geschichte von 1917 bis zur Gegenwart* (Berne, 1952).
Braunthal, Julius, *History of the International*, vols. I and II (London, 1966–1967).
Domenach, Jean-Marie, 'The French Communist Party', in: *Communism in Western Europe*. Mario Einaudi, ed. (Ithaca, 1951).
Ehrmann, Henry, *French Labor. From Popular Front to Liberation* (New York, 1947).
Einaudi, Mario, ed. *Communism in Western Europe* (Ithaca, 1951).
Frachon, Benoît, 'Une Étappe de la lutte des classes en France: Les grandes grèves de novembre–decembre 1947', in: *Cahiers du Communisme*, January 1948.
Graham, D. B., *The French Socialists and Tripartisme 1944–1947* (London, 1965).
Lecoeur, Auguste, *L'Autocritique attendue* (St Cloud, 1955).
Lefranc, Georges, *Le Mouvement socialiste sous la Troisième République: 1875–1940* (Paris, 1963).
Léon Blum before his Judges, with an Introduction by Félix Gouin and a Foreword by C. R. Attlee (London, 1943).
Lorwin, Val R., *The French Labor Movement* (Cambridge, Mass., 1954).
Marty, André, *L'Affaire Marty* (Paris, 1955).
Matthews, Ronald, *The Death of the Fourth Republic* (London, 1954).
Mayer, Daniel, *Les Socialistes dans la Résistance. Souvenirs et documents* (Paris, 1968).
Moch, Jules, *Le Parti Socialiste au peuple de France* (Paris, 1945).
Mottin, Jean, *Histoire politique de la presse: 1944–1949* (Paris, 1949).
Novick, Peter, *The Resistance Versus Vichy. The Purge of Collaborators in Liberated France* (London, 1968).
Pickles, Dorothy M., *France Between the Republics* (London, 1946).
    French Politics. The First Years of the Fourth Republic (London, 1953).

Rieber, Alfred J., *Stalin and the French Communist Party 1941–1947* (New York, 1962).
Taylor, O. R., *The Fourth Republic of France* (London, 1951).
Thomson, David, *Democracy in France: The Third Republic* (London, 1946).
Thorez, Maurice, '*Une Politique française; renaissance, démocratie, unité*', in *Rapport au Xe. Congrès du P.C.F.* (Paris, 1945).
Verdier, Robert, *La Vie clandestine du Parti Socialiste* (Paris, 1944).
Werth, Alexander, *France 1940–1955* (New York and London, 1956).
Willard, Germaine, *La Drôle de guerre et la trahison de Vichy* (Paris, 1960).
Williams, Philip, *Politics in Post-War France. Parties and the Constitution in the Fourth Republic* (2nd edition, London, 1958).
Wright, Gordon, *The Reshaping of French Democracy* (London, 1950).

3 UNITY AND DIVISION IN THE ITALIAN SOCIALIST MOVEMENT

Original sources:

S.I.L.O. Bulletin III, February 1947, Socialist Information and Liaison Office.

Literature:

Balabanoff, Angelica, *Erinnerungen und Erlebnisse* (Berlin, 1927).
Battaglia, Roberto, *The Story of the Italian Resistance* (London, 1957).
Blackmer, Donald L. M., *Unity in Diversity. Italian Communism and the Communist World* (Cambridge, Mass., 1968).
Borkenau, Franz, *Der europäische Kommunismus. Seine Geschichte von 1917 bis zur Gegenwart* (Berne, 1952).
Braunthal, Julius, *History of the International 1914–1943* (London, 1967).
Calamandrei, Piero, *Cenni introduttivi sulla Costituente e i suoi lavori* (Florence, 1950).
Crossman, R. H. S., ed. *The God that Failed* (London, 1950).
Deutscher, Isaac, *Stalin* (London, 1966).
Drachkovitch, Milorad M. and Branko Lazitch, eds., *The Comintern: Historical Highlights* (New York, 1966).
Einaudi, Mario, ed., *Communism in Western Europe* (Ithaca, 1951).
Galli, Giorgio, *Storia del Partito comunista italiano* (Milan, 1958).
Garosci, Aldo, 'The Italian Communist Party', in: *Communism in Western Europe*, Mario Einaudi, ed. (New York, 1951).
Hilton-Young, W., *The Italian Left. A Short History of Political Socialism in Italy* (London, 1949).
Hinterhäuser, Hans, *Italiener zwischen Schwarz und Rot* (Stuttgart, 1956).
Kommunistische Partei Italiens, Die (Berlin, 1952).
Neufeld, Maurice F., *Italy: School for Awakening. The Italian Labor Movement in its Political, Social and Economic Setting from 1800 to 1960* (New York, 1961).
Robotti, Paolo and Giovanni Germanetto, *Dreissig Jahre Kampf der italienischen Kommunisten 1921–1951* (Berlin, 1955).
Silone, Ignazio, *Fontamara* (London, 1934).
    Bread and Wine (London, 1934).
Valiani, Leo, *Dopo dieci anni* (Florence, 1946).
Vassart, Cecil and Albert, 'The Moscow Origin of the French "Popular Front"' in: *The Comintern—Historical Highlights*, Milorad M. Drachkovitch and Branko Lazitch eds. (New York, 1966).

4   THE PROBLEM OF UNIFICATION IN THE GERMAN LABOUR MOVEMENT

Original sources:

Dokumente und Materialien der deutschen Arbeiterbewegung, Reihe III, vol. I: May 1945–April 1946 (Berlin, 1959).
Kampf und Ziel des revolutionären Sozialismus. Die Politik der Sozialdemokratischen Partei Deutschlands (Prague, 1934).
Protokoll der Verhandlungen des Parteitages der Sozialdemokratischen Partei Deutschlands (Hamburg, 1947).
Wiedergeburt der deutschen Sozialdemokratie, Die. Bericht über die Vorgeschichte und den Verlauf der sozialdemokratischen Konferenz von Hannover vom 5. bis 7. Oktober 1945 (Roneotyped, London, 1945).
Zur Geschichte der Kommunistischen Partei Deutschlands. Eine Auswahl von Materialien und Dokumenten aus den Jahren 1914–1946 (Berlin, 1955).

Literature:

Abendroth, Wolfgang, *Aufstieg und Krise der deutschen Sozialdemokratie* (Frankfurt-am-Main, 1964).
Blumenberg, Werner, *Kämpfer für die Freiheit* (Berlin–Hanover, 1959).
Braunthal, Julius, *History of the International*, vols. I and II (London, 1966–1967).
Edinger, Lewis J., *Kurt Schumacher. A Study in Personality and Political Behaviour* (Stanford, 1965).
Gniffke, Erich W., *Jahre mit Ulbricht*, with a preface by Herbert Wehner (Cologne, 1966).
Grotewohl, Otto, *Wo stehen wir, wohin gehen wir? Der historische Auftrag der S.P.D.* (Berlin, 1945).
Hannak, Jacques, *Karl Renner und seine Zeit* (Vienna, 1965).
Heine, Friedrich, *Kurt Schumacher. Ein demokratischer Sozialist europäischer Prägung* (Göttingen, 1969).
Kaden, Albrecht, *Einheit oder Freiheit. Die Wiedergründung der S.P.D. 1945/46* (Hanover, 1964).
Kautsky, Benedikt, *Teufel und Verdammte. Erfahrungen und Erkenntnisse aus sieben Jahren in deutschen Konzentrationslagern* (Zürich, 1946).
Kertesz, Stephen D., ed., *The Fate of East Central Europe* (Notre Dame, Indiana, 1956).
Leonhard, Wolfgang, *Die Revolution entlässt ihre Kinder* (Cologne–Berlin, 1955).
Lipski, Horst, *Deutschland und die deutsche Arbeiterbewegung 1945–1949* (Berlin, 1963).
Migsch, Alfred, *Anschlag auf Österreich. Ein Tatsachenbericht über den kommunistischen Putschversuch im September–Oktober 1950* (Vienna, 1950).
Müller, Hans, *Die Entwicklung der S.E.D. und ihr Kampf für ein neues Deutschland 1945–1949* (Berlin, 1961).
Rath, R. John, 'Austria', in: *The Fate of East Central Europe*, Stephen D. Kertesz, ed. (Notre Dame, Indiana, 1956).
Renner, Karl, *Österreich von der Ersten zur Zweiten Republik* (Vienna, 1953).
Rieber, Alfred J., *Stalin and the French Communist Party 1941–1947* (New York, 1962).
Ritter, Waldemar, *Kurt Schumacher. Eine Untersuchung seiner politischen Konzeption* (Hanover, 1964).
Schärf, Adolf. *Österreichs Erneuerung 1945–1955* (Vienna, 1955).

...cholz, Arno and Walter G. Oschilewski, eds., *Turmwächter der Demokratie. Lebensbild von Kurt Schumacher.* 3 vols. (Berlin, 1953).

Schumacher, Kurt, *Politische Richtlinien* (Hanover, 1945).

Stern, Carola, *Porträt einer bolschewistischen Partei. Entwicklung, Funktion und Situation der S.E.D.* (Cologne, 1957).

Thomas, Siegfried, *Entscheidung in Berlin. Zur Entstehungsgeschichte der S.E.D. in der deutschen Hauptstadt 1945/46* (Berlin, 1964).

Weber, Hermann, *Von der S.B.Z. zur D.D.R. 1945–1958* (Hanover, 1966).

Wesemann, Fried, *Kurt Schumacher. Ein Leben für Deutschland* (Frankfurt-am-Main, 1952).

5   THE ORIGINS OF THE 'COLD WAR'

Original sources:

Circular No. 111, S.I.L.O.

COMISCO, Circular No. 15/49.

COMISCO, Circular No. 74/50.

Great Soviet Encyclopedia, vol. 34 (Moscow, 1955).

Report of the 42nd Annual Conference of the Labour Party (London, 1943).

Report of the 43rd Annual Conference of the Labour Party (London, 1944).

Soviet Documents on Foreign Policy, Jane Degras, ed., vol. III: 1933–1941 (London, 1953).

Trial of Polish Socialist Leaders, The. Report presented by the Polish Socialist Party to the International Socialist Conference, Copenhagen, 1950.

Literature:

Auty, Phyllis, 'Bulgaria', in: *Central and South-East Europe*, R. R. Betts, ed. (London, 1950).

Betts, R. R., ed., *Central and South East Europe 1945–1948* (London, 1950).

Braunthal, Julius, *History of the International 1914–1943* (London, 1967).

Bullock, Alan, *The Life and Times of Ernest Bevin*, vol. II: *Minister of Labour 1940–1945* (London, 1967).

Byrnes, James F., *Speaking Frankly* (New York, 1947).

Churchill, Winston S., *The Second World War.* vol. V: *Closing the Ring* (London, 1952). *The Second World War.* vol. VI: *Triumph and Tragedy* (London, 1954).

Ciolkosz, Adam, 'Poland', in: *The Curtain Falls*, Denis Healey, ed., with a Foreword by Aneurin Bevan (London, 1951).

Dallin, David J., *From Purge to Coexistence* (Chicago, 1964).

Dalton, Hugh, *High Tide and After. Memoirs 1945–1960* (London, 1962).

Dedijer, Vladimir, *Tito Speaks. His Self-Portrait and Struggle with Stalin* (London, 1953).

Dellin, L. A. D., ed., *Bulgaria* (London, 1957).

Djilas, Milovan, *Conversations with Stalin* (London, 1962).

Drachkovitch, Milorad, and Branko Lazitch, eds., *The Comintern: Historical Highlights* (New York, 1966).

Fleming, D. F., *The Cold War and its Origins 1917–1960*, 2 vols. (London, 1961).

Galati, Stephen Fischer, *The New Rumania. From People's Democracy to Socialist Republic* (Cambridge, Mass., 1967).

Gregoroyannis, A., 'The Socialist Movement in Greece', in: *Socialist World*, vol. I, March–May 1948.

Griffith, William, ed., *Communism in Europe* (Massachusetts, no date).

..y, Denis, ed., *The Curtain Falls*. With a Foreword by Aneurin Bevan (London, 1951).

..rowitz, David, *The Free World Colossus. A Critique of American Foreign Policy in the Cold War* (London, 1954).

..onescu, Ghita, *Communism in Rumania 1944–1962* (London, 1964).

Ireland, Brian, 'Poland', in: *Central and South East Europe 1945–1948*, R. R. Betts ed. (London, 1950).

Knapp, Wilfrid, 'The Partition of Europe', in: *The Cold War*, Evan Luard, ed. (London, 1964).

Lazitch, Branko, 'Stalin's Massacre', in: *The Comintern: Historical Highlights*. Milorad M. Drachkovitch and Branko Lazitch, eds. (New York, 1966).

Leahy, W. D., *I Was There* (London, 1950).

Luard, Evan, ed., *The Cold War* (London, 1964).

Macmillan, Harold, *The Blast of War 1939–1945* (London, 1967).

McNeill, William Hardy, *The Greek Dilemma. War and Aftermath* (London, 1947).

Meissner, Boris, *Russland, die Westmächte und Deutschland. Die sowjetische Deutschlandpolitik 1943–1953* (Hamburg, 1953).

Mikolajczyk, Stanislav, *The Pattern of Soviet Domination* (London, 1948).

Molotov, V. M., *Questions of Foreign Policy* (Moscow, 1949).

'R.', 'The Fate of Polish Socialism,' in: *Foreign Affairs* (New York), vol. XXVIII, October, 1949.

Reale, Eugenio, 'The Founding of the Cominform', in: *The Comintern: Historical Highlights*. Milorad M. Drachkovitch and Branko Lazitch eds. (New York, 1966).

Roosevelt, Elliot, *As He Saw It* (New York, 1946).

Seton-Watson, Hugh, *The East European Revolution* (London, 1951).

Sherwood, Robert E., *The White House Papers of Harry L. Hopkins*. vol. II (London, 1948).

 Roosevelt and Hopkins (New York, 1948).

Staar, Richard F., *Poland 1944–1962. The Sovietization of a Captive People* (Louisiana, 1962).

Stalin, J., *Über den Grossen Vaterländischen Krieg der Sowjetunion* (Moscow, 1946).

Stehle, Hansjakob, 'Polish Communism', in: *Communism in Europe*, William Griffith, ed., (Massachusetts, no date).

Stowe, Leland, *While Time Remains* (New York, 1946).

Tappe, E. D., 'Roumania', in: *Central and South-East Europe 1945–1948*. R. R. Betts, ed. (London, 1950).

Truman, Harry S., *Memoirs*, vol. I: *Year of Decisions, 1945* (New York, 1955).

Werth, Alexander, *Russia at War* (New York, 1964).

Woodhouse, C. M., *Apple of Discord* (London, 1948).

Zambrowski, Roman, 'The Party before the Elections', in: *Nowe Drogi*, vol. I, 1947.

PART TWO: THE REOPENING OF THE SPLIT

6 THE REVIVAL OF THE INTERNATIONAL

Original sources:

COMISCO, Circular No. 88/47.

Protokoll der Verhandlungen des Parteitages der Sozialdemokratischen Partei Deutschlands, Nürnberg, 29 Juni–2 Juli, 1947.

Report of the 44th Annual Conference of the Labour Party, 1945.

Report of the 46th Annual Conference of the Labour Party, 1947.

Literature:

Braunthal, Julius, *Need Germany Survive?* With an Introduction by Harold Laski (London, 1943).
    'The Socialist International and its President', in: *International Socialist Forum* (January 1945).
    '*Kurt Schumacher und die Sozialistische Internationale*', in: *Turmwächter der Demokratie*. vol. I: *Sein Weg durch die Zeit*. Arno Scholz and Walther Oschilewski, eds. (Berlin, 1954).
    History of the International 1914–1943 (London, 1967).
Langbein, Otto, '*Unsere Stellung zu Deutschland*', in: *Weg und Ziel* (January 1947).
Matthias, Erich, ed., *Mit dem Gesicht nach Deutschland. Eine Dokumentation über die sozialdemokratische Emigration. Aus dem Nachlass von Friedrich Stampfer* (Düsseldorf, 1968).
Röder, Werner, *Die deutschen sozialistischen Exilgruppen in Grossbritannien 1940–1945* (Hanover, 1968).
Scholz, Arno, and Walther Oschilewski, *Turmwächter der Demokratie. Ein Lebensbild von Kurt Schumacher*. 3 vols. (Berlin, 1954).

7 THE FOUNDING OF THE COMINFORM

Original sources:

Cahiers du Communisme, October 1947
Dějiny Komunisticki Straný Československá (Prague, 1961).
For a Lasting Peace and for a People's Democracy (Belgrade, 1947).
Foreign Affairs, vol. XXVI (July 1948) and vol. XXVIII (October 1949).
Socialist International Information, 17 May 1952.
Socialist World, vol. I, No. 4.
Statistical Yearbook of the Soviet Union (Moscow, 1963).
The White Terror in Hungary (London, 1921).
World News and Views, vol. XXVII.
Yearbook of the International Socialist Labour Movement 1956–1957, Julius Braunthal, ed. (London, 1956).

Literature:

Bán, Antal, 'Hungary', in: *The Curtain Falls*. Denis Healey, ed. (London, 1951).
    'The Last Months of Social Democracy in Hungary', in: *Socialist World*, vol. I.
Bernard, Vilem, 'Czecho-Slovakia: The Spurious Unification of the Labour Movement', in: *Labour's Call* (March, 1961).
Betts, R. R., ed., *Central and South-East Europe 1945–1948* (London, 1950).
Borkenau, Franz, *Der europäische Kommunismus* (Berne, 1952).
Braunthal, Julius, *History of the International 1914–1943* (London, 1967).
Ciolkosz, Adam, 'Poland', in: *The Curtain Falls*, Denis Healey, ed., with a Foreword by Aneurin Bevan (London, 1951).
Dedijer, Vladimir, *Tito Speaks. His Self-Portrait and Struggle with Stalin* (London, 1953).
Deutscher, Isaac, *Stalin* (2nd edition, London, 1966).
Diamond, W., *Czechoslovakia between East and West* (London, 1947).
Djilas, Milovan, *Conversations with Stalin* (London, 1962).

Domenach, Jean-Marie, 'The French Communist Party', in: *Communism in Western Europe*, Mario Einaudi, ed. (Ithaca, 1951).

Donnelly, Desmond, *Struggle for the World. The Cold War from its Origins in 1917* (London, 1965).

Drachkovitch, Milorad M. and Branko Lazitch, eds., *The Comintern: Historical Highlights* (New York, 1966).

Einaudi, Mario, ed., *Communism in Western Europe* (Ithaca, 1951).

Eliaš, Zdeněk, and Jaromir Netik, 'Czechoslovakia', in: *Communism in Europe*, William Griffith ed. (Massachusetts, no date).

Fierlinger, Zdeněk, *In the Service of the Czechoslovak Republic* (Prague, 1949).

Fontaine, André, *History of the Cold War. From the October Revolution to the Korean War, 1917–1950* (London, 1968).

Galli, Georgio, 'Italian Communism', in: *Communism in Europe*. William Griffith ed. (Cambridge, Mass., no date).

Griffith, William, *Communism in Europe* (Massachusetts, no date).

Halle, Louis J., *The Cold War as History* (London, 1967).

Healey, Denis, ed., *The Curtain Falls*. With a Foreword by Aneurin Bevan (London, 1951).

Hyde, Douglas, *I Believed* (London, 1951).

Illyés, Gyula, *People of the Puszta* (Budapest, 1967).

Kaplan, Karel, 'Class Struggle after February 1948', *Přispěvky*, No. 3, 1963.

Kennan, George F., *Memoirs 1925–1950* (London, 1968).

Lefranc, Georges, *Histoire du syndicalisme français* (Paris, 1947).

Lockhart, Robert Bruce, 'The Czechoslovak Revolution', in: *Foreign Affairs*, vol. XXVI (New York, 1948).

Lorwin, Val R., *The French Labor Movement* (Cambridge, Mass., 1954).

Majer, Václav, 'Czechoslovakia', in: *The Curtain Falls*, Denis Healey, ed., with a Foreword by Aneurin Bevan (London, 1951).

Masaryk, Thomas, *The Making of a State* (London, 1947).

Nagy, Ferenc, *The Struggle behind the Iron Curtain* (New York, 1948).

Nedved, Jaroslav, *Cesta ke slouceni socialni demokracie s kommunistockou stranou v roce 1948*', in: *Academica* (Prague), vol. 8, 1968.

Nollau, Günther, *International Communism and World Revolution* (London, 1961).

Pelling, Henry, *The British Communist Party* (London, 1958).

Trial of leadership of treasonable plot headed by Rudolf Slánsky: (Ministry of Justice, Prague, 1953).

Reale, Eugenio, 'The Founding of the Cominform', in: *The Comintern: Historical Highlights*. Milorad Drachkovitch and Branko Lazitch, eds. (New York, 1966). *Avec Jacques Duclos au Banc des Accusés* (Paris, 1958).

Révai, Joszef, 'On the Character of our People's Democracy', in: *Foreign Affairs*, vol. XXVIII (October 1949).

Révész, László, '*Die Liquidierung der ungarischen Sozialdemokratie*', in: *Die Zukunft* (June 1968).

Ripka, Hubert, *Le Coup de Prague* (Paris, 1949).

Smidt, Tana, *Anatomy of a Satellite* (Boston, 1952).

Souvarine, Boris, *Stalin. A Critical Survey of Bolshevism* (New York, 1939).

Storm, Walter, *The Crisis in Czechoslovakia* (Prague, 1948).

Stransky, Jan, *East Wind over Prague* (London, 1950).

Taborsky, Edward, *Communism in Czechoslovakia 1948–1960* (Princeton, 1961).

Taylor, A. J. P., *English History 1914–1945* (Oxford, 1965).

Werth, Alexander, *France 1940–1955* (New York–London, 1956).

What Happened in Czechoslovakia (Prague, 1948).

Zinner, Paul E., *Revolution in Hungary* (New York–London, 1962). *Communist Strategy and Tactics in Czechoslovakia 1918–1948* (London, 1963).

8 THE RECONSTITUTION OF THE SOCIALIST INTERNATIONAL

Original sources:

Report of the Special Conference in Socialism and Religion. Circular No. 80/53.
COMISCO, Circular No. 11/49.
COMISCO, Circular No. 27/49.
COMISCO, Circular No. 38/49.
COMISCO, Circular No. 3/49.
COMISCO, Italy File.
COMISCO, Circular No. 71/51.
COMISCO, Circular No. 65/52.
Limaye, Madhu, Report of the International Conference of the Socialist Parties, held at Antwerp, in *Report of the Sixth Annual Conference, Socialist Party, India* (Nasik, 1948).
Report of the First Congress of the Socialist International, Circular No. 100/51.
Report of the Second Congress of the Socialist International, Circular No. 1/53.
Report of the Third Congress of the Socialist International, Circular No. 115/53.
Socialist International Information (S.I.I.), vol. I, No. 2.
Socialist International Information, vol. I, No. 34, 1 Sept. 1951.
Socialist International Information, vol. II, No. 8.
Socialist International Information, vol. III, Nos. 12, 13, 14 and 15.
Soviet Press Translation, July 1949.
The Autobiography of Bertrand Russell, vol. III: 1944–1967 (London, 1969).
Yearbook of the International Socialist Labour Movement, Julius Braunthal, ed., 2 vols. (London, 1956–1957).

Literature:

Braunthal, Julius, ed., *Sozialistische Weltstimmen* (Berlin and Hanover, 1958).
    History of the International 1914–1943 (London, 1967).
Clay, Lucius, *Decision in Germany* (London, 1950).
Fleming, D. F., *The Cold War and its Origins 1917–1960.* 2 vols. (London, 1961).
Gaitskell, Hugh, '*Die ideologische Entwicklung des demokratischen Sozialismus in Grossbritannien,*' in: *Sozialistische Weltstimmen,* Julius Braunthal, ed. (Berlin and Hanover, 1958).
Kennan, George F., *Memoirs 1925–1950* (London, 1967).
Kogan, Norman, *A Political History of Postwar Italy* (New York, 1966).
Laski, Harold J., *Communist Manifesto: Socialist Landmark* (London, 1948).
Lorwin, Val R., *The French Labor Movement* (Cambridge, Mass., 1954).
Meissner, Boris, *Russland, die Westmächte und Deutschland. Die sowjetische Deutschlandpolitik 1943–1953* (Hamburg, 1953).
Millis, Walter, ed., *The Forrestal Diaries* (New York, 1951).
Molotov, V. M., *Problems of Foreign Policy* (Moscow, 1948).
Smith, Howard K., *The State of Europe* (New York, 1949).
Weber, Hermann, *Die Kommunistische Internationale. Eine Dokumentation* (Hanover, 1966).
Werth, Alexander, *France 1940–1955* (New York–London, 1956).
Zinner, Paul E., *Communist Strategy and Tactics in Czechoslovakia 1918–1948* (London, 1963).

PART THREE: SOCIALISM AND COMMUNISM IN ASIA

9   ORIENTAL KEY POSITIONS IN THE WORLD REVOLUTION

Original sources:

Soviet Documents on Foreign Policy Jane Degras, ed., vol. I (London, 1951).
The Communist International 1919–1943. Jane Degras, ed., vol. I (London, 1956).
Trotsky Papers 1917–1922, The, Jan M. Meijer, ed., vol. I: *1917–1919* (The Hague, 1964).
Weber, Hermann, *Die Kommunistische Internationale. Eine Dokumentation* (Hanover, 1966).

Literature:

Bauer, Otto, '*Orientalische Revolutionen*', in: *Der Kampf,* vol. V, 1911.
Braunthal, Julius, *History of the International,* vols. I and II (London, 1966, 1967).
Carr, Edward Hallet, *The Bolshevik Revolution 1917–1923.* vol. III (London, 1953).
Fischer, Louis, *The Soviets in World Affairs* (Princeton, 1951).
Haupt, Georges, and Madelaine Reberioux, '*L'Internationale et le Problème Colonial*', in: *La Deuxième Internationale et l'Orient* (Paris, 1967).
Laqueur, Walter Z., *Communism and Nationalism in the Middle East* (London, 1956).
Lenin, *Lieber weniger, aber besser. Ausgewählte Werke,* vol. II (Moscow, 1947).
Torr, Dona, ed., *Marx on China 1853–1860* (Bombay, 1951).
Trager, Frank N., ed., *Marxism in Southeast Asia* (Stanford, 1960).

10   BOLSHEVISM AND SOCIAL DEMOCRACY IN INDIA

Original sources:

Fourth Congress of the Communist International (London, 1923).
Praja Socialist Party. A Brief Introduction (Bombay, 1956).
Report of the Sixth Annual Conference of the Socialist Party (Nasik, 1948).
Report of the Eighth National Convention of the Socialist Party (Madras, 1950).
Report of the Special Convention of the Socialist Party, Pachmarhi, 1952 (Bombay, 1952).
Report of the Second National Conference of the Praja Socialist Party, Gaya, 1955 (New Delhi, 1956).
Second Five-Year Plan 1956. Government of India Planning Commission (Delhi, 1956).
Statement of Policy of the Socialist Party (Bombay, 1951).
We Build for Socialism (Bombay, 1951).

Literature:

Braunthal, Julius, *History of the International, 1914–1943* (London, 1967).
Carr, Edward Hallet, *Socialism in One Country 1924–1926,* vol. III, Part 2 (London, 1964).
Dandavate, M. R., *Three Decades of Indian Communism* (Bombay, 1959).

Dange, S. A., Ghosh, Ajoy and Ghate, S. V., *A Note on the Roots of our Mistakes After Calcutta.*
Das, Sitanshu, *The Future of Indian Democracy* (London, 1970).
Deva, Acharya Narenda, *Socialism and the National Revolution*, Yusuf Meherally, ed. (Bombay, 1946).
Facts and Fiction in Congress Manifesto. A Praja Socialist Publication (New Delhi, 1957).
Joshi, P. C., 'Letter to Foreign Comrades', in: *Views* (Calcutta, May 1950).
Kautsky, John H., *Moscow and the Communist Party of India. A Study in the Postwar Evolution of International Communist Strategy* (New York, 1956).
Lakhanpal, P. L., *History of the Congress Socialist Party.* With a Foreword by Prem Bhasin (Lahore, 1946).
Limaye, Madhu, *Evolution of Socialist Policy* (Hyderabad, 1952).
    Communist Party: Facts and Fiction (Hyderabad, 1951).
Masani, M. R., *The Communist Party of India* (London, 1954).
Mehta, Asoka, *The Political Mind of India* (Bombay, 1952).
Morris-Jones, W., 'The Indian Elections', in: *The Political Quarterly*, July–September, 1950.
Narayan, Jayaprakash, *Why Socialism* (Benares, 1936).
    Socialist Unity and the Congress Socialist Party (Bombay, 1941).
Nehru, Jawaharlal, *An Autobiography* (London, 1937).
    The Unity of India (London, 1941).
Ornati, Oscar, 'Indian Trade Unions Since Independence', in: *Far East Survey* (August 1954).
Overstreet, Gene D. and Marshall Windmiller, *Communism in India* (Berkeley–Los Angeles, 1959).
Praja Socialist Party. A Brief Introduction (Bombay, 1956).
Rose, Saul, *Socialism in Southern Asia* (London, 1959).
Shils, Edward, 'The Culture of the Indian Intellectual', in: *The Sewanee Review* (April–June 1959).
Singh, Hari Kishore, *A History of the Praja Socialist Party* (Lucknow, 1959).
Sitaramayya, B. P., *The History of the Indian National Congress* (Bombay, 1947).
Spratt, Philip, *Blowing up India. Reminiscences and Reflections of a Former Comintern Emissary* (Calcutta, 1955).
Troyanovsky, K., *Vostok i Revolyutsiya* (1918).

11 HINDU AND BUDDHIST SOCIALISM

Original sources:

Maha Bodhi and the United Buddhist World, vol. xv (August 1907).
Our Goal and Our Interim Programme (Rangoon, 1953).
Report of the Second National Conference of the Praja Socialist Party, Gaya, 1955 (New Delhi, 1956).
Second Five-Year Plan 1956, Government of India Planning Commission (Delhi, 1956).
The laws of Manu in the Sacred Books of the East, vol. xxv, 1.

Literature:

Bernstein, Eduard, *Sozialismus und Demokratie in der englischen Revolution* (Stuttgart, 1908).
Bhattacharyya, Buddhadeva, *Evolution of the Political Philosophy of Gandhi* (Calcutta, 1969).

Brailsford, H. N., *The Levellers and the English Revolution*, Christopher Hill, ed. (London, 1961).

Braunthal, Julius, '*Mahatma Gandhi und Indiens Revolution*', in: *Der Kampf*, vol. XVII (1924).

Christoph, James B., *Cases in Comparative Politics* (Boston-Toronto, 1965).

Cohn, Norman, *The Pursuit of the Millennium* (London, 1957).

Desai, Ishwarlal, 'Need for a New Dimension', in: *The New Socialist*, vol. I (Patna, 1958).

Furnivall, J. S., *Colonial Policy and Practice* (Cambridge, 1948).
    Introduction to the Political Economy of Burma (Rangoon, 1957).

Gandhi, Mahatma, *Jung-Indien. Aufsätze aus den Jahren 1919 bis 1922*. Romain Rolland and Madeleine Rolland, eds. (Erlenbach–Zürich, 1924).
    Towards Non-Violent Socialism. Bharatan Kumarappa, ed. (Ahmedabad, 1951).
    Economic and Industrial Life and Relations, V. B. Kher, ed., vol. I (Ahmedabad, 1957).

v. Glasenapp, Helmuth, *Der Hinduismus* (Munich, 1922).

Hall, D. G. E., *Burma* (London, 1950).

Kautsky, Karl, *Der Ursprung des Christentums* (Stuttgart, 1908).

Kennedy, Malcolm, D., *A Short History of Communism in Asia* (London, 1957).

Mashruwala, K. G., *Gandhi and Marx*. Introduction by Vinoba Bhave (Ahmedabad, 1954).

Maude, Angus, *South Asia* (London, 1960).

Mya, U, *The Two-Year Plan for Economic Development in Burma* (Rangoon, 1948).

Narayan, Jayaprakash, *Cultural Freedom in Asia*. Proceedings of a Conference held in Rangoon, February 1955 (Tokyo, 1956).
    From Socialism to Sarvodaya (Rajghat, 1958).

Nu, U, *Towards a Socialist State* (Rangoon, 1958).

Overstreet, Gene D., 'India', in: *Cases in Comparative Politics*, James B. Christoph, ed. (Boston–Toronto, 1965).

Passin, Herbert, 'The Jeevan Dani: A Profile of Jayaprakash Narayan', in: *Encounter*, June 1958.

Prasad, Narmadeshwar, *The Myth of the Caste System* (Patna, 1957).

Ramabhai, Suresh, *Vinoba and his Mission* (Sevagram, 1954).

Sarkisyanz, E., *Buddhist Backgrounds of the Burmese Revolution*. Preface by Dr Paul Mus (The Hague, 1965).

Swe, U Ba, *The Burmese Revolution* (Rangoon, 1952).

Thomas, Edward J., *The History of Buddhist Thought* (London, 1933).

Thomson, John Seabury, 'Marxism in Burma', in: *Marxism in Southeast Asia*. Frank N. Trager, ed. (Stanford, 1960).

Toofan, Birj Mohan, *The March of Science and Socialism and Indian Religious Society*. Paper of the Second Political Forum of the Asian Labour Institute (Tokyo, 1968).

Trager, Frank N., ed., *Marxism in Southeast Asia* (Stanford, 1960).

Weber, Max, *Hinduismus und Buddhismus. Gesammelte Aufsätze zur Religions-soziologie*, vol. II (Tübingen, 1923).

12   SOCIALIST AND COMMUNIST MOVEMENTS IN BUDDHIST COUNTRIES

Original sources:

Asian Socialist Conference. Information No. 4/1959.

Braunthal, Julius, *Report of the Bureau Meeting of the Asian Socialist Conference*, Tokyo, November 1954. Circular No. 60/54.

Burma Weekly Bulletin, 12 July 1956.
Joint Programme of the M.E.P. (Colombo, 1956).
Manifesto and Constitution of the Sri Lanka Freedom Party (Wellampitiya, 1951).
Nepali Congress. Manifesto Adopted at Birganj (Patna, 1956).
Report of the First Congress of the Socialist International. Circular No. 100/51.

Literature:

Beloff, Max, *Soviet Policy in the Far East 1914–1951* (London, 1953).
Braunthal, Julius, *History of the International 1914–1943* (London, 1967).
Brimmel, J. H., *Communism in South-East Asia. A Political Analysis* (London–New York, 1959).
Chatterji, Bhola, 'Nepal Today', in: *Janata*, October–November 1958.
Collis, M., *First and Last in Burma* (London, 1946).
Dallin, David J., *Soviet Russia and the Far East* (New Haven, 1948).
Dutt, R. Palme, *The International* (London, 1964).
Furnivall, J. S., 'Twilight in Burma', in: *Pacific Affairs* (March and June 1949).
Goonewardene, Leslie, *The Difference Between Trotskyism and Stalinism*. With an Introduction by Colvin R. de Silva (Colombo, 1954).
Jennings, Sir I., *The Constitution of Ceylon*. 3rd edition (Bombay, 1954).
Kennedy, Malcolm D., *A Short History of Communism in Asia* (London, 1957).
Lerski, George Jan, *Origins of Trotskyism in Ceylon. A Documentary History of Lanka Sama Samaya Party 1935–1942* (Stanford, 1968).
Nu, Thakin, *Towards Peace and Democracy* (Rangoon, 1949).
Rose, Saul, *Socialism in Southern Asia* (London, 1959).
Silva, Colvin R. de, *Their Politics—and Ours* (Colombo, 1954).
   Outline of the Permanent Revolution (Colombo, 1955).
Thomson, John Seabury, 'Marxism in Burma', in: *Marxism in Southeast Asia*, Frank N. Trager, ed., (Stanford, 1960).
Trager, Frank N., ed., *Marxism in Southeast Asia* (Stanford, 1960).
   'The Political Split in Burma', in: *Far East Survey*, vol. XXVII (October 1958).
Wickremasinghe, Dr S. A., *The Way Ahead. An Economic Policy for Ceylon* (Colombo, 1953).
Win, Sein, *The Split Story. An Account of Recent Political Upheaval in Burma* (Rangoon, 1959).

13   ISLAMIC SOCIALISM AND MARXISM IN INDONESIA

Original sources:

Foundation Manifesto of the Partai Socialis Indonesia (Manuscript in the International Institute for Social History in Amsterdam).
International Press Correspondence, November 1926.
Kepartaian dan Parlementaria di Indonesia (Djakarta, 1954).
Manifesto of Marhaenism (Djakarta, 1954).
Partai Socialis Indonesia (Djakarta, 1956).
Benda, Harry J., and Ruth T. McVey, eds., *The Communist Uprising of 1926–1927 in Indonesia: Key Documents* (Ithaca, 1960).
Semaon, 'The Situation in Indonesia. Co-Report before the 30th Session of the Comintern', in: *Inprecor*, 4 October 1928.

Literature:

Aidit, D. N., *A Short History of the Communist Party of Indonesia* (New Delhi, 1955).
   The Road to People's Democracy for Indonesia. Fifth National Congress of the Communist Party of Indonesia, March 1954 (Djakarta, 1955).
      Haridepan Gerankan Tani Indonesia, in: *Bitang Merah*, July 1953.
      Peladjaran dari Sedjarah P.K.I. (Djakarta, 1960).
Belenki, A. B., 'La Gauche Social-Démocrate Indonésienne et la Révolution Russe', in: *La Deuxième Internationale et l'Orient*, Georges Haupt and Madelaine Reberioux, eds. (Paris, 1967).
Brackman, Arnold C., *Indonesian Communism. A History* (New York, 1963).
Feith, Herbert, and Lance Castles, eds., *Indonesian Political Thinking 1945–1965* (Ithaca–London, 1970).
Gibb, H. A. R., *Modern Trends in Islam* (Chicago, 1947).
Haupt, Georges, and Madelaine Reberioux, eds., *La Deuxième Internationale et l'Orient* (Paris, 1967).
Hindley, Donald, *The Communist Party of Indonesia 1951–1963* (Berkeley–Los Angeles, 1964).
Hughes, John, *The End of Sukarno* (London, 1968).
Kahin, George Mcturnan, *Nationalism and Revolution in Indonesia* (New York, 1952).
Mintz, Jeanne S., *Mohammed, Marx and Marhaen. The Roots of Indonesian Socialism* (London, 1965).
Nieuwenhuyze, C. A. O., *Aspects of Islam in Post-war Indonesia* (The Hague and Bandung, no date).
Sjahrir, Soetan, *Indonesian Socialism* (Rangoon, 1956).
   Out of Exile. With an Introduction by Charles Wolf Jr. (New York, 1949).
Stalin, Joseph, *Marxism and the National and Colonial Question* (Moscow, 1940).
Suripno, *Why We Lost in Mutiara* (Djakarta, June 1949).
Tinker, H. and M. Walker, 'The First General Elections in India and Indonesia', in: *Far East Survey*, July 1956.

14   SOCIALISM AND COMMUNISM IN JAPAN

Original sources:

For a Lasting Peace and for a People's Democracy, 6 January 1950.
Official History of the J.C.P. (Tokyo, 1932).
Proceedings of the First Congress of the Toilers of the Far East (Petrograd, 1922).
Report of Activities (1951–1952), submitted to the Second Congress of the Socialist International (Milan, 1952).
Fourth Congress of the Labour and Socialist International 1931. Reports and Debate (Zürich, 1932).
Yearbook of the International Socialist Labour Movement 1956–1957 (London, 1956).

Literature:

Beckman, M., and Okubo Genji, *The Japanese Communist Party 1922–1945* (Stanford, 1969).
Braunthal, Julius, *History of the International 1864–1914* (London, 1966).
Colbert, E. S., *The Left Wing in Japanese Politics* (New York, 1952).
Cole, Allen B., George O. Totten and Cecil H. Uyehara, *Socialist Parties in Post-war Japan* (New Haven and London, 1966).
Katayama, Sen, *The Labor Movement in Japan* (Chicago, 1918).

Kublin, Hyman, *Asian Revolutionary: The Life of Sen Katayama* (Princeton, 1964).

Levine, Solomon B., *Industrial Relations in Post-war Japan* (Urbana, 1958).

Morris, Ivan, ed., *Japan 1931–1945: Militarism, Fascism, Nationalism* (Boston, 1963).

Scalapino, Robert A., *The Japanese Communist Movement, 1920–1966* (Berkeley and Los Angeles, 1967).

Stockwin, J. A. A., *The Japanese Socialist Party and Neutralism. A Study of a Political Party and its Foreign Policy* (London–New York, 1968).

Storry, Richard, *The Double Patriots: A Study of Japanese Nationalism* (London, 1957).

Swearingen, A. Rodger, and Paul F. Langer, *Red Flag in Japan: International Communism in Action, 1919–1951* (Cambridge, Mass., 1952).

Tokuda, Kyuichi, *Naigai josei to Nippon kyosanto no nimmu* (Tokyo, 1949).

Totten, George Oakley, *The Social Democratic Movement in Pre-war Japan* (New Haven, 1966).

15 THE CHINESE REVOLUTION

Original sources:

Mao Tse-tung, *Selected Works* (New York, 1954).

Literature:

Brandt, Conrad, John K. Fairbank and Benjamin Schwartz, *A Documentary History of Chinese Communism* (Cambridge, Mass., and London, 1952).

Braunthal, Julius, *History of the International 1914–1943* (London, 1967).

Clubb, O. Edmund, *Twentieth-Century China* (New York–London, 1964).

Creel, H. G., *Chinese Thought from Confucius to Mao Tse-tung* (London, 1954).

Fitzgerald, C. P., *China. A Short Cultural History* (London, 1935).

    Revolution in China (London, 1954).

Isaacs, Harold K., *The Tragedy of the Chinese Revolution* (Stanford, 1951).

Kennedy, Malcolm D., *A Short History of Communism in Asia* (London, 1957).

Latourette, Kenneth Scott, *A History of Modern China* (London, 1954).

Mao Tse-tung, *China's New Democracy*. With an Introduction by Earl Browder (New York, 1945).

    Problems of War and Strategy, Selected Works, vol. II (New York, 1954).

Rostow, W. W., *The Prospects for Communist China* (New York–London, 1954).

Schram, Stuart R., *Mao Tse-tung* (London, 1966).

Schwartz, B. I., *Chinese Communism and the Rise of Mao* (Harvard, 1951).

Sherwood, Robert E., *The White House Papers of Harry L. Hopkins*, vol. II (London, 1948).

Snow, Edgar, *Red Star Over China* (London, 1938).

Stilwell, Joseph M., *The Stilwell Papers*, Theodore W. White, ed. (New York, 1948).

Weber, Max, *Konfuzianismus und Taoismus. Die Wirtschaftsethik der Weltreligionen*, vol. I (Tübingen, 1922).

Yakhontoff, Victor H., *The Chinese Soviets* (New York, 1934).

16 SOCIALISM IN ISRAEL

Original sources:

Facts about Israel 1968. Ministry for Foreign Affairs (Jerusalem, 1968).

Palestina Events 1929 (London, 1929).

Socialist International Information, 10 February 1968.

The Arab Revolutionary Movement and the Tasks of the Proletariat (October 1929).
Yearbook of the International Free Trade Union Movement 1957–1958 (London, 1957).

Literature:

Abramovitch, Raphael, '*Zionismus, Judeufrage und Sozialismus*', in: *Der Kampf*, vol. XXII (1929).
Baratz, Joseph, *A Village by the Jordan. The Story of Degania* (London, 1954).
Bauer, Otto, *Die Nationalitätenfrage und die Sozialdemokratie* (Vienna, 1907).
Berger-Barseli, J., *Hatragedia shel Hamadafecha Hasovietit* (Tel Aviv, 1968).
Berlin, Isaiah, 'The Origins of Israel', in: Walter Z. Laqueur, ed., *The Middle East in Transition* (London, 1958).
Borochov, Ber, *Sozialismus und Zionismus. Eine Synthese.* Mendel Singer, ed. (Vienna, 1932).
   The Economic Development of the Jewish People (New York, 1916).
Braunthal, Julius, *The Significance of Israeli Socialism and the Arab-Israeli Dispute* (London, 1958).
Czudnowski, Moshe M., and Jacob Landau, *The Israeli Communist Party* (Stanford, 1965).
Herzel, Theodor, *Der Judenstaat* (Vienna, 1896).
Hess, Moses, *Rom und Jerusalem* (Leipzig, 1862).
Holloway, Mark, *Heavens on Earth. Utopian Communities in America 1680–1880* (London, 1951).
Johnston, Scott D., 'Communist Party Politics in Israel', in: Robert K. Sakai, ed., *Studies in Asia 1964* (Lincoln, 1964).
Laqueur, Walter Z., ed., *The Middle East in Transition* (London, 1958).
   Communism and Nationalism in the Middle East (London, 1956).
Levenberg, S., *The Jews and Palestine. A Study in Labour Zionism.* With a Preface by J. S. Middleton (London, 1945).
Malkosh, N., *Histadrut in Israel. Its Aims and Achievements* (Tel Aviv, 1961).
Marlowe, John, *Rebellion in Palestine* (London, 1946).
Meier-Cronemeyer, Hermann, *Kibbuzim, Geschichte, Geist und Gestalt* (Hanover, 1969).
Plunkett, Margaret, 'The *Histadrut.* The General Federation of Jewish Labour in Israel', in: *Industrial and Labour Relations Review*, vol. I (1958).
Preuss, W., *The Labour Movement in Israel, Past and Present* (New York, 1963).
Rolbant, Samuel, *MAPAI. The Israel Labour Party* (Tel Aviv, 1956).
Sakai, Robert K. ed., *Studies in Asia 1964* (Lincoln, 1964).
Sakharov, Andrei D., *Progress, Coexistence and Intellectual Freedom.* With an Introduction by Harrison F. Salisbury (London, 1968).
Spiro, M. E., *Kibbutz. Venture in Utopia* (New York, 1956).
Syrkin, Nachman, *Die Judenfrage und der sozialistische Judenstaat* (Berne, 1898).
Vilner, Meir, 'The 16th Congress of the Communist Party of Israel', in: *World Marxist Review* (May 1969).
Weingarten, Murray, *Life in a Kibbutz* (New York, 1955).
Williams, Rushbrook, L. F., *The State of Israel* (London, 1962).
Yaari, Meir, *From Vision to Reality* (Tel Aviv, 1963).
   What Faces Our Generation (Tel Aviv, 1958).

17   THE ASIAN SOCIALIST CONFERENCE

Original sources:

Report of the Third Congress of the Socialist International, Stockholm, 1953.
   Circular No. 115/53.

Resolutions of the First Asian Socialist Conference, Rangoon, 1953 (Rangoon, 1954).
Socialist Party of India. Report of the Sixth Annual Conference, Nasik 1948 (Bombay, 1948).
Socialist International Information, 17 November 1956.
Socialist International Information, 8 December 1956.
Socialist International Information, 22 December 1956.
Three Years of the Asian Socialist Conference (Bombay, 1956).

Literature:

Braunthal, Julius, *Report on Activities (1952–1953)*, submitted to the Third Congress of the Socialist International. Circular No. 90/53.
Sjahrir, Soetan, *Nationalism and Internationalism* (Rangoon, 1953).

PART FOUR: THE MORAL CRISIS OF COMMUNISM

18 YUGOSLAVIA'S REVOLT AGAINST MOSCOW'S HEGEMONY

Original sources:

For a Lasting Peace and for a People's Democracy, 29 November 1949.
Report of the International Socialist Conference, Copenhagen, 1950. Circular No. 155/50.
Socialist International. Circulars Nos. 3/53, 12/53, 13/53, 14/53, 15/53, 16/53, 18/53, 19/53, 21/53, 22/53, 23/53, 25/53, 26/53, 41/53, 45/53, 47/53, 49/53.
Soviet-Yugoslav Dispute, The (London, 1948).
The Dethronement of Stalin (London, 1956).
Zinner, Paul E. ed., *National Communism and Popular Revolt in Eastern Europe. A Selection of Documents on Events in Poland and Hungary, February–November 1956* (New York, 1956).

Literature:

Auty, Phyllis, *Tito: A Biography* (London, 1970).
Avakumovic, Ivan, *History of the Communist Party of Yugoslavia* (Aberdeen, 1964).
Braunthal, Julius, *History of the International 1914–1943* (London, 1967).
Burks, R. V., *Die Dynamik des Kommunismus in Osteuropa* (Hanover, 1969).
Churchill, Winston S., *The Second World War*, vol. v: *Closing the Ring* (London, 1952).
Clissold, Stephen, *Whirlwind. An Account of Marshal Tito's Rise to Power* (London, 1949).
Dedijer, Vladimir, *Tito Speaks. His Self-Portrait and Struggle with Stalin* (London, 1953).
Djilas, Milovan, *The New Class. An Analysis of the Communist System* (New York, 1957).
Dutt, R. Palme, *The International* (London, 1964)
Foster, William Z., *History of the Three Internationals* (New York, 1955).
Landauer, Carl, *Contemporary Economic Systems. A Comparative Analysis* (Philadelphia–New York, 1964).
Leonhard, Wolfgang, *Die Revolution entlässt ihre Kinder* (Cologne–Berlin, 1955).

Maclean, Fitzroy, *Eastern Approaches* (London, 1949).
Pijade, Mosa, *La fable de l'aide soviétique a l'insurrection nationale yougoslave* (Paris, 1950).
Ulam, Adam B., *Titoism and the Cominform* (Cambridge, Mass., 1952).

19   THE INSURRECTION IN EAST BERLIN

Literature:

Brant, Stefan, *Der Aufstand. Geschichte und Deutung des 17. Juni 1953* (Stuttgart, 1954).
Hildebrandt, Rainer, *Als die Fesseln fielen* . . . (Berlin–Grunewald, 1956).
Scholz, Arno, Werner Nieke and Gottfried Vetter, *Panzer am Potsdamer Platz* (Berlin–Grunewald, 1954).
Stamm, Eugen, *Juni 1953. Der Volksaufstand vom 17. Juni 1953* (Bonn, 1961).
Weber, Hermann, *Von der S.B.Z. zur D.D.R. 1945–1958* (Hanover, 1966).
Report of the Third Congress of the Socialist International, Stockholm, 1953. Circular No. 115/53.

20   THE DETHRONEMENT OF STALIN

Original sources:

History of the C.P.S.U. (Moscow, 1959).
Nuovi argomenti Nr. 20 (May–June 1956).
Socialist International Information, 10 March 1956.
The Dethronement of Stalin. Full Text of Khrushchev Speech (London, 1956).

Literature:

Banning, W., *Der Kommunismus als politisch-soziale Weltreligion* (Berlin, 1953).
Blackmer, Donald, L. M., *Unity in Diversity. Italian Communism and the Communist World* (Cambridge, Mass., 1968).
Conquest, Robert, *The Great Terror. Stalin's Purge of the Thirties* (London, 1968).
Fedenko, Panas, *Khrushchev's New History of the Soviet Communist Party* (Munich, 1963).
Nenni, Pietro, 'I "vergognosi fatte" del rapporto segreto di Krusciov', in: *Mondo Operaio*, June 1956.
Onofri, Fabrizio, *Classe operaia e partito* (Bari, 1957).
Sakharov, Andrei D., *Progress, Coexistence and Intellectual Freedom*. With an Introduction by Harrison E. Salisbury (London, 1968).

21   POLAND'S OCTOBER

Original sources:

Ciolkosz, Adam, '"Anti-Zionism" in Polish Party Politics', in: *Vienna Library Bulletin*, 1968.

Literature:

Bethell, Nicolas, *Gomulka: His Poland and His Communism* (London, 1969).
Braunthal, Julius, *History of the International 1914–1943* (London, 1967).

Brzezinski, Zbigniew K., *The Soviet Bloc: Unity and Conflict* (Cambridge, Mass., 1967).
Halecki, Oscar, 'Poland', in: *Eastern Central Europe and the World: Developments in the Post-Stalin Era*, Stephen D. Kertesz, ed. (Notre Dame, Indiana, 1962).
Hiscocks, Richard, *Poland: Bridge for the Abyss? An Interpretation of Developments in Post-War Poland* (Oxford, 1963).
Kertesz, Stephen D., ed., *Eastern Central Europe and the World: Developments in the Post-Stalin Era* (Notre Dame, Indiana, 1962).
Kuroń, Jacek, and Karol Modzelewski, *Monopolsozialismus. Offener Brief an die Polnische Vereinigte Arbeiterpartei.* Helmut Wagner, ed. (Hamburg, 1969).
Ulam, Adam B., *Expansion and Coexistence. The History of Soviet Foreign Policy 1917-1967* (London, 1968).
Zinner, Paul E., ed., *National Communism and Popular Revolt in Eastern Europe. A Selection of Documents on Events in Poland and Hungary February–November 1956* (New York, 1956).

22 THE TRAGEDY OF THE HUNGARIAN REVOLUTION

Original sources:

Zinner, Paul E., ed., *National Communism and Popular Revolt in Eastern Europe. A Selection of Documents on Events in Poland and Hungary February–November 1956* (New York, 1956).

Literature:

Aptheker, Herbert, *The Truth about Hungary* (New York, 1957).
Blackmer, Donald L. M., *Unity in Diversity. Italian Communism and the Communist World* (Cambridge, Mass., 1968).
Fryer, Peter, *Hungarian Tragedy* (London, 1956).
Kertesz, Stephen D. ed., *Eastern Central Europe and the World: Developments in the Post-Stalin Era* (Notre Dame, Indiana, 1962).
Molnar, Miklos, and Laszlo Nagy, *Imre Nagy: Réformateur ou Révolutionnaire* (Geneva, 1959).
Váli, Ference A., *Rift and Revolt in Hungary* (Cambridge, Mass., 1961).
Zinner, Paul E., *Revolution in Hungary* (New York–London, 1962).

23 'THE SPRING OF PRAGUE'

Original sources:

Bernard, Vilem, *Report to the Eleventh Congress of the Socialist International in Eastbourne, June 1969. Socialist International Information*, 4 October 1968.
Pelikán, Jiři, ed., *The Secret Vyscocany Congress—Minutes and Documents of the 14th Congress of the CP of 22 August 1968* (London, 1969).
Remington, Robin Alison, ed., *Winter in Prague. Documents on Czechoslovak Communism in Crisis* (London, 1969).
Socialist International Information, 21 September 1968.
The Current Digest of the Soviet Press, vol. xx, No. 39.
The Czech Black Book, ed., Robert Littell (New York–Washington–London, 1969).
The Times Literary Supplement, 18 July 1968.

Literature:

Bauer, Otto, *Zwischen zwei Weltkriegen?* (Bratislava, 1936).
Brahm, Heinz, *Der Kreml und die C.S.S.R. 1968–1969* (Stuttgart, 1970).
    Die Intervention in der C.S.S.R. Berichte des Bundesinstituts für Ostwissen-schaftliche und Internationale Studien, 15/1969.
Braunthal, Julius, *History of the International 1914–1943* (London, 1967).
Brown, J. F., *The New East Europe* (London, 1966).
Devlin, Kevin, 'The New Crisis in European Communism', in: *Problems of Communism*, November–December 1968.
Fetjo, François, 'Moscow and its Allies', in: *Problems of Communism*, November–December 1968.
Garaudy, Roger, *La Liberté en sursis-Prague 1968* (Paris, 1969).
Hamrin, Harold, 'Westeuropäischer Kommunismus und Prager August', in: *Geist und Tat, Nr. I, 1969*.
Hensel, K. Paul, *et al.*, *Die sozialistische Marktwirtschaft in der Tschechoslowakei* (Stuttgart, 1968).
Horlacher, Wolfgang, *Zwischen Prag und Moskau* (Stuttgart, 1968).
James, Robert Rhodes, *The Czechoslovak Crisis, 1968* (London, 1969).
    'Czechoslovakia: Invasion and Resistance', in: *Czechoslovakia 1968*.
Lenin, V. I., *Staat und Revolution. Ausgewählte Werke*, vol. II (Moscow, 1947).
    Sämtliche Werke, vol. XIX.
Löbl, Eugen, and Dusan Pokorný, *Die Revolution rehabilitiert ihre Kinder. Hinter den Kulissen des Slánsky-Prozesses* (Vienna, 1969).
Marschenko, Anatoli, *My Testimony* (New York–London, 1969).
Marx, Karl, *Debatten über Pressefreiheit und Publikationen der landständigen Verhandlungen*, in: *Gesammelte Schriften von Karl Marx und Friedrich Engels 1841–1850*, Franz Mehring, ed., vol. I (Stuttgart, 1913).
Sakharov, A. D., *Progress, Coexistence and Intellectual Freedom*. With an Introduction by Harrison E. Salisbury (London, 1968).
Schwartz, Harry, *Prague's 200 Days. The Struggle for Democracy in Czechoslovakia* (London, 1969).
Shawcross, William, *Dubcek* (London, 1970).
Solzhenitsyn, Alexander, *One Day in the Life of Ivan Denisovich* (London, 1963).
    The First Circle (London, 1970).
Stalin, J., *Problems of Leninism* (Moscow, 1947).
Windsor, Philip and Adam Roberts, *Czechoslovakia 1968. Reform, Repression and Resistance* (London, 1969).
    'Czechoslovakia, Eastern Europe and Détente', in: *Czechoslovakia 1968*.
Wolfe, Bertram D., *An Ideology in Power. Reflections on the Russian Revolution* (New York, 1969).
Wurmser, André, '*Le mois tragique*', in: *France Nouvelle*, September 1968.
Zeman, Z. A. B., *Prague Spring. A Report on Czechoslovakia* (London, 1969).

24   PEKING'S BREAK WITH MOSCOW

Original sources:

Brahm, Heinz, *Pekings Griff nach der Vormacht. Der chinesisch-sowjetische Konflikt vom Juli 1963 bis März 1965* (Cologne, 1966).
Dallin, Alexander, ed., *Diversity in International Communism. A Documentary Record 1961–1963* (New York–London, 1963).
Gittings, John, *Survey of the Sino-Soviet Dispute. A Commentary and Extracts from Recent Polemics 1963–1967* (London–New York, 1968).

Seven Letters. Correspondence between the Central Committee of the Communist Party of China and the Central Committee of the Communist Party of the Soviet Union (Peking, 1964).
Soviet Documents on Foreign Policy. vol. I: *1917–1924.* Jane Degras, ed. (London, 1951).
The Origin and Development of the Differences between the Leadership of the C.P.S.U. and Ourselves (Peking, 1963).
World Marxist Review, December 1960.

Literature:

Dedijer, Vladimir, *Tito Speaks* (London, 1953).
Fitzgerald, C. P., *Revolution in China* (London, 1954).
Griffith, William E., *Albania and the Sino-Soviet Rift* (Cambridge, Mass., 1963).
Löwenthal, Richard, *World Communism. The Disintegration of a Secular Faith* (New York, 1964).
Mao Tse-tung, *Problems of War and Strategy, Selected Works,* vol. II (New York, 1954).
Paasche, John, '*Mao Tse-tungs Theorie von den Zwischenzonen,*' in: *Osteuropa,* Nr. 1–2, 1965.
Stalin, J., *Economic Problems of Socialism in the U.S.S.R.* (New York, 1952).

PART FIVE: THE FIRST HUNDRED YEARS

25 DESTINY OF A VISION

Original sources:

Programme der Deutschen Sozialdemokratie (Bonn).
The Current Digest of the Soviet Press, 1 January 1958.

Literature:

Adler-Karlsson, G., *Functional Socialism: a Swedish Theory for Democratic Socialization* (1969).
Alliluyeva, Svetlana (Stalin), *Only One Year* (London, 1969).
Bauer, Otto, *Geistige Weltkrise. Der Kampf,* vol. XXIII (1930).
Braunthal, Julius, *History of the International,* vols. I and II (London, 1966–1967).
Chalmers, D., *The Social Democratic Party of Germany* (1964).
Cole, G. D. H., *A History of Socialist Thought,* vol. III: *The Second International 1889–1914* (London, 1956).
  World Socialism Restated (London, 1956).
  Is this Socialism? (London, 1954).
Crosland, Anthony, *The Future of Socialism* (London, 1956).
Crossman, R. H., ed., *New Fabian Essays* (London, 1952).
Deutscher, Isaac, *Stalin.* 2nd edition (London, 1966).
Eichler, Willi, '*Die politische Rolle des Programms*', in: *Geist und Tat,* 1969, Nr. 4.
Engels, Freidrich, '*Zur Kritik des sozialdemokratischen Programmentwurfs 1891*', in: *Die Neue Zeit,* Year XX, vol. I (1901–1902).
Fromm, Erich, *Das Menschenbild bei Marx. Mit den wichtigsten Teilen der Frühschriften von Karl Marx* (Frankfurt a. M., 1966).
Hammond, J. L. and Barbara, *The Bleak Age* (London, 1934).
Jay, Douglas, *Socialism in the New Age* (London, 1962).

Katz, Zev, 'After the Six-Day War', in: *The Jews in Soviet Russia since 1917*, Lionel
  Kochan, ed. (London, 1970).
Kichko, Trofin Koreyevich, *Judentum ohne Verzierung*.
Klenner, Fritz, *Das Unbehagen in der Demokratie. Ein Beitrag zu Gegenwarts-
  problemen der Arbeiterbewegung* (Vienna, 1956).
Kochan, Lionel, ed., *The Jews in Soviet Russia since 1917* (London, 1970).
Lauterbach, Albert, *Kapitalismus und Sozialismus in neuer Sicht* (Reinbek bei
  Hamburg, 1963).
Lenin, V. I., *Geschichtliches zur Frage der Diktatur. Sämtliche Werke*, vol. xxv.
  Staat und Revolution. Ausgewählte Werke, vol. ii (Moscow, 1947).
Lichtheim, George, *Marxism. An Historical and Critical Study* (London, 1961).
  A Short History of Socialism (London, 1970).
Luxemburg, Rosa, '*Die russische Revolution*', in: *Rosa Luxemburg, Politische
  Schriften*, Ossip K. Flechtheim, ed., vol. iii (Frankfurt, 1968).
März, Eduard, '*Zio-Imperialismus?*' in: *Neues Forum*, January 1970.
Marx, Karl, *Der Historische Materialismus. Die Frühschriften*, S. Landshut and
  J. P. Mayer, eds., 2 vols. (Leipzig, 1932).
  Der Bürgerkrieg in Frankreich (Berlin, 1952).
  Kritik des Gothaer Programms (1875).
  *Zur Judenfrage. Aus dem literarischen Nachlass von Karl Marx, Friedrich Engels
  und Ferdinand Lassalle*, Franz Mehring, ed. (Stuttgart, 1913).
  Das Kapital (1st edition 1867).
Karl Marx and Friedrich Engels, *Ausgewählte Schriften*, vol. ii (Berlin, 1953).
Mayer, Gustav, *Friedrich Engels. Eine Biographie* (The Hague, 1934).
Miliband, Ralph, *Parliamentary Socialism* (London, 1960).
Miller, Susanne, *Das Problem der Freiheit im Sozialismus* (Frankfurt a. M., 1964).
Namier, L. B., *1848: The Revolution of the Intellectuals* (London, 1946).
Pike, E. Royston, *Human Documents of the Age of the Forsytes* (London, 1969).
Rousset, David, 'The Class Nature of Stalinism', in: *Saturn*, vol. iii, No. 1, January/
  February 1957.
Sakharov, A. D., *Progress, Coexistence and Intellectual Freedom*. With an Intro-
  duction by Harrison E. Salisbury (London, 1968).
Schell, Kurt, *The Transformation of Austrian Socialism* (New York, 1962).
Schellenger, Harold Kent, Jr., *The S.P.D. in the Bonn Republic: A Socialist Party
  Modernizes* (The Hague, 1968).
Simmons, Harvey G., *French Socialists in Search of a Role 1956–1967* (Cornell,
  1969).
Solzhenitsyn, Alexander, *The First Circle* (London, 1970).
Stalin, J., *Problems of Leninism* (Moscow, 1947).
Strachey, John, 'Tasks and Achievements of British Labour', in: *New Fabian Essays*.
  R. H. Crossman, ed. (London, 1952).
Townsend, Peter, *Poverty, Socialism and Labour* (London, 1966).
Trotsky, L., *The Revolution Betrayed* (New York, 1937).
Tucker, Robert C., *Karl Marx. Die Entwicklung seines Denkens: von der Philosophie
  zum Mythos* (Munich, 1963).
  The Marxian Revolutionary Idea (London, 1970).

APPENDICES

Original sources:

Table I: *Socialist International Information*, vol. xx, No. 1. January 1970.
Table II: *World Strength of the Communist Party Organizations*, Department of
  State, Washington, 1969.
Keesing's Contemporary Archives, 4–11 October 1947.
The Czech Black Book (London, 1969).

List of Abbreviations

A.B.T.U.C.	All-Burma Trades Union Congress
A.F.P.F.L.	Anti-Fascist People's Freedom League (Burma)
A.I.T.U.C.	All-Indian Trade Union Congress
A.S.C.	Asian Socialist Conference
A.V.N.O.J.	*Antifašisticko Vjeće Narodnog Oslobodjenja Jugoslavije* (Antifascist National Liberation Council of Yugoslavia)
B.I.A.	Burma Independence Army
B.I.S.	*Bureau International Socialiste*
Bund	Jewish workers' organization in Russia, Lithuania and Poland
B.W.P.P.	Burma Workers' and Peasants' Party
C.A.S.	*Comité d'Action Socialiste*
C.D.U.	*Christlich-Demokratische Union*
C.F.T.C.	*Confédération Française des Travailleurs Chrétiens*
C.G.L.	*Confederazione Generale del Lavoro*
C.G.T.	*Confédération Générale du Travail*
Cheka	*Tschreswytschajnaja Kommissija* (Special Committee to fight the Counter-revolution)
C.I.A.	Central Intelligence Agency (United States)
C.I.O.	Congress of Industrial Organizations
C.N.L.	*Comité National de Liberation*
C.N.R.	*Conseil National de la Résistance*
Cominform	Communist Information Office
Comintern	Communist International
COMISCO	Committee of International Socialist Conferences
C.P.I.	Communist Party of India
C.P.S.U.	Communist Party of the Soviet Union
Č.S.D.	*Československá Sociálni Demokracie*
C.S.P.	Congress Socialist Party (India)
C.S.R.	Republic of Czechoslovakia
E.A.M.	*Ellenikos Apelevtherotikon Metopon* (National Liberation Front)
E.D.E.S.	*Ellenikos Dimikratikos Ethnikos Syndesmos*
E.L.A.S.	*Ellenikos Laikon Apelevtherotikon Straton* (National Liberation Army)
F.D.R.	*Front Demokrasi Rakjat* (People's Democratic Front, Indonesia)
F.I.L.	*Federazione Italiana del Lavoro*
F.N.	*Front National* (France)
F.N.D.	National Democratic Front (Romania)
F.O.	*Force Ouvrière—Confédération Générale du Travail*

F.T.P.F.	*Francs-Tireurs Partisans-Français*
Gestapo	Secret State Police (Germany)
G.T.I.	*Gerankan Tani Indonesia* (Indonesian Farmers' League)
H.M.S.	*Hind Mazdoor Sabha* (India)
I.C.F.T.U.	International Confederation of Free Trade Unions
I.F.T.U.	International Federation of Trade Unions
I.N.T.U.C.	Indian National Trade Union Congress
I.S.D.V.	*Indies Sociaal Democratic Vereeniging*
K.M.P.P.	*Kisan Mazdoor Praja Party* (India)
K.P.D.	Communist Party of Germany
K.P.Ö.	Communist Party of Austria
K.S.Č.	*Komunistická Strana Československá*
L.C.G.I.L.	*Libera Confederazione Generale Italiana del Lavoro*
L.S.I.	Labour and Socialist International
L.S.S.P.	*Lanka Sama Samaya Party* (Ceylon)
M.A.P.A.I.	*Mifleget Poale Eretz Israel* (Jewish Labour Party of Israel)
M.A.P.A.M.	*Mifleget Hapoalim Mameuhedet* (United Labour Party)
M.A.Q.I.	*Mifleget Qimunistit Isre'elit* (Communist Party of Israel)
M.A.S.J.U.M.I.	*Madjelis Sjaro Moslimin Indonesia*
M.E.P.	*Mahajama Eksath Peramuna* (United People's Front of Ceylon)
M.R.P.	*Mouvement Républicain Populaire*
M.V.D.	*Ministerij Vnutrennix Djel*
NATO	North Atlantic Treaty Organization
N.E.P.	New Economic Policy
N.K.V.D.	*Narodni Kommissariat Vnutrennix Djel*
N.U.F.	National United Front (Burma)
O.F.	*Otechestven Front* (Rumania)
O.G.P.U.	Name for former Cheka
P.C.F.	*Parti Communiste Français*
P.C.R.	*Partidul Comunist din Romania*
Pesindo	*Permuda Socialis Indonesia*
P.K.I.	*Partai Komunis Indonesia*
P.N.I.	*Partai Nasional Indonesia*
P.P.R.	*Polska Partia Robotnicza* (Polish Workers' Party)
P.P.S.	*Polska Partia Socjalistyczna* (Polish Socialist Party)
P.S.D.I.R.	*Partidul Social Democrat Independent din Romania*
P.S.I.	*Partito Socialista Italiano*
P.S.I.	*Partai Socialis Indonesia*
P.S.I.U.P.	*Partito Socialista Italiano di Unità Proletaria*
P.S.L.	*Polskie Stronnictwo Ludowe*
P.S.L.I.	*Partito Socialista dei Lavoratori Italiani*
P.S.P.	*Praja Socialist Party* (India)
P.V.O.	People's Volunteer Organization (Burma)
P.Z.P.R.	*Polska Zjednoczona Partia Robotnicza* (Polish United Workers' Party)
R.A.F.I.	*Reshimat Poale Israel*
R.P.F.	*Rassemblement du Peuple Français*
R.P.P.S.	*Robotnicza Partia Polskich Socjalistow* (Workers' Party of Polish Socialists)
Sanbetsu	*Zen Nihon Sangyobetsu Rodo Kumiai Kaigi* (National Congress of Industrial Organizations)
S.C.A.P.	Supreme Commander of the Allied Powers
S.E.D.	*Sozialistische Einheitspartei Deutschlands*
S.F.I.O.	*Section Française de l'Internationale Ouvrière—Parti Socialiste*
S.I.	*Serakat Islam* (Indonesia)
S.I.	Socialist International
S.I.L.O.	Socialist Information and Liaison Office

S.L.F.P.	Sri Lanka Freedom Party (Ceylon)
S.O.B.S.I.	*Sentral Organisasi Buruh Seluruh Indonesia* (Indonesian trade union Council)
Sodomei	*Nihon Rodo Kumiai Sodomei* (Japanese General Federation of Workers)
Sohyo	*Nihon Rodo Kumiai Sohyogikai* (General Council of Japanese Trade Unions)
S.P.D.	Social Democratic Party of Germany
S.P.Ö.	Socialist Party of Austria
S.S.P.	Samyukta Socialist Party (India)
T.U.C.	Trades Union Congress
U.N.	United Nations
U.N.P.	United National Party (Ceylon)
U.S.S.R.	Union of Soviet Socialist Republics
V.L.S.S.P.	*Viplavakari L.S.S.P.* (Ceylon)
W.F.T.U.	World Federation of Trade Unions
W.P.P.	Workers' and Peasants' Party (India)

Indexes

by Michael Gordon

SUBJECT INDEX